THAILAND
THE ROUGH GUIDE

THE ROUGH GUIDES

OTHER AVAILABLE ROUGH GUIDES
USA • FLORIDA • CALIFORNIA & WEST COAST USA • SAN FRANCISCO
NEW YORK • CANADA • EUROPE • ITALY • TUSCANY & UMBRIA
VENICE • SICILY • GREECE • CRETE • FRANCE • PARIS • PROVENCE
PYRENEES • BRITTANY & NORMANDY • PORTUGAL • SPAIN
BARCELONA • IRELAND • HOLLAND, BELGIUM & LUXEMBOURG
AMSTERDAM • SCANDINAVIA • GERMANY • BERLIN • HUNGARY
CZECHOSLOVAKIA • POLAND • EASTERN EUROPE • YUGOSLAVIA
ISRAEL • TURKEY • NEPAL • HONG KONG • EGYPT • WEST AFRICA
KENYA • TUNISIA • MOROCCO • ZIMBABWE & BOTSWANA • MEXICO
PERU • BRAZIL • GUATEMALA & BELIZE • WOMEN TRAVEL
MEDITERRANEAN WILDLIFE • NOTHING VENTURED

FORTHCOMING
BULGARIA • CYPRUS • WORLD MUSIC

Rough Guide Thailand Credits

Text Editors:	Jonathan Buckley and David Reed
Series Editor:	Mark Ellingham
Editorial:	Martin Dunford, John Fisher, Jack Holland, Richard Trillo, Kate Berens
Production:	Susanne Hillen, Andy Hilliard, Gail Jammy, Vivien Antwi
Financial:	Celia Crowley

The authors would both like to thank: Khun Sumontha, Khun Chaisong and Khun Peck at Bangkok TAT; Jeanne Muchnick; the late Peter Glencross; John Clewley and Charles de Ledesma; Ralph Mepham for proofreading; and most especially Jon and David.

Individually, the authors would also like to thank:

Paul – Prachuab Tangka-Aree and Lada Subhongsang in Khon Kaen; Wichok Angmanee and Manit Songsaengrit in Nakhon; Khun Wisut and Khun Chalermsak in Chiang Mai; Sunthorn Sidtrirueang at Doi Inthanon; Khun La-O on Ko Tarutao; Moo Zaikaen in Mae Hong Son; Khun Kannika in Narathiwat; the good samaritans, Somboon Sedaeng in Chiang Rai, and Khun Anake and Khun Ekasan in Mae Sariang; Preecha Thitichon for hospitality, friendship and red wine; Ron Emmons and Michael Barraclough for insight and good company; Bill and Sheila Gray, Bill and Maud Hall, Jack Grassby and David Johnson, and Ruth Derry, for their generous support and much else besides; and most of all Sarah, who makes everything possible.

Lucy – Chris Humphries for tramping undaunted across Ko Chang; Khun Nikhom at the Thailand Information Service; Boonchu Hankham of Phitsanulok and Khun Pirom of Surin; Cathy Bove for Mae Sot hospitality; Charlie Ridout for expert travel advice; Deb and Mark for weekend entertainment; Sonthida for Thai lessons; and finally, Ralph for inspirational companionship and unflagging support.

This first edition published October 1992 by Rough Guides Ltd, 1 Mercer Street, London WC2H 9QL. Distributed by Penguin Books, 27 Wrights Lane, London W8 5TZ.

Typeset in Linotron Univers and Century Old Style to an original design by Andrew Oliver.
Printed in the United Kingdom by Cox and Wyman Ltd (Reading).
Maps by Micromap, 1 Nursery Gardens, Romsey, Hampshire SO51 8UU.
Illustrations in Part One and Part Three by Ed Briant.
Illustrations on p.1 and p.431 by Henry Iles.
Illustrations in the guide by Ralph Mepham.

496pp. Includes index.

British Library Cataloguing in Publication Data.
A catalogue record for this book is available from the British Library.

ISBN 1-85828-016-8

THAILAND
THE ROUGH GUIDE

Written and researched by

Paul Gray
and Lucy Ridout

With additional contributions by
John R. Davies and Gavin Lewis

THE ROUGH GUIDES

CONTENTS

Introduction viii

| PART ONE | BASICS | 1 |

Getting to Thailand from the UK and Ireland 3
Getting to Thailand from North America 6
Getting to Thailand from Australasia 8
Red Tape and Visas 9
Information and Maps 10
Money, Banks and Costs 12
Health and Insurance 14
Getting Around 16
Accommodation 21
Food and Drink 23
Communications 29

Post, Phones and the Media 28
Trouble 30
Opening Hours and Holidays 31
Festivals 32
Entertainment and Sport 34
Meditation Centres and Retreats 37
Cultural Hints 37
Outdoor Pursuits 39
Gay Thailand 41
Disabled Travellers 41
Directory 42

| PART TWO | GUIDE | 43 |

■ 1   BANGKOK 45
■ 2   THE CENTRAL PLAINS 112
■ 3   THE NORTH 175
■ 4   THE EAST COAST 255
■ 5   THE NORTHEAST: ISAAN 278
■ 6   SOUTHERN THAILAND: THE GULF COAST 329
■ 7   SOUTHERN THAILAND: THE ANDAMAN COAST 365
■ 8   THE DEEP SOUTH 405

| PART THREE | CONTEXTS | 431 |

Historical Framework 433
Art and Architecture 447
Religion: Thai Buddhism 453
The Environment 457

Books 461
Language 465
A Thai Glossary 469

Index 471

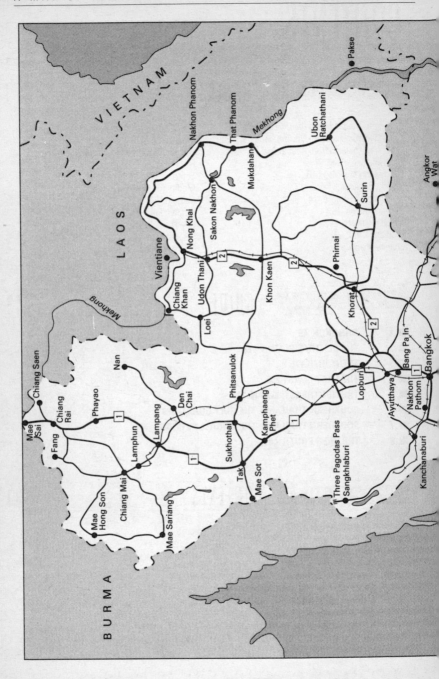

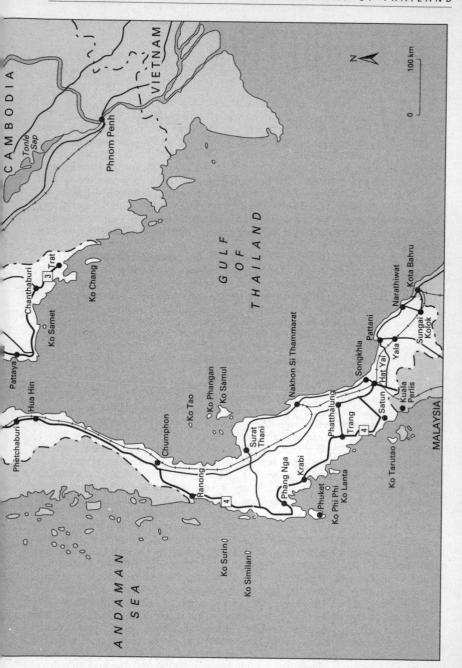

INTRODUCTION

With over five million foreigners flying into the country each year, **Thailand** has become Asia's primary holiday destination. The influx of tourist cash has played a large part in making this one of the world's fastest growing economies, yet Thailand's cultural integrity remains undamaged except for the largest resorts. In this country of fifty-three million people, over ninety percent are practising Theravada **Buddhists**, a unifying faith which colours all aspects of daily life – from the tiered temple rooftops that dominate every skyline, to the omnipresent saffron-robed monks and the packed calendar of festivals. Furthermore, though the high-rises and neon lights occupy the foreground of the tourist picture, the typical Thai community is the traditional **farming** village, and some ninety percent of Thais still earn their living from the land.

The clash of tradition and modernity is most intense in **Bangkok**, the first stop on almost any itinerary. Within the capital's historic core you'll find resplendent temples, canalside markets and the opulent indulgence of the eighteenth-century **Grand Palace**, while in downtown Bangkok lies the hub of the country's sex industry, the infamous strip known as **Patpong**. The political fault-lines of Thailand are inevitably most visible in Bangkok as well. Home of the revered King Bhumibol and the far less revered ministers who run this constitutional monarchy, it's the cockpit of the country's pro-democracy movement – which in May 1992 flared into open **demonstrations** and military violence that were witnessed on TV screens across the world.

After touchdown in Bangkok, much of the package-holiday traffic flows east to **Pattaya**, the country's first and most popular beach resort. Born as a rest-and-recreation base for the US military during the Vietnam War, it has grown into a concrete warren of hotels and strip joints that's just about the least authentic town in Thailand. For unpolluted beaches and clear seas, however, you have to venture just a little further afield, to the tiny unspoilt island of **Ko Samet**, with its superb sand and idyllic bamboo beach huts. Even fewer tourists strike north from the east coast into **Isaan**, the poorest and in some ways the most traditionally Thai region. Here, a trip through the gently modulating landscapes of the **Mekhong River** valley, which defines Thailand's northern and eastern extremities, takes in archetypal agricultural villages and a fascinating array of religious sites, while the southern reaches of Isaan hold some of the country's best-kept secrets – the magnificent stone temple complexes of **Phimai** and **Phanom Rung**, both built by the Khmers of Cambodia almost ten centuries ago. Closer to the capital, in the southwestern corner of Isaan, **Khao Yai National Park** encapsulates the phenomenal diversity of Thailand's flora and fauna, which here range from wild orchids to strangling figs, elephants to hornbills, tigers to macaques.

Attractively sited at the heart of the northern uplands, **Chiang Mai** draws tourists in almost the same quantities as Pattaya, but it has preserved its looks with far greater care, and appeals to a different kind of visitor. It's the vibrant cultural centre of a region whose overriding enticement is the prospect of **trekking** through villages inhabited by a richly mixed population of tribal peoples. With Chiang Mai so firmly planted on the independent tourist trail, the ancient cities of the intervening **central plains** tend to get short shrift. Yet the elegant ruins of former capitals **Ayutthaya** and **Sukhothai** embody a glorious artistic heritage, displaying Thailand's distinctive ability to absorb influences from quite different cultures. **Kanchanaburi**, stunningly located on the **River Kwai** in the western reaches of the central plains, tells a much darker episode of Thailand's past, for it was along the course of this river that the Japanese army built the Thailand–Burma Railway during World War II, at the cost of thousands of POW lives.

Sand and sea are what most Thailand holidays are about, though, and the pick of the coasts are in southern Thailand, where the **Samui archipelago**, off the **Gulf coast** is one of the highlights: its small resorts, desolate coves, immaculate sweeping beaches and dramatically eroded limestone formations draw teenage ravers and solitude seekers in equal parts. Across on the other side of the peninsula, the **Andaman coast** boasts even more exhilarating scenery and the finest **coral reefs** in the country. The largest resort, **Ko Phuket**, is packed with expensive highrises and threatens to go the way of Pattaya, but on nearby **Ko Phi Phi** the emphasis on budget travel persists, and the coral-rich sea remains an untainted azure. Neither of these, however, can match the spectacular **Ko Similan** island chain, some six hours out to sea, which ranks as one of the world's top diving destinations. Further down the Thai peninsula, in the provinces of the **deep south**, the teeming marine life and unfrequented sands of **Ko Tarutao National Marine Park** are the immediate attractions, though the edgy relationship between Thai sovereignty and Malaysian Islam – the kind of cultural brew that has characterised Thailand throughout its history – makes this region a rewarding one for the more adventurous traveller to explore.

When to go

The **climate** of most of Thailand is governed by three seasons: rainy (roughly June to October), caused by the southwest monsoon dumping moisture gathered from the Andaman Sea and the Gulf of Thailand; cool (November to February); and hot (March to May). The **rainy season** is the least predictable of the three, varying in length and intensity from year to year, but usually it gathers force between June and August, coming to a peak in September and October, when unpaved roads are reduced to mud troughs and whole districts of Bangkok are flooded. The **cool season** is the pleasantest time to visit, although temperatures can still reach a broiling 30°C in the middle of the day. In the **hot season**, when temperatures rise to 40°C, the best thing to do is to hit the beach.

TRANSLITERATION OF THAI WORDS

Because there's no standard system of **transliteration** of Thai script into Roman, you're sure to find that the Thai words and proper names in this book do not always match the versions written elsewhere. Maps and street signs are the biggest sources of confusion, so where possible we've used the transliteration that's most common on the spot; in less clear instances we've stuck to the most frequent national transliteration. However, it's sometimes necessary to practise a little lateral thinking when it comes to deciphering Romanised Thai, bearing in mind that a town such as Ubon Ratchathani, for example, could come out as Ubol Rajatani, or that Ayutthaya is synonymous with Ayudhia. As for street names, a classic variant would be Ratchawithi Road or Rajvithi Road – and it's not unheard of to find one spelling posted at one end of a road, with another at the opposite end.

Within this scheme, slight variations are found from region to region. The less humid **north** experiences the greatest range of temperatures: at night in the cool season the thermometer occasionally approaches zero on the higher slopes, and this region is often hotter than the central plains between March and May. It's **the northeast** which gets the very worst of the hot season, with clouds of dust gathering above the parched fields, and humid air too. In **southern Thailand**, temperatures are more consistent throughout the year, with less variation the closer you get to the equator. The rainy season hits the **Andaman coast** of the southern peninsula harder than anywhere else in the country – heavy rainfall usually starts in May and persists at the same level until October.

One area of the country, the **Gulf coast** of the southern peninsula, lies outside this general pattern – because it faces east, this coast and its offshore islands feel the effects of the northeast monsoon, which brings rain between October and January. This area also suffers less from the southwest monsoon, getting a relatively small amount of rain between June and September.

Overall, the **cool season** is generally the **best time** to come to Thailand: as well as having more manageable temperatures and less rain, it offers waterfalls in full spate and the best of the upland flowers in bloom. Bear in mind, however, that it's also the busiest season, so forward planning is essential.

THAILAND'S CLIMATE

Average daily maximum temperatures °C (°F) and Monthly Rainfall (Inches)

	Jan	Feb	Mar	Apr	May	June	July	Aug	Sept	Oct	Nov	Dec
Bangkok												
°C	32	34	35	36	34	33	32	32	32	32	31	31
(°F)	(90)	(93)	(95)	(97)	(93)	(91)	(90)	(90)	(90)	(90)	(88)	(88)
Inches	1	1	1	2	7	6	6	8	13	5	2	0
Chiang Mai												
°C	28	31	34	36	34	32	31	30	31	31	30	28
(°F)	(82)	(88)	(93)	(97)	(93)	(90)	(88)	(86)	(88)	(88)	(86)	(82)
Inches	1	1	1	2	6	6	7	10	10	5	1	1
Pattaya												
°C	33	33	33	34	33	33	32	32	32	32	32	32
(°F)	(91)	(91)	(91)	(93)	(91)	(91)	(90)	(90)	(90)	(90)	(90)	(90)
Inches	1	2	2	3	7	3	4	4	9	11	3	1
Ko Samui												
°C	27	27	28	29	29	28	28	28	28	27	27	26
(°F)	(81)	(81)	(82)	(84)	(84)	(82)	(82)	(82)	(82)	(81)	(81)	(79)
Inches	8	1	2	4	6	3	5	4	4	10	17	10
Ko Phuket												
°C	32	33	33	33	32	31	30	31	30	30	30	31
(°F)	(90)	(91)	(91)	91)	(90)	(88)	(86)	(88)	(86)	(86)	(86)	(88)
Inches	1	1	2	5	12	11	12	11	14	13	7	2

THE

BASICS

GETTING TO THAILAND FROM THE UK AND IRELAND

The fastest and most comfortable way of reaching Thailand from the UK is to **fly non-stop** from London to Bangkok with either *Qantas*, *British Airways* or *Thai International* – a journey time of about 12 hours. Many scheduled airlines operate **indirect flights** (ie flights with one or more connections), which usually take up to four hours longer, but work out significantly cheaper, particularly if you go with *Lauda Air* via Vienna, or *Finnair* via Helsinki. *Lauda Air* also fly London–Phuket with a change in Vienna. There are no non-stop flights from Glasgow, Manchester, Dublin or Belfast, only flights via other European cities, and fares sometimes work out about the same as for indirect flights from London – though with flights from Ireland it may be worthwhile getting a cheap flight or ferry to England then booking your flight to Bangkok from London. If you're really determined to get **rock bottom prices** and don't mind missing out on luxuries like in-flight movies, blankets and free alcohol, then plump for *Aeroflot* or *Tarom Romanian Air* – some agents refuse to deal with them, but they are generally the cheapest.

If you want to make extra use of all that flying time and **stop over** on the way there or back, you'll probably have to go with the associated national airline – eg *Air India* for stops in Delhi or Bombay. This is an option which most airlines offer at the same price as their direct flights. If you're continuing onward from Thailand, then consider buying a one-way London–Bangkok ticket and shopping around for the next leg of your trip once you arrive in Bangkok: because of lax governmental control, flights out of Thailand can be significantly cheaper than those bought in the West (see p.107). Remember though, that if you go into Thailand on a one-way ticket you must buy a sixty-day visa beforehand (see p.9). Alternatively, if planning a long trip with several stops in Asia or elsewhere, buying a **round-the-world ticket** makes a lot of sense: a typical one-year open ticket using *British Airways* and *Air New Zealand*, would depart and return to London, taking in Bangkok, Sydney, Honolulu and Los Angeles, and leaving you to cover the Bangkok–Singapore leg overland.

FARES

As there are currently no APEX fares to Thailand, there's very little point in buying direct from the airlines: any reliable specialist **agent** (see box) will be able to undercut airline prices by a hefty percentage. There are no advance booking restrictions on agency tickets, which means that theoretically you could book a discount ticket and fly out on the same day, but these discount deals nearly always carry **restrictions** on your length of stay in Thailand (generally 7–90 days) and sometimes require a fixed departure date from Thailand – check particulars with your agent.

The most expensive **times to fly** are between mid-June and the end of September and from the beginning of December to the end of January – you may have to book 2–3 months in advance for these peak periods. Check the airline's exact seasonal dates through an agent, as you could make major savings by shifting your departure date by as little as one day.

Discounted non-stop London–Bangkok return **fares** start at around £495 low season, rising to £605 during peak periods. For the cheaper indirect flights, *Lauda Air* flights via Vienna usually come out among the cheapest at £425 low season, £465 high season, with *Aeroflot* and *Tarom* sometimes dropping to as low as £383 in low season. Some agents offer special discounts (down to £399 return) with more reputable airlines for full-time students and/or under-26-year-olds. One-year open round-the-world tickets bought in London start at £700.

Before making a final decision on who to book with, it's always worth checking out the travel sections in the Sunday papers and, in London, the ads in *Time Out*, *City Limits*, the *Evening Standard*, and free travel magazines like *TNT*. Many of the companies advertising in these publications are **bucket shops** who are able to offer extremely cheap deals, but there's a risk attached to companies who don't belong to official travel associations such as ABTA or IATA – if your bucket shop goes bust you'll get no refund, even on a fully paid-up ticket. With associated agents, such as those listed below, ABTA and IATA will cover any debts in the case of bankruptcy.

Bear in mind that however much your ticket costs, you'll always have to pay a B200 airport **departure tax** when leaving Thailand on an international flight (B20 on domestic flights), payable when you check in.

MAJOR AIRLINES FROM THE UK TO THAILAND

Aeroflot, 70 Piccadilly, London W1 (☎071/355 2233). Four flights a week from Heathrow via Moscow; Delhi stopovers also possible. Very cheap, no frills, but fairly reliable. No direct sales to the public.

British Airways, 156 Regent St, London W1 (☎081/897 4000). Six non-stop flights a week from Heathrow.

Finnair, 14 Clifford St, London W1 (☎071/408 1222). Twice-weekly flights from Heathrow via Helsinki.

Lauda Air, 4th Floor, 7 Swallow St, London W1 (☎071/494 0702). Three flights a week from Gatwick via Vienna. Once-weekly flights from Gatwick to Phuket, also via Vienna.

Qantas, 182 The Strand, London W1 (☎0345/747767). Daily non-stop flights from Heathrow.

Royal Brunei, 49 Cromwell Rd, London SW7 (☎071/584 6660). Twice-weekly flights from Heathrow via Frankfurt and Dubai (one plane change in Frankfurt); no direct sales to the public.

Tarom Romanian Air, 17 Nottingham St W1 (☎071/224 3693). Twice-weekly flights from Heathrow via Bucharest. Not very reliable, but very cheap ; no direct sales to the public.

Thai International, 41 Albermarle St, London W1 (☎071/491 7953). Daily direct flights from Heathrow via Delhi with one non-stop flight a week.

DISCOUNTED FLIGHT AGENTS IN THE UK AND IRELAND

Airbreak Leisure, South Quay Plaza 2, 183 Marsh Wall, London E14 9SH (☎071/712 0303). Flights from Manchester and Gatwick.

Campus Travel, 52 Grosvenor Gardens, London SW1 (☎071/730 8111); 541 Bristol Rd, Selly Oak, Birmingham (☎021/414 1848); 39 Queen's Rd, Clifton, Bristol (☎0272/292494); 3 Emmanuel St, Cambridge (☎0223/324283); 53 Forest Rd, Edinburgh (☎031/225 6111); 13 High St, Oxford (☎0865/242067); also in YHA shops and on university campuses all over Britain.

Council Travel, 28a Poland St, London W1 (☎071/437 7767). General student discount agent.

South Coast Student Travel, 61 Ditchling Rd, Brighton BN1 4SD (☎0273/570 226). Plenty to offer non-students as well, and good associate agents in Bangkok.

STA Travel, 74 Old Brompton Rd, London SW7 (☎071/937 9962); 25 Queen's Rd, Bristol; 38 Sidney St, Cambridge; 88 Vicar Lane, Leeds; 75 Deansgate, Manchester; 36–38 George St, Oxford; and offices at the universities of Birmingham, Kent, London (all colleges) and Loughborough. All offices except London for personal callers only.

Trailfinders, 42–48 Earls Court Rd, London W8 (☎071/938 3366); 194 Kensington High St, London W8 (☎071/ 938 3939); 58 Deansgate, Manchester M3 (☎061/839 6969).

Travel Bug, 597 Cheetham Hill Rd, Manchester M8 (☎061/721 4000).

Travel Cuts, 295a Regent St, London W1 (☎071/ 255 2082).

UniqueTravel, Dudley House, 2nd floor 169 Piccadilly W1 (☎071/495 4848). The main *Aeroflot* outlet.

USIT, Aston Quay, O'Connell Bridge, Dublin 2 (☎01/778117) & 13b College St, Belfast BT1 6ET (☎0232/324073). Ireland's main outlet for discounted, youth and student fares.

PACKAGES

Package deals come in two varieties: those offering a return flight and a week or more's accommodation, and specialist tours which organise daytime activities and escorted tours – sometimes in addition to flights, sometimes instead of. **Flight and board deals** can work out good value if you're planning to base yourself in just one or two places, starting as low as £655 (excluding meals) for a week in a moderately to expensively priced hotel in Bangkok, Pattaya or Phuket (see below for the main operators). **Specialist tour** packages on the other hand work out pretty expensive compared to what you'd pay if you organised everything independently (from about £1000 including flight for a 12-day trip), but they do cut out a lot of hassle and the most adventurous ones in particular often feature activities that it wouldn't be easy to set up by yourself – such as rafting or canoeing. Before booking, make sure you know exactly what's included in the price.

PACKAGE COMPANIES IN THE UK

BA Speedbird, Speedbird House, Heathrow Airport, Hounslow, Middlesex (☎0293/613777). Beaches and cities (7 days from £655 including flights). Bookings through most travel agents.

Bales Tours, Bales House, Junction Rd, Dorking, Surrey RH4 3HB (☎0306/885991). High-quality escorted tours, including ten-day North Thailand Tour from £899 with flights and breakfasts.

Encounter Overland, 267 Old Brompton Rd (☎071/370 6845). 31-day overland trip from Bangkok to Bali and vice versa which includes ten days in Thailand (3-day trek in the Far North and visits to Sukhothai and Ko Samui or Ko Phuket). £1200 inclusive of flights and meals, staying in budget accommodation; book through major travel agents.

Exodus, 9 Weir Rd, London SW12 (☎071/675 5550). 17-day Golden Triangle (£590 excluding flights) and Classic Thailand (£750 excluding flights) adventure tours which cover Bangkok, Ayutthaya, Sukhothai, Chiang Mai, Mae Hong Song and Ko Samet. Bookings through major travel agents.

Explore Worldwide, 1 Frederick St, Aldershot, Hants GU11 1LQ (☎0252/319448). One of the best adventure tour operators. First-class tours of the Golden Triangle, Old Siam plus a hill-tribe trek, using a variety of transport and accommodation from £860 for 16 days.

Far East Travel Centre, 3 Lower John St, London W1 (☎071/734 9318). Beaches and cities (12 days from £865 including flights and breakfast) plus optional tours.

Hayes and Jarvis, Hayes House, 152 King St, London W6 0QU (☎071/748 5050). Tours and hotel-based holidays from under £600 inclusive.

Kuoni Travel Kuoni House, Dorking, Surrey (☎0306/740500). Beaches and cities (12 days from £669 including flights but no meals), and escorted tours to the Far North (12 days from £1000 including flights). Bookings through most travel agents.

Next Holidays, South Quay Plaza 2, 183 Marsh Wall, London E14 9SH (☎071/712 0505). Stylishly presented range of inexpensive packages using low-cost charter flights from *Airbreak Leisure*.

Thai Adventures, PO Box 82, Victoria St, Alderney, Channel Islands (☎0481/823 417). Small operator with a tailor-made approach focusing on hotel-based holidays.

Thomas Cook Holidays, PO Box 36, Thorpe Wood, Peterborough PE3 6SB (☎0733/332255). Range of flight and board deals from about £900 inclusive for a week, plus some tours.

Top Deck Travel, 131-35 Earl's Court Rd, London SW5 9RH (☎071/ 370 4555). Options include a 30-day trip starting in Bangkok, finishing in Singapore, including Chiang Mai trek and 9 days in Burma, from £1,349 excluding flights.

Trailrovers. Escorted small-group tours include a 4-day trek as part of their 12-day *North Thai Rover* holiday (£325 excluding flight). Book through *Trailfinders* (see "Flight Agents")

Travel Bag, 12 High St, Alton, Hants GU34 1BN (☎0420/80828). Thailand specialists selling tailor-made trips at varying prices direct to travellers only, not through agents.

GETTING TO THAILAND FROM NORTH AMERICA

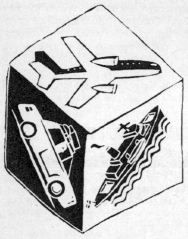

There are no non-stop **flights** from North America to Thailand, but *United Airlines* and *Japan Airlines* both run daily flights to Bangkok from major North American east and west coast cities, with one change in either Taipei, Tokyo or Seoul. Flying time is 22 hours from New York, 20 hours from Chicago and 16 hours from Seattle. West coast travellers can also go with *Thai International*, who do daily Bangkok flights departing from Los Angeles, and thrice weekly

flights from Seattle, both via Tokyo or Seoul. East coast travellers have the alternative option of flying with *Swissair* (change in Zurich; 17hr) or *Finnair* (change in Helsinki; 18hr).

Most major airlines offer "Circle Pacific" deals which allow four **stopovers** at no extra charge if tickets are bought 14–30 days in advance; for longer more complex itineraries, **round-the-world tickets** often work out good value, allowing several stops in Asia before continuing on through Europe and back to North America.

FARES

Fares obviously depend on where you're flying from, and when: the west coast works out cheapest, weekends are more expensive than weekdays, and peak periods slightly different for each airline, but generally the Christmas and New Year season and from June through August more expensive again. Prices quoted here are for roundtrip tickets bought **direct from the airlines** (midweek low season–weekend high season), and don't include tax, an additional fee of about $20: **Chicago** $1423–1530; **Los Angeles** $1124–2300; **Montréal** CAN$ 1695–2055; **New York** $1423–1630; **San Francisco** $1124–2300; **Seattle** $1124–1252; **Toronto** CAN$ 1695–2055.

MAJOR AIRLINES FROM NORTH AMERICA TO BANGKOK

Canadian Airlines, Suite 300-2912 Memorial Drive, Southeast Calgary, Alberta T2A 6R1 (☎403/235 1161). Six flights a week from **Vancouver** via Hong Kong.

Finnair, 10 East 40th St, New York 10016 (☎800/950 5000); 130 Blorr St West, Suite 601, Toronto, Ontario, M5S 1N5 (☎416/927 7400). Twice weekly flights from **New York** via Helsinki. Summertime connections only between **Toronto** and Helsinki.

Japan Airlines, 655 5th Avenue, New York 10022 (☎800/525 3663); 777 Hornby St, Vancouver, British Colombia V6Z 1S4 (☎604/688 6611). Daily one-stop flights via Tokyo from **Chicago**, **Los Angeles**, **New York** and **San Francisco**. Three flights a week from **Seattle** and **Toronto**.

Swissair, Swiss Centre, 608 5th Avenue, New York 10022 (☎800/221 4750); Confederation Building Suite 950, 1253 McGill College Avenue, Ste-Cathérine, Montréal, Québec (☎514/954 5600). Six weekly connections from **Montréal**, **New York** and **Toronto** via Zurich.

Thai International, 720 Olive Way, Suite 1400, Seattle, Washington 98101 (☎800/426 5204); The Atrium On Bay, Suite 1133 11th Floor, 20 Dundas St West, Toronto, Ontario M56 2CT (☎416/917 7907). Daily flights from **Los Angeles** via either Tokyo or Seoul and three weekly from **Seattle** via Taipei.

United Airlines, PO Box 66100, Chicago, IL 60666 (☎800/241 6522). Daily one-stop flights from **Chicago, Los Angeles, New York, San Francisco, Seattle** and **Toronto** via either Taipei or Tokyo; all flights routed via San Francisco.

The only reason to pay these prices, however, is if you need to travel at very short notice, or want to stay in the country for less than six days or over six months. For most tourists, the best option is to go for the much **cheaper** fares offered by **consolidators** and **discount agents** (see box, below) who buy in bulk from scheduled airlines and sell at rates up to fifty percent less than the quoted airline prices. You'll get a better bargain still if you can afford to be flexible over departure dates: **charter flights** average out at about sixty percent of official airline fares; charters advertise in the Sunday newspapers, but check companies' reputations with a travel agent before paying up. Students and under-26s may be able to make even larger savings through *STA Travel* (see box).

One thing to be wary of though when buying any discount or chartered flight, is that such low-price fares usually carry several restrictions, including heavy cancellation fees and immovable flying dates, with a minimum six days' and maximum six months' stay in Thailand, and in most cases they will need to be booked at least a week in advance.

DISCOUNT AGENTS & CONSOLIDATORS

Discount Club of America, 61–63 Woodhaven Blvd, Rego Park, NY 11374 (☎718/335 9612).

Moment's Notice, 425 Madison Ave, New York, NY 10017 (☎212/486 0503).

STA Travel, 48 East 11th St, New York, NY 10003 (☎212/477 7166); 166 Geary St, Suite 702, San Francisco, CA 94108 (☎415/391 8407).

Travel International, Ives Building, 114 Forrest Ave, Suite 205, Narbeth, PA 19072 (☎800/221 81390).

UniTravel, Box 12485, St Louis, MO 63132 (☎314/569 2501 or ☎800/325 2222).

PACKAGES

Relatively few operators in the US and Canada offer tours that concentrate solely on Thailand – many more feature a few places in Thailand (usually Bangkok, Chiang Mai and Phuket) as part of a two- or three-week round-Asia or round-southeast Asia trip. Before booking, confirm exactly what expenses are included, what class of hotel you're being offered and how large a group you'll be joining.

PACKAGE TOUR OPERATORS IN NORTH AMERICA

Abercrombie and Kent, 1420 Kensington Rd, Oak Brook, IL 60521 (☎708/954 2944 or ☎800/323 7308). Top-notch 7-day tours of major Thai cities ($1500 excluding flights), plus several 2–3-week round-Asia jaunts which include a few stops in Thailand (about $4450).

American Express, Box 5014, Atlanta, GA 30302 (☎800/282 0800 from Georgia, or ☎800/241 1700 from elsewhere). Huge choice of packaged combinations in and around Thailand from $1000 for a week-long trip.

Cultural Tours, 9920 La Cienega Blvd, Suite 715, Inglewood, CA 90301 (☎213/216 1332 or ☎800/282 8898). 15-day inclusive packages taking in major Thai cities, ancient sites and beaches from $2666.

Globus-Gateway, 9525 Queens Blvd, Rego Park, NY 11374 (☎718/268 1700 or ☎800/221 0090). Round-Asia tours from $1508 for eleven days.

Maupintour, 1515 St Andrews Drive, Lawrence, KS 66044-0807 (☎913/843 1211 or ☎800/255 4266). Round-Asia tours from $4654 for two weeks.

Mountain Travel Sobek, 6420 Fairmount Ave, El Cerrito, CA 94530 (☎800/227 2384). Range of active adventure tours such as 16-day hill-tribe treks through the north of Thailand (from $2290) and nine days' mountain biking, also in the north (from $1090).

Royal Orchid Holidays (☎800/426 5204). Subsidary of *Thai International* airlines with 7–15-day tours of Thai cities and beaches from $1215.

GETTING TO THAILAND FROM AUSTRALASIA

Direct flights from Australia to Thailand are available from *Thai International, Qantas, British Airways* and *Lauda Air* and from New Zealand on *Air New Zealand, Thai International* and *British Airways*. Return fares from Sydney or Melbourne start at around Aus$850 in low season rising to Aus$1070 during peak periods (with around 25 percent off if you fly out of Perth), and from Auckland range from NZ$1509–1748. Discounted fares for students and under-26s are sold by *STA* in Australia and New Zealand (see box).

OVERLAND ROUTES FROM ASIA

All **overland routes** enter Thailand from the south, via Malaysia and Singapore. Most Western tourists can pass through both Singapore and Malaysia without having bought a visa beforehand, but remember that to get into Thailand you need either an onward ticket or a sixty-day visa with you when you arrive at the Thai border (see opposite page).

The most comfortable way of covering the 1943km from Singapore to Bangkok is to take the daily **train**, a journey of 34 hours which costs about £20/$36 second class, with a change at Butterworth and again at Kuala Lumpur, and stops all the way up the line through Thailand, including at Surat Thani – access point for the popular island resort of Ko Samui. From November 1992, you'll also be able to make the overland journey in extreme luxury, when the *Eastern and Oriental Express* starts its once-weekly return trips between Singapore, Kuala Lumpur and Bangkok. A southeast Asian version of the *Orient Express*, the train has been refurbished in classic 1930s colonial style, with three classes of cabins, several restaurant and bar cars – complete with pianist – and an observation car. The full Singapore–Bangkok journey will take 41 hours, with two nights and one full day on board, and costs £530/$950 per person all-inclusive; you can also join or leave the train at Kuala Lumpur and Butterworth in Malaysia and at Surat Thani and Hua Hin in Thailand. For enquiries and bookings ask at major travel agents.

Buses also run from Singapore and Malaysia to destinations in south Thailand: the daily Singapore–Krabi bus takes about 24 hours and costs £10/$18; Kuala Lumpur–Krabi takes 15 hours (1 daily; £9/$16); and Penang–Krabi about 11 hours (2 daily; £8/$14). All buses pass through

Hat Yai, where you can change for a Bangkok connection. It's also possible to cross the Malaysian/Thai border by taking a longtail **boat** from the island of Lang Kawi to Satun in south Thailand and then a bus on to destinations further north (see p.415 for more on this).

RED TAPE AND VISAS

There are three basic visa categories for entering Thailand and once inside the country you have the additional options of extending your visa or applying for a re-entry permit.

For stays of **up to 15 days**, most foreign passport holders automatically get a free non-extendable transit visa when passing through immigration at Don Muang Airport or at the Malaysian border, but must show proof of onward travel arrangements: unless you have a confirmed bus, train or air ticket out of Thailand, you may well be put back on the next plane or sent back to get a tourist visa from the Thai Embassy in Kuala Lumpur.

Fifteen-day transit visas cannot be extended under any but the most exceptional circumstances. If you think you may want to stay longer, then from the outset you should apply for a **sixty-day tourist visa** from a Thai embassy or consulate (see below), accompanying your application with your passport and two photos. In the **UK** visa applications take two working days to process (ten if applied for by post), and the sixty-day visa costs £8. In the **US** it costs $15 and takes about 24 hours to process if you go to the embassy or consulate in person, or about five days by post. In **Canada** it costs Can$16.50 and takes three working days for personal applications, a week or more by post.

If entering on a sixty-day visa, you don't need to show proof of onward travel but, as in all countries, it's up to the immigration officials at the port of entry as to what expiry date they stamp on your visa, so it's always advisable to dress respectably (see p.38) when crossing borders. New Zealanders for some reason can stay in Thailand for up to three months with no visa at all.

Thai embassies will also accept applications for the slightly more expensive **ninety-day non-immigrant visas** as long as you produce a letter of recommendation from an official Thai source (an employer or school principal for example) that explains why you need to be in the country for three months.

As it's quite a hassle to organise a ninety-day visa from outside the country (and generally not feasible for most tourists), you're better off applying for a thirty-day **extension** to your sixty-day visa once inside Thai borders. All thirty-day tourist visas can be extended in Thailand for a further thirty days, at the discretion of officials; extensions cost B500 and are issued over the counter at immigration offices (*kaan khao muang*) in every provincial capital – most offices ask for one or two extra photos as well, plus two photocopies of the first four pages and latest Thai visa page of your passport. If you use up the three-month quota, the quickest and cheapest way of extending your stay for a further sixty days is to head down to Malaysia and apply for another tourist visa at the embassy in Kuala Lumpur.

Immigration offices also issue **re-entry permits** (B500) if you want to leave the country and come back again within sixty days. If you **overstay** your visa limits, expect to be fined B100 per extra day when you depart Don Muang Airport, though an overstayed period of a month or more could land you in trouble with immigration officials.

THAI EMBASSIES AND CONSULATES

Australia 111 Empire Circuit, Yarralumla, Canberra, ACT 2600 (☎62/273 1149).

Canada 180 Island Park Drive, Ottawa, ON K1Y 0A2 (☎613/722 4444); Scotia Plaza, 45th Floor, 40 King St West, Toronto, ON M5H 3Y4 (☎416/367 6750).

Malaysia 206 Jalan Ampang, Kuala Lumpur (☎03/248 8222).

Netherlands 1 Buitenrustweg, 2517 KD The Hague (☎070/345 2088).

New Zealand 2 Cook St, PO Box 17–226, Karori, Wellington (☎4/735538).

Singapore 370 Orchard Rd, Singapore 0923 (☎235 4175).

UK 29 Queens Gate, London SW7 5JD (☎071/589 2857); c/o Smith Keen Cutler, Exchange Bldgs, Stephenson Place, Birmingham B2 4NN (☎021/643 9977; 38 Station Rd, Llanishen, Cardiff CF4 5LT (☎0222/766993); Pacific House, 70 Wellington St, Glasgow G2 6SB (☎041/248 6677); 5 Spyvee St, Hull, HU8 7AD (☎0482/29925); 35 Lord St, Liverpool 2 (☎051/225 0504).

USA 35 E Wacker Drive, Chicago, IL 60601 (☎312/236 2447); 801 N La Brea Ave, Los Angeles, CA 90038 (☎213/937 1894); 351 E 52nd St, New York, NY 10022 (☎212/754 1770); 580 California St, San Francisco CA 94104 (☎415/781 1650); 2300 Kalorama Road NW, Washington, DC 20008 (☎202/483 7200).

INFORMATION AND MAPS

The efficient **Tourism Authority of Thailand** (**TAT**) maintains offices in several cities abroad, where you can pick up a few glossy brochures and get answers to general pre-travel questions, but these aren't a patch on the service it provides in-country. With headquarters in Bangkok and twelve other regional branches all open daily 8.30am to 4.30pm, TAT provides an array of information on everything from tennis courts and swimming pools in Bangkok to Thai rules of the road. Among their most useful stuff are the lists of TAT- and government-approved travel agents,

shops and restaurants – if pressed, staff will also give you names of those places de-listed because of malpractice. In addition, all TAT offices should have up-to-date info on local festival dates and regional transport schedules, but none of them offers accommodation booking services.

Independent **tour operators** and information desks crop up in tourist spots all over the country and will usually help with questions about the immediate locality, but be on the look-out for self-interested advice, given by staff desperate for commission. As with TAT offices, independent operators won't book accommodation – unless of course they happen to have business links with

TAT OFFICES ABROAD

Australia 12th Floor, Royal Exchange Building, 56 Pitt St, Sydney 2000 (☎02/247 7549) – also responsible for New Zealand.

UK 49 Albemarle St, London W1X 3FE (☎071/499 7679).

USA 5 World Trade Center, Suite 3443, New York, NY 10048 (☎212/432 0435) – also responsible for eastern Canada; 303 East Wacker Drive, Suite 400, Chicago, IL 60601 (☎312/819 3990); 3440 Wilshire Blvd, Suite 1100, Los Angeles, CA 90010 (☎213/382 2353) – also responsible for western Canada.

specific guest houses or hotels. For off-beat, enthusiastic first-hand advice, you can't do better than guest house **notice boards** – the best of these boast a whole range of travellers' tips, from anecdotal accounts of cross-country bike trips to recommendations as to where to get the perfect suit made.

MAPS

One thing neither TAT nor tour operators provides is a decent **map**. For most major destinations, the maps in this book should be all you need, though you may want to supplement them with larger-scale versions of Bangkok and the whole country. Bangkok bookshops are the best scource of maps, but if you want to buy one before you get there, go for *Bartholemew's* 1:500,000 map of Thailand, the most consistently accurate of those published abroad. The *Nelles* 1:500,000 is the other map of the country widely available outside Thailand, but this isn't nearly as reliable (for outlets, see box). Where appropriate, detailed local maps and their stockists are recommended in the relevant chapters of the guide.

Published by the Department of Highways in conjunction with Esso, the 1:1,600,000 *Thailand Highway Map* is especially good on **roads** – and has 23 schematic town plans as well. Sadly it's not widely available, however – try *Bangkok Books*. If you can't get hold of that one, go for the set of four 1:1,000,000 regional maps also produced by the Highway Department and sold for around B65 at *DK Books* all over the country, and in Bangkok at Hualamphong station and *Central* department stores. The drawback with this series is that much of the detail is written in Thai script. **Hiking maps** are hard to come by except in the most popular national parks, where you can pick up a free handout of the main trails on arrival.

MAP OUTLETS IN BRITAIN AND NORTH AMERICA

London *Daunt Books*, 83 Marylebone High St, W1 (☎071/224 2295); *National Map Centre*, 22–24 Caxton St, SW1 (☎071/222 4945); *Stanfords*, 12–14 Long Acre, WC2 (☎071/836 1321); *The Travellers' Bookshop*, 25 Cecil Court, WC2 (☎071/836 9132).

Chicago *Rand McNally*, 444 North Michigan Ave, IL 60611 (☎312/321 1751).

New York *The Complete Traveller Bookstore*, 199 Madison Ave, NY 10016 (☎212/685 9007); *Rand McNally*, 150 East 52nd St, NY 10022 (☎212/758 7488); *Traveller's Bookstore*, 22 West 52nd St, NY 10019 (☎212/664 0995).

San Francisco *The Complete Traveler Bookstore*, 3207 Filmore St, CA 92123; *Rand McNally*, 595 Market St, CA 94105 (☎415/777 3131).

Seattle *Elliot Bay Book Company*, 101 South Main St, WA 98104 (☎206/624 6600).

Montréal *Ulysses Travel Bookshop*, 4176 St-Denis (☎514/289 0993).

Toronto *Open Air Books and Maps*, 25 Toronto St, M5R 2C1 (☎416/363 0719); *Ulysses Travel Bookshop*, 101 Yorkville.

Vancouver *World Wide Books and Maps*, 1247 Granville St.

MONEY, BANKS AND COSTS

Thailand's unit of currency is the **baht** (abbreviated to "B"), which is divided into 100 satang. **Notes** come in B10 (brown), B20 (green), B50 (blue), B100 (red) and B500 (purple) denominations, inscribed with Arabic as well as Thai numerals, and increasing in size according to value. The **coinage** is more confusing, because new shapes and sizes circulate alongside older ones. Brass-coloured 25- and 50-satang pieces both come in two sizes but are rarely used, as most prices are rounded off to the nearest baht. Of the three silver one-baht coins, only the medium-sized one fits public call-boxes but all are legal tender; silver five-baht pieces come in two varieties, the larger round one distinguishable from the one-baht by a copper rim, while the smaller one is nine-sided; lastly, ten-baht coins have a small brass centre encircled by a silver ring.

The baht is a stable currency, tied to the US dollar. At the time of writing, **exchange rates** averaged out at B25 to $1 and B46 to £1, with more favourable rates for travellers' cheques. Daily rates are published in the *Bangkok Post* and the *Nation*, and at all foreign exchange counters and kiosks in Thailand. Thailand has no black market in foreign currency.

Banking hours are Mon–Fri 8.30am–3.30pm, but exchange kiosks are always open till at least 5pm, sometimes 10pm. Upmarket hotels will change money 24 hours a day and the **Don Muang airport exchange counter** also operates 24 hours, so there's little point buying baht before you arrive, especially as it takes seven working days to order from most banks outside Thailand.

TRAVELLERS' CHEQUES AND CREDIT CARDS

The safest and most economical way to carry your money is in **travellers' cheques**. Sterling and dollar cheques issued by *American Express* or *Visa* are accepted by banks, exchange booths and upmarket hotels in every sizeable Thai town, and most places also deal in a variety of other currencies. Everyone offers better rates for cheques than for straight cash and they generally charge a total of just B8 in commission and duty per cheque – though kiosks and hotels in isolated places may charge extra commission. All issuers give you a list of numbers to call in the case of **lost or stolen cheques** and will refund if you can produce the original receipts and a note of your cheque numbers; *American Express* usually reimburse straight away, while *Visa* and other issuers may take more time. In cases of loss or theft you should always notify the police first and then call the issuing company who will put you in touch with your nearest branch office.

American Express, *Visa*, *Mastercard* and *Diners Club* **credit cards** and **charge cards** are accepted at top hotels as well as in some posh restaurants, department stores, tourist shops and travel agents, but surcharging of up to 5% is rife, and theft and forgery are major industries – always demand the carbon copies and destroy them immediately, and never leave cards in baggage storage. The most useful cards are *Visa* and *Mastercard*, because with these you can also **withdraw cash** on your bank account from 650 ATMs around the country – most provincial capitals have at least one ATM. There's a handling fee of 1.5% on every withdrawal, but as an emergency or back-up facility this works out a cheaper and faster alternative to having money wired over.

Wiring money from overseas is the fastest way of obtaining extra funds if you don't have a credit card, but banks whack on a charge of around £20/$38 per transaction. Your home bank will need the addresses of the branch bank where you want to pick up the money and of the Bangkok head office, which will act as the clearing house; wired money normally takes two working days to arrive, and you'll need to show your passport to collect it.

LOST TRAVELLERS' CHEQUES AND CREDIT CARDS

American Express ☎02/273 0022 (24hr service).

Diners Club ☎02/238 2920–9 (Mon–Fri 8am–5pm), and ☎02/233 5775 (at other times).

Visa and Master Card c/o Thai Farmers Bank ☎02/271 0234 (Mon–Sun 7am–10pm); c/o Siam Commercial Bank ☎02/256 1361 (Mon–Fri 8.30am–4pm); c/o Bank of America ☎02/250 0795 (Mon–Fri 8.30am–8pm, Sat & Sun 10am–8pm).

EXCHANGE CONTROLS

Anyone entering Thailand is officially required to bring a **minimum amount of foreign currency** with them, a sum that varies with the class of visa: the equivalent of $125 per person or $250 per family for a fifteen-day transit visa; $250/$500 for a sixty-day tourist visa; and $500/$1000 for a ninety-day visa. Customs officials rarely take you up on this unless you're on a one-way ticket or look equipped to settle. There's no **maximum limit** to the amount of foreign currency you can import, but anything over the equivalent of $10,000 has to be declared.

If you do **import Thai money**, you're restricted to a paltry B2000 cash per person or B4000 per family; when you leave you're supposed to export no more than B500/B1000 without prior authorisation.

All non-residents who acquire income while in Thailand must get a **tax clearance certificate** from the Revenue Department on Chakrapong Road in Bangkok (☎02/282 9899). Theoretically, anyone who's stayed in Thailand for over ninety days within one calendar year also needs one of these certificates. Check with TAT or the Revenue Department on your specific case, but don't be surprised if they say you don't need one.

COSTS

You'll find Thailand an extremely inexpensive place. At the **bottom of the scale**, you could manage on a daily budget of about B250 if you're willing to opt for basic accommodation and eat, drink and travel as the locals do – spending B80 for a room (less if you share), around B100 on three meals, and the rest on travel and incidentals. With extras like air conditioning in rooms and on buses, taking tuk-tuks rather than buses for cross-town journeys, and a meal and a couple of beers in a more touristy restaurant, a day's outlay will rise to a minimum of B600. Staying in expensive hotels and eating in the more exclusive restaurants, you should be able to live in extreme comfort for around B2000 a day.

Travellers soon get so used to the low cost of living in Thailand that they start **bargaining** at every available opportunity, much as Thai people do. Although it's expected practice for a lot of commercial transactions, particularly at markets and when hiring tuk-tuks and taxis, bargaining is a delicate art that requires humour, tact and patience. If your price is way out of line, the vendor's vehement refusal should be enough to make you increase your offer: never forget that the few pennies you're making such a fuss over will go a lot further in a Thai's hands than in your own.

On the other hand, making a tidy sum off foreigners is sometimes official practice: at government-run museums and historical parks, for example, foreigners pay a B20 admission charge while Thais get in for B5. A number of privately owned tourist attractions follow a similar two-tier system, posting an inflated price in English for foreigners and a lower price in Thai for locals. This is perfectly legitimate, but overcharging tourists on fixed-fare public transport is definitely not acceptable – the best way to avoid getting stung by wily conductors on buses and trains is to watch or ask fellow passengers.

Few museums or transport companies offer student reductions, but in some cases **children** get discounts; these vary a lot, one of the more bizarre provisos being the state railways' regulation that a child of 3–12 only qualifies for half fare if under 150cm tall – in some stations you'll see a measuring scale painted onto the ticket hall wall.

HEALTH AND INSURANCE

There's no need to bring huge supplies of non-prescription medicines with you as Thai **pharmacies** (*raan khai yaa*; daily 8.30am–8pm) are well-stocked with local and international branded medicaments, and of course they are much cheaper. All pharmacies, whatever size the town, are run by highly-trained English-speaking pharmacists and they are usually the best people to talk to if your symptoms aren't acute enough to warrant seeing a doctor.

Hospital (*rong phayaabahn*) cleanliness and efficiency varies, but generally hygiene and health care standards are good and the ratio of medical staff to patients considerably higher than in most parts of the West. As with head pharmacists, doctors speak English. All provincial capitals have at least one hospital: ask at your accommodation for advice on and possibly transport to the nearest or most suitable. In the event of a major health crisis, get someone to contact your embassy (see p.110) or insurance company – it may be best to get yourself flown home.

TRAVEL INSURANCE

If you do have to undergo hospital treatment you'll have to pay, so taking out **travel insurance** is definitely worth it. Besides covering medical expenses and emergency flights home, a good policy should include insurance against loss and theft of money and personal belongings and possibly cover for damage to rented motorbikes and cars as well. Many bank and charge accounts include some form of travel cover, and insurance

is also sometimes included if you pay for your trip with a credit card. Among **UK** insurers, *Endsleigh* are about the cheapest, offering a month's cover for around £45 (£36 for under-35s). Their policies are available from most youth/student travel specialists or direct from their offices at 97–107 Southampton Row, London WC1 (☎071/436 4451). You must make sure you keep all medical bills, and, if you have anything stolen, get a copy of the police report when you report the incident – otherwise you won't be able to claim.

Travellers from the **US** should carefully check their current insurance policies before taking out a new one. You may discover that you're covered already for medical and other losses while abroad. Holders of **ISIC** cards are entitled to be reimbursed for $3000-worth of accident coverage and 60 days of in-patient benefits up to $100 a day for the period the card is valid – though this might not go far in the event of a serious setback. If you do want a specific travel insurance policy, there are numerous kinds to choose from: short-term combination policies covering everything from baggage loss to broken legs are the best bet and cost around $25 for ten days, plus $1 a day for trips of 75 days or more. Two companies you might try are *Travel Guard*, 110 Centrepoint Drive, Steven Point, WI 54480 (☎715/345-0505 or ☎1-800-826-1300), or *Access America International*, 600 Third Ave, New York, NY 10163 (☎212/949-5960 or ☎1-800-284-8300).

HEALTH PROBLEMS

Although Thailand's climate, wildlife and cuisine don't present Western travellers with as many health problems as many Asian destinations, it's as well to know in advance what the risks might be, and what preventive or curative measures you might take should some ailment strike.

INOCULATIONS

There are no **inoculation** requirements for Thailand, but it makes sense to ensure your polio and tetanus boosters are up to date (they last ten years); most doctors also advise vaccinations against typhoid and hepatitis A and, if you're intending to travel in rural areas, they might recommend protecting yourself against Japanese B encephalitis and rabies. If you do decide to have several injections, plan your course about four weeks in advance, as some combinations wipe each other out if given simultaneously and others come in two parts; the hepatitis serum lasts only three to six months, becoming less effective day by day and so should be taken as close to departure as possible.

In **North America** there's no way of reducing the prices charged by your local medical practitioner for inoculations, but in the **UK** the cheapest way of **getting immunised** is to buy the vaccines on prescription and have them administered for free by your doctor or health centre nurse. In England, you also have the option of going to a specialist travel clinic: these work out expensive at between £6 and £25 a shot, but have the advantage of being staffed by tropical disease specialists who should be clued up on very localised requirements. You don't need an appointment to attend the main *British Airways Travel Clinic* at 156 Regent St, London (☎071/439 9584), where patients are seen Mon–Fri 9am–4.15pm and Sat 10am–4pm; *BA* also have other clinics around the country (call ☎071/831 5333 for advice on your nearest). Alternatively, the Hospital for Tropical Diseases runs a clinic Mon–Fri 9am–5pm at 180–182 Tottenham Court Rd, London (☎071/637 9899); they also provide a recorded message on up-to-date immunisation and health advice in tropical countries on ☎0839/337722 – the code for Thailand on this message is 77.

MALARIA

Thailand is **malarial**, and general medical opinion holds that you'll need to take prophylactics if you plan to go anywhere in the country other than Bangkok, Phuket, Pattaya and Chiang Mai. Certain strains of malaria-bearing mosquitoes are, however, resistant to these drugs, and some doctors in Thailand believe that being tanked up on preventive medicines reduces the efficacy of their cures. Nevertheless, most travellers prefer to take the precautions, and **malaria prophylactics** can be bought without a prescription from all pharmacists. Start taking the pills a week before you enter a malarial zone, and continue the course for four weeks after you leave it; to reduce the side-effects of nausea and diarrhoea, take them at night.

Given the less than watertight reputation of preventive medicine, you should do your very best not to get bitten. Malarial mosquitoes are active from dusk until dawn and during this time you

should smother yourself and your clothes in **mosquito repellent**, reapplying regularly: shops, guest houses and department stores all over Thailand stock the stuff, so there's no need to take it over with you. At night you should either sleep under a **mosquito net** or in a room with screens across the windows. Accommodation in the most touristed spots usually provides screens or a net, but it's probably worth investing in your own net just in case – wait until you get to Bangkok to buy one, where they cost about an eighth of what you'd pay in the West. Mosquito coils – also widely available in Thailand – also help keep the insects at bay. The first **signs of malaria** are remarkably similar to flu: if you suspect anything go to a hospital or clinic immediately.

POISONOUS CUTS, BITES AND STINGS

Wearing protective clothing is a good idea when **swimming, snorkelling or diving**: a t-shirt will stop you from getting sunburnt in the water, while long trousers can guard against **coral grazes**. Should you scrape your skin on coral, wash the wound thoroughly with boiled water, apply antiseptic and keep protected until healed. Thailand's seas are home to a few dangerous creatures of which you should be wary, principally **jellyfish**, **poisonous sea snakes**, **sea urchins** and a couple of less conspicuous species – **sting rays**, which often lie buried in the sand, and **stone fish**, whose potentially lethal venomous spikes are easily stepped on because the fish look like stones and lie motionless on the sea bed.

If **stung or bitten** you should always seek medical advice as soon as possible, but there are a few ways of alleviating pain or administering your own first-aid in the meantime. If stung by a **jellyfish** the priority treatment is to remove the fragments of tentacles from the skin – without causing further discharge of poison – which is easiest done by applying vinegar to deactivate the stinging capsules. In the case of a poisonous **snake bite**, immobilise the limb and stay calm until medical help arrives: don't try sucking out the poison or applying a tourniquet. The best way to minimise the risk of stepping on the **toxic spines** of sea urchins, sting rays and stone fish is to wear thick-soled shoes, though these cannot provide total protection; sea urchin spikes should be removed after softening the skin with a special ointment, though some people recommend applying urine to help dissolve the spines;

for sting ray and stone fish stings, alleviate the pain by immersing the wound in very hot water – just under 50°C – while waiting for help.

DIGESTIVE PROBLEMS

By far the most common travellers' complaint in Thailand, **digestive troubles** are often caused by contaminated food and water, or sometimes just by an overdose of unfamiliar foodstuffs. Break your system in gently by avoiding excessively spicy curries and too much raw fruit in the first few days, and then use your common sense about choosing where and what to eat: if you stick to the most crowded restaurants and noodle stalls you should be perfectly safe. Furthermore, because most Thai dishes can be cooked in under five minutes, you'll rarely have to contend with stuff that's been left to smoulder and stew. You need to be a bit more rigorous about drinking the water, though: stick to bottled water, which is sold everywhere, or else opt for boiled water or tea.

Stomach trouble usually manifests itself as simple **diarrhoea**, which should clear up without medical treatment within three to seven days and is best combatted by drinking lots of fluids. If this doesn't work, you're in danger of getting **dehydrated** and should take some kind of rehydration solution, either a commercial sachet sold in all Thai pharmacies or a do-it-yourself version which can be made by adding a handful of sugar and a pinch of salt to every litre of boiled or bottled water (soft drinks are *not* a viable alternative). If diarrhoea persists for more than ten days, or if you have blood or mucus in your stools, you may have contracted bacillary or amoebic **dysentery**, in which case go to a doctor or hospital.

HEAT PROBLEMS

Aside from the obvious considerations about restricting your exposure to the searing midday sun, using high protection-factor sun creams, and protecting your eyes with dark glasses and your head with a hat, you should avoid **dehydration** by drinking plenty of water and occasionally adding a pinch of salt to fruit shakes. To prevent and alleviate heat rashes, prickly heat and fungal infections it's a good idea to use a mild antiseptic soap and to dust yourself with prickly heat talcum powder, both of which are sold cheaply in all Thai stores.

AIDS

Aids is spreading fast in Thailand, primarily because of the widespread sex trade. Condoms (*mechai*) substantially lower the risk of HIV infection through sexual contact, and are sold in pharmacists, department stores, hairdressers, even on street markets. Should you need to have a hypodermic injection at a hospital, try to check that the needle has been sterilised first; this is not always practicable, however, so you might consider carrying your own syringes. Don't even consider getting yourself tattooed in Thailand.

GETTING AROUND

Travel in Thailand is both cheap and efficient, if not exactly speedy. For long-distance travel between major towns you nearly always have the choice of a variety of buses, and in some cases a train or plane as well. Local transport comes in all sorts of permutations, both public and chartered, with relatively little to choose in terms of cost.

INTER-TOWN BUSES AND SONGTHAEWS

Buses, overall the fastest way of getting around the country, come in two categories: **ordinary** (*rot thammada*) and **air-conditioned** (*rot air*), with an additional air-con subsection known as **tour buses** (*rot tua*). The ordinary and air-con buses are run by *Baw Kaw Saw*, the government transport company, whereas the misleadingly named tour buses are privately owned and ply the most popular long-distance routes, with no tours involved.

The orange-coloured **ordinary buses** are incredibly cheap and cover most short-range routes between main towns (up to 150km) very frequently. Each bus is staffed by a team of two or three – the driver, the fare collector and the optional "stop" and "go" yeller – who often personalise the vehicle with stereo systems, stickers, jasmine garlands and the requisite Buddha image or amulet. With an entertaining team and eye-catching scenery, journeys can be fun, but there are drawbacks. For a start, teams work on a commission basis, so they pack as many people in as possible and might hang around for thirty minutes in the hope of cramming in a few extra. They also stop so often that their average speed of 60kmh can only be achieved by hurtling along at breakneck speeds between pick-ups, often propelled by amphetamine-induced craziness.

Air-conditioned buses stop a lot less often (if at all) and cover the distances faster and more comfortably: passengers are allotted specific seats and on long journeys get blankets, snacks and non-stop videos. On the downside, they cost almost twice as much (though that's still a paltry amount), depart less frequently, and don't cover nearly as many routes – and make sure you have some warm clothes if travelling air-con, as temperatures can get chilly, even with the blanket.

In a lot of cases **tour buses** are indistinguishable from air-cons, operating the busiest routes at similar prices and with comparable facilities. However, some tour buses – such as *VIP* – do offer a distinctly better service, with reclining seats and plenty of leg room. They do cost more than air-cons, but are worth every baht for mammoth journeys like Bangkok–Krabi.

Tickets for all buses can be bought from the departure terminals, but for ordinary buses it's normal to buy them on board. Air-con buses often operate from a separate station, and tickets for the more popular routes should be booked a day in advance. As a rough indication of **prices**, a trip from Bangkok to Chiang Mai should cost around B135 by ordinary bus, B242 by air-con and B370 by tour bus.

For a rough idea of frequency and duration of bus services between towns, check the **travel details** at the end of each chapter. **Timetables** do exist but are often ignored: for medium-length distances (150–300km) you can almost always turn up at a bus terminal and guarantee to be on your way within two hours. Long-distance buses often depart in clusters around the same time (early morning or late at night for example), leaving five or more hours during the day with no service at all.

SONGTHAEWS

In rural areas, the bus network is supplemented – or even substantially replaced – by **songthaews** (literally "two rows"), which are open-ended vans, or occasionally cattle-trucks, onto which the drivers squash as many passengers as possible on to two facing benches, leaving latecomers to swing off the running board at the back. (In the deep south they do things with a little more style – the longer-distance songthaews there are known as **share taxis**, and are usually clapped-out old limousines cars.) Songthaews ply set routes both within larger towns and out to the surrounding towns and villages: some have destinations written on in Thai, but few are numbered. In most towns you'll find the songthaew "terminal" near the market; to pick one up between destinations just flag it down, and to indicate to the driver that you want to get out, the normal practice is to rap hard with a coin on the metal railings as you approach the spot.

As a general rule, the cost of inter-town songthaews is comparable to that of air-con buses.

TRAINS

Although usually slower than buses, **trains** are safer and offer the possibility of sleeping during overnight trips; moreover, if travelling by day you're likely to follow a more scenic route by rail than by road.

Managed by the *State Railway of Thailand* (SRT), the rail network consists of four main lines and a few branch lines. The **Northern Line** connects Bangkok with Chiang Mai via Ayutthaya and Phitsanulok. The **Northeastern Line** splits into two just beyond Ayutthaya, the lower branch running eastwards to Ubon Ratchathani via Khorat and Surin, the more northerly branch linking the capital with Nong Khai via Khon Kaen and Udon Thani. You should have no reason to use the **Eastern Line**, which mainly ferries Cambodian refugees and refugee workers from Bangkok to the troubled border town of Aranyaprathet. The **Southern Line** extends to Hat Yai, close to the Malaysian border, where it branches to continue down the east coast of Malaysia via Sungai Kolok or down the west coast via Butterworth and Kuala Lumpur, before merging again to enter Singapore. At Nakhon Pathom a branch of this line veers off to Nam Tok via Kanchanaburi – this is all that's left of the Death Railway, of *Bridge Over the River Kwai* notoriety.

Fares depend on the class of seat, whether or not you want air conditioning, and on the speed of the train. Hard wooden **third-class** seats cost about the same as an ordinary bus (Bangkok–Chiang Mai B121), and are fine for about three hours, after which numbness sets in. For longer journeys you'd be wise to opt for the padded and often reclining seats in **second class** (Bangkok–Chiang Mai B255). On long-distance trains, you also usually have the option of **second-class berths** (for an extra B70, or B170 with air conditioning), with day seats that convert into comfortable curtained-off bunks in the evening. Travelling **first class** (Bangkok–Chiang Mai B537) means you automatically get a private one- or two-person air-conditioned compartment (add on B250–350 per person for a sleeping berth, complete with washbasin). All long-distance trains have **dining cars**, and rail staff will also bring meals to your compartment. Tourist menus are written in English but have inflated prices – ask for the similar but cheaper "ordinary" version, the *menu thammada*.

The speed supplements are as follows: Special Express (B50 extra), Express (B30), and Rapid (B20). The rare Special Diesel Railcars, whose speed is somewhere between Special Express and Express, operate on fares midway between those two categories.

Advance booking of at least one day is essential for second-class and first-class seats on all lengthy journeys, and for sleepers needs to be done as far in advance as possible. Unfortunately, with the exceptions of Ayutthaya and Surat Thani, you can reserve seats and berths only at the terminus – in other words, at Bangkok, Chiang Mai, Ubon Ratchathani, Udon Thani and Hat Yai – which makes it a pain trying to get anything other than a third-class seat from midway down the line. For details on how to book trains out of Bangkok, see p.106.

The SRT publishes two clear and fairly accurate free **timetables** in English, one for the North, Northeastern and Eastern lines and another for the South and Kanchanaburi lines. These detail types of trains and classes available on each route as well as fares and supplementary charges; the best place to get hold of them is over the counter at Bangkok's Hualamphong Station or, if you're lucky, the TAT office in Bangkok. The information desk at Hualamphong also stocks more detailed local timetables covering the Bangkok–Lopburi route via Don Muang airport and Ayutthaya.

FERRIES

Regular **ferries** connect all major islands with the mainland, and for the vast majority of crossings you simply buy your ticket on board. In tourist areas competition ensures that prices are kept low, and fares tend to vary with the speed of the crossing: thus Surat Thani–Ko Samui costs B95 if you do it in 2hr 30min or B40 for the six-hour crossing, while the two-hour Krabi–Ko Phi Phi route costs B95. Boats generally operate a reduced service during the monsoon season – from May through September along the east coast and Andaman coast and from November through April on the Gulf coast – while the more remote spots become inaccessible in these periods. Details on island connections are given in the relevant chapters.

FLIGHTS

The domestic arm of *Thai Airways* dominates the **internal flight** network, which extends to all extremities of the country, using a total of twenty-three airports. *Bangkok Airways* plies two additional routes. It's unlikely that you'll be tempted by the 65-minute Bangkok–Chiang Mai flight, which costs B1650 one-way, but in some instances a flight can save you days of travelling: the flight from Ubon Ratchathani to Surat Thani (B3000), for example, takes just over two hours, as against a couple of days by meandering train.

All towns served by an airport have at least one *Thai Airways* **booking** office; flights get booked a long way ahead, so reserve early if possible – but bear in mind it's far cheaper to book in Thailand than from abroad. Flight durations and frequencies are listed at the end of each chapter.

LOCAL TRANSPORT

In the midday heat, spending twenty-odd baht on local transport can be an awful lot more appealing than sweating it out on foot. In most sizeable towns you have two broad options – **fixed-route** or **chartered** transport. The former, such as buses, songthaews or even longtail boats, have set fares and routes, but not rigid timetabling: in most cases vehicles leave when they're full and run about every 10–20 minutes. Chartered transport – tuk-tuk, samlor, motorcycle, taxi or boat – is generally more expensive, but the increased cost is often so slight as to be completely offset by the added convenience. Whenever you charter a vehicle, always establish the **fare** beforehand: although drivers nearly always pitch their first offers too high, they do calculate with traffic and time of day in mind, as well as according to distance – if successive drivers scoff at your price, you know you've got it wrong.

BUSES AND SONGTHAEWS

Larger cities like Bangkok, Chiang Mai and Khorat have a **local bus** network which usually extends to the suburbs and operates from dawn till dusk (through the night in Bangkok); most are numbered in Arab numerals, and you pay the conductor B2–7 depending on your destination. As with inter-town routes, the more remote the area the greater is the role played by **songthaews** in the local transport stystem. Fares within towns range between B5 and B20, depending on distance.

TUK-TUKS AND SAMLORS

Named after the noise of its excrutiatingly unsilenced engine, the three-wheeled open-sided **tuk-tuk** is the classic Thai vehicle. Painted in primary colours, tuk-tuks blast their way round towns and cities on two-stoke engines, zipping around faster than any car, and taking corners on two wheels. They aren't as dangerous as they look, and can be an exhilarating way to get around, as long as you're not too fussy about exhaust fumes. They're also cheap: fares start at B10 (B20 in Bangkok) regardless of the number of passengers – three is the safe maximum, though six is not uncommon.

Tuk-tuks are also sometimes known as samlors (literally "three wheels"), but the real **samlors** are tricycle rickshaws propelled by pedal-power alone. Slower and a great deal more stately than tuk-tuks, samlors operate pretty much everywhere except in Bangkok. Forget any qualms you may have about being pedalled around by another human being: samlor drivers' livelihoods depend on a constant supply of passengers, so your most ethical option is to hop on and not scrimp on the fare. Drivers usually charge a minimum B10 fee and add B10 per kilometre, possibly more for a heavy load.

TAXIS

Even faster and more precarious than tuk-tuks, **motorbike taxis** feature both in big towns and out-of-the-way places. In towns – where the drivers are identified by coloured, numbered vests –

they have the advantage of being able to dodge traffic jams, but obviously they are only really suitable for the single traveller, and they aren't the easiest mode of transport if you're carrying luggage. In remote spots on the other hand, motorbike taxis are often the only alternative to hitching or walking and are especially useful for getting between bus stops on main roads and to national parks or ancient ruins. Within towns motorbike taxi fares are comparable to those for tuk-tuks, but for trips to the outskirts the cost rises steeply – about B80–100 for a twenty-kilometre round-trip. **Car taxis** are generally available only in the biggest towns, and charge fares that begin at around B40. In theory, some offer the benefit of air conditioning, but clapped-out air-con systems are probably more numerous than functioning ones.

LONGTAIL BOATS

Wherever there's a decent public waterway, there'll be a **longtail boat** ready to ferry you along it. Another great Thai trademark, these elegant streamlined boats are powered by deafening diesel engines – sometimes custom-built, more often adapted from cars or trucks – which drive a propeller mounted on a long shaft that is swivelled for steering. Longtails carry from ten to twenty passengers: in Bangkok most follow fixed routes, but elsewhere most are for hire at about B100 an hour per boat, more in tourist spots.

VEHICLE RENTAL

Take an look at the general standard of driving (dangerously reckless) and state of the roads (poor) before deciding to **rent a car or motorbike**, and then take time to get used to the more eccentric conventions. Of these, perhaps the most notable is the fact that a major road doesn't necessarily have right of way over a minor, but that the bigger vehicle *always* has right of way. Few vehicle owners stick to the roadside, preferring to hog the whole route by careering up the centre, and when it comes to lanes, speed distinctions are rarely adhered to. Also remember that most driving licences in Thailand are bought over the counter, so the general level of competence cannot be underestimated. The published **rules of the road** state that everyone drives on the left (which they do) and that they should keep to the speed limit of 60kmh within built-up areas and 80kmh outside them (which they don't).

Theoretically, foreigners need an international driver's licence to hire any kind of vehicle, but some companies accept national licences, and the smaller operations (especially bike rentals) may not ask for any kind of proof at all. **Petrol** (*nam man*, which also means oil) costs about B12–15 a litre; the big stations are the cheapest places, but most small villages have roadside huts where the fuel is pumped out of a large barrel.

CARS

If you decide to rent a car, go to a reputable dealer, preferably a *Hertz* or *Avis* branch or a rental company recommended by TAT, and make sure you get insurance from them. Prices for a small car range from B800 to B1200 per day, depending on the quality, which is generally not bad. If appropriate, consider the safer option of hiring a driver along with the car, which you can often do for the same price on day rentals. **Jeeps** are a lot more popular with farangs, especially on beach resorts and islands like Pattaya, Ko Phuket and Ko Samui, but they're no less dangerous; a huge number of tourists manage to roll their jeeps on steep hillsides and sharp bends. Jeep rental also works out somewhere between B800 and B1200. For all cars, the renters will often ask for a deposit of at least B2000, and will always want to hold onto your passport; you could offer an airline ticket if you're not happy about this.

MOTORBIKES

One of the best ways of exploring the countryside is to hire a **motorbike**, an especially popular option in the north of the country. Two-seater **80cc** bikes with automatic gears are best if you've never ridden a motorbike before, but aren't really suited for long slogs. If you're going to hit the dirt roads you'll certainly need something more powerful, like an **MTX 125** trail bike, though an inexperienced rider may find these machines a handful. The MTX 125 has the edge in gear choice and is the best bike for steep slopes, but the less widely available **Wing 125**s are easier to control and much cheaper on petrol.

Rental prices for the day usually work out at somewhere between B120 (for a fairly beat-up 80cc) and B250 (for a good MTX), though you can bargain for a discount on a long rental. As with cars, the renters will often ask for a deposit and a document as ransom. Insurance is not often available, so it's a good idea to make sure your travel insurance covers you for possible mishaps.

Before signing anything, **check the bike** thoroughly and preferably take it for a test run. Test the brakes, look for oil leaks, check the treads and the odometer, and make sure the chain isn't stretched too tight – a tight chain is likelier to break. As you will have to pay an inflated price for any damage when you get back, make a note on the contract of any defects such as broken mirrors, indicators and so on. Make sure you know what kind of petrol the bike takes as well.

As far as **equipment** goes, a helmet is essential – most rental places provide poorly made ones, but they're better than nothing. You'll need sunglasses if your helmet doesn't have a visor. Long trousers, a long-sleeved top and shoes, as well as being more culturally appropriate, will provide a second skin if you go over, which most people do at some stage. For the sake of stability, leave most of your luggage in baggage storage and pack as small a bag as possible, strapping it tightly to the bike with bungee cords – these are usually provided. Once on the road, **oil the chain** at least every other day, keep the **radiator** topped up, and fill up with oil every 300km or so.

BICYCLE

The safest and pleasantest way of conveying yourself around many towns and rural areas is by **bicycle**, except of course in Bangkok. You won't find bike rentals everywhere, but a lot of guest houses keep a few, and in certain bike-friendly tourist spots, like Kanchanaburi, Chiang Mai and Sukhothai, you'll find larger-scale rental places. They should charge around B20 a day. Mountain-biking doesn't seem to have hit Thailand in a big way yet, but there are a sprinkling of rental outlets in Chiang Mai and Chiang Rai, where the average fee is B60 per day.

HITCHING

Public transport being so cheap, you should only have to resort to **hitching** in the most remote areas, in which case you'll probably get a lift to the nearest bus or songthaew stop quite quickly. On routes served by buses and trains hitching is not standard practice, but in other places locals do rely on regular passers-by (such as national park officials), and as a farang you can make use of this "service" too. As with hitching anywhere in the world, think twice about hitching solo, especially if you're female. Truck drivers are notorious users of amphetamines (as are a lot of bus drivers), so you may want to wait for a better offer.

ACCOMMODATION

Accommodation is incredibly inexpensive all over Thailand: for the simplest double room prices start at around B80 in the outlying regions and B120 in Bangkok, rising to B250 in some resorts. Tourist centres invariably offer a huge range of more upmarket choices, and you'll have little problem finding luxury hotels of international standard in these places. Whatever the establishment, staff expect you to look at the room before taking it; in the cheaper ones especially, check for cockroaches and mosquitoes, and if you don't have your own mosquito net with you, make sure it's equipped with either a net or screens. In most resort areas rates fluctuate according to demand, rising at weekends throughout the year and plummeting during the off-season. Unless otherwise specified, rates quoted in this book are high season prices (Nov–Feb & July–Aug). In some towns, tuk-tuk and samlor drivers get a commission for bringing in customers and the extra baht will get slapped on your bill; to avoid this, either walk or make it clear to hotel or guest house staff that you asked to be brought there.

Showers and flush toilets are the norm only in moderately priced and expensive hotels: in the less touristed and budget places you'll be "showering" with a bowl dipped into a large water jar and using squat toilets.

GUEST HOUSES AND HOSTELS

Any place calling itself a **guest house** – which could be anything from a bamboo hut to a three-storey concrete block – is almost certain to provide cheap, basic accommodation specifically aimed at Western travellers and priced at around

B100–150 for a sparse double room with a fan and (usually shared) bathroom. You'll find them in all major tourist centres (in their dozens in Bangkok and Chiang Mai), on beaches, where they're also called **bungalows**, and even in the most unlikely backcountry spots.

In the main towns they tend to be concentrated in cheek-by-jowl farang ghettos, but even if you baulk at the world travellers' scene that often characterises these places, guest houses make great places to stay, with attached cafeterias and clued-up English-speaking staff. These days, they're providing more and more services and **facilities**, such as safes for valuables, baggage-keeps, travel and tour operator desks and their own poste restantes. Staying at one out in the sticks, you'll often get involved in local life a lot more than if you were encased in a hotel.

At the vast majority of guest houses check-out time is noon, which means that during high season you should arrive to check in at about 11.30am to ensure you get a room: few places will draw up a "waiting list" and they rarely take advance bookings unless they know you already.

Upmarket guest house is almost a contradiction in terms, but there are a few that charge between B300 and B800 for facilities that may include air conditioning, bathroom, TV and use of a swimming pool. Beware of pricey guest houses or bungalows in mega-resorts like Pattaya and Phuket, however, which often turn out to be low-quality fan-cooled establishments making a killing out of unsuspecting holidaymakers.

With fewer than ten officially registered **youth hostels** in the whole country, it's not worth becoming a YHA member just for your trip to Thailand, especially as card-holders get only about B20 discount anyway. In general, youth hostel prices work out the same as guest house rates and rooms are open to all ages, whether members or not.

CHEAP HOTELS

Few Thais use guest houses, opting instead for hotels offering rooms in the B80–B300 range. Beds in these places are large enough for a couple, and it's quite acceptable for two people to ask and pay for a single room (*hong diaw*). Usually run by Chinese-Thais, you'll find these three- or four-storey places in every sizeable town, often near the bus station. They're generally clean and usually come with attached bathroom, fan (or air conditioning) and boiled water, which makes them good value in terms of facilities. Unfortunately they also tend to be grim and unfriendly, staffed by brisk non-English speakers, and generally lacking in any communal seating or eating area, which makes them lonely places for single travellers. A number of cheap hotels also employ prostitutes, though as a farang you're unlikely to be offered this sideline, and may not even notice the goings-on anyway.

If the hotel's on a busy main road, as many of them are, try asking for a quiet room (*mii hong ngiap-kwaa mai?*). Advance bookings are accepted over the phone – if you can make yourself understood – but this is rarely necessary, as cheap hotels rarely fill up. The only time you may have difficulty finding a cheap hotel room is during Chinese New Year (a moveable three-day period in February), when many Chinese-run hotels close and the others get booked up fast.

MODERATE HOTELS

Moderate hotels – priced between B300 and B1000 – can sometimes work out good value, offering many of the trimmings of a top-end hotel (TV, fridge, air conditioning, pool), but none of the prestige. They're often the kind of places that once stood at the top of the range, but were downgraded when the multinational luxury class hotels hogged the poshest clientele. They make especially welcome alternatives to the cheap hotels in provincial capitals, but, like expensive guest houses, can turn out to be vastly overpriced in the resorts.

As with the cheap hotels, you're unlikely to have trouble finding a room on spec in one of these places, though advance bookings are accepted by phone. Bed size varies a lot more than in the Chinese-run places, though, with some making the strict Western distinction between singles and doubles.

UPMARKET HOTELS

Many of Thailand's **upmarket hotels** belong to international chains like *Hilton, Holiday Inn, Le Meridien* and *Sheraton*, maintaining top-quality standards in Bangkok and major resorts at prices of B2500 and upward for a double – rates far lower than you'd pay for such luxury accommodation in the West. Some of the best home-grown upmarket hotels are up to B1000 cheaper for

equally fine service, rooms equipped with TV, minibar and balcony, and full use of the hotel sports' facilities and swimming pools. Then of course, there's the *Oriental*, Bangkok's palatial riverside hotel which is ranked among the best ten hotels in the world and has rooms from B5300 – nothing short of an outright bargain. Prices quoted in this book don't include the 11 percent government tax and 10 percent service tax levied by all top hotels. All upmarket hotels can be booked in advance, an advisable measure in Chiang Mai, Phuket or Pattaya during peak season .

NATIONAL PARKS AND CAMPING

Unattractive accommodation is one of the big disappointments of Thailand's **national parks**. Generally built to a standard two-roomed format, these dismal concrete huts feature in 43 of the country's 60 parks, and cost an average B500 for four or more beds plus a probably malfunctioning shower. Because most of their custom comes from Thai family groups, park officials rarely discount these huts for lone travellers, even if you only use one bed, rendering them poor value for most farang visitors. In most parks, advance booking is unnecessary except on weekends and national holidays; if you do want to pre-book then either pay on the spot at the Forestry Department offices near Kasetsart University on Phaholyothin Road in Bangkok's Chatuchak district (☎02/579 0529) – which can be quite a palaver, so don't plan on doing anything else that day – or book on the phone, then send a baht money order and wait for confirmation. If you turn up without booking, check in at the park headquarters – which is usually adjacent to the visitors' centre.

In a few parks, private operators have set up low-cost guest houses on the outskirts and these make much more attractive and economical places to stay. Failing that, you can usually **camp** in a national park for a minimal fee of around B5, and some national parks also rent out tents at about B60. Unless you're planning an extensive tour of national parks though, there's little point in lugging a tent around Thailand: accommodation everywhere else is too cheap to make camping a necessity, and anyway there are no campgrounds inside town perimeters. Few travellers bother to bring tents for beaches either, opting for cheap bungalow accommodation or simply sleeping out under the stars. But camping is allowed on nearly all islands and beaches, many of which are national parks in their own right.

FOOD AND DRINK

Bangkok and Chiang Mai are the country's big culinary centres, boasting the cream of gourmet Thai restaurants and the best international cuisines. The rest of the country is by no means a culinary wasteland, however, and you can eat well and cheaply even in the smallest provincial towns, many of which offer the additional attraction of regional specialities. In fact you could eat more than adequately without ever entering a restaurant, as itinerant food vendors hawking hot and cold snacks materialise in even the most remote spots, as well as on trains and buses, and night markets serve customers from dusk until dawn.

Hygiene is a consideration when eating anywhere in Thailand, but being too cautious means you'll end up spending a lot of money and missing out on some real local treats. Wean your stomach gently by avoiding excessive amounts of chillies and too much fresh fruit in the first few days and by always drinking either bottled or boiled water.

You can be pretty sure that any noodle stall or curry shop that's permanently packed with customers is a safe bet, but if you're really concerned about health standards you could stick to restaurants displaying the TAT-approved symbol (also used for shops) which shows a woman seated between two panniers beneath the TAT logo. The *Thai Shell: Good Food Guide* also endorses a huge range of eating places: look for signs showing a rice bowl symbol with red, black or blue lettering underneath it.

WHERE TO EAT

Despite their obvious attractions, a lot of tourists eschew the huge range of Thai places to eat and opt instead for the much "safer" restaurants in **guest houses and hotels**. Almost all tourist accommodation has a kitchen, and while some are excellent, the vast majority serve up bland imitations of Western fare alongside equally pale versions of common Thai dishes. Having said that, it can be a relief to get your teeth into a processed cheese sandwich after five days' trekking in the jungle, and guest houses do serve comfortingly familiar Western breakfasts – most farangs quickly tire of eating rice three times a day.

Throughout the country most **cheap Thai restaurants and cafés** specialise in one general food type or preparation method – a "noodle shop" for example will do fried noodles and noodle soups, plus a basic fried rice, but they won't have curries, meat or fish dishes. Similarly, a restaurant displaying whole roast chickens and ducks in its window will offer these sliced or with chillis and sauces and served over rice, but their menu probably won't extend to noodles or fish, while in "curry shops" your options are limited to the vats of curries stewing away in the hot cabinet.

To get a choice of low-cost food, it's sometimes best to head for the wider array at the local **night market**, a term for the gatherings of open-air night-time kitchens found in every town. Operating from about 6pm to 6am, they are to be found on permanent patches close to the fruit and vegetable market or the bus station, and as often as not they're the best and most entertaining places to eat, not to mention the cheapest – after a lip-smacking feast of two savoury dishes, a fruit drink and a sweet you'll come away no more than B50 the poorer.

A typical night market has some thirty-odd "specialist" pushcart kitchens jumbled together, each fronted by several sets of tables and stools. Noodle and fried rice vendors always feature prominently, as do sweets stalls, heaped high with sticky rice cakes wrapped in banana leaves or thick with bags of tiny sweetcorn pancakes hot from the griddle – and no night market is complete without its fruit drink stall, offering banana shakes and freshly squeezed orange, lemon and tomato juices. In the best setups you'll find a lot more besides: curries, barbecued sweetcorn, fresh pineapple, watermelon and mango, and – if the town's by a river or near the sea, heaps of fresh fish. Having decided what you want, you order from the cook or the cook's dogsbody and sit down at the nearest table; there's no territorialism about night markets, so it's normal to eat several dishes from separate stalls and rely on the nearest cook to sort out the bill.

For a more relaxing ambience, Bangkok and Chiang Mai both have a range of gourmet restaurants specialising in **"royal"** Thai cuisine, which differs from standard fare mainly in the quality of the ingredients and the way the food is presented. As with the nouvelle cuisine of the West, great care is taken over how individual dishes look: they are served in small portions and decorated with carved fruit and vegetables in a way that used to be the prerogative of royal cooks, but has now filtered down to the common folk. The cost of such delights is not prohibitive, though – a meal in one of these places is unlikely to cost more than B500.

WHAT TO EAT

The repertoire of noodles, stir-fries, curries and rice dishes listed below is pretty much standard throughout Thailand. When you get out into the provinces, you'll have the chance to sample a few specialities as well, which have evolved either from the cuisines of neighbouring countries or from the crops best suited to that area. Bland food is anathema to Thais and restaurant tables everywhere come decked out with a condiment set featuring the four basic flavours: chopped chillis in watery fish sauce, chopped chillies in vinegar, sugar, and ground red pepper – and often extra bowls of ground peanuts and a bottle of chilli ketchup as well.

NOODLE AND RICE DISHES

Thais eat **noodles** (*kwetiaw* or *bamii*) when Westerners would dig into a sandwich – for lunch, as a late-night snack or just to pass the time – and at B10–15 they're the cheapest hot meal you'll find anywhere, whether bought from an itinerant street vendor or ordered in an air-conditioned restaurant. They come in assorted varieties (wide and flat, thin and transparent, made with eggs, soy-bean flour or rice flour) and get boiled up as soups (*kwetiaw nam*), doused in sauces (*kwetiaw rat na*), or stir-fried (*kwetiaw*

haeng or *kwetiaw pat*). All three versions include a smattering of vegetables, eggs and meat, but the usual practice is to order the dish with extra chicken, beef, pork or shrimps. Most popular of noodle dishes is **kwetiaw pat thai** (usually abbreviated to *pat thai*), a delicious combination of fried noodles, beansprouts, egg and tofu, sprinkled with ground peanuts and the juice of half a lime, and occasionally spiked with tiny shrimps.

Fried rice (*khao pat*) is the other faithful standby, guaranteed to feature on menus right across the country. Curries that come served on a bed of rice are more like stews, prepared long in advance and eaten more as a light meal than a main one; they are usually called *khao na* plus the meat of the chosen dish – thus *khao na pet* is duck curry served over rice.

CURRIES, STIR-FRIES, FISH AND SOUPS

Thai **curries** (*kaeng*) are based on coconut milk – which gives them a slightly sweet taste and a soup-like consistency – and get their fire from chilli peppers. The best curries are characterised by a subtle blend of freshly ground herbs and spices, but only the most practised palate can discern these beneath the mouth-blasting fire of the chillies. It's often possible to request one that's "not too hot" (*mai phet*); if you do bite into a chilli, the way to combat the searing heat is to take a mouthful of plain rice – swigging water just exacerbates the sensation.

Stir-fries tend to be a lot milder, often flavoured with ginger and whole cloves of garlic and featuring a pleasing combination of soft meat and crunchy vegetables or nuts. Chicken with cashew nuts (*kai pat met mamuang*) is a favourite of a lot of farang-oriented places as is sweet and sour chicken, pork or fish (*kai/muu/plaa priaw waan*). *Pat phak bung* – slightly bitter morning glory leaves fried with garlic in a black-bean sauce – makes a good vegetable side dish with any of these.

All seaside and most riverside restaurants rightly make a big deal out of locally caught **fish and seafood**. If you order fish it will be served whole, either steamed or grilled with ginger or chillies. Mussels often get stuffed into a viscous batter mixture and shrimps turn up in everything from soups to fried noodles.

You can't make a meal out of a Thai **soup** (*tom yam*), but it is an essential component in any shared meal, eaten simultaneously with other dishes, not as a starter. Watery and broth-like, soups are always flavoured with the distinctive tang of lemon grass and can be extremely hot if the cook adds liberal handfuls of chillis to the pot. It's best eaten in small slurps between mouthfuls of rice.

FRUIT AND SWEETS

The best way to round off a meal is with **fresh fruit** (*phonlamai*), as the country's orchards heave with an amazing variety, from papayas, mangoes, pineapples and watermelons to seventeen different types of banana, hairy red rambutans and the notoriously stinky durian. Restaurants often serve mixed platefuls of fresh fruit, while ready peeled and cut segments are sold on the street to be taken away in bags and eaten with a toothpick.

Sweets don't really figure on most restaurant menus, but a few places offer bowls of *luuk taan cheum*, a jellied concoction of lotus or palm seeds floating in a syrup scented with jasmine or other aromatic flowers. **Cakes** (*khanom*) are sold on the street and tend to be heavy sticky affairs made from glutinous rice and coconut cream pressed into squares and wrapped in banana leaves.

REGIONAL DISHES

Many of the specialities of the **north** originated over the border in Burma; one such is *khao soi*, now known as Chiang Mai noodles, in which egg noodles fried with beef or chicken are served under a thick coconut sauce. Also popular around Chiang Mai are thick spicey sausages (*Chiang Mai nam*) made from minced pork, rice and garlic left to cure for a few days and then eaten raw with spicy salad. Somewhat more palatable is the local curry *kaeng haeng lay* made from pork, ginger, coconut and tamarind.

The crop most suited to the infertile lands of **Isaan** is **sticky rice** (*khao niaw*), which replaces the standard grain as the staple diet for north-easterners. Served in its own special rattan "sticky rice basket" (the Isaan equivalent of the Tupperware lunchbox), it's usually eaten with the fingers, rolled up into small balls and dipped into chilli sauces and side dishes such as the local dish *somtam*, a spicey green-papaya salad. Although you'll find basted barbecued **chicken** on a stick (*kai yang*) all over Thailand, it originated in Isaan and it's even tastier in its home region. As with Chiang Mai, Isaan produces its own **sausages**, called *sai krog Isaan*, made from spiced and diced raw pork. Raw minced pork is

also the basis of another popular Isaan and northern dish called *larb*, when it is subtly flavoured with mint and served with vegetables.

Aside from putting a greater emphasis on seafood, **southern** Thai cuisine displays a marked Malaysian and Muslim aspect as you near the border. Satays feature more down here, but the two mainstays are the thick, rich but fairly mild Muslim **beef curry** (*kaeng matsaman*) and the **chicken curry** served over lightly spiced saffron rice, known as *kaeng Karii kai*. You'll find **rotis** in the south too – pancakes rolled with sickly sweet condensed milk and sugar and sold hot from pushcart griddles.

VEGETARIAN FOOD

Although very few Thais are **vegetarian,** it's rarely impossible to persuade cooks to rustle up a vegetable-only fried rice or noodle dish, though in more out-of-the-way places that's often your only option unless you eat fish – so you'll need to supplement your diet with the nuts, barbecued sweetcorn, fruit and other non-meaty goodies sold by food stalls. In tourist spots, vegetarians can happily splurge on specially concocted Thai and Western veggie dishes, and some restaurants will come up with a completely separate menu if requested. If you're **vegan** you'll need to stress that you don't want egg when you order, as eggs get used a lot; cheese and other dairy produce, however, don't feature at all in Thai cuisine.

DRINKS

Thais don't drink water straight from the tap, and nor should you: plastic bottles of drinking **water** (*nam plao*) are sold countrywide, even in the smallest villages, for about B10. Cheap restaurants and hotels generally serve free jugs of boiled water which should be fine to drink, though not as foolproof as the bottles.

Night markets, guest houses and restaurants do a good line in freshly-squeezed **fruit juices** such as lemon (*nam manao*) and orange (*nam som*), which come with salt and/or sugar if requested. The same places will usually do **fruit shakes** as well, blending bananas (*nam kluay*), papayas (*nam malakaw*), pineapples (*nam sapparot*) and others with liquid sugar or condensed milk (or yoghurt, to make *lassi*). Fresh **coconut milk** (*nam maprao*) is another great thirst-quencher – you buy the whole fruit dehusked, decapitated and chilled.

Bottled brand-name orange and lemon **soft drinks** are sold all over the place for B7–10 (on average a bit more expensive than fresh drinks), but only the big names like *Pepsi, Coca-Cola* and *Fanta* go by their names – the rest are known by the generic terms. Soft-drink bottles are returnable, so shops and drink stalls have an amazing system of pouring the contents into a small plastic bag (fastened with an elastic band and with a straw inserted) rather than charging you the extra for taking away the bottle. The larger restaurants keep their soft drinks refrigerated, but smaller cafés and shops add ice (*nam khaeng*) to glasses and bags. Most ice is produced commercially under hygienic conditions, but it might become less pure in transit so be wary in more remote places – and don't take ice if you have diarrhoea.

Weak Chinese **tea** (*nam chaa*) makes a refreshing alternative to water and often gets served in Chinese restaurants and roadside cafés. Posher restaurants keep stronger Chinese and western teas (*chaa*) and **coffee** (*kaafae*), which is mostly the local instant variety, blended with copious amounts of chicory.

Beer (*bia*) is one of the few consumer items in Thailand that's not a bargain – at B50–60 for a 355ml bottle it works out roughly the same as what you'd pay in the West. The two most popular beers are the slightly acrid locally-brewed *Singha*, and *Kloster*, which is brewed in Thailand under German licence and costs about B5–10 more than *Singha*, but is easier on the tongue. Some places also stock a lighter version of *Singha* called *Singha Gold* and another beer called *Amarit*, though that's not widely distributed.

At about B40–60 a 375ml bottle, the local **whisky** is a lot better value and Thais think nothing of consuming a bottle a night. The most palatable and widely available of these is *Mekhong*, which is very pleasant once you've stopped expecting it to taste like Scotch; distilled from rice, *Mekhong* is 35 percent proof , is deep gold in colour and tastes slightly sweet. Check the menu carefully when ordering a bottle of _Mekhong_ from a bar in a tourist area, as they often ask up to five times more than you'd pay in a guest house or shop

You can buy beer and whisky in food shops, guest houses and most restaurants at any time of the day; **bars** aren't really an indigenous feature as Thais rarely drink out without eating, but you'll find a fair number of western-style drinking holes in Bangkok and tourist centres elsewhere in the country.

A FOOD AND DRINK GLOSSARY

NOODLES (KWETIAW or BA MII)

Ba mii	Egg noodles	*Kwetiaw/ba mii rat na (muu)*	Rice noodles/egg noodles fried in gravy-like sauce with vegetables (and pork slices)
Kwetiaw (sen yai/ sen lek)	White rice noodles (wide/ thin)		
Ba mii krawp	Crisp fried egg noodles		
Kwetiaw/ba mii haeng	Rice noodles/egg noodles fried with egg, small pieces of meat and a few vegetables	*Pat thai*	Thin noodles fried with egg, beansprouts and tofu, topped with ground peanuts
Kwetiaw/ba mii nam (muu)	Rice noodle/egg noodle soup, made with chicken broth (and pork balls)	*Pat siyu*	Wide or thin noodles fried with soy sauce, egg and meat

RICE (KHAO) AND RICE DISHES (KHAO RAT NA)

Khao	Rice	*Khao niaw*	Sticky rice
Jok	Rice breakfast porridge	*Khao pat kai/muu/ kung/phak*	Fried rice with chicken/ pork/shrimp/vegetables
Khao man kai	Slices of chicken served over marinated rice	*Khao rat kaeng*	Curry over rice
Khao na kai/pet	Chicken/duck served with sauce over rice	*Khao tom*	Rice soup

STIR-FRIES, CURRIES (KAENG) AND SEAFOOD (AHAAN THALEH)

Hawy thawt	Omelette stuffed with mussels	*Pat phak bung*	Morning glory fried in garlic and bean sauce
Kaeng kai/nua/pet/ pladuk/som	Chicken/beef/duck/ catfish/fish and vegetable curry	*Pat phak lai yang*	Stir-fried vegetables
		Plaa (muu) priaw waan	Sweet and sour fish (pork)
Kai pat naw mai	Chicken with bamboo shoots	*Plaa neung pae sa*	Whole fish steamed with vegetables and ginger
Kai pat met mamuang	Chicken with cashew nuts		
Kai pat khing	Chicken with ginger	*Plaa rat phrik*	Whole fish cooked with chillies
Kung chup paeng thawt	Prawns fried in batter	*Plaa thawt*	Fried whole fish

FRUIT (PHONLAMAI)

Farang	Guava (year-round)	*Manao*	Lemon/lime (year-round)
Khanun	Jackfruit (year-round)	*Mangkut*	Mangosteen (April–Sept)
Kluay	Banana (year-round)	*Maprao*	Coconut (year-round)
Lamyai	Longan (July–Oct)	*Noina*	Custard apple (July–Sept)
Linjii	Lychee (April–May)	*Sapparot*	Pineapple (year-round)
Mamuang	Mango (Jan–June)	*Som*	Orange (year-round)
Ngaw	Rambutan (May–Sept)	*Som Oh*	Pomelo (Oct–Dec)
Malakaw	Papaya (year-round)	*Taeng moh*	Watermelon (year-round)
Makhaam	Tamarind (Dec–Jan)	*Thurian*	Durian (April–June)

THAI SWEETS (KHANOM)

Khanom beuang	Small crispy pancake folded over with coconut cream and strands of sweet egg inside	*Khao niaw thurian/ mamuang*	Sticky rice mixed with coconut cream, and durian/mango
		Kluay khaek	Fried banana
Khao laam	Sticky rice, coconut cream and black beans cooked and served in bamboo tubes	*Luk taan cheum*	Sweet palm kernels served in syrup
		Takoh	Squares of transparent jelly topped with coconut cream
Khao niaw daeng	Sticky red rice mixed with coconut cream		

DRINKS (KREUANG DEUM)

Bia	Beer	*Nam manao/som*	Fresh, bottled or fizzy lemon/orange juice
Chaa rawn	Hot tea		
Chaa yen	Iced tea	*Nam plao*	Drinking water (boiled or filtered)
Kaafae rawn	Hot coffee		
Mekhong	Thai brand-name rice whisky	*Nom jeud*	Milk
		Ohliang	Iced coffee
Nam kluay	Banana shake	*Sohdaa*	Soda water

ORDERING

I am vegetarian	*Phom (male)/dichan (female) pen mangsavirat; phom/dichan kin jeh*	I would like ... With /without Can I have the bill please?	*Khaw... Sai/mai sai Khaw bin?*
Can I see the menu?	*Khaw duu menu?*		

POST, PHONES AND THE MEDIA

With it's booming economy, it's hardly surprising that Thailand boasts a fast and efficient communications network. International mail services are relatively speedy, and phoning overseas is possible even from some small islands. To keep you abreast of world affairs there are several English-language newspapers, though a mild form of censorship affects the predominantly state-controlled media, even muting the English-language branches on occasion.

POST

Mail takes four to seven days to get between Bangkok and Europe or North America, and a little longer in the more isolated areas. Almost all **main post offices** across the country operate a **poste restante** service and will hold letters for two to three months. Mail should be addressed: Name (family name underlined or capitalised), Poste Restante, GPO, Town or City, Thailand. It will be filed by surname, though it's always wise to check under your first initial as well. The smaller post offices pay scant attention to who takes what, but in Bangkok you need to show your passport, pay B1 per item received and sign for them. The poste restante at Bangkok GPO opens Mon–Fri 8am–8pm and until 1pm on Sat; others follow regular post office hours – Mon–Fri 8am–4pm (some close from noon to 1pm and may stay open until 6pm) and Sat 8am–noon.

American Express in Bangkok also offers a poste restante facility of up to 30 days to holders of *Amex* credit cards or travellers' cheques. Mail should be addressed: c/o Amex, *C Tours Ltd*, Siam Centre, 965 Rama I Rd, Bangkok and can be collected Mon–Sat 8.30am–4.30pm from their office on the top floor of the Siam Centre, opposite Siam Square.

Post offices are the best places to buy **stamps**, though hotels and guest houses often sell them too, charging an extra baht per stamp. An airmail letter of under 10g costs B13 to send to Europe or Australia and B15 to North America; postcards cost B8 and B9 respectively, and aerogrammes are B8.50 regardless of where they're going to. All **parcels** must be officially boxed and sealed (for about B20) at special counters within main post offices or in a private outlet just outside – you can't just turn up with a package and buy stamps for it. In tourist centres (especially at Bangkok's GPO) be prepared to queue, first for the packaging, then for the weighing and then again for the buying of stamps. The surface rate for a parcel of up to 5kg is B530, and the package should reach Europe or North America in three months; the air mail parcel service is about twice as expensive and takes about a week.

PHONES

Every so often phone lines get jammed and a whole town becomes incommunicado for a few hours, but generally the phone system works well. Payphones are straightforward enough and generally come in two colours: red for **local calls** and blue for **long-distance calls within Thailand**. Red phones take the medium-sized one-baht coins and will give you three minutes per B1. The blue ones aren't very common outside Bangkok, so in smaller towns you usually have to go to a **private long-distance telephone office**, generally located opposite the post office, which will make the connection for you. Regional codes are given throughout the guide, but note that for some large hotels and government offices we've given several line numbers – thus ☎02/431 1802–9 means that there are eight lines and that you can substitute the last digit with any number between 3 and 9. One final local idiosyncrasy: Thai phone books list people by their first, not their family names.

The cheapest way of making an **international call** is to use the government telephone

INTERNATIONAL DIALLING CODES

If you're dialling from abroad, the international code for Thailand is 66. Calling out of Thailand, dial **001** and then the relevant country code:

Australia 61   **Ireland 353**   **New Zealand 64**   **USA 1**

Canada 1   **Netherlands 31**   **UK 44**

Bangkok is 7 hours ahead of GMT, 12 hours ahead of Eastern Standard Time and 3 hours behind Sydney.

For international directory enquires call 100

centre. Nearly always located within or adjacent to the town's main post office, and open daily from about 7am to 11pm (24hr in Bangkok), the government phone centres allot you an individual booth and leave you to do the dialling (in Bangkok) or call via the operator for you (in other towns). A five-minute IDD call to the UK costs B300, an operator-assisted call costs slightly more. If you can't get to one of the official places, try the slightly more expensive private international call offices in tourist areas (like Bangkok's Khao San Road), or the even pricier services offered by the posher hotels. Many guest houses on touristed islands like Ko Samet and Ko Phi Phi have radiophones which guests can use to call long distance and overseas (phone numbers for these are prefixed by ☎01).

NEWSPAPERS

Of the hundreds of Thai-language **newspapers** and magazines published every week, the sensationalist tabloid *Thai Rath* attracts the widest readership and the independent *Siam Rath* the most intellectual. Alongside these, two **daily English-language papers** – the *Bangkok Post* and the *Nation* – both adopt a fairly critical attitude to governmental goings-on and cover major domestic and international stories as well as tourist-related issues. Both detail English-language cinema programmes, TV schedules and expat social events, and are sold at most newstands in the capital as well as in major provincial towns and tourist resorts; the more isolated places receive their few copies at least one day late. You can also pick up foreign publications such as *Newsweek*, *Time* and the *International Herald Tribune* in Bangkok, Chiang Mai, Phuket and Pattaya; expensive hotels sometimes carry air-freighted copies of foreign national newspapers for at least B50 a copy.

TELEVISION

Channel 9 is Thailand's major TV station, transmitting a daily eighteen-hour dosage of news, quiz shows and predominantly imported dramas to all parts of the country. Four other networks broadcast to Bangkok – the privately run Channel 3, the military-controlled channels 5 and 7, and the Public Relations' Department Channel 11 – but not all are received in every province. The *Bangkok Post* and the *Nation* tell you which English-language programmes are dubbed in Thai; the English soundtracks are transmitted simultaneously on FM radio as follows – Channel 3: 105.5 MHz; Channel 7: 103.5 MHz; Channel 9: 107 MHz; Channel 11: 88 MHz.

A couple of cable stations show twenty-four-hour American and British programmes, mostly soaps and sitcoms, but with a fair amount of CNN news too; posh hotels usually pipe these into guests rooms.

RADIO

Radio Thailand broadcasts in several languages on shortwave bands 9655 kHz and 11905 kHz from 7am to 2pm and 4.30 to 10pm daily, with an uninterrupted English-language slot from 6 to 11.30am and again from 6.30 to 7.30pm. Similarly, the **Voice of Free Asia** transmits in English from 10 to 10.30pm on shortwave 1575 kHz.

With a shortwave radio, you can pick up the **BBC World Service** and the **Voice of America** on a variety of bands (depending on the time) right across the country. Times and wavelengths can change every three months, so get hold of a recent schedule just before you travel. Theoretically, you should also be able to receive the BBC World Service, relayed via Singapore on FM 88.9 MHz.

TROUBLE

As long as you keep your wits about you, you shouldn't encounter much trouble in Thailand. **Theft** and pickpocketing are the main problems – not surprising considering that a huge percentage of the local population scrape by on the minimum daily wage of B100. Most travellers prefer to carry their valuables with them at all times, either in a money belt, neck pouch or inside pocket, but it's also possible to leave your valuables in a hotel or guest house locker. The extra-safe option, and an advisable measure when trekking in the north, is to rent a safe-deposit box in a bank, which you can do over the counter at branches in the major cities for about B50 a week. **Padlock** your luggage when leaving it in hotel or guest house rooms, as well as when consigning it to storage or taking it on public transport. Padlocks also come in handy as extra security on your room, particularly on the doors of beachfront bamboo huts.

Never buy anything from **touts**, and in the case of travel agents call the relevant airline first to make sure you're holding a verified ticket before paying up. On a more dangerous note, beware of **drug** scams: either being shopped by a dealer (Chiang Mai samlor drivers are notorious) or having substances slipped into your luggage – simple enough to perpetrate unless all fastenings are secured with padlocks.

Violent crime against tourists is not common, but it does occur, usually to people making an ostentatious display of their belongings. Be wary of accepting food and drink from strangers, especially on long overnight bus or train journeys: it may be drugged so as to knock you out while your bags get nicked. This might

sound paranoid, but there have been enough drug-muggings for TAT to publish a specific warning about the problem. Finally, be sensible about **travelling alone** at night in a taxi or tuk–tuk and on no account risk jumping into an unlicensed taxi at Don Muang airport at any time of day: there have been some very violent robberies in these, so take the well-marked authorised vehicles instead. In the north you should be wary of motorbiking alone in uninhabited and politically sensitive border regions.

Drug smuggling carries a maximum penalty of death and will almost certainly get you from five to twenty years in a Thai prison. Don't expect special treatment as a farang: because of its reputation as a major source of drugs, Thailand works hard to keep on the right side of the US and makes a big show of dishing out heavy sentences. Even more alarming, drug enforcement squads receive 25% of the market value of seized drugs, so are liable to exaggerate the amounts involved

You're more likely to read about armed struggles than experience one, but nevertheless it's advisable to travel with a guide in certain **border areas**. As these regions are generally covered in dense unmapped jungle, you shouldn't find yourself alone in the vicinity anyway, but the main stretches to watch are the Burmese border north of Three Pagodas Pass – where villages, hideaways and refugee camps occasionally get shelled either by the Burmese military or by rebel Karen or Mon forces – and the border between Cambodia and southern Isaan, which is littered with unexploded mines.

REPORTING A CRIME OR EMERGENCY

TAT now has a special department for tourist-related crimes and complaints called the **Tourist Assistance Center** (TAC). Set up specifically to mediate between tourists, police and accused persons (particularly shopkeepers and tour agents), TAC has an office in the TAT headquarters on Rajdamnoen Nok Avenue, Bangkok (daily 8.30am–4.30pm; ☎02/281 5051). In **emergencies**, always contact the English-speaking **tourist police** (see box below) who have offices within or adjacent to many regional TAT offices – this is invariably more efficient than directly contacting the local police, ambulance or fire service.

TOURIST POLICE

Bangkok and the central plains (except Kanchanaburi) ☎02/225 7758 or ☎02/221 6206–10.

Kanchanaburi ☎034/512795.

Chiang Mai and the north ☎053/248974.

East coast and Isaan ☎038/429371.

Surat Thani and Ko Samui ☎077/421281.

Phuket and most of southern Thailand ☎076/212213.

Hat Yai and the deep south ☎074/246733.

SEXUAL HARASSMENT

On the whole, Thailand is a fairly hassle-free destination for women travellers. Though unpalatable and distressing, the high-profile sex industry is relatively unthreatening for Western women, with its energy focused exclusively on farang men; it's also quite easily avoided, being contained within certain pockets of the capital and a couple of beach resorts. As for harassment from Thai men, it's hard to generalise, but most Western tourists find it less of a problem in Thailand than they do back home. Outside of the main tourist spots, you're more likely to be of interest as a foreigner rather than a woman and, if travelling alone, as an object of concern rather than of sexual aggression.

OPENING HOURS AND HOLIDAYS

Most **shops** open at least Monday to Saturday from about 8am to 8pm, while **department stores** operate daily from around 9.30am to 9pm. Private office hours are generally Monday to Friday 8am–5pm and Saturday 8am–noon, though in tourist areas these hours are longer, with weekends worked like any other day. Government offices work Monday to Friday 8.30am–noon and 1–4.30pm, and national **museums** tend to stick to these hours too, but some close on Mondays and Tuesdays rather than at weekends.

Most tourists only register **national holidays** because trains and buses suddenly get extraordinarily crowded: although banks and government offices shut down on these days, most shops and tourist-oriented businesses carry on regardless, and TAT branches continue to dispense information. The only time an inconvenient number of shops, restaurants and hotels do close is during Chinese New Year, which, though not marked as an official national holiday, brings many businesses to a standstill for several days in February. You'll notice it particularly in the south, where most service industries are Chinese-managed.

A brief note on **dates**. Thais use both the Western Gregorian calendar and a Buddhist calendar – Buddha is said to have attained enlightenment in the year 543 BC, so Thai dates start from that point: thus 1992 AD becomes 2535 BE (Buddhist Era).

NATIONAL HOLIDAYS

January 1 Western New Year's Day .

February (day of full moon) *Maha Puja* – commemorates Buddha preaching to a spontaneously assembled crowd of 1250.

April 6 Chakri Day – founding of the Chakri dynasty.

April 13–15 *Songkhran* – Thai New Year.

May 5 Coronation Day.

May (day of full moon) *Visakha Puja* – the holiest of all Buddhist holidays, which celebrates the birth, enlightenment and death of Buddha.

July (day of full moon) *Asanha Puja* – commemorates Buddha's first sermon.

July (the day after *Asanha Puja*) *Khao Pansa* – the start of the annual three-month Buddhist rains retreat, when new monks are ordained.

August 12 Queen's birthday.

October 23 Chulalongkorn Day – anniversary of Rama V's death.

December 5 King's birthday.

December 10 Constitution Day.

December 31 Western New Year's Eve.

FESTIVALS

Hardly a week goes by without some kind of local or national festival being celebrated somewhere in Thailand, and most make great entertainment for participants and spectators alike. All the festivals listed below are spectacular or engaging enough to be worth altering your itinerary for, but bear in mind that for some of the more publicised celebrations (notably those in the northeast) you'll need to book transport and accommodation a week or more in advance.

Nearly all Thai festivals have some kind of religious aspect. The most theatrical are generally **Brahmin** in origin, honouring elemental spirits with ancient rites and ceremonial costumed parades. **Buddhist** celebrations usually revolve round the local temple, and while merit-making is a significant feature, a light-hearted atmosphere prevails, as the wat grounds are swamped with food and trinket vendors and makeshift stages are set up to show *likay* folk theatre, singing competitions and beauty contests.

Many of the secular festivals (like the elephant round-ups and the Bridge Over the River Kwai spectacle) are outdoor local culture shows, geared specifically towards Thai and farang tourists and so slightly artificial though no less enjoyable for that. Others are thinly-veiled trade fairs held in provincial capitals to show off the local speciality, which nevertheless assume all the trappings of a temple fair and so are usually worth a look.

Few of the **dates** for religious festivals are fixed, so check with TAT for specifics. The names of the most touristed celebrations are given here in English, the more low-key festivals are more usually known by their Thai name (*ngan* means "festival").

A FESTIVAL CALENDAR

JANUARY–MARCH

Chaiyaphum *Ngan Phrya Phakdi* – the founder of modern Chaiyaphum is feted with parades, music and dance (mid-Jan).

Chaiyaphum *Elephant round up* – smaller version of the more famous Surin round up (two days in mid-Jan, just before or after *Phraya Phakdi*).

Chiang Mai *Flower Festival* – enormous floral sculptures paraded through the streets (usually first weekend in Feb).

Nationwide, particularly Wat Benjamabophit in **Bangkok** and Wat Phra That Doi Suthep in **Chiang Mai** *Maha Puja* – a day of merit-making marks the occasion when 1250 disciples gathered spontaneously to hear Buddha preach, and culminates with a candle-lit procession round the local temple's bot (Feb full-moon day).

Phitsanulok *Ngan Phra Buddha Chinnarat* – Thailand's second most important Buddha image

is honoured with music, dance and *likay* performances (early Feb).

Phetchaburi *Phra Nakhon Khiri* fair – *son et lumière* at Khao Wang palace (mid-Feb).

Pattani *Ngan Lim Ko Niaw* – local goddess inspires devotees to walk through fire and perform other endurance tests in public (mid-Feb to March).

Nationwide, particularly Sanam Luang, **Bangkok** – *Kite fights and flying contests* (late Feb to mid-April).

Nakhon Si Thammarat *Hae Pha Khun That* – southerners gather to pay homage to the Buddha relics at Wat Mahathat, including a procession of long saffron cloth around the chedi (late Feb–early March).

Yala *ASEAN Barred Ground Dove festival* – international dove-cooing contests (first week of March).

Phra Phutthabat, near Ayutthaya *Ngan Phra Phutthabat* – pilgrimages to the Holy Footprint attracts food and handicraft vendors and travelling players (early to mid-March).

Khorat *Ngan Thao Suranari* – nineteenth-century local heroine is honoured with parades and exhibitions (late March).

APRIL AND MAY

Mae Hong Son *Poy Sang Long* – young Thai Yai boys precede their ordination into monkhood by parading the streets in floral headresses and festive garb (early April).

Nationwide, especially **Chiang Mai** *Songkhran* – the most exuberant of the national festivals welcomes the Thai New Year with massive water fights, sandcastle building in temple compounds and the inevitable parades and "Miss Songkhran" beauty contests (April 13–15).

Phanom Rung, near Surin *Ngan Phanom Rung* – daytime processions up to the eleventh-century Khmer ruins, followed by *son et lumière* (April full-moon day).

Nationwide, particularly **Bangkok's Wat Benjamabophit** *Visakha Puja* – the holiest day of the Buddhist year, commemorating the birth, enlightenment and death of Buddha all in one go; most public and photogenic part is the candlelit evening procession around the wat (May full-moon day).

Sanam Luang, Bangkok *Raek Na* – a royal ploughing ceremony to mark the beginning of the rice-planting season in which ceremonially clad Brahmin leaders parade sacred oxen and the royal plough, and interpret omens to forecast the year's rice yield (early May).

Yasothon *Rocket festival* (*Bun Bang Fai*) – beautifully crafted painted wooden rockets are paraded and fired to ensure plentiful rains; celebrated all over Isaan, but especially lively in Yasothon (weekend in mid-May).

JUNE–SEPTEMBER

Loei *Phi Ta Khon* – masked re-enactment of Buddha's penultimate incarnation (June).

Ubon Ratchathani *Candle Festival (Asanha Puja)* – Ubon citizens celebrate the nationwide festival to mark Buddha's first sermon and the subsequent beginning of the annual Buddhist retreat period (*Khao Pansa*) with parades of enormous wax sculptures (July, three days around the full moon).

Phra Phutthabat, near Ayutthaya *Tak Bat Dok Mai* – another merit-making festival at the Holy Footprint, this time on the occasion of the start of *Khao Pansa*, the annual three-month Buddhist retreat period (July around full-moon day).

Nakhon Pathom *Food and fruits fair* (*Ngan Phonlamai*) – cooking and fruit-carving demonstrations and folk theatre performances in the chedi compound (first week of Sept).

Nakhon Si Thammarat *Tamboon Deuan Sip* – merit-making ceremonies to honour dead relatives accompanied by a ten-day fair on the town field (late-Sept to early Oct).

OCTOBER–DECEMBER

Phuket and Trang *Vegetarian Festival (Ngan Kin Jeh)* – Chinese devotees become vegetarian for a nine-day period and then parade through town performing acts of self-mortification (Oct).

Nationwide, especially **Mae Hong Son** *Tak Bat Devo* – offerings to monks and general merrymaking to celebrate Buddha's descent to earth from *Tavatimsa* heaven and the end of the *Khao Pansa* retreat (Oct full-moon day).

Surat Thani *Chak Phra* – the town's chief Buddha images are paraded on floats down the streets and on barges along the river (mid-Oct).

Nan and Phimai *Boat races* – long-boat races and barge parades along town rivers (mid-Oct to mid-Nov).

Nationwide *Thawt Kathin* – the annual ceremonial giving of new robes by the laity to the monkhood at the end of the rains retreat (mid-Oct to mid–Nov).

Nationwide, especially **Sukhothai and Chiang Mai** *Loy Krathong* – baskets of flowers and lighted candles are floated to honour water spirits and celebrate the end of the rainy season; accompanied by *son et lumière* in Sukhothai and the release of balloons in Chiang Mai (late Oct or early Nov).

Wat Saket, Bangkok *Ngan Wat Saket* – probably Thailand's biggest temple fair, held around the Golden Mount with all the usual festival trappings (first week of Nov).

Surin *Elephant round up* – 200 elephants play team games, perform complex tasks and parade in battle dress (third weekend of Nov).

Nakhon Pathom *Ngan Phra Pathom Chedi* – week-long jamboree held in the grounds of the chedi with itinerant musicians, food vendors and fortune tellers (Nov).

Kanchanaburi *River Kwai Bridge festival* – spectacular *son et lumière* at the infamous bridge (last week of Nov & first week of Dec).

ENTERTAINMENT AND SPORT

Most travellers confine their experience of Thai traditional culture to a one-off attendance at a big Bangkok tourist show, but these extravaganzas are far less rewarding than authentic folk-theatre, music and sports performances. Traditional sport fits neatly into the same category as the more usual theatrical classifications, not only because it can be graceful, even dance-like, to watch, but because, in the case of Thai boxing, classical music plays an important role in the proceedings. Bangkok has one authentic fixed venue for dance and a couple for Thai boxing; otherwise it's a question of keeping your eyes open in upcountry areas for signs that a travelling troupe may soon turn up.

DRAMA

Drama pretty much equals **dance** in Thai theatre, and many of the traditional dance-dramas are based on the Hindu epic the *Ramayana*, a classic adventure tale of good versus evil which is taught in all the schools. Not understanding the plots can be a major disadvantage, so try reading an abridged version beforehand (see "Books" in *Contexts*) and check out the wonderfully imaginative murals at Wat Phra Kaeo in Bangkok, after which you'll certainly be able to sort the goodies from the baddies, if little else. There are three broad categories of traditional Thai dance-drama – khon, lakhon and likay – described below in descending order of refinement.

KHON

The most spectacular form of traditional Thai theatre is **khon**, a stylised drama performed in masks and elaborate costumes by a troupe of highly trained classical dancers. There's little room for individual interpretation in these dances, as all the movements follow a strict choreography that's been passed down through generations: each graceful, angular gesture depicts a precise event, action or emotion which will be familiar to educated *khon* audiences. The dancers don't speak, and the story is chanted and sung by a chorus who stand at the side of the stage, accompanied by a classical *phipat* orchestra.

A typical *khon* performance features several of the best-known **Ramayana** episodes, in which the main characters are recognised by their masks, headdresses and heavily brocaded costumes. Gods and humans don't wear masks, but it's generally easy enough to distinguish the hero Rama and heroine Sita from the action; they always wear tall gilded headdresses and often appear in a threesome with Rama's brother Lakshaman. Monkey masks are always open-mouthed, almost laughing, and come in several colours: monkey army chief Hanuman always wears white, and his two right hand men – Nilanol, the god of fire and Nilapat, the god of death – wear red and black respectively. In contrast, the demons have grim mouths, clamped shut or snarling out of usually green faces: Totsagan, king of the demons, wears a green face in battle and a gold one during peace, but always sports a two-tier headdress carved with two rows of faces.

Khon is performed regularly at Bangkok's National Theatre and nightly at various cultural shows staged by tourist restaurants in Bangkok, Chiang Mai and Pattaya. Even if you don't see a show you're bound to come across copies of the masks worn by the main *khon* characters, which are sold as souvenirs all over the country and constitute an art form in their own right.

LAKHON

Serious and refined, **lakhon** is derived from *khon* but is used to dramatise a greater range of stories including tales from the Buddhist *Jataka*, local folk dramas and of course the *Ramayana*. The form you're most likely to come across is *lakhon chatri*, which is performed at shrines like Bangkok's Erawan and Lak Muang shrines as entertainment for the spirits and a token of gratitude from worshippers. Usually female, the *lakhon chatri* dancers perform as a group rather than as individual characters, executing sequences which, like *khon* movements, all have minute and particular symbolism. They wear similarly decorative costumes but no masks, and dance to the music of a *phiphat* orchestra. Unfortunately, as resident shrine troupes tend to repeat the same dances over and over, it's rarely the sublime display it's cracked up to be. Occasionally the National Theatre features the more elegantly executed *lakhon nai*, a dance-form that used to be performed at the Thai court and often retells the *Ramayana*.

LIKAY

Likay is a much more popular derivative of *khon* – more lighthearted with lots of comic interludes, bawdy jokes and over-the-top acting and singing. Some *likay* troupes perform *Ramayana* excerpts, but a lot of them adapt pot-boiler romances or write their own. Depending on the show, costumes are either traditional as in *khon* and *lakhon*, modern and Western as in films, or a mixture of both. *Likay* troupes travel around the country doing shows on makeshift outdoor stages wherever they think they'll get an audience; temples sometimes hire them out for fairs and there's usually a *likay* stage of some kind at a festival. Performances are often free and generally last for about five hours, with the audience strolling in and out of the show, cheering and joking with the cast throughout. Televised *likay* dramas get huge audiences and always follow romantic plot-lines.

NANG

Nang or shadow plays are said to have been the earliest dramas performed in Thailand, but now are rarely seen except in the far south, where the Malaysian influence ensures an appreciative audience for *nang thalung* (see p.363). Crafted from buffalo hide, the two-dimensional *nang thalung* puppets play out scenes from popular dramas against a backlit screen, while the storyline is told through songs, chants and musical interludes. An even rarer *nang* form is the *nang yai*, which uses enormous cut-outs of whole scenes rather than just individual characters, so the play becomes something like an animated film.

MUSIC

Music is as integral a part of traditional and folk drama as dance is: you'll certainly have the chance to hear classical Thai music at a *khon* or *lakhon* performance, and *likay* shows upcountry nearly always feature folk music of some sort. Pop of course is ubiquitous, heard in shops and on public transport all over the country. If you want to take some home with you, the best places to buy Thai music tapes are at the street markets in any sizeable town.

CLASSICAL THAI MUSIC

Based on an eight-note scale of seven whole tones, **classical Thai music** sounds incomprehensible to Western ears and takes a lot of getting used to. You don't often hear it on its own, as instrumental music was developed specifically to accompany traditional dance-dramas and continues to play a vital part in *khon*, *lakhon* and *nang* performances as well as at Thai boxing matches. A *phipat* (classical orchestra) comprises an oboe-like reed instrument called a *phi nai* and a range of percussion instruments. A tiny pair of brass cymbals (*ching*) beats time, backed by several different drums, while the melody is played on two kinds of xylophone (*ranat ek*) and two semi-circular sets of gongs (the *gong wong yai* and the *gong wong lek*). Despite the fact that many of the performances are rigidly prescribed, *phipat* music depends a lot on improvisation and can't be notated: musicians memorise the melody and then work variations around that during the shows. In the last few years a band called Fong Nam have started a new trend in *phipat* music by adding modern instruments such as electric keyboards.

FOLK MUSIC

The most popular **folk music** (*luk thung* or *maw lam*) bands have their most enthusiastic audiences in the villages of the north and northeast where they precede *likay* theatre performances and produce highly theatrical shows of their own. In fact *luk thung* is often indistinguishable from *likay*, with vocalists singing tales of broken romances and big-time aspirations to the westernised music of electric keyboards, punctuating their songs with dances and comedy sketches. *Maw lam* singers tend to retain a more folksy element, favouring traditional instruments like the stringed *phin* and bamboo *khaen* reed pipes to accompany their narrative solos and duets, sung in fixed metre or extemporised to a rap beat.

PROTEST AND POP MUSIC

Folk and pop meet in Thai **protest songs** which first appeared in the 1960s under the banner category of "Songs for Life", with *luk thung* artists writing songs criticising the US military presence in Thailand. By the Seventies, the radical student band *Caravan* had a big following for their political lyrics sung to a mixture of western guitar and traditional folk sounds, which championed the pro-democracy movement and inspired other groups to focus on issues of poverty and the environment. Although officially split, *Caravan* do the occasional revival gig and their records still sell thousands.

Caravan's niche has now been partly filled by *Carabao*, Thailand's most famous rock band, who sing about Aids and other social issues. Sharing the limelight with *Carabao* is the Thai **pop** group *Bird* who you're bound to hear blasted over the loud speakers in buses, restaurants and shops. Like other local pop singers of the *string* (pop) genre, they're heavily influenced by current Western hits and compose everything from ballads to rock, disco to rap, generally with sentimental overtones.

FILM AND VIDEO

Fast-paced Chinese blockbusters dominate the Thai **movie** scene, serving up a low-grade cocktail of sex, spooks, violence and comedy. Not understanding the dialogue is rarely a drawback, as the storylines tend to be simple and the visuals more entertaining than the words. In the cities, Western films are also pretty big, and new releases often get subtitled rather than dubbed. All sizeable towns have a cinema or two and tickets generally start at around B40. Villagers have to make do with the travelling cinema, which sets up a mobile screen in wat compounds or other public spaces, and often entertains the whole village in one sitting.

Western **videos** come free with your evening meal in guest houses all over Thailand and dissuade many a traveller from venturing anywhere else of an evening. Even if you steer clear of them, you'll get back-to-back Chinese movies on long-distance air-con buses and in some trains too.

THAI BOXING

Thai boxing (*muay Thai*) enjoys a following similar to football in Europe: every province has a stadium and whenever it's shown on TV you can be sure that large noisy crowds will gather round the sets in streetside restaurants and noodle shops. The best place to see Thai boxing is at one of Bangkok's two stadiums, which between them hold bouts every night of the week and on some afternoons as well.

There's a strong spiritual and **ritualistic** dimension to *muay Thai*, adding grace to an otherwise brutal sport. Each boxer enters the ring to the wailing music of a three-piece *phipat* orchestra, often flamboyantly attired in a lurid silk robe over the statutory red or blue boxer shorts. The fighter then bows, first in the direction of his birthplace and then to the north, south, east and west, honouring both his teachers and the spirit of the ring. Next he performs a slow dance, claiming the audience's attention and demonstrating his prowess as a performer.

Any part of the body except the head may be used as an **offensive weapon** in *muay Thai*, and all parts except the groin are fair targets. Kicks to the head are the blows which cause most knockouts. As the action hots up, so the orchestra speeds up its tempo and the betting in the audience becomes more frenetic. It can be a gruesome business, but it was far bloodier before modern boxing gloves were made compulsory in the 1930s – combatants used to wrap their fists with hemp impregnated with a face-lacerating dosage of ground glass.

TAKRAW

You're very unlikely to stumble unexpectedly on an outdoor bout of *muay thai*, but you're sure to come across some form of **takraw** game at some point, whether in a public park, a wat compound or just in a backstreet alley. Played with a very light rattan ball (or one made of plastic to look like rattan), the basic aim of the game is to keep the ball off the ground. To do this you can use any part of your body except your hands, so a well-played *takraw* game looks extremely balletic, with players leaping and arching to get a good strike. There are at least five versions of competitive *takraw*, based on the same principles. The one featured in the South East Asian games and most frequently in school tournaments is played over a volleyball net and involves two teams of three; the other most popular competitive version has a team ranged round a basketball net trying to score as many goals as possible within a limited time period before the next team replaces them and tries to outscore them. Other *takraw* games introduce more complex rules (like kicking the ball backwards with your heels through a ring made with your arms behind your back) and many assign points according to the skill displayed by individual players rather than per goal or dropped ball. Outside of school playing fields, proper *takraw* tournaments are rare, though they do sometimes feature as entertainment at Buddhist funerals.

MEDITATION CENTRES AND RETREATS

Of the hundreds of **meditation temples** in Thailand, a few cater specifically for foreigners by holding meditation sessions and retreats in English. The meditation taught is **Vipassana** or "insight", which emphasises the minute observation of internal physical sensation, and novices and practised meditators alike are welcome. To join a one- or two-hour session in Bangkok, call to check times and then just turn up; for overnight and longer visits to wats in more remote areas, you must contact the monastery in advance, either directly or through the WFB (see below).

Longer retreats are for the serious-minded only. All the temples listed in the box below welcome both male and female English-speakers, but strict segregation of the sexes is enforced and many places observe a vow of silence. An average day at any one of these monasteries starts with a wake-up call at 3am and includes several hours of group meditation and chanting, as well as time put aside for chores and for personal reflection. All visitors are expected to keep the eight Buddhist precepts, however long their stay, the most restrictive of these being the abstention from food after midday and from alcohol, tobacco, drugs and sex at all times. Most wats ask for a minimal daily donation (B40–100) to cover accommodation and food costs. For more information and access details for particular temples, see the relevant sections in the guide.

MEDITATION CENTRES AND RETREAT TEMPLES

International Buddhist Meditation Centre (IBMC), 26/9 Soi Chumphon, Soi Lardprao 15, Bangkok (☎02/511 0439). Holds open meditation sessions three times a day and regular twice-monthly evening meditation classes and lectures in English at Bangkok's Wat Mahathat, as well as occasional longer retreats.

The World Fellowship of Buddhists (WFB), 33 Sukhumvit Rd, between sois 1 and 3 (☎02/251 1188). The main information centre for advice on English-speaking retreats in Thailand. Holds meditation sessions in English every Wednesday evening.

Wat Khao Tham, Ban Tai, Ko Pha Ngan (no phone). Frequent 10-day retreats led by a farang teacher.

Wat Pa Nanachat Beung Rai, Ban Beung Rai, Amphoe Warinchamrab, Ubon Ratchathani (no phone). An exclusively farang-run forest wat where all teachings are conducted in English. It has facilities for the ordination of men only, but both male and female guest are welcome for an initial period of three days. Male visitors are expected to shave their heads if staying for longer than three days.

Wat Ram Poeng, Canal Road, Chiang Mai (☎053/211620). Month-long courses held in English at the Northern Insight Meditation Centre. Before enrolling you need to show a certificate proving that you haven't contracted Aids – the documentation is available in Chiang Mai.

Wat Suan Mokkh, Amphoe Chaiya, Surat Thani (☎02/468 2857). Popular meditation course held on first ten days of every month.

CULTURAL HINTS

Tourist literature has so successfully marketed Thailand as the "Land of Smiles" that a lot of farangs arrive in the country expecting to be forgiven any outrageous behaviour. This is just not the case: there are some things so universally sacred in Thailand that even a hint of disrespect will cause deep offence. TAT publishes a special leaflet on the subject, entitled *Do and Don't in Thailand* – be sure to read it before you travel.

THE MONARCHY

The worst thing you can possibly do is to bad-mouth the **royal family**. The monarchy might be a constitutional one, but almost every household displays a picture of King Bhumibol and Queen Sirikit in a prominent position, and respectful crowds amass whenever either of them makes a public appearance. When addressing or speaking about royalty, Thais use a special language full of deferentials, called *rajasap* (literally "royal language").

Aside from keeping any anti-monarchy sentiments to yourself, you should be prepared to stand when the **national anthem** is played at the beginning of every cinema programme, and to stop in your tracks if the town you are in plays the national anthem over its public address system – many small towns do this twice a day at 8am and again at 6pm. A less obvious point: as the king's head features on all Thai currency, you should never step on a coin or banknote, which is tantamount to kicking the king in the face.

RELIGION

Almost equally insensitive would be to disregard certain religious precepts. Buddhism plays an essential part in the lives of most Thais, and Buddhist monuments should be treated accordingly – which basically means wearing long trousers or knee-length skirts, covering your arms, and removing your shoes whenever you visit one.

All **Buddha images** are sacred, however small, however tacky, however ruined, and should never be used as a backdrop for a portrait photo, clambered over, placed in a position of inferiority, or treated in any manner that could be construed as disrespectful. In an attempt to prevent foreigners from committing any kind of transgression the government requires a special licence for all Buddha statues exported from the country (see "Directory").

Monks come only just beneath the monarchy in the social hierarchy, and they too are addressed and discussed in a special language. If there's a monk around, he'll always get a seat on the bus, usually the back one. Theoretically, monks are forbidden to have any close contact with **women** which means, as a female, you mustn't sit or stand next to a monk, or even brush against his robes; if it's essential to pass him something, put the object down so that he can then pick it up – never hand it over directly. **Nuns**, however, get treated like women rather than like monks.

THE BODY

The Western liberalism embraced by the Thai sex industry is very unrepresentative of the majority Thai attitude to the body. **Clothing** – or the lack of it – is what bothers Thais most about tourist behaviour. As mentioned above, you need to dress modestly when entering temples, but the same also applies to other important buildings and all public places. Stuffy and sweaty as it sounds, you should keep shorts and vests for the real tourist resorts, and be especially diligent about covering up in rural areas. Baring your flesh on beaches is very much a Western practice: when Thais go swimming they often do so fully clothed, and they find **topless and nude bathing** extremely unpalatable. It's not illegal, but it won't win you many friends.

According to ancient Hindu belief the head is the most sacred part of the **body** and the feet the most unclean. This belief, imported into Thailand, means that it's very rude to touch another person's head or to point your feet either at a human being or at a sacred image – when sitting on a temple floor for example, you should tuck your legs beneath you rather than stretch them out towards the Buddha. These hierarchies also forbid people from wearing shoes (which are even more unclean than feet) inside temples and most private homes, and – by extension – Thais take offence when they see someone sitting on the "head", or prow, of a boat. On a more practical note, the **left hand** is used for washing after defecating, so Thais never use it to put food in their mouth, pass things or shake hands – as a farang though, you'll be assumed to have different customs, so left-handers shouldn't worry unduly.

SOCIAL CONVENTIONS

In fact, Thais very rarely shake hands anyway, using the **wai** to greet and say goodbye and to acknowledge respect, gratitude or apology. A prayer-like gesture made with raised hands, the *wai* changes according to the relative status of the two people involved: Thais can instantaneously assess which *wai* to use when, but as a farang your safest bet is to go for the "stranger's" *wai*, which requires that your hands be raised close to your chest and your fingertips placed just below your chin. If someone makes a *wai* at you, you should definitely *wai* back, but it's generally wise not to initiate.

Public displays of **physical affection** in Thailand are much more acceptable between friends of the same sex than between lovers of opposite sexes. Holding hands and hugging is as common among male friends as with females, so if you're given fairly intimate caresses by a Thai acquaintance of the same sex, don't assume you're being propositioned.

Finally, there are three specifically Thai **concepts** you're bound to come across and which may help you to comprehend a sometimes *laissez-faire* attitude to delayed buses and other inconveniences. The first, **jai yen**, translates literally as "cool heart" and is something everyone tries to maintain – most Thais hate raised voices, visible irritation and confrontations of any kind. Related to this is the oft-quoted response to a difficulty, **mai pen rai** – "never mind", "no problem" , or "it can't be helped" – the verbal

equivalent of an open-handed shoulder shrug which has its base in the Buddhist notion of karma (see "Religion" in *Contexts*). And then there's **sanuk**, the wide-reaching philosophy of "fun" which, crass as it sounds, Thais do their best to inject into any situation, even work. Hence the crowds of inebriated Thais who congregate at waterfalls and other beauty spots on public holidays, and the national waterfight which takes place every April on streets right across Thailand.

OUTDOOR PURSUITS

The vast majority of travellers' itineraries take in a few days' trekking in the north and a stint snorkelling or diving off the beaches of the south. The big beach resorts of Pattaya, Ko Phuket and Ko Samui also offer dozens of other water sports, and for the well-prepared wildlife enthusiast Thailand offers plenty of national parks to explore. What follows is a guide to the essentials of the outdoor activities you might pursue in various parts of the country – except for the small-scale operations in Kanchanaburi and Mae Sot, trekking is concentrated in the north, so we've covered the practicalities of trekking in that chapter (see pp.178–87), while details of water sports at the major resorts are given in the sections on those towns.

SNORKELLING AND DIVING

Coral reefs lie off all Thailand's mainland coasts and encircle many of the islands too, so snorkell-

ing and diving are extremely rewarding. Each coast has at least one resort with a number of equipment hire shops, diving schools and agencies who organise diving and snorkelling trips to outlying islands. You can dive all year round too, as the coasts are subject to different monsoon seasons: the diving seasons are from November to April along the Andaman coast, from May to October on the Gulf coast, and all year round on the East coast.

Whether you're snorkelling or diving you should be aware of your effect on the fragile reef structures. The bottom line is that any human contact with the reefs damages them in some way, and that if you're really concerned about saving these delicate ecosystems you should forgo the pleasure of seeing them. Obviously few people are willing to do that, so the next best thing is to minimise your impact by not touching the reefs or asking your boatman to anchor in the middle of one. And don't buy coral souvenirs, as tourist demand only encourages local entrepreneurs to dynamite reefs.

As far as **snorkelling equipment** goes, the most important thing is that you buy or rent a mask that fits. To check the fit, hold the mask against your face, then breathe in and remove your hands – if it falls off, it'll leak water. If you're buying equipment, you should be able to kit yourself out with a mask, snorkel and flippers for between B750–1000; few places rent flippers, but a mask and snorkel set usually costs about B50 a day to rent, and if you're going on a snorkelling day trip they are often included in the price. When renting equipment you'll nearly always be required to pay a deposit of around B200.

THAILAND'S BEST DIVES

The East Coast

Pattaya   see p.258

The Andaman Coast

Ko Phuket   see p.372
Ko Phi Phi   see p.395
Ko Similan   see p.371
Ko Surin   see p.369
Ko Racha   see p.383

The Gulf Coast

Ko Samui   see p.340
Ko Pha Ngan   see p.350
Ko Tao   see p.356
Chumphon   see p.335

Before you sign up for a **diving course** or expedition check that the diving centre has proof of membership of either **PADI** (Professional Association of Diving Instructors) or **NAUI** (National Association of Underwater Instructors) and ask other people who've done the course or expedition how they rate it. Ko Phuket is the best place to learn, Pattaya the second best, and dive centres at both offer a range of courses from beginner to advanced level, which all include equipment hire in the cost. The most popular are the one-day introductory or resort dive (a pep talk and escorted shallow dive fairly close to shore; B1650), and the four- or five-day open-water course (qualifying certificate course with lessons and at least one dive a day; B8000). Hiring a full set of diving gear, including wetsuit, from one of these dive centres costs about B600–700 a day.

NATIONAL PARKS

Over the last thirty years some sixty areas across Thailand have been singled out for conservation as **national parks**, with the dual aim of protecting the country's natural resources and creating educational and recreational facilities for the public, and these generally make the best places to observe wildlife. One of the best places for seeing larger animals is in **Khao Yai** (p.281), the most popular national park, some three hours northeast of Bangkok. If you join a night safari here, you could be rewarded with sightings of elephants, deer, civets, even tigers and leopards, while during the day you'll come across gibbons and hornbills at the very least. Bird-watchers consider the national park mountains of **Doi Suthep** (p.206) and **Doi Inthanon** (p.221) – both close to Chiang Mai – primary observation spots. Many of southern Thailand's protected reserves are marine parks, incorporating anything from a single beach, such as the turtle egg-laying-grounds on Ko Phuket (see p.379), to an entire archipelago, such as **Ko Phi Phi** (p.395).

All parks charge an entrance fee of about B5 and most have limited public facilities such as a set of bungalows (see "Accommodation", above) and a few signposted hiking trails. Not all of the parks are well-served by public transport – some can take a day to reach from the nearest large town, via a route that entails several bus and songthaew changes and a final lengthy walk. This factor, combined with the expense and poor quality of most national park accommodation, means that if you're planning to do a serious tour of the parks you should consider bringing a tent (all parks allow you to pitch for about B5) and be prepared to rent your own transport.

All the national parks are administered by the Royal Forestry Department on Phaholyothin Rd, Chatuchak District, Bangkok 10900 (☎02/579 0529), about forty minutes' bus ride north of Democracy Monument. To book national park bungalows in advance (advisable for weekends and public holidays) you need to pay up front.

GAY THAILAND

The most public aspect of Thailand's gay scene is the farang-oriented **sex industry**, which bears a gruesome resemblance to the straight sex trade, and is similarly most active in Bangkok and Pattaya, with smaller zones operating in Phuket and Chiang Mai. Paedophilia is rife in the gay sex bars that dominate these districts, with their tawdry floor shows and host services, and a significant number of gay prostitutes are gay by economic necessity rather than by inclination. The result of this racket is that gay foreigners have acquired a predatory reputation in certain quarters: many genuine Thai gay bars and clubs are hostile to farang customers, some going so far as to post "no farangs" notices above their doors. Also, Thailand's gay scene is very heavily male: lesbians are poorly catered for and, unless otherwise specified, gay means male throughout this guide. As with the straight sex scene we've eschewed mentioning the most flagrant of the gay sex bars, so those listed in the guide tend to be low-key meeting places for Thai and farang gay men.

For all the ill-will generated by the flesh industry, Thailand has a reputation for being open to homosexuality, exemplified by the fact that the age of consent is 15 years old, the same as for heterosexuals. Although excessively physical displays of affection are frowned upon for both heterosexuals and homosexuals, Western gay couples should get no hassle about being seen together in public. The Thai tolerance extends to cross-dressers and you'll find transvestites doing ordinary jobs even in upcountry towns.

Possibly because of the overall lack of homophobia in the country, there's no **gay movement** to speak of in Thailand – the nearest equivalent to an organised gay political force is the *Fraternity for Aids Cessation in Thailand (FACT)*, which runs Aids awareness campaigns, staffs a telephone counselling service (☎02/574 1100) and publishes a bilingual monthly newsletter.

DISABLED TRAVELLERS

Thailand makes few provisions for its disabled citizens and this obviously affects the **disabled traveller**. For example, wheelchair users will have a hard time negotiating the uneven pavements, which are high to allow for flooding and invariably lacking in dropped kerbs, and will find it difficult to board buses and trains. On the other hand, the country's top hotels are wising up to the need to provide decent facilities, and wherever you go there will always be people willing to help if necessary.

One way to cut down the hassle is to go with a **tour**: The extra money is often well-spent if it guarantees adapted facilities throughout your stay and enables you to explore otherwise inaccesible sights. In the **UK**, both *Kuoni* and *BA Speedbird* tour operators (see p.5 for addresses and phone numbers) are used to tailoring package deals to specific needs. For more general information on disabled travel abroad get in touch with the Royal Association for Disability and Rehabilitation (RADAR) at 25 Mortimer St, London W1 (☎071/637 5400). In the **US**, contact the Society for the Advancement of Travel for the Handicapped (SATH) at 26 Court St, Brooklyn, New York 11242 (☎718/858 5483) for information on suitable tour operators and travel agents, or Mobility International USA through PO Box 3551, Eugene, Oregon (☎503/343 1248).

For **independent travellers**, life is made a lot easier if you can afford to pay for more upmarket hotels (which should have lifts) and to shell out for taxis, the odd domestic flight and the occasional tour. Similarly, the more expensive international airlines tend to be the better equipped: *British Airways, Thai International, Emirates* and *Qantas* all carry aisle wheelchairs and have at least one toilet adapted for disabled passengers.

DIRECTORY

Addresses Thai addresses can be immensely confusing, mainly because property is often numbered twice, firstly to show which real estate lot it stands in, and then to distinguish where it is on that lot. Thus 154/7–10 Rajdamnoen Road means the building is on lot 154 and occupies numbers 7–10. There's an additional idiosyncracy in the way Thai roads are sometimes named too: in large cities a minor road running off a major road is often numbered as a soi ("lane" or "alley", though it may be a sizeable thorough-fare), rather than be given its own street name. Sukhumvit Road for example – Bangkok's longest – has minor roads numbered Soi 1 to Soi 103, with odd numbers on one side of the road and even on the other; so a Sukhumvit Road address could read something like 27/9–11 Soi 15 Sukhumvit Road, which would mean the property occupies numbers 9–11 on lot 27 on minor road number 15 running off Sukhumvit Road.

Contraceptives Condoms (known as *mechai*) are sold in all pharmacies and in many hairdressers

and village shops as well. You can get the Pill from the British Dispensary, Sukhumvit Road, Bangkok, but it's advisable to bring a sufficient supply of your own brand with you.

Customs To export an antique or a Buddha image from Thailand, you need to have a licence granted by the Fine Arts Department, which you can obtain through Bangkok's National Museum on Na Phra That Road (☎02/224 1370). Applications take about five days and need to be accompanied by two postcard-sized photos of the object, taken face on. Some antique shops will organise this for you.

Electricity Supplied at 220 volts AC and available at all but the most remote villages and basic beach huts.

Film There's little to be saved by buying your film in Thailand, but developing is a lot cheaper and in the main tourist areas is done in a couple of hours, to about the same quality as you'd get in the West.

Laundry services Guest houses and hotels all over the country run low-cost same-day laundry services.

Left luggage Few train stations have left-luggage facilities, but many guest houses and hotels offer a cheap and reliable service.

Tampons There's no need to haul box-loads of tampons into Thailand with you as you can stock up from department stores in every sizeable town and guest houses often sell them as well.

Women's groups The main political focus for Thai women is *Friends of Women* at 49 Phra Athit Rd, Bangkok (☎02/280 0429) which runs a counselling service and takes up women's rights issues, in particular fighting against the demeaning consequences of sex tourism .

PART TWO

THE
GUIDE

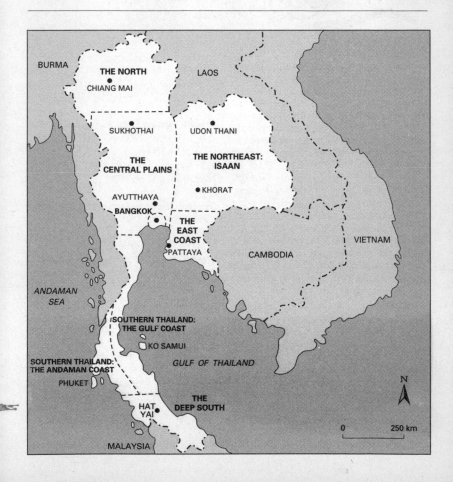

CHAPTER ONE

BANGKOK

The headlong pace and flawed modernity of **Bangkok** match few people's visions of the capital of exotic Siam. Spiked with high-rise blocks of concrete and glass, it's a vast flatness which holds a population of six million, and feels even bigger. But under the shadow of the skyscrapers you'll find a heady mix of chaos and refinement, of frenetic markets and hushed golden temples, of dispiriting, zombie-like sex shows and early-morning almsgiving ceremonies. One way or another, the place will probably get under your skin – and if you don't enjoy the challenge of slogging through jams of buses and tuk-tuks, which fill the air with a chain-saw drone and clouds of pollution, you can spend a couple of days on the most impressive temples and museums, have a quick shopping spree and then strike out for the provinces.

Most budget travellers head for the **Banglamphu** district, where if you're not careful you could end up watching videos all day long and selling your shoes when you run out of money. It's far from having a monopoly on Bangkok accommodation, but it does have the advantage of being just a short walk from the major sights in the **Ratanakosin** area: the dazzling ostentation of **Wat Phra Kaeo**, the grandiose decay of **Wat Po** and the **National Museum**'s hoard of

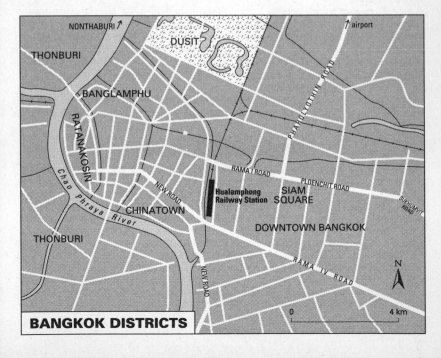

BANGKOK DISTRICTS

exquisite works of art. Once those cultural essentials have been seen, you can choose from a whole bevy of lesser sights, including **Wat Benjamabophit** (the "Marble Temple"), especially at festival time, and **Jim Thompson's House**, a small, personal museum of Thai design.

For livelier scenes, explore the dark alleys of **Chinatown**'s bazaars or head for the water: the great **Chao Phraya River**, which breaks up and adds zest to the city's landscape, is the backbone of a network of **canals and floating markets** that remains fundamentally intact in the west-bank Thonburi district. Inevitably the waterways have earned Bangkok the title of "Venice of the East", a tag that seems all too apt when you're wading through flooded streets in the rainy season; indeed, the city is year by year subsiding into the marshy ground, literally sinking under the weight of its burgeoning concrete towers.

Shopping on dry land varies from ubiquitous touristic stalls selling silks, handicrafts and counterfeit watches and clothes, to completely and sometimes undesirably authentic marketplaces – notably Chatuchak, where caged animals cringe among the pots and pans. As you might expect, the city offers the country's most varied **entertainment**, ranging from traditional dancing and the orchestrated bedlam of Thai boxing, through to the sex bars of the notorious Patpong district, a tinseltown Babylon that's the tip of a dangerous iceberg. Even if the above doesn't appeal, you'll inevitably pass through Bangkok once, if not several times – not only is it Thailand's main port of entry, it's also the obvious place to sort out **onward travel**, with agents offering some of the world's best deals on international air tickets as well as tours to restricted neighbouring countries.

A little history

Bangkok is a relatively young capital, established in 1782 after the Burmese sacked Ayutthaya, the former capital. A temporary base was set up on the western bank of the Chao Phraya, in what is now **Thonburi**, before work started on the more defensible east bank, where the French had built a grand, but short-lived fort in the 1660s. The first king of the new dynasty, Rama I, built his palace at **Ratanakosin**, within a defensive ring of two (later expanded to three) canals, and this remains the city's spiritual heart.

Initially, the city was largely **amphibious**: only the temples and royal palaces were built on dry land, while ordinary residences floated on thick bamboo rafts

---

CITY OF ANGELS

When Rama I was crowned in 1782, he gave his new capital a grand 43-syllable name to match his ambitious plans for the building of the city. Since then 21 more syllables have been added. Krungthepmahanakhornbowornrattanakosinmahintarayutthaya-mahadilokpopnopparatratchathaniburiromudomratchaniwetmahasathanamornpima navatarnsathitsakkathattiyavisnukarprasit is Guinness-certified as the longest place name in the world and roughly translates as "Great city of angels, the supreme repository of divine jewels, the great land unconquerable, the grand and prominent realm, the royal and delightful capital city full of nine noble gems, the highest royal dwelling and grand palace, the divine shelter and living place of the reincarnated spirits". Fortunately, all Thais refer to the city simply as Krung Thep, though plenty can recite the full name at the drop of a hat. Bangkok – "Village of the Plum Olive" – was the name of the original village on the Thonburi side; with remarkable persistence, it has remained in use by foreigners since the time of the French garrison.

on the river and canals, and even shops and warehouses were moored to the river bank. A major shift in emphasis came in the second half of the last century, first under Rama IV (1851–68), who as part of his effort to restyle the capital along European lines built Bangkok's first roads, and then under Rama V (1868–1910), who built a new residential palace in Dusit, north of Ratanakosin, and laid out that area's grand boulevards.

Since World War II, and especially from the mid-1960s onwards, Bangkok has seen an explosion of **modernisation**, which has blown away earlier attempts at orderly planning and left the city without an obvious centre. Most of the canals have been filled in, to be replaced by endless rows of cheap and functional concrete shophouses, sprawling over a built-up area of 330 square kilometres; these piles of drab boxes are now the capital's most prominent architectural feature. In the 1980s, most of the benefits of the **economic boom** were concentrated in Bangkok, which has attracted mass migration from all over Thailand and made the capital ever more dominant: Bangkokians own four-fifths of the nation's automobiles and the population is now forty times that of the second city, Chiang Mai.

ARRIVAL AND ACCOMMODATION

Finding a place to stay in Bangkok is usually no problem: the city has a huge range of **accommodation**, from the murkiest backstreet bunk to the plushest five-star riverside suite, and you don't have to spend a lot to get a comfortable place. Actually getting to your guest house or hotel, however, is unlikely to put you in a good mood, for there can be few cities in the world where **transport** is such a headache. Bumper-to-bumper vehicles create fumes so bad that a recent spot check revealed forty percent of the city's traffic policemen to be in need of hospital treatment. It's not unusual for residents to spend three hours getting to work – and these are people who know where they're going. No end to Bangkok's transport problems is in sight: the marshy ground is unsuitable for underground trains and the much-vaunted overhead train system has been in the planning stages for thirty years now. Water-borne transport provides the least arduous means of hopping from one site to another, but visitors are best advised to have low expectations of how much can be done in a day, and to find accommodation in the areas where you want to spend most time.

> The telephone code for Bangkok is ☎02.

Arriving in Bangkok

Unless you arrive in Bangkok by train, be prepared for a long slog into the centre. Most travellers' first sight of the city is the International Terminal at Don Muang Airport, a slow 25km to the north. Even if you arrive by coach, you'll still have a lot of work to do to get into the centre.

By air

Once you're through immigration at **Don Muang Airport** – queues are often horrendous, owing to the availability of free fifteen-day visas on the spot – you'll find 24-hour exchange facilities, a TAT information desk, a post office and cafés. Note that guest houses tend to shut their doors at 10pm, so if you're arriving after about 8pm you may have to resign yourself to shelling out for a hotel room for your first night: a round-the-clock accommodation desk can help with bookings.

Bus is the cheapest way of getting into the city, but is usually also the slowest. Head straight out from the northern end of arrivals to find the all-purpose bus shelter on the main highway. Ordinary buses run all day and night, with a reduced service after 10pm; pricier air-con buses stop running around 8.30pm, but are less crowded (see "City transport", below). The box below gives a rough sketch of the most useful routes – the TAT office in arrivals has further details.

USEFUL BUS ROUTES

#3 & #9 (a/c): Northern bus terminal–Sanam Luang (for Banglamphu guest houses).

#4 (a/c): Airport–Rajaprarop Rd–Silom Rd.

#10 (a/c): Airport–Northern bus terminal–National Library (guest houses)–Southern bus terminal-Thonburi.

#11 (a/c): Eastern bus terminal–Sanam Luang (for Banglamphu guest houses).

#13 (a/c): Airport–Northern bus terminal–Rajaprarop Rd–Sukhumvit Rd–Eastern bus terminal.

#29 (a/c & ordinary): Airport–Northern bus terminal–Siam Square–Hualamphong railway station.

#38 (ordinary): Northern bus terminal–Rajaprarop Rd–Eastern bus terminal.

#40 (ordinary): Southern bus terminal–Hualamphong railway station–Eastern bus terminal.

#53 (ordinary): Hualamphong Railway Station–Samsen Rd & Phra Athit Rd (for Banglamphu guest houses).

#59 (ordinary): Airport–Northern bus terminal–Sanam Luang (for Banglamphu guest houses).

#124 & #127 (ordinary): Southern bus terminal–Tha Pinklao (for ferry to Phra Athit and Banglamphu guest houses).

Thai Airways also runs a **minibus** service to the *Asia Hotel* near Siam Square and the *Viengthai Hotel* in Banglamphu, which at B80 is good value; the minibuses will run to other hotels on request, but expect to pay about half as much again.

The **train** to Hualamphong Station is the quickest way into town. To reach the station at Don Muang follow the signs from arrivals to the *Airport Hotel* across the main highway, carry on through the hotel foyer and the station is in front of you. About 25 trains a day make the 50-minute trip to Hualamphong for B5 (plus a surcharge on rapid and express trains), but they're concentrated around 7am and 5pm – at other times you might have to wait over an hour. Special airport shuttle trains are faster (35min) but more expensive (B80, or B100 a/c) and less frequent (6 daily), and you have to buy tickets at the *Thai Airways* limousine desk in arrivals – check the schedule there for the next departure before committing yourself.

Taxis to the centre are comfortable, air-conditioned and not too extravagantly priced, although the driving can be hairy. A wide variety is on offer, from a B300 *Thai Airways* limousine down to a B180 unlicensed cab – avoid these, as newly arrived travellers are seen as easy victims for robbery, and the cabs are untraceable. Licensed taxis are identifiable by their yellow and black number plates: for the best service, head for the airport-regulated taxi desk in the arrivals concourse, where you buy a ticket for the journey in advance for about B200.

If you're booked on a connecting **internal flight**, the domestic terminal at Don Muang is almost 1km away from the international terminal, but a *Thai Airways* minibus shuttles regularly between them. You can also spare yourself the trip into Bangkok if you're planning to head straight to **the north or northeast** by train or bus: all trains to these parts of the country stop at Don Muang train station, and all the city buses which pass the airport (except #4 and #69) also pass the Northern Bus Terminal on Phaholyothin Road. *Thai Airways* also runs an air-con bus from the airport direct to **Pattaya** twice a day.

By train and bus

Travelling to Bangkok by **train** from Malaysia and most parts of Thailand, you arrive at Hualamphong Station, which is centrally placed and is on numerous bus routes – the most useful being bus #53, which stops on the east side of the station and runs to the budget accommodation in Banglamphu. Trains from Kanchanaburi pull in at Bangkok Noi Station in Thonburi, which is on the express boat line (see below).

Buses come to a halt at a number of far-flung spots: services from Malaysia and the south use the Southern Terminal at the junction of Pinklao and Nakhon Chaisri roads in Thonburi; services from the north and northeast come in at the Northern Terminal on Phaholyothin Road (due for a temporary move soon round the corner to Kamphaeng Phet Road); and buses from the east coast use the Eastern Terminal at Soi 40, Sukhumvit Road. All of these will leave you with a long bus, tuk-tuk or taxi ride into town.

Orientation and information

Bangkok can be a tricky place to get your bearings as it's vast and flat, with largely featureless modern buildings and no obvious centre. The boldest line on the map is the **Chao Phraya River**, which divides the city into Bangkok proper on the east bank, and **Thonburi**, recently incorporated into Greater Bangkok, on the west.

The historical core of Bangkok proper, site of the original royal palace, is **Ratanakosin**, which nestles into a bend in the river. Three concentric canals radiate eastwards around Ratanakosin: the southern part of the area between the canals is the old-style trading enclave of **Chinatown** and Indian **Pahurat**, linked to the old palace by New Road; the northern part is characterised by old temples and the **Democracy Monument**. Beyond the canals to the north, **Dusit** is the site of many government buildings and the nineteenth-century palace, which is linked to Ratanakosin by Rajdamnoen Road.

"New" Bangkok begins to the east of the canals and beyond the main railway line, and stretches as far as the eye can see to the east and north. The main business district and most of the embassies are south of **Rama IV Road**, with the port of Khlong Toey at the southern edge. The diverse area north of Rama IV Road includes the sprawling campus of Chulalongkorn University, huge shopping centres around **Siam Square** and a variety of other businesses. Due north of Siam Square stands the tallest building in Bangkok, the *Baiyoke Tower Hotel* – with its distinctive rainbow colour scheme it makes a good point of reference. To the east lies the swish residential quarter off **Sukhumvit Road**.

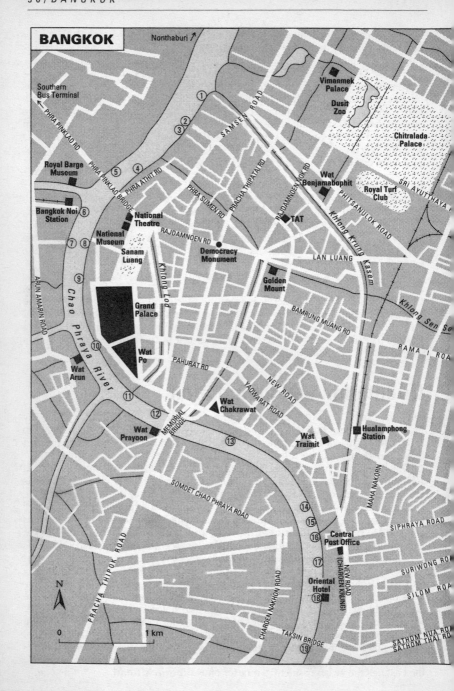

BANGKOK

Nonthaburi ↗

Southern Bus Terminal

PHRA PINKLAO RD

Royal Barge Museum

Bangkok Noi Station

PHRA PINKLAO BRIDGE

PHRA ATHIT RD

National Theatre

National Museum

Sanam Luang

ARUN AMARIN ROAD

Chao Phraya River

Wat Arun

Grand Palace

Wat Po

Wat Prayoon

MEMORIAL BRIDGE

SOMDET CHAO PHRAYA ROAD

PRACHA THIPOK ROAD

N

0   1 km

Khlong Lod

PHRA SUMEN RD

RAJDAMNOEN RD

Democracy Monument

Golden Mount

PAHURAT RD

Wat Chakrawat

YAOWARAT ROAD

NEW ROAD

SAMSEN ROAD

PRACHA THIPATAI RD

Vimanmek Palace

Dusit Zoo

Chitralada Palace

SRI AYUTTHAYA

Wat Benjamabophit

RAJDAMNOEN NOK RD

TAT

PHITSANULOK ROAD

Royal Turf Club

Khlong Krung Kasem

LAN LUANG

BAMRUNG MUANG RD

Khlong Sen Se

RAMA I ROAD

Hualamphong Station

Wat Traimit

MAHA NAKORN

SIPHRAYA ROAD

Central Post Office

NEW ROAD (CHAROEN KRUNG)

SURIWONG RD

SILOM ROAD

Oriental Hotel

CHAROEN NAKHON ROAD

TAKSIN BRIDGE

SATHOM NUA RD
SATHOM THAI RD

Information and maps

As well as the booth in the airport arrivals concourse, the **Tourism Authority of Thailand (TAT)** maintains an information office within walking distance of Banglamphu, at its headquarters on Rajdamnoen Nok Avenue (daily 8.30am–4.30pm; ☎282 1143–7). They're helpful and reliable, and have plenty of handouts about Bangkok and the provinces, as well as a guide to TAT-approved shops.

Two English-language **newspapers**, the *Nation* and the *Bangkok Post*, give limited information about what's on in Bangkok. More useful sources of information, especially about what to avoid, are the travellers' **notice boards** in many of the guest houses in Banglamphu.

To get around Bangkok cheaply, you'll need to buy a colour **bus map**: two similar versions, produced by rival map companies, are widely available in Bangkok, showing ordinary and a/c routes, as well as the names of dozens of streets and *sois* (side roads). Each costs around B40, although the price is hiked at the train stations and various other places where you need it most. Serious shoppers might also want to buy a copy of **Nancy Chandler's** idiosyncratic map of Bangkok, available in most tourist areas.

City transport

The main form of transport in the city are **buses**, and once you've mastered the labyrinthine complexity of the route map you'll be able to get to any part of the city, albeit slowly. Catching the various kinds of **taxi** can make a serious dent in your budget, and you'll still get held up by the daytime traffic jams. **Boats** are obviously more limited in their range, but they're regular and as cheap as buses, and you'll save a lot of time by using them whenever possible – a journey between Banglamphu and the GPO, for instance, will take around half an hour by water, half what it would take on land. **Walking** might often be quicker than travelling by road, but the heat can be unbearable, distances are always further than they look on the map and the engine fumes are stifling.

Buses

Bangkok has two types of bus service: the **ordinary** buses, on which you pay the conductor B2, or B3 for a long journey; and air-conditioned (a/c) buses, on which fares start at B5, rising to B15. As buses can only go as fast as the car in front, which at the moment is averaging 4kph, you'll probably be spending a long time on each journey, so you'd be well advised to pay the extra for cool air – and the air-con buses are usually less crowded too. Air-conditioned services stop at around 8.30pm, but most ordinary routes have a reduced service throughout the night.

Boats

Bangkok was built as an amphibious city around a network of canals – or khlongs – and the first streets were constructed only in the second half of the last century. Although most of the canals have been turned into roads on the Bangkok side, the Chao Phraya is still a major transport route for residents and non-residents alike, forming more of a link than a barrier between the two halves of the city.

There are two different kinds of boat on the Chao Phraya. The first are the **express boats** (*reua duan*), large, numbered water buses which run between Nonthaburi in the north and Krung Thep Bridge in the south during daylight hours, taking about ninety minutes for the whole route. Fares are B3, B5 or B7, depending on distance travelled, and tickets can be bought either at the pier or on board. Boats do not necessarily stop at every landing – they'll only pull in if people want to get on or off. Note also that during rush hours, certain boats (marked with a green flag) will stop only at certain busier piers – check the maps at the pier where you embark for further details. The important central stops are outlined in the box below and marked on our city map.

CENTRAL STOPS FOR THE CHAO PHRAYA EXPRESS BOAT

1 Thewes – for the National Library.

2 Wisut Kasat – for Samsen Road guest houses.

3 Wat Sam Phraya.

4 Phra Athit – for Khao San Road.

5 Pinklao.

6 Bangkok Noi.

7 Prannok.

8 Maharat – for Wat Mahathat.

9 Chang – for the Grand Palace.

10 Thien – for Wat Po.

11 Ratchini.

12 Saphan Phut (Memorial Bridge) – for Pahurat.

13 Rajavongs (Rajawong) – for Chinatown.

14 Harbour Department.

15 River City.

16 Si Phraya.

17 Wat Muang Kae – for GPO.

18 Oriental – for Silom Road.

19 Taksin – for Sathorn Road.

(Numbers correspond to those on the map on the previous page)

The other river boats are the slow **cross-river** ferries (*reua kham fak*), which shuttle back and forth between the same two points. Smaller than express boats, they can be found at every express stop and plenty of other piers in between. Fares are 50 satang or B1, which you usually pay at the entrance to the pier.

Longtail boats (*reua hang yao*) ply the khlongs of Thonburi like buses, stopping at designated shelters (fares are in line with those of express boats), and are also available for individual rental here and on the river (see p.80). On the Bangkok side, Khlong Sen Seb has been opened up to longtails, which run from the Phanfa pier at the Golden Mount (handy for Banglamphu, Ratanakosin and Chinatown), and head due east to Khlong Tan, with useful stops at Phrayathai Road, Pratunam, Witthayu (Wireless) Road, Soi Nana Nua and Soi 23 off Sukhumvit Road. This is your quickest and most interesting way of getting across town, if you can stand the stench of the canal. State your destination to the conductor when he collects your fare, which will be B5 or just over. A new longtail service is scheduled to plough along Khlong Krung Kasem around Ratanakosin.

Taxis

Bangkok **taxis** come in three forms, none of them metered, so always haggle before you set off. Rates rise after midnight, and during rush hours when each journey takes far longer. At most of the times of the day, there's a plentiful supply of all three kinds of taxi, so you can flag them down on most main streets.

Motorbike taxis are cheapest and quickest, though they require nerves of steel and are really only useful if you're on your own. Pick the riders out by their numbered, coloured vests or find their taxi rank, often at the entrance to a long soi; a short trip, say from Banglamphu to Wat Po, should cost B10. **Slightly more**

stable, **tuk-tuks** can carry three passengers comfortably and are the standard way of making short journeys (Banglamphu to Wat Po should cost around B30). Their passengers are fully exposed to the worst of Bangkok's pollution, but tuk-tuks are the least frustrating type of city transport – they are a lot nippier than taxi cabs, and the drivers have no qualms about taking semi-legal measures to avoid jams. Be aware, however, that tuk-tuk drivers tend to speak less English than taxi drivers – and there have been cases of robberies and attacks on women passengers late at night.

Top of the range are the air-conditioned **taxi cabs**. Fares start from about B50, with an average of B80, say from Siam Square to Hualamphong railway station. Unlicensed cabs (white and black plates) are no cheaper than licensed ones (yellow and black plates) and tend to be less reputable – you've got no comeback in the event of an accident – although outright rip-offs are confined mainly to the airport run.

Transport rental

Renting a car is possible in Bangkok (see p.110), but is best kept for out-of-town trips – city traffic jams are just too much to cope with, and parking is impossible. As there are some novel rules of the road, it would be better to get a car with driver from a travel agent or hotel for about B1000 a day. One place, outside the Malaysia Hotel on Soi Ngam Duphli, rents out **motorbikes**, but only big touring machines, from B500 per day. **Bicycles** are rarely available for rent in Bangkok.

Accommodation

For double rooms under B300 your widest choice lies with the **guest houses** of Banglamphu and the smaller travellers' ghetto that has grown up around Soi Ngam Duphli, off the south side of Rama IV Road. Bangkok guest houses are tailored to the independent traveller's needs and often have genuine single rooms with prices to match, a rarity elsewhere; many also have left-luggage rooms, available at minimal cost. Most rooms here are no-frills crash pads: small and usually windowless with thin walls and shared bathrooms. Bookings of any kind are rarely accepted by guest houses, but it's often useful to telephone just to establish whether a place is full already – note that during peak season (roughly Nov–Feb) you may have difficulty getting a room after noon.

Moderate and expensive lodgings are mainly concentrated downtown around Siam Square and in the area between Rama IV Road and New Road; along Sukhumvit Road, where the eastern suburbs start; and to a lesser extent in Chinatown. Air-conditioned rooms can be had for as little as B300, but for that you're looking at a pretty dingy cubicle; reckon on paying more like B1000 for a place with decent furnishings and a swiming pool. Remember that the top-whack hotels will add 11 percent tax and a 10 percent service charge to your bill.

Banglamphu

Banglamphu, Bangkok's cheapest and most popular accommodation centre, is within easy reach of the Grand Palace and other major sights in Ratanakosin, though food and entertainment options are almost entirely limited to guest house restaurants and their nightly video shows.

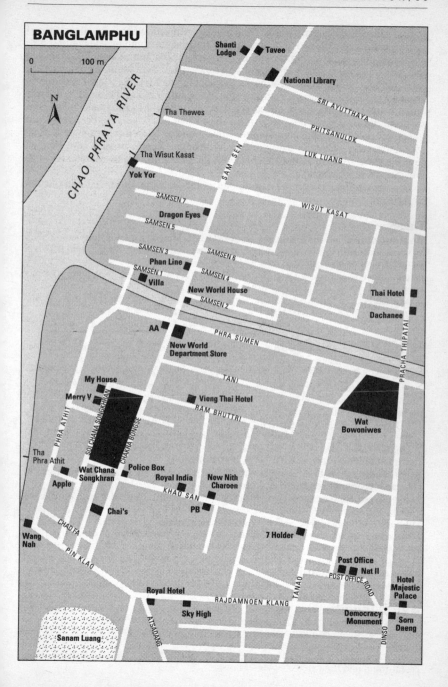

At the heart of Banglamphu is the legendary **Khao San Road** – almost a caricature, crammed with guest houses, dodgy travel agents and ethnic clothes stalls squashed between restaurants serving yoghurt shakes and muesli, racks of bootleg tapes, tattooists and hair-braiders. It's colourful, noisy and a good place to meet other travellers, but if you want the benefits of Khao San Road without the bustle, try the smaller roads running off it: **Soi Chana Songkhram, Phra Athit, Phra Sumen** and the **post office soi**, where the guest houses tend to be more modern. About ten minutes' walk north from Khao San Road, the **Samsen Road sois** offer more of a Thai atmosphere, while a further fifteen minutes' walk in the same direction will take you to **Sri Ayutthaya Road**, behind the National Library, the newest and best-value area in Banglamphu, where rooms are larger and guest houses smaller.

Banglamphu has only a few **upmarket** hotels and most of these don't live up to their price range.

Cheap

AA Guest House, 84–86 Phra Sumen Rd (☎282 9631). More like a hotel than a guest house in size and facilities, this is a good place to try if other places are full. Singles from B100 with fan to B300 with shower and a/c; doubles B200–350.

Apple Guest House, 10/1 Phra Athit (☎281 6838). An old building with some character; cheap but a bit grotty. B50 single, B80 double.

Chai's House, Soi Chana Songkhram. Large, clean, simple rooms, but a bit pricey – B100 single, B200 double. Very good restaurant, popular with government workers.

Merry V, 35 Soi Chana Songkhram (☎282 9267). Small, basic rooms, but clean and friendly. B70 single, B120 double.

My House, 37 Soi Chana Songkhram (☎282 9263). Ethnic furnishings, bamboo walls and good food make this a popular place despite its basic rooms. B70 single, B120 double.

Nat II, Post Office Rd. Large clean rooms; fairly quiet. B70–100 single, B120–150 double.

New Nith Charoen, Khao San Rd. Clean comfortable rooms; no singles. B200–290.

New World House, Samsen 2 (☎281 5605). Good-value, large, unadorned rooms with desks, shower and a/c; popular with long-stayers, but a bit souless. B300 double.

PB Guest House, 74 Khao San Rd. Archetypal world travellers' guest house: grotty rooms and hang-loose atmosphere. Snooker hall and boxing gym downstairs. B30 dorm; B80 double.

7 Holder Guest House, 216/2–3 Khao San Rd (☎281 3682). Clean and modern; simple rooms but a little overpriced. B100 single, B190 double.

Shanti Lodge, 37 Sri Ayutthaya Rd (☎281 2497). Quiet, attractively furnished and comfortable rooms; vegetarian restaurant. B100 single, B110 double.

Tavee Guest House, 83 Sri Ayutthaya Rd (☎282 5983). Good-sized rooms; quiet and friendly. B80 single, B110 double.

Villa, Samsen 1. Bangkok's most therapeutic guest house: a lovely old Thai house and garden with just ten large rooms. Fills up quickly, but worth going on the waiting list if you're staying a long time. From B80 single, B110 double.

Moderate and expensive

Hotel Majestic Palace, 97 Rajdamnoen Klang (☎280 5610). The best hotel in the area; near Democracy Monument. From B1800 single, B2400.

Royal Hotel, 2 Rajdamnoen Klang (☎222 9111). Nearest hotel to the Grand Palace; good facilities but not exactly plush for the price. From B841 single, B1070 double.

Thai Hotel, 78 Prajathipatai Rd (☎282 2831). Comfortable, but a little overpriced. From B850 double.

Viengthai Hotel, 42 Tani Rd (☎282 8672). Very near Khao San Rd; comfortable but a bit pricey. From B900 double.

Chinatown

Not far from the Ratanakosin sights and very convenient for Hualamphong Station, **Chinatown (Sampeng)** is one of the most vibrant and quintessentially Asian parts of Bangkok. Staying here can be noisy, but there's always plenty to look at. A lone travellers' guest house and a small range of moderate and expensive hotels jostle amongst a cluster of seedier places catering mainly to Thais.

Bangkok Center, 328 Rama IV Rd (☎238 4848). Handily placed opposite the railway station, but noisy. Rooms doubles from B1500.

Chinatown Hotel, 526 Yaowarat Rd (☎226 1267). Well-appointed with friendly staff and rooms from B1000 doubles.

New Empire Hotel, 572 Yaowarat Rd (☎234 6990). Average rooms, but right in the heart of Chinatown, with shower, a/c and use of swimming pool for B400 doubles.

TT Guest House, 138 Soi Wat Mahaphruttharam, off Mahanakhon Rd (☎236 3053). From the station, turn left along Rama IV, right down Mahanakhon and look for signs to the guest house. The cleanest place for the price in this area: the best rooms are in the wooden house rather than the depressing concrete block and cost B90–140 for a double.

Downtown: Siam Square and Ploenchit Road

Siam Square – not really a square, but a grid of shops and restaurants between Phrayathai and Henri Dunant roads – and nearby **Ploenchit Road** have no budget accommodation, but a few posh guest houses are springing up, providing extra comforts at moderate prices, alongside the expensive hotels. If any part of Bangkok is central, this is it, and it's especially handy for shopping, nightlife and Hualamphong Station.

A-One Inn, 25/13 Soi Kasemsan 1, Rama I Rd (☎215 3029). Justifiably popular upmarket guest house, in the next soi along from Jim Thompson's House. Quiet rooms with a/c and hot water from B400 double.

The Bed & Breakfast, 36/42 Soi Kasemsan 1, Rama I Rd (☎215 3004). Bright, clean and friendly, though the rooms are a bit cramped. Rooms with a/c and hot water B400 single, B500 double, continental breakfast included.

City Inn, 888/37–9 Ploenchit Rd (☎254 2070–1). Small, reliable hotel, popular with businessmen. Rooms with all facilities from B880 single, B960 double.

Hotel Siam Inter-Continental, 967 Rama I Rd (☎253 0355–7). Elegant, offbeat modern Thai building in huge, quiet gardens with a driving range and tennis. From B3200 single, B3400 double.

Jim's Lodge, 125/7 Soi Ruam Rudee (☎255 3100–3). Luxurious international standards on a smaller scale and at bargain prices. From B1404 single, B1500 double.

Regent, 155 Rajdamri Rd (☎251 6127). The stately home among Bangkok's top hotels. From B4200 double.

Downtown: south of Rama IV Road

South of Rama IV Road, the left bank of the river contains a full cross-section of places to stay. At the eastern edge there's **Soi Ngam Duphli**, a ghetto of budget guest houses which is choked with traffic escaping the jams on Rama IV Road – the neighbourhood is generally on the slide, although the best guest houses, tucked away on quiet Soi Saphan Khu, are as good as anything in Banglamphu.

Some medium-range places are scattered between Rama IV Road and the river, ranging from the notorious (the *Malaysian*) to the sedate (the *Bangkok Christian*

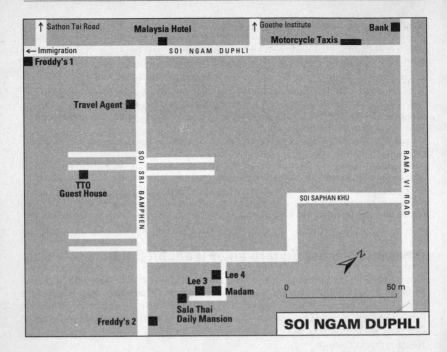

and the *YWCA*). The area also lays claim to the capital's biggest selection of top hotels, which are among the most opulent in the world. You can't get much farther away from the treasures of Ratanakosin, but this area is good for eating and shopping.

Cheap and moderate

Bangkok Christian Guest House, 123 Soi 2, Saladaeng (☎233 6303). Missionary house whose plain a/c rooms with hot water bathrooms surround a quiet lawn. B530 single, B760 double, breakfast included.

Freddy's 1 Guest House, Soi Ngam Duphli (☎286 6722). A maze of run-down rooms in a quiet block. B80 single, B150 double.

Freddy's 2, 27/40 Soi Sri Bamphen (☎286 7826). Popular, comfortable guest house with beer garden. Bit noisy. B80 single, B150 double.

Lee 3 Guest House, 13 Soi Saphan Khu (☎286 3042). The best of the Lee family (1–4) guest houses spread around this and adjoining sois. Decent, quiet, though stuffy. B100 single, B150–180 double.

Lee 4, 9 Soi Saphan Khu (☎286 7874). Simple, airy rooms in a dour modern tower. From B120 single, B180 double.

Madam Guest House, 11 Soi Saphan Khu (☎286 9289). Clean rooms in a warren-like wooden house. Friendly. From B80 single, B120 double.

Malaysia Hotel, 54 Soi Ngam Duphli (☎286 3582). Big, clean, dilapidated rooms with a/c and hot-water bathrooms. Swimming pool. Once a travellers' legend, now a bargain. From B414 single, B486 double.

Newrotel, 1216/1 New Rd, between the GPO and the *Oriental Hotel* (☎233 1406). Smart and clean, a bargain at B660 single, B770 double, including American breakfast.

River View Guest House, 768 Soi Panurangsri, Songvad Rd (☎235 8501). Great views over the bend in the river, especially from the top-floor restaurant. Large but unattractive rooms doubles at B400–600. Find it through a maze of crumbling Chinese buildings: head north for 400m from River City shopping centre (on the express-boat line) along Soi Wanit 2, before following signs to the guest house to the left.

Sala Thai Daily Mansion, 15 Soi Saphan Khu (☎287 1436). The pick of the area. A very clean and well-run place with a roof garden at the end of this quiet, shaded alley. From B150 double.

TTO Guest House, 2/48 Soi Sri Bamphen (☎286 6783). Rough, poorly designed but air-conditioned rooms, each with fridge. B300 single, B350 double.

YWCA Hostel, 13 Sathorn Thai Rd (☎286 1936). Bland but reliable upmarket hostel, with swimming pool and roller skating; a/c rooms with hot water bathrooms from B490 single, B590 double.

Expensive

Dusit Thani Hotel, Rama IV Rd, on the corner of Silom Rd (☎236 0450–9). Centrally placed top-class hotel, famous for its restaurants, including the *French Tiara*, with its spectacular top-floor views. B4500 single, B4900 double.

Montien Hotel, 54 Surawongse Rd, on the corner of Rama IV (☎233 7060–9). Grand, airy luxury hotel, famous for its lobby astrologers. From B3500 single, B3800 double.

Oriental Hotel, 48 Oriental Ave, off New Rd (☎236 0400). One of the world's best. Effortlessly stylish riverside hotel, with immaculate standards of service. From B5000 single, B5300 double.

Swissotel, 3 Convent Rd (☎233 5345). Swish and friendly top-notch small hotel, just off Silom Rd. Twin room designed for disabled visitors available. B2766 single, B3043 double.

YMCA Collins International House, 27 Sathorn Thai Rd (☎287 1900). First class facilities, no frills. Fitness club. From B960 single, B1060 double.

Sukhumvit Road

Sukhumvit Road is Bangkok's longest – it keeps going east all the way to Cambodia – but the best accommodation is between sois 1 and 21. Although this is not the place to come if you're on a tight budget, it's a good area for mid-range hotels, many of which have swimming pools and/or breakfast included. Staying here gives you a huge choice of restaurants, bars and shops, on Sukhumvit and on adjacent Ploenchit Road, and it's convenient for the Eastern Bus Terminal, but it does mean you're a long way from the main Ratanakosin sights.

Cheap and moderate

Bangkok Inn, Soi 11 (☎254 4834). A friendly, German-run place; rooms have a/c, shower, fridge and TV; rates include breakfast. B700 single, B800 double.

Best Inn, Soi 3 (☎253 0573). Reasonable rooms with a/c and shower for B350 double.

Golden Gate, Soi 2 (☎252 8126). B770 double, includes a/c, breakfast and use of pool.

Mermaid's Rest, Soi 8 (☎253 2400). Popular and well-run, with pool, garden and nightly Texan-style all-you-can-eat barbecues. Fan rooms from B325 single, B650 double.

Miami Hotel, Soi 13 (☎253 5611). Good value, large clean rooms with shower, a/c and use of pool. B500 double.

Ruamchit Inn, between sois 17 and 19. The cheapest place in the area with fair rooms (shared bathroom) for B150 single, B200 double.

SV Guest House, Soi 19 (☎253 1747). Adequate rooms with shared bathroom for B200 double.

Uncle Rey's Guest House, Soi 4 (☎252 5565). Quiet and friendly; good value a/c rooms with shower for B350 single, B400 double.

Expensive

Ambassador Hotel, between sois 11 and 13 (☎254 0444). The largest hotel in the area. Especially good restaurant. From B2178 double.

Boulevard Hotel, Soi 7 (☎255 2930). Small, unpretentious and friendly, with sizeable rooms and pool. From B3146 double.

Landmark Hotel, between sois 6 and 8 (☎254 0404). The best hotel on Sukhumvit. From B4961 double.

Rex Hotel, opposite Soi 49 (☎259 0106). Adequate rooms with all the trimmings. From B1111 double.

THE CITY

Bangkok is sprawling, chaotic and exhausting: to do it justice and keep your sanity, you need time, boundless patience and a bus map. The place to start is **Ratanakosin**, the royal island on the east bank of the Chao Phraya, where the city's most important and extravagant sights are to be found. On the edges of this enclave, the area around the landmark **Democracy Monument** includes some interesting and quirky religious architecture, a contrast with the attractions of neighbouring **Chinatown**, whose markets pulsate with the much more aggressive business of making money. Quieter and more European in ambience are the stately buildings of the new royal district of **Dusit**, two kilometres northeast of Democracy Monument. Very little of old Bangkok remains, but the back canals of **Thonburi**, across the river from Ratanakosin and Chinatown, retain a traditional feel quite at odds with the modern high-rise jungle of **downtown Bangkok**, which has evolved across on the eastern perimeter of the city and can take an hour to reach by bus from Ratanakosin. It's here that you'll find the best shops, bars, restaurants and nightlife, as well as a couple of worthwhile sights. Greater Bangkok now covers an area some thirty kilometres in diameter and though unsightly urban development predominates, an expedition to **the outskirts** is made worthwhile by several museums and the city's largest market.

Ratanakosin

When Rama I developed **Ratanakosin** as his new capital in 1782, after the sacking of Ayutthaya and a temporary stay across the river in Thonburi, he paid tribute to its precursor by imitating Ayutthaya's layout and architecture – he even shipped the building materials downstream from the ruins of the old city. Like Ayutthaya, the new capital was sited for protection beside a river and turned into an artificial island by the construction of defensive canals, with a central **Grand Palace** and adjoining royal temple, **Wat Phra Kaeo**, fronted by an open cremation field, **Sanam Luang**; the Wang Na (Palace of the Second King), now doing service as the **National Museum**, was also built at this time. **Wat Po**, which predates the capital's founding, was further embellished by Rama I's sucessors, who consolidated Ratanakosin's pre-eminence by building several grand European-style palaces (now housing government institutions), Wat Mahathat, the National Theatre and Thammasat University.

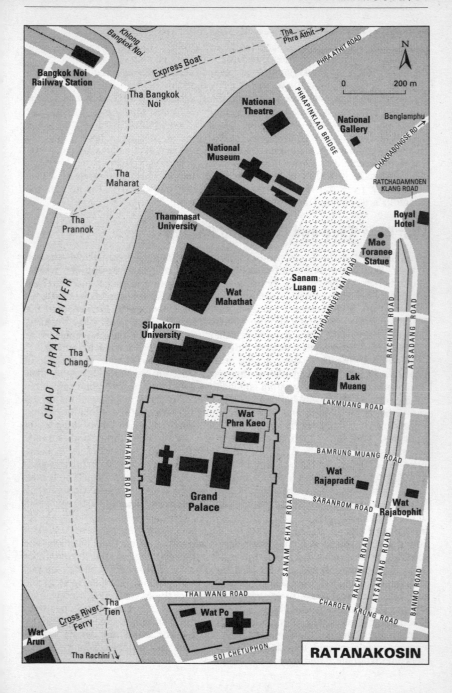

Bangkok has expanded eastwards away from the river, leaving the Grand Palace a good 5km from the city's commercial heart, and the royal family have long since moved their residence to Dusit, but Ratanakosin remains the ceremonial centre of the whole kingdom – so much so that it feels as if it might sink into the boggy ground under the weight of its own mighty edifices. The heavy, stately feel is lightened by noisy markets along the riverside strip and by Sanam Luang, still used for cremations and royal ceremonies, but also functioning as a popular open park and the hub of the modern city's bus system. Despite containing several of the country's main sights, the area is busy enough in its own right not to have become a swarming tourist zone, and strikes a neat balance between liveliness and grandeur.

Ratanakosin is within easy walking distance of Banglamphu, but is best approached from the river, via the express boat piers of Tha Chang (for the Grand Palace) or Tha Thien (for Wat Po).

Wat Phra Kaeo and the Grand Palace

Hanging together in a precarious harmony of strangely beautiful colours and shapes, **Wat Phra Kaeo** is the apogee of Thai religious art and the holiest Buddhist site in the country, housing the most important image, the **Emerald Buddha**. Built as the private royal temple, Wat Phra Kaeo occupies the northeast corner of the huge **Grand Palace**, whose official opening in 1785 marked the founding of the new capital and the rebirth of the Thai nation after the Burmese invasion. Successive kings have all left their mark, and the palace complex now covers sixty-one acres, though very little apart from the wat is open to tourists.

The only **entrance** to the complex in 2km of crenellated walls is the Gate of Glorious Victory in the middle of the north side, on Na Phra Lan Road. This brings you onto a driveway with a tantalizing view of the temple's glittering spires on the left and the dowdy buildings of the Offices of the Royal Household on the right: this is the powerhouse of the kingdom's ceremonial life, providing everything down to chairs and catering, and even lending an urn when someone of rank dies. Turn left at the end of the driveway for the ticket office and entrance turnstiles: **admission** to Wat Phra Kaeo and the palace is B100 (daily 8.30am–noon & 1–3.30pm), which includes a free brochure and invaluable map, as well as admission to the Vimanmek Palace in the Dusit area (see p.82). You'll be turned away if you're wearing shorts, but all need not be lost, as an enterprising stall-holder rents long trousers opposite the Gate of Glorious Victory.

Wat Phra Kaeo

Entering the temple is like stepping onto a lavishly detailed stage set, from the immaculate flagstones right up to the gaudy roofs. Although it receives hundreds of foreign sightseers and at least as many Thai pilgrims every day, the temple, which has no monks in residence, maintains an unnervingly santised look, as if it was built only yesterday. Its jigsaw of structures can seem complicated at first, but the basic layout is straightforward: the turnstiles in the west wall open onto the back of the bot, which contains the Emerald Buddha; to the left, the upper terrace runs parallel to the north side of the bot, while the whole temple compound is surrounded by arcaded walls, decorated with extraordinary murals of scenes from the *Ramayana*.

THE APPROACH TO THE BOT

Immediately inside the turnstiles, you'll be confronted by twenty-foot-tall *yaksha*, gaudy demons from the *Ramayana*, who watch over the Emerald Buddha from every gate of the temple and ward off evil spirits. Less threatening is the toothless old codger, cast in bronze and sitting on a plinth by the back wall of the bot, who represents a Hindu hermit credited with inventing yoga and herbal medicine. Skirting around the bot, you'll reach its **main entrance** on the eastern side, in front of which stands a cluster of grey **statues**, which have a strong Chinese feel: next to Kuan Im, the Chinese Goddess of Mercy, are a sturdy pillar topped by a lotus flower, which Bangkok's Chinese community presented to Rama IV during his 27 years as a monk, and two handsome cows which commemorate Rama I's birth, in the Year of the Cow. Worshippers make their offerings to the Emerald Buddha in amongst the statues, where they can look at the image through the open doors of the bot without messing up its pristine interior with candle wax and joss-stick ash.

Nearby in the southeastern corner of the temple precinct, look out for the beautiful country scenes painted in gold and blue on the doors of the **Chapel of the Gandhara Buddha**, a building which was crucial to the old royal rain-making ritual. Adorning the roof are thousands of nagas, symbolising water; inside the locked chapel – among the paraphernalia used in the ritual – is kept the Gandhara Buddha, a bronze image in the gesture of calling down the rain with its right hand, while cupping the left to catch it. In times of drought the king would order this week-long ceremony to be conducted, during which he was bathed regularly and kept away from the opposite sex while Buddhist monks and Hindu Brahmins chanted continuously. Traditional methods still have their place in Thai weather reading: 1991 was said to be a good wet year, with the rain measured at "five nagas".

THE BOT AND THE EMERALD BUDDHA

The **bot**, the largest building of the temple, is one of the few original structures left at Wat Phra Kaeo, though it has been augmented so often it looks like the work of a wildly inspired child. Eight *sema* stones mark the boundary of the consecrated area around the bot, each sheltering in a psychedelic fairy castle, joined by a low wall decorated with Chinese porcelain tiles which depict delicate landscapes. The walls of the bot itself, which sparkle with gilt and coloured glass, are supported by 112 golden garudas (birdmen) holding nagas (serpents) – representations of the god Indra saving the world by slaying the serpent-cloud which had swallowed up all the water. The symbolism reflects the king's traditional role as a rainmaker.

Inside the bot, a thirty-foot-high pedestal supports the tiny **Emerald Buddha**, a figure whose mystique draws pilgrims from all over Thailand – here especially you must act with respect, sitting with your feet pointing away from the Buddha. The spiritual power of the two-foot jadeite image comes from its legendary past. Reputed to have been created in Sri Lanka, it was discovered when lightning cracked open an ancient chedi in Chiang Rai in the early fifteenth century. The image was then moved around the north, dispensing miracles wherever it went, before being taken to Laos for two hundred years. The future Rama I snatched it back when he captured Vientiane in 1779, as it was believed to bring great fortune to its possessor, and installed it at the heart of his new capital as a talisman for king and country.

To this day the king himself ceremonially changes the Buddha's costumes, of which there are three, one for each season: the crown and ornaments of an Ayutthayan king for the hot season; a gilt monastic robe dotted with blue enamel for the rainy season, when the monks retreat into the temples; and a full-length gold shawl to wrap up in the cool season. (The spare outfits are displayed in the Coins and Decorations Pavilion outside the turnstiles leading into the temple.) Amongst the paraphernalia in front of the pedestal is the small, black, Victory Buddha, which Rama I always carried with him into war for luck. The two lowest Buddhas were both put there by Rama IX: the one on the left on his sixtieth birthday in 1987, the other when he became the longest-reigning Thai monarch in 1988.

THE UPPER TERRACE

The eastern end of the **upper terrace** is taken up with the **Prasat Phra Thep Bidorn**, known as the **Royal Pantheon**, a splendid hash of styles. The pantheon has its roots in the Khmer concept of *devaraja*, or the divinity of kings: inside are bronze and gold statues, precisely life-size, of all the kings since Bangkok became the capital. The building is open only on special occasions, such as Chakri Day (April 6), when the dynasty is commemorated.

From here you get the best view of the two **viharns** and the **library** to the north, any of which would take pride of place in any other wat, and, running along the east side of the temple, a row of eight bullet-like **prangs** which Somerset Maugham described as "monstrous vegetables": each has a different nasty ceramic colour and they represent, in turn, the Buddha, Buddhist scripture, the monkhood, the nunhood, the three Buddhas to come, and finally the king.

In the middle of the terrace, dressed in deep green glass mosaics, the **Phra Mondop** was built by Rama I to house the *Tripitaka*, or Buddhist scripture. It's famous for the mother-of-pearl cabinet and solid silver mats inside, but is never open. Four tiny **memorials** at each corner of the mondop show the symbols of each of the nine Chakri kings, from the ancient crown representing Rama I to the present king's sun symbol, while the bronze statues surrounding the memorials portray each king's lucky white elephants, labelled by name and pedigree. A contribution of Rama IV, on the north side of the mondop, is a **scale model of Angkor Wat**, the prodigious Cambodian temple which during his reign was under Thai rule. At the western end of the terrace, you can't miss the golden dazzle of the **Phra Si Ratana Chedi**, which Rama IV (1851–68) erected to enshrine a piece of the Buddha's breastbone.

THE MURALS

Extending for over a kilometre in the arcades which run inside the wat walls, the **murals of the Ramayana** depict every blow of this ancient story of the triumph of good over evil, using the vibrant buildings of the temple itself as backdrops, and setting them off against the subdued colours of richly detailed landscapes. Because of the damaging humidity, none of the original work of Rama I's time survives: maintenance is a never-ending process, so you'll always find an artist working on one of the scenes.

The story is told in 178 panels, labelled and numbered in Thai only, starting in the middle of the northern side: in the first episode, a hermit, while out ploughing, finds the baby Sita, the heroine, floating in a gold urn on a lotus leaf and brings her to the city. Panel 109 shows the climax of the story, when Rama, the hero, kills the ten-headed demon Totsagan, and the ladies of the enemy city weep at the demon's death. Panel 110 depicts his elaborate funeral procession, and in

THE RAMAYANA

The **Ramayana** is generally thought to have originated as an oral epic in India, where it appears in numerous dialects. The most famous version is that of the poet Valmiki, who as a tribute to his king drew together the collection of stories over 2000 years ago. From India, the *Ramayana* spread to all the Hindu-influenced countries of South Asia and was passed down through the Khmers to Thailand, where as the **Ramakien** it has become the national epic, acting as an affirmation of the Thai monarchy and its divine Hindu links. As a source of inspiration for literature, painting, sculpture and dance-drama, it has acquired the authority of holy writ, providing Thais with moral and practical lessons, while its appearance in the form of films and comic strips shows its huge popular appeal. The version current in Thailand was composed by a committee of poets sponsored by Rama I, and runs to 3000 pages.

The **central story** of the *Ramayana* concerns **Rama** (in Thai, Phra Ram), son of the King of Ayodhya, and his beautiful wife **Sita**, whose hand he wins by lifting and stringing a magic bow. The couple's adventures begin when they are exiled to the forest, along with Rama's good brother, **Lakshaman** (Phra Lak), by the hero's father under the influence of his evil stepmother. Meanwhile, in the city of Lanka (in Thai, Longka), the demon king **Totsagan** (also known as Ravana) has conceived a passionate desire for Sita and, disguised as a hermit, sets out to kidnap her. By transforming one of his subjects into a beautiful deer, which Rama and Laksmana go off to hunt, Totsagan catches Sita alone and takes her back to Lanka. Rama then wages a long war against the demons of Lanka, into which are woven many battles, spy scenes and diversionary episodes, and eventually kills Totsagan and rescues Sita.

The Thai version shows some characteristic differences from the Indian. Hanuman, the loyal monkey king, is given a much more playful role in the *Ramakien*, with the addition of many episodes which display his cunning and talent for mischief, but the major alteration comes at the end of the story, when Rama doubts Sita's faithfulness after rescuing her from Totsagan. In the Indian story, this ends with Sita being swallowed up by the earth so that she doesn't have to suffer Rama's doubts any more; in the *Ramakien* the ending is a happy one, with Rama and Sita living together happily ever after.

113 you can see the funeral fair, with acrobats, sword jugglers, and tightrope walkers. In between, Sita – Rama's wife – has to walk on fire to prove that she has been faithful during her fourteen years of imprisonment by Totsagan. If you haven't the stamina for the long walk round, you could sneak a look at the end of the story, to the left of the first panel, where Rama holds a victory parade and distributes thank-you gifts.

The palace buildings
The exit in the southwest corner of Wat Phra Kaeo brings you to the palace proper, a vast area of buildings and gardens, of which only the northern edge is on show to the public. Though the King now lives in the Chitrlada Palace in Dusit, the Grand Palace is still used for state receptions and official ceremonies, during which there is no public access to any part of the palace.

PHRA MAHA MONTHIEN
Coming out of the temple compound, you'll first be confronted by a beautiful Chinese gate covered in innumerable tiny porcelain tiles. The **Phra Maha Monthien**, which extends in a straight line behind the gate, was the grand resi-

dential complex of earlier kings. Only the **Phra Thinang Amarin Winichai**, the main audience hall at the front of the complex, is open to the public. The supreme court in the era of the absolute monarchy, it nowadays serves as the venue for the King's birthday speech; dominating the hall is the *busbok*, an open-sided throne with a spired roof, floating on a boat-shaped base. The rear buildings are still used for the most important part of the elaborate coronation ceremony, and each new king is supposed to spend a night there to show solidarity with his forefathers.

CHAKRI MAHA PRASAT AND INNER PALACE

Next door you can admire the facade – nothing else – of the "farang with a Thai hat", as the **Chakri Maha Prasat** is nicknamed. Rama V, whose portrait you can see over the entrance, employed an English architect to design a purely Neoclassical residence, but other members of the royal family prevailed on the king to add the three Thai spires. This used to be the site of the elephant stables: the large red tethering posts are still there and the bronze elephants were installed as a reminder. The building displays the emblem of the Chakri dynasty on its gable, which has a trident (*ri*) coming out of a *chak*, a discus with a sharpened rim.

The **Inner Palace**, which used to be the king's harem (closed to the public), lies behind the gate on the left-hand side of the Chakri Maha Prasat. The harem was a town in itself, with shops, law-courts and a police force for the huge all-female population: as well as the current queens, the minor wives and their servants, this was home to the daughters and consorts of former kings, and the daughters of the aristocracy who attended the harem's finishing school. Today, the Inner Palace houses a school of cooking, fruit-carving and other domestic sciences for well-bred young Thais.

DUSIT MAHA PRASAT

On the western side of the courtyard, the delicately proportioned **Dusit Maha Prasat**, an audience hall built by Rama I, epitomises traditional Thai architecture. Outside, the soaring tiers of its red, gold and green roof culminate in a gilded *mongkut*, a spire shaped like the king's crown which symbolises the 33 Buddhist levels of perfection. Each tier of the roof bears a typical *chofa*, a slender, stylised bird's head, and several *hang hong* ("swan's tails"), which represent three-headed nagas. Inside, you can still see the original throne, the **Phra Ratcha Banlang Pradap Muk**, a masterpiece of mother-of-pearl inlaid work. When a senior member of the royal family dies, the hall is used for the lying-in-state: the body, embalmed and seated in a huge sealed urn, is placed in the west transept, waiting up to two years for an auspicious day to be cremated.

To the right and behind the Dusit Maha Prasat rises a strange model mountain, decorated with fabulous animals and topped by a castle and prang. It represents **Mount Krailas**, a version of Mount Meru, the centre of the Hindu universe, and was built as the site of the royal tonsure ceremony. In former times, Thai children had shaved heads except for a tuft on the crown which, between the age of five and eight, was cut in a Hindu initiation rite to welcome adolescence. For the royal children, the rite was an elaborate ceremony that sometimes lasted five days, culminating with the king's cutting of the hair knot. The child was then bathed at the model Krailas, in water representing the original river of the universe flowing down the central mountain.

Wat Po

Where Wat Phra Kaeo may seem too perfect and shrink-wrapped for some, **Wat Po** (daily, 8am–5pm; B10), covering twenty acres to the south of the Grand Palace, is lively and shambolic, a complex arrangement of lavish structures which jostle with classrooms, basketball courts and a turtle pond. Coachloads of tourists disembark to see its colossal Reclining Buddha, but you'll leave them behind when you head off to explore the rest of the compound, where you'll more than likely be approached by friendly young monks wanting to practise their English.

Wat Po is the oldest temple in Bangkok and older than the city itself, having been founded in the seventeenth century under the name Wat Potaram. Foreigners have stuck to the contraction of this old name, even though Rama I, after enlarging the temple, changed the name in 1801 to Wat Phra Chetuphon, which is how it is generally known to Thais. The temple had another major over-haul in 1832, when Rama III built the chapel of the Reclining Buddha, and turned the temple into a public centre of learning by decorating the walls and pillars with inscriptions and diagrams on subjects such as history, literature, animal husbandry and astrology. Dubbed Thailand's first university, the wat is still an important centre for traditional medicine, notably **Thai massage**, which is used against all kinds of illnesses, from backaches to viruses. Thirty-hour training courses in English, held over either ten or fifteen days, cost B3000; alternatively you can simply go and suffer a massage yourself in the ramshackle buildings on the east side of the main compound, for B140 per hour.

The Eastern Courtyard

The visitors' **entrance** on Soi Chetuphon is one of a series of sixteen monumental gates around the main compound, each guarded by stone **giants**, many of them comic Westerners in wide-brimmed hats – ships which exported rice to China would bring these statues back as ballast.

The entrance brings you into the eastern half of the main complex, where a courtyard of structures radiate from the bot – the principal congregation and ordination hall – in a disorientating symmetry. To get to the bot at the centre, turn right and cut through the two surrounding cloisters, which are lined with 394 Buddha images, many of them covered with stucco to hide their bad state of repair – anyone can accrue some merit by taking one away and repairing it. The elegant **bot** has beautiful teak doors decorated with mother-of-pearl, showing stories from the *Ramayana* in minute detail. Look out also for the stone bas reliefs around the base of the bot, which narrate a longer version of the *Ramayana* in 152 action-packed panels. The plush interior has a well-proportioned altar on which ten statues of disciples frame a graceful Buddha image containing the remains of Rama I, the founder of Bangkok. Rama IV placed them there so that the public could worship him at the same time as the Buddha.

Back outside the entrance to the double cloister, keep your eyes open for a miniature mountain covered in statues of naked men in tall hats who appear to be gesturing rudely: they are *rishis* (hermits), demonstrating various positions of healing massage. Skirting the southwestern corner of the cloisters, you'll come to a pavilion between the eastern and western courtyards, which displays plaques inscribed with the precepts of traditional medicine, as well as anatomical pictures showing the different pressure points and the illnesses that can be cured by massaging them.

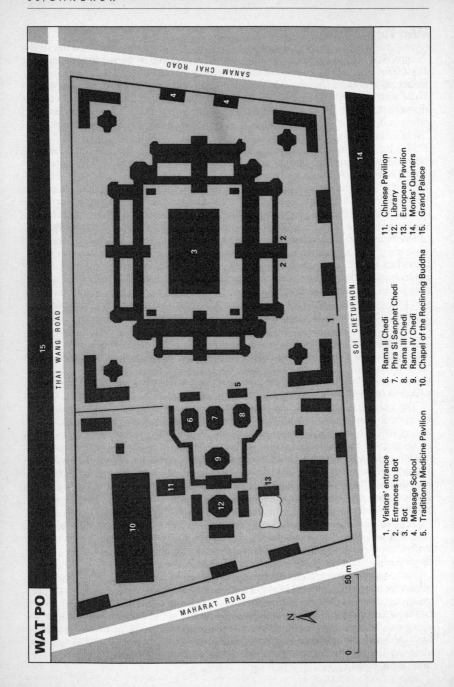

WAT PO

SANAM CHAI ROAD

THAI WANG ROAD

SOI CHETUPHON

MAHARAT ROAD

0   50 m

1. Visitors' entrance
2. Entrances to Bot
3. Bot
4. Massage School
5. Traditional Medicine Pavilion
6. Rama II Chedi
7. Phra Si Sanphet Chedi
8. Rama III Chedi
9. Rama IV Chedi
10. Chapel of the Reclining Buddha
11. Chinese Pavilion
12. Library
13. European Pavilion
14. Monks' Quarters
15. Grand Palace

The Western Courtyard

Amongst the 95 chedis strewn about the grounds, the four **great chedis** in the western courtyard stand out as much for their covering of garish tiles as for their size. The central chedi is the oldest, erected by Rama I to hold the remains of the most sacred Buddha image of Ayutthaya, the Phra Si Sanphet. (All chedis are supposed to hold the ashes of the Buddha or some other important religious figure.) Later, Rama III built the chedi to the north for the ashes of Rama II and the chedi to the south to hold his own remains. Rama IV built the fourth, with bright blue tiles, for an uncertain purpose.

In the northwest corner of the courtyard stands the chapel of the **Reclining Buddha**, a 45-metre-long gilded statue of plaster-covered brick which depicts the Buddha entering nirvana, a common motif in Buddhist iconography. The chapel is only slightly bigger than the statue – you can't get far enough away to take in anything but a surreal close-up view of the beaming five-metre smile. As for the feet, the vast black soles are beautifully inlaid with delicate mother-of-pearl showing the 108 *lakshanas* or auspicious signs which distinguish the true Buddha. Around the statue are 108 bowls which will bring you good luck and a long life if you put 25 satang in each.

Sanam Luang

Sprawling across thirty acres north of the Grand Palace, **Sanam Luang** represents one of the last open spaces left in Bangkok, a bare field where residents of the capital gather in the evening to meet, eat and play. The nearby pavements are the marketplace for some exotic spiritual salesmen: on the eastern side sit astrologers and palm readers, and sellers of bizarre virility potions and contraptions; on the western side and spreading around Thammasat University and Wat Mahathat, scores of small-time hawkers sell amulets, though the range and quality are not as good as at the main market at Wat Rajnadda. In the early part of the year, the sky is filled with kites, which every afternoon are flown in kite-fighting contests.

As it's in front of the Grand Palace, the field is also the venue for national ceremonies, such as royal funerals and the **Ploughing Ceremony**, held in May at a time selected by astrologers to bring good fortune to the rice harvest. The elaborate Brahmin ceremony is led by an official from the Ministry of Agriculture who stands in for the king, in case the royal power were to be reduced by any failure in the ritual. At the designated time, the official cuts a series of circular furrows with a plough driven by two oxen, and scatters rice which has been sprinkled with lustral water by the Brahmin priests of the court. When the ritual is over, spectators rush in to grab handfuls of the rice, which they then plant in their own paddies for good luck.

Lak muang

At 6.54am on April 21, 1782 – the astrologically determined time for the auspicious founding of Bangkok – a pillar containing the city's horoscope was ceremonially driven into the ground opposite the northeast corner of the Grand Palace. This pillar, the **lak muang** – all Thai cities have one, to provide a home for their guardian spirits – was made from a twelve-foot tree trunk carved with a lotus-shaped crown, and is now sheltered in an elegant shrine surrounded by immaculate gardens. It shares the shrine with the taller *lak muang* of Thonburi, which was recently incorporated into Greater Bangkok.

KITE FLYING

Flying intricate and colourful **kites** is now done mostly for fun in Thailand, but it has its roots in more serious activities. Filled with gunpowder and fitted with long fuses, kites were deployed in the first Thai kingdom at Sukhothai (1240–1438) as machines of war. In the same era, special *ngao* kites, with heads in the shape of bamboo bows, were used in Brahmin rituals: the string of the bow would vibrate in the wind and make a noise to frighten away evil spirits (nowadays noisy kites are still used, but only by farmers, to scare the birds). By the height of the Ayutthayan period (1351–1767) kites had become largely decorative: royal ceremonies were enhanced by fantastically shaped kites, adorned with jingling bells and ornamental lamps.

In the nineteenth century Rama V, by his enthusiastic lead, popularised kite flying as a clean-cut and fashionable recreation. **Contests** are now held all over the country between February and April, when winds are strong and farmers have free time after harvesting the rice. These contests fall into two broad categories: those involving manoeuvrable flat kites, often in the shapes of animals; and those in which the beauty of static display kites is judged. The most popular contest of all, which comes under the first category, matches two teams, one flying star-shaped *chulas*, six-foot-high "male" kites, the other flying the smaller, more agile *pakpaos*, diamond-shaped "females". Each team uses its skill and teamwork to ensnare the other's kites and drag them back across a dividing line.

Hundreds of worshippers come every day to pray and offer flowers, particularly childless couples seeking the gift of fertility. In one corner of the gardens you can often see short performances of **classical dancing**, paid for by well-off families when they have a piece of good fortune to celebrate.

Mae Toranee

In a tiny park by the hectic bus stops at the northeast corner of Sanam Luang stands the abundant but rather neglected figure of **Mae Toranee**, the earth goddess, wringing the water from her ponytail. Originally part of a fountain built here by Rama V's queen, Saowaba, to provide Bangkokians with fresh drinking water, the statue illustrates a Buddhist legend featured in the murals of many temples. While the Buddha was sitting in meditation at a crucial stage of his enlightenment, Mara, the force of evil, sent a host of earthly temptations and demons to try to divert him from his path. The Buddha remained cross-legged and pointed his right hand towards the ground – the most popular pose of Buddha statues in Thailand – to call the earth goddess to bear witness to his countless meritorious deeds, which had earned him an ocean of water stored in the earth. Mae Toranee obliged by wringing her hair and engulfing Mara's demons in the deluge.

The National Museum

Near the northwest corner of Sanam Luang, the **National Museum** (Wed–Sun 9am–4pm; B20) houses a colossal hoard of Thailand's chief artistic riches, ranging from sculptural treasures in the north and south wings, to bizarre decorative objects in the older buildings. The free **guided tours in English** (Wed & Thurs 9.30am) are worth making time for: they're generally entertaining and their explication of the choicest exhibits provides a good introduction to Thai religion and culture. Should you linger longer than anticipated – and most people do – the **cafeteria** serves good, cheap Thai food.

History and prehistory

The building which houses the ticket office provides a quick whirl through the **history** of Thailand, a display in which are hidden a couple of gems. The first is a black stone inscription, credited to King Ramkhamhaeng of Sukhothai, which became the first capital of the Thai nation in the thirteenth century. Discovered in 1833 by the future Rama IV, it's the oldest extant inscription using the Thai alphabet. This, combined with the description it records of prosperity and piety in Sukhothai's Golden Age, has made the stone a symbol of Thai nationhood. Further on is a four-foot-tall carved *kinnari*, a graceful half-human, half-bird creature said to live in one of the Himalayan heavens. This delicate masterpiece is from the best period of Thai woodcarving, the seventeenth and early eighteenth centuries, before the fall of Ayutthaya.

The **prehistory** room is entered through a separate door at the back end of the building. Prominent here are bronze artefacts from Ban Chiang in the northeast of Thailand, one of the earliest bronze-age cultures ever discovered, including the world's oldest socketed tool, an axe head set in a sandstone mould (3600–2300 BC).

The main collection: southern building

At the back of the compound, two large modern buildings, flanking an old converted palace, house the museum's **main collection**, kicking off on the ground floor of the **southern building**. Look out here for some historic sculptures from the rest of Asia, including one of the earliest representations of the Buddha, from Gandhara in northwest India. Alexander the Great left a garrison at Gandhara, which explains why the image is in the style of classical Greek sculpture: for example, the *ushnisha*, the supernatural bump on the top of the head which symbolizes the Buddha's intellectual and spiritual power, is rationalized into a bun of thick, wavy hair.

Upstairs, in the **Dvaravati** rooms (sixth to eleventh centuries), the pick of the stone and terracotta Buddhas is a small head in smooth, pink clay, whose downcast eyes and faintly smiling full lips typify the serene look of this era. You can't miss a voluptuous Javanese statue of elephant-headed Ganesh, Hindu god of wisdom and the arts, which, being the symbol of the Fine Arts Department, is always freshly garlanded. As Ganesh is known as the clearer of obstacles, Hindus always worship him before other gods, so by tradition he has grown fat through getting first choice of the offerings – witness his trunk jammed into a bowl of food in this sculpture.

Room 9 contains the most famous piece of **Srivijaya** art (seventh to thirteenth centuries), a bronze Bodhisattva Avalokitesvara found at Chaiya – according to Mahayana Buddhism, a *bodhisattva* is a saint who has postponed his passage into nirvana to help ordinary believers gain enlightenment. With its pouting face and sinuous torso, this image has become the ubiquitous emblem of southern Thailand. The rough chronological order of the collection continues back downstairs with an exhibition of **Khmer** and **Lopburi** sculpture (seventh to fourteenth centuries), most notably some dynamic bronze statuettes and stone lintels. Look out for an elaborate lintel which depicts Vishnu reclining on a dragon in the sea of eternity, dreaming up a new universe after the old one has been annihilated in the Hindu cycle of creation and destruction. Out of his navel comes a lotus, and out of this emerges four-headed Brahma, who will put the dream into practice. Nearby, a smooth, muscular stone statue with a sweet smile and downcast eyes shows King Jayavarman VII, last of the great Khmer emperors. Such royal statues are very rare and the features borrowed from Buddha images suggest that Jayavarman believed that he was close to Buddhahood himself.

The main collection: northern building

The second half of the survey, in the northern building, begins upstairs with the **Sukhothai** collection (thirteenth to fifteenth centuries), which is short on Buddha images but has some chunky bronzes of Hindu gods and a wide range of ceramics. The **Lanna** room (thirteenth to sixteenth centuries) includes a miniature set of golden regalia, including tiny umbrellas and a cute pair of filigree flip-flops, which would have been enshrined in a chedi. An ungainly but serene Buddha head, carved from grainy, pink sandstone represents the **Ayutthaya** style of sculpture (fourteenth to eighteenth centuries): the faintest incision of a moustache above the lips betrays the Khmer influences which came to Ayutthaya after its conquest of Angkor. A sumptuous scripture cabinet, showing a cityscape of old Ayutthaya, is a more unusual piece, one of a surviving handful of such carved and painted items of furniture.

Downstairs in the **Bangkok** rooms (eighteenth century onwards) a stiffly realistic standing bronze brings you full circle: in his zeal for Western naturalism, Rama V had the statue made in the Gandhara style of the earliest Buddha image displayed in the first room of the museum.

The funeral chariots

To the east of the northern building, beyond the café on the left, stands a large garage where the fantastically elaborate **funeral chariots** of the royal family are stored. Pre-eminent among these is the Vejayant Rajarot, built by Rama I in 1785 for carrying the urn at his own funeral. The forty-foot-high structure symbolises heaven on Mount Meru, while the dragons and divinities around the sides – piled in five golden tiers to suggest the flames of the cremation – represent the mythological inhabitants of the mountain's forests. Weighing 40 tons and pulled by 300 men, the teak chariot was used as recently as 1985 for the funeral of Queen Rambhai Bharni, wife of Rama VII.

Wang Na (Palace of the Second King)

The central building of the compound was originally part of the **Wang Na**, a huge palace stretching across Sanam Luang to Khlong Lod, which housed the "second king", appointed by the reigning monarch as his heir and deputy. When Rama V did away with the office in 1887, he turned the "Palace of the Second King" into a museum, which now contains a fascinating array of Thai *objets d'art*. Behind heavy iron bars, the display of sumptuous rare gold pieces includes a well-preserved armlet taken from the ruined prang of fifteenth-century Wat Ratburana in Ayutthaya. Nearby, an intricately carved ivory seat turns out, with gruesome irony, to be a *howdah*, for use on an elephant's back. Among the masks worn by *khon* actors, look out especially for a fierce Hanuman, the white monkey-warrior in the *Ramayana* epic, gleaming with mother-of-pearl.

The huge and varied ceramic collection includes some sophisticated pieces from Sukhothai, while the room above holds a riot of mother-of-pearl items, whose flaming rainbow of colours comes from the shell of the turbo snail from the Thai Gulf. It's also worth seeking out the display of richly decorated musical instruments, where you can hear tapes of the unfamiliar sounds they produce.

The Buddhaisawan Chapel
The second holiest image in Thailand, after the Emerald Buddha, is housed in the **Buddhaisawan Chapel**, the vast hall in front of the eastern entrance to the Wang Na. Inside, the fine proportions are enhanced by painted rows of divinities and converted demons, all turned to face the chubby, glowing **Phra Sihing Buddha**, which according to legend was magically created in Sri Lanka and sent to Sukhothai in the thirteenth century. Like the Emerald Buddha, the image was believed to bring good luck to its owner and was frequently snatched from one northern town to another, until Rama I brought it down from Chiang Mai in 1795 and installed it here in the second king's private chapel. Two other images (in Nakhon Si Thammarat and Chiang Mai) now claim to be the authentic Phra Sihing Buddha, but all three are in fact derived from a lost original – this one is in a fifteenth-century Sukhothai style. It's still much loved by ordinary people and at Thai New Year is carried out onto Sanam Luang, where worshippers sprinkle it with water as a merit-making gesture.

The careful detail and rich, soothing colours of the surrounding 200-year-old **murals** are surprisingly well-preserved; the bottom row between the windows narrates the life of the Buddha, beginning in the far right-hand corner with his parents' wedding.

The National Gallery and Silpakorn University Gallery
If the National Museum hasn't finished you off, two other lesser galleries nearby might. **The National Gallery**, on the north side of Sanam Luang at 4 Chao Fa Road (Wed–Sun 9am–4pm; B10), houses a permanent collection of largely uninspiring twentieth-century Thai art, most based on traditional Buddhist themes or the *Ramayana*. The gallery hosts some interesting temporary exhibitions, though, as does the **Silpakorn University Gallery** on Na Phra Lan Road, across the road from the entrance to the Grand Palace: see the *Bangkok Post* or the *Nation* for details.

The Democracy Monument area

The most interesting sights in the area stretching to the south and east of Democracy Monument – a district within walking distance of the Grand Palace and the guest houses of Banglamphu – are its temples. Though not as spectacular as the excesses of neighbouring Ratanakosin, all have some significant idiosyncratic feature to make them worth visiting.

Democracy Monument
Midway along Rajdamnoen Klang, the avenue that connects the Grand Palace and the new royal district of Dusit, looms the imposing **Democracy Monument**. Begun in 1939, it was conceived as a testament to the ideals that fuelled the 1932 revolution and the changeover to a constitutional monarchy, hence its symbolic positioning between the royal residences. Its dimensions are also significant: the four wings tower to a height of 24 metres, the same as the radius of the monument – allusions to June 24, the date the system was changed; the 75 cannons around the perimeter refer to the year, 2475 BE (1932 AD). The monument contains a copy of the constitution and is a focal point for public demonstrations – it was a rallying-point during the pro-democracy protests of May 1992.

It was designed by Corrado Feroci, an Italian sculptor who'd been invited to Thailand by Rama VI in 1924 to encourage the pursuit of western art. He changed his name to Silpa Bhirasi and stayed in Thailand until his death, producing many of Bangkok's statues and monuments – including the Rama I statue at Memorial Bridge and Victory Monument in the Phrayathai district – as well as founding the first Institute of Fine Arts.

Wat Rajnadda, Loh Prasat and the amulet market

Five minutes' walk southeast of Democracy Monument, at the point where Rajdamnoen Klang meets Mahachai Road, stands the assortment of religious buildings known collectively as **Wat Rajnadda**. It's immediately recognisable by the dusky pink, multi-tiered, castle-like structure called **Loh Prasat** or "Iron Monastery" – a reference to its numerous metal spires. The only structure of its kind in Bangkok, Loh Prasat is the dominant and most bizarre of Wat Rajnadda's components. Each tier is pierced by passageways running north–south and east–west (fifteen in each direction at ground level), with small meditation cells at each point of intersection. The Sri Lankan monastery on which it is modelled contained a thousand cells; this one probably has half that number. Until a couple of years ago, the elegant facade of Loh Prasat was completely hidden by the Chalerm Chai movie theatre; as the cinema was Thailand's first, there was some debate as to whether it merited conservation, but eventually Loh Prasat won out and the cinema was demolished.

An adjoining compound contains Bangkok's biggest **amulet market**, where at least a hundred stalls open up daily to sell tiny Buddha images of all designs, materials and prices. Alongside these miniature charms are statues, dolls and carved wooden phalluses, also bought to placate or ward off disgruntled spirits. While the amulet market at Wat Rajnadda is probably the best in Bangkok, you'll find cheaper examples from the streetside vendors who congregate daily along the pavement in front of Wat Mahathat. Prices start as low as B10 and rise into the thousands.

The Golden Mount

The dirty yellow hill crowned with a gleaming gold chedi just across the road from Wat Rajnadda is the grandiosely named Golden Mount, or Phu Khao Tong. It rises within the compound of **Wat Saket**, a dilapidated late eighteenth-century temple built by Rama I just outside his new city walls to serve as the capital's crematorium. During the following hundred years the temple became the dumping ground for some 60,000 plague victims – the majority of them too poor to afford funeral pyres, and thus left to the vultures.

The **Golden Mount** was a late addition to the compound and dates back to the early nineteenth century, when Rama III built a huge chedi on ground that proved too soft to support it. The whole thing collapsed into a hill of rubble, but Buddhist law states that a religious building can never be destroyed, however tumbledown, so fifty years later Rama V topped the debris with a more sensibly sized chedi in which he placed a few Buddhist relics, believed by some to be Buddha's teeth.

To reach the base of the mount, follow the renovated crenellations of the old city wall, past the small bird and antiques market skulking in one of the recesses, before veering left when signposted. Climbing to the top, you'll pass remnants of the collapsed chedi and plaques commemorating donors to the temple. The **terrace** surrounding the base of the new chedi is a good place for landmark-spotting: immediately to the west are the gleaming roofs of Wat Rajnadda and the

AMULETS

To gain protection from malevolent spirits and physical misfortune, Thais wear or carry at least one **amulet** at all times. The most popular **images** are copies of sacred statues from famous wats, while others show revered holy men, kings (Rama V is a favourite), healers or a many-armed monk depicted closing his eyes, ears and mouth so as to concentrate better on reaching nirvana – a human version of the hear-no-evil, see-no-evil, speak-no-evil monkeys. On the reverse side is sometimes inscribed a *yantra*, a combination of letters and figures also designed to ward off evil. Amulets can be made from bronze, clay, plaster or gold, and some even have sacred ingredients added, such as the ashes of burnt holy texts. But what really determines its efficacy is its history: where and by whom it was made, who or what it represents and who consecrated it. Monks are often involved in the making of the images and are always called upon to consecrate them – the more charismatic the monk, the more powerful the amulet. In return, the proceeds from the sale of amulets contributes to wat funds.

The **belief in amulets** is thought to have originated in India, where tiny images were sold to pilgrims who visited the four holy sites associated with Buddha's birth, enlightenment, first sermon and death. But not all amulets are Buddhist-related – there's a whole range of other enchanted objects to wear for protection, including tigers' teeth, rose quartz, tamarind seeds, coloured threads and miniature phalluses. Worn around the waist rather than the neck, the phallus amulets provide protection for the genitals as well as being associated with fertility, and are of Hindu origin.

For some people, amulets are not only a vital form of spiritual protection, but valuable **collectors' items** as well. Amulet-collecting mania is something akin to stamp collecting – there are at least six Thai magazines for collectors which give histories of certain types, tips on distinguishing between genuine items and fakes, and personal accounts of particularly powerful amulet experiences.

salmon-pink Loh Prasat, and behind them you should be able to see the spires of the Grand Palace and even further beyond, the beautifully proportioned prangs of Wat Arun on the other side of the river. To the northwest, look for the controversial *Banglamphu Department Store*, whose eleven storeys contravene the local building laws, which ordain that no structure in the vicinity should compete with the Grand Palace.

Wat Saket hosts an enormous annual **temple fair** in the first week of November when the mount is illuminated with coloured lanterns and the whole compound seethes with funfair rides, food sellers and travelling performers.

Wat Suthat and Sao Ching Cha

Located about 1km southwest of the Golden Mount, and a similar distance directly south of Democracy Monument along Thanon Dinso, **Wat Suthat** contains Bangkok's tallest **viharn**, built in the early nineteenth century to house the meditating figure of **Phra Sri Sakyamuni Buddha**. This eight-metre-high statue was brought all the way down from Sukhothai by river, and now sits on a glittering mosaic dais surrounded with surreal **murals** that depict the last twenty-four lives of the Buddha rather than the more usual ten. The courtyard and galleries around the bot are full of **Chinese statues**, most of which were brought over from China during Rama I's reign, as ballast in rice boats: check out the gormless western sailors and the pompous Chinese scholars. Note that the viharn is often locked on weekdays.

Sailor statue at
Wat Suthat

The area just in front of Wat Suthat is dominated by the towering, red-painted teak posts of **Sao Ching Cha**, otherwise known as the **Giant Swing**, once the focal point of a Brahmin ceremony to honour Shiva's annual visit to earth. Teams of two or four young men would stand on the outsized seat (now missing) and swing up to a height of 25 metres, to grab between their teeth a bag of gold suspended on the end of a bamboo pole. The act of swinging probably symbolised the rising and setting of the sun, though legend also has it that Shiva and his consort Uma were banned from swinging in their heavenly abode because doing so caused cataclysmic floods on earth – prompting Shiva to demand that the practice be continued on earth as a rite to ensure moderate rains and bountiful harvests. Accidents were so common with the terrestrial version that it was outlawed in the 1930s.

Wat Rajabophit

On Rajabophit Road, midway between Wat Suthat and the Grand Palace, stands **Wat Rajabophit**, one of the city's prettiest temples and another example of Chinese influence. It was built by Rama V and is characteristic of this progressive king in its unusual design, with the rectangular bot and viharn connected by a circular cloister that encloses a chedi. Every external wall in the compound is covered in the pastel shades of Chinese *bencharong* ceramic tiles, creating a stunning overall effect, while the bot interior looks like a tiny banqueting hall, with gilded Gothic vaults and intricate mother-of-pearl doors.

If you now head west towards the Grand Palace from Wat Rajabophit, you'll pass a gold **statue of a pig** as you cross the canal. The cute porcine monument was erected in tribute to one of Rama V's wives, born in the Chinese year of the pig.

Chinatown and Pahurat

When the newly crowned Rama I decided to move his capital across to the east bank of the river in 1782, the Chinese community living on the proposed site of his palace was given no choice but to relocate downriver, to the **Sampeng** area. Two hundred years on, **Chinatown** has grown into the country's largest Chinese district, a sprawl of narrow alleyways, temples and shophouses packed between New Road (Charoen Krung) and the river, separated from Ratanakosin by the Indian area of **Pahurat** – famous for its cloth and dressmakers' trimmings – and bordered to the east by Hualamphong railway station. Though it has a couple of noteworthy temples, Chinatown is chiefly interesting for its markets and shophouses, open-fronted warehouses, and remnants of colonial-style architecture.

Easiest **access** is to take the Express Boat to Tha Rajavongse (Rajawong) at the southern end of Rajawong Road, which runs through the centre of Chinatown, or to walk from Hualamphong station. This part of the city is also well served by buses from downtown Bangkok, as well as from Banglamphu and Ratanakosin.

Wat Traimit and the Golden Buddha

Chinatown's crowded alleyways can be disorienting, so it's worth starting at the eastern edge of Chinatown, just west of Hualamphong Station, with the triangle of land occupied by **Wat Traimit** (daily 8.30am–5pm; B10). Outwardly unprepossessing, the temple boasts a quite stunning interior feature: the world's largest solid-gold Buddha is housed here, fitting for a community so closely linked with the gold trade, even if the image has nothing to do with China's spiritual heritage. Over three metres tall and weighing five and a half tons, the **Golden Buddha** gleams as if coated in liquid metal, seated amidst candles and surrounded with offerings of lotus buds and incense. A fine example of the curvaceous grace of Sukhothai art, the beautifully proportioned figure is best appreciated by comparing it with the much cruder Sukhothai Buddha in the next-door bot, to the east.

THE CHINESE IN THAILAND

The **Chinese** have been a dominant force in the shaping of Thailand, and **commerce** is the foundation of their success. Chinese merchants first gained a toehold here in the mid-fourteenth century, when they contributed so much to the prosperity of the city-state of Ayutthaya that they were the only foreign community allowed to live within the city walls. Soon their compatriots were established all over the country, and when the capital was eventually moved to Bangkok it was to an already flourishing Chinese trading post.

The Bangkok era marked an end to the wars that had dogged Thailand and as the economy began to boom, both Rama I and Rama II encouraged Chinese immigration to boost the indigenous workforce. Thousands of migrants came, most of them young men eager to earn money that could be sent back to families impoverished by civil wars and persistently bad harvests. They saw their overseas stints as temporary measures, intending to return after a few years, though many never did. By the middle of the nineteenth century half the capital's population were of pure or mixed Chinese blood, and they were quickly becoming the masters of the new import-export trade, particularly the burgeoning tin and rubber industries. By the end of the century, the Chinese dominated Thailand's commercial and urban sector, while the Thais remained in firm control of the political domain, an arrangement that apparently satisfied both parties: as the old Chinese proverb goes, "We don't mind who holds the head of the cow, providing we can milk it."

Up until the beginning of this century, **intermarriage** between the two communities had been common, because so few Chinese women had emigrated – indeed, there is some Chinese blood in almost every Thai citizen, including the king. But in the early 1900s Chinese women started to arrive in Thailand, making Chinese society increasingly self-sufficient and enclosed. **Anti-Chinese feelings** grew and discriminatory laws ensued, including the restricting of Chinese-language education and the closing of some jobs to Chinese citizens, a movement that increased in fervour as communism began to be perceived as a threat. Since the late 1970s, strict immigration controls have been enforced, limiting the number of new settlers to 100 per nationality per year, a particularly harsh imposition on the Chinese.

The Chinese still dominate the commercial sector, as can be witnessed over the annual three-day holiday at **Chinese New Year**, when throughout the kingdom nearly all shops, hotels and restaurants shut down. This is the community's most important festival, but is celebrated much more as a family affair than in the Chinatowns of other countries. The Vegetarian Festival, observed by the Chinese residents of Phuket and Trang provinces, but not in Bangkok, is a more public celebration (see p.378).

Cast in the thirteenth century, the image was brought to Bangkok by Rama III, completely encased in stucco – a common ruse to conceal valuable statues from would-be thieves. The disguise was so good that no one guessed what was underneath until 1955 when the image was accidentally knocked in the process of being moved to Wat Traimit, and the stucco cracked to reveal a patch of gold. The discovery launched a country-wide craze for tapping away at plaster Buddhas in search of hidden precious metals, but Wat Traimit's is still the most valuable – it's valued, by weight alone, at $14 million. Sections of the stucco casing are now on display alongside the Golden Buddha.

Sampeng Lane, Soi Issaranuphap and Nakhon Kasem

Five minutes southwest of Wat Traimit, **Sampeng Lane** (signposted as Soi Wanit 1) used to thrive on opium dens, gambling houses and brothels, but now sticks to a more reputable trade in wholesale fabrics, shoes and household goods. Stretching southeast–northwest for about 1km, Sampeng Lane makes an interesting introduction to commercial Chinatown, but a walk along **Soi Issaranuphap**, which crosses it about halfway along, is a more sensual experience.

Packed with people from dawn till dusk, this dark alleyway is where you come in search of ginseng roots (essential for good health), still quivering fish heads, cubes of cockroach-killer chalk, and pungent piles of cinnamon sticks. You'll see Chinese grandfathers discussing business in darkened shops, ancient pharmacists concocting bizarre potions to order, alleys branching off in all directions to gaudy Chinese temples and market squares. Soi Issaranuphap finally ends at Plaplachai Road, where you'll find shops specialising in paper **funeral art**. Believing that the deceased should be well provided for in their afterlife, Chinese buy miniature paper replicas of necessities to be burned with the body: especially popular are houses, cars, suits of clothing and, of course, money.

A few hundred metres west of Soi Issaranuphap, there's an odd assortment of shops in the square known as **Nakhon Kasem** (Thieves' Market), bordered by New and Yaowarat roads to the north and south and Chakrawat and Boriphat roads to the east and west. In the sois that crisscross Nakhon Kasem outlets once full of illicitly acquired goods now stock a vast range of metal wares, from antique gongs to modern musical instruments and machine parts.

Wat Chakrawat

Before Sampeng Lane finally fizzles out at the western edge of Chinatown, turn left down Chakrawat Road (towards the river) to reach **Wat Chakrawat**, home to several long-suffering crocodiles, not to mention monkeys, dogs and chess-playing locals. **Crocodiles** have lived in the tiny pond behind the bot for about fifty years, ever since one was brought here after being hauled out of the Chao Phraya, where it had been endangering the limbs of bathers. (Unlikely as it sounds, crocodiles still occasionally turn up: a boy was attacked recently while playing in the Chao Phraya in Nonthaburi). The original crocodile, stuffed, sits in a glass case overlooking the current generation in the pond.

Across the other side of the wat compound is a grotto housing two unusual Buddhist relics. The first is a black silhouette on the wall, decorated with squares of gold leaf and believed to be the Buddha's shadow. Nearby, the statue of a fat monk looks on. The story goes that this monk was so good-looking that he was forever being tempted by the attentions of women; the only way he could deter them was to make himself ugly, which he did by gorging himself into obesity.

Pahurat

The ethnic emphasis changes one block west of Chakrawat Road. Cross Khlong Ong Ang and you're in **Pahurat** – here, in the small square south of the intersection of Chakraphet and Pahurat roads, is where the capital's sizeable Indian community congregates. Curiosity-shopping is not as rewarding here as in Chinatown, but if you're interested in buying **fabrics** other than thai silk this is definitely the place. Pahurat Road is chock-a-block with cloth merchants specialising in everything from curtain and cushion materials, through saree and sarong lengths to wedding outfits and *lakhon* dance costumes complete with accessories. Food is Pahurat's other speciality: a short stroll along Chakraphet Road will take you past a choice selection of bona fide **Indian restaurants** and street-vendors.

Thonburi

Bangkok really began across the river from Ratanakosin in the town of **Thonburi**. Devoid of grand ruins and isolated from central Bangkok, it's hard to imagine Thonburi as a former capital of Thailand, but so it was for fifteen years, between the fall of Ayutthaya in 1767 and the establishment of Bangkok in 1782. General Phrya Taksin chose to set up his capital here, strategically near the sea and far from the marauding Burmese, but the story of his brief reign is a chronicle of battles that left little time and few resources to devote to the building of a city worthy of its predecessor. When General Chao Phraya displaced the demented Taksin to become Rama I, his first decision as founder of the Chakri dynasty was to move the capital to the more defensible site across the river. It wasn't until 1932 that Thonburi was linked to its replacement by the **Memorial Bridge**, built to commemorate the one-hundred-and-fiftieth anniversary of the foundation of the Chakri dynasty and of Bangkok, and dedicated to Rama I, whose bronze statue sits at the Bangkok approach. Thonburi retained its separate identity for another forty years until, in 1971, it officially became part of Bangkok.

While Thonburi may lack the fine monuments of Thailand's other ancient capitals, it nevertheless contains some of the most traditional parts of Bangkok and makes a pleasant and evocative place to wander. As well as the imposing riverside structure of Wat Arun, Thonburi offers a fleet of royal barges and several moderately interesting temples. In addition, life on this side of the river still revolves around the khlongs, on which vendors of food and household goods paddle their boats through the residential areas and canalside factories transport their wares to the Chao Phraya artery. Canalside **architecture** ranges from ramshackle, makeshift homes balanced just above the water – and prone to flooding during the monsoon season – to villa-style residences where the river is kept at bay by lawns, verandahs and concrete. Modern Thonburi, on the other hand, sprawling to each side of Phra Pinklao Road, consists of the prosaic line-up of department stores, cinemas, restaurants and markets found all over urbanised Thailand.

Getting there is simply a matter of crossing the river – use one of the numerous bridges (Memorial and Phra Pinklao are the most central), take a cross-river ferry, or hop on the express ferry, which makes three stops around the riverside Bangkok Noi station, just south of Phra Pinklao Bridge. You might find yourself taking a train from Bangkok Noi, as this is the departure point for Kanchanaburi; the Southern Bus Terminal is also in Thonburi, on Pinklao–Nakhon Chaisri Road, and all public and air-con buses to southern destinations leave from here.

THONBURI CANAL RIDES

One of the most popular ways of seeing the sights of Thonburi is to embark on a canal tour by **chartering a longtail boat** from Tha Chang, in front of the Grand Palace. These tours follow a set route, taking in Wat Arun and the Royal Barge Museum and then continuing along Thonburi's network of small canals, and charge an average price of B250 per person. There are no official departure times: you just turn up at the pier, haggle with the boatman next in line and jump into his longtail.

A cheaper and equally satisfying alternative is to use the **public longtails** that run bus-like services along back canals from central Bangkok-side piers, departing every 10–30 minutes and charging B10–30 a round trip. No single route is more interesting than another, but the most accessible ones include: the Khlong Bangkok Noi service from Tha Chang; the Khlong Mon service from Tha Thien, in front of Wat Po; the Khlong Bang Waek service from Tha Saphan Phut, at Memorial Bridge; and the Khlong Om service from Tha Nonthaburi.

A fixture of the upper-bracket tourist round is the **organised canal tour** to see Thonburi's Wat Sai **floating market**. This has become so commercialised and land-based that it can't be recommended in preference to the two-hour trip out to the floating market of Damnoen Saduak (see p.118), but if you're short on time and set on seeing fruit- and flower-laden paddle boats, you can join longtail Wat Sai market tours from Tha Chang or from Tha Orienten (at the *Oriental Hotel*). Tours leave at around 7am and cost from B300 per person.

Wat Arun

Amost directly across the river from Wat Po rises the enormous five-pranged **Wat Arun** (daily 8.30am–5.30pm; B5), the Temple of Dawn, probably Bangkok's most memorable landmark and familiar as the silhouette used in the TAT logo. It's best seen from the river, as you head downstream from the Grand Palace towards the *Oriental Hotel*, but is ornate enough to merit stopping off for a closer look. All boat tours include half an hour here, but Wat Arun is also easily visited by yourself, although tour operators will try to persuade you otherwise: just take a cross-river ferry from Tha Thien (B2).

A wat has occupied this site since the Ayutthaya period, but only in 1768 did it become known as the Temple of Dawn – when General Phrya Taksin reputedly reached his new capital at the break of day. The temple served as his royal chapel and housed the recaptured Emerald Buddha for several years until the image was moved to Wat Phra Kaeo in 1785. Despite losing its special status after the relocation, Wat Arun continued to be revered and was reconstructed and enlarged to its present height of 104m by Rama II and Rama III.

The Wat Arun that you see today is a classic prang structure of Ayutthayan style, built as a representation of Mount Meru, the home of the gods in Khmer mythology. Climbing the two tiers of the square base that supports the **central prang**, you not only get a good view of the river and beyond, but also a chance to examine the tower's curious decorations. Both this main prang and the four minor ones that encircle it are covered in bits of broken porcelain, arranged to create an amazing array of polychromatic flowers. (Local people gained much merit by donating their crockery for the purpose.) Statues of mythical figures such as *yaksha* demons and half-bird, half-human *kinnari* support the different levels and on the first terrace, the mondops at each cardinal point contain statues of Buddha at the most important stages of his life: at birth (north), in meditation (east), preaching his first sermon (south) and entering nirvana (west). The second platform surrounds the base of the prang proper whose closed entranceways are guarded by four statues of the Hindu god Indra on his three-headed elephant Erawan. In the niches of the smaller prangs stand statues of Phra Pai, the god of the wind, on horseback.

Wat Prayoon

Downstream of Wat Arun, beside Memorial Bridge, **Wat Prayoon** is worth visiting for its unusual collection of miniature chedis and shrines, set on an artificial hill constructed on a whim of Rama III's, after he'd noticed the pleasing shapes made by dripping candle wax. Wedged in among the grottoes, caverns and ledges of this uneven mass are numerous shrines to departed devotees, forming a phenomenal gallery of different styles, from traditionally Thai chedis, bots or prangs to such obviously foreign designs as the tiny wild-west house complete with cactuses at the front door. Turtles fill the pond surrounding the mound – you can feed them with the banana and papaya sold nearby. At the edge of the pond stands a memorial to the unfortunate few who lost their lives when one of the saluting cannons exploded at the temple's dedication ceremony in 1836.

About ten minutes' walk upstream from Wat Prayoon, the Catholic church of **Santa Cruz** sits at the heart of what used to be Thonburi's **Portuguese quarter**. The Portuguese came to Thailand both to trade and to proselytise, and by 1856 had established the largest of the European communities in Bangkok: 4000 Portuguese Christians lived in and around Thonburi at this time, about one percent of the total population. The Portuguese ghetto is a thing of the distant past, but this is nonetheless an interesting patch to stroll through, comprising narrow backstreets and tiny shophouses stocked with all manner of goods, from two-baht plastic toys to the essential bottles of chilli sauce.

Royal Barge Museum

Until about fifteen years ago, the king would process down the Chao Phraya River to Wat Arun in a flotilla of royal barges at least once a year, on the occasion of Kathin, the annual donation of robes by the laity to the temple at the end of the rainy season. Fifty-one barges, filling the width of the river and stretching for almost a kilometre, drifted slowly to the measured beat of a drum and the hypnotic strains of ancient boating hymns, chanted by over 2000 oarsmen whose red, gold and blue uniforms complimented the black and gold craft.

The one-hundred-year-old boats are becoming quite frail, so such a procession is now a rare event – the last was in 1987, to mark the King's sixtieth birthday. The three elegantly narrow vessels at the heart of the ceremony now spend their time moored in the **Royal Barge Museum** on the north bank of Khlong Bangkok Noi (daily 8.30am–4.30pm; B10). Up to fifty metres long and intricately lacquered and gilded all over, they taper at the prow into magnificent mythical figures after a design first used by the kings of Ayutthaya. Rama I had the boats copied and, when those fell into disrepair, Rama V commissioned the exact reconstructions still in use today. The most important of the trio is *Sri Suphanahongse*, which bears the King and Queen and is instantly recognizable by the fifteen-foot-high prow representing a golden swan. In front of it floats *Anantanagaraj*, fronted by a magnificent seven-headed naga and bearing a Buddha image, while the royal children bring up the rear in *Anekchartphuchong*, which has a monkey god from the *Ramayana* at the bow.

The museum is a feature of all canal tours. To get there on your own, cross the Phra Pinklao Bridge and take the first left (Soi Wat Dusitaram), which leads to the museum through a jumble of walkways and houses on stilts. Alternatively, take a ferry to Bangkok Noi Station; from there follow the tracks until you reach the bridge over Khlong Bangkok Noi, cross it and follow the signs. Either way it's about a ten-minute walk.

Dusit

Connected to Ratanakosin via the boulevards of Rajdamnoen Klang and Rajdamnoen Nok, the spacious, leafy area known as **Dusit** has been a royal district since the reign of Rama V (1860–1910). The first Thai monarch to visit Europe, Rama V returned with radical plans for the modernisation of his capital, the fruits of which are most visible in Dusit: notably **Vimanmek Palace** and **Wat Benjamabophit**, the so-called Marble Temple. Today the peaceful Dusit area retains its European feel, and much of the country's decision-making goes on behind the high fences and impressive facades that line its tree-lined avenues: Government House is here, and the king lives on the eastern edge of the area, in the Chitrlada Palace.

Vimanmek Palace

Vimanmek Palace, at the end of the impressive sweep of Rajdamnoen Nok (daily 9.30am–4pm; compulsory free guided tours every 30min, last tour 3pm; B50, or free with Grand Palace ticket), was built by Rama V as a summer retreat on Ko Si Chang, from where it was transported bit by bit in 1901. Built entirely of golden teak without a single nail, the L-shaped "Celestial Residence" is encircled by verandahs that look out on to well-kept lawns, flower gardens and lotus ponds. Not surprisingly, Vimanmek soon became the king's favourite palace, and he and his enormous retinue of officials, concubines and children stayed here for lengthy periods between 1902 and 1906. All of Vimanmek's 81 rooms were out of bounds to male visitors, except for the king's own apartments, which were entered by a separate staircase.

A bronze equestrian statue of Rama V stands close to the entrance to the palace compound – walk to the right of the statue, around the Italian Renaissance-style Throne Hall (home of the National Assembly until the 1970s), and a little way past the entrance to Dusit Zoo (see below). Note that the same **dress rules** apply here as to the Grand Palace: no shorts or sleeveless tops.

On display inside is Rama V's collection of artifacts from all over the world, including *bencharong* ceramics, European furniture and bejewelled Thai betel-nut sets. Considered progressive in his day, Rama V introduced many newfangled ideas to Thailand: the country's first indoor bathroom is here, as is the earliest typewriter with Thai characters, and some of the first portrait paintings – portraiture had until then been seen as a way of stealing part of the sitter's soul.

Dusit Zoo

Nearby **Dusit Zoo** (daily 8am–6pm; B10), once part of the Chitrlada Palace gardens and now a public park, is nothing special but it does have a few rare animals in its small bare cages. Look out for the Komodo dragon, the world's largest reptile, which lives only on a small part of the Indonesian archipelago and in a few zoos in other parts of the world. The Dusit resident is relatively small as these monsters go: in the wild they can grow to a length of three metres and achieve a weight of 150kg. Also on show are cage-loads of white-handed gibbons, a favourite target of Thai poachers who make a lot of money by selling them as pets (and to zoos) via Chatuchak Weekend Market and other channels. The zoo used to house several royal white elephants, but at the time of writing they had all been returned to the stables in the grounds of Chitrlada Palace.

THE ROYAL WHITE ELEPHANTS

In Thailand the most revered of all elephants are the so-called **white elephants** – actually tawny brown albinos – which are considered so sacred that they all, whether wild or captive, belong to the king by law. Their special status originates from Buddhist mythology, which tells how the previously barren Queen Maya became pregnant with the future Buddha after dreaming one night that a white elephant had entered her womb. The thirteenth-century King Ramkhamhaeng of Sukhothai adopted the beast as a symbol of the great and the divine, and ever since, a Thai king's greatness is said to be measured by the number of white elephants he owns. The present king, Rama IX, has ten, the largest royal collection to date. An elaborate ceremony takes place every time a new white elephant is presented to the king: the animal is paraded with great pomp from its place of capture to Dusit, where it's annointed with holy water before an audience of the kingdom's most important priests and dignitaries, before being housed in the royal stables.

The expression "white elephant" probably derives from the legend that the kings used to present certain enemies with one of these exotic creatures. The animal required expensive attention but, being royal, could not be put to work in order to pay for its upkeep. The recipient thus went bust trying to keep it.

Wat Benjamabophit

Ten minutes' walk southeast from Vimanmek and the zoo along Sri Ayutthaya Road, **Wat Benjamabophit** (daily, 7am–5pm; B10) was the last major temple to have been built in Bangkok. It's an interesting fusion of classical Thai and nine-teenth-century European design, with its Carrara marble walls – hence the touris-tic tag "The Marble Temple" – complemented by the bot's unusual stained-glass windows, Victorian in style but depicting figures from Thai mythology. Inside, a fine replica of the highly revered Phra Buddha Chinnarat image of Phitsanulok presides over the small room containing Rama V's ashes. The courtyard behind the bot houses a gallery of Buddha images from all over Asia, set up by Rama V as an overview of different representations of Buddha.

Wat Benjamabophit is one of the best temples in Bangkok to see religious **festivals** and rituals. Whereas monks elsewhere tend to go out on the streets every morning in search of alms, at the Marble Temple the ritual is reversed, and merit-makers come to them. Between about 6am and 7.30am, the monks line up on Nakhon Pathom Road, their bowls ready to receive donations of curry and rice, lotus buds, incense, even toilet paper and Coca-Cola. The evening candlelight processions around the bot during the Buddhist festivals of Maha Puja (in February) and Visakha Puja (in May) are among the most entrancing in the country.

Downtown Bangkok

Extending east from the railway line and south to Sathorn Road, **downtown Bangkok** is central to the colossal expanse of Bangkok as a whole, but rather peripheral in a sightseer's perception of the city. This is where you'll find the main financial district, around Silom Road, and the chief shopping centres, around Siam Square, in addition to the smart hotels and restaurants, the embassies and airline offices. Scattered widely across the downtown area there are just a few attractions for visitors, including the noisy and glittering **Erawan Shrine** and three attractive museums housed in traditional teak buildings: **Jim Thompson's House**, the **Kamthieng House** and the **Suan Pakkad Palace Museum**. The infamous **Patpong** district hardly shines as a tourist sight, yet, lamentably, its sex bars provide Thailand's single biggest draw for farang men.

If you're heading downtown from Banglamphu, allow at least an hour to get to any of the places mentioned here by **bus**. To get to the southern part of the area, take an **express boat** downriver and then change onto a bus if necessary. For other parts of the downtown area, it's worth considering the regular **longtails** on Khlong Sen Seb, which runs parallel to Phetchaburi Road. They start at the Golden Mount, near Democracy Monument, and have useful stops at Phrayathai Road (for Jim Thompson's House), Pratunam (for Suan Pakkad and the Erawan Shrine) and Soi 23 off Sukhumvit Road (for Kamthieng House).

Siam Square to Sukhumvit Road

Though Siam Square has just about everything to satisfy the Thai consumer boom – big shopping centres, Western fast-food restaurants, cinemas – don't come looking for an elegant commercial piazza: the "square" is in fact a grid of small streets on the south side of Rama I Road, between Phrayathai and Henri Dunant roads, and the name is applied freely to the surrounding area. Further east, you'll find newer, bigger and more expensive shopping malls at Erawan corner, where Rama I becomes Ploenchit Road. Life becomes less frenetic along Ploenchit, which is flanked by several grand old embassies, and starts to become suburban once you pass under the expressway flyover and enter Sukhumvit Road, the broad avenue through the heart of the wealthy farang quarter.

Jim Thompson's House

Just off Siam Square at 6 Soi Kasemsan 2, Rama I Rd, **Jim Thompson's House** (Mon–Sat 9am–4.30pm; B100, under-25s B40) is a kind of Ideal Home in elegant Thai style, and a peaceful refuge from downtown chaos. The house was the residence of the legendary American adventurer, entrepreneur, art collector and all-round character whose mysterious disappearance in the jungles of Malaysia in 1967 has made him even more of a legend among Thailand's farang community. Apart from putting together this beautiful home, Thompson's most concrete contribution was to turn traditional silk-weaving from a dying art into the highly successful international industry it is today.

The grand, rambling **house** is in fact a combination of six teak houses, some from as far afield as Ayutthaya and most over 200 years old. Like all traditional houses, they were built in wall sections hung together without nails on a frame of wooden pillars, which made it easy to dismantle them, pile them onto a barge and float them to their new home. Although he had trained as an architect, Thompson had more difficulty in putting them back together again; in the end, he had to go back to Ayutthaya to hunt down a group of carpenters who still practised the old house-building methods. Thompson added a few unconventional touches of his own, incorporating the elaborately carved front wall of a Chinese pawn shop between the drawing room and the bedroom, and reversing the other walls in the drawing room so that their carvings faced into the room.

The impeccably tasteful **interior** has been left as it was during Thompson's life, even down to the cutlery on the dining table, and visitors are shown around on

THE LEGENDS OF JIM THOMPSON

Thai silk-weavers, art dealers and conspiracy theorists all owe a debt to **Jim Thompson**, who even now, 25 years after his death, remains Thailand's most famous farang. An architect by trade, Thompson left his New York practice in 1940 to join the Office of Strategic Services (later to become the CIA), a tour of duty which was to see him involved in clandestine operations in North Africa, Europe and, in 1945, the Far East, where he was detailed to a unit preparing for the invasion of Thailand. When the mission was pre-empted by the Japanese surrender, he served for a year as OSS station chief in Bangkok, forming links that were later to provide grist for endless speculation.

After an unhappy and short-lived stint as part owner of the *Oriental Hotel*, Thompson found his calling in the struggling **silk-weavers** of the area near the present Jim Thompson House, whose traditional product was unknown in the West and had been all but abandoned by Thais in favour of cheaper imported textiles. Encouragement from society friends and an enthusiastic write-up in *Vogue* convinced him there was a foreign market for Thai silk, and by 1948 he had founded the Thai Silk Company Ltd. Success was assured when, two years later, the company was commissioned to make the costumes for the Broadway run of *The King and I*. Thompson's celebrated eye for colour combinations and his tireless promotion – in the early days, he could often be seen in the lobby of the *Oriental* with bolts of silk slung over his shoulder, waiting to pounce on any remotely curious tourist – quickly made his name synonymous with Thai silk.

Like a character in a Somerset Maugham novel, Thompson played the role of Western exile to the hilt. Though he spoke no Thai, he made it his personal mission to preserve traditional arts and architecture at a time when most Thais were more keen to emulate the West, assembling his famous Thai house and stuffing it with all manner of Oriental *objets d'art*. At the same time he held firmly to his farang roots and society connections: no foreign gathering in Bangkok was complete without Jim Thompson, and virtually every Western luminary passing through Bangkok – from Truman Capote to Ethel Merman – dined at his table.

If Thompson's life was the stuff of legend, his **disappearance** and presumed death only added to the mystique. On Easter Sunday, 1967, Thompson, while staying with friends in a cottage in Malaysia's Cameron Highlands, went out for a stroll and never came back. A massive search of the area, employing local guides, tracker dogs and even shamans, turned up no clues, provoking a rash of fascinating but entirely unsubstantiated theories. The grandfather of them all, advanced by a Dutch psychic, held that Thompson had been lured into an ambush by the disgraced former prime minister of Thailand, Pridi Panyonyong, and spirited off to Cambodia for indeterminate purposes; later versions, supposing that Thompson had remained a covert CIA operative all his life, proposed that he was abducted by Vietnamese communists and brainwashed to be displayed as a high-profile defector to communism. More recently, an amateur sleuth claims to have found evidence that Thompson met a more mundane fate, having been killed by a careless truck driver and hastily buried.

guided tours in several languages. Complementing the fine artifacts from through-out Southeast Asia is a stunning array of Thai arts and crafts, including one of the best collections of traditional Thai paintings in the world. Thompson picked up plenty of bargains from the Thieves' Quarter in Chinatown, before collecting Thai art became fashionable and expensive. Other pieces were liberated from decay and destruction in upcountry temples, while many of the Buddha images were turned over by ploughs, especially around Ayutthaya. Some of the exhibits are very rare, such as a seventeenth-century Ayutthayan teak Buddha, but Thompson also bought pieces of little value and fakes simply for their looks – a shopping strat-egy that's all the more sensible in the jungle of today's Thai antiques trade.

The Erawan Shrine

For a break from high culture drop in on the **Erawan Shrine**, at the corner of Ploenchit and Rajdamri roads. Remarkable as much for its setting as anything else, this shrine to Brahma, an ancient Hindu gods, and Erawan, his elephant, squeezes in on one of the busiest and noisiest corners of modern Bangkok, in the shadow of the *Erawan Hotel* – whose existence is the reason for the shrine. When a string of calamities held up the building of the hotel in the 1950s, spirit doctors were called in, who instructed the owners to build a new home for the offended local spirits: the hotel was then finished without further mishap.

Be prepared for sensory overload: the main structure shines with lurid glass of all colours and the overcrowded precinct around it is almost buried under scented garlands and incense candles. You might also catch a lacklustre group of traditional **dancers** performing here to the strains of a small classical orchestra –

Merit-making

worshippers hire them to give thanks for a stroke of good fortune. To increase their future chances of such good fortune, visitors buy a bird or two from the flocks incarcerated in cages here; the bird-seller transfers the requested number of captives to a tiny hand-held cage, from which the customer duly liberates the animals, thereby accruing merit. People set on less abstract rewards will invest in a lottery ticket from one of the physi-cally handicapped sellers: they're thought to be the luckiest you can buy.

Kamthieng House

Another reconstructed traditional Thai residence, the **Kamthieng House** (Tues–Sat 9am–noon & 1–5pm; B20) was moved in the 1960s from Chiang Mai to 130 Soi Asoke, off Sukhumvit Road, and set up as an ethnological museum by the Siam Society. It differs from both Suan Pakkad and Jim Thompson's House in being the home of a commoner, and although the owner was by no means poor, the objects on display give a fair representation of rural life in northern Thailand.

The house was built on the banks of the River Ping in the mid-nineteenth century and the ground-level display of farming tools and fish traps evokes the upcountry practice of fishing in flooded rice paddies to supplement the supply from the rivers. Upstairs, the main rooms of the house are much as they would have been 150 years ago – the raised floor is polished and smooth, sparsely furnished with only a couple of low tables and seating mats, and a betel-nut set to hand. Notice how surplus furniture and utensils are stored in the rafters. The rectangular lintel above the door to the inner room is a *hum yon*, carved in floral patterns that represent testicles and designed to ward off evil spirits. Walking along the open verandah between the kitchen and the granary, you'll see betel-nut trees to your left: the garden too is as authentic as possible.

Next door to Kamthieng House, in the same compound, is the more recently acquired **Sangaroon House**, built here to house the folk-craft collection of Thai architect and lecturer Sangaroon Ratagasikorn. Upon his return to Thailand after studying in America under Frank Lloyd Wright, Sangaroon became fascinated by the efficient designs of rural utensils and began to collect them as teaching aids. Those on display include baskets, fishing pots and *takraw* balls, all of which fulfill his criteria of being functional, simple and beautiful, with no extraneous features.

Northern downtown

The area above Petchaburi Road, which becomes increasingly residential as you move north, is cut through by two major roads lined with monolithic company headquarters: Phaholyothin, which runs past the northern bus terminal and the weekend market, and Wiphawadi Rangsit, leading to the airport. The area's chief tourist attraction is Suan Pakkad, a museum of Thai arts and crafts set in a beautiful garden, but it also contains two of Bangkok's most famous landmarks and an important covered market.

Suan Pakkad Palace Museum

The **Suan Pakkad Palace Museum** (Mon–Sat 9am–4pm; B80), 352–4 Sri Ayutthaya Rd, stands on what was once a cabbage patch but is now one of the finest gardens in Bangkok. The private collection of beautiful Thai objects from all periods is displayed in five traditional wooden houses, which were transported to Bangkok from various parts of the country. You can either take a mediocre guided tour in English (free) or explore the loosely arranged collection yourself (some of the exhibits are labelled).

The highlight is the renovated **Lacquer Pavilion**, across the reedy pond at the back of the grounds. Set on stilts, the pavilion is actually an amalgam of two temple buildings, a *ho trai* (library) and a *ho khien* (writing room), one inside the other, which were found between Ayutthaya and Bang Pa-In. The interior walls are beautifully decorated with gilt on black lacquer: the upper panels depict the life of Buddha while the lower ones show scenes from the *Ramayana*. Look out especially for the grisly details in the tableau on the back wall, showing the earth goddess drowning the evil forces of Mara. Underneath are depicted some European dandies on horseback, probably merchants, whose presence suggests that the work was executed before the fall of Ayutthaya in 1767.

The carefully observed details of daily life and nature are skilful and lively, especially considering the restraints which the **laquering technique** places on the artist, who has no opportunity for corrections or touching up: the design has to be punched into a piece of paper, which is then laid on the panel of black lacquer (a kind of plant resin); a small bag of chalk dust is pressed on top so that the dust penetrates the minute holes in the paper, leaving a line of dots on the lacquer to mark the pattern; a gummy substance is then applied to the background areas which are to remain black, before the whole surface is covered in microscopically thin squares of gold leaf; thin sheets of blotting paper, sprinkled with water, are then laid over the panel, which when pulled off bring away the gummy substance and the unwanted pieces of gold leaf that are stuck to it, leaving the rest of the gold decoration in high relief against the black background.

The **Ban Chiang house** has a very good collection of elegant, whorled pottery and bronze jewellery, which the former owner of Suan Pakkad Palace, Princess Chumbot, excavated from tombs at Ban Chiang, the major Bronze Age settlement in the northeast. Scattered around the museum's other three traditional houses, you'll come across some attractive Thai and Khmer religious sculpture amongst an eclectic jumble of artifacts: fine ceramics as well as some intriguing kiln-wasters, failed pots which have melted together in the kiln to form weird, almost rubbery pieces of sculpture; beautiful betel-nut sets (see p.308); and some rich teak carvings, including a 200-year-old temple door showing episodes from *Sang Thong*, a folk tale about a childless king and queen who discover a handsome son in a conch shell.

Ban Chiang pottery

Baiyoke Tower, Pratunam Market and the Victory Monument

Fifteen minutes' walk southeast of Suan Pakkad is Thailand's tallest building, the **Baiyoke Tower Hotel**, distinguished by its rainbow colour scheme and sprouting out from a small enclave of hotels and shops. Extending southeast from the tower to the corner of Rajaprarop and Phetchaburi roads, **Pratunam Market** is famous for its cheap and low-quality casual clothes. The vast warren of stalls is becoming touristy near the tower, though there are still bargains towards the other end, amongst the amphetamine-driven sweatshops.

A good half hour north of Suan Pakkad, the stone obelisk of the **Victory Monument** can be seen from way down the broad Phrayathai and Rajwithi streets. It was erected after the Indo-Chinese War of 1940–41, when Thailand pinched back some territory in Laos and Cambodia while the French government was otherwise occupied in World War II, but nowadays it commemorates all of Thailand's past military glories.

Southern downtown

South of Rama I Road, commercial development gives way to a dispersed assortment of large institutions, dominated by Thailand's most prestigious centre of higher learning, Chulalongkorn University, and the green expanse of Lumphini Park. Rama IV Road marks another change of character: downtown proper, centring around the high-rise American-style boulevard of Silom Road, heart of the financial district, extends from here to the river. Alongside the smoked-glass banks and offices, the plush hotels and tourist shops, and opposite Bangkok's Carmelite convent, lies the dark heart of Bangkok nightlife, Patpong.

Carrying on to the river, the strip west of New Road reveals some of the history of Bangkok's early dealings with farangs in the fading grandeur of the old trading quarter. Here you'll find the only place in Bangkok where you might be able to eke out an architectural walk, though it's hardly compelling. Incongruous churches and "colonial" buildings (the best of these is the Authors' Wing of the *Oriental Hotel*, where nostalgic afternoon teas are served) are hemmed in by the spice shops and *halal* canteens of the growing Muslim area along New Road and the outskirts of Chinatown to the north.

The Museum of Imaging Technology

Chulalongkorn University's brand-new, hi-tech **Museum of Imaging Technology** (Sat & Sun 10am–4pm, B100), just south of the big entrance to the campus on the east side of Phrayathai Road, can compete with any museum of photography in the world, and is especially good for kids, with plenty of activities and things to take home. The impressive facilities have been made possible by corporate sponsors, who naturally capitalise on the PR potential of their bequests: in the Fuji Discovery Room you can set various machines going to make, process and develop a film (Fuji, of course), and the Canon Room allows you to handle the latest technology from – who else? – Canon. In addition to the activity rooms, the gallery of contemporary photography has a good permanent display, plus occasional temporary shows, of high-class works from around the world, and the gallery of Thai photography exhibits the best of local work.

The Snake Farm

The **Snake Farm**, at the corner of Rama IV and Henri Dunant roads, is a bit of a circus act, but an entertaining, informative and worthy one at that. Run by the Thai Red Cross, it has a double function: to produce snake-bite serums, and to educate the public on the dangers of Thai snakes. The latter mission involves putting on displays (Mon–Fri 10.30am & 2pm, Sat, Sun & holidays 10.30am; B70, free for children) that begin with a slick half-hour slide show illustrating, among other things, how to apply a tourniquet and immobilize a bitten limb. Things warm up

---

SNAKE'S BLOOD AND OTHER TREATS

In Thailand's big cities you'll occasionally come across obscure stalls offering restorative glasses of warm **snake's blood**, which appeals mostly to Malaysian, Chinese and Korean visitors. Not just any snake, of course: only poisonous varieties will do, with prices ranging from B200 for a common cobra, through B2000 for a king cobra, up to B30,000 for the rare albino cobra.

Once you've selected your victim from the roadside cages, the proprietor will take the snake behind the stall, hang it up by its head and slit it open with a razor blade. The major artery yields enough blood to fill a wine glass, and when it's been mixed with the bile from the snake's gall bladder, warm whisky and a dash of honey, you down the potion in one. If this doesn't satisfy, delicacies like dried gall bladder and pickled snake genitals might tempt you. But if your health is really in a bad way, all that's left is the shock cure of drinking the **venom**, after it's been mixed with whisky and left standing for quarter of an hour.

There's no evidence to support the claims made for the **medicinal properties** of snakes' innards, but there's no proof to the contrary either. While male impotence remains the main reason for the trade's persistence, the blood is also said to be good for the eyes, for backache, for malodorous urine, and simply to "make happy".

with a live demonstration of snake handling, which is well-presented and safe, and gains a perverse fascination from the knowledge that the strongest venoms of the snakes on show can kill in only three minutes. The climax of the display comes when, having watched a python squeezing great chunks of chicken through its body, the audience is invited to handle a docile Burmese constrictor.

Lumphini Park

If you're sick of cars and concrete, head for **Lumphini Park**, at the east end of Silom Road, where the air is almost fresh and the traffic noise dies down to a low murmur. Named after the town in Nepal where the Buddha was born, the park is arrayed around two lakes, where you can take out a pedalo or a rowing boat (B20 per half hour), and is landscaped with a wide variety of local trees and numerous pagodas and pavilions, usually occupied by Chinese chess players. The wide open spaces here are a popular area for gay cruising, and you might be offered dope,

---

THE SEX INDUSTRY

Bangkok owes its reputation as the carnal capital of the world to a highly efficient sex industry adept at peddling fantasies of cheap sex on tap. More than 1000 sex-related businesses operate in the city, employing perhaps as many as 200,000 women. But the gaudy neon fleshpots of Patpong give a misleading impression of an activity that is deeply rooted in Thai culture – the overwhelming majority of Thailand's 700,000 prostitutes of both sexes work with Thai men, not farangs.

Prostitution and polygamy have long been intrinsic to the Thai way of life. Until Rama VI broke with the custom in 1910, Thai kings had always kept a retinue of concubines around them, a select few of whom would be elevated to the status of wife and royal mother, the rest forming a harem of ladies-in-waiting and sexual playthings. The practice was aped by the status-hungry nobility and, from the early nineteenth century, by newly rich merchants keen to have lots of sons and heirs. Though the monarch is now monogamous, many men of all classes still keep mistresses, known as *mia noi* (minor wives), a tradition bolstered by the popular philosophy which maintains that an official wife (*mia luang*) should be treated like the temple's main Buddha image – respected and elevated upon the altar – whereas the minor wife is an amulet, to be taken along wherever you go.

The **farang sex industry** is a relatively new development, having had its start during the Vietnam War, when the American military set up seven bases around Thailand. The GIs' appetite for "entertainment" fuelled the creation of instant red-light districts near the bases, attracting women from surrounding rural areas to cash in on the boom; Bangkok joined the fray in 1967, when the US secured the right to ferry soldiers in from Vietnam for R&R breaks. By the mid-1970s, the bases had been evacuated but the sex infrastructure remained and tourists moved in to fill the vacuum, lured by advertising that diverted most of the traffic to Bangkok and Pattaya. Sex tourism has since grown to become an established part of the Thai economy – even the highly respectable *Bangkok Post* publishes a weekly column on sex-industry news and gossip – and, despite attempts by the tourist authorities to downplay the country's sleazy image, Bangkok attracts a growing international clientele, with some German and Japanese companies organising sex tours as a reward for high productivity.

The majority of the women who work in the Patpong bars come from the poorest rural areas of north and northeast Thailand. **Economic refugees** in search of a

though the police patrol regularly – for all that, it's not an intimidating place. To recharge your batteries, make for the garden restaurant, *Pop*, in the northwest corner, or you might be tempted by the snake's blood stall on the northern edge of the park, tucked away amongst a cluster of more conventional refreshment stalls.

Patpong

Concentrated into a small area between the eastern ends of Silom and Suriwong roads, the neon-lit go-go bars of the **Patpong** district loom like rides in a tawdry sexual Disneyland. In front of each bar, girls cajole passersby with a lifeless sensuality while insistent touts proffer printed menus detailing the degradations on show. Inside, bikini-clad or topless women gyrate to Western music and play hostess to the (almost exclusively male) spectators; upstairs, live shows feature women who, to use Spalding Gray's phrase in *Swimming to Cambodia*, "do everything with their vaginas except have babies".

better life, they're easily drawn into an industry where they can make in a single night what it takes a month to earn in the rice fields – in some Isaan villages, money sent home by prostitutes in Bangkok far exceeds financial aid given by the government. Women from rural communities have always been expected to contribute an equal share to the family income and it's hardly surprising that many opt for a couple of lucrative years in the sex bars and brothels as the most effective way of helping to pay off family debts and improve the living conditions of parents stuck in the poverty trap. Reinforcing this social obligation there's the pervasive Buddhist notion of **karma**, which holds that your lot, however unhappy, is the product of past-life misdeeds and can only be improved by making sufficient merit to ensure a better life next time round.

Despite its ubiquity, prostitution has been **illegal** in Thailand since 1960, but sex-industry bosses easily circumvent the law by registering their establishments as bars, restaurants, barbers, nightclubs or massage parlours, and making payoffs to the police. Sex workers, on the other hand, have no legal rights and will often endure exploitation and violence from employers, pimps and customers rather than face imprisonment and fines.

While most women enter the racket presumably knowing at least something of what lies ahead, younger girls definitely do not. **Child prostitution** is rife: an estimated ten percent of prostitutes are under fourteen, some no older than nine. They are valuable property: in the teahouses of Chinatown, a prepubescent virgin can be rented to her first customer for B5000, as sex with someone so young is believed to have rejuvenating properties. Most child prostitutes have been sold by desperate parents as **bonded slaves** to pimps or agents, and are kept locked up until they have fully repaid the money given to their parents, which may take two or more years.

The women who work with farangs attract over two million foreign men to the country a year – that's a foreign-exchange earnings potential of B50 billion. Small wonder then that the government remains happy enough to let rural Thai families sell their daughters into prostitution rather than come banging at the door of the agricultural subsidies department. But something drastic will have to be done soon: the current estimate of HIV carriers in Thailand is put at between 200,000 and 300,000, and if the current rate of infection continues, 2,000,000 Thais will be HIV-positive by the end of the century.

Patpong was no more than a sea of mud when the capital was founded on the marshy riverbank to the west, but by the 1960s it had grown into a flash district of nightclubs and dance halls for rich Thais, owned by a Chinese millionaire godfather who gave his name to the area. In 1969, an American entrepreneur turned an existing teahouse into a luxurious nightclub to satisfy the tastes of soldiers on R&R trips from Vietnam, and so began Patpong's transformation into a Western sex reservation. At first, the area was rough and violent, but over the years it has wised up to the desires of the affluent farang, and now markets itself as a packaged concept of Oriental decadence. Spread out on a number of parallel sois north of Silom Road, the layout of the area is kept simple for the average drunken tourist. The centre of the industrial skin trade lies along the interconnected sois of **Patpong 1 and 2**, where lines of go-go bars share their patch with respectable restaurants, a Christian bookstore and a 24-hour supermarket. By night, it's a thumping theme park, whose blazing neon promises tend towards self-parody, with names like *Pussy Galore* and *Love Nest*. Budget travellers, purposeful safari-suited businessmen and noisy lager louts throng the streets, and even the most demure tourists – of both sexes – turn out to do some shopping at the night market down the middle of Patpong 1, where hawkers sell fake watches and designer T-shirts alongside traditionally dressed Hmong women selling hill-tribe trinkets. By day, a relaxed hangover descends on the place. Bar-girls hang out at food stalls and cafés in respectable dress, often recognizable only by their faces, pinched and strained from the continuous use of antibiotics and heroin in an attempt to ward off venereal disease and boredom. Farang men slump at the bar beers on Patpong 2, drinking and watching videos, unable to find anything else to do in the whole of Bangkok.

Patpong 1 and 2 are flanked by two gay developments, **Soi Tantawan** and **Patpong 3**, the former more hard-core, with bar names like *Golden Cock* and *Mandate*, the latter more sophisticated and mixed. To the east of Patpong 3, **Thaniya Road**'s hostess bars and Bangkok's swishest shopping centre, Thaniya Plaza, cater mostly to Japanese tourists.

The outskirts

The amorphous clutter of Greater Bangkok doesn't harbour many attractions, but there are a handful of places – principally **Chatuchak Weekend Market**, the cultural theme park of **Muang Boran** and the upstream town of **Nonthaburi** – which make pleasant half-day escapes. Theoretically, you could also see any one of these sights en route to destinations north, east or west, though lumping luggage around makes negotiating city transport even more trying.

Chatuchak

Bangkok's weekly shopping extravaganza, the enormous **Chatuchak Weekend Market** (Sat & Sun 6am–6pm), is inconveniently relegated to a patch of waste ground in Chatuchak Park near the northern bus terminal, but with 6000 open-air stalls to peruse, and wares as diverse as Laotian silk, Siamese kittens and buffalo-horn catapults to choose from, it's well worth the effort. (Buses #2, #3, #9, #10 and #13 all go there). Though its primary customers are Bangkok residents in search of cheap clothes, home accessories and a strong dose of *sanuk*, Chatuchak also

---

ENDANGERED SPECIES FOR SALE

In April 1991 the Worldwide Fund for Nature (WWF) denounced Thailand as "probably the worst country in the world for the illegal trade in **endangered wildlife**", and branded Chatuchak Weekend Market "the wildlife supermarket of the world". Protected and endangered species traded at Chatuchak include gibbons, palm cockatoos, golden dragon fish, Indian pied hornbills – even tiger cubs and lions. Many of the animals are smuggled across from Laos and Cambodia and then sold at Chatuchak to private animal collectors and foreign zoos, particulary in eastern Europe. Those that don't make it alive to overseas destinations usually get there in some other form: leopard and reptile skins, ivory products and tiger claws are just a few of the goods for sale not only at Chatuchak, but throughout the city.

Although Thailand is a signatory to the **Convention on International Trade in Endangered Species** (CITES), until April 1991 it had failed to honour its membership with appropriate laws and penalties. WWF subsequently launched a campaign to boycott Thailand and Thai goods, and the US banned all Thai wildlife exports. In response, stringent amendments to Thailand's outdated and ineffective 1960 Wildlife Preservation Act were passed in November 1991. The Thai police have, meanwhile, become zealous in their pursuit of illegal traders, which is why you probably won't see rare species openly displayed at Chatuchak – though that doesn't mean the black market has folded. Vendors are hardly likely to forego the estimated $500,000 earned from trading wildlife at Chatuchak each year, and domestic demand will continue until it's no longer so amusing to have a cute white-handed gibbon chained to your tree or a myna bird screeching from a cage outside your front door.

---

has some collector- and tourist-oriented stalls and – highly controversially – a large wildlife section. It's unlikely that you'll see any endangered species on display, though you're bound to come across fighting cocks around the back (demonstrations are almost continuous), miniature flying squirrels being fed milk through pipettes, and iridescent red and blue Siamese fighting fish, kept in individual jars and shielded from each others' aggressive stares by sheets of cardboard. Best buys include antique and unusual silks and cottons, jeans, northern crafts, silver jewellery, basketware and ceramics, particularly the five-coloured *bencharong*. If you're going there to buy, take a copy of *Nancy Chandler's Map of Bangkok*, as it shows the location of all the specialist areas within the market.

There's no shortage of **food** stalls inside the market compound, but for really good vegetarian sustenance head for the open-air, cafeteria-style restaurant just outside on Kamphaeng Phet Road (across Kamphaeng Phet II Road, behind the air-con bus stop), set up by Bangkok's former governor as a service to the citizenry: good, wholesome food for B5 a plate (Tues–Sun 6am–2pm).

Nonthaburi

A trip to **NONTHABURI**, the first town beyond the northern boundary of Bangkok, is just about the easiest excursion you can make from the centre of the city, as it's the last stop upriver on the express boat, only forty-five minutes from Phra Athit (every 15min; B7 from Tha Si Phraya and points south, B5 from all other stops). The ride is half the fun in itself, weaving round huge, crawling rice barges and tiny canoes, and the slow pace of the boat gives you plenty of time to take in the sights on the way. Once out of the centre, you'll pass the royal boat house in front of the National Library on the east bank, where you can glimpse the minor ceremonial boats which escort the grand royal barges. The nearer you get to Nonthaburi, the less you see of the riverbanks, which are increasingly obscured by houses on stilts and houseboats – past the *Singha* brewery, you'll see a community of people who live on the huge teak vessels used to carry rice, sand and charcoal. A break in the journey can be made to explore the bizarre **Wat Khian**, two stops before Nonthaburi, where the bot and prangs are now half-submerged in the Chao Phraya and overgrown with river weeds.

Disembarking at Nonthaburi, you immediately get the feeling of being out in the sticks: the pier, on the east bank of the river, is overrun by a market that's famous for the quality of its fruit; the Provincial Office across the road, which houses a primitive but friendly tourist information office (Mon–Fri 8am–noon & 1–4pm), is covered in rickety old wooden lattice-work; and the short promenade, its lampposts hung with models of the town's famous durian fruit, lends a seaside atmosphere.

Two sights – a riverside wat and an oddball museum dedicated to Thai crime and punishment – will repay a few hours' wandering in the vicinity. To break up your trip with a slow, scenic drink or lunch, you'll find a floating restaurant at the end of the prom which, though a bit overpriced, is quiet and breezy. If you're thirsty for more cruising on the water, take a longtail boat from the pier up **Khlong Om** (round trip 45min, B10): the canal, lined with some grand suburban mansions, traditional wooden houses, temples and durian plantations, leads almost out into open country.

Wat Chalerm Phra Kiat

Set in relaxing grounds on the west bank of the river, elegant **Wat Chalerm Phra Kiat** injects a splash of urban refinement amongst a grove of breadfruit trees. From the Nonthaburi pier, you can either squeeze into one of the regular longtails going upriver (a five-minute ride) or take the ferry straight across the Chao Phraya then walk up the river bank for fifteen minutes. The beautifully proportioned temple, most of which has been lavishly restored, was built by Rama III in memory of his mother, whose family lived in the area. Entering the high, white walls of the temple compound, you feel as if you're coming upon a stately folly in a secret garden, and a strong Chinese influence shows itself in the unusual ribbed roofs and elegantly curved gables, decorated with pastel ceramics. The restorers have done their best work inside: look out especially for the simple, delicate landscapes on the shutters.

Museum of the Department of Corrections

Ghouls and social anthropologists might want to take a look at the **Museum of the Department of Corrections** (Mon–Fri 9am-4pm), a small collection of torture and execution instruments that's a ten-minute walk from the river. Take the road straight ahead from Nonthaburi pier, then turn first left – you'll then walk along the front of Bangkwang Central Prison on your right and find the museum signposted on the left. The display kicks off with pictures of grisly methods of execution used at Ayutthaya, such as scalping and burning. Even the game of *takraw*, a kind of foot-volleyball which you'll see played on any patch of open ground in Thailand, had its ugly side: an outsized version of the wicker *takraw* ball, with spikes inside, is on display here, into which an offender was placed before being thrown to the elephants for a kickaround. Numerous butchers'

DURIANS

The naturalist Alfred Russel Wallace, eulogising the taste of the **durian**, compared it to "rich butter-like custard highly flavoured with almonds, but intermingled with wafts of flavour that call to mind cream cheese, onion sauce, brown sherry and other incongruities". He neglected to discuss the smell, which is so bad – somewhere between detergent and dogshit – that durians are barred from Thai hotels and aeroplanes. The different **varieties** bear strange monikers which do nothing to make them more appetising: "frog", "golden pillow", "gibbon" and so on. However, the durian has fervent admirers, perhaps because it's such an acquired taste, and because it's considered a strong aphrodisiac. Aficionados discuss the varieties with as much subtlety as if they were vintage champagnes, and they treat the durian as a social fruit, to be shared around despite a price of up to B600 each.

Durian season is roughly April to June and the most famous durian orchards are around Nonthaburi, where the fruits are said to have an incomparably rich and nutty flavour due to the fine clay soil. If you don't smell them first, you can recognise durians by their sci-fi **appearance**: the shape and size of a rugby ball, but slightly deflated, they're covered in a thick, pale-green shell which is heavily armoured with short, sharp spikes (*duri* means thorn in Malay). By cutting along one of the faint seams with a good knife, you'll reveal a white pith in which are set a handful of yellow blobs with the texture of a bad soufflé: this is what you eat. The taste is best when the smell is at its highest, about three days after the fruit has dropped. Be careful when out walking: due to its great weight and sharp spikes, a falling durian can lead to serious injury, or even an ignominious death.

hooks and headsmen's axes are here to turn your stomach even more, along with photographs of recent executions: Thailand still has capital punishment, by machine gun, though it's rarely carried out.

Muang Boran Ancient City

The brochure for **Muang Boran Ancient City** (daily 8am–5pm; B50), 33km southeast of the city sells the place as a sort of cultural fast-food outlet – "a realistic journey into Thailand's past in only a few hours, saving you the many weeks of travel and considerable expense of touring Thailand yourself". The open-air museum is a considerably more authentic experience than its own publicity makes out, showcasing past and present Thai artistry and offering an enjoyable introduction to the country's architecture. To get there from Bangkok, take air-con **bus** #8 or #11 or regular bus #25 to SAMUT PRAKAN on the edge of built-up Greater Bangkok, then a songthaew.

Some of the 89 buildings are **originals**, such as the rare scripture library rescued from Samut Songkhram. Others are painstaking **reconstructions** from contemporary documents (the Ayutthaya-period Sanphet Prasat palace is a particularly fine example) or **scaled-down copies** of famous monuments such as the Grand Palace. A sizeable team of restorers and skilled craftspeople maintains the buildings and helps keep some of the traditional techniques alive; if you come here during the week you can watch them at work. Muang Boran also publishes a quarterly journal of the same name (in Thai and English) on Thai art, which is available from their Bangkok office on Rajdamnoen Klang Avenue, at the southwest corner of Democracy Monument.

A couple of kilometres east of Samut Prakan, the **Crocodile Farm** (daily 9am–6pm; B120) figures on tour group itineraries, but is a depressing place. The 30,000 reptiles kept here are made to "perform" for their trainers in hourly shows and are subsequently turned into handbags, shoes, briefcases and wallets, a selection of which are sold on site. Songthaews run from Samut Prakan.

Human Imagery Museum

Thirty-one kilometres west of Bangkok on Highway 4, the **Human Imagery Museum** (Mon–Fri 9am–5.30pm, Sat & Sun 8.30am–6pm; adults B140, kids B70) is a Thai version of Madame Tussaud's Wax Museum, but with a less global perspective than its London counterpart. The lifelike **figures**, complete with glistening tongues and dewy eyes, are skillfully cast in fibreglass – wax would melt – and for the most part represent key characters in Thailand's history. Aside from a group portrait of the first eight kings of the Chakri dynasty, there's a strong emphasis on revered monks, as well as several wry interpretations of everyday life in the kingdom. The upper floor is given over to temporary exhibitions on unusual aspects of Thai history – such as the story of slavery here – with informative English-language captions.

The regular **buses** from Bangkok's southern bus terminal to Nakhon Pathom will drop you outside the entrance, but to flag one down for the return journey you might have to enlist the help of the museum's car park attendant.

On the way to the Human Imagery Museum you'll see signposts for the nearby **Rose Garden Country Resort**, accessible only on tours from Bangkok, and a very synthetic experience. The lushly landscaped riverside resort makes big bucks from its hotel and golf course, but its main draw is the **Thai Village Cultural Show** (every afternoon; B190), an all-in-one cultural experience of Thai boxing, cockfighting, a wedding ceremony, elephant training and classical and hill-tribe dancing.

FOOD, ENTERTAINMENT, SHOPPING – AND MOVING ON

As you'd expect, nowhere in Thailand can compete with Bangkok's diversity when it comes to eating and entertainment, and although prices are generally higher here than in the provinces, it's still easy to have a good time while on a budget.

Bangkok boasts an astonishing 50,000 **places to eat** – that's almost one for every 100 citizens – ranging from grubby streetside noodle shops to the most elegant of restaurants. Despite this glut, though, an awful lot of tourists venture no further than their guest house's front doorstep, preferring the dining-room's ersatz Thai or Western dishes to the more adventurous fare to be found in even the most touristed accommodation areas. The section below is a run-through on the best of the city's indiginous eateries, with a few representatives of the capital's numerous ethnic minorities.

Except among the men who've come to Bangkok for the sex on sale in Patpong, guest-house inertia is prevalent when it comes to **nightlife** as well, with many travellers settling for an evening of videos. It's true that Bangkok's drinking bars and clubs are not the city's strongest suit, but there are some enjoyable spots, most of them staying open till at least 2am. Getting back to your lodgings is no problem in the small hours: most bus routes run a reduced service throughout the night, and tuk-tuks and taxis are always at hand – though it's probably best for unaccompanied women to avoid using tuk-tuks late at night.

Introductions to more traditional elements of Thai culture are offered by the raucous ambience of the city's **boxing arenas**, its **music and dancing** troupes and its profusion of **shops**, stalls and markets – all of them covered here. This section concludes with an overview of the options for **moving on from the city** – not only to elsewhere in Thailand, but to other countries too, as Bangkok is one of Asia's bargain counters when it comes to buying flights.

Eating

Thai restaurants of all types are found all over the city. The air-conditioned **standard Thai** places, patronised by office workers and middle-class families, almost always work out excellent value, with massive menus of curries, soups, rice and noodle dishes and generally some Chinese dishes as well; the Banglamphu and Democracy areas have a specially high concentration of these. The best **gourmet Thai** restaurants operate from the downtown districts around Sukhumvit and Silom roads, proffering wonderful royal, nouvelle and traditional cusines that definitely merit an occasional splurge. At the other end of the scale there are the **night markets** and **street stalls**, so numerous in Bangkok that we can only flag the most promising areas – but wherever you're staying, you'll hardly have to walk a block in any direction before encountering something edible.

Of the non-Thai cuisines, Chinatown naturally rates as the most authentic district for pure **Chinese** food; likewise neighbouring Pahurat, the capital's Indian enclave, is best for unadulterated **Indian** dishes – though here, as in Chinatown, most establishments are nameless and transient, so it's hard to make recommendations.

Fast food comes in two forms: the mainly Thai version which stews canteen-style in large tin trays on the upper floors of department stores all over the city, and the old western favourites like McDonalds and Kentucky Fried Chicken that mainly congregate around Siam Square and Ploenchit Road – an area that also has its share of good Thai and foreign restaurants.

The restaurants listed below are graded by three general price categories based on the cost of a main dish: cheap (under B40), moderate (B40–70) and expensive (over B70). In the more expensive restaurants you may have to pay a service charge and eleven percent government tax. All the restaurants have English menus unless stated; telephone numbers are given for the most popular, where bookings are advisable.

Banglamphu and Democracy area

Dachanee, 18/2 Prajathipatai Rd, near *Thai Hotel*. Standard Thai fare such as fiery *tom yam*, plus tasty extras like tofu- and beansprout-stuffed *khanom buang* (crispy pancakes), in air-conditioned restaurant. Cheap to moderate.

Dragon Eyes, Soi 7, Samsen Rd. Small restaurant popular with young Thai couples. Stylish renditions of standard Thai dishes – try the *khao pat* with added fruit and nuts (evenings only). Moderate.

Isaan restaurants, behind the Rajdamnoen Boxing Stadium on Rajdamnoen Nok Road. At least five restaurants in a row serving northeastern fare to hungry boxing fans: take your pick for hearty plates of *kai yang* and *khao niaw*. Cheap.

New World Food Centre, top floor of *New World* department store. Buy tokens and choose from Thai, Chinese and vegetarian food stalls; a bit school-dinnerish, but very cheap.

Phan Line, between sois 1 and 3, Samsen Rd. Good unwatered-down Thai food – try the snakefish – in a cosy atmosphere. Open evenings only. Moderate.

Royal India, off Khao San Rd. Excellent Indian food at this popular branch of the Pahurat original. Cheap to moderate.

Shogun, Phra Sumen Road, behind *New World* department store. Sukiyaki a speciality; family atmosphere. Cheap.

Sky High, Rajdamnoen Klang, not far from the *Royal Hotel*. Large menu of tasty Thai dishes, streetside and indoor seating. Cheap to moderate.

Sorn Daeng, southeast corner of Democracy Monument. Standard Thai dishes including unadulterated southern curries like the rich sweet beef *kaeng matsaman*. Cheap.

Wang Nah, Phra Athit Road, under Phra Pinklao Bridge. Sizeable seafood menu, riverside location. Cheap to moderate.

Yok Yor, Tha Wisut Kasat, Wisut Kasat Road. Riverside restaurant in two sections, which sends a boatload of diners down to Rama IX Bridge and back every evening: departs 8pm, returns 10pm. The food is nothing special – there's more choice before the boat sets off and leaves the main kitchen behind – but it's the cheapest of a host of similar operations, and the floodlit views of Wat Arun, Wat Phra Kaeo and others are worth the B50 cover charge. Moderate.

Chinatown and Pahurat

Chong Tee, 84 Soi Sukon 1, Traimit Road, between the station and Wat Traimit. Delicious pork satay and sweet toast. Cheap.

Royal India, just off Chakraphet Road. Serves the same excellent curries as its Banglamphu branch, but attracts an almost exclusively Indian clientele. Cheap to moderate.

White Orchid Hotel, 409–421 Yaowarat Rd. Great value lunch-time *dim sum* at about B10 per dish. Cheap.

Silom and New roads

Ban Chiang, 14 Srivieng Rd, between Silom and Sathorn roads (☎236 7045). Fine Thai cuisine in an elegant wooden house. Moderate to expensive.

Bussaracum, 35 Soi Pipat 2, Convent Road (☎235 8915). Superb classical Thai cuisine. Expensive, but well worth it.

Charuvan, 70–2 Silom Rd, near Patpong. Specialising in cheap and tasty duck on rice; the beer's cheap too.

Himali Cha-Cha, 1229/11 New Rd, just south of GPO (☎235 1569). Delicate north Indian food prepared by a character who has been chef to numerous Indian ambassadors; good vegetarian selection. Moderate.

Muslim Restaurant, 1360 New Rd, at the corner of Silom Road. Coffee-and-spittoons southern Thai canteen, serving up cheap and tasty food, including Indian and vegetarian dishes.

Ratstube, Goethe Institut, 18/1 Soi Ngam Duphli (Soi Attakarn Prasit). Delicious, moderately priced German food in elegant surroundings. There's also a good, cheap Thai cafeteria in the grounds outside.

Savoury, 60 Pan Rd, above the *Artist's Gallery* (☎236 4830). Excellent European food, highly recommended for a posh splurge; closed Sun. Expensive.

Tip Top, Patpong 1. Comfy air-conditioned diner serving reliable Thai and Western food 24 hours a day. Cheap.

Siam Square and Ploenchit Road

Bali, 15/3 Soi Ruam Rudee (☎250 0711). Top-notch Indonesian food in a cosy haven; closed Sun lunch. Moderate to expensive – blow out on seven-course *rijstaffel* for B160.

Ban Khun Por, 458/7–9 Soi 8, Siam Square. Rustic atmosphere and traditional music with good Thai specialities; food spiced to order. Moderate.

Isaan Krasing, Soi 11, Siam Square (no English sign). Decent Thai food, mostly northeastern, in a clean, institutional restaurant. Cheap.

Kirin Restaurant, 226/1 Soi 2, Siam Square. Swankiest and best of many Chinese restaurants in the area. Expensive.

Kroissant House, ground floor of *World Trade Centre*, corner of Rama I and Rajdamri roads. Fine Italian ice creams and cakes.

Kub Khum, Soi 1, Siam Square. Good Thai favourites with tacky folksy decor. Moderate.

Mah Boon Krong Food Centre, sixth floor of *MBK* shopping centre, corner of Rama I and Phrayathai roads. Increase your knowledge of Thai food: ingredients, names and pictures of dishes (including some vegetarian ones) from all over the country are displayed at the various stalls. Cheap.

Phai-boon, 219–223 Chulalongkorn Soi 50, near corner of Rama IV and Phrayathai roads. Busy, no-frills air-conditioned restaurant serving mostly seafood. Interesting combination dishes. Moderately priced.

Pop, northwest corner of Lumphini Park. Garden restaurant popular for breakfasts and *dim sum* lunches. Cheap.

Samyarn market, both sides of Phrayathai Road at corner of Rama IV. Fruitful area for stall-grazing, always busy with Chulalongkorn University students. Cheap.

Sarah Jane's, 36/2 Soi Langsuan. Unfussy restaurant, popular with Bangkok's Isaan population, serving excellent, simple northeastern food. Cheap.

TCBY – The Country's Best Yoghurt, Soi 7, at the east end of Siam Square. Consumer colonialism at its most bizarre: fat-free frozen yoghurt ("All the pleasure, none of the guilt"). Moderate.

Whole Earth, 93/3 Soi Langsuan. The best veggie restaurant in Bangkok, serving interesting and varied Thai food (plus some dishes for carnivores); twee but relaxing atmosphere. Moderate.

Sukhumvit Road

Cabbages and Condoms, Soi 12. Run by the Planned Parenthood Association of Thailand: safe eating in the Condom Room or the Vasectomy Bar. Good Thai food. Moderate.

Haus Munchen, Soi 15. German food, from pigs' knuckles to bratwurst. Moderate.

Lemongrass, Soi 24. Thai nouvelle cuisine in a converted traditional house; vegetarian menu on request. Moderate to expensive.

Mermaid's Rest, Soi 8. Nightly all-you-can-eat Texan-style barbecues are good value. Moderate.

Nipa, third floor of Landmark Plaza, between sois 6 and 8. Menu features an adventurous range of traditional Thai dishes, including a sizeable vegetarian selection; set meals are good value. Classical Thai music in the evening. Moderate to expensive.

Seafood Market, opposite Soi 21. More of a pink-neon supermarket than a restaurant: you pick your fish off the racks ("if it swims, we have it") and then choose how you want it cooked. Go for the novelty and choice rather than atmosphere or fine cuisine. Moderate.

Thai Ruam Ros, Soi 1. Mexican food a speciality – and it's not at all bad. Also Thai and European dishes available and a large vegetarian menu. A good place for lunch. Cheap to moderate.

Yong Lee, corner of Soi 15. One of the few unpretentious and refreshingly basic rice-and-noodle shops on Sukhumvit. Cheap, considering the competition.

Nightlife and entertainment

For many of Bangkok's visitors, nightfall in the city is the signal to hit the **sex bars**, the neon sumps that disfigure three distinct parts of town: along Sukhumvit Road's Soi Cowboy (between sois 21 and 23) and Nana Plaza (Soi 4), and, most notoriously, in the three small sois off the east end of Silom Road known as Patpong 1, 2 and 3. If you discount these red-light districts, Bangkok's night-time scene is active enough in certain downtown areas, but hardly thronging throughout the city. Overall, your best bet for a **drink** is to join the monied Thai youth and yuppie couples who pack out the **music bars** concentrated around Soi Langsuan and Sarasin Road, and scattered randomly over the rest of the city. The atmosphere in these places is as pleasant as you'll find in a Bangkok bar, but don't expect anything better than Western covers and bland jazz from the resident musicians, and look out for inflated drink prices – in the trendy bars a small bottle of Mekhong whisky can cost up to five times what a guest house would charge.

Bangkok's **clubs and discos** are similarly unenthralling, churning out a mix of current Thai and Western hits. Besides those listed below, most of the deluxe hotels – notably the *Ambassador, Dusit Thani* and *Oriental* – have nightclubs; all charge an admission price which often includes a couple of free drinks. The city's main **gay** areas are Patpong 3, nearby Soi Sukhumvit and the Pradiphat area near the weekend market. As with the straight scene, the majority of gay bars feature go-go dancers and live sex shows. Those listed here do not.

On the cultural front, **Thai dancing** is the most accessible of the capital's performing arts, particularly when served up in bite-size portions on tourist restaurant stages. **Thai boxing** is also well worth watching: the live experience at either of Bangkok's two main national stadiums far outshines the TV coverage.

Bars

Bobby's Arms, first floor of Patpong 2 car park. Naff imitation of an English pub (darts and horse brasses), but a quiet and cheap place for a draught beer. Dixieland band Sun nights.

Brown Sugar, Soi Sarasin. Chic but lively bar with nightly live music and occasional quality jazz from Tewan Sapsanyakorn. Pricey.

Focus, under *Bata* department store, Phra Pinklao Road, Thonburi. Small, dark but not at all seedy student hangout, with videos and nightly bands playing mostly Thai pop. Good atmosphere, reasonable prices.

The Glass, Soi 11, Sukhumvit Road. Usually packed out with Thai yuppies, but nothing special; nightly music from jazz-fusion band. Moderately priced drinks.

Gypsy Pub, west end of Phra Sumen Road. Banglamphu's only real bar has a predominantly Thai clientele, friendly staff and nightly live music of varying quality. Six nights of Latin-influenced pop, then loosely interpreted reggae and blues on Sunday night.

Hard Rock Café, Soi 11, Siam Square. Genuine outlet of the famous chain, better for drink than food. Big sounds and brash enthusiasm. Expensive.

Hyppordrome, Rajdamnoen Klang, next to *Majestic Hotel*, Banglamphu. Dreadful backroom bands make this place a laugh if you're not too fussy. Cheap beer.

Jai Yen, next to Phra Athit pier, Banglamphu. A good place for an early evening drink after 6pm, when the express boats stop running; riverside location, cheap beer, but the food is better for snacking. Moderate.

Manet Club, Renoir Club, Van Gogh Club, Soi 33, Sukhumvit Rd. Three very similar, unexciting, not-at-all-Parisian bars, all almost next door to each other, that are best visited during happy hour (4–8pm).

Old West, Soi Sarasin. Buzzing saloon with American country-rock band every night from 8pm; popular with Thai yuppies. Slightly expensive.

Round Midnight, 106/2 Soi Langsuan. Gimmicky decor and generally uninspiring live jazz and blues (nightly from 9pm), but the atmosphere is unpretentious. Moderate.

Saxophone, Phrayathai Rd, southeast corner of Victory Monument. Lively second-floor bar hosts nightly blues, folk and rock bands and attracts a good mix of Thais and farangs; relaxed drinking atmosphere and reasonable prices. There's a pool table on the first floor and a more sedate ground-floor bar with innocuous jazz bands.

Nightclubs and discos

Calypso Cabaret, between sois 24 and 26, Sukhumvit Road. Fairly tame transvestite show in theatre setting, twice nightly; B300.

Le Freak, Gaysorn Road, near to the *Meridian President Hotel* on Ploenchit Road. Plush, intimate club with good Thai and Western sounds. B150, including one drink.

Nasa, 999 Ramkhamhaeng Rd. Said to be Asia's largest disco, designed like an enormous spacecraft and featuring the nightly "lift-off" of a space capsule from the edge of the dance floor. B140 (B180 Fri & Sat), including three drinks. Open until 3am.

Rome Club, Patpong 3. Chic classical temple of a videotheque with a happy mix of gays and straights, Thais and farangs, heaving at weekends with Bangkok's sophisticated youth. The nightly transvestite show is reminiscent of a school pantomime. B200 (B300 Fri & Sat), including two drinks. *Rome Café*, opposite, serves pricey food and continues dispensing drinks after the club closes at 4am.

Gay bars and clubs

Aquarius, 243 Soi Hutavon, off Soi Suan Phlu, Sathorn Thai Road (near Immigration). Relaxed, civilized atmosphere in a traditional Thai house.

Ciro's, Soi Sukhumvit, Silom Road. One large bar, open until 4am.

Genesis, Patpong 3. Fairly quiet one-room bar.

Harrie's Bar, Soi Sukhumvit, Silom Road. Very popular exclusively gay bar and disco with nightly cabaret show. B150 admission (Fri & Sat) includes two drinks.

Puching, Patpong 3. Lively after-hours coffee shop and bar.

Telephone Bar, Patpong 3. Popular eating and drinking venue where each table has a telephone with a clearly displayed number so you can call up other customers.

Culture shows

Only in Bangkok can you be sure to catch a live display of non-tourist-oriented traditional dance or theatre; few of the outlying regions have resident troupes, so authentic performances elsewhere tend to be sporadic and may not coincide with your visit. The main venue is the *National Theatre* (☎224 1342) on the northwest corner of Sanam Luang which puts on special medley shows of **drama and music** from all over the country, performed by students from the attached College of the Performing Arts. These take place on the second Saturday and Sunday and the last Friday and Saturday of every month (more regularly Nov–May); tickets start at B20. Spectacular and authentic, the performances serve as a tantalising introduction to the theatre's full-length shows, which include *lakhon* (classical) and *likay* (folk) theatre and the occasional *nang thalung* (shadow-puppet play). Tickets for these start at B100 and programme details can be checked by calling the theatre.

Many tourist restaurants feature nightly **culture shows** – usually a hotchpotch of Thai dancing and classical music, with a martial-arts demonstration thrown in. Worth checking out are *Baan Thai*, a traditional teak house on Soi 32, Sukhumvit

Road, where diners are served a set meal during the show (performances at 9pm), and the outdoor restaurant in *Silom Village* on Silom Road, which does a nightly half-hour show (8pm) to go with its à la carte menu.

Thai dancing is performed for its original ritual purpose, usually several times a day, at the Lak Muang Shrine behind the Grand Palace and the Erawan Shrine on the corner of Ploenchit Road. Both shrines have resident troupes of dancers who are hired by worshippers to perform *lakhon chatri*, a sort of *khon* dance-drama, to thank benevolent spirits for answered prayers. The dancers are always dressed up in full gear and accompanied by musicians, but the length, number of dancers and complexity of the dance depends on the amount of money paid by the supplicant: a price list is posted near the dance area. The musicians at the Erawan Shrine are particularly highly rated, though the almost comic apathy of the dancers there doesn't do them justice.

Cinemas

Central Bangkok has over twenty **cinemas**, many of which show recent American and European releases with their original dialogue and Thai subtitles. Programmes are detailed every day in the *Nation* and *Bangkok Post*, and cinema locations are printed on *Nancy Chandler's Map of Bangkok*; seats start at about B40. The *Bata* cinema in the department store complex on Phra Pinklao Road in Thonburi is convenient for Banglamphu and there are four massive movie theatres in Siam Square. Western films are also occasionally shown at the British Council, Goethe Institut and Alliance Francaise: check the English-language press for details.

Thai boxing

The violence of the average **Thai boxing** match may be offputting to some, but spending a couple of hours at one of Bangkok's two main stadiums can be immensely entertaining, not least for the enthusiasm of the spectators and the ritualistic aspects of the fights.

Bouts are held in the capital every night of the week at the **Rajdamnoen Stadium**, next to the TAT office on Rajdamnoen Nok Avenue (Mon, Wed & Thurs 6pm; Sun 2pm & 6pm), and at **Lumphini Stadium** on Rama IV Road (Tues, Fri & Sat at 6pm). Tickets go on sale one hour before and start at B120. You might have to queue a few minutes, but there's no need to get there early unless there's a really important fight on. Sessions feature ten bouts, each consisting of five three-minute rounds (with two-minute rests in between each round), so if you're not a big fan it may be worth turning up an hour late, as the better fights tend to happen later in the billing. The most interesting place to sit is among the betting aficionados in the cheap seats.

Thai Boxing

Shopping

Bangkok has a justifiably good reputation for **shopping**, particularly for silk, tailored clothes and gems, where the range and quality is streets ahead of other Thai cities, and of many other Asian capitals as well. Antiques and handicrafts are good buys too, and some shops stock curiosities from the most remote regions of the country alongside the more typical standards. But as always, watch out for old, damaged goods being passed off as antiques: if you're concerned about the quality or authenticity of your purchases, stick to TAT-approved shops. Bangkok can also claim a healthy range of English-language bookshops.

For travellers, spectating, not shopping, is apt to be the main draw of Bangkok's neighbourhood **markets** – notably the bazaars of Chinatown and the massive Chatuchak Weekend Market (see p.92). If you're planning on some serious market exploration, get hold of *Nancy Chandler's Map of Bangkok*, an enthusiastically annotated creation which includes special sections on the main areas of interest. With the chief exception of Chatuchak, most markets operate daily from dawn till early afternoon; early morning is often the best time to go to beat the heat and crowds.

Fabrics and clothes

Thai silk became internationally recognised only about forty years ago after the efforts of American Jim Thompson (see p.85). Noted for its thickness and sheen, much of it comes from the northeast, but you'll find the lion's share of outlets and tailoring facilities in the capital. Prices start at about B250 per yard for single-ply silk, B500 for four-ply. *Jim Thompson's Thai Silk Company* at 9 Suriwong Rd is a good place to start looking, or at least to get an idea of what's out there – silk by the yard and ready-made items from dresses to cushion covers are well-designed and of good quality, but pricey. *Khanitha*, with branches at the Siam Centre, River City (near the *Sheraton* at the intersection of New and Si Phraya roads) and elsewhere, homes in on women's evening wear, for which Thai silk is probably best suited.

Traditional fabrics from the north and the northeast, as well as from Laos and Cambodia, are the speciality of *Prayer Textile Gallery*, at 197 Phrayathai Rd, on the corner of Rama I Road. The selection is good, but prices for these textiles are getting surprisingly high, particularly those now classified as antiques.

Bangkok can be a great place to have **tailored clothes** made: materials are cheap, and work is often completed in only 24 hours. On the other hand, you may find yourself palmed off with artificial silk and a suit that falls apart in a week. Cheap silk and tailoring shops crowd Silom, Sukhumvit and Khao San roads, but many people opt for hotel tailors, preferring to pay more for the security of an established business. Be wary of places offering ridiculous deals – when you see a dozen garments advertised for a total price of less than $200, you know something's fishy – and look carefully at the quality of samples before making any decision. If you're staying in Banglamphu, keep an eye on guest house noticeboards for cautionary tales from other travellers.

Designer fashions from big names as well as lesser-known labels are particularly good in the Siam Centre, across the road from Siam Square. The most exclusive designer wear fills the boutiques of Amarin Plaza on Ploenchit Road, Peninsula Plaza on Rajdamri Road and Thaniya Plaza on Silom Road. Wildly coloured **batik** clothes and artworks are sold at *Caspian Batik Art*, 552

> ### COUNTERFEIT CULTURE
>
> Faking it is big business in Bangkok, a city whose copyright regulations carry about as much weight as its anti-prostitution laws. Forged **designer clothes** and accessories are the biggest sellers; street vendors around the *Oriental Hotel* pier and along Silom, Sukhumvit and Khao San roads will flog you a whole range of cheap lookalikes, including Louis Vuitton bags, Benetton trousers, Levi 501s, Rayban sunglasses, YSL underpants and Lacoste shirts – even sew-it-on-yourself crocodiles to customise your existing wardrobe.
>
> Along Patpong, after dark, plausible would-be **Rolex and Cartier watches** from Hong Kong and Taiwan go for about B400 – and are fairly reliable considering the price. If your budget won't stretch to a phony Rolex Oyster, there's plenty of opportunities for smaller expenditure at the stalls concentrated along Khao San and Silom roads, where pirated **music and video cassettes** are sold at a fraction of their normal price. Quality is usually fairly high but the choice is often less than brilliant, with a concentration on mainstream pop and rock albums. Finally, a couple of holes-in-the-wall along Khao San Road even make up passable international **student and press cards** – though travel agencies and other organisations in Bangkok aren't so easily fooled.

Ploenchit Rd. Khao San Road is lined with stalls selling cheap **ready-mades**: the tie-dyed shirts, baggy cotton trousers, fake Levi's and ethnic-style outfits are all aimed at backpackers and New Age hippies; the stalls around *New World* department store have the best range of cheap Thai fashions in this area. **Shoes** and **leather goods** are good buys in Bangkok, being generally hand-made from high quality leather and quite cheap: check out the "booteries" along Sukhumvit Road.

Gems and stones

Bangkok boasts the country's best **gem and jewellery** shops, and some of the finest lapidaries in the world, making this *the* place to buy cut and uncut stones such as rubies, blue sapphires and diamonds. The most exclusive gem outlets are scattered along Silom Road, but many tourists prefer to buy from hotel shops, where reliability is assured.

While it's unusual for established jewellers to fob tourists off with glass and paste, a common sales technique is to charge a lot more than what the gem is worth based on its carat weight. Get the stone tested on the spot, and ask for a written guarantee and receipt. Be extremely wary of touts and the shops they recommend. Unless you're an experienced gem trader, don't even consider buying gems in bulk to sell at a supposedly vast profit elsewhere: many a gullible traveller has invested thousands of baht on a handful of worthless multi-coloured stones. If you want independent professional advice or precious stones certification, contact either the *Asian Institute of Gemological Sciences* at 484 Rajadapisek Rd (☎513 2112) or the *Geological Survey Division, Department of Mineral Resources* on Rama VI Road (☎246 1694).

The tiny *House of Gems* on New Road, near the GPO, deals almost exclusively in **fossils**, minerals and – no kidding – dinosaur droppings. Ranging from 60 million to 200 million years old, these petrified droppings (properly known as coprolite) were unearthed recently in Thailand's Isaan region; weighing from 10g to 8kg, they are sold at about B1 per gramme.

Handicrafts

Samples of nearly all regionally produced **handicrafts** end up in Bangkok, so the selection is phenomenal, if not quite exhaustive. Competition keeps prices in the city at upcountry levels, with the main exception of household objects – particularly wickerware and tin bowls and basins – which get palmed off relatively expensively in Bangkok.

Sukhumvit Road is full of touristy souvenir outlets, but one of the most interesting handicraft-antique shops is *Krishna's*, between sois 9 and 11. The four-storey building is crammed full of artifacts from all over Asia: many are unique and expensive collector's items, but there are also plenty of small curios for all budgets, including Balinese masks, Indian bedspreads, Thai and Burmese carvings and Nepalese jewellery. More specifically Thai is *Rasi Sayam* on Soi 23, opposite *Le Dalat* restaurant, which specialises in eclectic and fairly pricey decorative and folk arts such as tiny betel-nut sets woven from *lipao* fern. Less exclusive crafts and souvenirs are sold in the *Tourist Centre* under the expressway which divides Sukhumvit Road from Ploenchit Road.

On **Ploenchit Road**, on the second floor of Amarin Plaza (the *Sogo* building), *The Legend* stocks a small selection of well-made Thai handicrafts at reasonable prices including tableware made from coconut shells. Around the corner at 127 Rajdamri Rd, *Narayana Phand*, a government souvenir centre set up to ensure the preservation of traditional crafts and to maintain standards of quality, is packed with a huge variety of crafts at very reasonable prices, including *khon* masks, musical instruments, kites and celadon. Further north, off Rajaprarop Road, the *Bangkok Dolls Factory*, 85 Soi Rajatapan, makes and sells a range of dolls dressed in authentic traditional costumes.

In Thaniya Plaza, near Patpong on **Silom Road**, the small fourth-floor *Hyacinth Shop* focuses on high-quality crafts, including decorative boxes and unusual cushion covers, at reasonable prices. *Silom Village*, at 286/1 Silom Road, just west of Soi Decho, is a complex of wooden houses that attempts to create a relaxing, upcountry atmosphere as a backdrop for a variety of pricey fabrics and souvenirs, including some unusual finds.

Handicraft sellers in **Banglamphu**, particularly on Khao San Road, tend to tout a limited range compared to the shops downtown, but if you're interested in masks, try the shop on Chakrapong Road, between Khao San Road and Rajdamnoen Klang.

Antiques

Bangkok is the entrepôt for the finest Thai, Burmese and Cambodian **antiques**, but the market has long been sewn up, so don't expect to happen upon any undiscovered treasure. Even experts admit that they sometimes find it hard to tell real antiques from fakes, so the best policy is just to buy on the grounds of attractiveness. The River City shopping complex devotes its third and fourth floors to a bewildering array of pricey treasures and holds an auction on the first Saturday of every month (viewings held two Saturdays before). The other main area for antiques is the stretch of New Road that runs between the GPO and the bottom of Silom Road. Here you'll find a good selection of reputable individual businesses specialising in wood carvings, bronze statues and stone sculptures culled from all parts of Thailand and neighbouring countries as well. Remember that most antiques require an export permit (see p.42).

Books

English-language **bookshops** in Bangkok are always well stocked with everything to do with Thailand, and most carry fiction classics and popular paperbacks. *Asia Books*, an exclusively English-language Bangkok chain, covers all the usual bases and also keeps a good range of coffee-table tomes and reference works: branches on Sukhumvit Road between sois 17 and 19 and in Landmark Plaza near Soi 4; in Peninsula Plaza on Rajdamri Road; and in Thaniya Plaza near Patpong off Silom Road. *DK Books*, one of Thailand's biggest chains (Bangkok branches in Siam Square and on Patpong 1), is especially good for maps and books on Thailand. Behind *Narayana Phand* on Gaysorn Road, the unusual *Chalermnit* stocks an eclectic array, including books on Thailand written in English, French and German up to 200 years ago. *Central* department stores – the most convenient is on Silom Road – sell paperback fiction, maps and reference books in English.

The capital's few **second-hand** bookshops are surprisingly poor value, but you might turn up something worthwhile – or earn a few baht by selling your own cast-offs – in the shops and stalls along Khao San Road.

Travel from Bangkok

Despite Bangkok's numerous attractions, most travellers feel like getting out of it almost as soon as they arrive – and the city is full of tour operators and travel agents encouraging you to do just that. What's more, on any tour of Thailand you're bound to pass through the capital, as it's the terminus of all major highways and railway lines – there are no through Chiang Mai–Surat Thani links, for example. Fortunately, public transport between Bangkok and the provinces is cheap and plentiful, if not particularly speedy. This is also an unrivalled place to make arrangements for onward travel from Thailand – the city's travel agents can offer some amazing flight deals and all the major Asian embassies are here, so getting the appropriate visas should be no problem.

Travel within Thailand

Having to change trains or buses in Bangkok might sound a tiresome way to travel the country, but it has its advantages – breaking up what would otherwise be an unbearably long trip, and giving the chance to confirm plane tickets and stock up on supplies not so widely available elsewhere. It also means that you can store unwanted clothes in a guest house or hotel – very useful if coming from Chiang Mai (where you might need jumpers and walking boots) and going on to Ko Samui or Ko Phi Phi (T-shirts and swimwear).

Trains

All trains depart from **Hualamphong Station** except the twice-daily service to Kanchanaburi, which leaves from **Bangkok Noi Station** in Thonburi. **Tickets** for overnight trains and other busy routes should be booked at least a day in advance, either from the desk at Hualamphong (Mon–Fri 8.30am–6pm, Sat & Sun 8.30am–noon) or through an authorised train ticket agency, the most convenient being the *Trade Travel Service* at the *Viengthai Hotel* on Thani Road, Banglamphu (☎281 5788), and *Boon Vanit* at 420/9–10 Soi 1, Siam Square. Some hotels and guest houses will also book tickets for a commission of about B50.

Buses

Bangkok's three main bus terminals are distributed around the outskirts of town. The **Northern Bus Terminal** (*sathaanii moh chit*), on Phaholyothin Road near Chatuchak Weekend Market, is the departure point for northern and northeastern towns; there are plans to spruce up this terminal, during which time the buses will depart from nearby Kamphaeng Phet Road. The **Eastern Bus Terminal** (*sathaanii ekamai*), at Soi 40, Sukhumvit Road, serves east coast destinations. The **Southern Bus Terminal**, on Pinklao Road in Thonburi, handles departures to all points south and west of the capital. Regular and air-conditioned buses leave from different sections of the same terminals.

Regular buses don't need to be **booked** in advance, but air-con buses should be reserved ahead of time either at the relevant bus station or through an agent – much more widespread than train agencies, they can be found in many hotels and guest houses. Agencies sometimes provide transport to the bus station for an additional charge.

Planes

Domestic **flights** should be booked as far in advance as possible. *Thai Airways* flies to most major destinations; its main offices are on Silom Road (☎234 3100) and Larn Luang Road near Democracy Monument (☎280 0070). *Bangkok Airways* (☎253 4014–6), at 144 Sukhumvit Rd between sois 4 and 6, flies from Bangkok to Hua Hin and Ko Samui, and between Ko Samui and Phuket.

Tours

Many Bangkok outfits offer budget package **"tours"** to major tourist destinations (Chiang Mai, Phuket, Ko Samui, Ko Samet, Ko Phi Phi), which typically consist of a minibus ride to the train or bus station, a return ticket to your destination on standard public transport, and possibly a night's accommodation thrown in. It might be worth paying the extra if you haven't got time to make your own arrangements or can't face the hassle, but always be wary of unbelievably good deals: the free accommodation often has small print attached or will be miles from anywhere. **Day trips** to outlying destinations tend to be better value as they combine several places which would otherwise take a couple of days to see on your own: the most popular itinerary takes in Damnoen Saduak, Nakhon Pathom and Kanchanaburi.

Tour operators open up and go bust all the time, particularly in the Khao San Road area, so ask around for recommendations or make your arrangements through a reputable hotel or guest house; never hand over any money until you see the ticket.

Leaving Thailand

Whether you're moving on within Asia or just trying to get home, Bangkok is one of the best places in the world to buy **cheap international air tickets**, and there are hundreds of travel agents to buy them from. You'll get the very cheapest deals from agents who don't belong to the Association of Thai Travel Agents (ATTA), but as with their Western counterparts many of these are transient and not altogether trustworthy. Khao San Road is a notorious centre of such fly-by-night operations, some of which have been known to flee with travellers' money overnight: if you buy from a non-ATTA outlet it's a good idea to ring the airline and check your

RECOMMENDED TRAVEL AGENTS

Diethelm Travel, Kian Gwan Building II, 140/1 Wireless Rd (☎255 9150).

Educational Travel Centre, c/o *Royal Hotel*, 2 Rajdamnoen Rd (☎224 0043).

Pamela Tours and Travels, 888/18 Ploenchit Rd (☎253 8053).

STA Travel, c/o *Thai Hotel*, 78 Prajathipatai Rd, Banglamphu (☎281 5314).

Trade Travel Service, c/o *Viengthai Hotel*, 42 Thani Rd, Banglamphu (☎281 5788).

INTERNATIONAL AIRLINES

Aeroflot Regent House, 183 Rajdamri Rd (☎251 0617).

Air France Charn Issara Tower, 942/51 Rama IV Rd (☎233 9477).

Air India Amarin Plaza, 500 Ploenchit Rd (☎256 9614).

Air Lanka Charn Issara Tower, 942/34–35 Rama IV Rd (☎236 4981).

Biman Bangladesh Airlines Chongkolnee Building, 56 Suriwong Rd (☎235 7643).

British Airways Charn Issara Tower, 942/81 Rama IV Rd (☎236 0038).

Canadian Airlines Maneeya Building, 518/5 Ploenchit Rd (☎251 4521).

Cathay Pacific Charn Issara Tower, 942/135 Rama IV Rd (☎233 6105).

China Airlines Peninsula Plaza, 153 Rajdamri Rd (☎253 4438).

Egyptair 120 Silom Rd (☎231 0505).

Finnair Maneeya Building, 518/2 Ploenchit Rd (☎251 5012).

Garuda 944/19 Rama IV Rd (☎233 0981).

Gulf Air Maneeya Building, 518/5 Ploenchit Rd (☎254 7931).

Japan Airlines Wall Street Tower, 33/33–34 Suriwong Rd (☎233 2440).

KLM Patpong 2, Suriwong Rd (☎235 5155).

Korean Air Dusit Thani Building, 946 Rama IV Rd (☎235 9221).

Lauda Air Wall Street Tower, 33/37 Suriwong Rd (☎233 2565).

Lufthansa Pilot Pen Building, 331/1–3 Silom Rd (☎255 0370).

Malaysia Airlines 98–102 Suriwong Rd (☎236 4705).

Northwest Peninsula Plaza, 153 Rajdamri Rd (☎253 4822).

Pakistan International (PIA) 52 Suriwong Rd (☎234 2961).

Philippine Airlines Chongkolnee Building, 56 Suriwong Rd (☎233 2350).

Qantas Airways Charn Issara Tower, 942/51 Rama IV Rd (☎236 9163).

Royal Nepal 1/4 Convent Rd (☎233 3921).

Singapore Airlines Silom Centre, 2 Silom Rd (☎236 0440).

Swissair 1 Silom Rd (☎233 2935).

Thai International 485 Silom Rd (☎233 3810)

United Airlines Regent House, 183 Rajdamri Rd (☎253 0558).

reservation yourself – don't hand over any money until you've done that and have been given the ticket. The slightly more expensive ATTA agencies still work out good value by international standards: to check if an agency is affiliated either get hold of the TAT list, ask for proof of membership or call the ATTA office (☎252 0069). The box below lists some tried and tested companies.

All major airline offices are in downtown Bangkok, with a particularly dense concentration in the multi-storey office blocks along Ploenchit and Rajdamri roads and along Rama IV and Suriwong roads. There's absolutely no advantage in buying tickets directly off the airlines – their addresses and phone numbers are listed so you can check reservations and confirm bookings.

Tours to Burma, Laos, Vietnam and Cambodia

Bangkok is the best and cheapest place to arrange the tour packages which are required at the moment to get into **Burma**, **Laos**, **Vietnam** and **Cambodia**. It has the most efficient flight connections for the region, and travel agents here can arrange tourist visas more quickly, or at least less slowly. Entry formalities, lengths and prices of visas and permitted itineraries for all four countries change frequently: check with the relevant embassies for the latest story. Be very careful when arranging any kind of tour to this area of southeast Asia: read all small print, and try to confirm the travel details with the embassies. The **Burmese** embassy is at 132 Sathorn Nua Rd (☎234 4698); the **Laotian** is at 193 Sathorn Thai Rd (☎286 9244); the **Vietnamese** is at 83/1 Wireless Rd (☎251 7201). There is no Cambodian embassy.

Travel agent deals range from no-frills packages to Laos and Vietnam organised by *STA Travel* to *Diethelm Travel*'s expensive all-inclusive tours, which include such luxury oddities as flights from Chiang Mai to Pagan and Mandalay in Burma. A number of Khao San Road and other quick-fix agents also put together package deals to these countries. It's hard to recommend any as they come into the same category as the non-ATTA agents discussed above, but for information and help with getting to Laos you could try *Spangle Tours* at 205/1 Sathorn Thai Rd (☎211 3590) and for Burma *Copex Associated Travel Service* on the sixth floor of the Akaranupornpong Building, 130/2 Krung Kasem Rd, on the corner of Soi Thewes 1 (☎282 8131).

It's usually possible to extend your tourist visa in Laos, Vietnam and Burma at the end of an organised tour, though this may involve booking another tour with the local tourist authority.

Visas for other Asian countries

All foreign embassies and consulates with offices in Thailand are based in downtown Bangkok; the following list covers those countries that figure most frequently in onward Asian itineraries. Before heading off to the embassy, ring ahead to check on the documentation and photos you'll need for your visa application, and the probable waiting period.

China 57/2 Rajdapisek Rd (☎245 7032).
India 46 Soi 23, Sukhumvit Rd (☎258 0300).
Indonesia 600–602 Phetchaburi Rd (☎252 3135).
Korea Sathorn Thani Building, Sathorn Nua Rd (☎234 0723).
Malaysia 35 Sathorn Thai Rd (☎286 1390).
Nepal 189 Soi 71, Sukhumvit Rd (☎391 7240).
Pakistan 31 Soi 3, Sukhumvit Rd (☎253 0288).
Philippines 760 Sukhumvit Rd, opposite Soi 47 (☎259 0139).
Singapore 129 Sathorn Thai Rd (☎286 2111).
Sri Lanka 48/3 Soi 1, Sukhumvit Rd (☎251 2788).

Listings

Airport enquiries International departures ☎535 1254; international arrivals ☎535 1301; domestic services ☎535 1253.

Astrologers Mezzanine floor of the *Montien Hotel*, 54 Suriwong Rd; reduced menu of services is available in English, for B300 per half hour – palm reading Mon–Sat, card reading Sun & Mon.

American Express Top floor of the Siam Centre, opposite Siam Square, 965 Rama I Rd (☎273 0044; lost cards/cheques ☎273 0022). Amex credit card and travellers' cheque holders can use the office as a poste restante, but mail is only held for 30 days.

Car rental *Avis* 2/12 Wireless Road (☎255 5300–4) and 10/1 Sathorn Nua Rd (☎233 0397); *Hertz*, 987 Ploenchit Rd (☎252 4903) and 1620 New Phetchaburi Rd (☎251 7575); plus numerous others on Sukhumvit and Ploenchit roads.

Exchange The airport exchange desk and those in the upmarket hotels are open 24 hours; many other exchange desks stay open till 8pm, especially along Khao San, Sukhumvit and Silom roads.

Embassies and consulates *Australia*, 37 Sathorn Thai Rd (☎287 2680); *Canada*, Boonmitr Building, 138 Silom Rd (☎237 4126); *Great Britain*, 1031 Wireless Rd (☎253 0191); *Ireland*, 205 Rajawong Rd (☎223 0876); *Netherlands*, 106 Wireless Rd (☎254 7701); *New Zealand*, 93 Wireless Rd (☎251 8165); *US*, 95 Wireless Rd (☎252 5040). For visas to Asian countries, see previous page.

Emergencies For all emergencies, call the Tourist Police on ☎225 7758.

Hospitals and clinics *Bangkok Adventist Hospital*, 430 Phitsanulok Rd (☎281 1422); *Bangkok Christian Hospital*, 124 Silom Rd (☎233 6981); *Bangkok Nursing Home*, 9 Convent Rd (☎233 2610); *British Dispensary*, between sois 5 and 7, Sukhumvit Rd (☎252 8056); *VD International*, 588 Ploenchit Rd (☎250 1969); *Dental Polyclinic*, 211–3 New Phetchaburi Rd (☎314 5070).

Immigration office About 1km down Soi Suan Plu off Sathorn Thai Road (Mon–Fri 8am–noon & 1–4pm; ☎287 3101). Visa extension takes about an hour.

Language Courses AUA (☎252 8170) on Rajdamri Road runs regular Thai language courses.

Left luggage Both Don Muang airport and Hualamphong railway station have left luggage facilities (B20 per day); most hotels and guest houses will store bags by the week at much cheaper rates.

Libraries The National Library at the junction of Samsen and Sri Ayutthaya roads (Mon–Sat 9am–4.30pm) has a large collection of English-language books, as do AUA at 179 Rajdamri Rd (Mon–Fri 8.30am–6pm, Sat 9am–1pm) and the British Council in Siam Square (Tues–Fri 10am–7pm, Sat 10am–5pm).

Meditation A monthly meditation session in English is held at the headquarters of the World Fellowship of Buddhists, between sois 1 and 3, Sukhumvit Road – for details on these and other international Buddhist activities, call ☎511 0439. Wat Mahathat near Sanam Luang also holds regular meetings and introductory lectures, as well as meditation sessions in English led by farang monks (daily 7–10am, 1–4pm & 6–8pm; ☎222 2835).

Pharmacies English-speaking staff at the *British Dispensary*, between sois 5 and 7, Sukhumvit Road (☎252 8056).

Post The GPO is on New Road, just northeast of Wat Muang Kae express boat stop. Poste restante can be collected Mon–Fri 8am–8pm, Sat & Sun 8am–1pm; letters are kept for three months. The parcel packing service at the GPO operates Mon–Fri 8am–4.30pm, Sat 9am–noon.

Telephones The cheapest places to make international calls are the public telephone offices in or adjacent to post offices. The largest and most convenient of these is across Soi Praysanii from the New Road GPO (open 24 hours); the post offices at Hualamphong station and off Khao San Road in Banglamphu also have international telephone offices attached, but these close at 10pm.

travel details

Trains

From Bangkok Hualamphong station to Aranyaprathet (2 daily; 5hr); Ayutthaya (hourly; 1hr 30min); Chiang Mai (6 daily; 12hr 25min–14hr 15min); Hat Yai (4 daily; 16hr); Khon Kaen (5 daily; 7–8hr); Khorat (9 daily; 4–5hr); Lampang (6 daily; 11hr); Lamphun (4 daily; 13hr); Lopburi (12 daily; 2hr 30min–3hr); Nakhon Pathom (8 daily; 1hr 20min); Nakhon Si Thammarat (2 daily; 15hr); Nong Khai (3 daily; 11–12hr); Phatthalung (4 daily; 15hr); Phitsanulok (9 daily; 6hr 15min–9hr 30min); Surat Thani (8 daily; 9hr–11hr 30min); Surin (7 daily; 8–10hr); Trang (daily; 13hr 40min); Ubon Ratchathani (7 daily; 10hr 20min–13hr 15min); Udon Thani (6 daily; 10hr); Yala (3 daily; 18hr).

From Bangkok Noi station to Nam Tok (2 daily; 4hr 35min), via Nakhon Pathom (1hr 20min) and Kanchanaburi (2hr 40min).

Buses

From Northern Bus Terminal to Ayutthaya (every 10min; 2hr); Chiang Mai (28 daily; 9–10hr); Chiang Rai (15 daily; 12hr); Khon Kaen (23 daily; 6–7hr); Khorat (every 15min; 3–4hr); Lampang (10 daily; 8hr); Loei (17 daily; 10hr); Lopburi (every 15min; 3hr); Mae Hong Son (2 daily; 18hr); Mae Sai (8 daily; 13hr); Mukdahan (9 daily; 12hr); Nakhon Phanom (9 daily; 12hr); Nan (13 daily; 13hr); Nong Khai (10 daily; 11hr); Phitsanulok (up to 19 daily; 5–6hr); Sakhon Nakhon (5 daily; 11hr); Sukhothai (17 daily; 6–7hr); Surin (up to 20 daily;

8–9hr); Ubon Ratchathani (19 daily; 10–12hr); Udon Thani (every 20min; 10hr).

From Southern Bus Terminal to Damnoen Saduak (every 20min; 2hr); Hat Yai (9 daily; 14hr); Kanchanaburi (every 15min; 2–3hr); Krabi (at least 5 daily; 12–14hr); Nakhon Pathom (every 10min; 40min–1hr 20min); Nakhon Si Thammarat (12 daily; 12hr); Narathiwat (3 daily; 17hr); Pattani (2 daily; 16hr); Phang Nga (4 daily; 11hr–12hr 30min); Phatthalung (4 daily; 13hr); Phuket (at least 10 daily; 14–16hr); Ranong (7 daily; 9–10hr); Satun (2 daily; 16hr); Sungai Kolok (3 daily; 18hr); Surat Thani (11 daily; 12hr); Trang (8 daily; 14hr); Yala (3 daily; 16hr).

From Eastern Bus Terminal to Ban Phe (10 daily; 3hr); Pattaya (every 30min; 2hr 30min); Trat (14 daily; 6–8hr).

Flights

From Bangkok to Chiang Mai (9 daily; 1hr); Chiang Rai (2 daily; 1hr 20min); Hat Yai (5 daily; 1hr 30min); Hua Hin (one daily; 25min); Khon Kaen (2–3 daily; 50min); Khorat (one daily; 40min); Ko Samui (5 daily; 1hr 10min); Lampang (1 daily; 2hr); Loei (3 weekly; 2hr); Mae Hong Son (1 daily; 2hr); Nakhon Si Thammarat (4 weekly; 2hr); Nan (1 daily; 2hr); Narathiwat (3 weekly; 2hr 40min); Pattani (2 weekly; 2hr 30min); Phitsanulok (2–3 daily; 50min); Phuket (8–13 daily; 1hr 15min); Sakhon Nakhon (1 daily; 1hr); Trang (1 daily; 3hr); Ubon Ratchathani (1 daily; 1hr); Udon Thani (1–2 daily; 1hr).

CHAPTER TWO

THE CENTRAL PLAINS

North and west of the capital, the unwieldy urban mass of Greater Bangkok peters out into the vast well-watered **central plains**, a region that for centuries has grown the bulk of the nation's food and been a tantalising temptation for neighbouring power-mongers. The most densely populated region of Thailand, with sizeable towns sprinkled among patchworks of paddy and sugarcane fields, the plains are fundamental to Thailand's emergence as one of southeast Asia's healthiest economies. Its rivers are the key to this area's fecundity, especially the Nan and the Ping, whose waters flow from the Chiang Mai hills to irrigate the northern plains before merging to form the Chao Phraya which meanders slowly south through Bangkok and out into the Gulf of Thailand.

West of Bangkok, beyond the extraordinary religious site of **Nakhon Pathom**, the riverside town of **Kanchanaburi** has long attracted visitors to the notorious Bridge over the River Kwai and is now acquiring a reputation as a budget-travellers' hangout, for its unique and unpretentious raft-house accommodation. Few tourists venture further west except as passengers on the remaining stretch of the **Death Railway** – the most tangible wartime reminder of all – but the remote and tiny hilltop town of **Sangkhlaburi** holds enough understated allure to make the extra kilometres worthwhile.

On the plains north of Bangkok, the historic heartland of the country, the major sites are ruined ancient cities which cover the spectrum of Thailand's art and architecture. Closest to Bangkok, **Ayutthaya** served as the country's capital for the four centuries prior to the 1782 foundation of Bangkok, and its ruins evoke an era of courtly sophistication. A short hop north of here, the remnants of **Lopburi** hark back to an earlier time when the predominantly Hindu Khmers held sway over this region, building a constellation of stone temples across central and northeastern Thailand and introducing a complex grammar of sacred architecture that still dictates aspects of wat design today.

A separate nucleus of sites in the northern neck of the plains centres on **Sukhothai**, birthplace of the Thai kingdom in the thirteenth century. The buildings and sculpture produced during the Sukhothai era are the acme of Thai art, and the restored ruins of the country's first official capital are the best place to appreciate them, though two satellite cities – **Si Satchanalai** and **Kamphaeng Phet** – provide further incentives to linger in the area. West of Sukhothai, the Burmese border town of **Mae Sot** makes a therapeutic change from ancient history and is most easily reached from the northern plains, though it also forges a less predictable link between the northern plains and the far north.

Chiang Mai makes an obvious next stop after exploring the sights north of Bangkok, chiefly because the Northern Railway Line makes connections painless. A less common itinerary branches east into Isaan by bus from Lopburi, Sukhothai or Phitsanulok. Tying in the area west of Bangkok is a bit trickier: an irregular and convoluted bus service will eventually get you from Kanchanaburi to Lopburi, but the usual ploy is to treat Kanchanaburi as a mini-break from Bangkok and then backtrack to the city and proceed northwards.

WEST OF BANGKOK

Although the enormous chedi of **Nakhon Pathom** and the floating markets of **Damnoen Saduak** are easily seen in a day trip from the capital, the region west of Bangkok really merits a more extended stay, with at least a couple of nights spent on a raft house in **Kanchanaburi**. All tourist itineraries in this predominantly budget-traveller territory are dictated by the rivers – in particular the Kwai Noi, route of the Death Railway. At Kanchanaburi you reach the outer range of package tours from Bangkok, and following the Kwai Noi to its headwaters at **Sangkhlaburi** takes you into a forested and sparsely populated hill region that ten years ago was considered too dangerous to visit. These days it makes an attractive unhyped retreat worth a stay of a day or two, offering the possibility of a sidetrip to the nearby Burmese border at **Three Pagodas Pass**.

Highway 323 is the main artery of the region, branching northwest off Highway 4 just beyond Nakhon Pathom and running the length of the Mae Khlong and Kwai Noi valleys as far as Sangkhlaburi, a journey of some 400km from Bangkok; a dirt track connects Sangkhlaburi with the border. **Buses** bound for Nakhon Pathom and Kanchanaburi leave Bangkok's Southern Bus Terminal several times an hour; from then onwards services dwindle a little but never run less than once every two hours during daylight. The first 200km out of the capital is accessible by **train** along the remaining stretch of the Thailand–Burma Railway from Bangkok Noi to Nam Tok, via Nakhon Pathom and Kanchanaburi. Southbound trains also pass through Nakhon Pathom on their way to Phetchaburi, Surat Thani and eventually Malaysia.

Nakhon Pathom

Even if you're just passing through, you won't miss the star attraction of **NAKHON PATHOM**: the enormous **Phra Pathom Chedi** dominates the skyline from every direction, and forms the calm centre around which wheels the daily bustle of this otherwise unexceptional provincial capital, 56km west of Bangkok. Eye-catching in sunlight and floodlight, and imposing in all weathers, the chedi is well worth stopping off for, but there's little else to detain you here. Most people move on from Nakhon Pathom the same day, heading south to Damnoen Saduak to catch the next morning's floating markets or continuing west to Kanchanaburi and the River Kwai.

The only time you might want to stay overnight in Nakhon Pathom would be during either of its two annual **festivals**: for a week in early September the town hosts a food and fruits fair, featuring produce from Thailand's most fertile region and demonstrations of cooking and fruit-carving; then in mid-November the week-long Phra Pathom Chedi fair brings together itinerant musicians, food vendors and fortune tellers.

Nakhon Pathom (derived from the Pali for "First City") is probably Thailand's oldest town and is thought to be the point at which **Buddhism** first entered the region now known as Thailand, over 2000 years ago. Then the capital of a sizeable Mon kingdom, the settlement was deemed important enough to rate a visit from a pair of missionaries dispatched by King Ashoka of India, one of Buddhism's great early evangelists. Even today, the province of Nakhon Pathom retains a high Buddhist profile – aside from housing the country's most famous

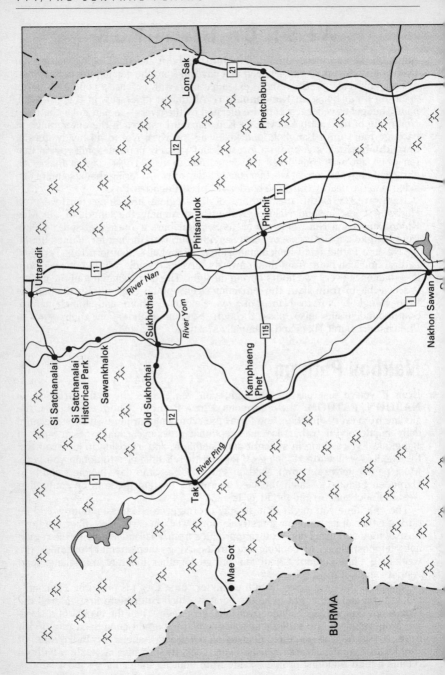

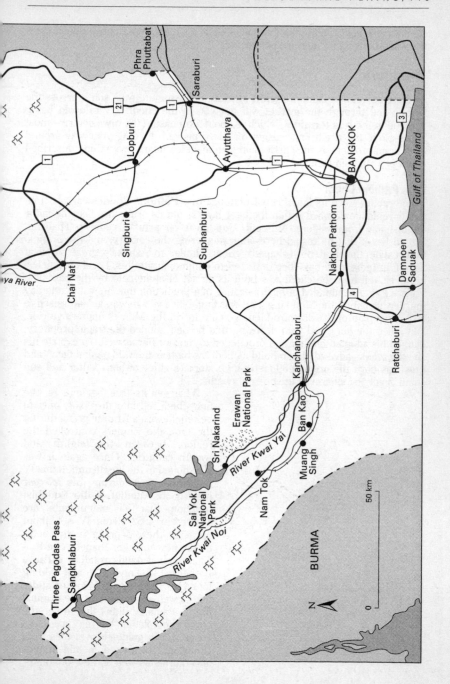

chedi, it also contains Phuttamonthon, Thailand's most important Buddhist sanctuary and home of its supreme patriarch.

The town

Arriving at Nakhon Pathom's **train station**, a five-minute walk south across the khlong and through the market will get you to the chedi. Try to avoid being dumped at the **bus terminal**, which is about 1km east of the town centre – most buses circle the chedi first, so get off there instead. Finding your way around town is no problem as the chedi makes an ideal landmark: everything described below is within ten minutes' walk of it.

Phra Pathom Chedi

Twice rebuilt since its initial construction, **Phra Pathom Chedi**'s earliest fragments remain entombed within the later layers, and its origin has become indistinguishable from folklore. Although Buddha never actually came to Thailand, legend has it that he rested here after wandering the country, and the original Indian-style (inverted bowl-shaped) chedi, similar to Ashoka's great stupa at Sanchi in India, may have been erected to commemorate this. Local chronicles, however, tell how the chedi was built as an act of atonement by the patricidal Phraya Pan. Abandonded at birth because of a prediction that he would one day murder his father, the Mon king, Pan was found by a village woman and raised to be a champion of the downtrodden. Vowing to rid the Mon of oppressive rule, Pan killed the king, and then, learning that he had fulfilled the tragic prophecy, blamed his adopted mother and proceeded to murder her as well. To expiate his sin, the monks advised him to build a chedi "as high as the wild pigeon flies", and thus was born the original 39-metre-high stupa. Statues of both father and son stand inside the viharns of the present chedi.

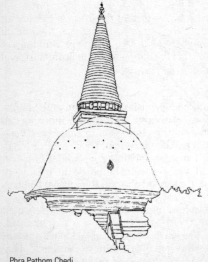

Whatever its true beginnings, the first chedi fell into disrepair, only to be rebuilt with a **Khmer** prang during the time the Khmers controlled the region, between the eighth and twelfth centuries. Once again it was abandoned to the jungle until Rama IV rediscovered it during his 27-year monkhood. Mindful of the Buddhist tradition that all monuments are sacred, in 1853 Rama IV set about encasing the old prang in the enormous new plunger-shaped **chedi** – 120m high, it stands as tall as St Paul's Cathedral in London – and adding four viharns, a circular cloister and a bot as well as a model of the original prang. Rama IV didn't live to see the chedi's completion, but his successors covered it in golden-brown tiles from China and continued to add statues and murals as well as new buildings.

Phra Pathom Chedi

A STUPA IS BORN

One of the more colourful explanations of the origin of the Buddhist **stupa** – chedi in Thai – comes from a legend describing the death of Buddha. Anxious about how to spread Buddha's teachings after his death, one of his disciples asked for a symbol of the Dharma philosophy. Notoriously lacking in material possessions, Buddha assembled his worldly goods – a teaching stick, a begging bowl and a length of cloth – and constructed the stupa shape using the folded cloth as the base, the inverted bowl as the central dome and the stick as the spire. Stupa design has undergone many changes throughout the Buddhist world since that first make-shift model, but Phra Pathom Chedi remains a robust facsimile of the original.

The most recent restoration was completed in 1981, when cracks were discovered in the dome, a job which clocked up a bill of over B24,000,000.

AROUND THE CHEDI

Approaching the chedi from the main (northern) staircase you're greeted by the eight-metre-high Buddha image known as **Phra Ruang Rojanarit**, recast in 1913 from a broken statue found among the ruins of Si Satchanalai near Sukhothai, and installed in front of the north viharn. Each of the viharns – there's one at each of the cardinal points – has an inner and an outer chamber containing tableaux of the life of Buddha. The figures in the outer chamber of the **north viharn** depict two princesses paying homage to the newly born Prince Siddhartha (the future Buddha), while the inner one shows a monkey and an elephant offering honey and water to Buddha at the end of a forty-day fast.

Proceeding clockwise around the chedi – as is the custom at all Buddhist monuments – look out for the red-lacquered Chinese **moon windows** punctuating the inner wall of the gallery before reaching the **east viharn**. Painted on the wall of the inner chamber, a clear cross-section of the chedi construction shows the incarcerated original. Flanking the staircase which leads up to the **south viharn** you can see a three-dimensional replica of the original chedi with Khmer prang (east side) and a model of the venerated chedi at Nakhon Si Thammarat (west side). The **west viharn** houses two reclining Buddhas: a sturdy nine-metre-long figure in the outer chamber and a more delicate portrayal in the inner one.

THE MUSEUMS

Two museums within the chedi compound vie for visitors' attention and, confusingly, both call themselves **Phra Pathom Museum**. The newer, more formal setup is clearly signposted from the bottom of the chedi's south staircase (Wed–Sun 9am–noon & 1–4pm; B5). It displays a good collection of Dvaravati-era (sixth to eleventh centuries) artifacts excavated nearby, including wheels of life – an emblem introduced by Theravada Buddhists before naturalistic images were permitted – and Buddha statuary with the U-shaped robe and thick facial features characteristic of Dvaravati sculpture.

For a broader, more contemporary overview, hunt out the other magpie's nest of a collection found near the east viharn (Wed–Sun 9am–noon & 1–4pm; free). More a curiosity shop than a museum, the small room is an Aladdin's cave of Buddhist amulets, seashells, gold and silver needles, Chinese ceramics, Thai musical instruments, world coins and banknotes, gems and ancient statues.

Sanam Chan Palace

A ten-minute walk west of the chedi along Rajdamnoen Road takes you through a large park to the **Sanam Chan Palace** complex. Built as the country retreat of Rama VI in 1907, the palace and pavilions were designed to blend Western and Eastern styles. Several of the elegant wooden structures still stand, complete with graceful raised walkways and breezy verandas. The main palace building has been converted into local government offices and so is officially out of bounds to tourists, but you can have a quick gander at the still sumptuous interior by going in to ask for a local (though not very useful) map. In the grounds, Rama VI erected a memorial statue of his favourite dog and a small shrine to the Hindu god Ganesh.

Practicalities

Nakhon Pathom's sights only merit half a day, and at any rate **accommodation** here is no great shakes. If you have to stay the night, probably the quietest of the cheapies is *Mitsampant Hotel* (☎034/241422), on the corner opposite the west gate of the chedi compound, where singles with fan and shower cost B90, doubles B120. Rooms at the *Mit Thawon* (☎034/243115), next to the railway station, are similarly priced – but don't take the one next to the generator. Rajvithee Road, which starts at the southwestern corner of the chedi compound, leads to the unbearably noisy *Muang Thong* and, further along, two good-value upmarket hotels: *Nakorn Inn Hotel* (☎034/251152) has air-conditioned singles and doubles for B450, while *Whale Hotel* (☎034/251020), down Soi 19 and signposted from the main road, has a disco (and cockfighting pit) and air-conditioned rooms with shower from B290.

Both the posh hotels have **restaurants** – the *Whale* does terrific American breakfasts – but for cheap Thai and Chinese dishes try *Thai Food*, on Phraya Gong Road just south of the khlong, or one of the garden restaurants along Rajdamnoen Road which runs west from the chedi's west gate. Night-time food stalls next to the *Muang Thong Hotel* specialise in noodle broth and chilli-hot curries, and during the day the market in front of the station serves up the usual takeaway goodies, including reputedly the tastiest *khao lam* (bamboo cylinders filled with steamed rice and coconut) in Thailand.

Damnoen Saduak floating markets

To get an idea of what shopping in Bangkok used to be like before all the canals were tarmacked over, make an early-morning trip to the **floating markets** (*talat khlong*) of **DAMNOEN SADUAK**, 60km south of Nakhon Pathom. Vineyards and orchards here back onto a labyrinth of narrow canals thick with paddle boats overflowing with fresh fruit and veg: local women ply these waterways every morning between 6am and 11am, selling their produce to each other and to the residents of weatherworn homes built on stilts along the banks. Many wear the deep blue jacket and high-topped straw hat traditionally favoured by Thai farmers. It's all richly atmospheric, which naturally makes it a big draw for tour groups – but you can avoid the crowds if you leave before they arrive, at about 9am.

The target for most groups is the main **Talat Khlong Ton Kem**, 2km west of the tiny town centre at the intersection of Khlong Damnoen Saduak and Khlong Thong Lang. Many of the wooden houses here have been expanded and converted into warehouse-style souvenir shops and tourist restaurants, dangerously diverting trade away from the khlong vendors and into the hands of large commercial enterprises. But, for the moment at least, the traditional water-trade continues, and the two bridges between Ton Kem and **Talat Khlong Hia Kui** (a little further south down Khlong Thong Lang) make rewarding and unobtrusive vantage points. Touts invariably congregate at the Ton Kem pier to hassle you into taking a **boat trip** around the khlong network (about B300 per hour) and while this may be worth it to get to the less accessible **Talat Khlong Khun Phitak** to the south, there are distinct disadvantages in being propelled between markets at top speed in a noisy motorised boat. For a less hectic and more sensitive look at the markets, explore the walkways beside the canals.

Practicalities

One of the reasons why Damnoen Saduak hasn't yet been totally ruined is that it's 109km and a two-hour **bus** journey from Bangkok. To make the trip in a day you'll have to catch one of the earliest #78 buses from Bangkok's Southern Bus Terminal (departures every 20min from 6am) or outside the *Nakorn Inn Hotel* on Rajvithee Road in Nakhon Pathom (from 7am onwards). From Kanchanaburi, take a bus to BAN PHE (1hr 15min), then change to the #78. Many tours from Bangkok combine the floating markets with a day trip to Phetchaburi (p.330), about 40km further south: to get from Damnoen Saduak to Phetchaburi by public bus, you'll have to change at SAMUT SONGKHRAM.

Damnoen Saduak's **bus terminal** is just north of Thanarat Bridge and Khlong Damnoen Saduak. Songthaews cover the 2km to Ton Kem, but walk if you've got the time: a walkway follows the canal, which you can get down to from Thanarat Bridge, or you can cross the bridge and take the road to the right (Sukhaphiban 1 Road, but unsignposted) through the orchards. The small **tourist information** office on the corner of this road keeps random hours and nobody there speaks much English.

The best way to see the markets is to **stay overnight** in Damnoen Saduak and get up before the buses and coach tours from Bangkok arrive. Try the *Floating Market Guest House* (☎032/251100), which has simple bamboo huts on the edge of Khlong Damnoen Saduak for B50 single, B80 double, and is just 200m from Ton Kem (signposted off Sukhaphiban 1 Road) – a perfect spot for exploring the canals on foot. If you don't fancy the huts, there are a couple of faceless cheap hotels near the bus terminal in the town centre where passable enough doubles go for B100.

Kanchanaburi and around

Set in a landscape of limestone hills 65km northwest of Nakhon Pathom, the provincial capital of **KANCHANABURI** unfurls along the left bank of the River Kwai Yai to reveal its most attractive feature: a burgeoning number of raft houses and riverside guest houses, any of which makes a wonderful place to unwind for a few days. With most of these catering mainly for modest budgets, Kanchanaburi has blossomed into quite a bustling independent travellers' centre. There's plenty to occupy several days here – the surrounding area offers numerous caves, waterfalls, wats and historical sites to explore, some of them easily reached by bicycle, and organised trekking and rafting trips to destinations further afield are also becoming popular.

Kanchanaburi's more official attractions, however, relate to its World War II role as a POW camp and base for construction work on the Thailand–Burma Railway. Day-trippers and tour groups descend in their hundreds on the infamous **Bridge over the River Kwai**, the symbol of Japanese atrocities in the region – though the town's **war museum** and **cemeteries** are much more moving. Many veterans returning to visit the graves of their wartime comrades are understandably resentful that others have in some cases insensitively exploited the POW experience – the commercial paraphernalia surrounding the bridge is a case in point. On the other hand, the museum provides a shockingly instructive account of a period not publicly documented elsewhere.

Kanchanaburi's history, of course, begins a lot further back – in the Stone Age – when small communities established themselves in the fertile river basin near the present-day town, an era documented in the **Ban Kao Museum** west of town. Several millennia later, the people of this area probably paid allegiance to the Mon kings of Nakhon Pathom and subsequently to the Khmers, whose sphere of influence spread north from what is now Cambodia – the temple sanctuary at **Muang Singh**, not far from Ban Kao, stands as a fine example of twelfth-century Khmer architecture. Over the next 500 years, Kanchanaburi's proximity to Thailand's aggressive Burmese neighbours gained it kudos as a key border stronghold; Rama III built walls around the town in 1743, and a small chunk of these can still be seen towards the western end of Lak Muang Road.

Arrival and accommodation

Trains from Bangkok Noi or Nakhon Pathom are the most scenic way to get to "Kanburi", if not always the most convenient – there are only two trains daily in each direction. The state railway also runs special day trips from Bangkok's Hualamphong station which include short stops at Nakhon Pathom, the Bridge over the River Kwai and Nam Tok, the terminus of the line (Sat, Sun & holidays only; advance booking is essential, see p.106). The station is on Saeng Chuto Road, about 2km north of the town centre – convenient for riverside lodgings along Soi Rong Heeb and Maenam Kwai roads, but a bit of a hike from Song Kwai Road accommodation. Samlor drivers armed with sheafs of guest house cards always meet the trains so you'll have no problem finding a ride, though getting to the guest house of *your* choice may take some firm negotiation.

Faster than the train are non-stop air-con **buses** from Bangkok's Southern Bus Terminal; slower regular services stop at Nakhon Pathom and several smaller towns en route. From Lopburi or points further north, you'll have to return to Bangkok or change buses at SUPHANBURI, about 70km north of Kanchanaburi. Arriving at the bus station at the southern edge of the town centre, it's a five-minute walk around the corner to the TAT office (daily 8.30am–4.30pm) and a ten- to twenty-minute walk or B10 samlor ride down Lak Muang Road to the raft houses off Song Kwai Road.

Accommodation

To get the best out of Kanchanaburi, you'll want to stay on or near the river, in either a raft house or a guest house. Most **raft houses** are little more than simple rattan and cane huts, partitioned into two or three sparsely furnished rooms and balanced on a raft of planks and logs moored close to the river bank. There's nothing romantic about sleeping in them, but the uninterrupted views of the river

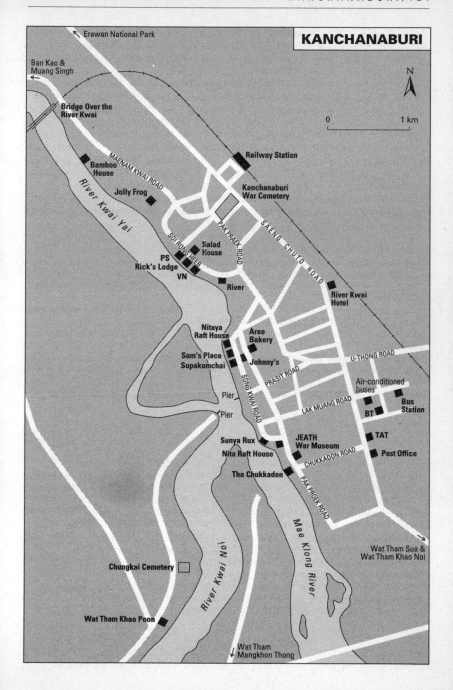

KANCHANABURI

N

0   1 km

Erawan National Park

Ban Kao &
Muang Singh

Bridge Over the
River Kwai

Railway Station

MAENAM KWAI ROAD

Bamboo
House

Kanchanaburi
War Cemetery

Jolly Frog

River Kwai Yai

SOI RONG HEEB

PAK PRAEK ROAD

SAENG CHUTO ROAD

Salad
House

PS
Rick's Lodge

VN

River

River Kwai
Hotel

Nitaya
Raft House

Aree
Bakery

Sam's Place
Supakomchai

Johnny's

SONG KWAI ROAD

PRASIT ROAD

U-THONG ROAD

Air-conditioned
buses

Bus
Station

BT

LAK MUANG ROAD

Pier

Pier

TAT

Sunya Rux

Nita Raft House

JEATH
War Museum

CHUKKADON ROAD

Post Office

Tha Chukkadon

PAK PRAEK ROAD

Wat Tham Sua &
Wat Tham Khao Noi

Chungkai Cemetery

River Kwai Noi

Mae Klong River

Wat Tham Khao Poon

Wat Tham
Mangkhon Thong

set against the blue silhouettes of the craggy hills can be magnificent. Not all **riverside guest houses** can offer such perfect vistas, but having a riverbank beneath you provides the option of an attached bathroom and sometimes the bonus of a grassy area to loll about on.

The river accommodation divides into two distinct areas. The noisier, brasher stretch of the river near **Song Kwai Road** is where holidaying Thais come – about half the rafts along here cater specifically for Thai families and package tours – so a party atmosphere prevails and it's not the place for peace and quiet. Development here has just about reached saturation point. Several hundred metres upriver, the accommodation along **Soi Rong Heeb and Maenam Kwai roads** offers a greater sense of isolation. There's really little point in coming to Kanburi and staying on dry land, but the town does have some non-aquatic accommodation; we've given details of a couple of places below.

Despite Kanchanaburi's increasing popularity, you're unlikely to have a problem finding a room except during the crazy ten days of the annual Bridge Festival (late Nov to early Dec).

SONG KWAI ROAD AREA

Nita Raft House (☎034/514521). Kanchanaburi's cheapest has very basic floating rooms away from the main fray near the museum. Relaxed seating/eating area offers some of the river's best views. Friendly management, well-organised day trips and tourist information. Singles B40, doubles B60.

Nitaya Raft House (☎034/513341). Some overpriced rooms on the riverfront with a/c and shower for B500, but cheaper ones further back with fan go for B150.

Sam's Place Middle-range raft houses. B70 single, B150 double (B250 double with shower and a/c).

Sunya Rux's Guest House (☎034/513868). Simple raft accommodation and raft trips featuring "master entertainer and daredevil Sunya", who owns a floating disco as well. Doubles B100.

Supakornchai Raft (☎034/512055). Fairly basic raft houses for B150 double (B250 a/c).

SONG RONG HEEB AND MAENAM KWAI AREA

Bamboo House (☎034/512532), down Soi Vietnam off the bridge end of Maenam Kwai Road. Kanburi's most secluded and peaceful digs, if a little inconvenient for shops and restaurants. A large and luscious lawn (good for kids) slopes down to simple floating huts. Singles B50, doubles B100; also a few air-conditioned rooms in the chalet-style house for B500.

Jolly Frog Backpackers (☎034/514579), just off the southern end of Maenam Kwai Road. Sizeable complex of comfortable bamboo huts ranged around a riverside garden, friendly and informative staff. Singles B40, doubles B70 (B100 with shower).

PS Guest House, Soi Rong Heeb (☎034/513039). Simple huts away from the river cost B40 single, B70 double; raft house with fan, B150.

Rick's Lodge, Soi Rong Heeb. Unusual two-storey A-frame bamboo huts with sleeping quarters in the roof section; rates are steep (B350 with fan and shower) but negotiable.

River Guest House, Soi Rong Heeb (☎034/512491). Beautifully located set of simple raft houses moored 30m from the bank. Singles B40, doubles B70.

VN Guest House, Soi Rong Heeb (☎034/514082). Well-run and attractively designed riverside huts with some of the thickest mattresses in town. Agent for treks in the Sangkhlaburi area. Singles B70, doubles B100 (B100/130 on the river).

SAENG CHUTO ROAD AREA

BT Guest House (034/511967) near the bus terminal, just east off Saeng Chuto Road. Fairly grotty, characterless single rooms with shared shower for B60, doubles B100.

River Kwai Hotel (aka *Rama of River Kwai*), 284/3–16 Saeng Chuto Road (☎034/511184). The town's top hotel, where facilities include a swimming pool and nightclub. Double rooms with shower and air-conditioning start at B640.

The Town

Strung out along the east bank of the River Kwai Yai, at the point where it joins the Kwai Noi to become Maenam Mae Khlong, Kanchanaburi is a long narrow ribbon of a town measuring about 5km from north to south. The war sights are sandwiched between the river and the busy main drag, Saeng Chuto Road, which along with the area around the bus station forms the commercial centre of Kanchanaburi. If you have the time, start with the museum and work your way northwards via the Kanchanaburi cemetery to the bridge, returning to one of the piers on Song Kwai Road for the ferry to the town's outlying sights.

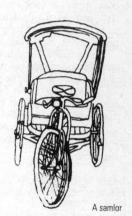

Walking around Kanchanaburi's main sights can be exhausting. By far the best way to see them, and the surrounding countryside, is by **bicycle**; most guest houses rent out bikes for about B20 per day and several also have **motorbikes** and jeeps for hire. Other outlets include the shop opposite *Aree Bakery* (see below), the house across from *VN Guest House*, or *BT Travel*, on the ground floor of the guest house of the same name. Alternatively, the standard **samlor** rate should be B10 per kilometre and there's a frequent **songthaew** service along Saeng Chuto Road between the bus terminal and the bridge (B5 per person).

A samlor

The JEATH War Museum

The **JEATH War Museum** (daily 8.30am–6pm; B20) gives the clearest introduction to local wartime history, putting the notorious sights of the Death Railway in context and painting a vivid picture of the gruesome conditions suffered by the POWs who worked on the line. JEATH is an acronym of six of the countries involved in the railway: Japan, England, Australia, America, Thailand and Holland. Notably lacking, though, is any real attempt to document the plight of the conscripted Asian labour force.

Set up by the chief abbot of the adjacent Wat Chaichumpon, the museum is housed in a reconstructed Allied POW hut of thatched palm beside the Mae Khlong, about 200m from the TAT office or a fifteen-minute walk southwest of the bus station. It's run by monks from the wat so, in accordance with Buddhist etiquette, women should remember to put the entrance fee on the table and not directly into the monk's hand.

The most interesting **exhibits** are the newspaper articles, paintings and photographs recording conditions in the camps. When things got really bad, photography was forbidden and any sketches had to be done in secret, on stolen scraps of toilet paper; some of those sketches, many by English POW Jack Chalker, were later reproduced as paintings. The simple drawings and paintings of torture methods are the most harrowing of all the evidence.

THE DEATH RAILWAY

Shortly after entering World War II in December 1941, Japan – fearing an Allied blockade of the Bay of Bengal – began looking for an alternative supply route to connect its newly acquired territories that now stretched from Singapore to the Burma–India border. In spite of the almost impenetrable terrain, they chose the River Kwai basin as the route for a new **Thailand–Burma Railway**, the aim being to join the existing terminals of Nong Pladuk in Thailand (51km southeast of Kanchanaburi) and Thanbuyazat in Burma – a total distance of 415km.

About 60,000 Allied POWs were shipped up from captured Southeast Asian territories to work on the link, their numbers later augmented by as many as 200,000 conscripted Asian labourers. Work began at both ends in June 1942. Three million cubic metres of rock were shifted and nine miles of bridges built with little else but picks and shovels, dynamite and pulleys. By the time the line was completed, fifteen months later, it had more than earned its nickname, the **Death Railway**: an estimated 16,000 POWs and 100,000 Asian labourers died while working on it.

The appalling conditions and Japanese brutality were the consequences of the samurai code: Japanese soldiers abhorred the disgrace of imprisonment – to them, ritual suicide was the only honourable option open to a prisoner – and considered that Allied POWs had forfeited any rights as human beings. Food rations were meagre for men forced into backbreaking eighteen-hour shifts, often followed by night-long marches to the next camp. Many suffered from beri-beri, many more died of dysentry-induced starvation, but the biggest killers were cholera and malaria, particularly during the monsoon. It is said that one man died for every sleeper laid on the track.

The two lines finally met at Konkuita, just south of present-day Sangkhlaburi. But as if to underscore its tragic futility, the Thailand–Burma link saw less than two years of active service: after the Japanese surrender on August 15, 1945, the Thais cut up the line between Nam Tok and Three Pagodas Pass and sold the rails as scrap.

The Kanchanaburi War Cemetery

Thirty-eight Allied POWs died for each kilometre of track laid on the Thailand–Burma Railway, and many of them are buried in Kanchanaburi's two war cemeteries. Of all the region's war sights, the cemeteries are the only places to have remained completely untouched by the tourist trade. Opposite the railway station on Saeng Chuto Road, the **Kanchanaburi War Cemetery** is the bigger of the two, with 6982 POW graves laid out in straight lines amidst immaculately kept lawns and flowering shrubs. Many of the identical stone memorial slabs state simply "A man who died for his country", others, inscribed with names, dates and regiments, indicate that the overwhelming majority of the dead were under 25 years old. A commemorative service is held here every year on April 25, ANZAC day. (The second cemetery, Chungkai, is just outside the town on the banks of the Kwai Noi – see below.)

Asian labourers on the Death Railway – who died in far higher numbers than the Allies – are remembered with rather less ceremony. In November 1990 a **mass grave** of Asians was discovered beneath a sugar cane field on the edge of town. The digging started after a nearby resident dreamt that the dead couldn't breathe and were asking for his help. The skeletons, many of them mutilated, have since been given a proper burial service, but the new graves are not for public viewing.

The Bridge over the River Kwai

For most people the plain steel arches of the **Bridge over the River Kwai** come as a disappointment: as a war memorial it lacks both the emotive punch of the museum and the perceptible drama of spots further up the line. As a bridge it looks nothing out of the ordinary – certainly not as awesomely hard to construct as it appears in David Lean's famous film of the same name. But it is the film, of course, that draws tour buses here by the dozen, and makes the bridge approach seethe with trinket-sellers and touts. For all the commercialisation of the place, however, you can't really come to the Kwai and not see it. To get here either take any songthaew heading north up Saeng Chuto Road, hire a samlor, or cycle – it's five kilometres from the bus station.

The fording of the Kwai Yai at the point just north of Kanchanaburi known as Tha Makkham was one of the first major obstacles in the construction of the Thailand–Burma Railway. Sections of a steel bridge were brought up from Java and reassembled by POWs using only pulleys and derricks. A temporary **wooden bridge** was built alongside it, taking its first train in February 1943; three months later the steel bridge was finished. Both bridges were severely damaged by Allied bombers in 1944 and 1945; only the stumps of the wooden bridge remain, but the steel bridge was repaired after the war and is still in use today. In fact the best way to see the bridge is by taking the train over it: the Bangkok–Kanchanaburi–Nam Tok train crosses it twice a day in each direction.

Some of the original World War II **railway engines** used on this stretch have been spruced up and parked beside the bridge; nearby, a memorial stone commemorates the Japanese soldiers who died while overseeing the construction work.

The bridge forms the dramatic centrepiece of the annual *son et lumière* **River Kwai Bridge Festival**, held over ten nights from the end of November to commemorate the first Allied bombing of the bridge on November 28, 1944. The hour-long show uses spectacular effects to sketch the history of the region's wartime role, liberally lacing the commentary with a stodgy anti-war message that doesn't quite square with the climactic go-get-'em pyrotechnics. Tourists of all nationalities, including Thais, flock here for the show, and the area around the bridge turns into an enormous funfair. Book accommodation and air-con buses well in advance, or join one of the many special tours operating out of Bangkok.

Chungkai Cemetery and Wat Tham Khao Poon

Several of Kanchanaburi's other sights lie some way across the river, and are best reached by bike (or by longtail boat, organised through your guest house). For Chungkai Cemetery and Wat Tham Khao Poon, on the left bank of the Kwai Noi, take the two-minute ferry ride (B2 for pedestrians and bikes) from the pier at the confluence of the two rivers on Song Kwai Road and follow the road on the other side. After about 2km you'll reach **Chungkai**, a peaceful cemetery built on the the banks of the Kwai Noi at the site of a former POW camp. Some 1750 POWs are buried here; most of the gravestone inscriptions include a name and regimental insignia, but a number remain unnamed – at the upcountry camps, bodies were thrown onto mass funeral pyres, making identification impossible.

One kilometre on from Chungkai Cemetery, at the top of the road's only hill, sits the cave temple **Wat Tham Khao Poon** (daily 8am–6pm; donation). This labyrinthine Santa's grotto is presided over by a medley of religious icons – the star being a Buddha reclining under a fanfare of flashing lights. The scenery around here makes it worth continuing along the road for another few kilometres; once over the hill, the prospect widens to take in endless square miles of sugar cane plantation (for which Kanchanaburi has earned the title "sugar capital of Thailand") fringed by dramatically looming limestone crags. Aside from the odd house, the only sign of human life along here is at the agricultural college in Somdech Phra Srinagarindra Park, 6km on from Wat Tham Khao Poon.

Wat Tham Mangkon Thong (Floating Nun Temple)

The impressive scenery across on the right bank of the Kwai Noi makes for an equally worthwhile bike trip, but the cave temple on this side – **Wat Tham Mangkon Thong**, otherwise known as the **"Floating Nun Temple"** – is fairly tacky. The attraction here is an elderly Thai nun who, clad in white robes, will get into the temple pond and float there, meditating – if tourists give her enough money to make it worth her while. It's difficult not to be cynical about such a commercial, and unspectacular, stunt, though Taiwanese visitors are said to be particularly impressed. The floating takes place on a round pond at the foot of the enormous naga staircase that leads up to the cave temple embedded in the hillside behind. The temple comprises an unexceptional network of low, bat-infested limestone caves, punctuated at intervals with Buddha statues.

To **get to** Wat Tham Mangkon Thong, take the ferry across the River Mae Khlong from the Chukkadon pier at the bottom of Chukkadon Road (near the museum) and then follow the road on the other side for about 4km.

Eating

All of Kanburi's guest houses and raft houses have **restaurants**, so independent eateries specialising in similar Western and toned-down Thai dishes have to be pretty outstanding to survive. Local food is of course cheaper and more authentic: cheap and tasty **noodle shops** abound, particularly down Pak Praek Road, and at night there's the ever reliable gastronomic delight of the **night market**, which sets up alongside Saeng Chuto Road near the air-con bus stop – the roar of the traffic is complemented by the jukebox that gets wheeled out every evening. For **seafood** try out the restaurants near *Johnny's* on Song Kwai Road. Don't bother with the **floating restaurants** at the confluence of the Kwai Yai and the Kwai Noi, which are overpriced, uninspired and cater for hapless tour groups; the same goes for the vast open-air restaurant next to the bridge.

Aree Bakery, Pak Praek Road. Especially popular for its German-made home-baked cakes; sandwiches, coffee and ice cream also served and there's usually a fluctuating pile of secondhand books to peruse or buy. Closes around 4pm.

Isaan, Saeng Chuto Road. Typical northeastern fare, including the excellent barbecued chicken (*kai yang*), sticky rice (*khao niaw*) and spicey papaya salad (*somtam*).

Johnny's, Song Kwai Road. Australian-run bar offers some food and is popular at night when it features live music (mostly local bands playing cover versions).

Saha 1, near the bus station (opposite the cinema and behind the clothes market). Huge menu of Thai dishes including a remarkably inventive vegetarian selection. Bar upstairs.

The Salad House, opposite *Rick's Lodge* on Soi Rong Heeb. Thai/Western-run garden restaurant with an emphasis on wholesome European food served up in massive portions. Impressive vegetarian menu. Prices reasonable, but not rock-bottom.

Around Kanchanaburi

The optimum way of getting to the main sights in the Kanchanaburi countryside – the temples of **Tham Sua** and **Tham Khao Noi**, the **Ban Kao Museum** and **Erawan National Park** – is by hiring a motorbike from one of the guest houses: the roads are good, but the public transport in the immediate vicinity of town is sporadic and wearisome at best. Alternatively, most guest houses in Kanchanaburi organise reasonably priced day trips to caves, waterfalls and historical sights in the surrounding area, as well as more adventurous and lengthier expeditions (see box below).

Wat Tham Sua and Wat Tham Khao Noi

A twenty-kilometre ride from the town centre gets you to the modern hilltop wats of **Tham Sua** and **Tham Khao Noi**, examples of the sort of rivalry that exists within all religious communities, even Buddhist ones. Take Highway 323 in the direction of Bangkok and follow signs for Wachiralongkorn Dam; cross the dam – at which point you should be able to see the wats in the distance – and turn right at the T-junction. If you have to rely on public transport, a tuk-tuk from the centre shouldn't cost more than B100.

Designed by a Thai architect, **Wat Tham Sua** was conceived in typical grandiose style around a massive chedi covered with tiles similar to those used at Nakhon Pathom. Twenty years on it is still unfinished, but alongside it has emerged the Chinese-designed **Wat Tham Khao Noi**, a fabulously gaudy seven-tiered Chinese pagoda whose more advanced state is an obvious indication of the differences in wealth between the Thai and Chinese communities. The differences between the temple interiors are equally pronounced: within Wat Tham Khao Noi, a laughing Buddha competes for attention with a host of gesturing and grimacing stone and painted characters, while next door a placid seated Buddha takes centre stage, his huge palms raised to show the wheels of life inscribed like stigmata across them. Common to both temples is the expansive view you get from their top storeys, which look down over the river valley and out to the mountains beyond.

DAY TRIPS, TREKKING AND RAFTING

Tours to Erawan National Park, the most popular organised day-tours from Kanchanaburi usually include transport to Phrathat Cave and the boat ride to Huay Khamin Falls. Trips run by *Nita Raft House* are particularly recommended, costing about B100 per person. If you're looking for a personal tour guide to more unusual destinations, try Mr Tom, a former Christian pastor turned samlor driver, who can be contacted through *Jolly Frog Backpackers'* guest house.

At the time of writing, *VN Guest House* had just introduced three-day **treks** to the Sangkhlaburi area (B1400 per person inclusive), which include rafting, elephant riding and a night in a Karen village. These could turn out to be refreshingly untouristed alternatives to treks in Chiang Mai and the far north, although the variety of hilltribe settlements in this region is nowhere near as great.

Except during the rainy season, *Nita Raft House* runs three-day **rafting** excursions up the Kwai Noi. Participants pole their own rafts, food is cooked over campfires and overnight accommodation is in tents.

Ban Kao Museum

Thirty-five kilometres west of Kanchanaburi, the **Ban Kao Museum** (Wed–Sun 9am–4pm; free) throws up some stimulating hints about an advanced prehistoric civilization that once settled along the banks of the Kwai Noi. The first evidence that a Stone Age community lived around here was uncovered during World War II, by the Dutch POW and former archaeologist Van Heekeren. Recognising that the polished stone axes he found might be several millennia old, he returned to the site in 1961 with a Thai–Danish team which subsequently excavated a range of objects that covered from around 8000BC to 1000 BC. Many of these finds are now displayed in the museum.

One of the most interesting discoveries was a group of some fifty **skeletons**, which had been buried with curiously designed pots placed significantly at the heads and feet. The graves have been dated to around 1770 BC and the terrracotta pot shards reassembled into tripod-shaped vessels of a kind not found elsewhere – they are thought to have been used for cooking over small fires. Polished stone tools from around 8000 BC share the display cabinets with inscribed bronze pots and bangles transferred from a nearby bronze culture site, which have been placed at around 1000 BC – somewhat later than the bronze artefacts from Ban Chiang in the northeast (p.309). The hollowed-out tree trunks just in front of the museum are also unusual: they may have been used as boats or as coffins – or possibly as a metaphorical combination of the two.

There's no public **transport** to the museum, so your best option is to hire a motorbike from Kanchanaburi, which also means that you can easily combine Ban Kao with a visit to Prasat Muang Singh, 8km west (see below).

Erawan National Park

Chances are that when you see a poster of a waterfall in Thailand, you'll be looking at a picture of the falls in **Erawan National Park**, 65km northwest of Kanchanaburi. The seven-tiered waterfall, topped by a triple cascade, is etched into the national imagination not solely by its beauty but also by its alleged resemblance to a three-headed elephant – the elephant (*erawan* in Thai) is the former national symbol and the usual mount of the Hindu god Indra. It makes a lovely setting for a picnic, especially just after the rainy season, and on Sundays and holidays Thais flock here to eat, drink and take family photographs against the falls; weekdays are generally a more peaceful time to come.

Access is along the well-maintained Highway 3199, which follows the Kwai Yai upstream, taking in fine views along the way. Buses stop at SRINAKARIND market, from where it's a one-kilometre walk to the national park **headquarters** and the trailhead. Although the park covers an area of 550 square kilometres, the only official trail is the one to the waterfalls. It's a fairly easy walk, though if you're aiming for the seventh and final level (2km), you'll have to negotiate a few dilapidated bridges and ladders, so wear strong shoes. Each level comprises a waterfall feeding a pool of invitingly clear water partly shaded by bamboos, rattans, lianas and other clotted vegetation – like seven sets for a Tarzan movie. The best pools for swimming are levels two and seven, though these inevitably get the most crowded.

If you follow the road from Srinakarind market for another 10km you'll reach Wat Phrathat, from where it's a 500-metre walk to **Phrathat Cave**. A songthaew from the market to the wat costs B200: buses don't come this far. The stalactite cave has several large chambers, but is of interest to geologists for the fault lines which run under the Kwai Noi and are clearly visible in the disjointed strata.

The Kwai Yai is dammed a few kilometres north of the turn-off to Erawan and broadens out into the scenic **Srinakarind Reservoir**, now a popular recreation spot and site of several resorts. From the dam you can hire boats to make the two-hour journey across the reservoir to **Huay Khamin Falls**, but as the boats cost at least B100 per person, you'd probably be better better off joining a tour from Kanchanaburi.

PRACTICALITIES

Buses to Erawan (#8170) leave Kanchanaburi every fifty minutes between 8am and 4pm and take two hours; if you miss the 4pm ride back you'll probably be there for the night. **Accommodation** is plentiful along the Kwai Yai valley, if a little select, most so-called "resorts" being fairly isolated communities of upmarket raft houses. The *Erawan Guest House Resort* (☎034/513001) is only ten minutes' drive from the park and has rafts starting from B600. On the reservoir, *Jungle Raft Resort* (☎02/253-4504) offers rooms and rafts from B700 and *Kwai Yai River Hut* (☎02/392-3286) has similar facilities from B600. It's also possible to stay in the *Erawan* national park bungalows, but these are pretty grim and cost a minimum of B500 for a two-bedroom hut that sleeps four. There are several **food** stalls, restaurants and shops selling snacks near the trailhead.

The Death Railway: to Nam Tok

The two-hour railway journey from Kanchanaburi to Nam Tok is one of Thailand's most scenic, and most popular. Leaving Kanchanaburi via the Bridge over the River Kwai, the train chugs through the Kwai Noi valley, stopping frequently at country stations decked with frangipani and jasmine to pick up villagers who tout their wares in the carriages before getting off at the nearest market. There are three **trains** daily in both directions, which means it's possible to make day trips from Kanchanaburi to Muang Singh and Nam Tok if you get the timing right; Kanchanaburi TAT keeps up-to-date timetables. Frequent **buses** also connect Kanchanaburi with Nam Tok via Highway 323.

Prasat Muang Singh

Eight hundred years ago, the Khmer empire extended west as far as Muang Singh ("City of Lions"), an outpost strategically sited on the banks of the Kwai Noi, 43km west of present-day Kanchanaburi. Thought to have been built at the end of the twelfth century, the temple complex of **Prasat Muang Singh** (daily 8am–4pm; B20) follows Khmer religious and architectural precepts (see p.288), but its origins are obscure – the City of Lions gets no mention in any of the recognised chronicles until the nineteenth century. If you're coming by train, get off at THA KILEN (1hr 15min from Kanchanaburi), walk straight out of the station for 500m, turn right at the crossroads and continue for another 1km. If you have your own transport, Muang Singh combines well with a trip to the Ban Kao Museum, 8km east of here (see above); both sites are on minor road 3445 which forks off from Highway 323 just north of Kanchanaburi.

Avalokitesvara

Prasat Muang Singh covers eighty acres, bordered by moats and ramparts which probably had cosmological as well as defensive significance, but unless you fancy a long stroll, you'd be wise to stick to the enclosed **shrine complex** at the heart of it all. Restoration work on this part has been sensitively done to give an idea of the crude grandeur of the original structure, which was constructed entirely from blocks of rough russet laterite.

As with all Khmer prasats, the pivotal feature of Muang Singh is the main prang, as always surrounded by a series of walls and a covered gallery, with gateways marking the cardinal points. The prang faces east, towards Angkor, and is guarded by a fine sandstone statue of **Avalokitesvara**, one of the five great *bodhisattvas* of Mahayana Buddhism, would-be-Buddhas who have postponed their entrance into Nirvana to help others attain enlightenment. He's depicted here in characteristic style, his eight arms and torso covered with tiny Buddha reliefs and his hair tied in a top-knot. In Mahayanist mythology, Avalokitesvara represents mercy, while the other statue found in the prasat, the female figure of **Prajnaparamita**, symbolises wisdom. When wisdom and mercy join forces, enlightenment ensues.

Just visible on the inside of the north wall surrounding the prang is the only intact example of the stucco carving that once ornamented every facade. Other fragments and sculptures found at this and nearby sites are displayed beside the north gate; especially tantalising is the single segment of what must have been a gigantic face hewn from several massive blocks of stone.

Nam Tok

Shortly after Tha Kilen the most hair-raising section of track begins: at **Wang Sing**, also known as **Arrow Hill**, the train squeezes through ninety-foot solid rock cuttings, dug at the cost of numerous POW lives; 6km further, it slows to a crawl at the approach to the **Wang Po viaduct**, where a 300-metre trestle bridge clings to the cliff face as it curves with the Kwai Noi – almost every man who worked on this part of the railway died. A couple of raft house operations have capitalised on the drama of this stretch of the river: on the viaduct side, *River Kwai Cabin* (☎02/412-4509) offers bungalows from B1250 (this is also the intended site for a new POW museum); on the other bank, *River Kwai Jungle House* (☎034/541052) has raft houses from B500.

Half an hour later, the train reaches **NAM TOK**, a small town that thrives chiefly on its position at the end of the line. Few foreign travellers stay here – daytrippers stay only until the train begins its return journey, while those on package tours are whisked downriver to pre-booked raft resorts. Nam Tok **railway station** is at the top of the town, 3km from the river and 500m north of Highway 323; **buses** usually stop near the T-junction of the highway and the station road.

On rainy season weekends, Thais flock to the town's roadside **Sai Yok Noi waterfall**, but if you're filling time between trains, you'd be better off stretching your legs on the short hike to the nearby Wang Badan Cave or taking a boat trip from Pak Saeng pier to Lawa Cave and Sai Yok Yai Falls (see below).

Best-value **accommodation** in town are the *Sai Yok Noi Bungalows*(☎034/ 512279), where a double room with fan and shower costs B120; to get there, turn northwest at the T-junction, walk five minutes and then turn right again. Down on the river, there are overpriced bungalows between Pak Saeng pier and the suspension bridge; not very clean huts for two, without shower, go for B200. The biggest resort on this section of the river is *River Kwai Jungle Rafts* (☎02/245-3069), about forty minutes upstream from Pak Saeng pier. A company called *River Kwai Floatel* runs the resort, organising overnight packages starting from Bangkok which include transport, trips along the river, French and Thai meals and raft accommodation. A two-day package costs B2000 per person; packages with only meals and accomodation cost B600 per person per day.

For **eating**, try the large open-air *Raena Restaurant* opposite the T-junction, which serves good food but sometimes caters to tour groups so is a little over-priced; the very friendly restaurant (no English sign) across the road offers the usual range of standard Thai dishes and is particularly lively in the evening.

Around Nam Tok

Impressive stalactites, fathomless chambers and unnerving heat make **Wang Badan Cave** (8.30am–4.30pm) one of the most exciting undergound experiences in the region. Located at the western edge of Erawan National Park (see p.128), the cave is reached by a trail that begins from Highway 323 about 1500m north-west of the T-junction (towards Sangkhlaburi). About 1km into the trail, you'll reach the park warden's office where you can rent feeble torches; better to bring your own or to pay the warden at least B50 to accompany you and turn on the generator – it's worth the money. From the office it's 2km of easy walking to the cave, but the descent should be made with care and sturdy shoes.

Longtail boats can be hired from Pak Saeng pier for the upstream **boat ride** to **Lawa Cave**, the largest stalactite cave in the area and home to three species of bat. To get to the pier from the T-junction, turn left towards Kanchanaburi, then take the first road on your right. The return journey to the cave takes roughly two hours, including half an hour there, and should cost about B500 for the eight-seater boat. Add on at least four more hours and another B700 if you want to continue on to Sai Yok Yai Falls (see below).

Nam Tok to Three Pagodas Pass

Although the rail line north of Nam Tok was ripped up soon after the end of the war, it casts its dreadful shadow all the way up the Kwai Noi valley into Burma. The remnants of track are most visible at **Hellfire Pass**, while many of the villages in the area are former POW sites – locals frequently stumble across burial sites, now reclaimed by the encroaching jungle. Small towns and vast expanses of impenetrable mountain wilderness characterise this stretch, a landscape typified by the dense monsoon forests of **Sai Yok National Park**. Most travellers drawn here will continue a further 160km to the border territory around **Sangkhlaburi**, 20km short of the actual border at **Three Pagodas Pass**, a notorious port of entry for smuggled goods and site of occasional skirmishes between Karen, Mon, Burmese and Thai factions. However, even if you have a visa you won't be allowed to enter Burma here, other than for the designated two-kilometre border stroll.

The only access to this region is via Highway 323, which runs almost to the border along a course dominated by the Tenasserim mountains to the west and the less extensive Mae Khlong range to the east. Five **buses** make the Nam Tok–Sangkhlaburi journey in both directions daily, so it's quite feasible to stop off for a couple of hours at either Hellfire Pass or Sai Yok National Park before resuming your trip northwards. As there's nowhere to stay at Hellfire Pass and the only decent accommodation at Sai Yok fills up fast, it's advisable to set off from Nam Tok reasonably early and aim to spend the night in Sangkhlaburi.

Hellfire Pass

To keep the Death Railway level through the uneven course of the Kwai valley the POWs had to build a series of embankments and trestle bridges and, at dishearteningly frequent intervals, gouge deep cuttings through solid rock. The most concentrated digging was at KONYU, 18km beyond Nam Tok, where seven separate cuttings were made over a 3.5-kilometre stretch. The longest and most brutal of these was **Hellfire Pass**, which got its name from the hellish lights and shadows of the fires the POWs used when working at night – it took three months of round-the-clock labour with the most primitive tools.

Hellfire Pass has now been turned into a **memorial walk** in honour of the POWs who worked and died on it. The ninety-minute circular trail follows the old rail route through the eighteen-metre-deep cutting and on to Hin Tok creek – then forded by a trestle bridge so unstable that it was nicknamed the Pack of Cards Bridge – along a course relaid with some of the original narrow-gauge track. The trail doubles back on itself, passing through bamboo forest and a viewpoint that gives some idea of the phenomenal depth of rock the POWs had to dig through. To get to the trailhead, take a Nam Tok–Sangkhlaburi bus and ask to be dropped off at the Army farm (*suan thahaan*) – Hellfire Pass is signposted on the lefthand side of Highway 323 as you face Sangkhlaburi.

Sai Yok National Park

Ten kilometres further up Highway 323, **Sai Yok National Park** also retains evidence of World War II occupation, but the chief attractions here are caves, waterfalls and teak forests. The park covers 500 square kilometres of uninhabited land stretching west of Highway 323 as far as the Burmese border, but the public has access only to the narrow strip between the Kwai Noi and the road, an area crisscrossed by short trails and dotted with caves and freshwater springs. It makes a refreshing resting point between Nam Tok and Sangkhlaburi, particularly if you have your own transport; accommodation and restaurant facilities are available, but cater primarily for Thai family groups.

Any of the Kanchanaburi–Sangkhlaburi **buses** will stop at the road entrance to Sai Yok (marked by the 104-kilometre stone), from where it's a three-kilometre walk to the **visitors' centre**, trailheads and river. The last buses in both directions pass the park at about 4pm. Motorbike-taxis sometimes hang around the road entrance waiting to transport visitors, but a more scenic way of visiting the park would be to join a longtail excursion from Nam Tok (see above).

All the trails start from near the visitors' centre and are clearly signposted from there as well as being marked on the map available from the centre. As in most of Thailand's national parks, Thais themselves come here for a waterfall. In this case it's the much-photographed **Sai Yok Yai Falls**, which tumbles right into the Kwai Noi in a powerful cascade – you can shower under it and bathe in the pools nearby, or gaze at it from the suspension bridge. If you come by longtail from Nam Tok, the boatman will probably also take you another 5km upstream to the stalactite-filled **Daowadung Caves**, a two-kilometre walk west of the river bank.

However, Sai Yok's most unusual feature is its dominant forests of **teak**, an endangered species in Thailand as a consequence of rapacious logging. During the war all the teak in this area was felled for railway sleepers – the present forests were replanted in 1954. The park's other rarity is the smallest known mammal in the world, the hog-nosed or **bumblebee bat**, discovered in 1973 and weighing only 1.75g, with a wingspan of 1.6cm. The bats live in twenty limestone caves in the Kanchanaburi area, of which Sai Yok's **bat cave** is the most accessible. Don't get too excited, though: it's almost impossible to see the bats unless you venture quite far inside with a powerful flashlight, and even then you'll need a fair amount of luck. On the way to the cave along the signposted trail, you might stumble across a few disintegrating railway sleepers which, together with the pile of bricks identified as the "Japanese cooking facility", constitute the park's only visible World War II remains. Although the camp kitchen is not worth making the effort for, follow its signposts from the visitors' centre for some secluded bathing spots in the crystal clear **natural springs** nearby.

Sai Yok has quite a few national park **bungalows**, which house a minimum of five people for B500. More inviting is the raft house near the waterfall, where doubles with shower cost B300; get there early if you want to be sure of a room. The raft house serves **food** and there are plenty of restaurants near the visitors' centre.

Sangkhlaburi

From Sai Yok, Highway 323 follows the Kwai Noi northwest, and beyond THONG PHA PHUM, the midway point between Sai Yok and Sangkhlaburi, the road affords increasingly spectacular views as it twists along the eastern shore of the vast Kreung Kra Wia Reservoir, whose creation fifteen years ago flooded several villages and a sizeable chunk of land. **SANGKHLABURI**, 160km from Sai Yok, now sits at the northernmost tip of this watery mass, overlooking an eerily beautiful post-holocaust scene of semi-submerged trees. One of those unassuming backwaters where there's nothing much to do except enjoy the scenery and observe everyday life, Sangkhlaburi has the rough feel of a mountain outpost and makes a charming place to hang out for a few days.

Sangkhlaburi's proximity to the border makes trade especially lucrative – the **early morning market** marks the town centre and is one of the best places for people-watching. During the cool season, when mist blankets the place until late morning, the townspeople – most of them Mon, Karen or Burmese, with the weathered skin and hardy bearing of mountain people – make their transactions wrapped in woolly hats and jumpers, sarongs and denim jackets. Among the many bargains, vendors stock a great selection of sarongs, running the range of styles from Indonesian batik and ikat to checked *longyis* from Burma. Also worth looking out for are ridiculously cheap bone jewellery and cakes of Burmese face powder which the villagers use both as protection against the elements and as a rejuvenating beauty aid.

A large Mon settlement of refugees from Burma has grown up across the water from Sangkhlaburi, connected to Sangkhlaburi by a spider's web of a wooden bridge, said to be the longest hand-made wooden bridge in the world. On the edge of the settlement, and dominating the far shore of the reservoir, stands the imposing modern structure of **Wat Wiwekaram**. Built in a composition of Thai, Indian and Burmese styles, its massive centrepiece is modelled on the stupa of India's Bodhgaya, revered site of Buddha's enlightenment. The wat occasionally gets embroiled in factional disputes. In December 1990 three monks from the temple set out to perform a ceremony for the Burmese army at the site of a new temple; seen as collaborators with the oppressive Saw Maung regime, they were attacked by Karen rebels inside the Burmese border, and one died of his injuries.

THE MON

Dubbed by some "the Palestinians of Asia", the **Mon** people – who number around four million in Burma and three million in Thailand – have endured an extended history of persecution, displacement and forced assimilation.

Ethnologists speculate that the Mon originated either in India or China, travelling south to settle on the western banks of the Chao Phraya valley in the first century BC. Here they founded the **Dvaravati kingdom** (sixth–eleventh centuries AD), building centres at U Thong, Lopburi and Nakhon Pathom and later consolidating a northern kingdom in Haripunchai (modern-day Lamphun). They probably introduced Theravada Buddhism to the region, and produced some of the earliest Buddhist monuments, particularly wheels of life and Buddha footprints.

Over on the Burmese side of the border, the Mon kingdom had established itself around the southern city of Pegu well before the Burmese filtered into the area in the ninth century, but over the next 900 years consistent harassment from the Burmese forced thousands to **flee** to Thailand. (As Burma was also engaged in an endless series of territorial battles with Thailand, the Mon got their own back by acting as spies and informers for the Thais.) Eventually, in the mid-eighteenth century, the Burmese banned the use of the Mon language in Burma, segregated Mon men and women by force, and decreed that they should be known as Talaings, a pejorative term implying bastardy. Stripped of their homeland, the Mon were once again welcomed into Thailand as a useful source of labour – in 1814, the future Rama IV arrived at the Kanchanaburi border with three royal warboats and a guard of honour to chaperone the exiles. Whole areas of undeveloped jungle were given over to them, many of which are still Mon-dominated today. Most of the Mon settlements in Thailand are in the western provinces of Kanchanaburi and Ratchaburi and in the central regions of Nonthaburi and Pathum Thani just north of Bangkok.

The assimilation of the Mon into Thai society was fairly smooth. Like Thais, they're a predominantly Buddhist, rice-growing people, but they also have strong animist beliefs. All Mon families have totemic **house spirits** such as the turtle, snake, chicken or pig, which carry certain taboos; if you're of the chicken spirit family, for example, the lungs and head of every chicken that you cook have to be offered to the spirits, and although you're allowed to raise and kill chickens, you must never give one away. Guests belonging to a different spirit group from their host are not allowed to stay overnight. Mon **festivals** also differ slightly from Thai ones – at Songkhran (Thai New Year), the Mon spice up the usual water-throwing and parades with a special courtship ritual in which teams of men and women play each other at bowling, throwing flirtatious banter around with their wooden discs.

Practicalities

If you're coming to Sangkhlaburi direct from Kanchanaburi, the most pleasant way to travel is by air-conditioned **minibus** (9 daily; 3hr), which departs from the privately run office at the back of Kanchanaburi bus station. The five daily **regular buses** are cheaper but may take twice as long: if you're coming from Nam Tok or Sai Yok, though, these are your only viable option, as the minibus is unlikely to stop and will in any case charge you the full fare. All buses stop in front of the marketplace at the heart of Sangkhlaburi.

Not many foreign tourists make it here, but those who do all seem to stay at *P Guest House* – not surprising, as it's perfectly sited on the sloping banks of the reservoir and has simple huts for B80, plus a restaurant. They also hire out rowing boats, which you can use to explore the reservoir and search for sunken chedis, and a couple of motorbikes for touring the locality. The guest house is about 1500m southeast of the bus terminal, clearly signposted all the way. If *P* is full you can try the central *Sri Daeng Hotel* (☎034/512996), just behind the market and opposite the army camp, which has large clean rooms with bathroom for B90.

Round the corner from *Sri Daeng* are several noodle shops, but the most popular **restaurant** is *No Name Restaurant*, on the road down to *P Guest House*, which serves good cheap Thai dishes under friendly management. *P*'s kitchen dishes up a tasty range of travellers' fare, including Western breakfasts and Thai rice and noodle standards. There's no bank in Sangkhlaburi and the post office is near *Sri Daeng Hotel*.

Three Pagodas Pass

Four kilometres before reaching Sangkhlaburi a dirt road branches off to **Three Pagodas Pass** (Sam Phra Chedi Ong), cutting through a couple of Karen and Mon villages and a police checkpoint where all foreigners must sign in. From here to the pass, it's an eighteen-kilometre ride through thick red dust – however you travel you'll get plastered in it, so think about taking a scarf and sunglasses for protection. Songthaews leave Sangkhlaburi bus station every forty minutes, cost B30 and take about an hour.

All **border trade** for hundreds of kilometres north and south has to come through Three Pagodas Pass: textiles, sandals, bicycles and medical supplies go out to Burma, in return for cattle and highly profitable teak logs – the felling of which has been illegal in Thailand since 1989. The Mon, the Karen and the Burmese government vie with each other for supremacy at the pass, the rebels relying on the tax on smuggled goods to finance their insurgency campaigns. An offensive is launched every dry season against the current holder of the pass: at the time of writing, the latest power wrestle had ended in 1990 with the Burmese government gaining command from the Mon. But smuggling continues at night, with soldiers turning a blind eye in return for bribes. Meanwhile, the Burmese want to turn the pass into a legal border **market** to encourage trade between Thailand, India and Bangladesh via the Burmese port of Moulmein. Under the current development plan, tempting incentives are being offered to Thais willing to set up shop here.

It must be the romantic image of a hilltop smuggling station that attracts the few foreign tourists to the 1400-metre-high pass, because there's nothing substantial to see here. The **pagodas** themselves are diminutive whitewashed structures unceremoniously encircled by a roundabout, though traffic is not exactly heavy

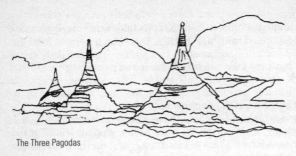

The Three Pagodas

up here. They are said to have been erected in the eighteenth century by the kings of Burma and Thailand as a symbolic commitment to peace between the traditionally warring neighbours. (During the Ayutthayan period, Burmese troops would regularly thunder through here on elephant-back on their way to attack the capital.) Each supposedly built a chedi on his own side of the border and, at the foot of the central, borderline pagoda they signed an agreement never to war with each other again.

All three are now on Thai soil, and Burmese land starts 50m away – you are allowed to cross **the border** provided you put your name in the book and proceed no further than the permitted 2km. At the time of writing, the village on the Burmese side was under reconstruction after being razed in the recent territorial struggles. The village on the Thai side is in better repair, but there's little of interest to look at and at present nowhere to stay. Nevertheless trade, official and unofficial, still goes on: if you get a kick out of crossing borders or want to buy *longyis* and cheroots then you probably won't be disappointed. There are moves afoot to entice tourists a little further into Burma to **Chengtoh Falls**, 12km from the pass; they are said to be a magnet for butterflies and a popular twilight watering hole for wild pigs and deer.

AYUTTHAYA AND THE CHAO PHRAYA BASIN

Bisected by the country's main artery, the **Chao Phraya River**, and threaded by a network of tributaries and canals, the fertile plain to the north of the capital retains a spectrum of attractions from just about every period of the country's history. The monumental kitsch of the nineteenth-century palace at **Bang Pa-In** provides a sharp contrast with the atmospheric ruins at the former capital of **Ayutthaya**, where ancient temples, some crumbling and overgrown, others alive and kicking, are arrayed in a leafy, riverine setting. **Lopburi**'s disparate remains, testimony to more than a millennium of continuous settlement, are less compelling, but you'll get a frenetic, noisy insight into Thai religion if you visit the nearby **Wat Phra Phutthabat** (Temple of the Buddha's Footprint), still Thailand's most popular pilgrimage site after three and a half centuries.

Each of the attractions of this region can be visited on a day trip from the capital – or, if you have more time to spare, you can slowly work your way through them before heading north or northeast. **Trains** are the most useful means of getting around, as plenty of local services run to and from Bangkok. The line from the capital takes in Bang Pa-In and Ayutthaya before forking at Ban Phachi: the northern branch heads for Lopburi and goes on to Phitsanulok and Chiang

Mai; the northeastern branch serves Isaan. **Buses** between towns are regular but slow, while Bang Pa-In and Ayutthaya can also be reached on scenic, but usually expensive **boat** trips up the Chao Phraya.

Bang Pa-In

Little more than a roadside market, the village of **BANG PA-IN**, 60km north of Bangkok, has been put on the tourist map by its extravagant and rather surreal **Royal Palace** (daily 8.30am–3.30pm; B50), even though most of the buildings can be seen only from the outside. King Prasat Thong of Ayutthaya first built a palace on this site, 20km downstream from his capital, in the middle of the seventeenth century and it remained a popular country residence for the kings of Ayutthaya. The palace was abandoned a century later when the capital was moved to Bangkok, only to be revived in the middle of the last century when the advent of steamboats shortened the journey time upriver. Rama IV (1851–68) built a modest residence here, which his son Chulalongkorn (Rama V), in his passion for Westernisation, knocked down to make room for the eccentric mélange of European, Thai and Chinese architectural styles visible today.

Set in manicured grounds on an island in the Chao Phraya River, and based around an ornamental lake, the palace complex is flat and compact – a free brochure from the ticket office gives a diagram of the layout. On the north side of the lake stand a two-storey colonial-style residence for the royal relatives and the Italianate **Warophat Phiman** ("Excellent and Shining Heavenly Abode"), which housed Chulalongkorn's throne hall and still contains private apartments where the present royal family sometimes stay. A covered bridge links this outer part of the palace to the **Pratu Thewarat Khanlai** ("The King of the Gods Goes Forth Gate"), the main entrance to the inner palace, which was reserved for the king and his immediate family. The high fence which encloses half of the bridge allowed the women of the harem to cross without being seen by male courtiers. You can't miss the photogenic **Aisawan Thiphya-art** ("Divine Seat of Personal Freedom") in the middle of the lake: named after King Prasat Thong's original palace, it's the only example of pure Thai architecture at Bang Pa-In. The elegant tiers of the pavilion's roof shelter a bronze statue of Chulalongkorn.

In the inner palace, the **Uthayan Phumisathian** ("Garden of the Secured Land") was Chulalongkorn's favourite house, a Swiss-style wooden chalet painted in bright two-tone green. After passing the **Ho Withun Thasana** ("Sage's Lookout Tower"), built so that the King could survey the surrounding countryside, you'll come to the main attraction of Bang Pa-In, the **Phra Thinang Wehart Chamrun** ("Palace of Heavenly Light"). A masterpiece of Chinese design, the mansion and its contents were shipped from China and presented as a gift to Chulalongkorn in 1889 by Chinese merchants living in Bangkok. You're allowed to take off your shoes and feast your eyes on the interior, which drips with fine porcelain and embroidery, ebony furniture inlaid with mother-of-pearl and fantastically intricate woodcarving. This residence was the favourite of Rama VI, whose carved and lacquered writing table can be seen on the ground floor.

The simple marble **obelisk** behind the Uthayan Phumisathian was erected by Chulalongkorn to hold the ashes of Queen Sunandakumariratana, his favourite wife. In 1881, Sunanda, who was then 21 and expecting a child, was taking a trip on the river here when her boat capsized. She could have been rescued quite easily, but the laws concerning the sanctity of the royal family left those around her no option: "If a boat founders, the boatmen must swim away; if they remain near the boat [or] if they lay hold of him [the royal person] to rescue him, they are to be executed." Following the tragedy, King Chulalongkorn became a zealous reformer of Thai customs and strove to make the monarchy more accessible.

Turn right out of the main entrance to the palace grounds and cross the river on the small cable car, and you'll come to the greatest oddity of all: **Wat Nivet Dhamapravat**. A grey Buddhist viharn in the style of a Gothic church, it was built by Chulalongkorn in 1878, complete with wooden pews and stained-glass window.

Practicalities

There's nowhere to stay in the village, but it can easily be visited on a day trip from Bangkok or Ayutthaya. The best way of getting to Bang Pa-In **from Bangkok** is on one of the hourly **trains** from Hualamphong station. The journey takes just over an hour and all trains continue to Ayutthaya, with half going on to Lopburi. From Bang Pa-In station (notice the separate station hall built by Chulalongkorn for the royal family) it's a two-kilometre hike to the palace, or you can take a samlor for about B20. Slow **buses** leave Bangkok's northern terminal every twenty minutes and stop at Bang Pa-In market, a samlor ride from the palace.

Every Sunday, the *Chao Phraya Express Boat Company* runs a **river tour** to Bang Pa-In, taking in a shopping stop at a folk arts and handicrafts centre. The boat leaves Bangkok's Maharat pier at 8am, stopping also at Phra Athit pier, and returns at 5.30pm. Tickets, available from the piers, are B180, not including lunch and admission to the palace. Luxury cruises to Ayutthaya (see below) also stop here.

From Ayutthaya, the hourly fifteen-minute train journey is the best option, though dawdling buses depart from Chao Phrom Road every hour.

Ayutthaya

In its heyday as the booming capital of the Thai kingdom, **AYUTTHAYA** was so well-endowed with temples that sunlight reflecting off their gilt decoration was said to dazzle from three miles away. Wide, grassy spaces today occupy most of the atmospheric site 80km north of Bangkok, which now resembles a graveyard for temples: grand, brooding red-brick ruins rise out of the fields, satisfyingly evoking the city's bygone grandeur while providing a soothing contrast to the brashness of modern temple architecture. A few intact buildings help form an image of what the capital must have looked like, while three fine museums flesh out the picture.

The core of the ancient capital was a four-kilometre-wide **island** at the confluence of the Lopburi, Pasak and Chao Phraya rivers, which was once encircled by a twelve-kilometre wall, crumbling parts of which can be seen at the Phom Phet fortress in the southeast corner. A grid of broad roads now crosses the island, with recent buildings dotted about uneasily: the main part of the small, grim and lifeless modern town rests on the northeast bank of the island around the corner of U Thong and Chao Phrom roads, although the most recent development is off the island to the east.

The hourly **train**, taking ninety minutes, is the best way of getting to Ayutthaya from Bangkok; trains continue on to the north and the northeast, making connections to Chiang Mai (5 daily), Nong Khai (3 daily) and Ubon Ratchathani (7 daily). To get to the centre of town from the station on the east bank of the Pasak, take the one-baht ferry from the jetty 100m west of the station (last ferry 8pm); it's then a five-minute walk to the junction of U Thong and Chao Phrom roads. The station has a left luggage service (5am–10pm) and, helpfully, sells onward first- or second-class tickets (9am–noon & 1–4pm).

Though frequent, **buses** to Ayutthaya are slower and much less convenient, as they depart from Bangkok's remote northern terminal. A small lane off Chao Phrom Road, right in the centre of Ayutthaya new town, is used as the bus station. Buses to Bangkok from the north stop on Highway 32, 5km east of town, from where you can catch a local bus or tuk-tuk to the centre.

It's also possible to get here by scenic **boat tour** from Bangkok via Bang Pa-In Palace: the *Oriental Hotel* (☎02/236 0400), among others, runs swanky day trips for B1000 per person, and a plushly converted teak rice barge called the *Mekhala* (☎02/235 4100) does overnight cruises.

Some history

Ayutthaya takes its name from Ayodhya (Sanskrit for "invincible"), the city of Rama, hero of the *Ramayana* epic. It was founded in 1351 by U Thong – later King Ramathibodi I – after Lopburi was ravaged by smallpox, and rose rapidly through exploiting the expanding trade routes between India and China. Stepping into the political vacuum left by the decline of the Khmer empire at Angkor and the first Thai kingdom at Sukhothai, Ayutthaya by the mid-fifteenth century controlled an empire covering most of the area of modern-day Thailand. Built entirely on canals, few of which survive today, Ayutthaya grew into an enormous amphibious city, which by 1685 had one million people – roughly double the population of London at the same time – living largely on houseboats in a 140-kilometre network of waterways.

Ayutthaya's great wealth attracted a swarm of foreign traders, especially in the seventeenth century. At one stage forty different nationalities, including Chinese, Portuguese, Dutch, English and French, were settled here, many of whom lived in their own ghettos and had their own docks for the export of rice, spices, timber and hides. With deft political skill, the kings of Ayutthaya maintained their independence from outside powers, while embracing the benefits of their cosmopolitan influence: they employed foreign architects and navigators, used Japanese samurai as royal bodyguards, and even took on outsiders as their prime ministers, who could look after their foreign trade without getting embroiled in the usual court intrigues.

In 1767, this 400-year-long golden age of stability and prosperity came to an abrupt end. After over two centuries of recurring tensions, the Burmese captured and ravaged Ayutthaya, taking tens of thousands of prisoners back to Burma with them. With even the wats in ruins, the city had to be abandoned to the jungle, but its memory endured: the architects of the new capital on Ratanakosin island in Bangkok perpetuated Ayutthaya's layout in every possible way.

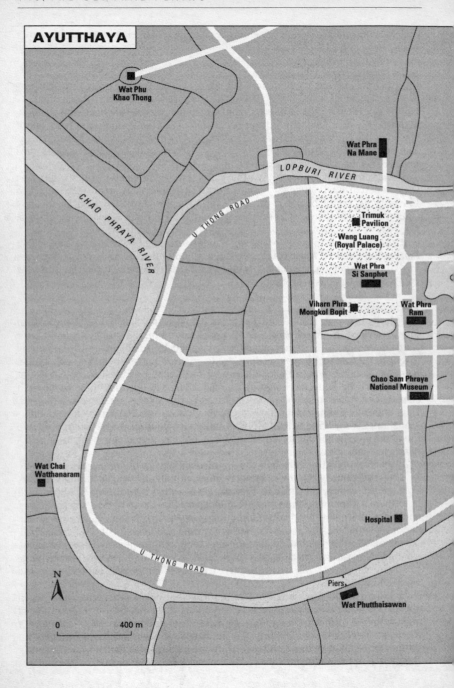

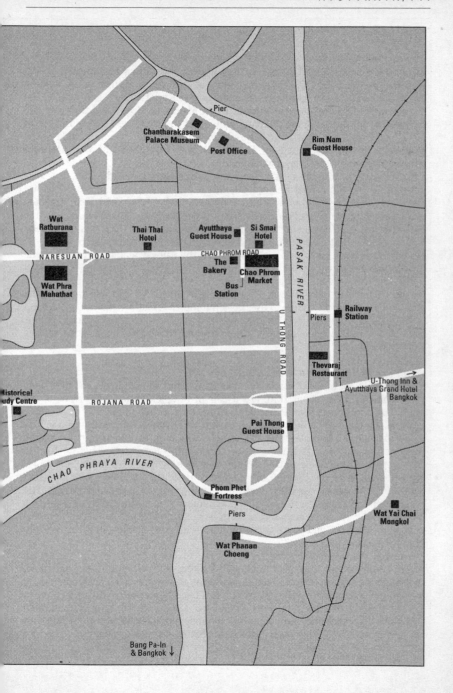

Pier

Chantharakasem
Palace Museum

Post Office

Rim Nam
Guest House

Wat
Ratburana

Thai Thai
Hotel

Ayutthaya
Guest House

Si Smai
Hotel

PASAK RIVER

NARESUAN ROAD

CHAO PHROM ROAD

The
Bakery

Chao Phrom
Market

Wat Phra
Mahathat

Bus
Station

U THONG ROAD

Piers

Railway
Station

Thevaraj
Restaurant

Historical
udy Centre

ROJANA ROAD

U-Thong Inn &
Ayutthaya Grand Hotel
Bangkok

Pai Thong
Guest House

CHAO PHRAYA RIVER

Phom Phet
Fortress

Piers

Wat Yai Chai
Mongkol

Wat Phanan
Choeng

Bang Pa-In
& Bangkok ↓

The City

The majority of Ayutthaya's ancient remains are spread out across the western half of the island in a kind of large historical park: **Wat Phra Mahathat** and **Wat Ratburana** stand near the modern centre at the park's eastern edge, while a broad band runs down its middle, containing the **Royal Palace** and temple, the most revered Buddha image at **Viharn Phra Mongkol Bopit**, and the two main **museums**. To the north of the island you'll find the best-preserved temple, **Wat Na Phra Mane**, and **Wat Phu Khao Thong**, the "Golden Mount", while to the southeast lie the giant chedi of **Wat Yai Chai Mongkol** and **Wat Phanan Choeng**, still a vibrant place of worship.

Coachloads of tourists descend on the sights during the day, but the area covered by the old capital is large enough not to feel swamped. Distances are deceptive, so it's best not to walk everywhere if you're doing a full visit: **bicycles** can be hired at the guest houses for B30–40 per day, or it's easy enough to hop on a **tuk-tuk** – B3 for a short distance if you're sharing, B10 if you're on your own. If you're short on time you could hire a tuk-tuk for a whistle-stop tour of the old city for around B100 an hour, either from the railway station or from outside the *Si Smai Hotel*.

Big tour **boats** can be chartered from the pier outside the Chantharakasem Palace or from the *Pai Thong Guest House*. A one-hour trip will take in Wat Phanan Choeng and a couple of overgrown temples (B300 for the boat). Because of the lack of bridges, small **ferries** also ply across the river at specific points, such as at Wat Phanan Choeng, charging around B1 and leaving as soon as they have passengers.

Wat Phra Mahathat and Wat Ratburana

Heading west out of the new town centre along Chao Phrom Road, the first ruins you'll come to, after about 1km, are a pair of temples on opposite sides of the road. The overgrown **Wat Phra Mahathat**, on the left (daily 8.30am–4.30pm; B20), is the epitome of Ayutthaya's nostalgic atmosphere of faded majesty. The name "Mahathat" indicates that the temple was built to house remains of the Buddha himself: according to the royal chronicles – never renowned for historical accuracy – King Ramesuan (1388–95) was looking out of his palace one morning when ashes of the Buddha materialised out of thin air here. A gold casket containing the ashes was duly enshrined in a grand 38-metre-high prang. The prang later collapsed, but the reliquary was unearthed in the 1950s, along with a horde of other treasures including a gorgeous marble fish which opened to reveal gold, amber, crystal and porcelain ornaments – all now on show in the Chao Sam Phraya Museum (see below).

You can climb what remains of the prang to get a good view of the broad, grassy complex, with dozens of brick spires tilting at impossible angles and headless Buddhas scattered around like spare parts in a scrapyard – and look out for the serene head of a stone Buddha which has become nestled in the embrace of a bo tree's roots. To the southwest you'll see a lake where King Ramathibodi (1351–69) discovered an auspicious conch shell, symbol of victory and righteousness, which confirmed his choice of site for his new city. Nowadays you can hire pedalos for B20 per hour from the western side of the lake, behind the crumbling remains of Wat Phra Ram.

Across the road from Wat Phra Mahathat, the towering **Wat Ratburana** (daily 8am–4.30pm; B20) was built in 1424 by King Boromraja II to commemorate his elder brothers Ay and Yi, who managed to kill each other in an elephant-back duel over the succession to the throne, thus leaving it vacant for Boromraja. Four elegant Sri Lankan chedis lean outwards as if in deference to the main prang, on which some of the original stucco work can still be seen, including fine statues of garudas swooping down on nagas. It's possible to go down steep steps inside the prang to the crypt, where on two levels you can make out fragmentary murals of the early Ayutthaya period. Several hundred Buddha images were buried down here, most of which were snatched by grave robbers, although some can be seen in the Chao Sam Phraya Museum. They're in the earliest style that can be said to be distinctly Ayutthayan – an unsmiling Khmer expression, but on an oval face and elongated body that show the strong influence of Sukhothai.

Wat Phra Si Sanphet and the Wang Luang (Royal Palace)
Further west you'll come to **Wat Phra Si Sanphet** (8.30am–4.30pm; B20), built in 1448 by King Boromatrailokanat as his private chapel. Formerly the grandest of Ayutthaya's temples, and still one of the best preserved, it took its name from the largest standing metal image of the Buddha ever known, the **Phra Si Sanphet**, erected here in 1503. Towering 16m high and covered in 173kg of gold, it did not survive the ravages of the Burmese, though Rama I rescued the pieces and placed them inside a chedi at Wat Po in Bangkok. The three remaining grey chedis in the characteristic style of the old capital were built to house the ashes of three kings and have now become the most hackneyed image of Ayutthaya.

The site of this royal wat was originally occupied by Ramathibodi's wooden palace, which Boromatrailokanat replaced with the bigger **Wang Luang (Royal Palace)**, stretching to the Lopburi River on the north side. Successive kings turned the Wang Luang into a vast complex of pavilions and halls with an elaborate system of walls designed to isolate the inner sanctum for the king and his consorts. The palace was destroyed by the Burmese in 1767 and plundered by Rama I for its bricks, which he needed to build the new capital at Bangkok. Now you can only trace the outlines of a few walls in the grass and inspect an unimpressive wooden replica of an open pavilion – better to consult the model of the whole complex in the Historical Study Centre (see below).

Viharn Phra Mongkol Bopit and the cremation ground
Viharn Phra Mongkol Bopit (8.30am–5.30pm), on the south side of Wat Phra Si Sanphet, attracts tourists and Thai pilgrims in about equal measure. The pristine hall – a replica of a typical Ayutthayan viharn with its characteristic chunky lotus-capped columns around the outside– was built in 1956, with help from the Burmese to atone for their flattening of the city two centuries earlier, in order to shelter the revered **Phra Mongkol Bopit**, one of the largest bronze Buddhas in Thailand. The powerfully plain jet-black image, with its flashing mother-of-pearl eyes, was cast in the fifteenth century, then sat exposed to the elements from the time of the Burmese invasion until its new home was built. During restoration, the hollow image was found to contain hundreds of Buddha statuettes, some of which were later buried around the shrine to protect it.

The car park in front of the viharn used to be the **cremation site** for Ayutthayan kings and high-ranking members of the royal family. Here, on a propitious date decided by astrologers, the embalmed body was placed on a towering *meru* (funeral pyre), representing Mount Meru, the centre of the Hindu-Buddhist universe. These many-gabled and pinnacled wooden structures, which had all the appearance of permanent palaces, were a miracle of architectural technology: the *meru* constructed for King Phetracha in 1704, for example, was 103m tall and took eleven months to raise, requiring thousands of tree trunks and hundreds of thousands of bamboo poles. The task of building at such great heights was given to *yuan-hok*, a special clan of acrobats who used to perform at the top of long poles during special festivals. Their handiwork was not consigned to the flames: the cremation took place on a pyramid erected underneath the central spire, so as not to damage the main structure, which was later dismantled and its timber used for building temples. The cremation ground is now given over to a picnic area and a clutch of souvenir and refreshment stalls.

The museums

A ten-minute walk south of the viharn brings you to the largest of the town's three museums, the **Chao Sam Phraya National Museum** (Wed–Sun 9am–4pm; B10), where most of the movable remains of Ayutthaya's glory – those which weren't plundered by treasure-hunters or taken to the National Museum in Bangkok – are exhibited. Apart from numerous Buddhas, it's bursting with gold treasures of all shapes and sizes – betel-nut sets and model chedis, a royal wimple in gold filigree, a model elephant dripping with gems and the original relic casket from Wat Mahathat. A second gallery, behind the main hall, explores foreign influences on Thai art and is particularly good on the origins of the various styles of Buddha images. This room also contains skeletons and artefacts from the site of the Portuguese settlement founded in 1540 just south of the town on the banks of the Chao Phraya. The Portuguese were the first Western power to establish ties with Ayutthaya, when in 1511 they were granted commercial privileges in return for supplying arms.

The **Historical Study Centre** (Mon–Fri 9.30am–3.30pm, Sat & Sun 9.30am–4.30pm; B100), five minutes' walk away along Rotchana Road, is the town's spanking new showpiece, with a hefty admission charge to go with it. The visitors' exhibition upstairs puts the ruins in context, dramatically presenting a wealth of background detail through videos, sound effects and reconstructions – temple murals and model ships, a peasant's wooden house and a small-scale model of the Royal Palace – to build up a broad social history of Ayutthaya.

In the northeast corner of the island, the museum of the **Chantharakasem Palace** (Wed–Sun 9am–noon & 1–4pm; B10) was traditionally the home of the heir to the Ayutthayan throne. The Black Prince, Naresuan, built the first *wang na* ("palace of the front") here in about 1577 so that he could guard the area of the city wall which was most vulnerable to enemy attack. Rama IV (1851–68) had the palace rebuilt and it now displays many of his possessions, including a throne platform overhung by a white *chat*, a ceremonial nine-tiered parasol which is a vital part of a king's insignia. The rest of the museum is a jumble of beautiful ceramics, Buddha images and random artefacts.

Wat Na Phra Mane

Wat Na Phra Mane, on the north bank of the Lopburi River opposite the Wang Luang, is Ayutthaya's most rewarding temple, as it's the only one from the town's golden age which survived the ravages of the Burmese. The story goes that when the Burmese were on the brink of capturing Ayutthaya in 1760, a siege gun positioned here burst, mortally wounding their king and prompting their retreat; out of superstition, they left the temple standing when they came back to devastate the city in 1767.

The main **bot**, built in 1503, shows the distinctive features of Ayutthayan architecture – outside columns topped with lotus cups, and slits in the walls instead of windows to let the wind pass through. Inside, underneath a rich red and gold coffered ceiling representing the stars around the moon, sits a powerful six-metre-high Buddha in the disdainful, overdecorated royal style characteristic of the later Ayutthaya period.

In sharp contrast is the dark green **Phra Khan Thavaraj** Buddha which dominates the tiny viharn behind to the right. Seated in the "European position", with its robe delicately pleated and its feet up on a large lotus leaf, the gentle figure conveys a reassuring serenity. It's advertised as being from Sri Lanka, the source of Thai Buddhism, but more likely is a Mon image from Wat Phra Mane at Nakhon Pathom dating from the seventh to ninth centuries.

Wat Phu Khao Thong

Head 2km northwest of Wat Na Phra Mane and you'll be in open country, where the fifty-metre chedi of **Wat Phu Khao Thong** rises steeply out of the ricefields. In 1569, after a temporary occupation of Ayutthaya, the Burmese erected a Mon-style chedi here to commemorate their victory. Forbidden by Buddhist law from pulling down a sacred monument, the Thais had to put up with this galling reminder of the enemy's success until it collapsed nearly two centuries later, when King Borommakot promptly built a truly Ayutthayan chedi on the old Burmese base – just in time for the Burmese to return in 1767 and flatten the town. This "Golden Mount" is now cracked, overgrown and grey, but you can still climb 25m of steps to the top of the base to look out over the countryside and the town, a view that's best appreciated in the wet season, when the paddies are flooded. In 1956, to celebrate 2500 years of Buddhism, the government placed on the tip of the spire a ball of solid gold weighing 2500g, of which there is now no trace.

Wat Yai Chai Mongkol

To the southeast of the island, if you cross the suspension bridge over the Pasak River and the railway line, then turn right at the major roundabout, you'll pass through Ayutthaya's new business zone and some rustic suburbia before reaching the ancient but still functioning **Wat Yai Chai Mongkol**, nearly 2km from the bridge (B10). Surrounded by decidedly un-Asian formal lawns and flower beds, the wat was established by King Ramathibodi in 1357 as a meditation site for monks returning from study in Sri Lanka. King Naresuan put up the celebrated **chedi** to mark the decisive victory over the Burmese at Suphanburi in 1593, when he himself had sent the enemy packing by slaying the Burmese crown prince in a duel. Built on a colos-

Reclining Buddha

sal scale to outshine the Burmese Golden Mount on the opposite side of Ayutthaya, the chedi has come to symbolise the prowess and devotion of Naresuan and, by implication, his descendants down to the present king.

By the entrance, a **reclining Buddha**, now gleamingly restored in toothpaste white, was also constructed by Naresuan; elsewhere in the grounds, the wat maintains its contemplative origins with some highly topical maxims pinned to the trees such as, "Cut down the forest of passion not real trees".

Wat Phanan Choeng

In Ayutthaya's most prosperous period the docks and main trading area were located near the confluence of the Chao Phraya and Pasak rivers, to the west of Wat Yai Chai Mongkol. This is where you'll find **Wat Phanan Choeng**, the oldest and liveliest working temple in town. If you can get here during a festival, especially Chinese New Year, you'll be in for an overpowering experience. The main viharn is filled with the sights, sounds and smells of an incredible variety of merit-making activities, as devotees burn huge pink Chinese incense candles, offer food and rattle fortune sticks. It's even possible to buy tiny golden statues of the Buddha to be placed in one of the hundreds of niches which line the walls, a form of votive offering peculiar to this temple.

The nineteen-metre-high Buddha, which almost fills the hall, has survived since 1324, shortly before the founding of the capital, and tears are said to have flowed from its eyes when Ayutthaya was sacked by the Burmese. However, the reason for the temple's popularity with the Chinese is to be found in the early eighteenth-century shrine by the pier, with its image of a beautiful Chinese princess who drowned herself here because of a king's infidelity: his remorse led him to build the shrine at the place where she had walked into the river.

Practicalities

Although Ayutthaya is usually visited on a day trip, there is a slim choice of **budget accommodation** for those who want to make a little more of it. The friendly *Ayutthaya Guest House*, 16/2 Chao Phrom Rd (☎035/251468), on a quiet lane in the town centre, has decent rooms for B50 per person and is a good source of information. On the east bank of the Pasak River, 1km north of the train station, is the *Rim Nam Guest House*, a traditional riverside compound with peaceful rooms also for B50. It's a long way from the island by road, but you can nip straight across by boat for B3. The *Pai Thong Guest House* (☎035/241830), also on the river, just south of the Pridi Damrong Bridge at 8 U Thong Road, has simple two-berth cubicles for B60.

Slightly **more upmarket**, the motel-like *Thai Thai Hotel* (☎035/251505), is conveniently placed on Naresuan Road between the modern town and Wat Mahathat; air-conditioned rooms are B250, fan rooms B120, each with its own cold-water bathroom. The *Si Smai Hotel* on Chao Phrom Road is uncomfortable and overpriced – one to avoid. At the top end but way out east of town are *U-Thong Inn*, 210 Rojana Rd (☎035/242618), with air-conditioned rooms from B500, and at 55/5 Rojana Rd, *Ayutthaya Grand Hotel* (☎035/244483), which is better value, with rooms with all facilities from B600.

The best of a bad bunch of **places to eat** is the moderately priced *Lumpang Restaurant*, at 1/10–11 Chao Phrom Shopping Centre, down a short lane directly opposite the *Si Smai Hotel*. The mostly Chinese fare is delicious. Riverside restaurants in Ayutthaya are slightly expensive and generally disappointing: the most popular is the sprawling *Thevaraj*, south of the train station, which has live singers, lousy service and a floating terrace. *The Bakery* by the bus station at 9/3 Chao Phrom Road does good cakes, ice cream and breakfasts. Around the central ruins are a few pricey restaurants if you're in need of air conditioning with your lunch.

Lopburi and around

Mention the name **LOPBURI** to a Thai and the chances are that he or she will start telling you about monkeys – the central junction of this tidy provincial capital, 150km due north of Bangkok, swarms with them. So beneficial are the beasts to the town's tourist trade that a local hotelier treats 600 of them to a sit-down meal every year, complete with menus, waiters and napkins, as a thank you for the help. In fact, the monkeys can be a real nuisance, but at least they add some life to the town's central **Khmer buildings**, which, though historically important, are rather unimpressive sights. More illuminating is the **Narai National Museum**, housed in a partly reconstructed palace complex dating from the seventeenth century, and distant Wat Phra Phutthabat, a colourful eye-opener for non-Buddhists.

Originally called Lavo, Lopburi is one of the longest-inhabited towns in Thailand, and was a major centre of the Mon (Dvaravati) civilization from around the sixth century. It maintained a tenuous independence in the face of the advancing Khmers until as late as the early eleventh century, when it was incorporated into the empire as the provincial capital for much of central Thailand. Increasing Thai immigration from the north soon tilted the balance against the Khmers and Lopburi was again independent from some time early in the thirteenth century until the rise of Ayutthaya in the middle of the fourteenth. Thereafter, Lopburi was twice used as a second capital, first by King Narai of Ayutthaya in the seventeenth century, then by Rama IV of Bangkok in the nineteenth, because its remoteness from the sea made it less vulnerable to European expansionists. Rama V downgraded the town, turning the royal palace into a provincial government office and museum; Lopburi's modern role is as the site of several huge army barracks.

As it's on the main line north to Chiang Mai, Lopburi is best reached by **train**. Twelve trains a day run from Bangkok (3hr) via Ayutthaya (1hr 30min): a popular option is to arrive in Lopburi in the morning, leave your bags at the conveniently central station while you look around the town, then catch one of the night trains to the north. **Buses** from Ayutthaya take up to three hours, as do services from Bangkok's northern bus terminal (every 15min). The long-distance bus terminal is on the south side of the huge Sakeo roundabout, 2km east of the town centre: a city bus or a songthaew will save you the walk.

The town

The centre of Lopburi sits on an egg-shaped island between canals and the Lopburi River, with the rail line running across it from north to south. Most of the hotels and just about everything of interest lie to the west of the line, within walking distance of the train station. The main street, Wichayen Road, crosses the railway tracks at the town's busiest junction before heading eastwards through the newest areas of development to Highway 1. If you're tempted by a gleaming samlor, it'll cost you about B100 per hour to get around the sights.

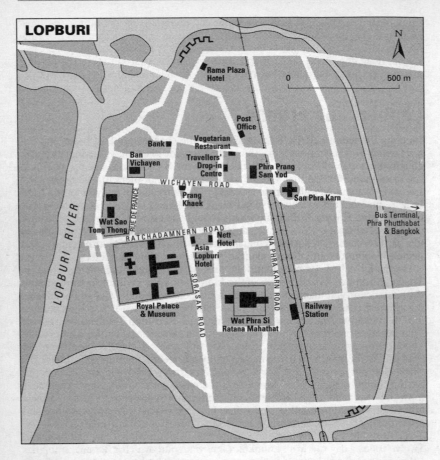

Wat Phra Si Ratana Mahathat

Coming out of the railway station, the first thing you'll see are the sprawled grassy ruins of **Wat Phra Si Ratana Mahathat** (daily, 8am–4.30pm; B20), where the impressive centrepiece is a laterite prang in the Khmer style of the twelfth century, decorated with finely detailed stucco work and surrounded by a ruined cloister. Arrayed in loose formation around this central feature are several more rocket-like Khmer prangs and a number of graceful chedis in the Ayutthaya style, among them one with a bulbous peak and faded bas-reliefs of Buddhist saints. On the eastern side of the main prang, King Narai added to the mishmash of styles by building a "Gothic" viharn, now roofless, which is home to a lonely, headless stone Buddha, draped in photogenic saffron.

Phra Narai Ratchanivet (King Narai's palace)

The imposing gates and high crenellated walls of the **Phra Narai Ratchanivet**, a short walk northwest of the ruins, might promise more than the complex delivers, but the museum in its central courtyard is outstanding, and the grounds are a green and relaxing spot. King Narai built the heavily fortified palace in 1666 as a precaution against any possible confrontation with the Western powers, and for the rest of his reign he was to spend eight months of every year here, entertaining foreign envoys and indulging his love of hunting. After Narai's death, Lopburi was left forgotten until 1856, when Rama IV – worried about British and French colonialism – decided to make this his second capital and lavishly restored the central buildings of Narai's palace.

THE OUTER COURTYARD
The main **entrance** to the palace complex (free) is through the Phayakkha Gate on Sorasak Road. You'll see the unusual lancet shape of this arch again and again in the seventeenth-century doors and windows of Lopburi – just one aspect of the Western influences embraced by Narai. Around the **outer courtyard**, which occupies the eastern half of the complex, stand the walls of various gutted buildings – twelve warehouses for Narai's treasures, stables for the royal hunting elephants, and a moated reception hall for foreign envoys.

THE CENTRAL COURTYARD AND THE NARAI NATIONAL MUSEUM
Straight ahead from the Phayakkha Gate another arch leads into the **central courtyard**, where the typically Ayutthayan **Chanthara Phisan Pavilion** contains a fascinating exhibition on Narai's reign – check out the pointed white cap typical of those worn by noblemen of the time, which increased their height by no less than eighteen inches.

To the left is the colonial-style Phiman Mongkut Hall, now the **Narai National Museum** (Wed–Sun 9am–noon & 1–4pm; B10), whose exhibits span the whole of Lopburi's existence, from simple, elegant prehistoric pottery to modern Thai abstract painting. On the ground floor, a rubbing taken from a Dvaravati bas-relief, showing the Buddha preaching to Shiva and Vishnu, eloquently illustrates how Buddhism lived side by side with Hinduism in Thailand in the second half of the first millennium. Details of Arab costume in some fragments of eighth-century architectural decoration show the extent of Lopburi's early trade routes – from the third century onwards the town had links with the Middle East as well as with China. Inevitably there's a surfeit of Buddhas, most of them fine examples of the Khmer style and the distinctive **Lopburi style**, which emerged in the thirteenth and fourteenth centuries, mixing traditional Khmer elements – such as the conical *ushnisha* or flame on the crown of the Buddha's head – with new features such as a more oval face and slender body.

On the south side of the museum lies the shell of the **Dusit Sawan Hall**, where foreign dignitaries came to present their credentials to King Narai. Inside you can still see the niche, raised twelve feet above the main floor, where the throne was set. The whole building is divided in two around the throne: the front half has "foreign" doors and windows with pointed arches; the rear part, from where the king would have made his grand entrance, has traditional Thai openings. The hall used to be lined with French mirrors, in imitation of Versailles, with Persian carpets and a pyramidal roof of golden glazed tiles rounding off the most majestic building in the palace.

THE PRIVATE COURTYARDS
King Narai's private courtyard, through whose sturdy walls only the trusted few were admitted, occupied the southwest corner of the complex. During Narai's time, hundreds of lamps used to be placed in niches around the walls of

this courtyard by night, shedding a fairy-like light on the palace. Now there's not much more than the foundations left of his residence, the **Sutha Sawan Hall**, and its bathing ponds and artificial grotto.

Rama IV's private courtyard was built to house his harem in the northwest corner of the grounds, behind the present site of the museum. In what used to be the kitchen there's now a small folk museum, containing a bamboo house, a loom and various pieces of farming and fishing equipment. In front, you can consult a crude model of the palace as it looked in Narai's time.

Wat Sao Tong Thong and Ban Vichayen

The north entrance to the palace is called the Vichayen Gate after Constantine Phaulkon, who took the title *ookya vichayen* (prime minister) under King Narai. It leads directly to the aptly named Rue de France, the approach to the remains of his grand residence. Halfway along this road, set back on the left, you'll pass a building whose plain terracotta roof tiles and whitewashed exterior give it a strangely Mediterranean look. This is in fact the viharn of **Wat Sao Tong Thong**, and is typical of Narai's time in its combination of Thai-style tiered roof with "Gothic" pointed windows. Erected as either a Christian chapel or a mosque for the Persian ambassador's residence, it was later used as a Buddhist viharn and has now been tastefully restored, complete with brass door-knockers and plush red carpet. Inside there's an austere Buddha image of the Ayutthaya period and, in the lamp niches, some fine Lopburi-style Buddhas.

The complex of **Ban Vichayen** (daily, 8am–4.30pm; B20) was built by Narai as a residence for foreign ambassadors, complete with a Christian chapel incongruously stuccoed with Buddhist flame and lotus-leaf motifs. Though now just a nest of empty shells, it still succeeds in conjuring up the atmosphere of court intrigue and dark deeds which, towards the end of Narai's reign, centred on the colourful figure of **Constantine Phaulkon**. A Greek adventurer who had come to Ayutthaya with the English East India Company in 1678, Phaulkon entered the royal service as interpreter and accountant, rapidly rising to the position of Narai's prime minister. It was chiefly due to his influence that Narai established close ties with Louis XIV of France, a move which made commercial sense but also formed part of Phaulkon's secret plan to turn Narai and his people to Christianity with the aid of the French.

Two missions were sent from Versailles, but both failed in their overt aim of signing a political alliance and their covert attempt at religious conversion. (It was around this time that the word for Westerner, *farang*, entered the Thai language, derived from *français* which the Thais render *farangset*.) In 1688, a struggle for succession broke out, and leading officials persuaded the dying Narai to appoint as regent his foster brother, Phetracha, a great rival of Phaulkon's. Phetracha promptly executed Phaulkon on charges of treason, and took the throne himself when Narai died. Under Phetracha, Narai's open-door policy towards foreigners was brought to a screeching halt and the Thai kingdom returned to traditional, smaller-scale dealings with the outside world.

East of Narai's palace

By the northeast corner of the palace, the junction of Vichayen and Sorasak roads is marked by an unusual traffic island, on which perch the three stubby red-brick towers of **Prang Khaek**, a well-preserved Hindu shrine possibly dating from as early as the eighth century. The nearby **Phra Prang Sam Yod**, at the top of Na

Phra Karn Road, seems also to have been a Hindu temple, later converted to Buddhism under the Khmers. The three chunky prangs, made of dark laterite with some restored stucco work, are Lopburi's most photographed sight, though they'll only detain you for a minute or two – at least check out some carved figures of seated hermits at the base of the door columns. The shrine's grassy knoll, a popular meeting place for Lopburians, is good for monkey-watching – they run amok all over this area, so keep an eye on your bags and pockets. Across the railway line at **San Phra Karn**, there's even a monkey's adventure playground for the benefit of tourists, beside the base of what must have been a huge Khmer prang.

Wat Phra Phutthabat (Temple of the Buddha's Footprint)

Seventeen kilometres southeast of Lopburi along Highway 1 stands the most important pilgrimage site in central Thailand, **Wat Phra Phutthabat**, which is believed to house a footprint made by the Buddha. From Lopburi, any of the frequent buses to Saraburi or Bangkok from Lopburi's Sakeo roundabout will get you there in half an hour. The souvenir village around the temple, which is on the western side of Highway 1, includes plenty of food stalls for day-trippers.

The **legend** of Phra Phutthabat dates back to the beginning of the seventeenth century, when King Song Tham of Ayutthaya sent some monks to Sri Lanka to worship the famous Buddha's footprint of Sumankut. To the monks' surprise, the Sri Lankans asked them why they had bothered to travel all that way when, according to the ancient Pali scriptures, the Buddha had passed through Thailand and had left his footprint in their own backyard.

As soon as Song Tham heard this he instigated a search for the footprint, which was finally discovered in 1623 by a hunter named Pram Bun, when a wounded deer disappeared into a hollow and then emerged miraculously healed. The hunter pushed aside the bushes to discover a foot-shaped trench filled with water, which immediately cured him of his terrible skin disease. A temple was built on the spot, but was destroyed by the Burmese in 1765 – the present buildings date from the Bangkok era.

A staircase flanked by nagas leads up to a marble platform, where pilgrims make a cacophony by whacking the bells with walking sticks, many of them bought from the stalls below. It's said that if you ring all 93 bells, and count them correctly, you will live that number of years. In the centre of the platform, a gaudy mondop with mighty doors inlaid with mother-of-pearl houses the **footprint**, which in itself is not much to look at. Sheltered by a mirrored canopy, the stone print is five feet long and is obscured by layers of gold leaf presented by pilgrims; people also throw money into the footprint, some of which they take out again as a charm or merit object. The hill behind the shrine, which you can climb for a fine view over the gilded roofs of the complex to the mountains beyond, is covered in a plethora of shrines. The small bot, which elsewhere would be the centrepiece of a temple, is where pilgrims go for a nap.

During the dry season in January and February – the free time in the rice-farming calendar, between harvesting and sowing – a million pilgrims from all over the country flock to the **Ngan Phrabat** (Phrabat Fair), when other pilgrims are making their way to the other major religious sites at Doi Suthep, Nakhon Si Thammarat and Nakhon Phanom. During the fair, the stalls selling souvenirs and traditional medicines around the entrance swell to form a small town, and traditional entertainments, magic shows and a Ferris wheel are laid on.

The fair is still a major religious event, but before the onset of industrialisation it was the highlight of social and cultural life for all ages and classes. It was an important place of courtship, for example, especially for women at a time when their freedom was limited. Another incentive for women to attend the fair was the belief that visiting the footprint three times would ensure a place in heaven – for many women, the Phrabat Fair became the focal point of their lives, as Buddhist doctrine allowed them no other path to salvation. Up to the reign of Rama V even the king used to come, performing a ritual lance dance on elephant-back to ensure a long reign.

Lopburi practicalities

Lopburi has a poor choice of **accommodation**. The concept of the guest house hasn't arrived yet, though there is the *Travellers' Drop-In Centre* on Ratchadamnern Road, Soi 3, with quiet, bare rooms above a language school at B60 for a single, B70 double. The owner of the school dispenses local information and encourages travellers to come into his classes to speak English; the students also enjoy taking foreigners out sightseeing or for a meal. Na Phra Karn Road is a minefield of seedy **hotels**, with rooms from B80, but a far better option is the clean and friendly *Nett Hotel* at 17/1–2 Ratchadamnern Rd (☎036/411738) – rooms with bathroom start at B100 for a double. Opposite the entrance to the Royal Palace, the *Asia Lopburi Hotel* (☎036/411892) is good value at B120 for a double room with fan and bathroom, B170 with air-conditioning and hot water. Uptown and upmarket is the new *Rama Plaza* at 4 Ban Pom Rd (☎036/411484), where large, well-furnished rooms with bathroom are B150 with fan and B220 with air-conditioning.

For **food**, good breakfast doughnuts and coffee are served on the corner of Na Phra Karn and Ratchadamnern roads; later in the morning, up to 1pm, the simple vegetarian restaurant at 26/47 Soi Manora is well worth seeking out – inventive Thai food at stunningly cheap prices. The surprisingly clean night market on Na Phra Karn Road is the best place to eat in the evening. At about 6pm, the stall-holders don their blue aprons and chef's hats to rustle up a wide variety of popular dishes – *khanom beuak* (a kind of veggie omelette), *pat thai* and *hawy thawt* (mussels in batter omelette). For a classier meal, try the open-air *White House Garden Restaurant*, on Praya Kumjud Road (parallel to and south of Ratchadamnern), which specialises in rich seafood dishes at moderate prices.

THE NORTHERN PLAINS

Most tourists bypass the lush northern reaches of the central plains, fast asleep in an overnight train from Bangkok to Chiang Mai, yet it was here, during the thirteenth, fourteenth and fifteenth centuries, that the kingdom of Thailand first began to cohere and assume its present identity. Some of Thailand's finest buildings and sculpture were produced in **Sukhothai**, once the most powerful city in Thailand. Abandoned to the jungle by the sixteenth century, it has now been extensively restored, the resulting historical park making an attractive open-air museum. Less complete renovations have made Sukhothai's satellite cities of **Si Satchanalai** and **Kamphaeng Phet** worth visiting, both for their relative wildness and lack of visitors.

With so many ruins on offer, it's sensible to interweave days of history with days out in the wilds. The nearest hills in which to clear the cobwebs are in the rugged Phu Hin Rongkla National Park (see p.313), but to get there you'll need to hire a motorbike or base yourself in **Phitsanulok.** By public transport from Sukhothai an easier option is the longer expedition to the Burmese border town of **Mae Sot**, which offers excellent trekking.

Phitsanulok stands at the hub of an efficient **transport** network that works well as a transit point between Bangkok, the far north and Isaan. Nearly every Bangkok–Chiang Mai train stops here, and assorted buses head east towards the Isaan towns of Loei, Khon Kaen and Chaiyaphum. It's also possible to fly in and out of the northern plains, through the tiny airstrips at Phitsanulok, Tak and Mae Sot. Within the region, local buses and songthaews ferry tourists between sights, though a less time-consuming way of doing things would be to hire a car or motorbike from Phitsanulok or Sukhothai.

Phitsanulok

Heading north from Lopburi, road and railway plough through a landscape of lurid green paddies interrupted only by the unwelcoming sprawl of NAKHON SAWAN, sited at the confluence of the Ping and the Nan. A prosperous city of about 100,000 predominantly Chinese inhabitants, Nakhon Sawan plays a vital role as the region's main market and the distribution centre for rice, but about the only reason you'd ever want to set foot in the place would be to change buses for Kamphaeng Phet, Phitsanulok or Chaiyaphum. The bus station is in the town centre and there are a couple of passable cheap hotels close by as a last resort. All Bangkok–Chiang Mai trains stop here, but as the station is 10km out of town, with skeletal local transport and no station hotels, breaking your journey 130km further north at Phitsanulok makes much more sense.

Well equipped with hotels and pleasantly located on the east bank of the River Nan, **PHITSANULOK** makes a handy base for exploring the historical centres of Sukhothai and Kamphaeng Phet. Phitsanulok itself, however, has been basically a one-temple town since fire destroyed most of its old buildings thirty-odd years ago: the country's second most important Buddha image is housed here in Wat Mahathat, drawing pilgrims from all over Thailand. This modest town harks back to a heyday in the late fourteenth and early fifteenth centuries when, with Sukhothai waning in power, it rose to prominence as the favoured home of the crumbling capital's last rulers. After supremacy was finally wrested by the emerging state of Ayutthaya in 1438, Phitsanulok was made a provincial capital, subsequently becoming a strategic army base during Ayutthaya's wars with the Burmese and adoptive home to Ayutthayan princes.

Seven **trains** a day pass through Phitsanulok on their way between Bangkok and Chiang Mai; the railway station is in the town centre. **Buses** are more frequent, but you'll need to catch a local bus into town from the bus station, 2km east on Highway 12. If you're short on time you could even **fly** here: by air, Phitsanulok is fifty minutes from Bangkok or Chiang Mai. **Local buses** all start from the city bus centre on Ekathosarot Road, a few hundred metres south of the train station, and cover five routes: #1 serves the bus station, #2 goes to villages on the southeastern edge of town, #3 heads west over the river, #4 is the airport shuttle, and #5 runs to villages to the southwest.

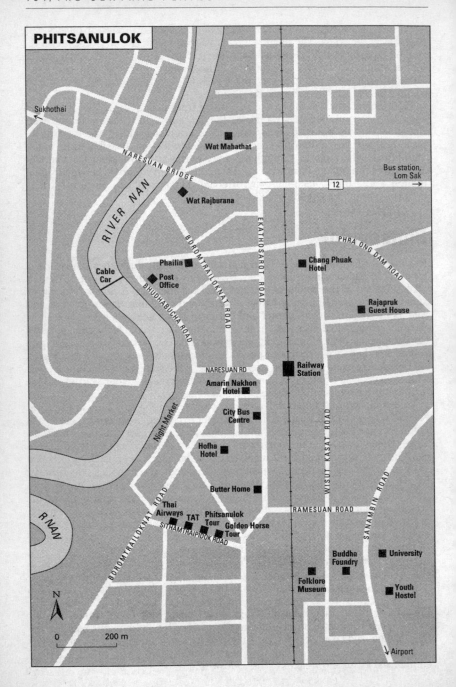

PHITSANULOK

Sukhothai

NARESUAN BRIDGE

RIVER NAN

Wat Mahathat

Bus station,
Lom Sak

12

Wat Rajburana

EKATHOSAROT ROAD

PHRA ONG DAM ROAD

Phailin

Chang Phuak
Hotel

Cable
Car

Post
Office

BHUDHABUCHA ROAD

BOROMTRAILOKNAT ROAD

Rajapruk
Guest House

NARESUAN RD

Railway
Station

Amarin Nakhon
Hotel

City Bus
Centre

WISUT KASAT ROAD

Night Market

Hofha
Hotel

Butter Home

SANAMBIN ROAD

R. NAN

BOROMTRAILOKNAT ROAD

Thai
Airways

TAT

Phitsanulok
Tour

Golden Horse
Tour

RAMESUAN ROAD

SITHAMTRAIPIDOK ROAD

Buddha
Foundry

University

Folklore
Museum

Youth
Hostel

N

0   200 m

↓Airport

The Town

Typically for a riverside town, "Phi-lok" is long and narrow, and while the centre is small enough to cover on foot, the two main sights lie at opposite extremities. You'd be hard pressed to find more than a half-day's worth of attractions to detain you here, though an evening stroll along the river – past the ramshackle house-boats which are illegal everywhere but Phitsanulok – and the prospect of a fresh fish dinner eaten on its banks may entice you.

Wat Mahathat

Officially called **Wat Phra Si Ratana Mahathat** (and known locally as **Wat Mahathat** or **Wat Yai**), this fourteenth-century temple was one of the few buildings to miraculously escape Phitsanulok's great fire. Standing at the northern limit of town on the east bank of the River Nan, it receives a constant stream of worshippers eager to pay homage to the highly revered Buddha image inside the viharn. Because the image is so sacred, a **dress code** is strictly enforced – shorts and skimpy clothing are forbidden – and there's an entrance fee of B10.

Delicately inlaid mother-of-pearl doors mark the entrance to the viharn, opening onto the low-ceilinged interior, painted mostly in dark red and black and dimly lit by narrow slits along the upper walls. In the centre of the far wall sits the much-cherished **Phra Buddha Chinnarat**; late Sukhothai in style, and probably cast in the fourteenth century, this gleaming, polished-bronze Buddha is one of the finest of the period and, for Thais, second in importance only to the Emerald Buddha in Bangkok. Tales of the statue's miraculous powers have fuelled the devotion of generations of pilgrims – one legend tells how the Buddha wept tears of blood when Ayutthayan princes arrived in Phitsanulok to oust the last Sukhothai regent. The Phra Buddha Chinnarat stands out among Thai Buddha images because of its *mandorla*, the flame-like halo that frames the upper body and head like a chair-back, tapering off into nagas at the arm rests, which symbolises extreme radiance and makes any reproductions immediately recognisable. Not surprisingly, the image has spawned several copies, including an almost perfect replica commissioned for Bangkok's Marble Temple by Rama V in 1901. Every February, Phitsanulok honours the Phra Buddha Chinnarat with week-long festivities which include *likay* folk theatre performances and dancing.

Behind the viharn, the gilded mosaic **prang** houses the holy relic that gives the wat its name (Mahathat means "Great Relic") – though which particular remnant lies entombed here is unclear – and the cloister surrounding both structures contains a gallery of Buddha images of different styles. As in all such popular pilgrimage spots, the courtyard is crammed with amulet stalls, trinket sellers and lottery ticket vendors.

Also spared by the fire was the nearby **Wat Rajburana**, just south of Naresuan Bridge and five minutes' walk from Wat Mahathat. Recognisable by the dilapidated brick-based chedi that stands in the compound, the wat is chiefly of interest for the *Ramayana* murals that cover the bot's interior walls. Quite well preserved, they were probably painted in the mid-nineteenth century.

The Folklore Museum and Buddha foundry

Across town on Wisut Kasat Road, southeast of the railway station, the **Dr Thawi Folklore Museum** (daily 8.30am–noon & 1–4.30pm; donation) puts a different slant on the region's culture with an engaging display of crude but ingenious traditional farm implements and domestic tools. The collection belongs to former sergeant-major Dr Thawi, who has pursued a lifelong personal campaign to preserve and document a way of life that's gradually disappearing. Among the exhibits, his roomful of traps is unparallelled in any other ethnology museum in Thailand – it showcases an amazing assortment of specialised contraptions designed to ensnare everything from cockroaches to birds perched on water buffaloes' backs. Amongst the home accessories, check out the masochistic aid for "improving blood circulation" and the range of simple wooden games.

Cross the road from the museum for a rare chance to see Buddha images being forged at the **Buranathai Buddha Bronze-Casting Foundry** (soon to be moved to new premises next door to the museum). The foundry, which also belongs to Dr Thawi, is open during working hours and anyone can drop in to watch the stages involved in moulding and casting a Buddha image. It's a fairly lengthy procedure, based on the lost-wax method, and best assimilated from the illustrated explanations inside the foundry. Images of all sizes are made here, from thirty-centimetre-high household icons the size of sporting trophies to mega-models destined for wealthy temples. The Buddha business is quite a profitable one: worshippers can earn a great deal of merit by donating a Buddha statue, particularly a precious one, to their local wat, so demand rarely slackens.

Practicalities

Rajapruk Guest House, just east of Wisut Kasat Road (☎055/258477), offers the best value in **budget accommodation**: a scaled-down version of the adjoining *Rajapruk Hotel*, it has large, clean doubles with hot showers starting at B180 (B280 a/c). In a similar vein but a cut beneath, rooms at *Chang Phuak Hotel*, next to the railway line on Phra Ong Dam Road (☎055/252822), cost B140 with fan and shower. Cheaper and more atmospheric – but unfortunately a great deal noisier because of heavy traffic – *Phitsanulok Youth Hostel* (☎055/242060) occupies a lovely old wooden building furnished with carved beds and chairs and featuring a communal eating/sitting area on ground level; rooms are B50 dorm, B100 single, B120 double – slightly less for IYHA members. It's located on the busy Sanambin (Airport) Road about 1500m southeast of the centre: to get there, take bus #4 (bikes can be borrowed from the hostel). More central and cheaper still, but a lot dingier, *Hohfa Hotel* (☎055/258484) on Phayalithai Road charges B90 and up for rooms with fan and shower.

Top-end hotels include the *Amarin Nakhon* on Chaophraya Road near the station (☎055/258588), with rooms from B420; the *Phailin* on Boromtrailoknat Road (☎055/252411), where rooms start at B600; and the *Rajapruk* on Wisut Kasat Road (☎055/258788), from B700.

Good, cheap Thai, Chinese and European **food** features on the meticulously coded menu at *Butter Home*, a couple of blocks south of the station on Ekathosarot Road, and if that doesn't appeal, you only have to walk back up the same road to pass five or six curry and noodle shops. In the evening, the place to head for is the lively **night market** along the east bank of the river, which gets started at about 6pm: fish and mussels are a speciality – along with cassette tapes, souvenirs and clothes. If you want to eat on the water and don't mind paying for the privilege, try the cruising **restaurant boats** run by *Song Kwae* and *Tharn Thip*, which leave fairly regularly throughout the day from near the post office and travel upriver and back for an hour or two at a time. The nearby floating restaurants also overcharge for their unexceptional food, but – if you miss the boats – it's probably worth forking out the extra money for the breezy riverside location. Restaurants serving **"flying vegetables"** are also perennial crowd-pullers: the vegetable in question is the strong-tasting morning-glory (*phak bung*), which is stir-fried before being tossed flamboyantly in the air towards the plate-wielding waiter or customer. Several restaurants around the *Rajapruk Hotel* on Phra Ong Dam Road do the honours, and stall-holders at the night market put on occasional performances.

Should you need to contact Phitsanulok's highly efficient **TAT** (daily 8.30am–4.30pm; ☎055/252742), it's east off Boromtrailoknat Road, in a row of travel businesses that includes *Thai Airways* (☎055/258020) and **car hire** companies *Golden Tour* (☎055/259973) and *Phitsanulok Tour Centre* (☎055/242206). To rent a **motorbike**, go to *Landi Motor* on Phra Ong Dum Road (☎055/242687).

Sukhothai

For a brief but brilliant 150 years (1238–1376), the walled city of **SUKHOTHAI** presided as the capital of Thailand, creating the legacy of a unified nation of Thai peoples and a phenomenal artistic heritage. Now an impressive assembly of elegant ruins, **Muang Kao Sukhothai (Old Sukhothai)**, 58km northwest of Phitsanulok, has been designated a historical park and has grown into one of Thailand's most visited ancient sites.

There's only one good hotel near the historical park, so most travellers stay in **"New" Sukhothai**, a small and friendly town 12km to the east, which is also better for restaurants and travel connections. Aside from the necessities, the new town has little of interest, but makes a peaceful base for visiting not only the historical park but also the outlying ruins of Si Satchanalai and Kamphaeng Phet.

Sukhothai can be done as a day trip from Phitsanulok easily enough, with **buses** to New Sukhothai running every half hour. From Bangkok it's a six- or seven-hour journey; from Chiang Mai it takes between five and six hours. Frequent **songthaews** shuttle between the new and old towns, departing from behind the police box on Charodvithitong Road, west of the river.

Some history

Prior to the thirteenth century, the land now known as Thailand was divided into a collection of petty principalities, most of which owed their allegiance to the Khmer empire and its administrative centre Angkor (in present-day Cambodia). With the Khmers' power on the wane, two Thai generals joined forces in 1238 to oust the Khmers from the northern plains, founding the kingdom of **Sukhothai** ("Dawn of Happiness" in Pali) under the regency of one of the generals, Intradit. In short order they had extended their control over much of present-day Thailand, including parts of Burma and Laos.

The third and most important of Sukhothai's eight kings, Intradit's youngest son **Ramkhamhaeng** (c. 1278–1299) laid the foundations of a unique Thai identity by establishing Theravada (Hinayana) Buddhism as the common faith and introducing the forerunner of the modern Thai alphabet; of several inscriptions attributed to him, the most famous, known as Ramkhamhaeng's Stele and housed in Bangkok's National Museum, tells of a utopian land of plenty ruled by a benevolent monarch. Ramkhamhaeng turned Sukhothai into a vibrant spiritual and commercial centre, inviting Theravada monks from Nakhon Si Thammarat and Sri Lanka to instruct his people in the religion that was to supplant Khmer Hinduism and Mahayana Buddhism, and encouraging the growth of a ceramics industry with the help of Chinese potters. By all accounts, Ramkhamhaeng's successors lacked his kingly qualities and, paying more attention to religious affairs, squandered much of Sukhothai's political capital. By the second half of the fourteenth century, Sukhothai had become a vassal state of the newly emerged kingdom of Ayutthaya and finally, in 1438, was forced to relinquish all vestiges of its independent identity.

Traditionally, the **Sukhothai era** has always been viewed as the golden age of Thai history: the beginning of the kingdom of Thailand as we know it, the cornerstone of all things Thai, and a happy and prosperous time for all. Recently, however, the importance of Ramkhamhaeng's Stele, upon which this rose-tinted view is based, has been reappraised. Some historians consider the stele's inscription a fake or at best an outrageous exaggeration, but whatever the authenticity of the stele, Sukhothai-era ruins provide compelling evidence of a time of great prosperity, strong Buddhist faith and a refined artistic sensibility.

Old Sukhothai: Sukhothai Historical Park

In its prime, **OLD SUKHOTHAI** boasted some forty separate temple complexes and covered an area of about seventy square kilometres between the River Yom and the low range of hills to the west. At its heart stood the walled royal city, protected by a series of moats and ramparts. **Sukhothai Historical Park** (daily 6am–6pm) covers all this area and is divided into five zones, each costing B20 to enter. All of the most important temples lie within the central zone, as does the museum (which charges a separate admission fee); the ruins outside the city walls are spread out over a sizeable area and divided into north, south, east and west zones. There's an official entrance gate for the central zone, but in the other zones you generally buy your ticket at the first temple you visit.

With the help of UNESCO, the Fine Arts Department has restored the most significant ruins and replaced the retreating jungle with lawns, leaving some trees for shade, unclogging a few ponds and moats, and clearing pathways between the wats. The result reveals the original town planners' keen aesthetic sense, especially their astute use of water to offset and reflect the solid monochrome contours of the stone temples. Nevertheless, there is a touch of the too perfectly packaged theme park about the central zone and it still takes a determined imagination to visualise the ancient capital as it must once have looked. Noticeably absent are the houses and palaces which would have filled the spaces between the wats: like their Khmer predecessors, the people of Sukhothai constructed their secular buildings from wood, believing that only sacred structures merited such a durable and costly material as stone.

Songthaews from New Sukhothai stop about 300m inside the east walls, close to the museum and central zone entrance point. The best way to avoid being overwhelmed (or bored) by so many ruins is to hire a **bicycle** from one of the numerous outlets near the museum. Paths crisscross the park and circle most of the ruins, particularly in the central zone, which means you'll be able to appreciate some of the more spectacular settings from all angles without having to explore every individual site – and you'll have a jump on the tour groups.

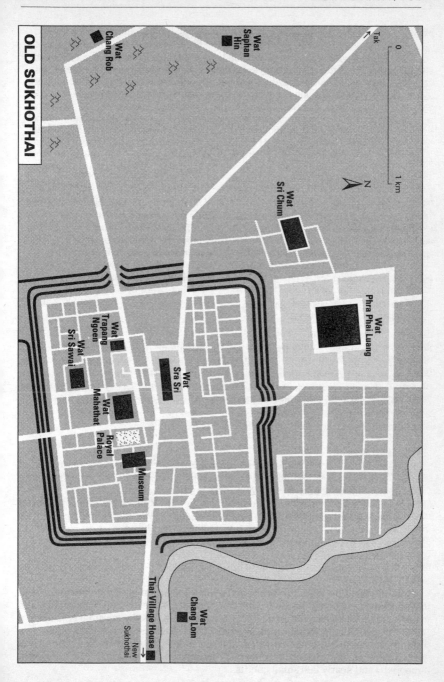

OLD SUKHOTHAI

Tak

0

1 km

N

Wat Saphan Hin

Wat Chang Rob

Wat Sri Chum

Wat Phra Phai Luang

Wat Trapang Ngoen

Wat Sri Sawai

Wat Sra Sri

Wat Mahathat

Royal Palace

Museum

Thai Village House

Wat Chang Lom

New Sukhothai

THE SUKHOTHAI BUDDHA

The classic Buddha images of Thailand were produced towards the end of the Sukhothai era. Ethereal, androgynous figures with ovoid faces and feline expressions, they depict not a Buddha meditating to achieve enlightenment – the more usual representation – but an already **enlightened Buddha**: the physical realisation of a philosophical abstract. Though they produced mainly seated Buddhas, Sukhothai artists are renowned for having pioneered the **walking Buddha**, one of four postures described in ancient Pali texts but without precedent in Thailand. These texts also set down a list of the marks of greatness by which future Buddhas could be recognised; of all Thai schools of art, Sukhothai sculptors stuck the most literally to these precepts, as you can see by checking the **features** below against any Sukhothai statue:

Legs like a deer's.
Thighs like the trunk of a banyan tree.
Shoulders as massive as an elephant's head.
Arms tubular like an elephant's trunk, and long enough to touch each knee without bending.
Hands like lotus flowers about to bloom.
Fingertips turned back like petals.
A head shaped like an egg.

A flame to signify fiery intellect.
Hair like scorpion stings.
A chin like a mango stone.
A nose like a parrot's beak.
Eyebrows like drawn bows.
Eyelashes like a cow's.
Earlobes elongated by the heavy earrings worn by royalty.
Skin so smooth that dust couldn't stick to it.

If you want to **eat** inside the park, try the large (and pricey) restaurant near the museum, or buy cold drinks and snacks from the vendors who congregate under the trees near Wat Mahathat. Tour groups all eat at *Thai Village House*, just east of the city walls on the road to New Sukhothai – enough said. **Accommodation** at *Thai Village House* (✆055/611049) is much better value than the food, however, with air-conditioned wooden bungalows in the landscaped garden behind the restaurant costing B350 single, B500 double.

The central zone

Only four of the eleven ruins in the **central zone** are worth dwelling on, and of these Wat Mahathat should definitely not be missed. The area covers three square kilometres: a bike is recommended, but not essential.

Just outside the entrance to the central zone, the **Ramkhamhaeng National Museum**'s (Wed–Sun 9am–4pm; B10) collection of locally found artifacts is neither particularly inspiring nor informatively displayed, but if you haven't already seen King Ramkhamhaeng's famous stele in Bangkok, you might want to look at the copy kept here.

WAT MAHATHAT
Turn left inside the gate for Sukhothai's most important site, the enormous **Wat Mahathat** compound, packed with the remains of scores of monuments and surrounded, like a city within a city, by a moat. This was the spiritual epicentre of the city, the king's temple and symbol of his power; eager to add their own stamp, successive regents restored and expanded it so that by the time it was abandoned in the sixteenth century it numbered ten viharns, one bot, eight mondops and nearly 200 small chedis.

Looking at the wat from ground level, it's hard to distinguish the main structures from the minor ruins. Remnants of the viharns and the bot dominate the present scene, their soldierly ranks of pillars (formerly supporting wooden roofs) directing the eye to the Buddha images seated at the far western ends.

The one component you can't overlook is the principal chedi complex which houses the Buddha relic (*mahathat*): it stands grandly – if a little cramped – at the heart of the compound, built on an east-west axis in an almost continuous line with two viharns. Its elegant centrepiece follows a design termed **lotus-bud chedi** (after the bulbous finial ornamenting the top of a tower), and is classic late-Sukhothai in style. This lotus bud reference is no mere whimsy but an established religious symbol; though Sukhothai architects were the first to incorporate it into building design – since when it's come to be regarded as a hallmark of the era – the lotus bud had for centuries represented the purity of Buddha's thoughts battling through the clammy swamp and finally bursting out into flower. The chedi stands surrounded by eight smaller towers on a square platform decorated with a procession of walking Buddha-like monks, another artistic innovation of the Sukhothai school, here depicted in stucco relief. The two square mondops flanking the chedi were built for the colossal standing Buddhas still inside them today.

The grassy patch across the road from Wat Mahathat marks the site of the former palace, of which nothing now remains.

Wat Mahathat

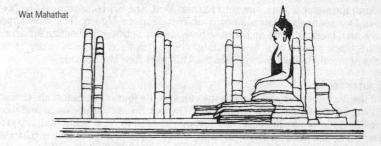

AROUND WAT MAHATHAT

A few hundred metres southwest of Wat Mahathat, the triple corn-cob-shaped prangs of **Wat Sri Sawai** make an interesting architectural comparison. Just as the lotus-bud chedi epitomises Sukhothai aspirations, the prang represents Khmer ideals – Wat Sri Sawai was probably conceived as a Hindu shrine several centuries before the Sukhothai kingdom established itself here. The stucco reliefs decorating the prangs feature a few weatherworn figures from both Hindu and Buddhist mythology, which suggest that the shrine was later pressed into Buddhist service; the square base inside the central prang supported the Khmer Shiva lingam (phallus), while the viharn out front is a later, Buddhist addition.

Just west of Wat Mahathat, the particularly fine lotus-bud chedi of **Wat Trapang Ngoen** rises gracefully against the backdrop of distant hills. Aligned with the chedi on the symbolic east–west axis are the dilapidated viharn and, east of that, on an island in the middle of the "silver pond" after which the wat is named, the remains of the bot. It's worth walking the connecting plank to the bot to appreciate the setting from the water. North of the chedi, notice the fluid lines of the walking Buddha mounted onto a brick wall – a classic example of Sukhothai sculpture.

LOY KRATHONG: THE FESTIVAL OF LIGHTS

Every year on the evening of the full moon of the twelfth lunar month (between late October and mid-November), Thais celebrate the end of the rainy season with the festival of **Loy Krathong**. One of the country's most beautiful festivals, it's held to honour the spirits of the water at a time when all the fields are flooded and the khlongs and rivers are overflowing their banks. To thank and appease Mae Khong Kha, the goddess of water, Thais decorate **krathong** – miniature basket-boats fashioned from banana leaves – with flowers, load them with burning incense sticks, lighted candles and coins, and set them afloat on the nearest body of water. The bobbing lights of thousands of floating *krathong* make a fantastic spectacle.

Loy Krathong is celebrated all over Thailand, but nowhere more magically than on the ponds of Old Sukhothai. It is here that the festival is said to have originated 700 years ago, when the consort of a Sukhothai king adapted the ancient Brahmin custom of paying homage to the water goddess, and began the tradition of placing *krathong* on the lotus ponds. In recent history, Sukhothai has magnified the original "festival of lights" so that, for the three nights around the full moon, not only are the pond surfaces aglow with candles, but the ruins are wreathed in lights and illuminated during a nightly *son et lumière* performance, and spectators are dispatched home amidst a massive panoply of fireworks.

Taking the water feature one step further, **Wat Sra Sri** commands a fine position on two connecting islands north of Wat Trapang Ngoen. The bell-shaped chedi with a tapering spire and square base shows a strong Sri Lankan influence, and the black replica of a freestanding walking Buddha displays many of the "marks of greatness" as prescribed in the Pali texts (see box above).

The outer zones

You'll need a bicycle or car to get to the ruins in the four outer zones; all sites are signposted from the city wall boundaries. The north zone is the closest and most rewarding, followed by the east zone just off the road to New Sukhothai. If you're feeling energetic, head for the west zone, which requires a much longer bike ride and some hill climbing. The ruins to the south just aren't worth the effort.

THE NORTH ZONE

Continuing north of Wat Sra Sri, cross the city walls into the **north zone** and carry on for a further 500m to reach **Wat Phra Phai Luang**, one of the ancient city's oldest structures. The three prangs (only one of which remains intact) were built by the Khmers before the Thais founded their own kingdom here and, as at the similar Wat Sri Sawai, you can still see some of the stucco reliefs showing both Hindu and Buddhist figures. It's thought that Phra Phai Luang was at the centre of the old Khmer town and that it was as important then as Wat Mahathat later became to the Thais. When the shrine was converted into a Buddhist temple, the viharn and chedi were built to the east of the prangs: the reliefs of the (now headless and armless) seated Buddhas are still visible around the base of the chedi. Also discernible among the ruins are parts of a large reclining Buddha and a mondop containing four huge standing Buddhas in different postures.

About 500m west from Wat Phra Phai Luang, **Wat Sri Chum** boasts Sukhothai's largest surviving Buddha image. The enormous brick and stucco seated Buddha, measuring over 11m from knee to knee and almost 15m high, peers through the slit in its custom-built mondop. Check out the elegantly tapered fingers, complete with gold-leaf nail varnish and mossy gloves. A passage-way – rarely opened up, unfortunately – runs inside the mondop wall, taking you from ground level on the lefthand side to the Buddha's eye level and then up again to the roof, affording a great bird's-eye view of the image. Legend has it that this Buddha would sometimes speak to favoured worshippers, and this staircase would have enabled tricksters to climb up and hold forth, unseen; one of the kings of Sukhothai is said to have brought his troops here so as to spur them on to victory with encouraging words from the Buddha.

THE EAST ZONE
About 1km east of the city walls, the only temple of interest in the **east zone** is **Wat Chang Lom**, just off the road to New Sukhothai, near *Thai Village House*. Chang Lom, which also transliterates as Chang Rob, means "Surrounded by Elephants": the main feature here is a large Sri Lankan-style bell-shaped chedi encircled by a frieze of elephants.

THE WEST ZONE
Be prepared for a long haul out to the **west zone**, in the forested hills off the main road to Tak. Marking the western edge of Old Sukhothai almost 5km west of the city walls, the hilltop temple of **Wat Saphan Hin** should – with sufficiently powerful telescopic lenses – afford a fantastic panorama of the old city's layout, but with the naked eye conjures up only an indistinct vista of trees and stones. If you make it this far, chances are you'll share the view only with the large stand-ing Buddha at the top. The wat is reached via a steep pathway of stone slabs (hence the name, which means "Stone Bridge") that starts from a track running south from the Tak road. This is the easiest approach if you're on a bike as it's completely flat; the shorter route, which follows a lesser, more southerly, road out of the old city, takes you over several hills and past the elephant temple of **Wat Chang Rob**, 1km short of Saphan Hin, where it joins the other track.

New Sukhothai practicalities

Straddling the River Yom, **NEW SUKHOTHAI** offers a reasonable choice of **budget accommodation** options, most no more than ten minutes' walk from the water. *Somprasong Guest House*, on the west bank at 32 Pravetnakorn Rd, affords good views from its riverfront balcony, and the affable managers are good sources of information on the surrounding area; rooms in the large wooden house cost B50 single, B80 double. Another converted family home 100m down-river, *Yupa Guest House* has large bare rooms – some with balconies – from B60. Facing *Somprasong* across the river, the popular *Chinawat Hotel* (☎055/611031) on Nikhon Kasem Road offers adequate rooms with fan and shower for B80 (a/c from B200). *Sukhothai Hotel* (☎055/611133) on Singhawat Road is another good option: clean rooms with fan and shower here go for B80 single, B120 double. Further down Singhawat Road, rooms at the slightly swisher *Sawaddipong Hotel* (☎055/611567) start at B120 (a/c from B220).

Top of the range is the luxurious *Northern Palace* (☎055/611193), also on Singhawat Road, where rates start at B850 single, B950 double (discount negotia-ble in low season) and facilities include pool tables and swimming pool.

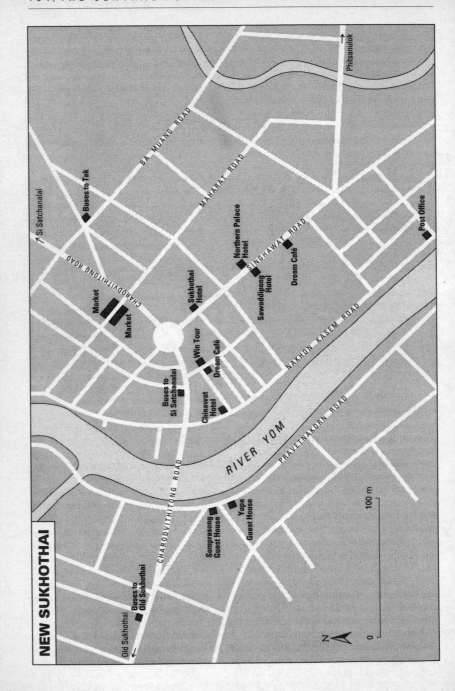

NEW SUKHOTHAI

Phitsanulok

Si Satchanalai

BA MUANG ROAD

MAHARAT ROAD

Buses to Tak

CHAROD VITHITONG ROAD

Northern Palace Hotel

SINGHAWAT ROAD

Post Office

Market

Sukhothai Hotel

Sawaddipong Hotel

Dream Café

Market

Win Tour

Dream Café

NAKHON KASEM ROAD

Buses to Si Satchanalai

Chinawat Hotel

RIVER YOM

PRAVETNAKORN ROAD

CHAROD VITHITONG ROAD

Samprasong Guest House

Yupa Guest House

100 m

Old Sukhothai

Buses to Old Sukhothai

N

0

The *Chinawat Hotel*'s **restaurant** sports a large menu of good Thai and Western fare (dinner only) that runs the range from *pla rat prik* (fish grilled with chillis) down to cheese sandwiches. Next door, *Dear House* serves up the standards: *pat thai*, *kwetiaw ratna* and *khao pat kai*. Further down Nikhon Kasem Road, *Duck Restaurant* (aka *Kho Jung Hong*) specialises, as you'd expect, in duck meals, cooked to Chinese recipes such as the stewed and mildly spiced *pet phalo*, or the roasted *pet yang*, and to Thai specifications as in the thick *kaeng pet* curries. The cosy *Dream Café*, with branches on Ramkhamhaeng Road and Singhawat Road opposite the *Bangkok Bank*, fosters a coffee-shop atmosphere with its walls and windowsills of curios and knick-knacks and a menu of espressos and ice-creams, but it also does hearty savoury plates of curries, omelettes and seafood, making a pleasant place to while away an evening until 10pm closing. The **night market** near the *Dream Café* on Ramkhamhaeng Road offers the usual open-air selection of soups, curries, rice and noodle dishes.

If you're short on time or prefer seeing the sights with a guide, reasonably priced **tours** (from B2000) to Muang Kao Sukhothai and Si Satchanalai can be arranged through the *Chinawat Hotel*, *Somprasong Guest House* or *Sky Tour* (☎055/612236) on Prasertpong Road.

Si Satchanalai and around

In the mid-thirteenth century, Sukhothai cemented its power by establishing several satellite towns, of which the most important was **SI SATCHANALAI**, 57km upriver from Sukhothai on the banks of the Yom. Now a historical park, the restored ruins of **Muang Kao Si Satchanalai** have a quieter ambience than the grander models at Old Sukhothai, and the additional inducements of the riverside wat in nearby Chalieng and the Sawankhalok pottery kilns in Bang Ko Noi combine to make the area worth exploring.

Si Satchanalai is for all intents and purposes a day trip from Sukhothai as local accommodation is thin on the ground, and isn't even very local. Don't attempt to do Si Satchanalai and Sukhothai in a single day – a lot of tour outfits offer this option, but seeing so many dilapidated facades in seven or eight hours is mind-numbing. Half-hourly buses bound for Si Satchanalai depart from opposite the *Chinawat Hotel* on Charodwithitong Road in New Sukhothai: get off at the signpost for Muang Kao Si Satchanalai (1hr) and follow the track southwest over the River Yom for about 500m to a **bicycle rental** place, conveniently planted at the junction for the historical park (1500m northwest) and Chalieng (1km southeast); the kilns are a further 2km north of the park. Hiring a bike makes sense as even the walk to the park can be exhausting in the heat; the park itself is fairly compact. If cycling isn't your cup of tea, you could either rent a motorbike from next to the *Chinawat Hotel* in New Sukhothai or join a half-day tour from there.

The historical park stands pretty much on its own with only a couple of hamlets in the vicinity, where you'll be able to buy cold drinks, but won't get much in the way of food or a place to stay. If you're really determined to see Muang Kao Si Satchanalai on your way elsewhere (like Phrae or Lampang for example) you'll need to proceed to the old city's modern counterpart at Si Satchanalai proper, 11km north along Highway 101 and the terminus of the Sukhothai buses. Accommodation here is limited to the B100 rooms at the *Kruchang Hotel* near the *Bangkok Bank* in the town centre.

Muang Kao Si Satchanalai

Muang Kao Si Satchanalai (daily 8.30am–4.30pm; B20) was built to emulate its capital, but Si Satchanalai is much less hyped than Sukhothai, sees fewer tourists and, most significantly, has escaped the sometimes overzealous landscaping of the more popular sight. It's also a lot less strung out, though lacking in the watery splendour of Sukhothai's main temples.

The ruins are numbered and it makes sense to do them in order. Begin with the elephant temple of **Wat Chang Lom**, whose centrepiece is a huge Sri Lankan-style bell-shaped chedi set on a square base which is studded with 39 life-sized elephant buttresses. Many of the elephants are in good repair, with most of their stucco flesh still intact; others now have their laterite skeletons exposed. According to a contemporary stone inscription, the chedi was built to house sacred Buddhist relics originally buried in Chalieng. Contrary to the religious etiquette of the time, King Ramkhamhaeng of Sukhothai put the relics on display for a year before moving them – a potentially blasphemous act that should have been met with divine retribution, but Ramkhamhaeng survived unscathed and apparently even more popular with his subjects.

Across the road from Wat Chang Lom, **Wat Chedi Jet Taew**'s seven rows of small chedis probably enshrine the ashes of Si Satchanalai's royal rulers, which makes this the ancient city's most important temple. One of the chedis is a scaled-down replica of the hallmark lotus-bud chedi at Sukhothai's Wat Mahathat; some of the others are copies of other important wats from the vicinity.

Following the road a short way southeast of Chedi Jet Taew you reach **Wat Nang Phya**, remarkable for the original stucco reliefs on its viharn wall that remain in fine condition. The balustraded wall has slit windows and is entirely covered with intricate floral motifs. Stucco is a hardy material which sets soon after being first applied, and becomes even harder when exposed to rain – hence its ability to survive 700 years in the open. To the right on the way back to Wat Chang Lom, **Wat Suan Utayan Noi** contains one of the few Buddha images still left in Si Satchanalai.

North of Chang Lom, the hilltop ruins of Wat Khao Phanom Pleung and Wat Khao Suan Khiri afford splendid aerial views of different quarters of the ancient city. The sole remaining intact chedi of **Wat Khao Phanom Pleung** sits atop the lower of the hills and used to be flanked by a set of smaller chedis built to entomb the ashes of Si Satchanalai's important personages – the ones who merited some special memorial, but didn't quite make the grade for Wat Chedi Jet Taew. The temple presumably got its name, which means "mountain of sacred fire", from the cremation rituals held on the summit. **Wat Khao Suan Khiri**'s huge chedi, which graces the summit 200m northwest, has definitely seen better days, but the views from its dilapidated platform – south over the main temple ruins and north towards the city walls and entrance gates – are worth the climb.

Chalieng

Before Sukhothai asserted control of the region and founded Si Satchanalai, the Khmers governed the area from **CHALIENG**, just over 2km to the east of Si Satchanalai. Cradled in a bend in the River Yom, all that now remains of Chalieng is a single temple, Wat Phra Si Ratana Mahathat, the most atmospheric of all the sights in the Sukhothai area. Left to sink into graceful disrepair, the wat has escaped the perfectionist touch of restorers and now serves both as playground to the kids from the hamlet across the river and grazing patch for their parents' cows.

Originally a Khmer temple and later adapted by the kings of Sukhothai, **Wat Phra Si Ratana Mahathat** forms a compact complex of two ruined viharns aligned east–west each side of a central chedi. Of the western viharn only two Buddha images remain, seated one in front of the other on a daïs overgrown with weeds, and staring folornly at the stumps of pillars that originally supported the roof over their heads: the rest has long since been buried under grass, efficiently grazed by the cows. A huge standing Buddha, similar to the one in Sukhothai's Wat Mahathat, gazes out from the nearby mondop. The more important viharn adjoins the central Sri Lankan-style chedi to the east, and is surrounded by a sunken wall of laterite blocks. Entering it through the semi-submerged eastern gateway, you pass beneath a sizeable carved lintel, hewn from a single block of stone. The seated Buddha in the centre of the western end of the viharn is typical Sukhothai style, as is the towering stucco relief of a walking Buddha to the left, which is regarded as one of the finest of its genre.

The Sawankhalok kilns

Endowed with high-quality clay, the area around Si Satchanalai – known as Sawankhalok during the Ayutthayan era – commanded an international reputation as a ceramics centre from the mid-fourteenth to the end of the fifteenth century, producing pieces still rated among the finest in the world. Over 200 kilns have been unearthed in and around Si Satchanalai to date, and it's estimated that there could once have been a thousand in all. Two kilometres upstream of Muang Kao Si Satchanalai in BAN KO NOI, the **Sawankhalok Kiln Preservation Centre** (daily 9am–noon & 1–4pm; B20) showcases an excavated production site, with a couple of kilns roofed over as museum pieces.

Unfortunately, there are no English signs to explain how the kilns worked, though a small display of **Sawankhalok ceramics** gives an idea of the pieces that were fired here. Works fall into three broad categories: domestic items such as pots, decorated plates and lidded boxes; decorative items like figurines, temple sculptures and temple roof tiles; and items for export, particularly to Indonesia and the Philippines, where huge Sawankhalok storage jars were used as burial urns. Most Sawankhalok ceramics were glazed – the grey-green celadon, probably introduced by immigrant Chinese potters, was especially popular – and typically decorated with fish or chrysanthemum motifs. Several of Thailand's major museums feature collections of ceramics from both Si Satchanalai and Sukhothai under the umbrella label of Sawankhalok.

Sawankhalok dish

Kamphaeng Phet

KAMPHAENG PHET, 77km south of Sukhothai, was probably founded in the fourteenth century by the kings of Sukhothai as a buffer city between their capital and the increasingly powerful city-state of Ayutthaya. Its name, which translates as "Diamond Wall", refers to its role as a garrison town. Strategically sited 100m from the east bank of the Ping, the ruined old city has, like Sukhothai and Si Satchanalai before it, been partly restored and opened to the public as a historical park. The least visited of the three, it should nevertheless rival Si Satchanalai for your attentions, mainly because of the eloquently weathered statues of its main temple. A new city has grown up on the southeastern boundaries of the old, the usual commercial ugliness offset by a riverside park, plentiful flowers and traditional wooden houses.

Highway 1, the region's main north–south route, skirts Kamphaeng Phet on the western side of the river – the town is served by direct **buses** from Bangkok and Chiang Mai, but most travellers come here as a day trip from Sukhothai or Phitsanulok. Arriving from either of these two, you'll enter from the east and should ask to be dropped off inside the old city walls rather than wait to be dumped across the river at the terminal 2km west of town on Highway 1. If you are coming from the bus terminal, you'll need to hop on a town songthaew which will take you to the Tesa Road roundabout just east of the river (the most convenient disembarkation point for the ruins), or further into the town centre for most of the hotels and restaurants.

Muang Kao Kamphaeng Phet

Ruins surround modern Kamphaeng Phet on all sides, but **Muang Kao Kamphaeng Phet** (daily 8.30am–4.30pm; B20) takes in the two most interesting areas: the oblong zone inside the old city walls and the forested area just north of that. A tour of both areas involves a five-kilometre round trip; there's no public transport, so if you don't feel like walking you'll have to strike a deal with a samlor driver or rent a motorbike from the shop on the road between the Tesa Road roundabout and the old city walls.

The ruins that dot the landscape west of the roundabout, across the Ping River, belong to the even older city of Nakhon Chum, but are now too overgrown, tumbledown and difficult to reach to be worth the effort.

Inside the city walls

Parts of the **city walls** that gave Kamphaeng Phet its name are still in good condition, though Highway 101 to Sukhothai now cuts through the enclosed area and a few shops have sprung up along the roadside, making it hard to visualise the fortifications as a whole.

Approaching from the Tesa Road roundabout, you enter the compound from the western side and come in at the back end of **Wat Phra Kaeo**. Built almost entirely of laterite and adorned with laterite Buddhas, this was the city's central and most important structure, and given the name reserved for temples that have housed the kingdom's most sacred image: the Emerald Buddha, now in the wat of the same name in Bangkok, is thought to have been set down here to rest at some point. Seven centuries later, the Buddha images have been worn away into attractive abstract shadows of their originals – often aptly compared to the pitted,

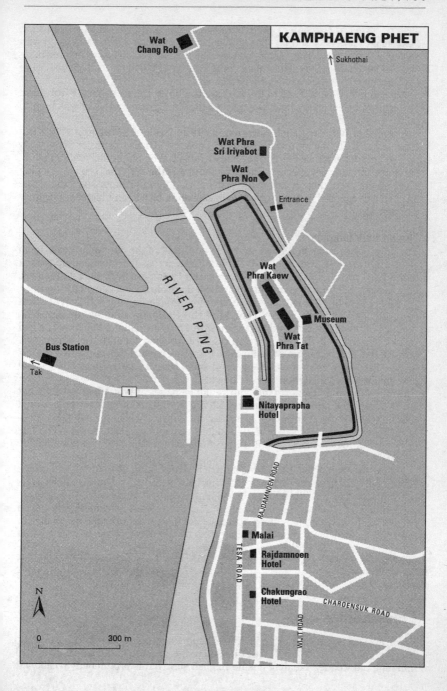

KAMPHAENG PHET

↑ Sukhothai

Wat
Chang Rob

Wat Phra
Sri Iriyabot

Wat
Phra Non

Entrance

Wat
Phra Kaew

RIVER PING

Museum

Wat
Phra Tat

Bus Station

Tak

1

Nitayaprapha
Hotel

RAJDAMNOEN ROAD

Malai

TESA ROAD

Rajdamnoen
Hotel

Chakungrao
Hotel

CHAROENSUK ROAD

WIJIT ROAD

N

0   300 m

spidery forms of Giacometti sculptures – and the slightly unkempt feel to the place makes a perfect setting. The statues would originally have been faced with stucco, and restorers have already patched up the central tableau of one reclining and two seated Buddhas. The empty niches that encircle the principal chedi were once occupied by statues of bejewelled lions.

Adjoining Wat Phra Kaeo to the east are the three chedis of **Wat Phra That**. The central bell-shaped chedi is typical of the Sri Lankan style and was built to house a sacred relic.

Just east of Wat Phra That, **Kamphaeng Phet National Museum** (Wed–Sun 10am–4pm; B10) houses a clear, succinct survey of Thailand's major art periods on the ground floor and a comprehensive display of Sukhothai-era sculpture, ceramics and utensils upstairs. The prize exhibit is the very fine bronze standing Shiva on the ground floor: cast in the sixteenth century in Khmer style, the statue has had a chequered history, including decapitation by a keen nineteenth century German admirer.

The arunyik temples

The dozen or so ruins in the forested area northeast of the city walls – east 100m along Highway 101 from behind Wat Phra Kaeo, across the moat and up a track to the left – are all that remains of Kamphaeng Phet's **arunyik** (forest) temples, built here by Sukhothai-era monks in a wooded area to encourage meditation.

Passing through the entrance gate, the first temple on your left is **Wat Phra Non**, otherwise known as the Temple of the Reclining Buddha, though little remains of the enormous Buddha figure save for a few chunks helpfully labelled "neck", "head" and the like. Gigantic laterite pillars support the viharn that houses the statue; far more ambitious than the usual brick-constructed jobs, these pillars were cut from single slabs of stone from a nearby quarry and would have measured up to eight metres in height.

A relic's throw to the north, the four Buddha images of **Wat Phra Sri Iriyabot** are in better condition. With cores of laterite and skins of stucco, the restored standing and walking images tower over the viharn, while the seated (south-facing) and reclining (north-facing) Buddhas remain indistinct masses. The full-grown trees rooted firmly in the raised floor are evidence of just how old the place is.

Follow the path around the bend to reach **Wat Chang Rob**, crouched atop a laterite hill 1km from the entrance gate. Built to the same Sri Lankan model as its sister temples of the same name in Sukhothai and Si Satchanalai, this "temple surrounded by elephants" retains only the square base of its central bell-shaped chedi. Climb one of its four steep staircases for a view out over the mountains in the west, or just for a different perspective of the 68 elephant buttresses that encircle the base. Sculpted from laterite and stucco, they're dressed in the ceremonial garb fit for such revered animals; along the surfaces between neighbouring pachyderms you can just make out floral reliefs – the lower level was once decorated with a stucco frieze of flying birds.

Practicalities

Few travellers spend the night in Kamphaeng Phet, but if you do want to **stay**, *Nitayaprapha Hotel* (☎055/711381) has the edge in price and convenience. The rambling old wooden building has no English sign, but is prominently positioned over a restaurant on the southwest corner of the Tesa Road roundabout; basic rooms with fan and shower cost B80. Nearer the new town centre, on the corner of Soi 9 and Rajdamnoen Road, *Rajdamnoen Hotel* (☎055/711029) has fair rooms for B120 with fan and B160 with air-conditioning. *Chakungrao Hotel* (☎055/711315), between sois 11 and 13 on Tesa Road, is the poshest choice in town, though the large air-conditioned rooms are a touch shabby for the price (B300, negotiable).

Food in Kamphaeng Phet rarely rises above the noodles-and-curry level, but *Malai*, just north of Soi 9 on Tesa Road, serves up a reliable range of northeastern food – *khao niaw, kai yang* and *somtam* – at very reasonable prices. (There's no English sign, or menu, but you can recognise the place by the enormous sticky-rice baskets hanging up outside.) Otherwise you're best off with the noodle shops near *Nitayapraphya Hotel* or seeking out the **nightmarket** on Wijit Road. The big outdoor restaurants along Tesa Road are the kind that have singers-with-synthesizers as evening-long entertainment and menus tailored for large Thai groups, which work out expensive for individuals.

West of Sukhothai

Highway 12 heads west from Sukhothai, crossing the westernmost reaches of the northern plains before arriving at the provincial capital of **TAK** (79km), on the east bank of the Ping River. Historically important only as the birthplace of King Taksin of Thonburi (who appended the name of his hometown to the one he was born with), Tak is of little interest to tourists except as a place to change **buses** for continuing north to Lampang and Chiang Mai, south to Kamphaeng Phet and Bangkok, or west to Mae Sot and the Burmese border. You might also find yourself touching down here on a flight between Phitsanulok and Chiang Mai – four flights a week make the journey via Tak and Mae Sot. The bus terminal and airfield are both about 3km east of the town centre. If you need to break your journey overnight, try the *Mae Ping* (☎055/511807) or *Sa Nguan Thai* (☎055/511265) **hotels**: both are near the lively central market and have rooms from B90.

Better to hold out for Mae Sot, reached by either of two roads through the stunning western mountain range that divides the northern plains from the Burmese border. Highway 105, the more direct route, is served by cramped song-thaews that leave Tak approximately hourly and take ninety minutes; rickety but roomy regular buses take twice as long to ply Route 1175, which follows a winding and at times hair-raising course across the thickly forested range, affording great views over the valleys on either side and passing through makeshift roadside settlements built by hill tribes. (Returning along either of these routes to Tak, most public vehicles are stopped at an army checkpoint in an attempt to prevent Burmese entering Thailand illegally.) Much of this whole area is conserved as a national park, the most accessible stretch of which falls within **Langsang National Park** and is signposted off Highway 105, 20km west of Tak.

Route 1175 eventually descends into the valley of the **River Moei** – which forms the Thai–Burmese border here – and joins Route 1085 at the lovely, traditional village of MAE RAMAT before continuing south to Mae Sot. Route 1085 carries on northwards, reaching Mae Sariang (see p.224) after six hours and three songthaew changes – a rough, bumpy journey through rugged border country where law enforcement is intermittent at best.

Mae Sot and the border

Located 100km west of Tak and only 6km from the Burmese border, **MAE SOT** boasts a rich ethnic mix (Burmese, Karen, Hmong and Thai), thriving trade (legal and illegal) and a laid-back atmosphere. There's little to see in the small town apart from several glittering Burmese-style temples, but it's a relaxed place to hang out, and the short ride to the border market provides additional, if low-key, entertainment. Arriving by road, you'll either be dropped off near the police box on Indharakiri Road – one of just two main thoroughfares running parallel through the centre – or just around the corner in front of *First Hotel*. The airport is a couple of kilometres west of town, between Mae Sot and the border.

Mae Sot also makes a good starting point for untouristed **treks** into the area around UMPANG, 100km to the south. These generally include trips to caves and waterfalls, nights in Lisu, Akha, Karen or Lahu villages, and rafting and elephant-back excursions. If you're wary of overpackaged, commercialised treks, then Mae Sot is a great place to go from. *Mae Sot Guest House* in particular organises small trekking groups and will tailor-make itineraries; *Siam Hotel* runs slightly less adventurous treks. If you haven't got time for an overnight trek, there are plenty of **waterfalls** within day-tripping distance of Mae Sot: Nam Tok Mae Kasa, about 20km north of town, and Nam Tok Phra Charoen, 41km south, are both accessible by songthaew.

Practicalities

You won't go wrong with either of Mae Sot's two **guest houses**, both of which can provide a wealth of information on the scenic and political shape of the area. *Mae Sot Guest House*, ten minutes' walk east of the bus terminal on Indharakiri Road, is very much a private residence, with only four simple rooms (B50 single, B80 double) and cooking and laundry facilities. The owner, Khun Too, organises three-day treks from here, and if he can't get help during the low season he sometimes closes the guest house while he's away. At the other, western, end of Indharakiri Road (15min walk from the bus terminal), *No. 4 Guest House* is a little larger and more comfortable, with rooms from B60 single, B90 double.

If you'd rather stay in a **hotel**, sizeable, clean rooms at the *Siam* (☎055/ 531376), centrally located in amongst the gem and jade shops on Prasat Vithi Road, start at B120 with shower; treks can also be arranged from here. *First Hotel* (☎055/531233), just north of Indharakiri Road, where Tak-bound songthaews leave from, has similar rooms from B140. *Mae Sot Hills Hotel* (☎055/532601), away from the centre on Asia Road (Highway 1085), seems strangely upmarket for such an isolated town. Rooms here start at B580, with free use of the swimming pool. Non-guests can use the pool for B25.

For good Thai and Western **food** at very reasonable prices – and certainly the biggest menu in town – head for *Pim Hut* on Tang Kim Chang Road, which is popular with locals as well as Thai and farang tourists. You could also try out the two large open-air restaurants near *Mae Sot Guest House* which, wreathed in strings of coloured light bulbs and loud with the wails of teenage singers, entertain partying groups of Thais with slightly pricey menus of mostly *tom yam*, fish-and-meat-over rice dishes, and vast quantities of Mekhong whisky. For authentic, cheap no-frills meals, check out the noodle shops and night-market stalls along Prasat Vithi Road, the street parallel to Indharakiri Road.

THE BURMESE JUNTA AND THE KAREN

With a population of five million, the **Karen** are Burma's largest ethnic minority, but their numbers have offered no protection against persecution by the Burmese. This mistreatment has been going on for centuries, and entered a new phase after World War II, when the Karen remained loyal to the British. As a reward, the Karen were supposed to have been granted a special settlement when the British left, but were instead left to fend for themselves. Fifteen years after the British withdrawal, the **Burmese army** took control, setting up an isolationist state run under a bizarre ideology compounded of militarist, socialist and Buddhist principles. In 1988, opposition to this junta peaked with a series of pro-democracy demonstrations which were suppressed by the slaughter of thousands.

The army subsequently felt obliged to hold elections, which resulted in an overwhelming majority for the **National League for Democracy**, led by **Aung San Suu Kyi**, recipient of the 1991 Nobel Peace Prize. In response, the military placed Aung San Suu Kyi under house arrest and declared all opposition parties illegal. The disenfranchised MPs then joined the thousands who, in the face of the savagery of the Burmese militia against the country's minorities, had fled east to the **refugee villages** set up north and south of Mae Sot.

It is in this area that Karen's armed struggle for their **independent state of Kawtulay** is focused, and every so often the Burmese army launches a headline-making assault on the Karen strongholds just across the border, the most important of which is at **Manerplaw**, upriver from Mae Sot on the Burmese bank of the River Moei. Armed by the Karen guerrillas, all resistance activities are centred on this jungle camp, home of the democratically elected government and command centre of the Karen National Liberation Army.

The war for democracy and a Karen homeland is locked into a cycle to which no imminent end is visible. Every dry season the Burmese army makes territorial gains, but when the rains arrive at the end of April the Karen recapture most of their strongholds, ready for the next round of battles in October. The Thai government never openly condemns the neighbouring regime but supports the rebel camps by tolerating their presence and sending in the troops whenever the Burmese army sneaks across the border to try and attack Manerplaw from Thai soil. Meanwhile, in the Burmese heartlands the murderers and rapists wreak their frustrated revenge on unarmed villagers, and every year, half of Burma's GNP is spent on weaponry. The entrenched virulence of the Burmese attitude to the Karen – and by extension, their allies – can be gauged by the recent comment of a senior Burmese soldier: "I want my country to be at peace; I want to extinguish all the minority peoples".

(For more on the Karen, see p.184.)

Rim Moei border market

Frequent songthaews ferry Thai traders and a meagre trickle of tourists the 6km from Mae Sot to the border at **RIM MOEI**, where a thriving market for Burmese goods has grown up on the banks of the River Moei. Burmese currency is accepted at the border and at some places in Mae Sot, and Burmese villagers from MYAWADDY on the opposite bank seem to be granted unquestioned leave to cross the narrow river and trade both at Rim Moei and in the markets of Mae Sot. Farangs, however, are on no account allowed into Burma at this point. As at most gateways along this border, Burmese and Thai officials reap juicy payoffs from the contraband loads – in this instance, mainly teak and jade – which get smuggled into Mae Sot at night so to avoid Thai taxes.

Despite the touristy nature of many of its wares, Rim Moei's large and colourful market is not a bad place to pick up Burmese **handicrafts**, particularly the distinctive brightly coloured lacquerware, checked *longyis*, silverware and jewellery. Jade and other gems are a big feature too, though you'll probably get better bargains in the more competitve Mae Sot jewellery shops. As in Mae Sot, half the fun is watching the goings-on and enjoying the multi-cultural fashion show – best done from the small restaurant overlooking the river.

travel details

Trains

From Ayutthaya to Bangkok Hualamphong (hourly; 1hr 30min), via Bang Pa-In (15min); Chiang Mai (6 daily; 12hr), via Lopburi (1hr–1hr 30min) and Phitsanulok (5hr); Nong Khai (4 daily; 5hr); Ubon Ratchathani (7 daily; 10hr).

From Kanchanaburi to Bangkok (2 daily; 2hr 40min); Nam Tok (3 daily; 2hr).

From Lopburi to Bangkok (12 daily; 2hr 30min–3hr), via Ayutthaya (1hr–1hr 30min); Chiang Mai (6 daily; 11hr), via Phitsanulok (4hr).

From Nakhon Pathom to Bangkok (10 daily; 1hr 20min); Nam Tok (2 daily; 1hr 20min), via Kanchanaburi (3hr 20min); Nakhon Si Thammarat (up to 9 daily; 15hr), via Phetchaburi (2hr 50min–3hr 15min) and Surat Thani (9hr–11hr 30min).

From Nam Tok to Bangkok Noi (2 daily; 4hr 35min).

From Phitsanulok to Bangkok (9 daily; 6hr 15min–9hr 30min); Chiang Mai (4 daily; 7hr 10min–8hr).

Buses

From Ayutthaya to Bangkok (every 10min; 2hr); Bang Pa-In (hourly; 40min); Lopburi (every 10min; 3hr).

From Bang Pa-In to Bangkok (every 20min; 1hr 30min).

From Damnoen Saduak to Bangkok (every 20min; 2hr).

From Kamphaeng Phet to Tak (hourly; 1hr).

From Kanchanaburi to Bangkok (every 15min; 2–3hr); Sai Yok (every 30min; 2hr 30min), via Nam Tok (1hr 30min); Sangkhlaburi (14 daily; 3–5hr).

From Lopburi to Bangkok (every 15min; 3hr), via Wat Phra Phutthabat (30min).

From Nakhon Pathom to Bangkok (every 10min; 40min–1hr 20min); Damnoen Saduak (every 20min; 1hr); Kanchanaburi (every 10min; 1hr 20min).

From Nam Tok to Sangkhlaburi (5 daily; 3hr 30min).

From Phitsanulok to Bangkok (up to 19 daily; 5–6hr); Chiang Mai (up to 18 daily; 5–6hr); Kamphaeng Phet (hourly; 3hr); Khon Kaen (4 daily; 5hr); Phrae (hourly; 3hr); Sukhothai (every 30min; 1hr); Tak (hourly; 3hr).

From Sukhothai to Bangkok (up to 17 daily; 6–7hr); Chiang Mai (up to 16 daily; 5–6hr); Kamphaeng Phet (hourly; 2hr); Si Satchanalai (every 30min; 1hr); Tak (every 90min; 2hr).

From Tak to Mae Sot (hourly; 1hr 30min–3hr).

Flights

From Phitsanulok to Bangkok (2–3 daily; 50min); Chiang Mai (1–2 daily; 50min–2hr 35min); Mae Hong Son (3 weekly; 2hr); Nan (daily; 1hr 45min), via Phrae (45min); Mae Sot (4 weekly; 1hr 20min), via Tak (35min).

CHAPTER THREE

THE NORTH

Travelling up through the central plains, there's no mistaking when you've reached the **north** of Thailand: somewhere between Uttaradit and Den Chai, the train slows almost to a halt, as if approaching a frontier post, to meet the abruptly rising mountains, which continue largely unbroken to the borders of Burma and Laos. Beyond this point the climate becomes more temperate, nurturing the fertile land which gave the old kingdom of the north the name of **Lanna**, "the land of a million ricefields". Although only one-tenth of the land can be used for rice cultivation, the valley ricefields here are three times more productive than those in the dusty northeast, and the higher land yields a great variety of fruits, as well as beans, groundnuts, tobacco and – notoriously – opium.

Until the beginning of this century, Lanna was a largely independent region. On the back of its agricultural prosperity, it developed its own styles of art and architecture, which can still be seen in its flourishing temples and distinctive handicraft traditions. The north is also set apart from the rest of the country by its exuberant way with festivals, a cuisine which has been heavily influenced by Burma and a dialect quite distinct from central Thai. Northerners proudly call themselves *khon muang*, "people of the principalities", and their gentle sophistication is admired by the people of Bangkok, whose wealthier citizens build their holiday homes in the clean air of the north's forested mountains.

Chiang Mai, the capital and transport centre of the north, is a place to relax before setting off into the hills. For many travellers, this means joining a trek to visit one or more of the **hill tribes**, who comprise one-tenth of the north's population and are just about clinging on to the ways of life which distinguish them from each other and the Thais around them. For those with qualms about the exploitative element of this ethnological tourism, there are plenty of other, more independent options. To the west, the trip to **Mae Hong Son** takes you through the most stunning mountain scenery in the region into a land with its roots across the border in Burma. Heading north from Chiang Mai brings you to **Chiang Rai**, which is making a bid to rival Chiang Mai as a base for exploring the countryside. Above Chiang Rai, the northernmost tip of Thailand is marked by the fascinating, schizophrenic border town of **Mae Sai**, and the junction of Laos and Burma at **Sop Ruak**. Fancifully dubbed the "Golden Triangle", Sop Ruak is a must on every coach party's itinerary – you're more likely to find peace and quiet among the ruins of nearby **Chiang Saen**, set on the leafy banks of the Mekhong River. Few visitors backtrack south from Chiang Mai, even though the towns of **Lamphun** and **Lampang** are packed with artistic and historical goodies. Further out on a limb to the east, **Nan** is even less popular, but combines rich mountain scenery with eclectic temple art.

Transport routes are necessarily roundabout and bus services often slow, though frequent: in some cases, it's worth considering hopping over the mountains by plane. To appreciate the landscape fully, many people take to the open roads on rented **motorbikes**, which are available in most northern towns and relatively inexpensive – Chiang Mai has the best choice, followed by Chiang Rai.

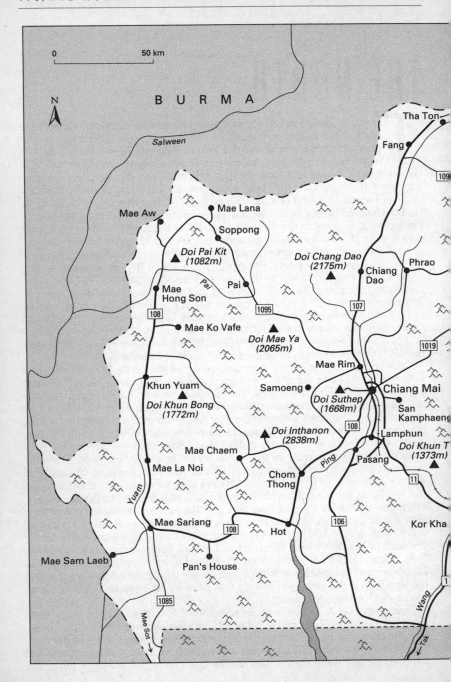

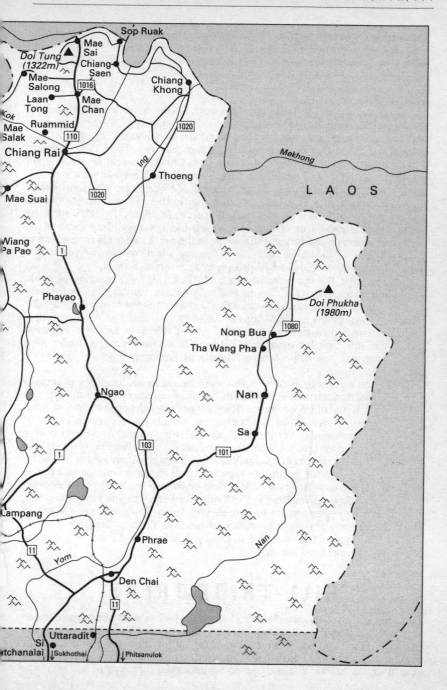

You should be cautious about biking in the north, however. The border police may stop you from venturing into an area that's considered too dangerous, but don't ride alone on any remote trails – there have been incidents where lone riders have been shot or harassed.

Some history

The first civilisation to leave an indelible mark on the north was **Haripunjaya**, the Mon (Dvaravati) state which was founded at Lamphun in the ninth century. Maintaining strong ties with the Mon kingdoms to the south, it remained the cultural and religious centre of the north for four centuries. The Thais came onto the scene after the Mons, migrating down from China between the seventh and the eleventh century and establishing small principalities around the north. The prime mover for the Thais was **King Mengrai** of Ngon Yang, who shortly after the establishment of a Thai state at Sukhothai in the middle of the thirteenth century, set to work on a parallel unified state in the north. By 1296, when he began the construction of Chiang Mai, which has remained the capital of the north ever since, he had brought the whole of the north under his control and at his death in 1317 he had established a dynasty which was to oversee a two-hundred-year period of unmatched prosperity and cultural activity.

However, after the expansionist reign of Tilok (1441–87) a series of weak, squabbling kings came and went, while Ayutthaya increased its unfriendly advances. But it was the **Burmese** who finally snuffed out the Mengrai dynasty by capturing Chiang Mai in 1558, and for most of the next two centuries, they controlled Lanna through a succession of puppet rulers. In 1767, the Burmese sacked the Thai capital at Ayutthaya, but the Thais soon regrouped under King Taksin who with the help of **King Kawila** of Lampang gradually drove the Burmese northwards.

Kawila was succeeded as ruler of the north by a series of incompetent princes for much of the nineteenth century, until colonialism reared its head. After the British took control of Upper Burma, **Rama V** of Bangkok began to take an interest in the north to prevent its annexation. He forcibly moved large numbers of ethnic Thais northwards, in order to counter the British claim of sovereignty over territory occupied by Thai Yai (Shans), who also make up a large part of the population of Upper Burma. In 1877 Rama V appointed a high commissioner in Chiang Mai, and since then the north has built on its agricultural richness to become relatively prosperous. However, the recent economic boom has been concentrated, as elsewhere in Thailand, in the towns, due in no small part to the increase in tourism. The eighty percent of Lanna's population who live in rural areas, of which the vast majority are subsistence farmers, are finding it increasingly difficult to earn a living off the soil, due to rapid population growth and land speculation for tourism and agro-industry.

HILL-TRIBE TREKS

Trekking in the mountains of north Thailand – which is what brings most travellers here – differs from trekking in most other parts of the world, in that the emphasis is not primarily on the scenery but on the region's inhabitants. Northern Thailand's **hill tribes**, now numbering over half a million people living in as many as 10,000 villages, have so far preserved their way of life with little change over thousands of years. Visiting their settlements is not an easy enterprise, as only a few of the villages are near enough to a main road to be reached on a day trip from a major town: to get to the other, more traditional villages usually entails joining a hastily assembled guided party for a few days, roughing it in a different place each night. For most, however, encountering peoples of so different a culture, travelling through beautiful tropical countryside and tasting the excitement of elephant riding and river rafting are experiences that far outweigh these considerations.

On any trek you are necessarily confronted by the **ethics** of your role. Around 80,000 travellers now go trekking each year, the majority of them heading to certain well-trodden areas such as the Mae Tang valley (40km northwest of Chiang Mai), the region to the north of Pai and the hills between Chiang Rai and Mae Salong. Beyond the basic level of disturbance caused by any tourism, this steady flow of trekkers creates pressures for the traditionally insular hill tribes. Foreigners unfamiliar with hill-tribe customs can easily cause grave offence, and opium-smoking farangs have tended to increase the habit amongst the locals. Tourism also provides a distraction from the tribes' traditional way of life, though this last problem can easily be exaggerated – the effects of tourism are minimal in comparison to the major problems caused by exploitation by lowland Thais, lack of land rights, poor health provision and minimal educational services. Most tribespeople are genuinely welcoming and hospitable to foreigners, appreciating the contact with Westerners and the material benefits which trekking brings them. Nonetheless it must be stressed that to keep disruption to a minimum it is important to take a responsible attitude when trekking – always go with a sensitive and knowledgeable guide who has the welfare of the hill tribes in mind, and follow the basic guidelines on etiquette outlined below.

Trekking practicalities

The hill tribes are big business in northern Thailand: in Chiang Mai there are over 200 agencies, which between them cover just about all the trekkable areas in the north. Chiang Rai is the second biggest trekking centre, and agencies can also be found in Mae Hong Son, Pai and Nan, which usually arrange treks only to the villages in their immediate area. For the independent traveller, a dozen or so rural guest houses have been set up either in or near to hill-tribe villages, specifically for those who want to explore the countryside by themselves.

The basics

The right **clothing** is the first essential on any trek. Strong boots with ankle protection are the best footwear, although in the dry season training shoes are adequate. Long trousers should be worn, to protect against thorns and, in the wet season, leeches. Wear thin, loose clothing and a hat, and cover your arms if prone to sunburn. Antiseptic, antihistamine, anti-diarrhoea **medicine** and insect repellant are essential, and a mosquito net is a good idea. At least two changes of clothing are needed, plus a sarong or towel.

If you're going on an organised trek, **water** is usually provided by the guide, as well as a small backpack. **Blankets** are also supplied, but rarely enough in the cool season, when night-time temperatures can dip to freezing – you should bring a sleeping bag, and a sweater, to be sure of keeping the chill off.

TREKKING ETIQUETTE

As the guests, it's up to farangs to adapt to the customs of the hill tribes and not to make a nuisance of themselves. Apart from keeping an open mind and not demanding too much of your hosts, a few simple rules should be observed.

● Dress modestly, with long trousers or skirt and a T-shirt or shirt.

● Loud voices and boisterous behaviour are out of place. Smiling and nodding establishes good intent.

● Most hill-tribe houses contain a religious shrine. Do not touch or photograph this shrine, or sit underneath it.

● Some villagers like to be photographed, most do not. Point at your camera and nod if you want to take a photograph. Never insist if the answer is an obvious "no". Be particularly careful with pregnant women and babies – most tribes believe cameras affect the soul of the foetus or new-born.

● Taking gifts is dubious practice: writing materials for children are very welcome, but sweets and cigarettes may encourage begging.

● Smoking opium on a trek is a big attraction for many travellers, but there is evidence of increased addiction rates among hill-tribe villagers who are regularly visited by trekkers.

It's wise not to take anything valuable with you – most banks in the north have safe-deposit boxes where you can leave small items. Trekkers have occasionally been robbed by bandits, although the Border Patrol Police have recently increased their activities in trekking areas to provide better security. If there is a robbery attempt, don't resist.

Organised treks

Organised treks can be as short as two days or as long as fifteen, but are typically of four days' duration. Each trek usually follows a regular itinerary established by the agency, although they can sometimes be customised, especially for smaller groups and with agencies in the smaller towns. Some itineraries are geared towards serious hikers while others go at a much gentler pace, but on all treks much of the walking will be up and down steep forested hills, often under a burning sun, so a minimum fitness level is required. Many treks now include a ride on an elephant and a trip on a bamboo raft – exciting to the point of being dangerous if the river is running fast. The typical trek costs about B1800 in Chiang Mai, often less in other towns, and much less without rafting and elephant riding.

Between eight and ten people is a standard size for a trekking group, but a **party of four** is preferable, enabling you to strike a more informative relationship with your guide and with the villagers. Everybody in the group usually sleeps on a bamboo floor or platform in the headman's hut, with a guide cooking communal meals, for which the food is generally brought from outside, since the effects of hill-tribe food are unpredictable.

When **choosing a trek**, there are several features to look out for. If you want to trek with a small group, get an assurance from your agency that you won't be tagged onto a larger group. A trek should have at least two guides – a leader and a back-marker; tourists have got lost for days by losing touch with the rest of the group. Ask about transport from base at the beginning and end of the trek, since sometimes the trip can include a long public bus ride. Meet the guides, who should speak reasonable English, and should be able to inform trekkers about hill-tribe culture and especially the details of etiquette in each village. Finally, ask what food will be eaten, check how much walking is involved per day, and get a copy of the route map to gauge the terrain.

Recommending particular **agencies** is difficult, as names change and standards rise and fall. TAT recommends using agencies which are members of local clubs such as the Jungle Tour Club and the Professional Guide Association of Chiang Mai, lists of which are obtainable from the TAT office in Chiang Mai. Alternatively, if you hear of a good one by word of mouth, try it. Each trek should be **registered** with the Tourist Police, stating the itinerary, the duration and the participants, in case the party encounters any problems – it's worth checking with the Tourist Police that your agency has done this before departure.

Independent trekking

Unfortunately, the options for independent trekking are limited, chiefly by the poor mapping of the area. Only Hongsombud's widely available *Guide Map of Chiang Rai* (Bangkok Guides) offers adequate detail, as it includes 1:1000 maps of the more popular chunks of the province. For other areas of the north, you can consult the maps at the **Hill Tribe Research Institute** at Chiang Mai University (Mon–Fri 9am–4pm), between Huai Kaeo and Suthep roads, which mark the villages where people can stay.

For most independent travellers, the only feasible approach is to use as a base one of the half-dozen or so **guest houses** specifically geared for farangs in various parts of the north. They're generally set deep in the countryside, within walking range of several hill-tribe villages, about which the owner can give information in English. Conditions in these guest houses are usually spartan, but the food should be safe to eat. All these guest houses are covered in the relevant parts of this chapter, and a checklist is provided in the box below.

If you're confident about finding your way round, it's possible to find **accommodation in hill-tribe villages**. It helps if you speak some Thai, but most villagers, if you hang around for any time, will ask if you want to stay with the usual "sleep" gesture. It is usual to stay in the headman's house on a guest platform, but increasingly villages are building small guest houses. Expect to pay B50 per night – for this, you will often be offered dinner and breakfast. It's safe to accept plain rice, boiled drinks and food that's bolied or fried in your prescence, but you're taking a risk with anything else, as it's not unusual for foreigners to suffer food poisoning.

Most villages are safe to stay in, but trekking this way leaves you particularly vulnerable to armed bandits who sporadically rob foreigners. If possible check with the Hill Tribe Research Institute, and with local guides and the district police in the area where you intend to trek. Furthermore, the lone trekker will learn very little without a guide as intermediary, and is far more likely to commit an unwitting offence against the local customs.

GUEST HOUSES FOR INDEPENDENT TREKKING

East of Mae Sariang: *Pan's House.*
Between Mae Hong Son and Pai: *Wilderness Lodge*; *Mae Lana Guest House* at Mae Lana; *Cave Lodge* at Ban Tum.
Between Chiang Mai and Chiang Rai: *Trekker House.*
North of Chiang Rai: *Mountain View* at Huai Khom; *Laan Tong Lodge*; *Akha Guest House* on Doi Tung.

The Hill Tribes

Originating in various parts of China and Southeast Asia, the hill tribes are often termed Fourth World people, in that they are migrants who continue to migrate without regard for established national boundaries. Most arrived in Thailand during this century, and many of the hill peoples are still also found in other parts of Southeast Asia – in Vietnam, for example, where the French used the *montagnards* in their fight against communism.

Called **chao khao** (mountain people) by the Thais, the tribes are mostly pre-literate societies, whose sophisticated systems of customs, laws and beliefs have developed to harmonise relationships between individuals and their environment. In recent years, with the effects of rapid population growth and ensuing competition for land, of discrimination and exploitation by lowland Thais, and of tourism, their ancient culture has come under threat, but the integrity of their way of life is as yet largely undamaged, and what follows is the briefest of introductions to an immensely complex subject. If you want to learn more, the small museum and library at the Tribal Research Institute in Chiang Mai are worth a visit (see previous page), as is the *Hill Tribe Museum and Handicrafts Shop* in Chiang Rai.

Agriculture

Although the hill tribes keep some livestock such as pigs, poultry and elephants, the base of their economy is **slash-and-burn farming**, a crude form of shifting cultivation also practised by many Thai lowland farmers. At the beginning of the season an area of jungle is cleared and burned, producing ash to fertilise rice, corn, chillies and other vegetables, which are replanted in succeeding years until the soil's nutrients are exhausted. This system is sustainable with a low population density, which allows the jungle time to recover before it is used again. However, with the increase in population over the last thirty years, ever greater areas are being exhausted and the decreasing forest cover is leading to erosion and micro-climatic change.

As a result, many villages have taken up the large-scale production of **opium** to supplement the traditional subsistence crops. With some success the government has attempted to stamp out opium cultivation, but the cash crops which have been introduced in its place have often led to further environmental damage, as these low-profit crops require larger areas of cultivation, and thus greater deforestation. Furthermore, the water supplies have become polluted with chemical pesticides, and although more environmentally sensitive agricultural techniques are being introduced, they have yet to achieve widespread acceptance. Meanwhile, progress towards long-term solutions is hindered by the resentment of neighbouring Thais against whatever projects are set up to help the hill tribes, and the uncertainty of the tribes' legal position: few have identity cards, and without citizenship they have no rights to the land they inhabit.

Religion and festivals

Although some have taken up Buddhism and others – especially among the Karen, Mien and Lahu – have been converted by Christian missionaries bringing the material incentives of education and modern medicine, the hill tribes are predominantly **animists**. In this belief system, all natural objects are inhabited by spirits, which, along with the tribe's ancestor spirits and the supreme divine spirit, must be propitiated to prevent harm to the family or village. Most villages have two religious leaders, a priest who looks after the ritual life of the community, and a shaman who has the power to mediate with the spirits and prescribe what has to be done to keep them happy. If a member of the community is sick, for example, the shaman will be consulted to determine what action has insulted which spirit, and will then carry out the correct sacrifice.

The most important festival, celebrated by all the tribes, is at **New Year**, when whole communities take part in dancing, music and rituals particular to each tribe: Hmong boys and girls, for instance, take part in a courting ritual at this time, while playing catch with a ball. The New Year festivals are not held on fixed dates, but at various times during the cool-season slack period in the agricultural cycle from January to March.

Costumes and handicrafts

The most conspicuous characteristics of the hill tribes are their exquisitely crafted **costumes** and adornments, the styles and colours of which are particular to each group. Although many men and children are adopting Western clothes for everyday wear, most women still wear the traditional attire at all times, and it's the women who make the clothes – most still spin their own cotton, but some Hmong, Lisu and Mien women are prosperous enough to buy materials from itinerant traders. Other distinctive hill-tribe artefacts – tools, jewellery, weapons and musical instruments – are the domain of the men, and specialist **blacksmiths** and **silversmiths** have such high status that some attract business from villages many kilometres away. Jewellery, the chief outward proof of a family's wealth, is displayed most obviously by women at the New Year festivals, and is commonly made from silver melted down from Indian and Burmese coins, though brass, copper and aluminium are also used.

Clothing and handicrafts were not regarded as marketable products until the early 1980s, when co-operatives were set up to manufacture and market these goods, which are now big business in the shops of Thailand. The hill tribes' deep-dyed coarse cloth, embroidered with simple geometric patterns in bright colours, has become popular among middle-class Thais as well as farang visitors. Mien material, dyed indigo or black with bright snowflake embroidery, is on sale in many shops, as is the simple but very distinctive Akha work – coarse black cotton, with triangular patterns of stitching and small fabric patches in rainbow colours, usually made up into bags and hats. The Hmong's much more sophisticated embroidery and appliqué, added to jacket lapels and cuffs and skirt hems, is also widely seen – Blue Hmong skirts, made on a base of indigo-dyed cotton with a white geometric batik design and embroidered in loud primary colours, are particularly attractive.

Besides clothing, the hill tribes' other handicrafts, such as knives and wooden or bamboo musical pipes have found a market amongst farangs, the most saleable product being the intricate engraving work of their silversmiths, especially in the form of chunky bracelets. For a sizeable minority of villages, handicrafts now provide the security of a steady income to supplement their income from farming.

The main tribes

Within the small geographical area of northern Thailand there are at least ten different hill tribes, many of them divided into distinct sub-groups – the following are the main seven, listed in order of population and under their own names, rather than the sometimes derogatory names used by Thais. (The Shan – or Thai Yai – the dominant group in most of the west of the region, are not a hill tribe, but a subgroup of Thais.) Beyond the broad similarities outlined above, this section sketches their differences in terms of history, economy and religion, and describes elements of dress by which they can be distinguished.

Karen

The **Karen** (called Kaliang or Yang in Thai) form by far the largest hill-tribe group in Thailand with a population of about 300,000, and are the second oldest after the Lawa, having begun to arrive here from Burma and China in the seventeenth century. The Thai Karen, many of them refugees from Burma (see p.173), mostly live in a broad tract of land west of Chiang Mai, which stretches along the border from Mae Hong Son province all the way down to Kanchanaburi, with scattered pockets in Chiang Mai, Chiang Rai and Phayao provinces.

The Karen traditionally practise a system of rotating cultivation which is ecologically far more sensitive than slash-and-burn in the valleys of this region and on low hills. Their houses are small (they do not live in extended family groups) and are very similar to those of lowland Thais: built on stilts and made of bamboo or teak, they're often surrounded by fruit gardens and neat fences. As well as farming their own land, they often hire out their labour to Thais and other hill tribes, and they keep a variety of livestock including elephants, which used to be employed in the teak trade but are now often found giving rides to trekking parties.

Unmarried Karen girls wear loose white or undyed V-necked blouses, decorated with grass seeds at the seams. Married women wear blouses and skirts in bold colours, predominantly red or blue. Men generally wear blue, baggy trousers with red or blue shirts, a simplified version of the womens' blouse.

Karen woman

Hmong

Called the Meo by the Thais (a term meaning "barbarian"), the **Hmong** ("free people") originated in central China or Mongolia and are now found widely in northern Thailand. There are two subgroups: the **Blue Hmong**, who live around and to the west of Chiang Mai; and the **White Hmong**, who are found to the east. A separate group of White Hmong live in refugee camps along the border with Laos: they fled from Laos after the end of the Vietnam War, during which they had sided with the Americans. Their overall population in Thailand is about 70,000, making them the second largest hill-tribe group.

Of all the hill tribes, the Hmong have been the quickest to move away from subsistence farming. Many villages grow opium for sale, although many others have eagerly embraced the newer cash crops. Hmong clothing has become much in demand in Thailand, and Hmong women will often be seen at markets throughout the country selling their handicrafts. The women in fact are expected to do most of the work on the land and in the home.

Hmong villages are usually built at high altitudes, below the crest of a protecting hill. Although wealthier families sometimes build the more comfortable Thai-style houses, most stick to the traditional house, with its dirt floor and a roof extending almost to ground level. They live together in extended families, with two or more bedrooms and a large guest platform.

The Blue Hmong dress in especially striking clothes. The women wear intricately embroidered pleated skirts decorated with parallel horizontal bands of red, pink, blue and white; their jackets are of black satin, with wide orange and yellow embroidered cuffs and lapels. White Hmong women wear black baggy trousers and simple jackets with blue cuffs. Men of both groups generally wear baggy black pants with colourful sashes round the waist, and embroidered jackets closing over the chest with a

Hmong child

button at the left shoulder. All the Hmong are famous for their chunky silver jewellery, which the women wear every day and the men only on special occasions: they believe silver binds a person's spirits together, and wear a heavy neckring to keep the spirits weighed down in the body.

Lahu

The **Lahu** originated in southwest China and have migrated into Thailand from northern Burma since the end of the last century. They're called Muser, "hunters", by the Thais, because many of the first Lahu to reach northern Thailand were professional hunters. Most of their settlements are concentrated close to the Burmese border, in Chiang Rai, northern Chiang Mai and Mae Hong Son provinces, but families and villages change locations frequently. The Lahu language has become the *lingua franca* of the hill tribes, since the Lahu often hire out their labour. About one third of Lahu have been converted to Christianity, and many have abandoned their traditional way of life as a result. The remaining animist Lahu believe in a village guardian spirit who is often worshipped at a central temple that is surrounded by banners and streamers of white and yellow flags. Ordinary houses are built on high stilts with walls of bamboo or wooden planks, thatched with grass.

Some Lahu women wear a distinctive black cloak with diagonal white stripes, decorated in bold red and yellow at the top of the sleeve, but traditional costume has been supplanted by the Thai shirt and sarong amongst many Lahu groups. The tribe is famous for its richly embroidered *yaam* (shoulder bags), which are widely available in Chiang Mai.

Mien

The **Mien** (called Yao in Thai) consider themselves to be the aristocrats of the hill tribes. Originating in southern China, where they used to have such power that at one time a Mien princess was married to a Chinese emperor, the Mien are now widely scattered throughout the north, with concentrations around Nan, Phayao and Chiang Rai. The Mien are the only hill tribe to have a written language, and a

Mien woman

codified religion based on medieval Chinese Taoism, although in recent years there have been many converts to Christianity and Buddhism.

In general, the Mien strike a balance between integration into Thai life and maintenance of their separate cultural base. Many earn extra cash by selling exquisite embroidery and religious scrolls, painted in bold Chinese style, and the number of villages which grow opium is declining rapidly, as the Mien begin to adopt new cash crops.

Mien villages, which are never sited below those of other tribes, are not especially distinctive: their houses are usually built of wooden planks on a dirt floor, with a guest platform of bamboo in the communal living area. The clothes of the women, however, are instantly recognisable: long black jackets with lapels of bright scarlet wool, heavily embroidered loose trousers in intricate designs which can take up to two years to complete, and a similarly embroidered black turban. The caps of babies are also very beautiful, richly embroidered with red or pink pom-poms. On special occasions, women and children wear silver neck rings, with silver chains decorated with silver ornaments extending down the back.

Akha

The poorest of the hill tribes, the **Akha** (Kaw or Eekaw in Thai) migrated from Tibet over 2000 years ago to Yunnan in China, where at some stage they had an organized state and kept written chronicles of their history – these chronicles, like the Akha written language, are now lost. From the 1910s they began to settle in Thailand, mostly in Chiang Rai and northern Chiang Mai province.

The Akha are less open to change than the other hill tribes, and have maintained their old agricultural methods – though many Akha villages grow opium for their own consumption, creating a major problem of addiction, especially amongst the older men. The Akha's form of animism – *Akhazang*, "the way of life of the Akha" – has also survived in uncompromised form. As well as spirits in the natural world, *Akhazang* encompasses the worship of ancestor spirits: some Akha can recite the names of over sixty generations of forebears.

Every Akha village is entered through ceremonial gates decorated with carvings of human activities and attributes – even cars and aeroplanes – to indicate to the spirit world that beyond here only humans should pass. To touch any of these carvings, or to show any lack of respect to them, is punishable by fines or sacrifices. The gates are rebuilt or replaced every year, so many villages have a series of gates, the older ones in a state of disintegration. Another characteristic of all Akha villages is its giant swing, used every August in a swinging festival in which the whole population takes part.

Akha houses are recognisable by their low stilts and steeply pitched roofs. Even more distinctive is the elaborate headgear which women wear all day: it frames the entire face and usually consists of a conical wedge of white beads interspersed with silver coins and topped with plumes of red taffeta. The rest of their heavy costume is made up of hooped leggings, a short black skirt with a white beaded centrepiece, and a loose fitting black jacket with heavily embroidered cuffs and lapels.

Lisu

The **Lisu** (Lisaw in Thai), who originated in eastern Tibet, first arrived in Thailand in 1921 and are found mostly in the west, particularly between Chiang Mai and Mae Hong Son, but also in western Chiang Rai, Chiang Mai and Phayao provinces. Whereas the other hill tribes are led by the village headman or shaman, the Lisu are organised into patriarchal clans which have authority over many villages, and their strong sense of clan rivalry often results in public violence. Many Lisu villages are involved in the opium trade, but addiction rates are declining and the Lisu are turning increasingly to alternative cash crop production.

The Lisu live in extended families at moderate to high altitudes, in houses built on the ground, with dirt floors and bamboo walls. Both men and women dress colourfully. The women wear a blue or green parti-coloured knee-length tunic, split up the sides to the waist, with a wide black belt and blue or green pants. At New Year, dazzling outfits are worn by the women, including waistcoats and belts of intricately fashioned silver and turbans with multi-coloured pom-poms and streamers. Men wear green, pink or yellow baggy pants and a blue jacket.

Lawa

The history of the **Lawa** people (Lua in Thai) is poorly understood, but it seems likely that they have inhabited Thailand since at least the eighth century and they were certainly here when the Thais arrived 800 years ago. The Lawa believe that they migrated from Cambodia, but some archaeologists think that their origins lie in Micronesia, which they left perhaps 2000 years back.

This lengthy cohabitation with the Thais has produced large-scale integration, so that most Lawa villages are indistinguishable from Thai settlements and most Lawa speak Thai as their first language. However, in an area of about 500 square kilometres between Hot, Mae Sariang and Mae Hong Son, the Lawa still live a largely traditional life, although even here the majority have adopted Buddhism and Thai-style houses. The basis of their economy is subsistence agriculture, with rice grown on terraces according to a sophisticated rotation system.

Unmarried Lawa girls wear distinctive strings of orange and yellow beads, loose white blouses edged with pink, and tight skirts in parallel bands of blue, black, yellow and pink. After marriage, these brightly coloured clothes are replaced with a long fawn dress, but the beads are still worn. All the women wear their hair tied in a turban, and the men wear light-coloured baggy pants and tunics or, more commonly, Western clothes.

Lawa woman

OPIUM AND THE GOLDEN TRIANGLE

The production of **opium** has been illegal in Thailand since 1959, and with concerted attempts by the government to eliminate it, the size of the crop has been reduced by eighty percent in the last decade, to around twenty tonnes per year. Opium nevertheless remains an important cash crop of the Hmong, Yao, Lahu and Lisu hill tribes, and Thailand has now become an important conduit for opium from Burma and Laos, where production stands at 2500 tonnes per year and is still rising.

For the hill farmers, the attractions of the opium poppy are difficult to resist. It's an easy crop to grow, even on almost barren land; it's a highly productive plant, with each flower pod being tapped several times for its sap; and it yields a high value for a small volume – around B500 per kilo at source. Refined into heroin and transported to the US – the world's biggest market – the value of the powder is as much as 10,000 times greater.

The small-scale heroin refineries in the lawless region on the borders of Thailand, Burma and Laos have become so successful that the area has earned the nickname the "**Golden Triangle**". Two "armies" operate most of the trade within this area. The **Shan United Army**, which is fighting the Burmese government for an independent state for the Shan people, funds its weapons and manpower from the production of heroin. Led by the notorious warlord Khun Sa, the Shan United Army attempted to extend their influence inside Thailand during the 1960s, where they came up against the **Kuomintang** (KMT). These refugees from China, who fled after the communist takeover there, were at first befriended by the Thai and Western governments, who were pleased to have a fiercely anti-communist force patrolling this border area. The Kuomintang were thus able to develop the heroin trade, while the authorities turned a blind eye.

The Kuomintang and Shan Armies were once powerful enough to operate unhindered. In the last ten years, though, the danger of communist incursion into Thailand has largely disappeared, and the government has been able to concentrate on the elimination of the crop. In 1983 the Shan United Army were pushed out of their stronghold at Ban Hin Taek near Mae Salong, and over the border into Burma, and the Kuomintang in the surrounding area have been put on a determined "pacification" programme. With the destruction of huge areas of poppy fields, it has been necessary for the Thai government to give the hill tribes an alternative livelihood through the introduction of more legitimate cash crops. Yet opium cultivation continues in remote valleys, hidden from the Thai authorities, and opium abuse among the hill tribes themselves is if anything getting worse: over thirty percent of Hmong men, for example are addicted.

CHIANG MAI

Although rapid economic progress in recent years – due largely to tourism – has brought its share of problems, **CHIANG MAI** manages to preserve the irresistible atmosphere of an overgrown village. A population of 150,000 makes this the country's second city, but the contrast with the maelstrom of Bangkok could scarcely be more pronounced: the people are famously easy-going and even speak more slowly than their cousins in the capital, while the old quarter, set within a two-kilometre-square moat, has retained many of its traditional wooden houses and quiet, leafy gardens. Chiang Mai's elegant temples are the primary tourist sights, but these are no pre-packaged museum pieces – they're living community centres, where you're quite likely to be approached by monks keen to chat and practise their English. Inviting craft shops, rich cuisine and riverside bars further enhance the city's allure, making Chiang Mai a place that detains many travellers longer than they expected.

Chiang Mai – "New City" – was **founded** as the capital of Lanna in 1296, on a site indicated by the miraculous presence of deer and white mice, and it has remained the north's most important city ever since. Lanna's golden age under the Mengrai dynasty, when most of the city's notable temples were founded, lasted until the Burmese captured Chiang Mai in 1556. Two hundred years passed before the Thais pushed the Burmese back beyond Chiang Mai to roughly where they are now, and the **Burmese influence** is still strong – not just in art and architecture, but also in the rich curries and soups served here, which are better "Burmese" food than you can find in modern-day Burma. After the recapture of the city, the *chao* (princes) of Chiang Mai remained nominal rulers of the north until 1939, but with communications rapidly improving from the beginning of this century, Chiang Mai was brought firmly into Thailand's mainstream as the region's administrative and service centre.

In the past few years, concern has grown about Chiang Mai's traffic jams and fumes, and a solution whereby the city would be split in two is being seriously considered; most businesses would move out to a new site while the present town and its ancient temples would be preserved as a tourist enclave. As it is, the city remains bounded by a huge ring road, the Superhighway, and divides roughly into two main parts: the **old town**, bounded by the well-maintained moat and occasional remains of the city wall, where you'll find most of Chiang Mai's traditional wats, and the **new town centre**, between the moat and the Ping River to the east, for hotels, shops and travel agents. The main concentration of guest houses and restaurants hangs between the two, centred on the landmark of Pratu Tha Pae (**Tha Pae Gate**) in the middle of the east moat.

The main tourist activities in Chiang Mai – apart from eating, drinking and relaxing – are visiting the **temples** and **shopping** for handicrafts, pursuits which many find more appealing here than in the rest of Thailand. A pilgrimage to **Doi Suthep**, the mountain to the west of town, should not be missed, however, to see the sacred temple and the views over half of northern Thailand. Beyond the city limits, a number of other day trips can be made, such as to the ancient temples of Lamphun or to the orchid farms and elephant shows of the Mae Sa valley – and, of course, Chiang Mai is the main centre for hill-tribe **trekking**.

Arrival, information and transport

Most people **arrive** at the **train station** on Charoen Muang Road, just over 2km from Tha Pae Gate on the eastern side of town, or at the Arcade **bus station** on Kaeo Nawarat Road, 3km out to the northeast. Getting from either of these to the centre is easy by bus, songthaew or tuk-tuk (see below). Some private air-con buses between Bangkok and Chiang Mai use the central Anusarn Market, off Chang Klan Road, whereas if you've come south from Fang or Tha Ton, you'll wind up at the Chang Puak bus station on Chotana Road, 2km north of Tha Pae Gate. If you've bought a cheap package deal on Khao San Road in Bangkok, you should be dropped at the guest house you've paid for.

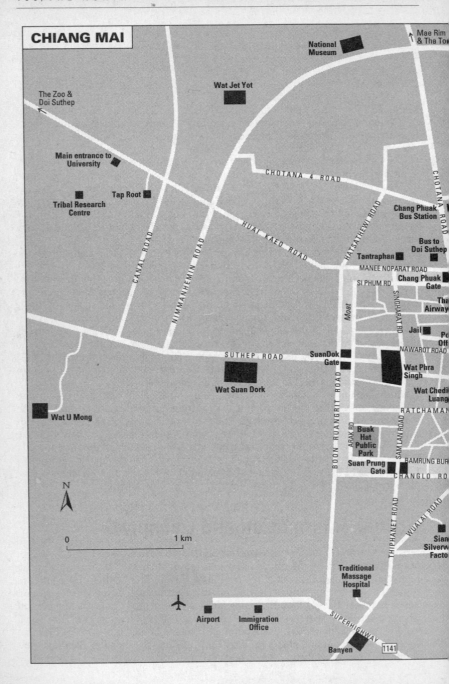

CHIANG MAI

National Museum

Mae Rim & Tha Ton

Wat Jet Yot

The Zoo & Doi Suthep

CHOTANA 4 ROAD

CHOTANA ROAD

Main entrance to University

HUAI KAED ROAD

Chang Phuak Bus Station

Tap Root

HATSATHEWI ROAD

Bus to Doi Suthep

Tribal Research Centre

CANAL ROAD

NIMMANHEMIN ROAD

Tantraphan

MANEE NOPARAT ROAD

SI PHUM RD

Chang Phuak Gate

Moat

SINGHARAT RD

Tha Airway

Jail

Po Off

NAWAROT ROAD

SUTHEP ROAD

SuanDok Gate

Wat Phra Singh

Wat Suan Dork

Wat Chedi Luang

RATCHAMAN

Wat U Mong

BOON RUANGRIT ROAD

ARAK RD

SAM LAN ROAD

N

Buak Hat Public Park

Suan Prung Gate

BAMRUNG BUR

CHANGLO RO

0   1 km

THIPHANET ROAD

WUALAI ROAD

Sian Silverw Facto

Traditional Massage Hospital

Airport   Immigration Office

SUPERHIGHWAY

Banyen   1141

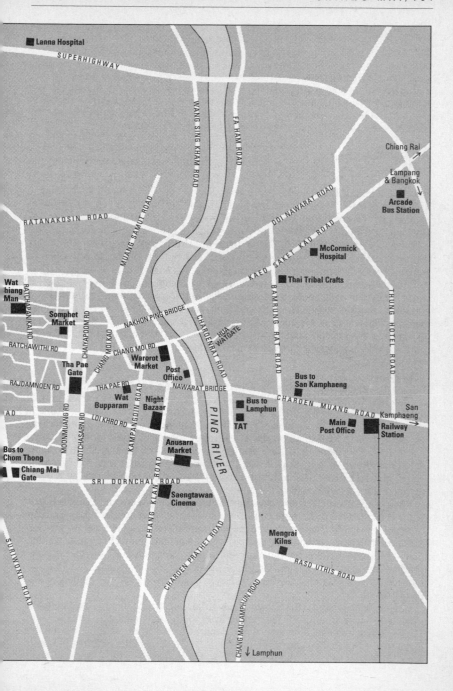

> The telephone code for Chiang Mai is ☎053.

Arriving at the **airport**, 3km southwest of the centre, you'll find a bank, a post office with an overseas phone, and a TAT office. A *Thai Airways* minibus to any destination in town should cost B30, while a taxi will run B70 for the car or B30 per person for three or more passengers. The #6 bus, which stops outside the airport compound, follows a tedious route around the outskirts.

Information

TAT operates out of a swish new **information** office (daily 8.30am–4.30pm; ☎235334) at 105/1 Chiang Mai–Lamphun Road, on the east bank of the river just south of Nawarat Bridge, where you can pick up various handouts and a simple free **map** of the city. Perhaps their most valuable service, however, is their information about recommended **trekking agencies** – the TAT lists are the most reliable guide through the morass of competing companies. Equally important for any trekker is the **Hill Tribe Research Institute** at Chiang Mai University (Mon–Fri 9am–4pm), between Huai Kaeo and Suthep roads, where you can consult detailed maps and generally get clued up on the cultures of the north.

Nancy Chandler's Map of Chiang Mai, sold in many shops all over the city, is very handy for a detailed exploration: like her Bangkok map, it highlights a personal choice of sights, shops, restaurants and various oddities, as well as local transport information. Of many other inferior city maps, the *BP* map is widely available, and up-to-date, and also features one of the least inaccurate maps of the north on the reverse side – useful for onward travel.

Transport

Although you can comfortably walk between the most central temples, **bicycles** are the best way of looking round the old town and, with a bit of legwork, getting to the attractions outside the moat. Trusty sit-up-and-beg models are available at many outlets on the roads along the eastern moat for about B30 a day, and dealers along Chang Klan Road proffer a few ropey mountain bikes for B60 a day. If you don't fancy pedalling through the heat and pollution, Chiang Mai has plenty of **motorbikes** for rent, though they really come into their own for exploring places around Chiang Mai and in the rest of the north (see "Listings" at the end of this section for addresses of outlets).

The cheapest form of public transport is the small, often crowded yellow **buses** (B2 flat fare), which, although routes are sometimes eccentric, all pass Tha Pae Gate at some stage. The most useful services are given in the box below. Quicker and more efficient are the **songthaews**, which will take you right to your destination – red ones shuttle around the city, other colours serve outlying villages. They charge according to how far you're going and you may well have to bargain – expect to pay B10 for a medium distance, say from the railway station to Tha Pae Gate.

Chiang Mai is also stuffed with **tuk-tuks**, for which heavy bargaining is expected – allow around B30 for getting from the railway station to Tha Pae Gate. They're quick and useful on arrival and departure, and work out quite reasonable if you're in a group. You can hire a tuk-tuk for a day for as little as B100, but there are strings attached: half the day will be spent sightseeing, the other half shopping along the San Kamphaeng Road at stores chosen by the driver, where he'll pick up a commission for bringing you there. If you fancy really mixing it with the traffic, you could treat yourself to a **self-drive tuk-tuk** for B400 a day from *PC Travel*, 56 Chaiyapoom Rd.

The town still has a few cheap **samlors**, but they're really too dangerous on the busy, fast streets, and the drivers are notorious for dealing dope to farangs and then shopping them to the police.

BUS ROUTES

#1 Charoen Muang Road–railway station–Tha Pae Gate–Wualai Road–Phra Pokklao Road–NW corner of the moat–Suthep Road.

#2 Chotana Road–Chang Puak bus station–Tha Pae Gate–Chang Klan Road–Charoen Prathet Road–Lamphun Road.

#3 Railway station–Arcade bus station–Tha Pae Gate–Wat Phra Singh–Huai Kaeo Road.

#4 Kaeo Nawarat Road–Arcade bus station–Tha Pae Gate–Wat Phra Singh–Suthep Road

---

Accommodation

Chiang Mai is well stocked with all kinds of **accommodation** and usually there are plenty of beds to go around, but many places fill up from December to February and at festival time. For expensive hotels you'll need a booking at these times, and for guest houses it's a good idea to phone ahead – you may not be able to book a place, but you can save yourself a journey if the place is full. Many touts at the bus and train stations offer a free ride if you stay at their guest house, but you'll probably find that the price of a room is bumped up to pay for your ride. Be sure that you can trust your proprietor before you leave valuables in one of the **left-luggage rooms** while you go off trekking, because the hair-raising stories of theft and credit-card abuse are often true. (Most of the banks have cheap safe-deposit boxes.)

Cheap

In all ways that matter, the choice of **budget guest houses** is better in Chiang Mai than in Bangkok: they're generally more comfortable, friendly and quiet, and often have their own outdoor cafés. Many of the cheaper places make their money from hill-tribe trekking, which can be convenient, as a trek often needs a lot of organising beforehand.

Most cheap places are gathered around the eastern side of the old moat, along **Moonmuang** and **Chaiyapoom roads** and on the surprisingly quiet adjoining sois. This puts you between the old city and the new shopping centre, in the middle of a larder of Thai and travellers' restaurants. A more bucolic alternative is the string of riverside places along **Charoenrat Road**, away from it all on the east bank of the river.

Chiang Mai Guest House, 91 Charoen Prathet Rd (☎276501). Rambling old house with overgrown garden café by the river. Spotless, airy doubles with shared hot showers from B150.

Chiang Mai Youth Hostel 1, 21/8 Chang Klan Rd (☎236737). Very clean, quiet and reliable, but 1500m from the Night Bazaar. Dorm beds B50, tiled rooms with hot showers and fans B150 single, B200 double (B300 a/c).

Chiang Mai Youth Hostel 2, Soi 3, Phra Pokklao Rd (☎210455). Cheap and adequate, with reductions for IYHA members. B30 dorm bed, singles from B50, doubles from B60.

Chang Moi Guest House, 29 Chang Moi Kao, behind Chaiyapoom Rd (☎251839). Clean, family-run house, with doubles from B50 (shared hot showers).

Gold Riverside, 282/3 Charoenrat Rd. Quiet and remote, in a leafy compound. Brick chalets with bathrooms from B80.

Hollanda Montri, 365 Charoenrat Rd (☎242450). Clean and friendly with spacious modern block by river. B100 single, B140 double, all with hot-water bathrooms.

Kent Guest House, Soi 1 Ratchamanka (☎217578). Clean and well-run. Rooms with bathrooms B100 single, B120 double.

Lamchang House, 24 Soi 7, Moonmuang Rd (☎210586). Gloomy, adequate rooms with shared hot showers in a peaceful, shady compound. B60 single, B80 double.

Lek House, 22 Chaiyapoom Rd. Central and set back from the road, with clean rooms round a shaded garden from B70 single, B80 double.

Northland House, Soi 2, Talat Ton Phayom, off Suthep Rd (☎249115). Large, clean rooms with hot showers for B100. Way out west, but free transport from their booth at the train station.

Somsook Minicourt, 56 Chaiyapoom Rd (☎251294). Modern, friendly place opposite *Lek House*; comfy rooms with bathrooms B80 single, B100 double.

Thana Guest House, 27/8 Soi 4, Tha Pae Rd (☎279794). Popular rowdy hangout. Clean rooms for B70 single, B100 double (shared hot showers).

Times Square, Soi 6, Tha Pae Rd (☎232448). High standards, but situated on the noisy corner of Kotchasarn Rd. Clean singles with shared hot showers from B60, doubles from B100.

Moderate

For a little over B300 for a double, you can buy yourself considerably more comfort than the bottom-bracket accommodation provides. By far the best of these **moderate** places are the upmarket guest houses and lodges, which as well as providing good facilities (hot water and often air-conditioning) do a good line in decor and atmosphere. Chiang Mai is also scattered with dozens of bland, no-frills hotels in the same price range, of which the best few are included here.

Chiang Mai Phucome, 21 Huai Kaeo Rd (☎211026). Relaxed hotel, popular with businessmen. Basic luxury facilities from B540 per room.

Galare Guest House, 7 Charoen Prathet Rd (☎273885). Smart, popular place with terrace and shady lawn overlooking river. Clean, quiet rooms for B400 fan, B500 a/c.

Gap's House, 3 Soi 4, Ratchdamnoen Rd (☎278140). Best deal in town, especially welcoming to lone travellers. Plush a/c rooms with hot showers in a relaxing, leafy compound strewn with antiques. B175 single, from B300 double, including American breakfast. Free bicycles.

Montri Hotel, 2–6 Ratchdamnoen Rd (☎211069). Beside noisy Tha Pae Gate, but good value. Smart, clean doubles for B320 fan, B370 a/c.

Once Upon A Time Lodge, 385/2 Charoen Prathet Rd (☎274932). Camp nostalgia in a traditional house with riverside garden on the south side of town. Rooms from B800.

River View Lodge, 25 Soi 2, Charoen Prathet Rd (☎271109). Tasteful alternative to international-class hotels with beautiful riverside garden and bags of character. Quiet rooms from B650.

Top North Guest House, 15 Soi 2, Moonmuang Rd (☎278900; Bangkok ☎02/251 8448). Modern, unpretentious place with a swimming pool, in a quiet enclave of guest houses. A/c rooms B400, fan rooms B300.

Expensive

Clustered around the night bazaar and out towards Doi Suthep, Chiang Mai's **expensive hotels** aren't quite up to Bangkok's very high standards, but the best of them lay on all the expected luxuries plus traditional Lanna architectural touches. In general, top-end room prices are more reasonable here than in Bangkok.

Chiang Mai Orchid, 100 Huai Kaeo Rd (☎222099; Bangkok ☎02/245 3973). Grand, tasteful hotel on the northwest side of town. From B1700 single, B2000 double.

Chiang Mai Plaza, 92 Sri Dornchai Rd (☎270036; Bangkok ☎02/253 1276). Sprawling and unfussy hotel, but ragged at the edges. From B1600 single, B1800 double.

Dusit Inn, 112 Chang Klan Rd (☎281033; Bangkok reservations ☎02/238 4790). Tidy, centrally located hotel with impeccable standards. Elegant rooms from B1900 single, B2300 double.

Mae Ping Hotel, 153 Sri Dornchai Rd (☎270160; Bangkok reservations ☎02/235 1350). Chiang Mai's newest luxury hotel in the former red-light area. Massive and characterless with rooms at B1200 single, B1400 double.

CHIANG MAI'S FESTIVALS

Chiang Mai is the best and busiest place in the country to see in the Thai New Year, **Songkhran**, which takes over the city between April 13 and 16. The most obvious role of the festival is as an extended "rain dance" in the driest part of the year, when huge volumes of canal water are thrown about in a communal water fight that spares no one a drenching. The other elements of this complex festival are not as well known but no less important. Communities get together to build sand castles in the shape of chedis in the temple compounds, which they cover with coloured flags – this bestows merit on any ancestors who happen to find themselves in hell and may eventually release them from their torments, and also shows an intent to help renovate the wat in the year to come. Houses are given a thorough spring-clean to see out the old year, while Buddha images are cleaned, polished and sprinkled with lustral water, before being ceremonially carried through the middle of the water fight, to give everyone the chance to throw water on them and receive the blessing of renewal. Finally, younger family members formally visit their elders during the festival to ask for their blessings, while pouring scented water over their hands.

Loy Krathong, on the night of the full moon in November, has its most showy celebration at Sukhothai, but Chiang Mai is not far behind. While a spectacular but unnerving firework fiesta rages on the banks, thousands of candles are gently floated down the Ping River in beautiful lotus-leaf boats. People hope in this way to float away any sins or ill luck they have incurred, and give thanks to Mae Kong Kha, the ancient water goddess, for the rainy season. In northern Thailand, the parallel event of **Loy Khome** takes place during the daytime, when brightly coloured paper hot-air balloons (*khome fai*), often with fireworks attached, are released to carry away problems and bad luck, and honour the Buddha's top-knot, which he cut off when he became an ascetic. According to legend, the top-knot is looked after by the Buddha's mother in heaven.

Chiang Mai's brilliantly colourful **flower festival**, usually on the first weekend of February, also attracts huge crowds. The highlight is a procession of floats, modelled into animals, chedis, and even scenes from the *Ramayana*, which are then covered in flowers.

The City

Chiang Mai feels less claustrophobic than most large towns in Thailand, being scattered over a wide plain and broken up by waterways: in addition to the moat encircling the old town, the gentle Ping River brings a breath of fresh air to the eastern side of the new centre. A good place to watch the river, whose east bank remains largely green and rural, is from the footbridge over the river at the east end of Chang Moi Road, near the noisy, pungent food markets on the west bank. To the south spreads the modern and hectic shopping area around Tha Pae and Chang Klan roads, while the great wats lie mostly in the quieter parts away to the west.

Wat Phra Singh

If you see only one temple in Chiang Mai it should be **Wat Phra Singh**, at the far western end of Ratchadamnoen Road in the old town (bus #3 or #4), perhaps the single most impressive array of buildings in the city. The largest structure, a colourful modern viharn fronted by naga balustrades, hides from view a rustic wooden bot, a chedi constructed in 1345 to house the ashes of King Kam Fu, and the beautiful **Viharn Lai Kam**, the highlight of the whole complex. This wooden gem from the early nineteenth century is a textbook example of Lanna architecture, with its squat, multi-tiered roof and exquisitely carved and gilded pediment: if you feel you're being watched as you approach, it's the sinuous double arch between the porch's central columns, which represents the Buddha's eyebrows.

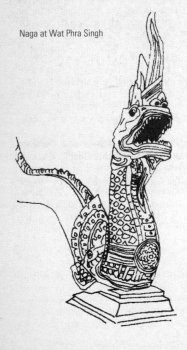

Naga at Wat Phra Singh

Inside sits one of Thailand's three **Phra Singh** (or Sihing) Buddha images (see p.73), a portly, radiant and much-revered bronze in a fifteenth-century Lanna style. The image's setting is enhanced by the colourful **murals** of action-packed tableaux, which give a window on life in the north a hundred years ago: courting scenes and piggyback fights, merchants, fishermen and children playing. The murals illustrate two different stories: on the right-hand wall is an old folk tale, the *Sang Thong*, about a childless king and queen who are miraculously given a beautiful son, the "Golden Prince", in a conch shell; those on the left, which have been badly damaged by water, show the story of the mythical swan Suwannahong, who forms the magnificent prow of the principal royal barge in Bangkok. Incidentally, what look like Bermuda shorts on the men are in fact **tattoos**: in the last century, all boys in the north were tattooed from navel to kneecap, an agonising ordeal undertaken to show their courage and to make themselves beautiful to women.

Wat Chedi Luang

From Wat Phra Singh a ten minute walk east along a quiet stretch of Ratchadamnoen Road brings you to **Wat Chedi Luang** on Phra Pokklao Road, where an enormous chedi, toppled from 90m to its present 60m by an earthquake in 1545, presents an intriguing spectacle – especially in the early evening when the resident bats flit around. You'll need a titanic leap of the imagination, however, to picture the chedi as it was in the fifteenth century, when it was covered in bronze plates and gold leaf, and housed the Emerald Buddha – the crumbling structure is at present covered in wooden scaffolding, which gives it the appearance of a kneeling giant undergoing acupuncture. In an unprepossessing modern building by the main entrance stands the city's navel pillar, the *lak muang*, sheltered by a stately eucalyptus tree which, the story has it, will stand for as long as the city's fortunes prosper.

If you've got time, pop in on **Wat Pan Tao** next door to see the wonderfully gnarled wooden viharn, a classic of graceful Lanna architecture.

Wat Chiang Man

From Wat Chedi Luang, the old town's main commercial street, Phra Pokklao Road, heads north past a monument to King Mengrai, the founder of Chiang Mai, and the conspicuous old provincial office, set in its own small piazza. Turn right along Wiang Kaeo Road to reach the oldest temple in Chiang Mai, **Wat Chiang Man**, fifteen minutes' walk from Chedi Luang.

Erected by Mengrai on the site where he first pitched camp, the wat is most notable for two dainty and very holy Buddha images housed in the viharn to the right of the entrance: the **Phra Sila**, a graceful stone work carved in northern India in the sixth century BC, stands in the typical *tribunga* or hipshot stance; its partner, the **Phra Setangamani** (or Crystal Buddha), made four centuries later probably in Lavo (modern Lopburi), is much revered by the inhabitants of Chiang Mai for its rain-making powers and is carried through the streets during the Songkhran festival to help the rainy season on its way. Neither image is especially beautiful, but a powerful aura is created by making them difficult to see, high up behind three sets of iron bars. Check out the chedi at the back of the compound, for the herd of stone elephants on whose backs it sits.

Chiang Mai National Museum

For a fuller picture of Lanna art and culture, head for the grand **National Museum** (9am–4pm Wed–Sun; B10), on the northwestern outskirts of Chiang Mai: leave the old town through Chang Puak Gate on the northern moat, then go up Chotana Road, a crowded shopping street, for 2km, before turning left along the Superhighway to reach the museum after about 1km. The #2 bus will get you to the junction of Chotana and the Superhighway, where you could switch to the #6 bus or start walking (about 15min); otherwise bike it, or charter a tuk-tuk or songthaew from the centre of town.

The museum's neat lawns and impressive architecture, mixing modern materials with traditional stylistic elements, contrast palatially with the tedium of the Superhighway. Inside, the airy rooms are cool enough for a long browse, and the collection, though it doesn't quite match the grandness of its setting, is engrossing and liberally labelled. The ground floor supports a wide range of beautiful **Buddha images**, including a humble, warmly smiling sandstone head from Haripunjaya (Lamphun), representing the earliest northern style, and many statues from the golden age of Lanna sculpture in the fifteenth and sixteenth centuries, when images were produced in two contrasting styles.

One group, which resembles images from northern India, has been called the **"lion-type"**, after the Shakyamuni ("Lion of the Shakyas") archetype at the great Buddhist temple at Bodhgaya, the site of the Buddha's enlightenment. It's been conjectured that a delegation sent by King Tilok to Bodhgaya in the 1450s brought back not only a plan of the temple to be used in the building of Wat Jet Yot, but also a copy of the statue, which became the model for hundreds of Lanna images. These broad-shouldered and plump-bellied Buddhas are always seated with the right hand in the touching-the-earth gesture, while the face is well-rounded with pursed lips and a serious, majestic demeanour: typical of this style is the massive bronze head with chubby cheeks and disdainfully hooded eyes which dominates one end of the downstairs hall. The second type is the **"Thera Sumana"** style named after the monk Mahathera Sumana, who came from Sukhothai in 1369 to establish his Sri Lankan sect in Lanna. The museum is well stocked with this type of image – though confusingly, they're labelled "late Chiang Saen" – which show strong Sukhothai influence, with an oval face and a flame-like *ushnisha* on top of the head. A number of crude wooden Buddhas round off the story of Lanna styles – they were carved after 1556, when, under Burmese domination, the region's sculpture became little more than popular folkcraft.

Also on this floor there's a fine exhibition of **ceramics**, including simple wares for everyday use, some dainty porcelain and Sawankhalok-style celadon (see p.167) – much of it produced at the local kilns near San Kamphaeng – the latter typified by a muddy green plate decorated with wriggling fish. And if you've ever wondered what the **relics** enshrined in Thailand's chedis look like, the answer is revealed here in a humble brass bowl containing some highly venerable black pellets. Upstairs, a free-form "local history" room contains everything from early photos of the town and giant ceremonial drums to intricately carved opium weights and musty hill-tribe costumes.

Wat Jet Yot

Set back from the Superhighway ten minutes' walk west of the museum, the peaceful garden temple of **Wat Jet Yot** is named after the "seven spires" of its unusual chedi, which lean together like brick chimneys at crazy angles. The temple was built in 1455 by King Tilok, to represent the seven places around Bodhgaya in India which the Buddha visited in the seven weeks following his enlightenment. Around the base of the chedi, delicate stuccos portray cross-legged deities serenely floating in the sky, a role model for all yogic fliers; their faces are said to be those of King Tilok's relatives.

The zoo and arboretum

About 1km beyond Wat Jet Yot, the Superhighway ends at the junction with Huai Kaeo Road, a broad avenue of posh residences and hotels, which starts out from the northwest corner of the moat and ends at the foot of Doi Suthep. Bus #3 runs up Huai Kaeo, past the sprawling campus of Chiang Mai University to **Chiang Mai Zoo** (daily 8am–6pm; B10 adults, B5 children), at the base of the mountain. Started as a menagerie of a missionary family's pets, the zoo now extends over an attractive 36-acre park, run by the municipality. Despite a disorientating layout, it makes a diverting visit, especially for kids: housed in modern, relatively comfortable conditions is a huge collection of colourful Asian birds, monkeys and larger mammals, including the most popular attraction, Thai elephants.

An unprepossessing park next door, where you'll often see joggers toiling in the heat and itinerant monks sleeping or meditating under their parasols, is in fact a small **arboretum** (daily 8.30am–4.30pm; free), with name tags stuck to the plants and trees, so you can mug up on them before going upcountry.

Wat Umong

More of a park than a temple, **Wat Umong** makes an unusual, charming place for a stroll in the western suburbs. If you're coming from the zoo, it's best to take a tuk-tuk or songthaew around the university campus. From the centre of town, you can take bus #4 or #1, or a songthaew along Suthep Road for about 2km; ask for the wat and, from where you're dropped off, it's a fifteen-minute walk down a winding lane to the left.

According to legend the wat was built in the 1380s by King Ku Na for a brilliant but deranged monk called Jan, who was prone to wandering off into the forest to meditate. Because Ku Na wanted to be able to get Jan's advice at any time, he founded this wat and decorated the **tunnels** (*umong*) beneath the chedi with paintings of trees, flowers and birds to simulate the monk's favoured habitat. Some of the old tunnels can still be explored, where obscure fragments of paintings and one or two small modern shrines can be seen. Above the tunnels, frighteningly lavish nagas guard the staircase up to the overgrown **chedi** and a grassy platform supporting a grotesque black statue of the Buddha, all ribs and veins: it shows him during his six years of self-mortification, before he realized that he should avoid extremes along the Middle Path to enlightenment. Behind the chedi, the ground slopes away to a **lake** inhabited by hungry carp, where locals come to study and talk. On a tiny island here, reached by a concrete bridge, stands a statue of Buddhadasa Bhikkhu, whose eclectic philosophy is followed at Wat Umong. Meditation classes in English are sometimes held here on Sunday afternoons, when a German monk is in residence.

Throughout the tranquil wooded grounds, the temple's diverse philosophy comes stridently alive: educational signs are pinned to nearly every tree, displaying outrageous cartoons of sinning dogs and simple Buddhist maxims. Colourful and surreal didactic paintings also cover the modern hall near the entrance. At the entrance gate, handicrafts are sold by the community of disabled people who have a house and workshop in the wat.

Fasting Buddha

Wat Suan Dork

From the turn-off to Wat Umong, Suthep Road heads back towards town, meeting the western moat at Suan Dork Gate. Halfway along this stretch of the road, the *Hill tribe Products Foundation* (see below) sits in front of **Wat Suan Dork**, the "Flower Garden Temple", which was later surrounded by walls as part of Chiang Mai's fortifications. Legend says that Mahathera Sumana, when he was invited to establish his Sri Lankan sect here in 1369, brought with him a miraculous glowing relic. The king of Chiang Mai ordered a huge chedi – the one you see today – to be built in his flower garden, but as the pea-sized relic was being placed inside the chedi, it split into two parts: one half was buried here, the other found its way to Doi Suthep, after more miracles.

The brilliantly whitewashed chedi now sits next to a garden of smaller, equally dazzling chedis containing the ashes of the Chiang Mai royal family – framed by Doi Suthep to the west, this makes an impressive and photogenic sight, especially at sunset. Standing in the way of a panoramic shot of all the chedis, the huge, open-sided viharn on the east side has been crudely restored, but the bot at the back of the dusty compound is more interesting – decorated with lively *Jataka* murals, it enshrines a 500-year-old Buddha.

Wat Bupparam

On the east side of town at the mid-point of the main shopping drag, Tha Pae Road, **Wat Bupparam** makes for a mildly interesting stroll from the main guest house area around Tha Pae Gate. The new wedding-cake structure at the centre of the temple houses a magnificent black Buddha, which was apparently made for King Naresuan of Ayutthaya nearly 400 years ago from a single piece of teak. The **temple well** (off-limits for women) was used for watering the Buddha relics enshrined in the chedi and is also Chiang Mai's representative in the *murathaphi-sek* ceremony, when holy waters are gathered from Thailand's most auspicious localities for the ritual bathing of a new king.

Shopping

Shopping is an almost irresistible pastime in Chiang Mai, a hotbed of traditional cottage industries whose prices are low and standards of workmanship generally high. Two main shopping areas, conveniently operating at different times of the day, sell the full range of local handicrafts.

The **road to San Kamphaeng**, which extends due east from the end of Charoen Muang Road for 13km, is the main daytime strip, lined with every sort of shop and factory, where you can usually watch the craftsmen at work. The biggest concentrations are at Bo Sang, the "umbrella village", 9km from town, and at San Kamphaeng itself, once important for its kilns but now dedicated chiefly to silk-weaving. Red and white **buses** to San Kamphaeng leave Chiang Mai every fifteen minutes from in front of the *Bangkok Bank* on Charoen Muang Road – or you can pick one up on its inner-city circuit, which extends west down Tha Pae Road, along the east and south moats, past Wat Phra Singh, along the north moat and down Charoenrat Road. Numerous **tuk-tuk** drivers offer cheap (B100 or less) excursions, but the catch is that you go to the shops they choose, where they'll pick up a commission.

The other shopper's playground is the **night bazaar** on Chang Klan Road, which starts up at around 5pm. It's an unatmospheric modern shopping centre, surrounded by department stores, but it sells just about anything produced in Chiang Mai, plus crafts from other parts of Thailand, bootleg tapes and counterfeit designer goods. You're more likely to get ripped off or palmed off with junk or fakes here, but then again it's one of the few things to do at night in Chiang Mai.

For those with a serious interest in traditional crafts, **Tap Root**, tucked away behind the *Phucome Hotel* at 46/13 Soi 3, Huai Kaeo Rd (☎217945), is worth checking out – phone first to see if any activities are scheduled during your stay. Primarily a cooperative of artists, it arranges tours to surrounding villages to learn about local crafts such as pottery, woodcarving and the making of musical instruments, and organises craft workshops, performances and exhibitions around Chiang Mai.

Silk and cotton

The **silk** produced out towards SAN KAMPHAENG is richly coloured and hard-wearing, with an attractively rough texture. Bought off a roll, the material is generally cheaper than in Bangkok, though more expensive than in the northeast – prices vary from around B300 a metre for two-ply (for thin shirts and skirts) to B400 a metre for four-ply (suitable for suits). Ready-made clothes and made-to-measure tailoring, though cheap, are generally staid and more suited to formal wear. With branches 5km out of Chiang Mai and in San Kamphaeng itself, *Piankusol* is the best place to follow the silk-making process right from the cocoon. If you've got slightly more money to spend on better quality silk, head for *Shinawatra* (branches 7km out and in San Kamphaeng), which was once graced by no less a personage than Princess Diana.

Shops in San Kamphaeng and Chiang Mai sell the coarse, pale-coloured **cotton** made around Pa Sang, near Lamphun, starting at B80 per metre, which is nice for furnishings. Chiang Mai is also awash with geometric *mut mee* cloth and techni-colour Thai Lue weaves, but both are far better and cheaper in their place of origin: the former in the northeast, the latter around Chiang Khong and Nan.

At the **top end of the market**, *The Loom*, at 27/3 Ratchamanka Rd, specializes in gorgeous and very pricy "antique" silk and cotton weaves from the north, the northeast and Laos. For expensive, sumptuous clothes, ready-made by traditional northern methods, try *Classic Lanna Thai*, on the first floor of the night bazaar and on Moonmuang Road – gold-embroidered minidresses go for B18,000.

A more responsible way of spending your money is to take your custom to one of the **non-profit making shops**, whose proceeds go to the hill tribes. These include *The Hill Tribe Products Foundation*, on Suthep Road in front of Wat Suan Dork, which sells beautiful lengths of cotton and silk and a variety of hill-tribe gear, and *Thai Tribal Crafts*, 204 Bamrungrat Rd off Kaeo Nawarat Rd – *yaam*, the embroidered shoulder bags popular with Thai students, are particularly good here (around B250).

Woodcarving

Chiang Mai has a long tradition of **woodcarving**, which expresses itself in everything from salad bowls to half-size elephants. In the past the industry has relied on the cutting of Thailand's precious teak, but manufacturers are now beginning to use other hardwoods, while bemoaning their inferior quality.

The best place for carving is *Banyen*, 201 Wualai Rd at the junction with the Superhighway: the workmanship is topnotch and the wood is treated to last, although prices are quite high – a statue of a chubby, reclining boy of the kind found all over Chiang Mai will set you back B500 here. With refreshing honesty, the proprietors explain that a lot of their stuff is left outside for a few rainy seasons to give it a weathered look – elsewhere, pieces that have been weathered in this way are often passed off as antiques. *Banyen* also has an absorbing folk museum of wooden objects collected from around the north. If you're a real aficionado and have your own transport, head for BAN TAWAI, a large village of shops and factories where prices are low and you can watch the woodworkers in action – to get there, follow Highway 108 south from Chiang Mai 13km to Hang Dong, then head east for 2km .

Lacquerware

Lacquerware can be seen in nearly every museum in Thailand, most commonly in the form of betel-nut sets, which used to be carried ceremonially by the slaves of grandees as an insignia of rank and wealth (see p.308). Betel-nut sets are still produced in Chiang Mai according to the traditional technique, whereby a woven bamboo frame is covered with layers of rich red lacquer and decorated with black details. A variety of other objects, such as trays and jewellery boxes, are also produced, some decorated with gold leaf on black gloss. Just about every other shop in town sells lacquerware: *Napa Lacquerware*, 3km towards San Kamphaeng, is the best place to see the intricate process of manufacture, where gold-leaf trinket boxes cost around B500.

Celadon

Celadon, sometimes known as greenware, is a delicate variety of stoneware which was first made in China over 2000 years ago and was later produced in Thailand, most famously at Sukhothai and Sawankhalok. Several kilns in Chiang Mai have revived the art, the best of them being *Mengrai Kilns*, whose showroom at 31/1 Rasd Uthis Rd is quite hard to find – take Chiang Mai–Lamphun Road down the east bank of the river, turn left after 1km at the tree roundabout, and the showroom is on the left after 100m. Sticking to the traditional methods, *Mengrai* produces beautiful hand-crafted vases, boxes and plates, thrown in elegant shapes and covered with transparent green and blue glazes from as little as B200.

Umbrellas and paper

The village of BO SANG bases its fame on souvenir **umbrellas** – made of silk, cotton or mulberry paper and decorated with bold, painted colours (from about B100 for a kid's parasol) – but the artists who work here will also paint a small motif on your bag or camera in two minutes flat. The grainy mulberry **paper** (*sa*) is sold in Chiang Mai's night bazaar opposite *Novotel*, beautifully bound into cheap sketch pads.

Jade

Chinese soft **jade** and nine colours of hard jade from Burma are worked into a great variety of objects, from chopsticks (B3000) to *trompe l'oeil* bunches of grapes (B8500), but the finest, translucent, hard jade is reserved for jewellery, usually deep green in colour, which is supposed to bring the wearer good health. You can watch the stone being cut, decorated and polished at *Chamchuree Lapidary*, about 8km towards San Kamphaeng – but for the very best workmanship and prices you need to visit Mae Sai on the Burmese border (see p.248).

Silver

Of the traditional craft quarters, only the **silversmiths'** area on Wualai Road remains in its original location. The *Siam Silverware Factory* on Soi 3 – a ramshackle and sulphurous compound loud with the hammering of hot metal – gives you a whiff of what this zone must have been like in its heyday. Attractive, chunky jewellery is sold cheaply at B25 per gramme here, while plates, bowls and cups are priced individually.

Eating

The main difficulty with eating in Chiang Mai is knowing when to stop. All over town there are cheap and enticing restaurants serving typically northern food, which has been strongly influenced by Burmese cuisine, especially in curries such as the spicy *kaeng hang lay* (or "Chiang Mai curry"), made with pork, ginger and coconut cream, often with added tamarind. Another favourite local dish is Chiang Mai *nam*, spicy pork sausage – although the uncooked, fermented varieties are probably not a wise move. At lunchtime the thing to do is to join the local workers in one of the simple cafés that put all their efforts into producing just one or two special dishes – the traditional meal at this time of day is *khao soi*, a thick broth of curry and coconut cream, with egg noodles and a choice of meat.

None of the Western food in Chiang Mai is brilliant, and it's generally more expensive than Thai, but sometimes it's very hard to resist. Easier to refuse are the restaurants which lay on touristy **cultural shows** with *khan toke* dinners, a selection of northern dishes eaten on the floor off short-legged lacquer trays. There are better places to sample the region's food, and the hammy dancing displays, often with embarrassing audience participation, are a dubious diversion.

Thai

Anusarn Market, Chang Klan Rd. Happy night-time hunting ground of open-air stalls and restaurants. The landmark is *King Prawn Jumping Fatty*, a vibrant restaurant with excellent seafood. On the same side, you'll find a stall serving very good *pat thai*, on the opposite side there's tasty grilled chicken with honey, mussel omelettes cooked up with great panache, and lots more.

Aroon Rai, 43 Kotchasarn Rd. Excellent northern food in popular no-frills restaurant, one of many open-air places on this stretch. Cheap to moderate.

AUM Vegetarian Food, on the corner of Ratchadamnoen and Moonmuang roads. Noisy and dingy, but cheap and interesting veggie dishes.

The Gallery, 25 Charoenrat Rd. Refined eaterie on soothing riverside terraces, behind a gallery for local artists. Interesting selection, slow service. Moderate to expensive, but big portions.

New Lamduon Fahharm Khao Soi, 352/22 Charoenrat Rd. Excellent *khao soi* prepared to a secret recipe, which was once cooked for no less a personage than King Bhumibol. Also satay, waffles and *somam* (spicy papaya salad). Way up the east bank of the river; open 9am–3pm only.

Pat Thai stall, alleyway on Tha Pae Rd, near *Roong Ruang Hotel*. Best *pat thai* in town, prepared with flaming theatricality. Worth queueing for. Open 6–9pm.

Sala Kai, 41 Nawarot Rd, off Phra Pokklao Rd. Delicious and very popular satay and *khao man kai* – boiled chicken breast served with broth and garlic rice. This and the surrounding cafés are especially handy if you're looking round the old town. Open 5am–2pm.

Suthasinee, 164/10 Chang Klan Rd. Great, creamy *khao soi*, and good *som tam* ordered from the stall outside. Lunch time only.

Ta-krite Restaurant, 17 Soi 1, Sam Lan Rd, on the south side of Wat Phra Singh. Delicious and varied cuisine, in a maze of rooms and balconies around a green and pleasant courtyard. Cheap to moderate.

Thanom Restaurant, Chaiyapoom Rd, near Tha Pae Gate. Great introduction to northern Thai and Burmese-style cooking, in startlingly clean surroundings. Moderate prices; closes 8pm.

European and all-rounders

Daret, 4 Chaiyapoom Rd. *The* cheap travellers' hangout with outdoor trestles and a friendly buzz. Famous fruit shakes, good breakfasts and back-home staples; pass over the Thai food. Cheap to moderate.

JJ Coffee Shop and Bakery, *Montri Hotel*, corner of Ratchadamnoen and Moonmuang roads. All kinds of food, but best for breakfast, with bread and croissants baked in front of your eyes. Sanitized atmosphere with air-conditioning and camp indoor garden. Moderate to expensive.

Old Banrai Steak House, Wiang Kaeo Rd, between Wat Chiang Man and *Thai Airways*. Nicely prepared slabs of buffalo steak and baked potatoes, which hit the spot after a hard trek. Moderate to expensive.

Papillon, 12/1 Rotfai Rd, by the railway station. Screw up your eyes and you could be in a French station restaurant. Honest but pricey food, reasonable wine by the glass. Good for breakfast off the train.

Pensione La Villa, 145 Ratchadamnoen Rd. Relaxing barn-style restaurant with good salads and the best pizzas in town. Expensive but good value. Closed Tues.

Times Square Guest House, Soi 6, Tha Pae Rd. Roof garden above Tha Pae Gate with good views to get your bearings. Tasty if sanitized Thai dishes, good French food and breakfasts. Moderate to expensive.

Nightlife

Although there's a clutch of subdued hostess bars bordering the east moat and a few gay sex bars offering go-go shows scattered around the outskirts, Chiang Mai's **nightlife** generally avoids Bangkok's excesses – most of the places below are bar-restaurants, geared to a relaxing night out. If your heart's set on dancing, some of the big hotels have predictable, Westernized night clubs: *Bubbles* at the *Porn Ping*, *77* at the *Orchid*, *The Wall* at *Chiang Inn*, *Plaza* at the *Plaza* all charge about B100 admission, including one drink.

Chiang Mai Tea House, Chiang Mai–Lamphun Rd, near TAT. Balconied teak house with live "country" music and unstuffy atmosphere. Good for drinks, especially cocktails; forget the food.

Heritage, 8 Soi 1, Hua Watgate (off Soi 2, Kaeo Nawarat Rd). Eccentric place for an expensive night out, where kitsch fountains and neon signs clash with the immaculate trappings of a teak-wallah's mansion. Classy Thai restaurant on back terrace, drinks at a gorgeous teak bar, or in the lounge to the sounds of weird Beatles imitators.

Old West, Manee Noparat Rd, next to *Tantraphan* department store. Bar of the moment with young Thais. Lively scene, with rock bands and sprawling outdoor terraces.

The Pub, 88 Huai Kaeo Rd. Homely, relaxing ex-pat hangout, rated by *Newsweek* as one of the world's best bars. As the name suggests: draught beer, darts, old-fashioned landlord.

The River, 239/1 Charoenrat Rd. Outside, tables on an unappealing stretch of river; inside, typical Thai night club till 4am – dark and friendly, with an impossibly loud MOR band.

Riverside, 9 Charoenrat Rd. Archetypal farang bolthole: candlelit terraces by the water, reliable Western and Thai food (moderate to pricey), extensive drinks list and cheap draught beer. Live bands perform slavish folk-rock covers. *Rim Ping* next door is an extension, with mostly Thai clientele. Usually packed.

Listings

Airlines *Thai Airways*, 240 Phra Pokklao Rd (☎277782).

Banks Dozens of banks are dotted around Tha Pae Rd, many of which offer safe-deposit boxes: those on Chang Klan Rd stay open for evening shoppers. *Bangkok Bank*, Chotana Rd (☎221306) handles refunds of lost *American Express* traveller's cheques.

Books *Suriwong* at 54/1 Sri Dornchai Rd and *DK* on Tha Pae Rd have a predictable selection of books in English. The *Library Service* at 21/1 Soi 2, Ratchamanka Rd (nearer Moonmuang Rd) trades second-hand books as well as selling advice on motorbike trekking (B50 – no charge if you buy breakfast there). The owner, David Unkovich, has also written *The Pocket Guide to Motorcycle Touring in Northern Thailand*.

Car rental Many outlets around Tha Pae Gate rent out cars and 4-wheel drives, from around B800 a day, although it's probably worth paying the extra at *AVIS*, which has an office at the *Dusit Inn* (☎281033) and charges B1200, including limited insurance.

Cinema Thai and Hong Kong romantic action comedies are standard fare at the *Saengtawan*, on the corner of Sri Dornchai and Chang Klan roads, but for American films, the English soundtrack is relayed into a separate room at the back of the auditorium.

Directory enquiries (in English) ☎13 for Chiang Mai, ☎183 for other areas.

Hospitals *Lanna*, at 103 Superhighway (☎211037–41, 215020–2), east of Chotana Road, is Chiang Mai's top hospital, with a 24-hour emergency service and dentistry department. *McCormick* (☎241107) is also used to farangs and is nearer, on Kaeo Nawarat Road.

Immigration On the southern leg of the Superhighway, 300m before the airport on the left (☎277510).

Jail Amongst the prisoners at the jail on Ratchawithi Rd are dozens of farangs, usually serving unimaginably long sentences for drugs offences. With no family or friends at hand, they rely on casual visits to get them out of their cells. If you make a visit, soap, toothpaste, newspapers, cigarettes and just about anything else are appreciated. Check the guest house notice boards for the latest.

Laundry *Nulvarat*, 29/1 Chang Moi Kao (behind Chaiyapoom Rd), which has machines and charges by the kilo, is cheap and reliable.

Meditation *Northern Insight Meditation Centre*, at Wat Ram Poeng on Canal Rd near Wat Umong (☎211620), holds month-long *vipassana* courses and has a resident farang instructor.

Motorbike rental Motorbikes can be rented from about B120 per day for an old 80cc step-through to B200 for a 125cc trail bike. The most reliable places are *65*, 65 Moonmuang Rd, and *AP*, 191 Moonmuang Rd. (See also "Books", above.)

Post and telephones The GPO is on Charoen Muang Rd near the railway station. Poste restante and other postal services are available downstairs at the usual times (a private packing service operates outside on Charoen Muang Rd); the overseas phone service upstairs is open 24hr. Many private agencies in town, for example in the basement of the Night Market, sell overseas calls, but at a higher rate. Chiang Mai's other post offices are on Praisanee Rd by Nawarat Bridge, on Phra Pokklao Rd and on Chotana Rd.

Thai boxing Dechanukrau Stadium, Khong Say Rd (off Charoen Muang Rd); Sat & Sun 8pm.

Tourist Police 105/1 Chiang Mai–Lamphun Rd; helpline ☎232508 6am–midnight, ☎222977 midnight–6am.

Traditional massage *Traditional Hospital*, 78/1 Soi Moh Shivagakomarpaj, off Wualai Rd opposite the *Old Chiang Mai Cultural Center* (daily 8.30am–4.30pm; ☎275085).

Around Chiang Mai

You'll never feel cooped up in Chiang Mai, as the surrounding countryside is dotted with day-trip options in all directions. Dominating the skyline to the west, **Doi Suthep** and its eagle's-nest temple are hard to ignore, and a wander around the pastoral ruins of **Wiang Kum Kam** on the southern periphery has the feel of fresh exploration. Further south, the quiet town of **Lamphun** offers classic sightseeing in the form of historically and religiously significant temples and a museum. In sharp contrast to the north, the **Mae Sa valley** is a kind of rural theme park and too artificial and exploitative for many tastes – for honest, unabashed commerce, head for the shopping strip which stretches east towards San Kamphaeng (described in the "Shopping" section above). All the trips described here can be done in half a day; longer excursions are dealt with later in the chapter.

Doi Suthep

A jaunt up **DOI SUTHEP**, the mountain which rises steeply at the city's western edge, is the most satisfying brief trip you can make from Chiang Mai, chiefly on account of beautiful **Wat Phra That Doi Suthep**, which dominates the hillside and gives a towering view over the goings-on in town. This is the north's holiest shrine, which takes its pre-eminence from a magic relic enshrined in its chedi and the miraculous legend of its founding. The original chedi here was built by King Ku Na at the end of the fourteenth century, after the glowing relic of Wat Suan Dork had self-multiplied just before being enshrined. A place had to be found for the clone, so Ku Na put it in a travelling shrine on the back of a white elephant and waited to see where the sacred animal would lead: it eventually climbed Doi Suthep, trumpeted three times, turned round three times, knelt down and died, thereby indicating that this was the spot. Ever since, it's been northern Thailand's most important place of pilgrimage, especially for the candlelit processions on **Maha Puja**, the anniversary of the sermon to the disciples, and **Visakha Puja**, the anniversary of the Buddha's birth, enlightenment and death.

Frequent **songthaews** leave the corner of Manee Noparat and Chotana roads for the sixteen-kilometre trip up the mountain (B30 to the wat). The road, although steep in places, is paved all the way and well-suited for **motorcycles**. At the end of Huai Kaeo Road, a statue of Khruba Srivijaya, the monk who organised the gargantuan effort to build the road from here to the wat, points the way to the temple.

A checkpoint halfway up is about the only sign that Doi Suthep is a **national park**: despite the nearness of the city, its rich mixed forests support 330 species of birds, and the area is a favoured site for nature study, second in the north only to the larger and less disturbed Doi Inthanon National Park. On the higher slopes there's a **campsite** (two-person tents can be rented for B50 a night) and large, simple **bungalows** (B1000 for 12 people), which can only be reached if you have your own transport – ask for a map at the checkpoint.

About 1km beyond the checkpoint, a good unpaved road on the right leads 3km to **Mon Tha Than Falls**, a beautiful and rarely visited spot, believed by some to be home to evil spirits. Camping is possible beside the pretty lower cascade, where a refreshment stall is open during the day. The higher fall is an idyllic five-metre drop into a small bathing pool, completely overhung by thick, humming jungle.

KHRUBA SRIVIJAYA

Khruba Srivijaya, the most revered monk in northern Thailand, was born in 1877 in a small village 100km south of Chiang Mai. His birth coincided with a supernatural thunderstorm and earthquake, after which he was named In Fuan, "Great Jolt", until he joined the monkhood. A generous and tireless campaigner, he breathed life into Buddhist worship in the north by renovating over a hundred religious sites, including Wat Phra That Haripunjaya in Lamphun and Wat Phra That Doi Tung near Mae Sai. His greatest work, however, was the construction in 1935 of the paved road up to Wat Phra That Doi Suthep, which beforehand could only be reached after a climb of at least five hours. The road was constructed entirely by the voluntary labour of people from all over the north, using the most primitive tools. The project gained such fame that it attracted donations of B20 million, and on any one day as many as 4000 people worked on it. So that people didn't get in each other's way, Khruba Srivijaya declared that each village should contribute 50 feet of road, but as more volunteers flocked to Chiang Mai, this figure had to be reduced to 10 feet. After just six months, the road was completed and Khruba Srivijaya took the first ride to the temple in a donated car.

When Khruba Srivijaya died in 1938, Rama VIII was so moved that he sponsored a royal cremation ceremony, which was held in 1946. The monk's relics were divided up and are now enshrined at Wat Suan Dork in Chiang Mai, Wat Phra Kaeo Don Tao in Lampang and at many other holy places throughout the north.

Wat Phra That Doi Suthep

Opposite a car park and souvenir village, a flight of 300 naga-flanked steps is the last leg on the way to Wat Phra That Doi Suthep – a nearby funicular (B5) provides a welcome alternative. From the temple's **lower terrace**, the magnificent views of Chiang Mai and the surrounding plain, 1000m below, are best in the early morning or late afternoon, though peaceful contemplation of the view is frequently shattered by people sounding the heavy, dissonant bells around the terrace – it's supposed to bring good luck.

Before going to the **upper terrace** you have to remove your shoes – and if you're showing a bit of knee or shoulder, the temple provides wraps to cover your impoliteness. This terrace is probably the most harmonious piece of temple architecture in Thailand, a dazzling combination of red, green and gold in the textures of carved wood, filigree and gleaming metal – even the tinkling of the miniature bells and the rattling of fortune sticks seem to keep the rhythm. A cloister, decorated with gaudy murals, tightly encloses the terrace, leaving room only for a couple of small minor viharns and the altars and ceremonial gold umbrellas which surround the central focus of attention, the **chedi**. This dazzling gold-plated beacon, a sixteenth-century extension of Ku Na's original, was modelled on the chedi at Wat Phra That Haripunjaya in Lamphun – which previously had been the region's most significant shrine – and has now become a venerated emblem of northern Thailand.

A small *hong*, or swan, on a wire stretching to the pinnacle is used to bless the chedi: a cup in the swan's beak is filled with water, a pulley draws the swan to the spire where the water is tipped out over the sides of the chedi. Look out also for a wooden statue at the northwestern corner of the chedi, showing a cockerel which used to peck the feet of visitors who entered with their shoes on.

Beyond the wat

Songthaews continue another 4km up the paved road to **Phuping Palace**, the residence for the royals when they come to visit their village development projects in the north. A viewpoint over the hills to the south, a rose garden and some pleasant trails through the forest are open to the public when the family is not in residence, but only from Friday to Sunday (8am–4pm).

About 3km from the palace along a dirt side road, BAN DOI PUI is a highly commercialized Hmong village, only worth visiting if you don't have time to get out into the countryside – seeing the Hmong is about all you'll get out of it.

Wiang Kum Kam

The well-preserved and rarely visited ruins of the ancient city of **WIANG KUM KAM** – traditionally regarded as the prototype for Chiang Mai – are hidden away in the picturesque, rural fringe of town, 5km south of the centre. According to folklore, Wiang Kum Kam was built by King Mengrai as his new capital of the north, but was soon abandoned because of inundation by the Ping River. Recent excavations, however, have put paid to that theory: Wiang Kum Kam was in fact established much earlier, as one of a cluster of fortified satellite towns that surrounded the Mon capital at Lamphun. After Mengrai had conquered Lamphun in 1281, he resided at Kum Kam for a while, raising a chedi, a viharn and several Buddha statues before moving on to build Chiang Mai. Wiang Kum Kam was abandoned sometime before 1750, probably as a result of a Burmese invasion.

The ancient city, which is about 3km square, can only be explored on a bicycle or a motorbike. The best way to approach it without getting lost is from Highway 1141, the southern leg of the Superhighway, which links the airport to Highway 11: immediately to the east of the Ping River bridge, take the signposted turning to the south.

About half of Wiang Kum Kam's twenty-two known temple sites have now been uncovered, along with a unique stone slab (now housed in the Chiang Mai National Museum) inscribed in a unique forerunner of the Thai script and a hoard of terracotta Buddha images. It's easiest to head first for **Chedi Si Liam**, reached 1km after the Ping River bridge, which provides a useful landmark: this much-restored Mon chedi, in the shape of a tall, squared-off pyramid with niched Buddha images, was built by Mengrai on the model of Wat Kukut in Lamphun, and is still part of a working temple.

Backtracking along the road you've travelled down from Chiang Mai, take the first right turn, turn right again and keep left through a scattered farming settlement to reach, after about 2km, **Wat Kan Thom** (aka **Chang Kham**), the centre of the old city and still an important place of worship. Archaeologists were only able to get at the site after much of it had been levelled by bulldozers building a playground for the adjacent school, but they have managed to uncover the brick foundations of Mengrai's viharn. The modern spirit house next to it is where Mengrai's soul is said to reside. Also in the grounds are a white chedi and a small viharn, both much restored, and a large new viharn displaying fine craftsmanship.

The real joy now is to head off along the trails through the thick foliage of the longan plantations to the northwest of Wat Kan Thom, back towards Chedi Si Liam. You'll come across surprisingly well-preserved chedis and red brick walls of Wiang Kum Kam's temples in a handful of shady clearings, with only a few stray cows and sprouting weeds for company.

Lamphun

Though capital of its own province, **LAMPHUN** is a small, disconsolate place,
living in the shadow of the tourist attention (and baht) showered on Chiang Mai,
26km to the north. The town's largely drab architecture is given some character
by the surrounding waterways, beyond which stretch lush ricefields and *lam yai*
(longan) plantations – the sweetness of the local variety is celebrated every year
in early August at the **Ngan Lam Yai** (Longan Festival), when the town comes
alive with processions of fruity floats, a drum-beating competition and a Miss Lam
Yai beauty contest. In welcome contrast with the rest of downtown Lamphun,
however, the ancient but lively working temples of Wat Phra That Haripunjaya
and Wat Kukut are worth aiming for on a half-day trip from Chiang Mai.

Lamphun's history dates back to the early ninth century, when the ruler of the
major Dvaravati centre at Lopburi sent his daughter, Chama Thevi, to found the
Buddhist state of **Haripunjaya** here. Under the dynasty established by Chama
Thevi, Haripunjaya flourished as a link in the trade route to Yunnan in southwest
China, although it eventually came under the suzerainty of the Khmers at
Angkor, probably in the early eleventh century. In 1281, after a decade of schem-
ing, King Mengrai of Chiang Mai conquered Lamphun and integrated it once and
for all into the Thai state of Lanna, which by then covered all of the north country.

The town

Chama Thevi's planners are said to have based their design for the town on the
shape of an auspicious conch shell. The rough outcome is a rectangle, narrower at
the north end than the south, with the Khuang River running down its kilometre-
long east side, and moats around the north, west and south sides. The main street,
Inthayongyot Road, bisects the conch from north to south, while the road to Wat
Kukut (Chama Thevi Road) heads out from the middle of the west moat.

One of the north's grandest and most important temples, **Wat Phra That
Haripunjaya** (Wat Hari for short) has its rear entrance on Inthayongyot Road
and its bot and ornamental front entrance facing the river. The earliest guess at
the date of its founding is 897, when the king of Haripunjaya is said to have built a
chedi to enshrine a hair of the Buddha. More certain is the date of the main
rebuilding of the temple, under King Tilokaraja of Chiang Mai in 1443, when the
present ringed chedi was erected in the then-fashionable Sri Lankan style (later
copied at Doi Suthep and Lampang). Clad in brilliant copper plates, it has since
been raised to a height of 50m, crowned by a gold umbrella.

The plain open courtyards around the chedi contain a compendium of religious
structures in a jarring mix of styles and colours. On the north side, the tiered
Haripunjaya-style pyramid of **Chedi Suwanna** was built in 1418 as a replica of
the chedi at nearby Wat Kukut. You get a whiff of southern Thailand in the open
space beyond the Suwanna chedi, where the **Chedi Chiang Yan** owes its resemblance to a pile of flattened pumpkins to the Srivijayan style. On either side of the
viharn (to the east of the main chedi) stand a dark red **belltower**, containing
what's claimed to be the world's largest bronze gong, and a weather-beaten
library on an ochre-coloured base. Just to add to the temple's mystique, an open
pavilion at the southwestern corner of the chedi shelters a stone indented with
four overlapping **footprints**, which are believed by fervent worshippers to
confirm an ancient legend that the Buddha once passed this way. Next to the
pavilion can be seen the **Phra Chao Tan Jai**, a graceful standing Buddha, and a

small **museum**, which houses bequests to the temple, including some beautiful Buddha images in the Lanna style.

Across the main road from Wat Hari's back entrance, the **National Museum** (Wed–Sun 9am–noon & 1–4pm; B10) contains a well-organised but not quite compelling collection of religious finds, and occasionally stages some interesting temporary exhibitions. The terracotta and bronze Buddha images here give the best overview of the distinctive features of the Haripunjaya style: large hair curls above a wide, flat forehead, bulging eyes, incised moustache and enigmatic smile.

Art-history buffs will get the most out of **Wat Kukut** (aka Wat Chama Thevi), though they'll bemoan the neon lights which decorate the tiers of the main chedi. Queen Chama Thevi is supposed to have chosen the site by ordering an archer to fire an arrow from the city's western gate – to retrace his epic shot, follow the road along the National Museum's southern wall to the west gate at the city moat, and keep going for nearly 1km along Chama Thevi Road. The two brick **chedis**, dated to 1218, are the only complete examples not just of Haripunjaya architecture, but of the whole Dvaravati style. The main chedi – Suwan Chang Kot – is tiered and rectangular, the smaller one octagonal, and both are inset with niches sheltering beautiful, wide-browed Buddha images in stucco, typical of the Haripunjaya style. Suwan Chang Kot, believed to enshrine Chama Thevi's ashes, lost its pinnacle at some stage, giving rise to the name Wat Kukut, the "topless" wat.

Practicalities

The direct (and scenic) route to Lamphun is Highway 106, for much of the way a stately avenue lined by thirty-metre-tall *yang* trees. Frequent white and blue **buses** from in front of the Chiang Mai TAT office make the journey (45min), stopping outside the back entrance of Wat Hari. If you turn up at Lamphun by **train**, it's a half-hour walk or a samlor ride southwest to the town centre.

An attractive nineteenth-century teak house and the former residence of the Prince of Lamphun, *Khum Ton Kaew*, behind the National Museum on Wangsai Road, now contains an expensive handicrafts shop downstairs and a good but overpriced **restaurant** on the balcony and in the garden. Basic cheap Thai food is served at cafés on Inthayongyot Road to the south of Wat Hari. It's unlikely you'll want to **stay overnight** in Lamphun, but if you do you'll probably end up in *Sri Lamphun*, 50m south of Wat Hari's back entrance, where noisy, grubby rooms start at B60; or try *Haw Pak Sawat Ari*, out towards Wat Kukut on the south side of Chama Thevi Road, which is not a regular hotel but keeps a few rooms for visiting archaeologists (B50 a night).

The Mae Sa valley

On the north side of Chiang Mai, Chotana Road turns into Highway 107, which heads off through a flat, featureless valley, past a golf course and an army camp, before reaching the small market town of MAE RIM after 16km. Turn left at Mae Rim to enter the **Mae Sa valley**, a twenty-kilometre strip of touristy sideshows, including a butterfly farm, a rose garden, several upmarket "hill station" resorts and a couple of unexciting waterfalls. The most interesting attractions are the orchid nurseries and the two elephant camps, where you can see logging shows in the morning and take an expensive elephant ride into the countryside (from B300 for 30min). If any of this takes your fancy, it's best to go on a tour from one of Chiang Mai's many travel agents, or on a rented motorbike.

EAST OF CHIANG MAI

From Chiang Mai, visitors usually head west to Mae Hong Son or north to Chiang Rai, but a trip eastwards to the ancient city-states of Lampang and Nan can be just as rewarding, not only for the dividends of going against the usual flow, but also for the natural beauty of the region's upland ranges and its eccentric variety of Thai, Burmese and Laotian art and architecture. Congenial **Lampang** contains Thai wats to rival those of Chiang Mai for beauty – in Wat Phra That Lampang Luang it has the finest surviving example of traditional northern architecture anywhere – and is further endowed with pure Burmese temples and some fine old city architecture. More difficult to reach but a more intriguing target is **Nan**, with its heady artistic mix of Thai and Laotian styles and steep ring of scenic mountains.

A few major **roads**, served by regular through buses from Chiang Mai, cross the region: Highway 11 heads southeast through Lampang and the junction town of Den Chai, before plummeting south to Phitsanulok; from Lampang Highway 1 heads north to Chiang Rai, and from Den Chai Highway 101 carries on northeast to Nan, almost on the border with Laos. The northern **railway** follows a course roughly parallel with Highway 11 through the region, and although trains here are generally slower than buses, the Lampang and Den Chai stations are useful if you're coming up from Bangkok.

Lampang and around

Slow passes and long tunnels breach the narrow, steep belt of mountains between Chiang Mai and **LAMPANG**, 100km to the southeast. The north's second largest town and an important transport hub – Highway 11, Highway 1 and the northern railway line all converge here – Lampang's attractions are undeniably low-key, and nearly all travellers sail through it on their way to the more trumpeted sights further north. But unlike most provincial capitals, it has the look of a place where history has not been completely wiped out: many notable temples and some houses survive in the traditional style, and the town makes few concessions to tourism. Out of town, the beautiful complex of Wat Phra That Lampang Luang is the main event in these parts, but while you're in the neighbourhood you could also stop by to watch a logging show at the Young Elephant Training Centre, on the road from Chiang Mai.

Founded as Kelang Nakhon by the ninth-century Haripunjaya queen, Chama Thevi, Lampang became important enough for one of her two sons to rule here after her death. After King Mengrai's conquest of Haripunjaya in 1281, Lampang suffered much the same ups and downs as the rest of Lanna, enjoying a burst of prosperity as a **timber** town at the end of the last century, when it supported a population of 20,000 people and 4000 working elephants. Many of its temples are financially endowed by the waves of outsiders who have settled here: refugees from Chiang Saen (who were forcibly resettled here by Rama I at the beginning of the last century), Burmese teak-loggers and workers, and, more recently, rich Thai pensioners attracted by the town's sedate charm.

The whole town can be covered on foot without trouble, though to get out to Wat Phra Kaeo Don Tao you might want to hop on one of the many **songthaews** which cruise the streets. **Horse-drawn carriages**, which have become a hack-

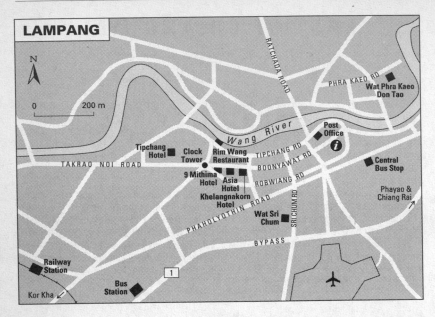

neyed symbol of Lampang, can be hired in the centre (starting from B50 for 15min), but locals only use them in the very early morning when songthaews are banned from the main streets.

The town

The modern centre of Lampang sprawls along the south side of the Wang River, with its most frenetic commercial activity taking place along Boonyawat and Robwiang roads near Ratchada Bridge, where you'll find stalls and shops selling the famous local pottery, a kitsch combination of whites, blues and browns, made from the area's rich kaolin clay. The town's few sights are well scattered, the best place to start being the leafy suburbs on the north side of the river – the site of the original Haripunjaya settlement – which today contain the most important and interesting temple, **Wat Phra Kaeo Don Tao**, a grand, rather forbidding complex on Phra Kaeo Road, 1km northeast of the Ratchada Bridge (B10 admission fee for farangs). The temple was founded in the fifteenth century to enshrine the Phra Kaeo Don Tao image, now residing at Wat Phra That Lampang Luang (see below), and for 32 years also housed the Emerald Buddha – which local stories aver to be a copy of Phra Kaeo Don Tao – when an elephant carrying the holy image from Chiang Rai to Chiang Mai made an unscheduled and therefore auspicious halt here in 1436.

The clean, simple lines of the white **chedi**, which is reputed to contain a hair of the Buddha, form a shining backdrop to the wat's most interesting building, a Burmese **mondop** stacked up in extravagantly carved tiers. A Thai prince, whose British-style coat-of-arms can be seen on the ceiling inside, employed craftsmen from the local Burmese community to build the mondop in 1909. The interior decoration, all gilt and gaudy coloured glass, is a real fright, mixing Oriental and European influences, with some incongruously cute little cherubs on the ceiling. The mondop's boyish bronze centrepiece has the typical features of a Mandalay Buddha, with its jewelled headband, inset black and white eyes, and exaggerated, dangling ears, which denote the Buddha's supernatural ability to hear everything in the universe. The image in front of the Buddha, dripping with gold leaf offerings, is of Khruba Srivijaya, the north's most venerated monk (see p.207). A small, gloomy **museum** opposite the mondop displays some dainty china and a humorous *nagadan*, a carved supporting panel showing a man being given a piggyback to hold up the roof.

Sited in a small grove of bodhi trees five minutes' walk south of Robwiang Road, **Wat Sri Chum** is the most interesting of Lampang's Burmese temples and is still home to a community of Burmese monks. After the British conquest of Upper Burma in the late nineteenth century, timber companies expanded their operations into northern Thailand, bringing with them many Burmese workers. Fearing that the homeless spirits of fallen trees would seek revenge, the Burmese often sponsored the building of temples to gain merit and appease the spirits. Built in 1900, the carpeted **viharn**, where the monks have their sleeping quarters, feels like a cosy library. Burmese craftsmen were brought over from Mandalay to carve the delicate floral work over the entrance and on the ceiling inside. The highlight here is a vivid **mural**, done in gold on a red lacquer background, which shows Lampang as it was early this century. The wat is pictured in detail, surrounded by palm trees, elephants and teak traders' houses, and you can make out some farang tourists, having a drink on their way to visit the temple by car.

If you've had your fill of temples, the streets of the **Talat Khao**, the "Old Market" (also known as Talat Jiin, "Chinese Market") around Tipchang Road are good for a stroll, especially in the evening. It's now a quiet area of shophouses and mansions, which show a mixture of Burmese, Chinese and European influence, with intricate balconies, carved gables and unusual sunburst designs carved over some of the doors. Small lanes on the north side of the Talat Khao lead down to the Wang River, whose waters are as green as its overgrown banks – what used to be the main thoroughfare for trading boats and huge rafts of felled timber has been reduced almost to stagnation by an upriver dam.

Practicalities

Buses from Nawarat Bridge in Chiang Mai run to Lampang every half hour for most of the day, the majority of which then trundle on up Highway 1 to Chiang Rai. Ten buses a day from Chiang Mai's Arcade station also stop at Lampang on their way to Nan. Only six **trains** a day stop here in each direction, though if you're coming from Bangkok the railway is more convenient than direct buses to Lampang. The train and bus stations lie to the southwest of town, but many buses also stop on Phaholyothin Road in the centre. The small, primitive **tourist information** centre (Mon–Fri 9am–4pm) at the Provincial Office, at the corner of Boonyawat and Pakham roads, can help with advice on excursions to the elephant training centre and the like.

Lampang's cheapest **hotels**, which queue up to the west of the centre along Boonyawat Road, are generally dismal, dirty affairs. Best of them is *9 (Kao)*

Mithima Hotel, far out and set back from the road at 285 Boonyawat Rd (☎054/217438), where single rooms go for B90, doubles B120. If this is full, try *Romsri Hotel* at 142 Boonyawat Rd (☎054/217054), with singles at B80, doubles B120. For a little more cash, standards improve markedly: *Khelangnakorn Hotel*, at 719 Suandok Rd, a side road off Boonyawat (☎054/226137), has decent rooms with attached bathrooms for B130 single, B180 double, and smart air-conditioned rooms with hot showers for B260/B340. Rooms at the plusher *Asia Hotel*, a few doors away at 229 Boonyawat Rd (☎054/217844), are also good value at B260 single, B340 double, all with air-conditioning and hot water. At the top end is the tacky luxury of the *Tipchang Hotel*, to the west at 54/22 Takrao Noi Rd (☎054/226501–6), which has a swimming pool and rooms from B780.

The **place to eat and drink** is the *Rim Wang* (aka the *Riverside*) at 328 Tipchang Rd, a cosy, relaxing spot on terraces overlooking the water. A wide variety of excellent Thai and Western food is served to the strains of live acoustic music.

Wat Phra That Lampang Luang

If you've made it as far as Lampang, a visit to **Wat Phra That Lampang Luang**, a grand and well-preserved capsule of beautiful Lanna art and architecture, is a must. However, although the wat is a busy pilgrimage site, **getting there** without your own transport isn't easy: catch a songthaew from Lampang's Sri Chum Road (south of the junction with Boonyawat Road) for KOR KHA, 10km south on Highway 1; songthaews covering the last 5km from there to the wat are rare, so you'll probably have to hire a motorcycle taxi (about B50 round trip) or walk (cross the bridge over the Mae Nam Wang and turn right, heading north on a paved road).

The wat was built early in the Haripunjaya era as a *wiang* (fortress), one of a satellite group around Lampang – you can still see remains of the threefold ramparts in the farming village around the temple. Getting into the *wiang* is easier nowadays: a naga staircase leads you up to a wedding cake of a gatehouse, richly decorated with stucco, which is set in the original brick boundary walls. Just inside, the oversized **viharn** is open on all sides in classic Lanna fashion, and shelters a spectacular centrepiece: known as a *ku*, a feature found only in the viharns of northern Thailand, this gilded brick tower looks like a bonfire for the main Buddha image sitting inside, the Phra Chao Lan Thong. Watch your head on the panels hanging from the low eaves, which are decorated with attractive early-nineteenth-century paintings of battles, palaces and nobles in traditional Burmese gear.

This central viharn is snugly flanked by three others. In front of the murky, beautifully decorated viharn to the left, look out for a wooden *tung chai* carved with flaming, coiled nagas, which was used as a heraldic banner for northern princes. The battered, cosy **Viharn Nam Tame**, second back on the right, is possibly the oldest wooden building in Thailand, dating back to the early sixteenth century. Its drooping roof configuration is archetypal: divided into three tiers, each of which is divided again into two layers, it ends up almost scraping the ground. Under the eaves you can just make out fragments of panel paintings, as old as the viharn, illustrating a story of one of the exploits of the Hindu god Indra.

Hundreds of rainy seasons have turned the copper plates on the wat's huge central **chedi** into an arresting patchwork of greens, blues and purples: safe inside are supposed to be a hair of the Buddha and ashes from his right forehead and neck. By the chedi's northwest corner, a sign points to a drainage hole in the wat's boundary wall, once the scene of an unlikely act of derring-do: in 1736, local hero Thip Chang managed to wriggle through the tiny hole and free the *wiang* from the occupying Burmese, before going on to liberate the whole of Lampang.

A gate in the south side of the boundary wall leads to a spreading **bodhi tree** on crutches: merit-makers have donated hundreds of supports to prop up its drooping branches. The tree, with its own small shrine standing underneath, is believed to be inhabited by spirits, and the sick are sometimes brought here in search of a cure.

Don't miss the small, unimpressive viharn to the west of the bodhi tree – it's the home of **Phra Kaeo Don Tao**, the much-revered companion image to Bangkok's Emerald Buddha, and the wat's main focus of pilgrimage. Legend has it that the statuette first appeared in the form of an emerald found in a watermelon presented by a local woman to a venerated monk. The two of them tried to carve a Buddha out of the emerald, without much success, until the god Indra appeared and fashioned the marvellous image, at which point the ungrateful townsfolk accused the monk of having an affair with the woman and put her to death, thus bringing down upon the town a series of disasters which confirmed the image's awesome power. In all probability, the image was carved at the beginning of the fifteenth century, when its namesake wat in Lampang was founded. Peering through the dim light and the rows of protective bars inside the viharn, you can just make out the tiny meditating Buddha – it's actually made of jasper, not emerald – which on special occasions is publicly displayed wearing a headdress and necklace. To cash in on its supernatural reputation, a dusty shop in the viharn sells monkeys' skulls, turtle shells and other exotic charms.

Young Elephant Training Centre

The **Young Elephant Training Centre,** which has recently moved to a site 25km west of Lampang on Highway 11, is the most authentic place to see elephants being trained for logging work and, being more out of the way, is less touristy than the elephant showgrounds to the north of Chiang Mai (June–Feb daily 9–11am). It's best visited en route from Chiang Mai to Lampang: take an early bus (before 7am) to get there in time for the 9am start, and ask for Suan Pa ("Forest Park") Thung Kwian. On a day trip from Lampang, a bus towards Lamphun or Chiang Mai should get you there in around half an hour. Note that the centre closes for every conceivable religious holiday, of which there are about fifty a year, so you'd do well to check with TAT in Chiang Mai or the tourist information centre in Lampang before setting off.

Run by the veterinary section of the Thai forestry organization, the training centre was the earliest of its kind in Thailand and is now home to around 100 elephants. The daily **shows** put the young elephants through their paces with plenty of amusing showmanship and loud trumpeting for their audience: after some photogenic bathing, they walk together in formation and go through a long routine of pushing, dragging, carrying and piling logs. If you want to get a closer look, bring some bananas or sugar cane to feed the animals.

THE ELEPHANT IN THAILAND

To Thais the **Asian elephant** has profound **spiritual significance**, derived from both Hindu and Buddhist mythologies. Carvings and statues of **Ganesh**, the Hindu god with an elephant's head, feature on ancient temples all over the country and, as the god of knowledge and remover of obstacles, Ganesh has been adopted as the symbol of the Fine Arts Department – and is thus depicted on all entrance tickets to historical sights. The Hindu deity Indra rarely appears without his three-headed elephant mount **Erawan**, and miniature devotional elephant effigies are sold at major Brahmin shrines, such as Bangkok's Erawan shrine. In Buddhist legend, the future **Buddha's mother** was able to conceive only after she dreamt that a white elephant had entered her womb: that is why elephant balustrades encircle many of the Buddhist temples of Sukhothai, and why the rare white elephant is accorded royal status (see p.83) and regarded as a highly auspicious animal.

The **practical** role of the elephant in Thailand is almost as great as its symbolic importance. The kings of Ayutthaya relied on elephants to take them into battle against the Burmese – one king assembled a trained elephant army of 300 – and during the last century King Rama IV offered Abraham Lincoln a male and a female to "multiply in the forests of America" and to use in the Civil War. In times of peace, the phenomenal stength of the elephant has made it invaluable as a beast of burden: elephants hauled the stone from which the gargantuan Khmer temple complexes of the north and northeast were built, and for centuries they have been used to clear forests and carry timber.

By a terrible irony, the **timber industry** has been the animal's undoing. Mechanised logging has destroyed their preferred river-valley habitats, forcing them into isolated upland pockets. As a result, Thailand's population of wild elephants is perhaps only half the size of the domesticated population of 5000, many of which are trained for environmentally less damaging forms of logging. Most are bred in captivity, spending the first three years of their lives with their mothers (who get five years' maternity leave), before being forcefully separated and raised with other calves in training schools. From the age of three each elephant is assigned its own **mahout** – a trainer, keeper and driver rolled into one – who will stay with it for the rest of its working life. Training begins gently, with mahouts taking months to earn the trust of their charge; over the next thirteen years the elephant is taught about forty different commands, from simple "stop" and "go" orders to complex instructions for hooking and passing manoeuvres with the trunk. By the age of sixteen an elephant is ready to be put to work and is expected to carry on working until it reaches fifty or so. Today, however, the domesticated elephant is becoming less useful. The government ban on teak logging has reduced the role of the working elephant to such an extent that training schools concentrate as much on perfecting shows for tourists as on honing their practical skills.

Nan

From Lampang, most travellers head north for Chiang Rai, but remote and little-visited Nan – recently designated a tourist development area for its historic hybrid temples and stunning mountainous countryside – provides a strong incentive to carry on eastwards. **Buses** from Lampang follow Highway 11 to the junction town of DEN CHAI (Bangkok–Chiang Mai trains also stop here), 83km to the southeast, then veer northeastwards on Highway 101 through the tobacco-rich Yom valley, dotted with distinctive brick curing houses. PHRAE, 20km on, is famous for woodcarving and the quality of its *seua maw hawm*, the deep blue, baggy working shirt seen all over Thailand. After leaving the Yom, the highway gently climbs through rolling hills of cotton fields and teak plantations to its highest point, framed by limestone cliffs, before descending into the high, isolated valley of the Nan River, one of the two great tributaries of the Chao Phraya. Coming direct from Chiang Mai, you might want to weigh up the seven-hour bus journey to Nan against the one-hour **flight** (B400).

Ringed by high mountains, the sleepy but prosperous provincial capital of **NAN**, 225km east of Lampang, rests on the grassy west bank of the Nan River, where traditional floating houses moored to the bank add to the rustic ambience. This stretch of river really comes alive during the **Lanna boat races**, usually held in the second week of October, when villages from around the province send teams of up to fifty oarsmen here to race in long, colourfully decorated canoes with dragon prows. The lush surrounding valley is noted for its cotton-weaving, sweet oranges and the attractive grainy paper made from the bark of local *sa* (mulberry) trees.

Although it has been kicked around by Burma, Laos and Thailand, Nan province has a history of being on the fringes, distanced by the encircling barrier of mountains. Rama V brought Nan into his centralisation programme at the turn of the century, but left the traditional ruling house in place, making it the last province in Thailand to be administered by a local ruler (it remained so until 1931). During the troubled 1970s, communist insurgents holed up in this twilight region and proclaimed Nan the future capital of the liberated zone, which only succeeding in bringing the full might of the Thai Army down on them. Though the insurgency faded after the government's 1982 offer of amnesty, roadside checkpoints betray a continued large military presence in the province. Nan still has a slight reputation for lawlessness, but most of the bandits nowadays are illegal loggers.

The town

No more than 1km square, Nan comprises a disorienting grid of crooked streets, most of them tree-lined and marked by a welcome scarcity of cars. A small core of shops and businesses centres on the corner of Mahawang and Sumondhevaraj roads, to the north of which, beyond the *Dhevaraj Hotel*, you'll find *Jantragul*, with its excellent selection of colourful clothes made from locally woven cotton.

A khut

The best place to start an exploration of the town is the **National Museum** (Wed–Sun 9am–4pm; B10), located in a tidy palace with superb teak floors, which used to be home to the rulers of Nan. Informative, user-friendly displays give you a bite-sized introduction to Nan, its history and its peoples. The prize exhibit is a talismanic elephant tusk with a bad

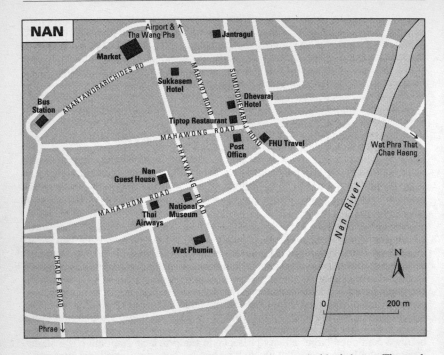

case of brown tooth decay, which is claimed to be magic black ivory. The tusk was discovered over 300 years ago and now sits on a colourful wooden *khut*, a mythological eagle. The museum also houses elegant pottery and woodcarving, gorgeously wrought silverware and some rare Laotian Buddhas.

Nearby on Phakwang Road, **Wat Phumin** will grab even the most over-templed traveller. Its 500-year-old centrepiece is an unusual cruciform building, combining both the bot and the viharn, which balances some quirky features in a perfect symmetry. Two giant nagas (serpents) pass through the base of the building, with their tails along the balustrades at the south entrance and their heads at the north, representing the sacred oceans at the base of the central mountain of the universe. The doors at the four entrances, which have been beautifully carved with a complex pattern of animals and flowers, lead straight to the four Buddha images arranged around a tall altar in the centre of the building – note the Buddhas' piercing onyx eyes and pointed ears, showing the influence of Laos, 50km away. What really sets the bot apart are the recently restored **murals**, whose bright, simple colours seem to jump off the walls. Executed in 1857, the paintings take you on a whirlwind tour of heaven, hell, the Buddha's previous incarnations, local legends and incidents from Nan's history, and include stacks of vivacious, sometimes bawdy, detail, which provides a valuable pictorial record of that era.

Wat Phra That Chae Haeng, on the opposite side of the river 2km southeast of town, is another must, as much for its setting on a hill overlooking the Nan valley as anything else. The wat was founded in 1300, at a spot determined by the Buddha himself when he passed through this way – or so local legend would have it. The nagas here outdo even Wat Phumin's: the first you see of the wat across the fields is a wide driveway flanked by monumental serpents gliding down the slope from the temple. A magnificent gnarled bodhi tree with hundreds of spreading branches and roots guards the main gate, set in high boundary walls. Inside the walls, the highlight is a slender, 55-metre-high golden chedi, surrounded by four smaller chedis and four carved and gilded umbrellas, as well as small belfries and stucco lions. Close competition comes from the viharn roof, which has no less than fifteen Laotian-style tiers, stacked up like a house of cards and supported on finely carved *kan tuei* (wood supports) under the eaves.

Practicalities

Coming by bus you'll arrive at the **bus station** on the west side of town, which leaves a manageable walk or a samlor ride to the central accommodation area. A free *Thai Airways* minibus runs passengers from the **airport** on the north side of town to the hotels. A bicycle is handy for getting around town – try *FHU Travel* at 453/4 Sumondhevaraj Rd (B20 a day; they also rent battered motorbikes for B170).

For the time being, Nan's lone **budget accommodation** offering is the *Nan Guest House*, 57/16 Mahaphom Rd (☎054/771148), where plain, clean box rooms start at B30 per bed; the owner speaks English and can help with local info. Fairly representative of local **hotels**, the *Sukkasem*, 119 Anantaworarichides Rd (☎054/710141), has shabby rooms for B120 single, B180 double (B200 with a/c, singles only). The best in town is the *Dhevaraj*, 466 Sumondhevaraj Rd (☎054/710094), which does little to justify its billing as a luxury hotel: rooms with hot water are B250 single, B350 double (B500/B700 with a/c).

In addition to the usual simple Thai **restaurants** along Sumondhevaraj Road, Nan's big culinary surprise is the *Tiptop* at 99/6–7 Mahawong Rd (closed Sundays). Run by a Swiss-Italian chef, it serves some of the best Western food in the north – pastas, meat in creamy sauces and the like – as well as very good Thai fare, all at reasonable prices.

Around Nan

The remote, mountainous countryside around Nan runs a close second to the headlong scenery of Mae Hong Son province, but its remoteness means that Nan has even worse transport and is even more poorly mapped than Mae Hong Son. It's worth making the effort. Your best option is to head for the reliable *FHU Travel*, the only fixer in town at 453/4 Sumondhevaraj Rd (☎054/710636), which organises slightly pricey but popular and enjoyable trekking and rafting trips. **Treks** of two days (B1100 per person) or three days (B1400) generally head west, through tough terrain of thick jungle and high mountains, visiting at least one Phi Tong Luang village (see box) and nearby Hmong and Mien villages where they work. *FHU*'s **raft trips** (B900 per person per day) start from SA, 25km south of Nan, and head further south along an exciting, rocky stretch of the Nan River, tightly enclosed by hills – swimming is possible, as well as camping by the river, if you want to turn this into a two-day trip.

If you want to go it alone, *FHU* also rents out motorbikes: the easiest and most varied day trip out of Nan is to the north, heading first for **THA WANG PHA**, a famous weaving centre 40km up Highway 1080. The village and the surrounding area are largely inhabited by Thai Lue people, distant cousins of the Thais who've

SPIRITS OF THE YELLOW LEAVES

Inhabiting the remote hill country west of Nan, the **Phi Tong Luang – "Spirits of the Yellow Leaves"** – represent the last remnant of nomadic hunter-gatherers in Thailand, and their way of life, like that of so many other indigenous peoples, is rapidly passing. Believing that spirits will be angered if the tribe settles in one place, grows crops or keeps animals, the Phi Tong Luang build only temporary shelters of branches and wild banana leaves and move on to another spot in the jungle as soon as the leaves turn yellow, thus earning their poetic Thai name. They call themselves Mrabri – "Forest People" – and traditionally eke out a hard livelihood from the forest, hunting with spears, trapping birds and small mammals, digging roots and collecting nuts, seeds and honey.

Recent deforestation by logging and slash-and-burn farming have eaten into the tribe's territory, however, and many of the Phi Tong Luang have been forced to sell their labour to Hmong and Mien farmers (the spirits apparently do not get angry if the tribe settles down and works the land for other people). They are paid only with food – because of their docility and their inability to understand and use money, they often get a raw deal for their hard work. They are also particularly ill-equipped to cope with curious and often insensitive tourists, although one of the American missionaries working with the tribe believes that occasional visits help the Phi Tong Luang to develop by teaching them about people in the outside world. Their susceptibility to disease (especially malaria) is high and life expectancy low, however, and at the last count there were only 107 members of the tribe alive.

migrated from China in the past 150 years and produce beautiful cotton garments in richly coloured geometrical patterns. Beyond Tha Wang Pha the road forks to the right, before passing **Wat Nong Bua**, the sister temple to Wat Phumin, set in a pretty, traditional village of teak houses on stilts. The murals here were executed by the Wat Phumin painters, and although more damaged, they're still worth seeing for their humour and vivid detail.

A right turn, 16km further along Highway 1080, leads into **DOI PHUKHA NATIONAL PARK**, where a good access road heads up through Lawa villages and fertile countryside dotted with salt-wells towards the cool 1980-metre summit. The highest point of the road, after 10km, leaves you with a 300-metre climb to the peak, but the views from the road, over the steep slopes of thick virgin forest, speckled with bare green patches left by loggers, are just as spectacular.

THE MAE HONG SON LOOP

Two roads from Chiang Mai head over the western mountains into Mae Hong Son, Thailand's most remote province, offering the irresistible prospect of tying them together into a 600-kilometre loop. The towns en route give an appetising taste of Burma to the west, but the journey itself, winding over implausibly steep forested mountains and through tightly hemmed farming valleys, is what will stick in the mind.

The southern leg of the route, Highway 108, first passes **Doi Inthanon National Park**, with its lofty views over half of northern Thailand and enough waterfalls to last a lifetime, then **Mae Sariang**, an important town for trade across the Burmese border. The provincial capital, **Mae Hong Son**, at the midpoint of the loop, still has the relaxing atmosphere of a big village and makes the best base for exploring the area's mountains, rivers and waterfalls. The northern leg, Highway 1095, heads northeast out of Mae Hong Son into an area of beautiful caves and stunning scenery around **Mae Lana** and **Soppong**: staying at one of the out-of-the-way guest houses here will enable you to hike independently around the countryside and the local hill-tribe villages. **Pai**, halfway back towards Chiang Mai from Mae Hong Son, is a cosy travellers' hangout with some gentle walking trails in the surrounding valley.

We've taken the loop in a clockwise direction here only because Doi Inthanon is best reached direct from Chiang Mai – apart from that consideration, you could just as easily go the other way round. Travelling the loop is straightforward, although the mountainous roads go through plenty of bends and jolts. Either way, Mae Hong Son is about eight hours' travelling time from Chiang Mai by **bus**, although services along the newly paved northern route are slightly less frequent and entail a change at Pai. The one-hour **flight** to Mae Hong Son is surprisingly cheap (B330), and is worth considering for one leg of the journey, especially if you're short on time. Above all, though, the loop is made for **motorcycles** and **jeeps**: the roads are quiet (but watch out for huge logging trucks) and you can satisfy the inevitable craving to stop every five minutes and admire the mountain scenery.

Highway 108: Chiang Mai to Mae Hong Son

Bus drivers who ply **Highway 108** are expected to have highly sharpened powers of concentration and the landlubber's version of sea legs – the road negotiates almost two thousand curves in the 349km to Mae Hong Son, so if you're at all prone to travel sickness plan to take a breather in Mae Sariang. Buses to Mae Sariang and Mae Hong Son depart from Chiang Mai's Arcade bus station; services to Chom Thong (for Doi Inthanon National Park) leave from the bottom of Phra Pokklao Road (Chiang Mai Gate).

Doi Inthanon National Park

Covering a huge area to the southwest of Chiang Mai, **DOI INTHANON NATIONAL PARK**, with its hill-tribe villages, dramatic waterfalls and panoramas over rows of wild, green peaks to the west, gives a pleasant, if sanitised, whiff of northern countryside, its attractions and concrete access roads kept in good order by the Thai Forestry Department. The park, named after the highest mountain in the country and so dubbed the "Roof of Thailand", is geared mainly to wildlife conservation and also contains a hill-tribe agricultural project and a drug rehabilitation centre. Often shrouded in mists, Doi Inthanon's temperate forests shelter a huge variety of flora and fauna which make this one of the major destinations for naturalists in Southeast Asia. The park supports about 380 species of birds, the largest number of any site in Thailand – among them the ashy-throated warbler and a species of the green-tailed sunbird, both unique to Doi Inthanon – and, near the summit, the only red rhododendrons in Thailand (in bloom Dec–Feb) and a wide variety of ground and epiphytic orchids. The waterfalls, birds and flowers are at their best in the cool season, but night-time temperatures sometimes drop below freezing, making warm clothing a must.

Getting there

The gateway to the park is CHOM THONG, 58km southwest of Chiang Mai on Highway 108, a drab town with little to offer apart from the attractive **Wat Phra That Si Chom Thong**, whose impressive brass-plated chedi dates from the fifteenth century. The nearby bo tree has become an equally noteworthy architectural feature: dozens of Dalí-esque supports for its sagging branches have been sponsored by the devoted in the hope of earning merit. Inside the gnarled sixteenth-century viharn, a towering, gilded *ku* housing a Buddha relic just squeezes in beneath the ceiling, from which hangs a huge, sumptuous red and green umbrella. Weaponry, gongs, umbrellas, thrones and an elephant-tusk arch carved with delicate Buddha images all add to the welcoming clutter.

The main road through the park leaves Highway 108 1km north of Chom Thong, winding generally northwestwards for 48km to the top of Doi Inthanon; a second paved road forks left 10km before the summit, reaching the riverside market of MAE CHAEM, southwest of the park, after 20km. For a detailed park map, bird lists and other information, stop at the **visitors' centre**, 9km up the main road, or the **park headquarters**, a further 22km on. Sticking to public transport, you'll be limited to the **songthaews** that shuttle between Chom Thong and Mae Chaem along the mountain's lower slopes – to get to the summit you'll have to hitch the last 10km (generally manageable) or hike up a trail from the park headquarters, either of which will entail overnighting. By **motorbike** or jeep you could do the park justice in a day trip from Chiang Mai, or treat it as the first stage of a longer trip to Mae Hong Son, either picking up Highway 108 south again or following rough roads beyond Mae Chaem.

The park

Three sets of waterfalls provide the main roadside attractions on the way to the park headquarters: overrated **Mae Klang Falls**, 8km in, which with its picnic areas and food vendors gets overbearingly crowded, especially at weekends; **Vachiratharn Falls**, a misty long drop down a granite escarpment 11km beyond; and the twin cascades of **Siriphum Falls**, backing the park headquarters a further 11km on. With your own wheels you could reach a fourth and much more beautiful cataract, **Mae Ya**, which is believed to be the highest in Thailand – the dusty, bumpy fourteen-kilometre track to it heads west off the main park road 2km north of Highway 108. Another unpaved side road, dubbed the **Karen Village Circuit Road**, takes a roundabout but culturally more enlightening route to the headquarters, leaving the main road 3km beyond Vachiratharn Falls and takes in four traditional and unspoilt Karen villages before rejoining the main road at the more developed Hmong village of BAN KHUN KLANG, 500m before the HQ.

For the most spectacular views in the park, continue 11km along the summit road or hike the steep trail (about 4hr – ask for a guide at the HQ) to the sleek, modern **Napamaytanidol Chedi**, looming incongruously over the misty green hillside: on a clear day you can see the mountains of Burma to the west. Starting a short distance up the road from the chedi, the rewarding **Gew Mae Pan Trail**, a two-hour circular walk, wanders through sun-dappled forest and open savannah as it skirts the steep, western edge of Doi Inthanon, where violent red rhododendrons are framed against open views over the canyoned headwaters of the Pan River; at the time of writing, a guide from the headquarters was needed, although work on signposting and marking the trail had started.

Doi Inthanon's **summit** (2565m), 6km beyond the chedi, is a big disappointment – from the car park you can see little beyond the radar installation. A small, still-revered stupa on the right contains the ashes of King Inthanon of Chiang Mai (after whom the mountain was renamed): at the end of the last century he was the first to recognize the importance of this watershed area in supplying the Ping River and ultimately the Chao Phraya, the queen of Thailand's rivers. One hundred metres back down the road, it's an easy walk to the bog which is the highest source of these great waterways. The cream and brown sphagnum mosses which spread underfoot and hang off the trees give a creepy, primeval atmosphere, offset by the brash rhododendrons.

The paved **Mae Chaem road** skirts yet another set of waterfalls, 7km after the turnoff: look for a steep, unpaved road to the right, leading down to a ranger station and, just to the east, the dramatic long drop of **Huai Sai Luaeng Falls**. A circular two-hour trail from the ranger station takes in creeks and small waterfalls as well as **Mae Pan Falls**, a series of short cascades in a peaceful, shady setting. Continuing southwest, the paved road affords breathtaking views as it helter-skelters down to the sleepy valley of Mae Chaem. Hardy bikers can push on south from here towards Highway 108, though this involves 45km of tough dirt road; an even hairier route heads northwest from Mae Chaem straight towards Mae Hong Son, joining Route 108 at Khun Yuam.

Practicalities

Accommodation in the park is not as rough and ready as you might expect. Sturdy national park bungalows, set in a pleasant wooded compound near the headquarters, come with electricity, cold showers, mattresses and bedding – these are sometimes booked up at weekends, but at other times you should be all right turning up on the day. Prices start from B300 for a four-person bungalow, but on weekdays it's possible to take one room in a large bungalow at a lower rate. Elsewhere, the *Little Guest House and Restaurant*, 500m after the turnoff to Mae Ya Falls on the main park road, has clean, breeze-block huts with inside bathrooms for B150 with fan, B200 with air conditioning, and the *Guest House* at Mae Chaem also has very basic huts at B30 per person.

Camping, an often chilly alternative, is permitted in the headquarters compound and at Mae Pan Falls. Two-person tents can be rented at the headquarters for B50 per night, as can blankets at B10 each per night.

Daytime **food** stalls operate at Mae Klang Falls and at the headquarters, and the restaurant in the national park bungalow compound serves cheap evening meals as long as you request them earlier in the day.

West to Mae Sariang

Highway 108 parallels the Ping River downstream as far as HOT, a dusty, forgettable place 27km from Chom Thong, before bending west and weaving through pretty wooded hills up the valley of the Chaem River. If you're ready for a stopover at this point, the twee *Hot Resort*, 4km west of Hot, has well-appointed chalets with hot water for B400 per night. The resort's riverside restaurant does tasty food at moderate prices.

Another 13km brings you to **Ob Luang Gorge National Park**, billed with wild hyperbole as "Thailand's Grand Canyon". A wooden bridge over the short, narrow channel lets you look down on the Chaem River bubbling along 50m below; upstream from the bridge, you can relax at the roadside food stalls and swim in the river when it's not too fast, and the shady park contains a campsite. West of Ob Luang the highway gradually climbs through pine forests, the road surface deteriorating and the countryside becoming steeper and wilder. A tranquil, isolated **guest house** in the hills 3km south of the highway, *Pan's House*, offers the opportunity of **trekking** to Karen and Lawa villages, and can arrange elephant riding and rafting trips – reach it via an uphill track signposted from the highway 68km from Hot, which takes nearly an hour to walk and is navigable on a motorbike (if you're travelling by bus, ask to be let off at BAN MAE WAEN).

After a nerve-wracking hairpin descent into the broad, smoky valley of the Yuam River, Highway 108's westward progress ends at **MAE SARIANG**, 183km from Chiang Mai, a quietly industrious market town showing a marked Burmese influence in its temples and its rows of low wooden shophouses. If you need a stopover between Chiang Mai and Mae Hong Son, this is an obvious place as it's halfway along the southern route. From here you can make an intriguing but uncomfortable day trip to the trading post of Mae Sam Laeb on the river border with Burma, and it's also possible (though not recommended) to strike off south on an even more bone-rattling journey to Mae Sot. Buses enter Mae Sariang from the east along the town's main street, Wiang Mai Road, and pull in at the terminal on Mae Sariang Road, one of two north–south streets; the other, Laeng Phanit Road, parallels the Yuam River to the west.

The town and around

There's nothing pressing to do apart from soaking up the atmosphere in this border outpost, which is regularly visited by local hill tribes and dodgy traders from Burma. If you want something more concrete to do, stroll around a couple of temples off the north side of Wiang Mai Road, whose Burmese features provide a glaring contrast to most Thai temples. The first of these, **Wat Si Boonruang**, sports a fairy-tale bot done out in lemon, ochre and red, with an intricate, tiered roof piled high above. Topped with lotus buds, the unusual *sema* stones, which delineate the bot's consecrated area, look like old-fashioned street bollards. The open viharns here and next door at the lop-sided **Wat Utthayarom** are mounted on stilts, with broad teak floors that are a pleasure to get your feet onto. Both enshrine the hard-faced white Buddhas of Burma.

All this is pretty tame stuff compared to a trip to **MAE SAM LAEB**, about 50km to the southwest on the Salween River, which forms the border with Burma at this point. It's not the easiest way to see Burma – the 7.30am songthaew from Mae Sariang takes four jolting hours and includes sixty river fordings for your B50, though the route is undeniably scenic. (*River Side Guest House* also organises more comfortable day trips, if enough people are interested.) Mae Sam Laeb is no more than a row of bamboo stores and restaurants, ending in a gambling den by the river, which swarms with smuggling traffic and floating teak logs. In the dry season, it's possible to hire an expensive longtail boat (figure on B400 for an hour) on the river to view the steep, wooded banks on both sides of the frontier. As the Burmese army has in the past mounted attacks against the Karen insurgents in the area of Mae Sam Laeb, you should check that all is quiet before leaving Mae Sariang.

A more relaxing way of seeing the countryside around Mae Sariang is to walk to the nearest Karen village, **PAMALOR**, about 5km northwest of town. Follow Laeng Phanit Road as far as it's paved, then keep bearing left until you come to a bamboo bridge over the river, which leads to the village. Many of the villagers now work in Mae Sariang and some even speak a little English, so a friendly soul should be able to point you back to Mae Sariang a different way, through the tree-lined rice fields on the western side of the river.

Practicalities

The best **place to stay** in town is the *See View Guest House*, run by a young and friendly staff, where big, comfortable rooms, each with a bathroom and hot water, go for B120 – it's located across the river from the town centre, but call in at the office at 70 Wiang Mai Rd and they'll take you from there. Outside of town, in an idyllic riverside setting, the simple chalets of the *Mae Sariang Resort* cost B150 for a single, B200 for a double – to get there, go 2km out towards Chiang Mai, then follow the signs to the left for a further 1km. Mae Sariang's other travellers' hangout, the *River Side Guest House* on Laeng Phanit Road, with dingy B60 singles (B120 for doubles), would only be worth considering in a pinch, though it does have a popular riverside restaurant. Located 50m east of the post office on Wiang Mai Road (15min from Laeng Phanit Road by foot), the *Mittaree Guest House* is as noisy as accommodation gets in Mae Sariang, but it offers clean rooms with attached baths from B120 single, B150 double, some with views (B280/B350 with a/c).

When it's time for **food**, don't be put off by the shabby appearance of the *Inthira Restaurant* on Wiang Mai Road, the locals' favourite, which dishes up excellent Thai dishes at moderate prices. At lunchtime, the Islamic food stall opposite serves cheap and tasty *khao mok kai*, chicken soup with spiced rice. *The Bakery* on the same road near the corner of Laeng Phanit Road serves delicious versions of all your travellers' favourites (including breakfast) in pleasant surroundings.

South from Mae Sariang: Highway 1085 to Mae Sot

Highway 1085, which drops south for 230km to Mae Sot, makes a scenic and quiet link between the north and the central plains, though it has some major drawbacks. Setting off through the Yuam valley, the road winds over a range of hills to the Burmese border, formed here by the Moei River, which it then hugs all the way down to Mae Sot; along the way, you'll pass through traditional Karen villages which still keep some working elephants, and dense forests with occasional forlorn stands of teak.

The major deterrent against travelling this way is the standard of public transport: the route involves two changes of **songthaew** and a total journey time of six hours or more, which is really too much on a rattling bench seat, especially considering that the first 50km or so is unpaved and bumpy. Each songthaew waits to connect with the previous one, but this leaves no time for a breather or refreshments. In addition to the discomfort, this border area is rather remote and lawless, and the scene of occasional **skirmishes** between the Burmese Army and the opposition freedom fighters – most of the fighting is conducted on the Burmese side, but check that the coast is clear before leaving Mae Sariang.

North to Mae Hong Son

North of Mae Sariang, wide, lush valleys alternate with tiny, steep-sided glens – some too narrow for more than a single rice paddy – turning Highway 108 into a winding roller coaster with a surface that can be dangerous on a motorbike. The market town of **KHUN YUAM**, 95km north of Mae Sariang, is a popular resting place, especially for bikers who've taken the tough, direct route over the mountains from Mae Chaem. The excellent *Ban Farang* **guest house** here, just off the main road at the north end of town and well-signposted, can put you up in fine style: beds in an airy dorm cost B30, and large triple rooms with bathrooms start at B80, all set in an ornamental garden. The restaurant serves up good French food, including homemade bread, at reasonable prices, and cheap Thai food.

Ten kilometres north of Khun Yuam, the landscape broadens for the river crossing at BAN MAE SURIN, gracefully complemented by a typical Burmese temple and chedi. A steep, paved side road, 35km north of Khun Yuam, leads 10km to **BAN MAE KO VAFE** (a distortion of "microwave" – a reference to the radio mast on the peak above the settlement), perched high in the mountains to the east. This Hmong village of low, wooden houses, with one or two poppy fields dotted around, commands breathtaking views of layer upon layer of forested mountains stretching across to Burma in the west. The villagers are used to tourists by now and it's possible to stay with the headman, but the only way to get there is by motorbike or jeep, or on a tour from Mae Hong Son.

After the side road to Mae Ko Vafe, Highway 108 climbs for 10km to a **viewing area**, with stunning vistas of the sheer, wooded slopes and the Pha Bong Dam in the valley far below, before making a dramatic, headlong descent towards Mae Hong Son. Twelve kilometres north of the viewing area (10km before Mae Hong Son), a set of **hot springs** on the north side of BAN PHA BONG are great for bathing, especially after a long journey or trek.

Mae Hong Son and around

MAE HONG SON, capital of Thailand's northwesternmost province, sports more nicknames than a town of 6000 people seems to deserve. In Thai, it's Muang Sam Mok, the "City of Three Mists": set deep in a mountain valley, Mae Hong Son is often swathed in mist, the quality of which differs according to the three seasons (in the hot season it's mostly composed of unpleasant smoke from slash-and-burn agriculture). In former times, the town, which wasn't connected to the outside world by a paved road until 1968, was known as "Siberia" to the troublesome politicians and government officials who were exiled here from Bangkok. Nowadays, thanks to its mountainous surroundings, it's increasingly billed as the "Switzerland of Thailand": 80 percent of Mae Hong Son province is on a slope of more than 45 degrees.

To match the hype, Mae Hong Son has become one of the fastest-developing tourist centres in the country, sporting dozens of backpacker guest houses and more latterly, for Thais and farangs who like their city comforts, luxury hotels. Most travellers come here for **trekking** and day-hiking in the beautiful countryside, others just for the cool climate and lazy upcountry atmosphere. The town is still small enough and sleepy enough to hole up in for a quiet week, but there's no telling how long this can last – if local civic boosters had their way, Mae Hong Son would reverberate every week with the lucrative sounds of explosions and machine-gun fire, as it did during the 1990 filming of *Air America*, starring Mel Gibson.

Mae Hong Son was founded in 1831 as a training camp for elephants captured from the surrounding jungle for the princes of Chiang Mai (Jong Kham Lake, in the southeastern part of the modern town, served as the elephants' bathing spot). The hard work of hunting and rearing the royal elephants was done by the **Thai Yai** (or Shan), an ethnic group related to the Thais who account for half the population of the province and bring a strong Burmese flavour to Mae Hong Son's temples and festivals. The other half of the province's population is made up of various hill tribes (a large number of Karen, as well as Lisu, Hmong and Lawa), with a tiny minority of Thais concentrated in the provincial capital.

The latest immigrants to the province are **Burmese refugees**: as well as rural Karen, driven across the border when the Burmese army razed their villages, many urban students and monks, who formed the hard core of the brutally

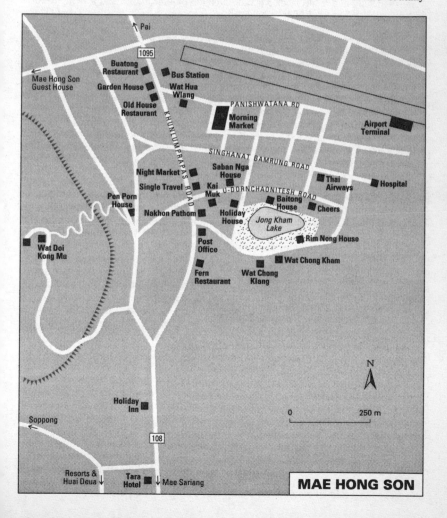

FESTIVALS IN MAE HONG SON

Mae Hong Son's most famous and colourful festival is **Poy Sang Long**, held at the beginning of April, which celebrates the ordination into the monkhood, for the duration of the schools' long vacation, of Thai Yai boys between the ages of seven and fourteen. Similar rituals take place all over Thailand at this time, but the Mae Hong Son version is given a unique flavour by its Thai Yai elements. On the first day of the festival, the boys have their heads shaved and are anointed with turmeric and dressed up in the gay colours of a Thai Yai prince, with traditional accessories: long white socks, plenty of jewellery, a headcloth decorated with fresh flowers, a golden umbrella and heavy face make-up. They are then announced to the guardian spirit of the town and taken around the temples. The second day brings general merry-making and a spectacular parade, headed by a drummer and a richly decorated riderless horse, which is believed to carry the town's guardian spirit. The boys, still in their finery, are each carried on the shoulders of a chaperone, accompanied by musicians and bearers of traditional offerings. In the evening, the novices tuck into a sumptuous meal, waited on by their parents and relatives, before the ordination ceremony in the temple on the third day.

Tak Bat Devo, which is part of the Kathin period observed all over Thailand and falls on the full moon at the start of the eleventh lunar month (usually October), commemorates the Buddha's descent to earth from heaven, where he had spent the rainy season preaching to his mother. In Mae Hong Son, the ceremony, held at Wat Doi Kong Mu on the hill above town, closely re-enacts the descent: in the early morning the townspeople leave offerings of food all the way down the hillside path, and the monks, who spend the rainy season confined to the temple, walk down the path and collect the food (you can get a good view of the procession from the airstrip).

---

repressed 1988 uprising, have fled to this area to join the resistance forces; the latter are susceptible to malaria and generally suffer most from the harsh jungle conditions here. Many refugees live in camps between Mae Hong Son and the border, but these do not encourage visitors as they've got quite enough on their plates without having to entertain onlookers.

The Burmese army has been known to attack villages and camps along the border, and there is occasional fighting over opium on the northern frontier beyond Mae Aw, so if you're planning any trips other than those described below, you should check with one of the travel agents in town first.

Arriving at Mae Hong Son's **bus station** towards the north end of Khunlumprapas Road puts you within walking distance of the guest houses. Tuk-tuks run from the **airport** to the centre, or if you're booked into a resort or hotel you can arrange for a car to pick you up. Motorcycle taxis also operate in and around the town: the local transport hub is the north side of the morning market.

Accommodation

At the cheap end of the accommodation spectrum, Mae Hong Son's roster of **guest houses** is swelling almost by the day, most of them being good-value, rustic affairs built of bamboo or wood and set in their own quiet gardens; many have ranged themselves around Nong Jong Kham (Jong Kham Lake) in the southeast corner of town, which greatly adds to their scenic appeal. If you've got a little more money to spend, you can get out into the countryside to one of several self-contained **resorts** on the grassy banks of the Pai River, though staying at one of these is not exactly a wilderness experience – they're really designed for weekending Thais travelling by car. Finally, two **luxury hotels** on the southern edge of town have latched onto the area's meteoric development, offering all the usual international standard facilities.

One hindrance to the farang traveller is that many of Mae Hong Son's guest houses, restaurants and travel agents don't advertise themselves with English signs, as this would incur extra local taxes – you'll just have to refer to the map to home in on them.

GUEST HOUSES

Baitong House, Fitness Park. A small, intimate and tranquil lakeside place, where clean bamboo rooms go for B50 single, B80 double.

Holiday House, Pradit Jongkham Road. Clean and friendly, with shared hot-water bathroom and its own small garden; a good deal at B100 doubles.

Mae Hong Son Guest House, Phachachon U-Tish Road. Relaxing old-timer that's moved out to the suburbs for a view over the town. Clean single huts are B50 and bare wooden double rooms start at B80.

Pen Porn House, 16/1 Padunomuaytaw Rd (☎053/611577). Clean, smart doubles with hot showers from B300, and a quiet terrace café overlooking town.

Rim Nong House, on the south side of the lake. The cheapest bed in town is in the cosy dorm here (B40); also has cramped bungalows for B100.

Saban Nga House, 14 U-Dornchaonitesh Rd (☎053/611581). Clean, friendly and a good deal: B100 for a double with shared hot shower.

RESORTS

Golden Pai Resort, 5km north of town, signposted to the left of the road towards Pai (☎053/611523, or ☎053/273198 in Chiang Mai). Clean, well-appointed chalets arranged around a smart swimming pool; B850 with fan, B1200 with air conditioning.

Mae Hong Son Resort, 6km south of town, on the road to Huai Deua (☎053/611504, or ☎053/251121 in Chiang Mai). Poshest of the resorts – a friendly and quietly efficient place, where rooms are B970, chalets B1300.

Rim Nam Klang Doi, 5km along the road to Huai Deua, with an office at 70/5 Khunlumprapas Rd (☎053/611142). The best situated of the resorts, with rambling gardens sloping down to the Pai River and swimming, fishing and boating. Comfortable, well-maintained rooms with hot-water bathrooms start at B400; two-person tents on the banks of the Pai for B140.

HOTELS

Holiday Inn, 114/5–7 Khunlumprapas Rd (☎053/611231; Bangkok reservations ☎02/254 2614). At the south end of town on the road out towards Mae Sariang. Has a swimming pool, tennis courts and a discotheque; rooms start at B1800 single, B2000 double.

Tara Hotel, 149 Moo 8, Tambon Pang Moo (☎053/611473; Bangkok reservations ☎02/254 0023). Further out by the turn-off for Huai Deua, this grand building is set in pretty landscaped gardens, with a swimming pool; single rooms are B1700, doubles B2200.

The town

Running north to south, laid-back shops and businesses line Mae Hong Son's main drag, Khunlumprapas Road, intersected by Singhanat Bamrung at the only traffic lights west of Chiang Mai (a landmark which locals are very proud of). Beyond the typical concrete boxes around the central junction, the town sprawls lazily across the valley floor and up the lower slopes of Doi Kong Mu to the west, with trees and untidy vegetation poking through at every possible opportunity to remind you that open country is only a stone's throw away. Plenty of traditional Thai Yai buildings remain – wooden shophouses with balconies, shutters and corrugated-iron roof decorations, thatched homes with herringbone-patterned window panels – though they take a severe beating from the weather and may soon be replaced by cheap, all-engulfing concrete.

Mae Hong Son's classic picture-postcard view is of its twin nineteenth-century Burmese-style temples from the opposite bank of Jong Kham Lake, their gleaming white chedis and the multi-tiered spires of their viharns reflected in the lily-strewn water. In the viharn of **Wat Chong Kham** you'll find two huge sermon thrones, one decorated with the *dharmachakra* (wheel of the doctrine) in coloured glass on gold; the pink building on the left houses the temple's most revered Buddha image, the benign, inscrutable Luang Pho To. Next door, **Wat Chong Klang** is famous for its *Jataka* pictures, showing stories from the Buddha's previous incarnations; crudely painted on glass, they are displayed on the left-hand wall of the viharn. A small room beyond (usually locked – ask around for the key) houses an unforgettable collection of **teak statues**, brought over from Burma in the middle of the last century. The dynamically expressive, often humorous figures are characters from the *Jataka*, but the woodcarvers have taken as their models people from all levels of traditional Burmese society, including toothless emaciated peasants, butch tattooed warriors and elegant upper-class ladies.

The town's vibrant, smelly **morning market**, just south of the bus station, is worth dragging your bones up at dawn to see. People from the local hill tribes often come down to buy and sell, and the range of produce is particularly weird and wonderful, including, in season, porcupine meat, displayed with quills to prove its authenticity. Next door, **Wat Hua Wiang** is guaranteed to make your guest house look like a palace: the rusty iron panels pile up in crazy, sagging tiers like a Hollywood haunted house. Inside, under a lace canopy, is one of the most beautiful Buddha images in northern Thailand, the Chao Palakeng. Copied from a famous statue in Mandalay, the strong, serene bronze has the regal clothing and dangling ears typical of Burmese Buddhas.

For a godlike overview of the area – especially at sunset – climb up to **Wat Doi Kong Mu** on the steep hill to the west: from the temple's two chedis, which enshrine the ashes of respected nineteenth-century monks, you can look down on the town and out across the sleepy farming valley north and south. Behind the chedis, the dilapidated viharn contains an unusual and highly venerated white marble image of the Buddha, surrounded in gold flames. If you've still got the energy, hike up to the new lemon-coloured bot on the summit, where the view extends over the Burmese mountains to the west.

Around Mae Hong Son

Once you've exhausted the few obvious sights in town, the first decision you'll have to grapple with is whether to visit the **"long-neck" women** – our advice is don't, though many travellers do. Less controversial, **boat and raft trips** on the babbling Pai River are fun, and the bumpy dirt-road excursion to **Pha Sua Falls** and the soaring viewpoint at **Mae Aw** makes a satisfying day out. If all that sounds too easy, Mae Hong Son is now Thailand's third largest centre for **trekking**. Other feasible targets include the hot springs at Ban Pha Bong and the hilltop village of Mae Ko Vafe (described in "North to Mae Hong Son", above) and, at a push, Tham Lot (see "Highway 1095", below).

LONG-NECK WOMEN

The most famous – and notorious – of the Mae Hong Son area's spectacles is its contingent of **"long-neck" women**, members of the tiny Padaung tribe of Burma who have come across to Thailand to escape Burmese repression. Though the women's necks appear to be stretched to twelve inches and more by a column of brass rings, the "long-neck" tag is a technical misnomer: a *National Geographic* team once X-rayed one of the women and found that instead of stretching out her neck, the pressure of eleven pounds of brass had simply squashed her collarbones and ribs. Girls of the tribe start wearing the rings from about the age of six, adding one or two each year up to the age of sixteen or so. Once fastened, the rings are for life, for to remove a full stack would cause the collapse of the neck and suffocation – in the past, removal was a punishment for adultery. Despite the obvious discomfort, and the laborious daily task of cleaning and drying the rings, the tribeswomen, when interviewed, say that they're used to their plight and are happy to be continuing the tradition of their people.

The **origin** of the ring-wearing ritual remains unclear, despite an embarrassment of plausible explanations. Padaung legend says that the mother of their tribe was a dragon with a long, beautiful neck, and that their unique custom is an imitation of her. Tour guides will tell you the practice is intended to enhance the women's beauty. In Burma, where it is now outlawed as barbaric, it's variously claimed that ring-wearing arose out of a need to protect women from tiger attacks or to deform the wearers so that the Burmese court would not kidnap them for concubines.

In spite of their handicap (they have to use straws to drink, for example), the women are able to carry out some kind of an ordinary life: they can marry and have children, and they're able to weave and sew, although these days they spend most of their time posing for photographs, displayed like circus freaks by unscrupulous managers. Only half of the Padaung women – about twenty – now lengthen their necks; left to its own course, the custom would probably die out, but the influence of tourism may well keep it alive for some time yet.

Local transport, in the form of songthaews from the morning market, is thinly spread and unreliable, so for all of these excursions it's best to take a motorbike or join an organized tour. **Motorbikes** can be hired from several places in town, probably the most trustworthy being *Garden House*, opposite the bus station on Khunlumprapas Road (B150 for a street model, B200 for a trail bike). Mae Hong Son's **travel agents** do some good deals on tours: *Single Travel* on Khunlumprapas (☎053/611092) is helpful and reputable, and can lay on some unusual activities like horse riding and landscape painting.

Nai Soi

The original village of long-neck Padaung women in the Mae Hong Son area, **NAI SOI**, 25km northwest of town, has effectively been turned into a human zoo for snap-happy tourists. The Padaung here have fallen under the control of fellow refugees in the Burmese Karen Army, who extract a B300 entrance fee from tourists. The "long necks" pose in front of their huts and looms, every now and then getting it together to stage a good-luck song – all a visitor can do is stand and stare in embarrassed silence or click away with a camera (no video cameras allowed). All in all it's a disturbing spectacle, offering no opportunity to discover anything about Padaung culture, though at least some of the money collected is used to buy medicine and school books for the Karens.

Without your own transport, you'll have to hitch up with an expensive tour (about B700) from a travel agent in town. By motorbike, head north along Highway 1095 for 2km and turn left at the police box into TUNG KONG MOO; through the village, the unpaved road narrows down to a trail before crossing a narrow suspension bridge near SOP SOI, then widens out again to lead to Nai Soi.

Trips on the Pai River

Scenic **boat trips** on the Pai River start from HUAI DEUA, 8km southwest of town near the *Mae Hong Son Resort*. No need to go on an organised tour: take a motorcycle taxi, tuk-tuk or one of the infrequent song-

A Padaung woman

thaews from Mae Hong Son market to Huai Deua and approach the owners at the boat station. Twenty minutes downriver from Huai Deua will get you to HUAI PHU KAENG, where five long-neck women are ruthlessly exploited for their tourist potential by Thai entrepreneurs (B300, plus B300 admission charge to the village). You're better off enjoying the river for its own sake, as it scythes its way between cliffs and forests to the Burmese border, another ten minutes beyond (B400), or travelling upriver to SOPPONG (B400), a pretty, quiet Thai Yai village 5km due west of Mae Hong Son (not to be confused with the Soppong on Highway 1095, northeast of Mae Hong Son). **Elephant rides** into the surrounding jungle can also be arranged at the Huai Deua boat station (B200 per hour for two people).

A small stretch of the Pai River between SOP SOI, 10km northwest of Mae Hong Son, and Soppong is clear enough of rocks to allow safe clearance for bamboo **rafts**. The journey takes two hours at the most, as the rafts glide down the gentle river, partly hemmed in by steep wooded hills. Most of Mae Hong Son's travel agents can fix this trip up for you, including travel to Sop Soi and from Soppong, charging around B100 each for a party of six.

Pha Sua Falls and Mae Aw

North of Mae Hong Son, a trip to Pha Sua Falls and the border village of Mae Aw takes in some spectacular and varied countryside. The easiest way of doing it is to join a tour – *Single Travel*, for example, charges B250 per person, which includes a visit to a nearby cave – as there are only occasional expensive (B100 to Mae Aw) songthaews from the market in the morning, and it's murder on a motorbike (the road is manageable as far as the falls).

Pha Sua Falls, 17km north on Highway 1095 and then 9km up a dusty side-road to the left, is a wild, untidy affair, crashing down in several cataracts through a dark, overhung cut in the limestone. The waterfall is in full roar in October after the rainy season, but has plenty of water all year round. Take care when swimming, as several people have been swept to their deaths here.

Above the falls the road is steep and rutted, and impassable during the rainy season. After 13km it reaches **MAE AW**, a settlement of Kuomintang anti-communist Chinese refugees (see p.245), and neighbouring NAPAPAK, a Hmong village, both right on the Burmese border. In the past, this area has seen fighting between the Kuomintang and the army of Khun Sa, the opium warlord who, having been kicked out of the Mae Salong area by the Thai Army in 1983, set up his present base somewhere in the uncharted mountains across the border northeast of Mae Aw. The 22-kilometre road up here was recently built by the Thai military to help the fight against the opium trade and all has been quiet for a couple of years, but it might be worth checking in Mae Hong Son before setting out. Mae Aw is the highest point on the border which visitors can reach, commanding stunning open views down over the serried peaks and thick forests of Burma, interrupted only by Doi Lan (1936m) to the northwest, whose summit marks the frontier here. Day-trippers can get simple **food** in the next-door village of NAPAPAK, where there's also a primitive **guest house** with rooms from B40, if you're stuck.

TREKKING AROUND MAE HONG SON

There's no getting away from the fact that **trekking** up and down Mae Hong Son's steep inclines is tough, but the hill-tribe villages are generally unspoilt and the scenery is magnificent. To the west, trekking routes tend to snake along the Burmese border, occasionally nipping over the line for a quick thrill, and can sometimes get a little crowded as this is the more popular side of Mae Hong Son. Nearly all the hill-tribe villages here are Karen, interspersed with indigenous Thai Yai (Shan) settlements. To the east of Mae Hong Son the Karens again predominate, but you'll also be able to visit Hmong, Lisu and Lahu — many villages here are very traditional, having little contact with the outside world. If you're very hardy, you might want to consider the seven-day route to Chiang Mai, which by all accounts has the best scenery of the lot.

About a dozen guest houses and travel agencies run treks out of Mae Hong Son, among which the *Mae Hong Son Guest House*, *Single Travel* and *Mae Hong Son Travel Agency* (20 Singhanat Bamrung Rd) are known to be reliable; all three charge around B300 per person per day. One small advantage of trekking out of Mae Hong Son is that many of the guides are Burmese who speak very good English, in addition to knowing the tribes well.

Eating and drinking

Nobody comes to Mae Hong Son for the **food** – the available options are limited, although a few good restaurants have sprung up in order to cater specifically to foreigners.

If you fancy a change from guest-house **breakfasts**, head for the morning market, where a wizened old man rustles up excellent *roti*: pancakes with condensed milk and sugar for B2 a throw. At 34 Khunlumprapas Rd, *Buatong* has the best deal on Western breakfasts in town and does cheapish Thai food, in simple surroundings with a few frills. For breakfast and lunch (tasty pork on rice and noodle soup), *Nakhon Pathom* is a cheap, local favourite at 67/1 Khunlumprapas Rd.

For excellent, simple **restaurant** meals that won't burn a hole in your money belt, try *Kai Muk* on U-Dornchaonitesh Road, where the house specialities are chicken in lemon sauce and *seeda somroop*, a Chinese version of a Scotch egg. At *Old House*, 44 Khunlumprapas Rd, the Norwegian-trained chef does surprisingly good and reasonably priced imitations of worldwide dishes, from Mexican to Italian and Israeli, all to the strains of Fifties country-and-western. For a bit of posh, try *Fern*, at 87 Khunlumprapas Rd, a showy, tourist-oriented eatery with a nice candlelit terrace, which offers a huge range of dishes, including some local specialities. The **night market** on Khunlumprapas Road does the standard Thai dishes at cheap prices, and is a good place to meet other travellers.

A good place for a **drink** is *Cheers Food and Drink* on U-Dornchaonitesh Road, where you can relax on a wooden balcony overlooking Jong Kham Lake and the wats behind.

Highway 1095: Mae Hong Son to Chiang Mai

Highway 1095, the 243-kilometre northern route between Mae Hong Son and Chiang Mai, is every bit as wild and scenic as the southern route through Mae Sariang – if anything it has more mountains to negotiate, with a greater contrast between the sometimes straggly vegetation of the slopes and the thickly cultivated valleys. Much of the route was established by the Japanese army to move troops and supplies into Burma after their invasion of Thailand during World War II. The labour-intensive job of paving every hairpin bend has only recently been completed, but ongoing repair work can still give you a nasty surprise if you're riding a motorbike. If you're setting off along this route from Chiang Mai by public transport, catch a Pai-bound bus at Chiang Mai's Arcade station.

Mae Suya and Mae Lana

The first stretch north out of Mae Hong Son weaves up and down the west face of Doi Pai Kit (1082m), giving great views over the lush valley to the north of town. Beyond the turn-off for Mae Aw (see "Around Mae Hong Son") and the much-touted but pretty useless Fish Cave, the highway climbs eastward through many hairpin bends before levelling out to give tantalising glimpses through the trees of the Burmese mountains to the north, then passes through a hushed valley of paddy-fields, surrounded by echoing crags, to reach the Kuomintang village of **MAE SUYA**, 40km from Mae Hong Son. Take the left turning 1km east of the village to reach *Wilderness Lodge* after a further 1km of dirt road; set in wild countryside, the friendly guest house offers primitive bungalows and dorm beds in the barn-like main house for B35, and does set vegetarian meals.

The owner of the lodge can give you directions for easy day walks: either via a Lahu village to **Tham Nam Pha Daeng**, an airy 1.6-kilometre-long cave which, like Tham Lot (see below) is dotted with unexplained coffins; or to Susa Falls and **Tham Nam Lang**, a spectacular nine-kilometre-long cave which can be explored between November and May (for the rest of the year the river which emerges from the cave is too high, though you can get into the towering entrance chamber).

Another remote guest house lies in the sleepy valley of **MAE LANA**, a Thai Yai village 6km north of the highway, reached by a dirt road which branches off to the left 56km from Mae Hong Son and leads uphill through dramatic countryside. The clean and cosy *Mae Lana Guest House* has dorm beds for B30, single rooms for B50 and doubles for B80, and serves good Thai and French food. Mae Lana is within easy walking of Lahu and Lisu villages, plus Tham Nam Pha Daeng and several other caves.

Soppong, Ban Tum and Tham Lot

The small, lively market town of **SOPPONG**, 68km from Mae Hong Son, gives access to the area's most famous cave, Tham Lot, 9km north in **BAN TUM** (or Ban Tham). There's no public transport along the gentle forest road to the village, so if you haven't got your own wheels, you'll have to hitch or walk.

Turn right in the village to find the entrance to the Forestry National Park recently set up to look after the cave, where you can hire a large, bright gas lantern and a guide for B50 each, both of which are recommended. A short walk through the forest brings you to the entrance of **Tham Lot**, where the Lang River begins a 400-metre subterranean journey through the cave, requiring you to wade across the knee-deep water half a dozen times. Three hours should allow you enough time for walking through the broad, airy tunnel, and for the main attraction, climbing up into the sweaty caverns in the roof.

The first of these, **Column Cavern**, 50m from the entrance on the right, seems to be supported on the metre-thick stalagmites which snake up towards the ceiling. Another 50m on the left, bamboo ladders lead up into **Crystal Cave**, which has a glistening, pure white wall and a weird red and white formation shaped like a Wurlitzer organ. Just before the vast exit from the cave, wooden ladders on the left lead up into **Coffin Cave**, named after the remains of five crude burial caskets discovered here, one of them preserved to its full length of 5m. Hollowed out from tree trunks, they are similar to those found in many of the region's caves: some are raised 2m off the ground by wooden supporting poles, and some still contain bones, jewellery and other artefacts. The coffins date back over 2000 years, but anthropologists are at a loss to explain the custom. Local people attribute them to *pi man*, the cave spirits. It's worth hanging round the cave's main exit at sunset, when thousands upon thousands of tiny black chirruping swallows pour into the cave in an almost solid column, to find their beds for the night.

Practicalities

Cave Lodge, on the other side of Ban Tum from the cave, makes an excellent and friendly base for exploring the area. The owners, a former trekking guide and her Australian husband, have plenty of useful information about Tham Lot and some of the sixty other caves in the region, and organise occasional guided trips through the more interesting ones. Walking to local Karen, Lahu, Lisu and Hmong villages from the lodge is possible, as well as river rafting and tubing. Dorm beds are B35, bungalows B80, and the communal meals are delicious.

Jungle Guest House is the most popular of several places along the main road at the western end of Soppong, and can organise trekking trips into the quiet region south of the village. Dorm beds here are B30, single huts B50, doubles B80.

Pai and beyond

Beyond Soppong, the road climbs through the last of Mae Hong Son province's wild landscape before descending into the broad, gentle valley of **PAI**, 43km from Soppong, where you'll have to change buses. There's nothing special to do in Pai, but the atmosphere is relaxing and the guest houses and restaurants have tailored themselves to the steady trickle of travellers who make the four-hour bus journey out from Chiang Mai. The small town's traditional buildings spread themselves liberally over the west bank of the Pai River, but everything's still within walking range of the bus station at the north end.

Several undemanding **walks** can be made around Pai's broad, gently sloping valley. The easiest – one hour there and back – takes you across the river on the east side of town and up the hill to Wat Mae Yen, which commands a great view over the whole district (the much-touted hot springs, 7km south of the wat, are a big disappointment). To the west of town, an unpaved road (accessible by motorbike) heads out from Pai Hospital, passing, after 3km, Wat Nam Hu, whose Buddha image has an unusual hinged top-knot containing holy water, before gradually climbing through comparatively developed Kuomintang, Lisu and Lahu villages to Mo Pang Falls, about 10km west of Pai.

Pai makes a good base for **trekking**, which can be arranged cheaply through the guest houses. Karen, Lisu and Lahu villages are within range, and the terrain has plenty of variety: jungles and bamboo forests, hills and flat valleys. The area north of town, where trekking can be combined with **rafting** and **elephant riding**, is rather touristy now, but the countryside to the south is very quiet and unspoilt: hardened walkers could arrange a trek to Mae Hong Son, six days away to the southwest.

Practicalities

Opposite the bus station at the north end of town, *Duang Guest House* is a welcoming, relaxing **place to stay**, with clean singles from B30, doubles from B60. On the river bank to the east of *Duang*, *Pai Resort* has tidy bungalows with shared hot-water bathrooms for B100. *Charlie's Guest House* at 9 Rungsiyanon Road, the main street running south from the bus station, offers a variety of rooms around a lush garden, all of them clean (Charlie is the district health officer). Dorm beds are B30, singles start at B50, doubles at B60, all with shared hot-water bathrooms – or you might fancy the kitsch honeymoon suite, for B200 with all mod cons. Turn left south of *Charlie's* to reach *PS Riverside* by the Pai River bridge, which has a friendly terrace restaurant and simple huts on the river for B40.

In a beautiful setting by the river to the east of the bus station, *Rim Pai Cottage* is as posh as Pai gets. Comfortable rooms and rustic log cabins, all with hot showers, go for B300, including American breakfast.

Best of the travellers' **restaurants** is *Thai Yai* at 12 Rungsiyanon Rd, where the Scottish chef rustles up generous portions of back-home favourites at surprisingly cheap prices. On the street which leads to the bridge, *Own Home Vegetarian Restaurant* is also popular, serving good, moderately priced Western and Thai food. The unnamed eatery at 39/1 Chaisongkhram Rd (west from the bus station) does cheap and tasty *khao man kai* (boiled chicken with rice and broth) in the daytime only.

Northern Green, by the bus station, rents out small **motorbikes** and a few ropey mountain bikes.

Beyond Pai

Once out of the Pai valley, Route 1095 climbs for 35km of hairpin bends, with beautiful views north to 2175-metre Doi Chiang Dao at each turn. Once over the 1300-metre pass, the road steeply descends the south-facing slopes in the shadow of Doi Mae Ya (2065m), before working its way along the narrow, more populous lower valleys. Mokfa Falls makes an appealing setting for a break – it's 2km south of the main road, 76km from Pai. At MAE MA LAI, you'll turn right onto the busy Route 107 for the last 34km across the wide plain of rice paddy to Chiang Mai.

CHIANG RAI AND THE BORDERS

The northernmost tip of Thailand, stretching from the Kok River and **Chiang Rai** to the border, is a schizophrenic place, split in two by Highway 110, the continuation of Thailand's main north–south road. In the western half, rows of wild, shark's-tooth mountains jut into Burma, while to the east, low-lying rivers flow through Thailand's richest rice-farming land to the Mekhong River, which forms the border with Laos here. Although this is the end of the line (the overland crossings to Burma and Laos are closed to Western travellers), the region is well-connected and has been thoroughly opened up to tourism. Chiang Rai now has well over 2000 hotel rooms, catering mostly to upmarket fortnighters, who plough through the countryside in air-conditioned Scenicruisers in search of quaint, photogenic primitive life. What they get – fairground rides on boats and elephants, a santised presentation of the Golden Triangle's opium fields, and colourfully dressed hill people performing artificial folkloric rituals – generally satisfies expectations, but has little to do with the harsh realities of life in the north.

Chiang Rai itself pays ever less attention to independent travellers, so although you have to pass through the provincial capital, you should figure on spending most of your time in the border areas to the north, exploring the dizzy mountain heights, frenetic border towns and ancient ruins. Trekking, the prime domain of the backpacker, has also taken the easy route upmarket, and is better embarked on elsewhere in the north.

Chiang Mai to Chiang Rai

From Chiang Mai you can choose from three main approaches to Chiang Rai. The quickest and most obvious is Highway 1019, a fast 185-kilometre road that swoops through rolling hill country. Tourist coaches make the run in three hours, and most travellers end up passing this way once – it's best saved for the return journey, when you may well want to speed back to the comforts of Chiang Mai. For do-it-yourself **trekking**, this route has the benefit of running close to the primitive *Trekker House*, set in a beautiful landscape among a plethora of hill-tribe settlements: get off at the signpost 64km from Chiang Mai, just before BAN SOB PONG, and then it's a seven-kilometre walk up a dirt road. But unless you're in a desperate hurry getting to and from Chiang Rai, you'll probably opt for one of the scenic routes to Chiang Rai described below. The westerly of the two follows Highway 107 to **Tha Ton** and then completes the journey by longtail boat or bamboo raft down the **Kok River**. The other heads east as far as Lampang (see p.211) before barrelling north on Highway 1 via **Phayao**.

Tha Ton and the Kok River

You should set aside two days for this road and river journey along the **Kok River**, allowing for the almost inevitable overnight stay in Tha Ton. **Buses** between Chiang Mai's northern Chang Puak bus station and Tha Ton take about five hours, but many buses go only as far as Fang, 23km and an hour short of Tha Ton, in which case you'll have to do the final leg by songthaew. The standard **boat** trip takes the better part of the following afternoon. If you're on a motorbike, once at Tha Ton you have the choice of meandering up to Mae Salong by a scenic but testing minor road, or stowing your bike on the longtail for Chiang Rai.

Chiang Mai to Fang

From Chiang Mai the route heads north along Highway 107, retracing the Mae Hong Son loop in the early going and, after 56km, passing an **elephant training centre** on the right, which puts on logging shows daily at 9am and 10am (June–April; B40). It's a tourist trap, though – you're better off visiting the less hyped equivalent near Lampang. CHIANG DAO, an oversized market village, stretches on and on along the road around the 72km marker, as the crags and forests of the mountain after which the village is named loom up on the left. Before descending into the flat plain around Fang and the Kok River, the road shimmies over a rocky ridge, which marks the watershed separating the catchment areas of the Chao Phraya River to the south and the Mekhong River ahead.

The ugly frontier town of **FANG**, 153km from Chiang Mai, is made more appealing by the *Crocodile Dundee Guest House*, at the far south end of the main street. Clean, simple rooms in the wooden house are B50 single, B80 double; the friendly and informative proprietor leads treks and dirt-biking trips in the area west of the town. If you're travelling by bike you can cut east 5km before Fang on Highway 109 for Chiang Rai (125km), but this route misses out the beautiful Kok valley and is no easy option as much of it is unpaved.

Tha Ton

The tidy, leafy settlement of **THA TON**, 176km north of Chiang Mai, huddles each side of a bridge over the Kok River, which flows out of Burma four kilometres upstream. The main attractions here are boat and raft rides, but if you've got a morning to kill while waiting to go downriver, the ornamental gardens of **Wat Tha Ton** on the west side of the village are well worth the short climb. From the pavilion in front of the colossal, brilliant white Buddha, the view up the narrow green valley towards Burma and downstream across the sun-glazed plain is heady stuff.

Thip's Traveller House (☎053/245538), by the foot of the path to the wat, is the best budget **place to stay**, with dorm beds at B40, rooms from B80, and good food. The formidable Mrs Thip can fix raft trips to Chiang Rai, scenic longtail-boat trips to the Burmese border (half an hour upstream), treks to the wide variety of hill-tribe villages nearby, elephant riding, or various combinations of the above (phone bookings accepted). If *Thip's* is full, *Thaton House* on the north side of the river is next best: rooms with cold-water bathrooms cost B60 single, B80 double.

With its own gardens and swimming pool further along the same bank, *Mae Kok River Lodge* is incongruously **upmarket**. Comfy but tiny rooms in a cramped, traditional teak building start at B500: guests might empathise with the caged animals which the owner has rescued from illegal hunters and brought to the officially condoned wildlife refuge in the grounds.

Beyond Tha Ton, a difficult dirt road, beginning on the north bank of the river, winds its way up towards Mae Salong (see p.245), 40km to the northeast. Public transport on this route is provided by open-bed pickups, which make the two-hour trip every morning except in the rainy season, and experienced bikers might relish the challenge (all this might improve soon, as the road is scheduled to be paved). Mrs Thip has opened a second guest house 4km along the road on a farm above the river, where huts start at B100.

Along the Kok River

Travelling down the hundred-kilometre stretch of the **Kok River** to Chiang Rai gives you a chance to soak up a rich diversity of typical northern landscapes, which you never get on a speeding bus. Heading out of Tha Ton, the river traverses a flat valley of ricefields and orchards, where it's flanked by high reeds inhabited by flitting swallows – be sure to take a look back for the best view of Wat Tha Ton's beacon-like Buddha, which remains in sight for at least the first half-hour of the trip. About the same time as the statue disappears, you'll pass **Wat Phra That Sop Fang**, with its small hilltop chedi and a slithering naga staircase leading up from the river bank. After a twenty-minute break in MAE SALAK, 20km from Tha Ton, where dozens of Akha women and children beg and hawk necklaces, the river starts to meander between thickly forested slopes. From amongst the banana trees and giant wispy ferns, kids come out to play, adults to bathe and wash clothes, and water buffaloes emerge simply to enjoy the river.

About two and a half hours out of Tha Ton the hills get steeper and the banks rockier, leading up to a half-hour stretch of small but feisty rapids, where you might well get a soaking. Here and there, denuded slopes studded with burnt tree stumps attest to recent deforestation. Beyond the rapids, crowds of boats suddenly appear, ferrying camcorder-toting tour groups from Chiang Rai to the Karen village of RUAMMID, 20km upstream, for elephant riding. From here on, the landscape deteriorates as the bare valley around Chiang Rai opens up.

The best time of year to make this trip is in the cool season (roughly Nov–Feb), when the vegetation is lushest and the rapids most exciting; during the hot season (March–June) services are sometimes suspended because the water level falls too far – phone *Thip's* (see above) to check. Cramped **longtail boats** leave Tha Ton every day at 12.30pm for the trip to Chiang Rai, which takes four or five hours. The fare is B170, with motorcycles charged at B2 per cubic centimetre of engine. The slower, less crowded journey upriver gives an even better chance of appreciating the scenery – the longtails leave Chiang Rai at 10.30am.

If you have more time, the **bamboo rafts** which glide downriver to Chiang Rai in three days and two nights almost make you part of the scenery. Rafts can fit up to eight paying passengers – there are usually plenty of travellers to hitch up with during the high season, when you shouldn't have to wait more than a day for a full complement – and the price (B3500) includes mats, blankets and food. Each party is accompanied by two steersmen, who recycle the raft in Chiang Rai by selling the bamboo off as building material. Raft trips can be organised through *Thip's* and other guest houses in Tha Ton.

River boats used to be easy pickings for bandits – an English woman was shot dead in a longtail in 1987 – but the police have clamped down by setting up riverside checkpoints. The most important is at Mae Salak, where you'll be asked to show your **passport**.

To Chiang Rai via Phayao

The only substantial reason to consider the old 337-kilometre route from Chiang Mai to Chiang Rai along highways 11 and 1 is to stop off at Lampang (see p.211), as the full journey takes around seven hours, over twice as long as the new Highway 1095. Northeast of Lampang, Highway 1 winds over a forested range, after 50km passing through the narrow gulley called **Pratu Pa** ("Gateway of the Cliffs"), where bus drivers invariably honk at a small spirit shrine. Beyond, the road descends to the unremarkable junction town of NGAO, before speeding over a low pass to Phayao.

Facing the 1800-metre peak of Doi Bussaracum, the ancient town of **PHAYAO**, 140km from Lampang, is worth a break in the journey to visit its bizarre wat or to have lunch on the east bank of its hyacinth-strewn lake. Buses pull in at the station on central Donsanam Road – where, at no. 55, the *Tharn Thong Hotel* has clean rooms with hot water from B150.

According to legend, the lakeside position of **Wat Sri Khom Kham** – a two-kilometre walk or songthaew north along the main road from the bus station – was chosen by the Buddha himself, when, wilting in the notorious Phayao heat, he received shelter from a tree which miraculously sprouted from a seed planted by a passing bird. The main object of worship here is the Phra Chao Ton Luang, a huge pointy-nosed Buddha in the crude, angular local style of the fifteenth century. Outside the central image hall, various Buddha bits in crumbling sandstone are forlornly piled together on the grass like a spare-parts shop. Their limelight has been stolen by a gruesome modern **statue garden** at the north end of the temple: standing next to a children's playground, the supposedly educational statues, which look like special-effects models from a particularly nasty fright movie, are inspired by the Buddhist scriptures and represent the torments of hell. In contrast to these horrors, a modern **viharn**, which has been built on stilts over the lake at the south end of the wat, is all elegance and good taste. The interior has been vibrantly decorated with murals by Angkarn Kalyanapongsa, a famous artist and poet, who has followed traditional Lanna styles and included typically homely comic detail but added a sharp, modern edge.

Chiang Rai

Having lived in the shadow of Chiang Mai for all but thirty years of its existence, **CHIANG RAI** – sprawled untidily over the south bank of the Kok River – is now coming up on the rails to make a challenge as an upmarket tourist centre, with all the hype and hustle that goes with it. The long arm of the package-tour industry has reached this northern outpost, bringing snap-happy coach potatoes and well-heeled honeymooners, who alight for a couple of days of excursions and then shoot off again. Paradoxically, this leaves the town to get on with its own business during the day, when the trippers are out on manoeuvres, but at night the neon lights flash on and souvenir shops and ersatz Western restaurants are thronged. Meanwhile, the town keeps up its reputation as a dirty-weekend destination for Thais, a game given away by just a few motels and carports – where you drive into the garage and pay for a discreet screen to be pulled across behind you. Budget travellers have been sidelined, but they still turn up for the trekking and for the excellent handicraft shopping.

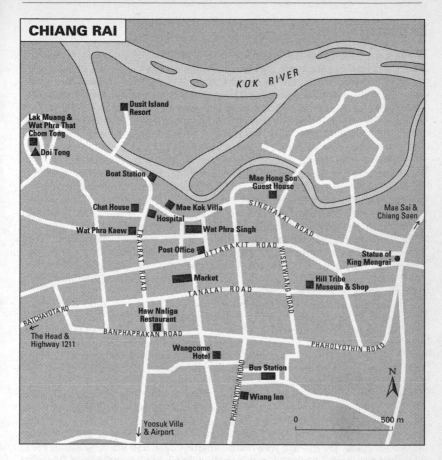

CHIANG RAI

KOK RIVER

Dusit Island Resort

Lak Muang & Wat Phra That Chom Tong

▲ Doi Tong

Boat Station

Mae Hong Son Guest House

Chat House   Mae Kok Villa
             Hospital

SINGHAKAI ROAD

Mae Sai & Chiang Saen

Wat Phra Kaew   Wat Phra Singh

Post Office   UTTARAKIT ROAD

TRAIRAT ROAD

WISETWIANG ROAD

Statue of King Mengrai

Market

Hill Tribe Museum & Shop

TANALAI ROAD

RATCHAYOTA RD

Haw Naliga Restaurant

BANPHAPRAKAN ROAD

The Head & Highway 1211

PHAHOLYOTHIN ROAD

Wangcome Hotel

PHAHOLYOTHIN ROAD

Bus Station

Wiang Inn

N

0   500 m

Yoosuk Villa
↓ & Airport

   Chiang Rai is most famous for the things it had and lost. It was founded in 1263 by King Mengrai of Ngon Yang who, having recaptured a prize elephant he'd been chasing around the foot of Doi Tong, took this as an auspicious omen for a new city. Tradition has it that Chiang Rai prevailed as the capital of the north for thirty years, but historians now believe Mengrai moved his court directly from Ngon Yang to the Chiang Mai area in the 1290s. Thailand's two holiest images, the Emerald Buddha (now in Bangkok) and the Phra Singh Buddha (now perhaps in Bangkok, Chiang Mai or Nakhon Si Thammarat, depending on which story you believe), also once resided here before moving on – at least replicas of these can be seen at Wat Phra Kaeo and Wat Phra Singh.
   Arriving at the **bus station** on Phaholyothin Road on Chiang Rai's south side leaves a long walk to most of the guest houses, so you might want to bundle into a samlor, the main form of transport around town. Longtails from Tha Ton dock at the **boat station**, situated at the top end of Trairat Road northwest of the centre and handy for the best guest houses. Taxis run into town from the **airport**, 3km south, for B50.

The town

A walk up to **Doi Tong**, the hummock to the northwest of the centre, is the best way to get your bearings and, especially at sunset, offers a fine view up the Kok River as it emerges from the mountains to the west. On the highest part of the hill stands the most interesting of Chiang Mai's few sights, a kind of phallic Stonehenge centred on the town's new **lak muang**, representing the Buddhist layout of the universe. The erection of a *lak muang* marks the official founding of a Thai city, and in Chiang Rai's case this has been precisely dated to January 26, 1263. To commemorate King Bhumibol's sixtieth birthday, this *lak muang* and the elaborate stone model around it were erected 725 years later to the day. The *lak muang* itself represents Mount Sineru (or Meru), the axis of the universe, while the series of concentric terraces, moats and pillars represent the heavens and the earth, the great oceans and rivers, and the major features of the universe. Sprinkling water onto the garlanded *lak muang* and then dabbing your head with the water after it has flowed into the basin below brings good luck.

The old wooden *lak muang* can be seen in the viharn of **Wat Phra That Chomtong**, the city's first temple, which sprawls shambolically over the eastern side of the hill. Look out for the small teetering prang, the old-fashioned wooden spirit house and the Chinese shrine, with which the wat shares the hillside in a typically ecumenical spirit.

The Emerald Buddha, Thailand's most important image, was discovered when lightning cracked open the chedi (since restored) at **Wat Phra Kaeo** on Trairat Road. A beautiful replica, which was carved in China from 300kg of milky green jade and presented by a Chinese millionaire in 1991, can now be seen here. It's not an exact copy, however: according to religious protocol, the replica could not have exactly the same name, materials or appearance as the original. At 47.9cm wide and 65.9cm high, the model is millimetres smaller.

As Chiang Rai is surrounded by such a variety of hill tribes and visited by such a weight of tourists, there are plenty of **handicraft shops**, though most of those lined up along Phaholyothin Road are merely trinket stalls. For a more authentic selection, head for the *Hill Tribe Museum and Handicrafts Shop* at 620/25 Tanalai Rd, which stocks tasteful and well-made hill-tribe, Thai and Burmese handicrafts. The shop was started by the country's leading development campaigner, Meechai Viravaidya, and all proceeds go to village projects. The upstairs museum is an excellent place to learn about the hill tribes before going on a trek – ask to see the slick, informative slide show (a small donation is requested to cover costs). The *Akha Cultural Education Centre* on the north bank of the river (take the left turn 200m after the bridge on the Mae Sai road and then it's down a lane to the left after 1km) sells a small but cheap range of bags and clothes in characteristic black and red patterns, and the profits are used to help Akha students. The *Handicraft Centre*, 2km north of town on the Mae Sai road, is the biggest souvenir shop, but it's pricey and the quality isn't up to much.

Practicalities

What Chiang Rai lacks in sights it more than makes up for with accommodation, if only in terms of quantity. That said, one or two guest houses compare with Chiang Mai's finest, and in the *Dusit* it boasts one of the north's finest hotels. You can eat well in Chiang Rai too, as long as you're prepared to shell out a bit. **TAT** plan to open a new office on Singakai Road near Wat Phra Singh – it may be open by now, but these things do take time.

Accommodation

Chiang Rai is overstuffed with **places to stay** of all categories, but many offer poor quality for the price – the ones listed below are those that stand out. Much of the more expensive accommodation is clustered around the commercial centre on Phaholyothin Road, while the guest houses can be found along the south bank of the river and on the fringes.

CHEAP AND MODERATE

Chat House, 3/2 Soi Sangkaew, Trairat Rd (☎053/711481). Located behind its own garden café, this is Chiang Rai's best travellers' hangout; modern rooms for B50 single, B80 double with shared hot showers, and bargain B100 doubles with own hot-water bathroom.

Mae Hong Son Guest House, 126 Singhakai Rd. Another laid-back establishment where decent singles start at B45, doubles B80, with shared hot showers.

Mae Kok Villa (aka *Chiang Rai Youth Hostel*), 445 Singhakai Rd (☎053/711786). An offbeat bargain, sprawling across an overgrown compound around an old, crumbly riverside mansion: dorm beds are B30, clean rooms with their own bathrooms (some with hot water) start at B100 single, B120 double.

The Head, 279 Soi 2, Ratchayota Rd. Quiet location at the western outskirts (free bicycles); bamboo bungalows from B40 single, B60 double, and shared hot showers.

YMCA, 70 Phaholyothin Rd (☎053/713785–6). Ever-reliable with air-con singles for B300, doubles for B400 (B220/B260 with fan, B70 for a dorm bed) and a swimming pool for children and accompanying adults.

Yoosuk Villa, 952/13 Ruamjitthawai Rd (☎053/711913). A good deal in the moderate price range, charging B395 for neat rooms with air conditioning, TV, fridge and hot water.

EXPENSIVE

Dusit Island Resort Hotel, 1129 Kraisorasit Rd (☎053/715777). Set on a 10-acre island in the Kok River, with unbeatable views of the valley, this is the top of the top end. Facilities include a health club, tennis courts, swimming pool and children's playground, with high standards of service and rates from B2200 single, B2600 double.

Wangcome, 869/90 Pemawibhata Rd (☎053/711800). Chintzy luxury hotel, not quite up to international standards. Singles from B900, doubles B1100.

Wiang Inn, 893 Phaholyothin Rd (☎053/711543). Almost identical to the *Wangcome*, but with a swimming pool and Chiang Rai's premier nightspot, *The Hill Discotheque*. Singles start at B900, doubles B1100.

Eating

Chiang Rai's restaurants congregate along Banphaprakan and Phaholyothin roads, with a growing number of unimpressive Western places scattered around. The **Thai** cheapies are a disappointing bunch: try *Khun*, by the clocktower at 528/8–9 Banphaprakan Rd, a popular, rough-hewn night-time restaurant which serves tasty Thai and Chinese standards and has a few pavement tables. For an even cheaper lunch-time buffet, make for the red canopy of *Siwachai*, a few doors away. Also on Banphaprakan Road, to the west of the clocktower after which it's named, *Haw Naliga* is a touch upmarket, but justifiably popular. At the top end, the elegant, open-sided pavilion in the grounds of the *Dusit Island Resort* is well worth a splurge for its wide range of delicious Thai cuisine.

TREKKING FROM CHIANG RAI

Communities from all the hill tribes have settled around Chiang Rai and the region offers the full range of terrain for **trekking**, from gentle walking trails near the Kok River to tough mountain slopes further north towards the Burmese border. The Kok River both to the west and the east of town is deep enough for rafts, and elephant-riding is also included in most treks. However, this natural suitability has attracted too many agencies and trekkers, and many of the hill-tribe villages, especially between Chiang Rai and Mae Salong, have become weary of the constant to-ing and fro-ing. Some of the agencies in Chiang Rai have recently widened their net to include the rest of the province, such as Chiang Khong, where there's a large population of Hmong and Mien, and other provinces like Nan, 270km to the south-east. All guest houses in Chiang Rai can fix you up with a trek – *Chat* and *Mae Hong Son* are responsible and reliable.

For comprehensive and accurate coverage of trails and hill-tribe villages in Chiang Rai province, the widely available *Guide Map of Chiang Rai* by V. Hongsombud (Bangkok Guides) is essential.

The enterprising director of the *Alliance Française*, 585 Wisetwiang Rd, serves up excellent **French** meals until 9pm, and also puts on a weekly film night (in French with English subtitles); if you're just looking for a daytime slice of café society, take coffee at the outdoor tables with a newspaper and a game of petanque. The *Bierstube*, south on Phaholyothin Road beyond the *Wiang Inn*, is a well-run and easygoing watering hole, with cheap draft beer and good **German** food.

North of Chiang Rai

At a push, any one of the places described in this section could be visited on a day trip from Chiang Rai, but if you can devote three or four days, you'd be better off moving camp to make a circuit of **Mae Salong** with its mountaintop Chinese enclave, **Mae Sai**, an intriguing border town, and **Chiang Saen**, whose atmospheric ruins by the banks of the Mekhong contrast sharply with the commercialism of nearby **Sop Ruak**. Given more time and patience, you could also stop over on the way to Mae Sai at **Doi Tung** to look down over Thailand, Laos, Burma, and China, and continue beyond Chiang Saen to the sleepy, little-visited town of **Chiang Khong** on the banks of the Mekhong.

Chiang Rai province is unique in being so well-mapped, which opens it up to independent exploration: the *Guide Map of Chiang Rai* (see box above) is indispensable for getting the most out of a rented motorbike, and even if you're not on a bike, might well give you some ideas for day walks away from the major attractions. For renting a **motorcycle**, *Soon* at 197/2 Trairat Rd (☎053/714068) is the most reliable place in Chiang Rai and has the best choice. If you just want to hop around the main towns by **public transport**, the set-up is straightforward enough: frequent buses to Mae Sai run due north up Highway 110; to Chiang Saen, they start off on the same road before forking right onto Highway 1016; for most other places, you have to make one change off these routes onto a songthaew.

Huai Khom and Laan Tong

The peaceful Karen village of **HUAI KHOM**, 15km northwest of Chiang Rai, sports a set of new, inexpensive bungalows, *Mountain View*, from which you can walk to several Lahu, Akha and Mien villages. Some of these villages, however, have become so used to trekkers that they are interested in farangs only for the money they can extract from them. Songthaews make the trip (40min) every half hour from the morning market on Chiang Rai's U-Tarakit Road, following a secondary road to the west off Highway 110, just north of the bridge over the Kok.

Far preferable is the **Laan Tong Lodge**, about 35km north of Chiang Rai, which has opened up the gentle, green valley of the Chan River, populated by Lisu, Akha, Mien and Lahu, to independent travellers. Set in an idyllic riverside meadow, the lodge has clean, cute bamboo bungalows with shared hot showers, starting at B70. From the lodge, you can walk to a small waterfall with a quiet bathing pool in two hours, while Mae Salong is a hard day's walk to the northwest (the owner can also organise cheap guided trekking). To get there from Chiang Rai, take any northbound bus along Highway 110 to MAE CHAN, a market town for the hill tribes that's famous for the quality of its lychees, and then board one of the buses that head westwards up the partially paved road every hour until early afternoon – the whole operation should take a little over one hour. Instead of backtracking to Mae Chan, hardened trail bikers could press on to Tha Ton from here, 75km away on a bad road.

Mae Salong (Santikhiri)

Perched 1300m up on a ridge with commanding views of sawtoothed hills, the Chinese Nationalist outpost of **MAE SALONG** lies at the end of a roller coaster of a road that plows 36km into the harsh border country west of Highway 110. Songthaews ply the freshly paved route frequently, starting from BAN PA ZANG, 32km north of Chiang Rai on Highway 110, and take ninety minutes to make the journey. A few marginally interesting attractions might tempt you to hop off en route – notably the Hill Tribe Training Centre, where local minorities are taught how to farm cash crops other than opium, and a couple of Mien and Akha souvenir villages – you should have no trouble flagging down another pickup when you're done.

Mae Salong is the focal point for the area's 14,000 **Kuomintang**, who for two generations now have held fast to their cultural identity, if not their political cause. The ruling party of China for twenty-one years, the Kuomintang (Nationalists) were swept from power by the communist revolution of 1949 and fled in two directions: one group, under party leader Chiang Kai-shek, made for Taiwan, where they founded the Republic of China; the other, led by General Li Zongren, settled in northern Thailand and Burma. The Nationalists' original plan to retake China from Mao Zedong in a two-pronged attack never came to fruition, and the remnants of the army in Thailand became major players in the heroin trade. Over the last ten years, the Thai government has worked hard to "pacify" the Kuomintang by a mixture of force and more peaceful methods, such as crop programmes to replace opium. Around Mae Salong at least, their work seems to have been successful, as evidenced by the slopes to the south of the settlement, which are covered with a carpet of rich green tea bushes. Since its rehabilitation, Mae Salong is now officially known as SANTIKHIRI ("Hill of Peace").

The town and beyond

Though it has a new temple, a church, a wat and a mosque, it's the details of Chinese life – the low-slung bamboo houses, the pictures of Chiang Kai-shek, ping pong tables, the sounds of Yunnanese conversation punctuated with throaty hawking – that make the village absorbing. Mae Salong gets plenty of Thai visitors, especially at weekends, who come to buy such delicacies as sorghum whisky (pickled with ginseng, deer antler and centipedes) and locally grown Chinese tea and herbs. If you want to sample the wares for yourself, take the left fork which skirts along the hill at the western end of the main street to reach the **traditional medicine shop**, on the right after 100m. The septuagenerian teacher who runs it will explicate in wild sign language the teas, pellets and biscuits which are good for the various parts of the body. It's also worth braving the dawn chill to get to the **morning market**, held at the fork in the road between 6 and 8am, which pulls them in from the surrounding Akha, Lisu and Mien villages.

The right fork which passes the wat at the west end of town leads after an hour to a clutch of very traditional and conservative **Akha villages** – notably BAN MAE DO – whose inhabitants moved here from Burma only in the last few years. Guided **trekking** from Mae Salong is expensive, but the Kuomintang live up to their Thai nickname – *jiin haw*, meaning "galloping Chinese" – by offering trekking on horses, a rare sight in Thailand. Trips can be arranged at the *Mae Salong Guest House* (see below) from B400 a day.

Beyond Mae Salong, a rough road judders 40km southwestwards to THA TON; songthaews make the two-hour journey from the market every day (less reliably in the rainy season). North of Mae Salong lies BAN THERD THAI, although to get to it by road you'd have to backtrack down the main road 12km to SAM YAEK and then make your own way up a nasty side road a further 13km into the hills. In its former incarnation as Ban Hin Taek, this mixed village was the opium capital of the notorious Khun Sa (see p.188): the Thai Army drove Khun Sa out after a pitched battle in 1983, and the village has now been renamed and "pacified" with the establishment of a market, school and hospital, but it's still dangerous to go any further north up the road.

Practicalities

The bottom end of Mae Salong's **accommodation** is *Rainbow*, a friendly guest house on the left beyond the traditional medicine shop, which serves reasonable Thai food and Western breakfasts and has primitive rooms for B70. The right fork at the market leads up a steep bank to the *Mae Salong Guest House* (☎053/711264) where decent rooms with attached bathrooms and shared hot showers cost B150. The better of the upmarket places is the *Mae Salong Villa* (☎053/713444) on the main road at the eastern end of the village: functional rooms are B500, comfy wooden bungalows with balconies facing the Burmese mountains are B700, and they all have hot-water bathrooms. The terrace **restaurant** shares the same view and cooks up the best food in town, including delicious but expensive Chinese specialities like *het haam* (wild mushrooms) and *kai dam* (black chicken).

Doi Tung

Steep, wooded hills rise abruptly from the plains west of Highway 110 as it approaches the Burmese border. Crowned by a thousand-year-old wat, the central peak here, 1300-metre **DOI TUNG**, makes a worthwhile outing just for the journey. Two paved roads run up the mountainside, intermittently criss-crossing and joining up, which can cause confusion: the older, less direct road begins in BAN HUAI KHRAI, 33km north of Chiang Rai on Highway 110, while the better new one starts 1km to the south. Songthaews make the eighteen-kilometre ascent up the old road from Ban Huai Khrai about every half an hour.

Both roads ascend through Akha and Lahu villages, pass over a precarious saddle with some minor temple buildings and refreshment stalls 2km before the top, and finally climb through a tuft of thick woods to **Wat Phra That Doi Tung** – look out for the strange collection of small Indian, Chinese and Thai statues, brought as offerings by pilgrims, in a rocky glade just before you reach the main temple buildings. Pilgrims to the wat earn themselves good fortune by clanging the rows of dissonant bells around the temple compound and by trying to throw coins into the gaping bellybutton of a giant Chinese Buddha: even if they miss they earn merit, because an attendant monk scoops up the misdirected money for temple funds. For non-Buddhist travellers, the reward for getting this far is the stunning view out over the cultivated slopes and half of northern Thailand. The wat's most important structures are its twin **chedis**, erected to enshrine relics of the Buddha in 911. When the building of the chedis was complete, King Achutaraj of Ngon Yang ordered a giant flag (*tung*), reputedly 2km long, to be flown from the peak, which gave the mountain its name.

More recently, Doi Tung has become the site of the Queen Mother's country seat, built in 1988 11km up the old road, and her hill-tribe project which has helped to develop local villages by introducing new agricultural methods: the slopes which were formerly blackened by the fires of slash-and-burn farming are now used to grow teak, pine and strawberries.

A steep, rocky and possibly dangerous **back road** north to Mae Sai (22km) begins at the saddle beneath the peak, by the refreshment stalls. This area has been the scene of conflict among the Kuomintang, the hill tribes and others involved in the opium trade, and although the road is now regulated by army and police checkpoints they can't keep a constant watch over every inch. After a right turn to a forestry camp and a left fork towards the southwest, you'll reach the two pavilions at the pinnacle of **Doi Chang Moob**, an even higher and better view-point than Doi Tung – on a clear day, you can make out the Mekhong River and the triangular outline of 2600-metre Loi Pangnao, on the border between Burma and China. The track then follows the sharp ridge north to BAN PHA HEE and then snakes down to BAN PHA MEE – both of these Akha villages have shops selling drinks. From Ban Pha Mee, the left fork goes directly to Mae Sai (7km) or you can descend for 5km to the main Highway 110, 4km south of the town.

Practicalities

There's no need to stay overnight on Doi Tung, but if you're taking things slowly, the two **guest houses** here are cheap and quiet. About 1500m from the bottom of the new road, the clean and friendly *Khwan Guest House* has bamboo shacks for B60 and some nice posh huts for B150, although the setting is dull. For better views make for the pleasant Akha village of BAN PAKHA, 7km up on a section of the old road, where the primitive bamboo bungalows of the *Akha Guest House* (no sign because of restrictions imposed by the palace) go for B40 per person, and cheap **trekking** to the well-developed villages of Doi Tung can be arranged.

Mae Sai

MAE SAI, with its hustling tourist trade and bustling border crossing, is not to everyone's taste, but it can be an intriguing place to watch the world go by, and with some good-value guest houses it can also be used as a base for exploring Doi Tung or Sop Ruak. Thailand's most northerly town lies 61km from Chiang Rai at the dead end of Highway 110, which forms the town's single north–south street and is the site of the bus stop. Wide enough for an armoured battalion, this ugly boulevard still has the same name – Phaholyothin Road – as at the start of its journey north in the suburbs of Bangkok.

Phaholyothin Road ends at a short but commercially important **bridge** over the Mae Sai River, which forms the border with Burma. During daylight hours, Thais and Burmese are allowed to travel up to 5km into each other's territory, which attracts swarms of Thai day-trippers, especially at weekends, who shop in the Burmese town of THAKHILEK for souvenirs, herbs and Chinese wares. The Burmese mostly come to Mae Sai for work, and for serious shopping at the **morning market** in the centre of town, while a few gem merchants cross over to entertain potential buyers in a house near the bridge. As elsewhere, farangs are not permitted to enter Burma by land, but you are allowed onto the bridge which forms the no-man's-land between the frontier posts. A handful of Burmese hawk handicrafts and cheap Western cigarettes here, and on Buddhist holidays and other special days the bridge hosts a full-blown **market** of weird and wonderful Burmese goods. In the evening, the town becomes peaceful and eerie, especially when the wind blows down the narrow valley, and you get the chance to enjoy the riverside location of many of the guest houses.

Shopping is what brings tourists to Mae Sai by the coachload; the stores around the bridge duly cash in by selling a lot of "Burmese" handicrafts made in the factories of Chiang Mai and coloured glass posing as gems. On the left 100m before the bridge, *Village Product* offers more interesting stuff, such as hill-tribe fabric and clothes from both Thailand and Burma. *Thong Tavee*, further south at 17 Phaholyothin Rd, is the place to buy good quality jade and to watch the delicate process of cutting, decorating and polishing the stone in the workshop behind.

Climb up to the chedi of **Wat Phra That Doi Wao**, five minutes' walk from the bridge (behind the *Top North Hotel*), for a better perspective on the town. As well as Doi Tung to the south and the hills of Laos in the east, you get a good view up the steep-sided valley and across the river to Thakhilek – far from being an exotic forbidden land, the Burmese town looks surprisingly similar to Mae Sai.

Most travellers staying in Mae Sai end up making **day trips** out to Doi Tung (see above) and Sop Ruak (below). A third, less compelling choice would be **Tham Luang**: this "Royal Cave" has an impressive entrance cavern, flooded with natural light, and 7km of low, sweaty passageways beyond (weak lanterns can be hired by the entrance for B20). Without a bike you'll have to hop on a bus south on Highway 110 for 5km, to where a row of roadside stalls sell strawberries in the cool season; the cave is a signposted 3km from there. On the way, look out for the elaborate mausoleums of Mae Sai's Chinese cemetery, 2km south of town.

Practicalities

A handful of **cheap guest houses** are strung out along the river bank west of the bridge. The best of these is the furthest away: *Mae Sai* (☎053/732021) is a beautiful, relaxing place to stay, wedged between a steep hill and the river, ten minutes from the main road. A variety of bungalows start at B50 single, B80 double. *Chad Guest House* on Soi Wiangpan (look out for the signpost on the left, 1km before the bridge) scores low for location but is the classic travellers' rest: the family is welcoming and well-informed about the area, the food is good and it's an easy place to meet people. Dorm beds are B40, and clean, quiet rooms are B80 single, B90 double, with shared hot showers. Most of the guest houses have **motorbikes** for rent, though the price is usually slightly higher than in Chiang Rai.

The *Tai Tong* at 6 Phaholyothin Rd (☎053/731976) is Mae Sai's best **hotel**, if you go by the thickness of its carpets; air-conditioned rooms start at B500. Much better value is the *Mae Sai Hotel* at 125/5 Phaholyothin Rd (☎053/731462), where simple, clean rooms with attached bathrooms are B180 with fan, B280 with air conditioning.

Mae Sai's top **place to eat** is *Rabieng Kaew*, a wooden house with an open-air terrace, opposite the *Krung Thai Bank* – the menu lists a wide choice of excellent Thai cuisine, though it's not cheap by local standards. The terrace of the *Riverside*, under the western side of the bridge, is crowded during the day with tourists watching the border action, but the Thai dishes are surprisingly good and generous, and not too pricey. The night market, across the main road from the *Sri Wattana Hotel*, is cheap and very popular. *JoJo* (daytime only) serves up decent Western breakfasts and fancy ice creams at a price: look out for the cuckoo clock opposite the *Sri Wattana Hotel*.

The *Frontier Saloon* by the entrance to Soi Wiangpan is good for a laugh: it's a real end-of-the-world **bar**, dark and run-down, with entertainment provided by an abysmal band.

Sop Ruak

The Golden Triangle, which actually denotes a huge opium-producing area spreading across Burma, Laos and Thailand, has, for the benefit of tourists, been artificially concentrated into the precise spot where the borders meet, 57km northeast of Chiang Rai. Don't come to the village of **SOP RUAK**, at the confluence of the Ruak and Mekhong rivers, expecting to run into sinister drug-runners, addicts or even poppy-fields – instead you'll find souvenir stalls, pay toilets and a huge sign saying "Golden Triangle" which pops up in a million photo albums around the world.

The meeting of the waters is undeniably monumental, but to get an unobstructed view of it you need to climb up to **Wat Phra That Phu Khao**, a 1200-year-old temple perched on a small hill above the village: to the north, beyond the puny Ruak (Mae Sai), the mountains of Burma march off into infinity, while eastwards across the mighty Mekhong spread the hills and villages of Laos. The scene will soon be transformed, however, as planning permission has been obtained for a Thai luxury hotel to be built on the uninhabited strip of land immediately upstream of the confluence. The attached casino will bypass Thai laws against gambling, and the usually strict border formalities will be waived for visitors coming from Thailand.

For B250, you can have the thrill of stepping on Laotian soil. A longtail boat from *Sri Wan Restaurant* on the north side of the village will give you a kiss-me-quick tour of the "Golden Triangle", including five minutes on an island in the Mekhong which belongs to Laos.

To get to Sop Ruak you'll have to go via Chiang Saen or Mae Sai. **From Chiang Saen** you can go by regular songthaew (departing from the south side of the T-junction), rented bicycle (an easy 14-km ride on a paved road, though not much of it runs along the river bank) or longtail boat up the Mekhong (B350 round trip). **From Mae Sai**, songthaews make the one-hour trip from the side of the *Sri Wattana Hotel* on Phaholyothin Road (they leave when they're full); if you're travelling by your own transport, be sure to turn left at the police box in BAN MAE MA, at the start of the unpaved section 21km from Mae Sai.

Practicalities

Budget travellers are better off **staying** in Chiang Saen. The grotty B60 cubicles at the *Golden Triangle Guest House* are typical of Sop Ruak's cheapies, but you might be tempted by the *Golden Hut* (contact reception at the *Golden Triangle Resort Hotel* opposite), where clean riverside rooms with their own bathrooms cost B150, including continental breakfast on the hotel terrace.

For a touch of luxury, try *Northern Villa* at the south end of the village. Rustic bungalows with balconies overlooking the river and hot-water bathrooms are B600, including American breakfast. For all the luxury you'll ever want, *Baan Boran* (☎053/716678; Bangkok reservations ☎02/2514707), 1km north out of Sop Ruak, is probably northern Thailand's finest hotel. Tastefully designed in impeccable traditional style, all the rooms and the swimming pool have great views over the countryside to the Mekhong; singles B2400, doubles B2700.

Chiang Saen

Combining tumbledown ruins with sweeping Mekhong River scenery, **CHIANG SAEN**, 60km northeast of Chiang Rai, makes a rustic haven and a good base camp for the border region east of Mae Sai. The town's focal point, where the Chiang Rai road meets the main road along the banks of the Mekhong, is a lively junction thronged by buses, songthaews and longtails, with a small day market on its south side. Turning left at this junction will soon bring you to Sop Ruak, but you may well share the road with the tour buses that sporadically thunder through; very few tourists turn right in Chiang Saen along the rough road to Chiang Khong, even though this is the best way to appreciate the slow charms of the Mekhong valley.

The region around Chiang Saen, originally known as Yonok, seems to have been an important Thai trading crossroads from some time after the seventh century. The much-romanticised chronicles of the region maintain that Chiang Saen ruled as the capital of northern Thailand from the twelfth century, but most historians now reserve that distinction for the lost principality of Ngon Yang. The city whose remains you see now was founded around 1328 by the successor to the renowned King Mengrai of Chiang Mai, Saen Phu, who gave up his throne to retire here. Coveted for its strategic location, guarding the Mekhong, Chiang Saen was passed back and forth between the kings of Burma and Thailand for nearly 300 years until Rama I razed the place to the ground in 1804. The present village was established only in 1881, when Rama V ordered a northern prince to resettle the site with descendants of the old townspeople mustered from Lamphun, Chiang Mai and Lampang.

Buses from Chiang Rai and **songthaews** from Sop Ruak stop just short of the T-junction of Phaholyothin Road and the river road, no more than a stone's throw from Chiang Saen's main guest houses. **Longtail boats** from Sop Ruak dock just east of this junction. If you're travelling by **bike or car**, follow Highway 110 north as far as MAE CHAN (30km), then bear northeastwards along a secondary route (Highway 1016) for the last 30km to Chiang Saen. **Bicycles** can be borrowed or rented from the guest houses to get around the ruins and the surrounding countryside.

The town

The layout of the old, ruined city is defined by the Mekhong River running along its east flank; a tall rectangle, 2.5km from north to south, is formed by the addition of the ancient ramparts, now fetchingly overgrown, on the other three sides. The grid of leafy streets inside the ramparts is now too big for the modern town, which is generously scattered along the river road and across the middle on Phaholyothin Road.

The **National Museum** (Wed–Sun 9am–4pm; B5), announced by the primitive stone bell at the western end of Phaholyothin Road, makes an informative starting point. As well as a disparate collection of exhibits from elsewhere, including unusual silver Buddhas and a transparent phallic lingam, the museum houses some impressive Buddha images and architectural features rescued from the surrounding ruins. The art of northern Thailand was once dubbed "Chiang Saen style" because the town had an important school of bronze casting. The more appropriate name "Lanna style" is now preferred, though you'll still come across the traditional term. As in many of Thailand's museums, the back end is given over to a curious jumble of folk objects, one highlight being the beautiful wooden lintel carved with *hum yon* (floral swirls representing testicles), which would have been placed above the front door of a house to ward off evil. **Wat Phra That Chedi Luang**, originally the city's main temple, is worth looking in on next door for its imposing octagonal chedi, now decorated with weeds and a huge yellow ribbon.

Beyond the ramparts to the west, **Wat Pa Sak**'s brick buildings and laterite columns have been excavated and restored by the Fine Arts Department, making it the most accessible and impressive of Chiang Saen's many temples (there's an entrance fee of B20 whenever the custodian is about). The wat's name is an allusion to the thousand (or so) teak trees which Saen Phu planted in the grounds when he built the chedi in 1340 to house some Indian Buddha relics. The central chedi owes its eclectic shape largely to the grand temples of Pagan in Burma: the square base is inset with niches housing alternating Buddhas and *deva* (angels) with flowing skirts, and above rises the tower for the Buddha relic, topped by a circular spire. Beautiful carved stucco covers much of the structure, showing intricate floral scrolls and stylised lotus patterns as well as a whole zoo of mythical beasts.

The open space around modern Chiang Saen, which is dotted with trees and another 140 overgrown ruins (both inside and outside the ramparts), is great for a carefree wander. A spot worth aiming for is the hapless leaning chedi of **Wat Phra That Chom Kitti**, which gives a good view of the town and the river from a small hill outside the northwest corner of the ramparts.

Practicalities

Most of Chiang Saen's **guest houses** are spread along the river road. The *Chiang Saen Guest House*, 250m north of the main T-junction, is a friendly family affair with a scenic terrace restaurant overlooking the river and clean, comfy rooms starting at B40 single, B60 double (bicycles are free); the owners can also organise treks. Prices at the *Siam Guest House*, two minutes' walk to the north, are much the same, and the management is helpful and runs treks to the area around Chiang Khong. In *Lanna*'s pleasant garden, on the south side of the junction, the cheapest scruffy bungalows are B40 single, B60 double, and the restaurant is good. **Eat** at your guest house or at the touristy *Sala Thai*, which hogs the view over the Mekhong from the main junction.

East to Chiang Khong

Several routes lead from Chiang Saen to Chiang Khong, 70km downriver, a peaceful and rarely visited backwater which is the only other town on the Mekhong before it enters Laos. The most scenic way to get there is by **motorbike**, following the northward kink in the river for three hours along bumpy, unpaved roads. An exciting but expensive alternative – about B1500 – is to run the rapids on a hired longtail boat, which will also take about three hours. Public transport between the two towns is limited to one **songthaew** a day, which heads off along the river before cutting across country on Highway 1129 to reach Chiang Khong after two hours. If you're going straight to Chiang Khong from Chiang Rai, direct hourly **buses** cover the ground in two hours; more frequent buses go through THOENG, but they take three hours.

Heading out of Chiang Saen by the river road, you'll pass through tobacco fields and, after 4km, see the brick gate of **Wat Phra That Pha Ngao** on the right. The tenth-century temple contains a supposedly miraculous chedi perched on top of a large boulder, but the real attraction is the view from the new chedi on the hillside above: take the one-kilometre paved track which starts at the back of the temple and you can't miss the lumbering **Chedi Ched Yod**, designed by an American in the style of a concrete bunker and built over and around a ruined brick chedi. From here the panorama takes in Chiang Saen's ruins, the wide plain and the slow curve of the river. To the east, the Kok River, which looks so impressive at Chiang Rai, seems like a stream as it pours into the mighty Mekhong.

Around 40km from Chiang Saen, **BAN HAT BAI**, inhabited by the Thai Lue minority, is famous for weaving brightly coloured cotton. Beyond, the hills close in and the river enters a stretch of rocky rapids, forcing the road to climb up the valley side and making for some dramatic vantage points.

Chiang Khong

CHIANG KHONG achieved its greatest fame among travellers as the starting point for the old Laotian loop, lost since the Pathet Lao government closed the country in 1975. Thais are still allowed to cross over from the passenger pier at the north end of the riverside town to trade and shop in the Laotian town of BAN HUAI SAI, with its old French-built fort, directly opposite. For trading boats, the port is BAN HAT KHRAI, just south of town, which springs to life during the annual giant catfish hunt: at this time the good but pricey restaurant above the port is the place to sample catfish. In between these two boat landings, Chiang Khong is strung out along a single north–south street on a high, steep bank above the river. Once you've admired the view of Laos and the traffic on the Mekhong from this elevated position, there's little to do but relax and enjoy the fact that none of the hustle is directed at you.

PRACTICALITIES

The two **guest houses** in Chiang Khong are welcome relief if you've made the tough trip down from Chiang Saen – both are easygoing and restful, with ringside views over the water. *Ban Tam-Mi-La*, at the north end of the main street, at 8/1 Sai Klang Rd (☎053/791234), has smart wooden bungalows with shared hot showers, overlooking the river, for B60 single and B100 double. The helpful owner can arrange longtail boat trips up or down the Mekhong for B200 per hour. The slightly more refined *Wiang Kaew* (☎053/791140), further down Sai Klang Road towards the centre, is a pretty wooden house with a riverside garden, where very clean rooms with shared hot showers go for B100 single, B200 double.

Trekking around Chiang Khong is still in its infancy, but it's possible to take in some good walking in the scenic mountains on the Thailand–Laos land border and to visit Hmong, Lahu and Mien settlements – *Ban Tam-Mi-La* can organise treks, but only at weekends as the owner is a teacher.

GIANT CATFISH

The **giant catfish** (*pla buk*), found only in the Mekhong, is said to be the largest freshwater fish in the world, measuring up to 3m in length and weighing in at 300kg. Chiang Khong is the catfish capital of the north, attracting fish merchants and restaurateurs from Chiang Rai and Chiang Mai – the tasty meat of the *pla buk* is prized for its fine, soft texture and can fetch up to B400 a kilo. The hunting season is officially opened at the port of Ban Hat Khrai on April 18 with much pomp, including an elaborate ceremony to appease Chao Por Pla Buki, the giant catfish god. Around 100 fishing boats then set out, as they do every morning before dawn for the rest of the season, from both the Thai and Laotian banks, vying with each other to see who can make the first catch. Gone is the old challenge and excitement of harpooning the fish, however: the fishermen now trawl the river over several kilometres of its course with 250-metre nylon nets. The season's haul is usually between thirty and sixty fish all told, but recent years have been so disappointing that Thailand's Fishery Department has begun an artificial spawning programme.

---

travel details

Trains

From Chiang Mai to Bangkok (6 daily; 13hr).

From Den Chai to Bangkok (8 daily; 9hr); Chiang Mai (6 daily; 4hr).

From Doi Khun Tan to Bangkok (5 daily; 12hr); Chiang Mai (5 daily; 1hr).

From Lampang to Bangkok (6 daily; 11hr); Chiang Mai (6 daily; 2hr).

From Lamphun to Bangkok (4 daily; 13hr); Chiang Mai (4 daily; 20min).

Buses

From Chiang Khong to Bangkok (3 daily; 13–14hr).

From Chiang Mai to Bangkok (28 daily; 9–10hr); Chiang Rai (22 daily; 3–4hr); Chom Thong (every

30min; 1hr); Fang (every 30min; 4hr); Khon Kaen (11 daily; 11–12hr); Khorat (10 daily; 11–12hr); Lampang (21 daily; 2hr); Lamphun (every 30min; 30min); Loei (6 daily; 9–10hr); Mae Hong Son (8 daily; 8hr); Mae Sai (10 daily; 4–5hr); Nan (13 daily; 7–8hr); Pai (6 daily; 4hr); Phayao (12 daily; 3hr); Phitsanulok (9 daily; 10hr); Rayong (3 daily; 12hr); San Kamphaeng (every 15min; 30min); Sukhothai (6 daily; 5hr); Tak (6 daily; 4hr); Tha Ton (6 daily; 5hr); Ubon (4 daily; 15–17hr); Udon Thani (6 daily; 11–12hr).

From Chiang Rai to Bangkok (15 daily; 12hr); Chiang Khong (hourly; 2hr); Chiang Saen (every 15min; 1hr 30min); Khorat (3 daily; 12hr); Mae Sai (every 15min; 1hr 30min); Nan (1 daily; 7hr); Pattaya (3 daily; 16hr); Phayao (21 daily; 2hr); Phitsanulok (3 daily; 7hr).

From Lampang to Bangkok (10 daily; 8hr); Chiang Rai (21 daily; 5hr); Nan (10 daily; 5hr); Phayao (21 daily; 3hr).

From Mae Hong Son to Bangkok (2 daily; 18hr).

From Mae Sai to Bangkok (8 daily; 13hr).

From Nan to Bangkok (13 daily; 13hr).

From Pai to Mae Hong Son (4 daily; 4hr).

From Phayao to Nan (3 daily; 5hr).

Flights

From Chiang Mai to Bangkok (9 daily; 1hr); Chiang Rai (2 daily; 40min); Khon Kaen (2 weekly; 1hr 40min); Mae Hong Son (2 daily; 40min); Mae Sot (4 weekly; 1hr); Nan (3 weekly; 1hr); Phitsanulok (9 weekly; 1hr 30min); Phuket (4 weekly; 2hr); Surat Thani (2 weekly; 2hr); Tak (4 weekly; 2hr).

From Chiang Rai to Bangkok (2 daily; 1hr 20min).

From Lampang to Bangkok (1 daily; 2hr); Phitsanulok (5 weekly; 35min).

From Loei to Bangkok (3 weekly; 2hr); Phitsanulok (3 weekly; 1hr).

From Mae Hong Son to Bangkok (1 daily; 2hr).

From Nan to Bangkok (1 daily; 2hr); Phitsanulok (3 weekly; 1hr); Phrae (1 daily; 30min).

CHAPTER FOUR

THE EAST COAST

Billed over-optimistically by tour operators as Thailand's riviera, the **east coast** is a five-hundred-kilometre string of predominantly dull, grey beaches blotched with expensive, over-packaged family resorts. Worse still, the discovery of oil and natural gas fields in these coastal waters has turned pockets of the first one-hundred-kilometre stretch into an unsightly industrial landscape of refineries and depots. Off-shore, however, it's an entirely different story, with island beaches as peaceful and unsullied as many of the more celebrated southern retreats.

The first worthwhile stop comes 100km east of Bangkok at Si Racha, a less than scintillating town but the point of access for diminutive **Ko Si Chang**, whose dramatically rugged coastlines and low-key atmosphere make a restful getaway. In complete contrast, **Pattaya**, just half an hour south, is Thailand's number-one package-tour destination, its customers predominantly middle-aged Western males enticed by the resort's sex-market reputation and undeterred by its notoriety as the country's most polluted beach. Things soon look up though, as the coast veers sharply eastwards towards Ban Phe, revealing the island of **Ko Samet**, the loveliest of all beach resorts within a comfortable bus ride radius of Bangkok. Primarily geared towards budget travellers, Samet strikes a perfect pitch between unspoilt rough-living and well-equipped comfort.

East of Ban Phe the scenery starts to get more lush and hilly as the coastal highway nears **Chanthaburi**, the dynamo of Thailand's gem trade and the only one of the region's provincial capitals worth visiting. Another 80km brings you to **Ko Chang**, a huge island still barely developed for the tourist trade, with long, fine beaches. Ko Chang marks the easternmost limit of the tourist trail: although it looks tantalisingly easy to get into Cambodia from here, you won't get beyond the border posts, whatever touts might tell you.

Highway 3 extends almost the entire length of the east coast – beginning in Bangkok as Sukhumvit Road, and known by the same name when cutting through towns – and hundreds of **buses** ply the road, connecting all major mainland destinations. Buses from Bangkok's Eastern Bus Terminal serve all the provincial capitals and tourist spots, but it's also possible to travel between the east coast and the northeast without passing back through the capital: the most direct routes start from Pattaya and Chanthaburi.

Ko Si Chang

Almost thirty kilometres southeast out of Bangkok, Highway 3 finally emerges from the urban spread at the fishing town of SAMUT PRAKAN, from where it follows the edge of the plain for a further 50km before reaching the prosperous but dull provincial capital of CHONBURI. The road divides here, Route 344 making a diagonal short-cut to the coastal stretch between Rayong and Chanthaburi, and Highway 3 continuing to follow every kilometre of the L-shaped

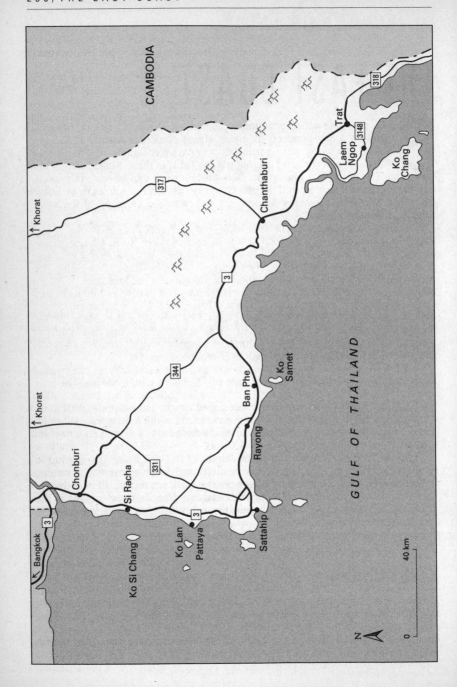

coastline to Rayong. Thai holidaymakers are very keen on the expensive beach resort of BANG SAEN, 10km south of Chonburi, particularly as a day-trip getaway from Bangkok. As an off-the-beaten-track experience, however, the small nearby island of **KO SI CHANG** is incomparably more rewarding.

The unhurried pace and the absence of consumer pressures make this tiny rocky island a satisfying place to hang out for a few days. Unlike most other east-coast destinations, Ko Si Chang offers no real beach life – fishing is the major source of income, and there's little else to do here except explore the craggy coastline and gaze at the horizon. Yet there is some night-time action: the island caters for the crews of the cargo ships which choke the deep channel between Ko Si Chang and the mainland – hence the transformation at night, when the apparently unsophisticated village is enlivened by the strains of singing hostesses.

Getting to Ko Si Chang

Access to Ko Si Chang is from the fishing port and refinery town of SI RACHA, a two-hour bus journey from Bangkok. **Buses** leave the capital every twenty-five minutes: air-con buses stop near *Laemtong* department store on Si Racha's Sukhumvit Road, from where you'll need to take a samlor to the pier, whereas most regular buses stop nearer the pier on Chermchompon Road. **Boats** leave four times a day (last one about 4.30pm) from the pier at the end of Soi 14, Chermchompon Road. The hop should take about forty minutes, but the time varies according to how many passengers need to be transferred to and from the cargo ships between which the ferry weaves. If you miss the last boat and have to stay in Si Racha overnight, try either the *Samchai*, *Sri Wattana*, or *Siwichai* hotels: all overlook the sea from just off Chermchompon Road, and have adequate rooms from B100.

The island

Most of the islanders live along Asadang Road, which runs parallel to the east coast and harbour – where you'll also find the market, shops, bank (with exchange facilities) and post office. Asadang Road is part of a small ring road that encircles the northeast corner of Ko Si Chang and extends down to the southeast coast; the rest of the island is accessible only by paths. It's easy enough to walk from place to place, or to jump in one of the island's fleet of motorcycle samlors, which have the roads virtually to themselves – there are probably fewer than ten private cars on Ko Si Chang. The easiest point of reference for orientation is *Tiew Pai Guest House*, which stands at the southwest "corner" of the ring road, at the point where it branches off down the southeast coast, about 750m from the pier.

Because of its relative inaccessibility, the **southern part** of the island is the more interesting area to explore, and it also holds the best beach. From *Tiew Pai* the road veers left, passing a Marine Research Centre before coming to an end at pebbly **Hat Tha Wang** – fine for picnics but useless for swimming. If you follow the paths west from here, uphill through trees, you'll see the overgrown foundations of **Rama V's summer palace**, built here in the 1890s but moved piece by piece to Bangkok in 1901, where it was reconstructed as Vimanmek Palace (see p.82). Aside from the stone steps and balustrades which still cling to the shallow hillside, the only intact structure on the site is the circular **Wat Asadang Nimitr**, right at the top and surmounted by a crumbling chedi.

The paths diverge just beyond the old palace. One heads southeast to the island's most swimmable and sheltered beach, **Hat Sai Kaew** (2km from *Tiew Pai*), which is sandy and secluded; there's coral amongst the shells on the adjoining beach, but not much in evidence underwater. The other track snakes through the savannah-like grassland of the interior, affording glimpses of the rugged western coastline, but giving no direct access to it; this quiet part of the island is a good place to observe wildlife, particularly butterflies and yellow squirrels.

The main beach on the southern stretch of the **west coast** is **Hat Tam Pang** – a great place for perching on the cliff-tops and watching the seagulls, but again, too rocky for swimming, and in the monsoon season too green with algae. You can only get there via the unmetalled road opposite the Marine Research Centre (paying B3 to cross the landowner's property) – a half-hour walk.

Spectacular views can also be enjoyed from the rocky **northwest** headland of **Khao Khat** – a classic sunset spot, and safe enough for cliffside scrambling. The ring road runs close by: take the right fork at the *Tiew Pai Guest House*, walk beneath the gaze of the large modern Buddha seated on the western hillside, and Khao Khat is less than a kilometre away. From here, the ring road veers eastwards to reach the gaudy multi-tiered **Chinese Temple** at the northern end of Asadang Road, stationed at the top of a steep flight of steps and commanding a good view of the harbour and the mainland coast. Boatloads of Chinese pilgrims make their way here, particularly over Chinese New Year.

Practicalities

Disembarking at the pier on Asadang Road, it's less than a ten-minute walk to your left to the island's cheapest **accommodation**: *Tiew Pai Guest House* (☎038/216084). It has simple rooms from B90 to B450, dorm beds for B45, a good menu, friendly manager and nightly entertainment from teenage girls hired to sing Thai pop and folk songs karaoke-style. Further towards the centre of the island, near the hillside Buddha, *Champ Bungalows* (☎038/216105) has more of a resort feel, with fairly well-appointed B300 bungalows and open-air bar and restaurant, which also features adolescent crooners. The island's also good for **camping**: the cliffs at Khao Khat are a particularly popular spot, though quite exposed.

Aside from the **nightlife** on offer at *Tiew Pai* and *Champ*, there's a lively open-air restaurant south of the pier on Asadang Road and an outdoor *likay* stage near the Chinese temple which puts on frequent performances by travelling folk-theatre players.

Pattaya

Voted by *Which Holiday* magazine in 1992 as one of the world's ten worst beach resorts, **PATTAYA** – 30km south of Si Racha – is the epitome of exploitative tourism gone mad. Visibly polluted sea, narrow, rubbish-strewn beaches and streets packed with high-rise hotels combine to make it visually Thailand's least attractive holiday spot. But for most Pattaya tourists it doesn't matter that the place looks like Torremolinos nor that most buildings dump their sewage straight into the bay – what they are here for is **sex**. The town swarms with male and female prostitutes, spiced up by a sizeable population of transvestites (*katoey*), and plane loads of Western men flock here to enjoy their services in the rash of go-go bars and massage parlours for which "Patpong-on-Sea" is notorious. It has the largest gay scene in Thailand, too, with several exclusively gay hotels and a whole area given over to gay sex bars.

Pattaya's evolution into sin city began with the Vietnam War, when Pattaya got fat on selling sex to American servicemen. Tempted by the dollars, outside investors moved in, local landowners got squeezed out, and soon the place was unrecognisable as the fishing village it once was. When the soldiers and sailors left in the mid-Seventies, western tourists were enticed to fill their places, and as the seaside Sodom and Gomorrah boomed, ex-servicemen returned to run the sort of joints they had once blown their dollars in. Almost half the bars, cafés and restaurants are Western-run, specialising in home-from-home menus of English breakfasts, sauerkraut and bratwurst, hamburgers and chips.

Yet Pattaya does have its good points even if you don't fit the lecherous profile of the average punter, as proved by the number of families who choose to spend their packaged fortnights here. Pattaya's water sports facilities are the best in the country, and though holidaying here might not be cheap – there are no makeshift low-budget bamboo huts for backpackers and few bargain food stalls – there are several relatively low-cost hotels with their own pools. You won't learn much about Thailand in Pattaya, but you could have quite a good time here.

Arrival, orientation and information

Most people **arrive** in Pattaya direct **from Bangkok**, either by public bus from the Eastern Bus Terminal, or by air-con tour bus from a Bangkok hotel or Don Muang airport. All public buses stop at the bus station just north of Soi 1, off Pattaya Beach Road in North Pattaya; tour buses have drop-off points all over town. **From Si Racha** it's a thirty-minute ride in one of the frequent songthaews and you'll probably get dropped just east of the resort on Sukhumvit Road, from where Pattaya songthaews will ferry you into town; a few Si Racha songthaews will take you all the way. It's also possible to get to Pattaya direct **from Isaan** – Pattaya-bound buses leave Khorat four times a day, arriving at the bus station in North Pattaya.

Pattaya comprises three separate bays. At the centre is the four-kilometre **Pattaya Beach**, the noisiest, most unsightly zone of the resort, crowded with yachts and tour boats and fringed by a sliver of sand. **Pattaya Beach Road** runs the length of the beach and is connected to the parallel Pattaya 2 Road by a string of sois numbered from 1 in the north to 17 in the south. The core of this block, between sois 6 and 13, is referred to as **Central Pattaya** and is packed with hotels, restaurants, bars, fast-food joints, souvenir shops and tour operators. During the day this is the busiest part of the resort, but after dark the neon zone south of Soi 13 – **South Pattaya** – takes over. Known locally as "the strip", this is what Pattaya's really about, with sex for sale in go-go bars, discos, massage parlours and "bar beers". The town's enclave of gay sex bars is here too, focused mainly on the interlinked network of small lanes numbered as Pattayaland sois 1, 2 and 3, between the wider Beach Road sois 13 and 14. **North Pattaya**, between Central Road and North Pattaya Road, also has its "bar beers", but is a more sedate up market district.

The southerly bay, **Jomtien Beach**, though fronted by enormous high-rises, is the only one where swimming and sunbathing is actually enjoyable. Fourteen kilometres long, it is cleaner and safer than Pattaya Beach, and is considered Thailand's number one windsurfing spot. The northernmost end has become a gay cruising beach.

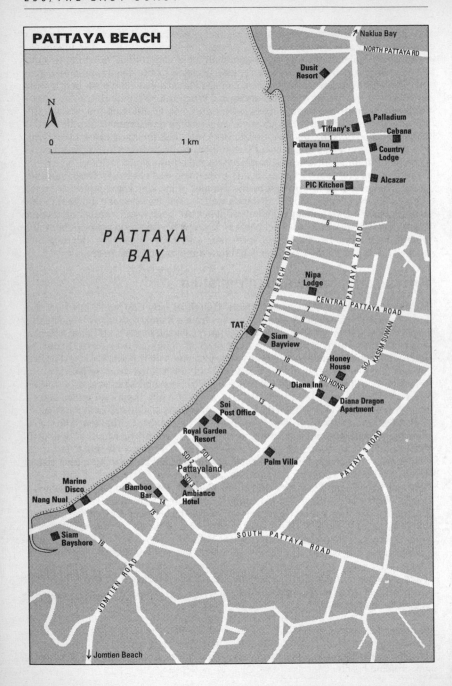

PATTAYA BEACH

PATTAYA BAY

N

0   1 km

Naklua Bay

NORTH PATTAYA RD

Dusit Resort

Palladium

Tiffany's

Cabana

Pattaya Inn

Country Lodge

PIC Kitchen

Alcazar

PATTAYA 2 ROAD

PATTAYA BEACH ROAD

CENTRAL PATTAYA ROAD

Nipa Lodge

TAT

Siam Bayview

Honey House

SOI KASEM SUWAN

SOI HONEY

Diana Inn

Diana Dragon Apartment

Soi Post Office

Royal Garden Resort

SOI 1

SOI 2

Pattayaland

SOI 3

Palm Villa

PATTAYA 3 ROAD

Marine Disco

Bamboo Bar

Ambiance Hotel

Nang Nual

Siam Bayshore

SOUTH PATTAYA ROAD

JOMTIEN ROAD

Jomtien Beach

Naklua Bay, around the northerly headland from Pattaya Beach, is the quietest of the three, and has managed to retain its fishing harbour and indigenous population despite the onslaught of condominiums and holiday apartments. On the downside, much of the accommodation is so far off the main road that it's inaccessible for tourists without private transport and there's no decent beach.

The easiest way to **get around** Pattaya is by **songthaew** – though on all routes beware of being overcharged. Most follow a standard anti-clockwise route up Pattaya 2 Road as far as North Pattaya Road and back down Pattaya Beach Road, for a fixed fee of B5 per person. Songthaews to Jomtien leave from the junction between Pattaya 2 Road and South Pattaya Road and cost B5 to the beginning of the beach, B10 beyond. To get to Naklua you need to negotiate with your driver to take you further up Pattaya 2 Road. The alternative is to rent your own transport: Pattaya Beach Road is full of **motorbike and jeep** rental places.

The **TAT** office at 382/1 Beach Rd, Central Pattaya (daily 8.30am–4.30pm), has lots of information on the area, including up-to-date price lists, and will give you trustworthy advice on pollution levels. The **Tourist Police** headquarters is next door (☎038/429371).

Accommodation

Most of Pattaya's cheap and moderately priced hotels offer similar facilities, notably swimming pools or the use of pools in neighbouring hotels – an essential asset considering the dreadful beaches. Those listed below as "cheap" are the best of the under-B400 range; there's no point paying more than that unless you're looking for the plush facilities of the top-end hotels, which start at around B1500. Bear in mind that prices in the expensive hotels can plummet when demand is slack, and that the high-profile sex industry ensures that all rooms have beds large enough for at least two people; rates quoted here are for "single" rooms with one big double bed (a "double" room will have two big double beds and cost more). Though hotels are easy-going about gay couples, we've listed a few exclusively gay hotels as well, for which it may be worth paying over B400.

Cheap

Cabana, Pattaya 2 Rd, North Pattaya (☎038/421223). Comfortable rooms in the quieter area of town from B250.

Country Lodge, 78/12 Pattaya 2 Rd, North Pattaya (☎038/428484). Same low key atmosphere as nearby *Cabana*. From B250.

Diana Dragon Apartment, 198/16 Soi Buakhao, off Pattaya 2 Rd at the end of the soi opposite Soi 11, Central Pattaya (☎038/429550). Enormous rooms with fridge, and use of the pool at *Diana Inn*, 100m away; favoured by long-stay tourists. Very good value at B200.

Diana Inn, 216/3–9 Pattaya 2 Rd, opposite Soi 11, Central Pattaya (☎038/429675). Upmarket atmosphere and good rooms. B300.

Honey House, Soi Honey, opposite Soi 10, Pattaya 2 Rd, Central Pattaya (☎038/424396). Friendly, clean and the best value in Pattaya at B150 (B250 a/c) for a room with bathroom.

Palm Villa, 485 Pattaya 2 Rd, opposite Soi Post Office, Central Pattaya (☎038/429099). Peaceful haven close to the nightlife, with small garden. Sizeable rooms for B350.

Expensive

Asia Pattaya, 325 Cliff Rd, South Pattaya (☎038/428602). Well placed in private bay between the *Royal Cliff* and Jomtien beach. Extensive facilities including nine-hole golf course, tennis courts, swimming pool and snooker tables. Quality rooms from B2662.

Dusit Resort, 240/2 Pattaya Beach Rd, North Pattaya (☎038/425616). In the thick of the high-rises; has an excellent reputation for high-quality service and facilities: two pools, a gym and tennis courts. Rooms from B2000.

Royal Cliff, Royal Cliff Bay, between South Pattaya and Jomtien (☎038/421421). Pattaya's most luxurious retreat, with landscaped gardens, private bay, three pools and tennis courts. Rooms from B2600.

Royal Garden Resort, 218 Pattaya Beach Rd, South Pattaya (☎038/428126). Facilities include floodlit tennis courts, a huge pool, a tropical garden and a certified dive centre. Well-equipped rooms from B2057.

Siam Bayshore, 559 Pattaya Beach Rd, South Pattaya (☎038/428678). Set in a secluded wooded spot overlooking the beach; many rooms with balconies and sea view. Two pools, tennis courts, snooker, table tennis and badminton facilities. From B1694.

Gay hotels

Ambiance Hotel, 325/91 Pattayaland Soi 3, South Pattaya (☎038/424099). Right in the heart of the gay area. Well-appointed rooms from B600.

Homex Inn, 157/24–30 Pattaya Naklua Rd, North Pattaya (☎038/429039). Small hotel built around a pool in quiet area of town. From B450.

Pattaya Inn, 380 Soi 2, North Pattaya (☎038/428400). Lots of facilites and good rooms from B600.

Daytime activities

Most tourists in Pattaya spend the days recovering from the night before: not much happens before midday, breakfasts are served until early afternoon, and the hotel pool generally seems more inviting than a tussle with water-skis. But the energetic are well provided for, with a massive range of water sports and a fair choice of land-based activities.

Jomtien Beach is the place for **water sports** enthusiasts, particularly windsurf-ers, water-skiers, jet-ski riders and parasailors: you can either book up in the outlets along Beach Road or head down to Jomtien and sign up there. Average prices start at about B1000 per hour for water-skiing; B200 for windsurfing; and B250 for parasailing.

Snorkelling and **scuba diving** are also big here, though if you've got the choice between diving here or off the Andaman Coast (see p.365), go for the latter – the waters are a lot more spectacular. TAT-approved dive shops that run certificate courses and diving expeditions include *Dave's Divers Den* on Soi 6, Beach Road, *Steven's Dive Shop* on Soi 4, Beach Road and *Seafari Sports Center* at the *Royal Garden Resort* hotel on Beach Road, South Pattaya. One-day introduc-tory dives start at about B2000. Several companies along Beach Road run snor-kelling trips to nearby Ko Larn and Bamboo Island, though mass tourism has taken its toll on the coral and the islands.

All top-end hotels have **tennis courts** and some offer badminton and gym facilities too, though these are generally only open to guests. The *Pattaya Bowl*, just north of Soi 5, Pattaya 2 Road, has twenty **bowling** lanes (B30 per game) and ten **snooker** tables (B100 per hour) and opens daily from 10am to 2am; if you're more of a gung-ho type, head for the **shooting range** at *Tiffany's* on Pattaya 2 Road, North Pattaya (daily 9am–9pm; B120), the **go-kart circuit** in Jomtien (daily 10am–6pm), or the **archery range** at Nong Nooch 18km south of Pattaya along Highway 3 (daily 10am–6pm). And at weekends there's always the prospect of a

speedway race at the Bira International Circuit, 14km northeast of Pattaya on Route 36 (B80–150 admission).

If you're really stuck for something to do, you could visit **Mini Siam**, just north of the North Pattaya Road/Sukhumvit Road intersection, which is just what it sounds like: two hundred of Thailand's most precious monuments reconstructed to 1:25 scale. Mini Europe is coming soon. Alternatively, **Nong Nooch Village**, 18km south of Pattaya off Sukhumvit Road, serves life-sized Thai culture in the form of traditional dancing and elephant rides against the backdrop of an attractively landscaped park. It's on all tour group itineraries, but it's worth coming here if you're into flowers: the **orchid garden** is said to be the world's largest.

Plenty of agents·fix up day trips to tourist spots further afield, like Ko Samet (B600), the River Kwai (B1200) and Ayutthaya (B1800), though for all these the journey times are so long as to make them hardly worth the effort.

Eating

The scores of expat restaurateurs in Pattaya have made western food more of a feature than Thai cuisine, a generally dismal situation made worse by the host of fast-food joints along Pattaya Beach Road – *Shakey's, Kentucky Fried Chicken, Mr Donut* and so on. For cheap **Thai food**, hunt out the curry and noodle vendors on Soi Kasem Suwan – they are concentrated between Central Pattaya Road and Soi Honey, but might pitch up anywhere. Top quality Thai restaurants are a bit thin on the ground – not surprisingly given the setting, there's more of an emphasis on seafood than on classical cuisine, though the traditional Thai place listed below ranks alongside the best of Bangkok's.

Blue Parrot, Soi 2 Pattayaland, Central Pattaya. Mexican café and bar, good for lunch-time tacos, enchildas and chilli. Moderate prices.

Café India, Soi Post Office, Central Pattaya. Authentic Indian standards at moderate prices.

Dolf Riks, signposted just north of Soi 5, off Pattaya 2 Rd, North Pattaya. High-class international cuisine, with Indonesian food a speciality. The *rijstaffel* – a set of eighteen different dishes – is well worth B190; some vegetarian dishes too. Moderate to expensive.

Flying Vegetable, opposite Welcome Plaza on Pattaya 2 Rd. Named after the speciality dish from Phitsanulok – stir-fried greens tossed theatrically from the pan to the customer's plate. Also on offer are standard Thai rice, noodle and curry dishes. Cheap.

Nang Nual, Pattaya Beach Rd, South Pattaya. Pattaya's most popular seafood restaurant, where you get to choose your fish from the iceblocks out front before eating it on the seafront terrace. Moderate.

PIC Kitchen, Soi 5, North Pattaya. One of Pattaya's finest traditional Thai restaurants, set in a stylish series of teak buildings. Mouthwatering menu of elegantly presented curry, seafood, rice, noodle and vegetarian dishes. A classical dance show is sometimes included. Moderate.

Schwarzwaldstübe, Soi 15, Central Pattaya. Hearty Swiss and German dishes with lots of steak and an unusually good cheese selection. Moderate.

Nightlife

Entertainment is Pattaya's *raison d'être* and the **nightlife** is what most tourists come for – as do oilfield workers from the Gulf and US marines on R&R – "Pattaya Suffers Mother of all Hangovers" was one of the *Bangkok Post*'s more memorable Gulf War headlines. Of the 400-odd **bars** in Pattaya, the majority are the so-called "bar beers", relatively innocent open-air drinking spots staffed by hostesses whose primary job is to make you buy beer not bodies. However, sex makes more money than booze in Pattaya – depending on who you believe, there are between six and twenty thousand Thais working in Pattaya's sex industry, a workforce that includes children as young as ten years old. It's an all-pervasive trade: the handful of uninspiring discos depend more on prostitutes than on ravers, while the cabarets attract audiences of thousands to see their huge casts of transvestites.

Bars

Pattaya's often nameless outdoor "**bar beers**" group themselves in clusters all over North, Central and South Pattaya. The set-up is the same in all of them: the punters – usually lone males – sit on stools around a brashly lit circular bar, behind which the hostesses keep the drinks, bawdy chat and well-worn jokes flowing. Beer is generally quite cheap at these places, the atmosphere low-key and good-humoured, and couples as well as single women drinkers are almost always made welcome.

Drinks are a lot more expensive in the **go-go bars** on the South Pattaya "strip" where almost-naked hostesses serve the beer and live sex shows keep the boozers hooked through the night. The scene follows much the same pattern as in Patpong, with the women dancing on a small stage in the hope they might be bought for the night – or the week.

There's not a great deal of demand for bars where the emphasis is on simple companiable drinking, but *Bamboo Bar*, at the seafront end of South Pattaya Road, pulls in a fair crowd to listen to the exuberant in-house band, and the cosy pub-style *Green Bottle*, adjacent to *Diana Inn* on Pattaya 2 Road, has forged a studiously unsleazy atmosphere.

Go-go dancers, shower shows and striptease are the mainstays of the gay scene and to date there are no **gay bars** which don't feature some sort of show. The gay area centres around Pattayaland Soi 3, South Pattaya.

Discos

Pattaya's **discos** tend to be pick-up joints with few frills, no admission charges, cheapish beer, and a large number of unattached women hanging round the edges. The house scene hasn't hit the discos yet, so expect old Western hits rather than sophisticated club sounds. The huge and sleazy *Marine Disco*, in the heart of "the strip", is the ultimate meat market, with its cramped upstairs dance-floor encircled by ringside seats, and a more official boxing ring downstairs, starring prepubescent boys. The more hi-tech *Pattaya Palladium*, at the intersection of Soi 1 and Pattaya 2 Road in North Pattaya, boasts a more salubrious ambiance, but is not exactly intimate – it's supposed to have a capacity of six thousand and is popular with tour groups.

Cabarets

Tour groups – and families – also constitute the main audience at the **transvestite cabarets**. Glamorous and highly professional, these shows are performed three times a night at two theatres in North Pattaya: *Alcazar*, opposite Soi 4 on Pattaya 2 Road, and *Tiffany's*, north of Soi 1 on Pattaya 2 Road. Each theatre has a troupe of sixty or more transvestites who run through twenty musical-style numbers in fishnets and crinolines, ball gowns and leathers, against ever more lavish stage sets. All glitz and no raunch, the shows cost B300.

Ko Samet

With its sparkling seas, bamboo huts and limited electricity and water supply, **KO SAMET**, 80km southeast of Pattaya, is the east coast's high spot. Backpackers and Thai students flock to the island for low-budget fun, attracted by its proximity to Bangkok and its powdery white sand – the island's former name, Ko Kaew Phitsadan, means "the place with sand of crushed crystal". Only six kilometres long, Ko Samet was declared a **national park** in 1981 (hence the B5 entrance fee), but typically the ban on building has been ignored and there are now over forty bungalow operations here, albeit unobtrusive one-storey affairs. In May 1990 the authorities decided to flex their muscles a bit – national park officials raided the island, arresting 38 bungalow managers for encroachment upon protected areas, and banning tourists from staying on Samet overnight. Notices were posted, threatening a fine of B1000 or one month's imprisonment for violators. The signs are still there, but tourists have returned in force – the only tangible change being that bungalow operators now pay rent to the Royal Forestry Department. There's unlikely to be another raid in the near future, but it may be worth checking the current situation with TAT all the same.

Samet's **beaches** fall into three broad categories: the popular backpackers' bays along the northern stretch of the east coast; the upmarket resort-oriented area in the middle of the east coast; and the increasingly isolated retreats towards the southern tip. All beaches get packed on weekends and national holidays, so you'd be sensible to take the first available **room** and if necessary change early the following day. Many bungalow managers raise their rates by fifty percent during such peak periods, but if all affordable accommodation is booked up, you can always **camp** – in accordance with national park rules, camping is permissible on any of the beaches, despite what you might be told. At other times, there's a lot of low-cost space in simple **bamboo huts**: usually containing a large well-worn mattress, a blanket and mosquito net, they cost from around B70. The more upmarket you go, the more solid – but not necessarily more attractive – your hut is. Samet has no fresh water, but water is trucked in from the mainland, and most sets of bungalows offer at least a few huts with attached bathroom. Electricity in the more basic places is rationed for evening consumption only, but even these outfits have video shows after dark to help keep the beer flowing.

Finally, Samet is said to be **malarial**, so you should take precautions even though bungalows are routinely sprayed with DDT; the health centre on the island will administer blood tests if you think you've come down with it.

Getting to the island

The mainland departure point for Ko Samet is the tiny fishing port of BAN PHE, about 200km from Bangkok. Ten regular **buses** make the daily three-hour journey from the Eastern Bus Terminal to the Ban Phe pier. Buses from Pattaya also leave ten times a day and take ninety minutes. **Boats** depart at least every two hours between 8am and 4pm, take thirty minutes to get to Samet and charge B30 one way. Some boats are owned by individual resorts and ferry both pre-paid package tourists and fare-paying independent travellers, others make the crossing as soon as they have enough passengers or sufficient cargo to make it worth their while; during peak periods there can be as many as eight boats a day. All boats stop at **Na Dan** pier, which is close to Hat Sai Kaew, the most popular beach; the resort boats continue to their bungalows at the more central Ao Cho and Ao Wong Deuan. Your best option is to take the first available boat – if it terminates at Na Dan and you want to go further you'll be able to hop on one of the island's **songthaews**, which meet the Na Dan boats and drive down the centre of the island as far as Wong Deuan for about B20.

Several tour operators organise **through-trips** from Bangkok to Ko Samet: the fares include the air-con minibus journey from your Bangkok guest house to Ban Phe and the boat trip, and are good value at B260 return, especially considering that the minibuses are timed to link up with resort-boat departures. *Sea Horse Tours* (☎02/282 1574), bookable through most low-budget Bangkok tour operators, offer a good deal whereby you can exchange your return ticket for an onward ticket to Ko Chang further east along the coast (see below).

The island

Most of the islanders not associated with the tourist trade live in the **northeast** of the island, near Na Dan, where there are a few shops and food stalls, as well as the island's only school, health centre and wat. Samet's best **beaches** are along the **east coast**, and this is where you'll find most of the bungalow resorts. A rough track connects some of them, otherwise it's a question of walking along the beach at low tide or over the low, rocky points at high water. Long stretches of the **west coast** are well-nigh inaccessible, though at intervals the coastal scrub has been cleared to make way for a track. The views from these clifftop clearings can be magnificent, particularly around sunset time, but you can only safely descend to sea level at the bay up near the northwest headland.

A few narrow tracks cross the island's forested central ridge to link the east and west coasts, but much of the **interior** is dense jungle, home of hornbills, gibbons, spectacular butterflies, and of course the ubiquitous **gecko**. Even if you don't venture inland, you'll see and hear geckos in every beachfront restaurant, and more than likely a few will turn up in your bungalow as well. Samet harbours a huge population of the largest and most vociferous gecko, the **tokay**, named after the disconcertingly loud sound it makes. Tokays can grow to an alarming 35cm, but they are completely harmless to humans – in fact they're welcomed by most householders, as they devour insects and mice, and Thais consider it auspicious if a baby is born within earshot of a crowing tokay.

Tokay gecko

Samet has no large or spectacular coral reefs of its own, so you'll have to take a boat trip to the islands of Ko Kuti and Ko Thalu, off the northeast coast, to get good **snorkelling**. At least one bungalow outfit on each of the main beaches runs daily excursions for about B200, including mask and lunch.

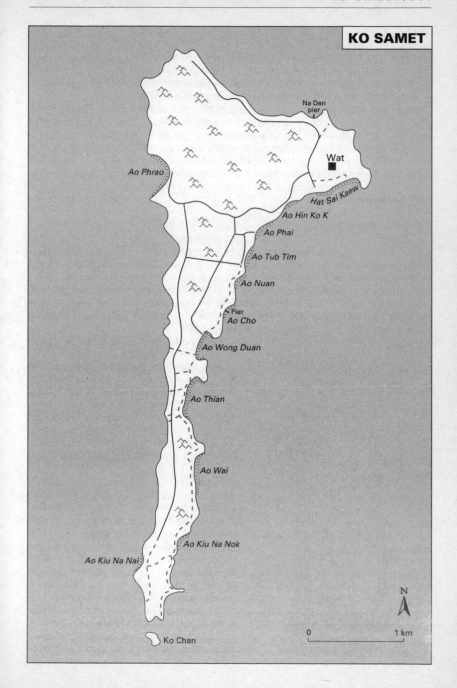

KO SAMET

Na Dan pier

Wat

Ao Phrao

Hat Sai Kaew

Ao Hin Ko K

Ao Phai

Ao Tub Tim

Ao Nuan

Pier
Ao Cho

Ao Wong Duan

Ao Thian

Ao Wai

Ao Kiu Na Nok

Ao Kiu Na Nai

Ko Chan

N

0   1 km

Hat Sai Kaew

Arriving at **Na Dan** pier, a ten-minute walk south along the track, past the health centre and school, will bring you to **HAT SAI KAEW** or Diamond Beach, named after its luxuriant sand. The longest and most developed beach on Samet, this is the only part of the island where the beachfront is lined with a continuous stretch of bungalows, restaurants, beach-wear stalls, deck chairs and parasols.

Diamond Beach, covering a long expanse at the northern end of the strand (☎01/321 0814), is the largest bungalow operation here, and has a huge choice of huts from B100 to B600. You're most likely to get an uninterrupted sea-view if you stay here, and the bungalows are well-spaced and away from the main fray. Huts belonging to the other six operations are mostly priced between B100 and B200, and there's little to distinguish between them. The restaurant attached to *White Sand* serves good fish dishes and *Toy*'s restaurant is a popular place to hang out in the evening.

Ao Hin Kok and Ao Phai

Separated from Hat Sai Kaew by a low promontory on which sits a mermaid statue – a reference to an eighteenth-century poem set on Samet – **AO HIN KOK** is smaller and less cluttered than its neighbour. There are only two bunga-low outfits here, both looking over the beach from the grassy slope on the far side of the track. English-run *Naga* (☎01/321 0732) has simple huts from B60 and a restaurant specialising in home-made bread and cakes. There's also a **poste restante** here, the only one on the island. Next-door *Odds Little Hut* (☎01/323 0264) offers slightly less basic bungalows for B150.

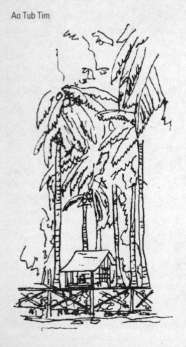
Ao Tub Tim

Beach life gets a little more active around the next collection of rocks on **AO PHAI**, where evenings are enlivened by the outdoor bar and an occasional disco. *Sea Breeze* (☎01/321 1397) is the largest set of bungalows here, with huts from B80 to B200, plus telephone, boat ticket and money-exchange facilities. *Samet Villa* has sturdy chalet-style bungalows, a little too close together, from B250.

Ao Tub Tim

Also known as Ao Pudsa, **AO TUB TIM** is a lovely white-sand bay sandwiched between rocky points, partly shaded with palms and backed by a wooded slope. It feels secluded and peaceful, but is only a short stroll from Ao Phai and the other beaches further north, so you get the best of both worlds. Of the two bungalow oper-ations here, *Tub Tim* (☎038/611279) offers the greatest choice of accommoda-tion, from simple bamboo huts for B70 through to concrete bungalows for B300. Huts at the next-door *Ao Pudsa* cost from B50.

Ao Nuan

Clamber up over the next headland to reach Samet's smallest and most laid-back beach, **AO NUAN**. The atmosphere here teeters somewhere between hippy and New Age, but it's relaxed and friendly, and the mellow restaurant of the *Ao Nuan* (nine huts from B80) – decked out with huge floor cushions and shell mobiles – has the best veggie food on the island. The tiny enclosed bay is not brilliant for swimming, but the rocky shore reveals a good patch of sand when the tide withdraws, and Tub Tim's only five minutes' walk away.

Ao Cho and Ao Wong Deuan

A five-minute walk south along the track from Ao Nuan brings you to the unappealing **AO CHO**: the sand's not so good and the sea gets crowded with supply boats, so there's not a vast amount of pleasure to be had here. But if everywhere else is booked up, you've got the choice between the very basic *White Shark* (from B80) and the well-designed but overpriced *Tantawan* (B400).

The horseshoe-bay of **AO WONG DEUAN**, round the next headland, is dominated by upmarket bungalow resorts, and though the beach isn't bad it suffers a plague of revving jet-skis and crowds arriving and leaving on the ferries. *Wong Deuan Villa* (☎01/321 0789) offers the poshest accommodation (B600–2000), complete with mini-golf, snooker and TVs in the best rooms. *Wong Deuan Resort* (☎038/651777) comes a close second, featuring a swimming pool and flower garden; bungalows here range from B600 to B1200. *Seahorse* (☎01/323 0049) is the cheapest, at B250 for passable huts.

Ao Thian

Off nearly all beaten tracks, **AO THIAN** is a good choice if you want seclusion. Ten minutes' walk from Wong Deuan, the bay is divided by outcrops that create several distinct beaches, and as it curves outwards to the south you get a great view of the east coast, including the impressively long Hat Sai Kaew. At the northern end, the friendly *Lung Dam Den* has about thirty basic huts from B60 and a simple restaurant; its only competition comes from the less good *Lung Dum Hut* (from B100), much further down the beach.

Ao Kiu

You have to really like the solitary life to plump for Samet's most isolated beach, **AO KIU**, over an hour's walk south of Ao Thian through unadulterated wilderness – the track begins behind *Wong Deuan Resort* and can be joined at the back of *Lung Dum Hut* at Ao Thian. It's actually two beaches: Ao Kiu Na Nok on the east coast and Ao Kiu Na Nai on the west, separated by a few hundred metres of scrub and coconut grove. The few bungalows here belong to *Coral Beach* (☎02/ 579 6237), and start from B100; most are set in among the palms on the east shore, but a couple look down on the tiny west-coast coral beach. The most convenient way of getting here is by direct boat from the mainland; at least one *Coral Beach* boat makes the run daily – call to check departure times.

Ao Phrao

Across on the west coast, the rugged, rocky coastline only softens into beach once and that's at the run-down **AO PHRAO**, misleadingly known as Paradise Bay, on the northwestern stretch, some 4km north of Ao Kiu. The most direct route from the east coast beaches is via the inland track from behind *Sea Breeze* on Ao Phai, though the track from the back of *Tub Tim* will also get you there. Ao Phrao doesn't get that many overnight visitors (though Thai students camp here sometimes) and accommodation is uninviting.

Chanthaburi

For over five hundred years precious stones have drawn prospectors and traders to the provincial capital of **CHANTHABURI**, 80km east of Ban Phe, and it's the town's pivotal role within Thailand's most lucrative **gem mining** area that makes it the only major east coast town worth visiting. Seventy percent of the country's gemstones are mined in the hills of Chanthaburi and Trat provinces, a fruitful source of sapphires and Thailand's only known vein of rubies. Since the fifteenth century hopefuls of all nationalities have flocked here, particularly the Shans from Burma, the Chinese and the Cambodians, many of them establishing permanent homes here. The largest ethnic group, though, are Catholic refugees from Vietnam, vast numbers of whom have arrived here since the eighteenth century. The French too have left their mark: during their occupation of Chanthaburi from 1893–1905, when they held the town hostage against the fulfilment of a territorial treaty on the Laotian border, they undertook the restoration and enlargement of the town's Christian cathedral.

This cultural diversity makes Chanthaburi an engaging place, even if there's less than a day's worth of sights here. Built on the wiggly west bank of the Maenam Chanthaburi, the town fans out westwards for a couple of kilometres, though the most interesting parts are close to the river, in the district where the Vietnamese families are concentrated. Here, along the soi running parallel to the river, the town presents a mixture of pastel-painted colonial style housefronts and traditional wooden shophouses, some with finely carved latticework.

Continuing south along this soi, you'll reach a footbridge across which stands Thailand's largest **cathedral**: the Church of the Immaculate Conception. There's thought to have been a church on this site ever since the first Christians arrived in town, though the present structure was revamped in French style in the late nineteenth century. West of the bridge, the **gem dealers' quarter** begins, where shopkeepers sit sifting through great mounds of tiny coloured stones, peering at them through microscopes and classifying them for resale. Some of these shops also cut, polish and set the stones: Chanthaburi is as respected a cutting centre as Bangkok, and Thai lapidaries are considered amongst the most skilled – not to mention cheapest – in the world. Most of Chanthaburi's market-trading is done on weekend mornings, when buyers from Bangkok descend in their hundreds to sit behind rented tables and haggle with local dealers.

Chanthaburi has a reputation for high-grade fruit too, notably durian, rambutan and mangosteen, all grown in the orchards around the town and sold in the daily **market**, a couple of blocks northwest of the gem quarter. Basketware products are also good buys here, mostly made by the Vietnamese.

West of the market and gem quarter, the landscaped **Taksin Park** is the town's recreation area and memorial to King Taksin of Thonburi, the general who reunited Thailand between 1767 and 1782 after the sacking of Ayutthaya by the Burmese. Chanthaburi was the last Burmese bastion on the east coast – when Taksin took the town he effectively regained control of the whole country. The park's heroic bronze statue of Taksin is featured on the back of the B20 note.

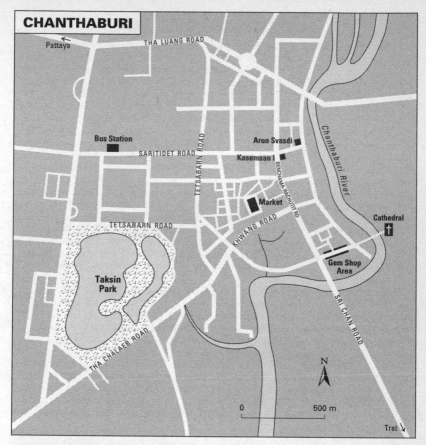

Practicalities

Buses from Bangkok, Ban Phe and Trat all arrive at the bus station on Saritidet Road, about 750m northwest of the town centre and market. Chanthaburi also makes a handy connection point between the east coast and Isaan: twelve daily buses make the six-hour Chanthaburi–Khorat journey in both directions.

The two best **accommodation** options are both near the river. The small and basic *Arun Svasdi* at 239 Sukha Phiban Rd (☎039/311082), down a soi off the eastern end of Saritidet Road, has quiet rooms with fan and bathroom for B80 and is in the heart of the Vietnamese part of town. Around the corner at 98/1 Benchama-Rachutit Rd, the much larger *Kasemsan 1* (☎039/312340) offers sizeable, clean rooms with fan and bathroom for B150 on the noisy streetside, and similar air-con ones in the quieter section for B250. The **restaurant** next door to *Kasemsan 1*, called *Chanthon Pochana* (no English sign), serves a range of standard rice and seafood dishes. Otherwise, check out the food stalls in the market and along the riverside soi for Vietnamese spring rolls (*cha gio*) served with sweet sauce, and for the locally made Chanthaburi rice noodles (*kwetiaw Chanthaburi*).

RUBIES AND SAPPHIRES

As long ago as the fifteenth century, European travellers noted the abundance of precious stones in Chanthaburi and Trat, but the first **gem mining rush** happened in 1857, when stories of farmers ploughing up cartloads of rubies and fishermen trawling precious stones from the sea bed brought in hundreds of prospectors from ruby-rich Burma. Before long they had been joined by Cambodians and Vietnamese, and then the British mine companies from Burma came over to organise the industry. By 1900, *Sapphires and Rubies of Siam Ltd* had bought up nearly all the mining fields in eastern Thailand, but it proved an unwise move, as most immigrant miners refused to work for the colonials and moved on elsewhere. When Thailand lost many of its best sapphire mines in a border dispute with Cambodia, the company decided to pull out, leaving the Chanthaburi fields once more to independent self-employed miners.

The next great transformation came half a century later, as a consequence of the upheavals in Burma, which until then had been the world's main supplier of **corundum** – the term for all crystalline forms of aluminium oxide, such as ruby and sapphire. In 1962 the Burmese effectively sealed their country against the outside world, ousting all foreign companies and ceasing all external trade. The Thai dealers promptly muscled in to fill the gap in the world corundum market, and rapidly achieved their current dominant status by forcing the government to ease import and export duties.

Locally produced stones account for a small fraction of the total trade in and around Chanthaburi, whose mines have now been exploited for so long that high-cost mechanical methods are the only viable way of getting at the rocks. Self-employed panhandlers have rushed to work on new veins in Cambodia, while Thai dealers pull the strings in Vietnam's embryonic industry, and regularly buy up the entire annual production of some of Australia's gem fields.

Though artificially produced stones are now used where formerly only the genuine article would do – the glasses of most high-quality watches are nowadays made from synthetic sapphire – the demand for top-notch natural stones from jewellers and watchmakers is virtually limitless. In view of the profits to be made – an uncut 150-carat ruby sold for $1.2 million in 1985 – it's inevitable that sharp practice should be commonplace.

Doctoring the classification of a stone is a common act of skulduggery. A low-quality rough stone from Africa might emerge from the cutter's workshop with a label identifying it as Burmese or Kashmiri, the top rank in the gem league. But perhaps the most prevalent form of fraud involves **heating the stones** to enhance their colour, a cosmetic operation recorded as long ago as the first century, when Pliny the Elder described the technique of enhancing the quality of agate by "cooking" it. Trace elements are what give corundums their colour – in the case of blue sapphires it's titanium and iron that create the hue. To convert a weakly coloured sapphire into an expensive stone, factories now pack the low-grade rocks with titanium and iron oxide, heat the lot to within a whisker of 2050°C – the melting point of sapphire – and thereby fuse the chemicals into the surface of the stone to produce an apparently flawless gem. As long as the cutter and polisher leave the new "skin" intact when they do their work, only an expert will be able to tell whether the highly priced end product is a sham. It takes a lot less effort to fool the gullible Westerners who reckon they can make a killing on the Chanthaburi market: tumble the red glass of a car tail-light in a tub of gravel, and after an hour or two you've got a passable facsimile of a ruby.

Trat and around

If you need to stock up on essentials, change money, make long-distance telephone calls or extend your visa before hitting Ko Chang, **TRAT**, 80km east of Chanthaburi and a half-hour ride from the dock at Laem Ngop, is the place to do it. A small and lively market town, it's served by regular buses from Bangkok and Chanthaburi, which arrive on the main Sukhumvit Road, one block away from the central commercial area. The very helpful **tourist information** office on Soi Sukhumvit, which skirts the southern edge of the day market, will fill you in on the boat schedules to Ko Chang (see below) and on the current state of **accomodation** in Trat.

Guest houses open and close with little warning in this town, and the tourist market is distinctly seasonal, but you should be able to count on *Foremost Guest House* (☎039/511923), a short signposted walk southeast of the bus stop, at 49 Thoncharoen Rd. Large, basic rooms cost B50 single, B70 double, with dorm beds for B30. Even more convenient are the small but comfortable B80 singles and B100 doubles at *Max and Tick's*, less than fifty metres north of the bus stop on Sukhumvit Road, but rumour has it that the owners are uprooting to Bangkok. The best **places to eat** in Trat are at the day market on the ground floor of the Sukhumvit Road shopping centre, and the night market between Soi Vichidanya and Soi Kasemsan, east of Sukhumvit Road. *Golf Pub and Restaurant* near the bus stop serves breakfasts and good northeastern dishes and is popular with young locals in the evenings.

Khlong Yai

The one worthwhile land-based excursion from Trat is to travel 74km east to the small, thriving fishing port of **KHLONG YAI**, just a few kilometres from the Cambodian border. The journey into this narrow tail of Thailand passes through some of the most gripping countryside in the region, with seaviews to the south and a continuous range of forested mountains to the north, pierced by a couple of sheer waterfalls so mighty you can see them from the road. Khlong Yai itself boasts a great setting, the town's long pier jutting way out to sea and partly flanked by rows of stilt houses that form a shelter for the fishing boats. It's a dramatic place to visit during rough weather, when the turbulent seas lash against the housefronts and the end of the pier disappears beneath low-lying storm clouds. **Songthaews** to Khlong Yai leave Trat about every thirty minutes from behind the shopping centre, take an hour and a quarter and cost B25.

Laem Ngop

The mainland departure point for Ko Chang is **LAEM NGOP**, 17km southwest of Trat and served by songthaews every twenty minutes or so (B10). If you do miss the boat or the seas are too rough to cross, it's no great hardship to be stuck in this tiny port, which consists of little more than a wooden pier, one main road, an exchange booth and a small collection of traditional houses inhabited mainly by fisherfolk, a number of them Muslim. If you happen to be in the area between January 13 and 17, it may be worth staying here anyway for the festival commemorating the time when French forces were repelled from Laem Ngop in the nineteenth century. The *Isaan Guest House*, less than five minutes' walk from the pier, is a welcoming **place to stay**; simple rooms are B50 single, B100 double.

Ko Chang

Part of a national marine park archipelago of fifty-two islands, **KO CHANG** offers miles of beaches as yet fronted only by bamboo and wooden huts, and a hilly interior of barely penetrable virgin forest. It's Thailand's second largest island, 30km north to south and 8km across, but has just 3000 inhabitants, most of whom make their living from fishing and live in the hamlets scattered around the fringes of the island. As a tourist destination Ko Chang is still in its infancy, and much of its small-scale accommodation is shut down from May to October, when Ko Chang is subject to quite fierce storms.

Although a wide dirt track now runs almost all the way round the island, leaving only the southeastern and southwestern coasts out of bounds to vehicles, **getting round** Ko Chang remains problematic – time-consuming and exhausting if you walk, pricey and hair-raising by motorbike. Thus it makes life a lot easier if you decide which beach you want to stay on before leaving the mainland, and catch the most direct boat.

Several of the other much **smaller islands** in the archipelago have been built on, but most are the domain of expensive resorts patronised by Thai businessmen; if you can get to them though, camping is allowed on any island within the national marine park. It's sometimes possible to get a lift with a fishing boat from Laem Ngop or on one of the coconut boats which come up the canal into Trat; alternatively you could try to persuade the staff on Ko Chang's Hat Bang Bao, the most southerly beach and the closest to the islands, to run a trip out to them.

Getting to Ko Chang

Boat departures **from Laem Ngop** vary according to the day, the tide, and the time of year, but during peak season there should be at least two daily boats to the west coast and one to each of the east coast beaches. During this season, the **west coast boats** depart Laem Ngop at around noon and 3pm and head for the main pier at Hat Khlong Phrao (2–3hr), dropping passengers for Hat Sai Khao and Hat Kai Bai into waiting longtail boats on the way, as both those beaches are too shallow for the ferry. There's also a sporadic direct service to Hat Bang Bao on the far southwestern tip, but this doesn't always run daily. The two daily **east coast boats** both depart Laem Ngop at 1pm: one goes straight across to Hat Sai Tong (45min), the other heads down to Hat Yao (Long Beach) on the southeastern tip (1hr 45min). All boats cost B70 and tickets should be bought from the pier in Laem Ngop.

If schedules run according to plan, it's possible to do the whole **Bangkok** to Ko Chang trip in a day, catching the earliest public bus at 7am, arriving in Trat about 1pm, and making the short connection to Laem Ngop in time for the 3pm west-coast boat. Budget tour operators in Bangkok also offer **air-con minibus** rides from Khao San Road through to Laem Ngop for B260, and *Seahorse Tour* do Ko Samet to Laem Ngop minibus connections for B130.

The island

Ko Chang's **west coast** has the best beaches and is the more developed, though the further south you go the less crowded the resorts become. The **east coast** is closer to the mainland and less exposed to storms, but only has a couple of beaches, one of which is very small, the other extremely remote.

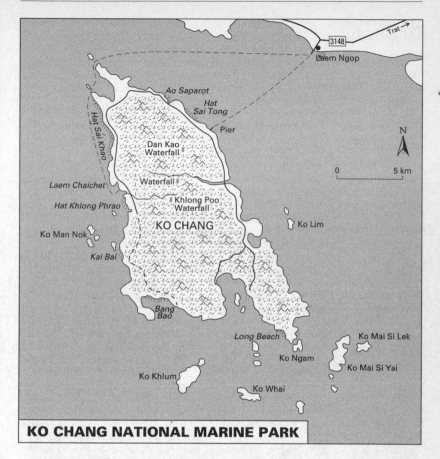

KO CHANG NATIONAL MARINE PARK

Much of the island's pot-holed, undulating track is more suitable for scrambling than for a quiet afternoon's bike ride, but most bungalows rent out a couple of **motorbikes** at the inflated rate of B80 per hour or B400 per day. If you don't fancy braving the route yourself, motorcycle taxis will ferry you between most spots, but again prices are not good value: from Hat Sai Khao in the northwest across to Hat Sai Tong on the northeast coast costs B150, for example. During high season, a minibus runs most mornings between the east coast *Ko Chang Cabana* and the west coast *Ko Chang Resort* on Hat Khlong Phrao, charging non-guests B50.

There is no bank on the island and few shops, so buy any necessities before you leave Trat. These should include mosquito repellent and a net, as the island is notoriously **malarial**. (Both Laem Ngop and Trat have malaria clinics.) Sand fleas are also a problem, but there's not a lot you can do about them except soothe your bites with calamine; apart from that, watch out for **jellyfish**, which plague the west coast in April and May, and for **snakes** sunbathing on the overgrown paths into the interior.

The west coast

The northernmost **west-coast** beach of **HAT SAI KHAO** (White Sand Beach) is
the island's longest and busiest, but that means just a dozen bungalow operations. The fine sand might not be exactly white, but it's littered with beautiful
shells, divided by low rocks into individual bays at high tide and is good for swimming. Many huts along here have neither electricity nor running water, so it's
paraffin lamps after dark and Thai-style bathing in the mornings.

At the northern end, *White Sand Resort* (aka *Hat Sai Khao Resort*) is quite a
distance from the other **bungalows** on the beach and thus quite secluded.
Efficiently managed, if not overly friendly, the resort offers simple bamboo huts
from B80 single, B100 double. Access at high tide is down a long, steep path
through the forest, signposted from the track; if you're carrying a lot you'd be
advised to wait till low tide and walk down the beach. There's little to choose
between the more central bungalows, all of which offer basic huts from around
B50 single, B80 double. Further south, and away from the crowd, the very
congenial *Honey* has adequate huts from B50 and an excellent restaurant; a few
hundred metres beyond, *Ploloma Cliff Resort* is the poshest place on the beach,
with fan-cooled bungalows for B500 single, B800 double.

Following the track south for another four kilometres or so, you come to **Laem
Chaichet**, a small cape topped by *Chaichet Bungalows*, where huts go for B80.
The boats dock at the pier just around the cape, at the northernmost stretch of
HAT KHLONG PHRAO (Coconut Beach), a pretty sweep of fine, clean sand
with only a few bungalows. Closest to the pier, *Coconut Beach* has good single
huts for B100, doubles for B120–400; at the nearby *Ko Chang Resort* (☎01/211
5193) luxury air-con bungalows go for B1500–2000, making them the island's
most expensive accommodation. An estuary cuts the beach in half; cross it by
boat (for B5) to get to *Magic*, which has good food and fair huts for B50 single,
B100–300 double, and *Chog Dii*, which has better huts for B80 but poorer food.

The rocky **HAT KAI BAI**, an hour's walk south around the headland from Hat
Khlong Phrao, is lined with half a dozen indistinguishable bungalow outfits
strung out between the estuaries at each end. Some are set back from the beach
and all offer basic huts from B80 single and B110 double: the friendly *Nan Muang*
has notably good huts for the price, but avoid *Kai Bai Beach Bungalows*, as it
backs on to a mosquito-ridden, stagnant pond. Swimming's not so good here –
head south for about twenty minutes along the path from behind *Siam Bay*
restaurant at the southernmost end of Kai Bai to get to a more secluded, sandy
and nameless beach.

From Kai Bai, the track narrows down into a path which wiggles its way
through inland forest until, three hours' walking later, it reaches the southernmost beach of **HAT BANG BAO** and its village. Boats sometimes come direct
here from Laem Ngop, otherwise you'll have to walk. Three sets of bungalows
share this isolated, clean and sandy stretch. Near the village, *Bang Bao Viewside*
and *Bang Bao Cottage* both offer quite good single huts for B80, doubles for
B100. Across on the other end of the beach, *Bang Bao Beach Bungalows* are
slightly better and cost B100 single, B150 double; staff here sometimes organise
boat trips to the islands of Ko Khlum, Ko Rung and Ko Mak.

The east coast

If you're walking between the east and west coasts, you'll pass along the back of
KHLONG SON village, built mainly on stilts in the deep bay carved out of the

island's northwestern tip. There's no beach to speak of, though if you want to break a long round-island hike, try putting up at *Mannee Guest House*, tucked away alongside the more rickety of the two piers, which offers tasty home-cooking and rooms for B50.

The daily **east coast** boat docks at a pier about fifteen minutes' walk north of the nearest beach, **HAT SAI TONG**. Close by the pier, the upmarket *Ko Chang Cabana* has fan-cooled bungalows for B600, and because this coast is fairly grotty it runs a daily minibus service to west coast beaches if enough guests want to go there. The one set of bungalows at Hat Sai Tong itself, also called *Hat Sai Tong*, has comfortable huts, with beds for B60 single and B100 double, ranged around a garden-cum-menagerie, complete with caged squirrels, monkeys and an aviary.

There's little to entice you into making the two and a half-hour hike down to **THAN MAYOM**, site of the National Park office and predictably unattractive national park bungalows, except perhaps the prospect of a long walk along the base of a forested hillside, punctuated by occasional seaviews. South of Than Mayom the track continues another 4km to the equally untempting south-coast **HAT SALAKPET**, cutting inland and bypassing the whole southeast headland.

The southeast headland actually holds the best beach on this coast, **HAT YAO** (Long Beach), but the only access is via direct boat from Laem Ngop. Another fine, isolated spot, Hat Yao is excellent for swimming and has some coral close to shore. Depending on the sea conditions, some boats will take you directly into Hat Yao, while others will drop you just around a small promontory close to *Tantawan House*, which has a couple of very basic B80 huts. For slightly better accommodation, follow the path westwards for ten minutes to the beachfront *Long Beach Bungalows*, where large huts equipped with fans and electric lights go for B100.

travel details

buses

From Ban Phe to Bangkok (10 daily; 3hr); Chanthaburi (6 daily; 1hr 30min); Trat (6 daily; 3hr).

From Chanthaburi to Bangkok (18 daily; 5–7hr); Khorat (12 daily; 6hr); Trat (every 90min; 1hr 30min).

From Pattaya to Bangkok (every 40min; 2hr 30min); Ban Phe (10 daily; 1hr 30min); Chanthaburi (6 daily; 3hr); Khorat (4 daily; 5–6hr); Trat (6 daily; 4hr 30min).

From Si Racha to Bangkok (every 25min; 2hr); Ban Phe (10 daily; 2hr); Chanthaburi (6 daily; 3hr 30 min); Pattaya (every 20min; 30min); Trat (6 daily; 5hr).

From Trat to Bangkok (16 daily; 6–8hr).

Ferries

From Ban Phe to Ko Samet (4–8 daily; 30min).

From Laem Ngop to Ko Chang (at least 2 daily; 45min–3hr).

From Si Racha to Ko Si Chang (4 daily; 40min).

CHAPTER FIVE

THE NORTHEAST: ISAAN

Bordered by Laos and Cambodia on three sides, the tableland of **northeast Thailand** – known as **Isaan**, after the Hindu god of death and the northeast – comprises a third of the country's land area and is home to nearly a third of its population. This is the least visited region of the kingdom, and the poorest: eighty percent of Isaan villagers earn less than the minimum wage of B100 a day. Farming is the livelihood of virtually all northeasterners, despite appallingly infertile soil – the friable sandstone contains few nutrients and retains little water – and long periods of drought punctuated by downpours and intermittent bouts of flooding. In the 1960s, government schemes to introduce hardier crops set in motion a debt cycle that has forced farmers into monocultural cash-cropping to repay their loans for fertilizers, seeds and machinery. With so much time and energy going into raising the cash crops, little is left over for growing and making everyday necessities, which farmers then have to buy. For many families, there's only one way off the treadmill: each January and February, Bangkok-bound trains and buses are crammed with northeasterners leaving in search of seasonal or short-term work; of the eighteen million who live in Isaan, an average of two million seasonal economic refugees leave the area every year, and northeasterners now make up the majority of the capital's lowest paid workforce.

Most northeasterners speak a dialect that's more comprehensible to residents of Vientiane than Bangkok, and Isaan's historic allegiances have tied it more closely to Cambodia and Laos than to Thailand. Between the eleventh and thirteenth centuries, the all-powerful **Khmers** covered the northeast in magnificent stone temple complexes, the remains of which constitute the region's most satisfying tourist attractions. During subsequent centuries the territories along the Mekhong River changed hands numerous times, until the present border with Laos was set at the end of World War II. In the 1950s and 1960s, **communist insurgents** played on the northeast's traditional ties with Laos; a movement to align Isaan with the Marxists of Laos gathered some force, and the Communist Party of Thailand, gaining sympathy amongst poverty-stricken northeastern farmers, established bases in the region. At about the same time, major US air bases for the **Vietnam War** were set up in Khorat, Ubon Ratchathani and Udon Thani, fuelling a sex industry that has plagued the region ever since. When the American military moved out, northeastern women turned to the tourist-oriented Bangkok flesh trade instead, and nowadays the majority of prostitutes in the capital come from Isaan.

These cities, like Isaan's other major population centres, are chaotic, exhausting places, with precious little going for them apart from accommodation and onward transport. **Khorat**, the inescapable hub of southern Isaan, is nevertheless worth enduring as a springboard for the majestic Khmer ruins of **Prasat Hin Phimai**, which adorns an otherwise insignificant outlying village, and **Prasat Hin Khao Phanom Rung**, perched on a hilltop miles from anywhere. Congenial guest houses make the provincial capitals of **Surin** and **Chaiyaphum** rewarding

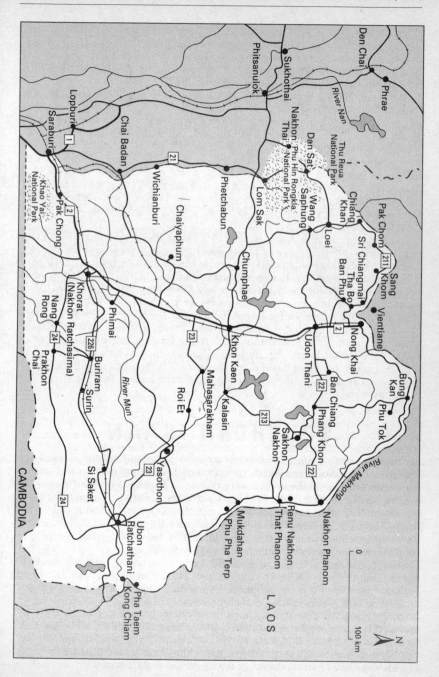

targets at any time of year, especially in November (in the case of Surin) and January (Chaiyaphum), when they host their flamboyant – though inevitably touristy – "elephant round-ups". Festivals also put two other Isaan cities on the map: **Ubon Ratchathani**, focal point of the extravagant candle festival in July, and **Yasothon**, with its bawdy rocket festival in May.

Isaan's only mountain range of any significance divides the uninspiring town of **Loei** from the central plains and offers some stiff walking, awesome scenery and the possibility of spotting unusual birds and flowers in the **national parks** which spread across its heights. Due north of Loei, the **Mekhong River** begins its leisurely course around Isaan with a lush stretch where a sprinkling of guest houses have opened up the river countryside to travellers. Marking the eastern end of this reach, the fast-developing border town of **Nong Khai** is surrounded by possibly the most outlandish temples in Thailand. The grandest and most important religious site in the northeast, however, is **Wat Phra That Phanom**, way downstream beyond Nakhon Phanom, a town which affords some of the finest Isaan vistas.

The most comfortable **time of year** in Isaan is the cool season (Nov–Feb), which is also when the waters of the Mekhong are highest and the scenery greenest – but if you want to catch the region's most exciting festivals you'll have to brave the hot season, when temperatures can soar to 40°C. **Getting around** can be time-consuming, as northeastern bus drivers are particularly nonchalant about timetables, but most sizeable places are connected by public transport. Many of the roads through Isaan were built in the 1960s and 1970s by a government desperate to quash the spread of communism in these hitherto isolated parts; the United States helped with much of the finance, and was also responsible for the so-called Friendship Highway (Highway 2), which connects Bangkok with the Laotian border at Nong Khai. The two rail lines which skirt the edges of Isaan are more useful for the long journey up from Bangkok than for short hops between towns.

SOUTHERN ISAAN

For tourists, Isaan divides conveniently into three regions, dictated primarily by transport routes. **Southern Isaan**, described in this section, more or less follows one of two branches of the northeastern railway as it makes a beeline towards the eastern border, skirting the edge of Khao Yai National Park before entering Isaan proper to link the major provincial capitals of Khorat, Surin and Ubon Ratchathani. The railway is handy enough for entering the region, but once here it's as well to follow a route that takes in smaller towns and villages wherever possible, which means switching to buses and songthaews.

Even if your time is limited, you shouldn't leave this part of Isaan without visiting at least one set of **Khmer ruins**: Prasat Hin Phimai and Prasat Hin Khao Phanom Rung are the most accessible examples. Relics of an even earlier age, prehistoric **cliff paintings** also draw a few visitors eastwards to the border town of Kong Chiam, but crowds only mass for southern Isaan's spectacular calendar of **festivals**, most notably Surin's elephant round-up, Ubon Ratchathani's candle festival and Yasothon's Bun Bang Fai rocket festival. To get the best out of Isaan you need to meet English-speaking locals – the small **guest houses** in Surin, Phimai and Kong Chiam are some of the friendliest in the country.

Khao Yai National Park

About 120km northeast of Bangkok, the unrelieved cultivated lushness of the central plains gives way to the thickly forested Phanom Dongrek mountains. A 2168-square-kilometre chunk of this sculpted limestone range has been conserved as **KHAO YAI NATIONAL PARK**, one of Thailand's most rewarding preserves, and certainly its most popular. Spanning five distinct forest types – including one of the largest tropical forests in Asia – Khao Yai ("Big Mountain") sustains 300 bird and 20 large land-mammal species, and offers a plethora of waterfalls and several undemanding walking trails.

Although Khao Yai can be done as a day trip from Bangkok, it really deserves an overnight stop – night safaris are a highlight here. If the resort-style accommodation inside the park is beyond your means, consider staying in PAK CHONG, the nearest town to the park, from where a couple of guest houses run budget tours. If possible try to avoid Khao Yai at weekends, when trails and waterfalls get ridiculously crowded and the animals make themselves scarce. Even at quiet times, don't expect it to be like a safari park – patience, a soft tread and a keen-eyed guide are generally needed.

Access and accommodation

Direct buses from Bangkok's northern bus terminal go straight to the park visitors' centre, departing daily at 9am and returning at 3pm (3hr; B74 one way) – which doesn't leave much time unless you're staying overnight in the park. All Bangkok–Khorat **trains** and **buses** stop at PAK CHONG, 37km north of the park visitors' centre on Highway 2, a cheaper base and better for onward connections; there's only an irregular songthaew service from Pak Chong to the park, but you'll probably end up joining a tour anyway (see below). On weekends and holidays, you can pick up **rail excursions** from Bangkok that include a day-return to PRACHINBURI (50km south of the visitors' centre), connecting transport to the park, and lunch; trains leave Hualamphong at 6am and the fare is B130.

Budget accommodation boils down to two guest houses in Pak Chong, *Jungle Adventure* (☎044/312877) and *Jungle Camp* (☎044/313055), both near the bus terminal on Highway 2 (signposted from the railway station) and charging B60 per person for basic but adequate rooms. Their best features are their **tours** of the park, each featuring one and a half days of guided daytime treks and a three- to four-hour night safari for B500 inclusive. **Camping** is permitted in the park in designated areas near the visitors' centre for the usual fee.

In early 1992, Khao Yai's two **luxury resorts** became a political football, when interim Prime Minister Anand suddenly decided to enforce laws against private concessions in national parks and ordered them to be dismantled. The park was duly closed to overnight guests for several months, but nothing was pulled down and the subsequent political turmoil left national parks on the back burner. If they're still operating, bungalows at *Juldis Khao Yai Resort* (☎02/255 2480, ext 413) are from B2000, and those at *Sophanaves Resort* (☎044/311347) start at B750 (B950 at weekends); both will arrange transport from Bangkok. The less luxurious bungalows at *Khao Yai Motor Lodge* (☎02/281 3041), costing B500 per person, should be exempt from any political wranglings; they can be booked at the Bangkok TAT office. The *Motor Lodge* puts on hour-long safaris every night for B25 per person, but these don't compare with the longer ones organised by the Pak Chong guest houses. For **food** in the park, expect no more than basic fried rice variations at the restaurant next door to the visitors' centre.

The park

During the daytime you're bound to hear some of the local wildlife even if you don't catch sight of them. Noisiest of all are the white-handed and crowned **gibbons**, the **macaques** and the long-tailed and pig-tailed **monkeys**, who hoot and whoop from the tops of the tallest trees. **Hornbills** also create quite a racket, calling attention to themselves by flapping their enormous wings; Khao Yai harbours large flocks of four different hornbill species, which makes it one of the best places in Southeast Asia to observe these creatures. The Great Hornbill in particular is an incredibly beautiful bird, with brilliant yellow and black undersides; the equally magnificent Indian Pied Hornbill boasts less striking black and white colouring, but is more commonly seen at close range because it swoops down to catch fish, rats and reptiles. You might also see silver pheasants, woodpeckers and Asian fairy-bluebirds, and – from November to March – several species of **migrant birds**, including the yellow-browed warbler from North Asia and the red-breasted flycatcher from Europe.

Night safaris, organised by the hotels and guest houses, are definitely worth the time and money for the excitement of following trails of tiger tracks, fresh elephant dung, or whatever else you happen to come across – but be sure to wear warm clothes. A herd of about 200 Asian **elephants** lives in the park and its members are often seen at night – this is the only place in Thailand where you have much likelihood of spotting wild elephants. **Tigers** and **leopards** are less commonly sighted, but you're almost certain to spot **civets**, and barking **deer** and sambar deer are less nervous after dark. **Bats** assemble en masse at sunset, especially at the cave entrance on Khao Roobchang (Elephant Head Mountain), which every evening disgorges millions of them on their nightly forage.

Great Indian Hornbill

Several well-worn **trails** – originally made by elephants and other park species, and still used by these animals – radiate from the area around the visitors' centre at kilometre stone 37, and a few more branch off from the roads that traverse the park. Although the Bangkok TAT office stocks a sketchy trail map of the park, don't rely on finding copies of it at the park visitors' centre; you shouldn't need a map anyway, as paths in the central area are well-signposted and colour-coded. If you want to explore the remoter parts, hire a guide from the park headquarters (next to the visitors' centre) for B100 a day.

The two most popular trails, **Kaeng Kaeo** (about 1km one way) and **Haew Sawat** (a further 6km) start just beside the visitors' centre and pass through tropical forest and grassland. Even on the short hike east to Kaeng Kaeo you may encounter gibbons, woodpeckers and kingfishers, and the route on to Haew Sawat runs close to an area used by roosting hornbills from June to August. The more rewarding

Beung Phai/Khlong E Taw trail is a circular hike of 11km (beginning north of the visitors' centre near kilometre stone 32) that takes you west through a forested area thick with large strangling figs, across the Beung Phai grasslands, over Khlong E Taw and eventually to the **Nong Pak Chee observation tower**. The tower stands just 1km west of the road, linked by a trail which starts between kilometre stones 35 and 36. The fruits of the figs attract all manner of birds and animals, including hornbills, barbets and mynah birds, macaques and palm civets, while barking deer come to graze the grassland. Khlong E Taw also entices birds such as the silver pheasant, but only the observation tower gives you the cover necessary for several hours' of wildlife-spotting: stay here long enough and you'll see needletails dive-bombing the nearby pond and maybe some otters playing in the water; elephants and gaurs sometimes come to drink here too, and you're almost certain to see deer and hornbills – possibly tigers as well.

Khorat (Nakhon Ratchasima) and around

Beyond Pak Chong, Highway 2 and the railway diverge to run either side of picturesque Lam Takhong Reservoir, offering a last taste of undulating, forested terrain before gaining the largely barren Khorat Plateau. They rejoin at **KHORAT** (now officially renamed NAKHON RATCHASIMA) – literally, "Frontier Country" – which is still considered the gateway to the northeast.

If this is your first stop in Isaan, it's not a particularly pleasant introduction: Khorat's streets are far too narrow for the traffic they're expected to cope with, the town seems constantly under construction (a situation worsened in the run-up to Thai Expo '92), and there's little that merits the term "tourist attraction". But Khorat is at the centre of a good transport network and makes an obvious base for exploring the potteries of Ban Dan Kwian; the Khmer ruins of Phimai, Phanom Rung and Muang Tham are also within striking distance.

Khorat can be a confusing place to get to grips with: the commercial centre used to be contained within the old city moat, at the eastern end of town, but it has spilt over westwards and there are shops and markets as well as hotels and restaurants in both areas. Regular **buses** stop at the main bus station on Suranari Road, close to the town centre and most hotels; the terminal for air-con buses is on Mitraphap Road, ten minutes' walk to the northwest. Aside from serving Bangkok and all the main centres within Isaan, Khorat's bus network also extends south along Highway 304 to the east coast, enabling you to travel directly to Pattaya and Chanthaburi without going through the capital. Arriving at the **train** station on Mukkhamontri Road, you're midway between the commercial centre to the east (1km) and the town's best guest house to the west (1km). It's also possible to **fly** to Khorat from Bangkok; the airport is about 5km southwest of town on Highway 304.

Local buses travel most of the main roads and cost B2 a ride within the town (the exact money is required on some of the most ancient buses). The most useful routes are #1, which heads west along Chumphon Road, past the station and out to the *Doctor's Guest House* and returns east via Yommarat Road, and #2, which runs between TAT in the west and beyond the *lak muang* (city pillar) to the east.

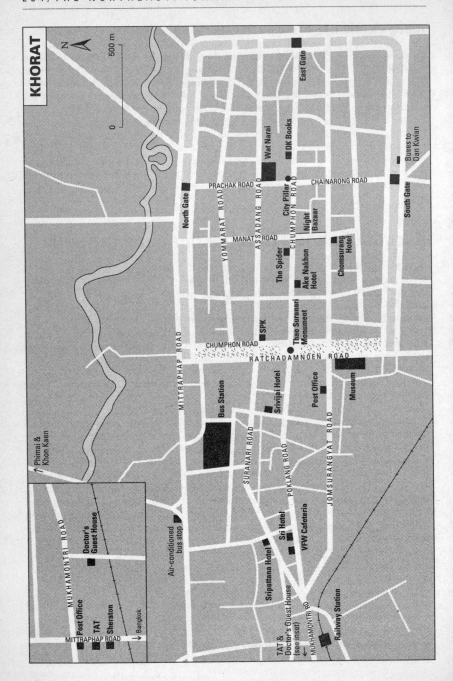

The city

Sights are thin on the ground in Khorat, but if you spend more than a couple of hours in the city you're bound to come across the landmark statue at the western gate of the old city walls. This is the much-revered **Thao Suranari Monument**, erected to commemorate the heroic actions of the wife of the deputy governor of Khorat, during an attack by the kingdom of Vientiane – capital of modern-day Laos – in 1826. Local chronicles proffer several versions of her feat: some say she organised a feast for the Laotian army and enticed them into bed, where they were then slaughtered by the Thais; another tells how she and the other women of Khorat were carted off as prisoners to Vientiane, whereupon they attacked and killed their guards with such ferocity that the Laotians retreated out of fear that the whole Thai army had arrived. At any rate, Thao Suranari saved the day and still is feted by the citizens of Khorat, who lay flowers at her feet, light incense at her shrine and even dance around it. At the end of March, the town holds a week-long **festival** in her honour, with parades through the streets and the usual colourful trappings of Thai merry-making.

The closest Khorat has to a public **park** is the strip of grass that runs north and south of the monument, between Chumphon and Ratchadamnoen Roads. It's a great place for hanging out with the local populace: all sorts of things happen here, from haircuts and massages to chess tournaments and picnics.

Otherwise, check out the city's **Maha Veeravong Museum** (Wed–Sun 9am–4pm; B5), which houses a small and unexceptional collection of predominantly Dvaravati- and Lopburi-style Buddha statues found at nearby sites. It's in the grounds of Wat Suthachinda, on Ratchadamnoen Road. Modern Khorat's main attraction, especially for kids, is **Tarn Hiran** (Silver Lake Water Park), south of TAT on Mitraphap Road, an outdoor leisure complex with a huge swimming pool, water slides and artificial-wave machines as well as restaurants and nightly performances of local folk dances.

Tourist shops and crafts outlets don't really feature in Khorat, but if you're not going further east to Surin, or north to Chaiyaphum, this is a good place to buy **silk**, much of which is produced in Pak Tong Chai, an uninteresting and over-exploited town 32km south of Khorat on Highway 304; the specialist shops along Chumphon Road sell at reasonable prices and stock a bigger range than places in Pak Tong Chai. The reverse is true of **ceramics**: there's far more choice at the local pottery village of Dan Kwian (see below) than at Khorat's night bazaar.

Practicalities

There's a small tourist information booth at the railway station, but if you're basing yourself in Khorat for more than a night you'd do well to trek out to the main **TAT office** (☎044/243751; daily 8.30am–4.30pm), on the western edge of town, to pick up a free map of the convoluted city bus network and get advice on transport to sights out of town. A branch of *DK Books* east of the *lak muang* on Chumphon Road stocks the whole range of regional Survey Department maps, plus lots of English-language novels and reference books.

Accommodation

Khorat isn't short of **accommodation**, and at the time of writing several new hotels (most notably a *Sheraton* near TAT on Mitraphap Road) were going up in anticipation of large numbers of Thai Expo visitors. Hopefully the added competition will encourage hoteliers to spruce up existing rooms, because apart from a couple of notable exceptions recommended here, the city's budget places currently rate as pretty poor value. Noise is the main problem in the cheaper central hotels – best to request a room away from the main road. If you're planning a visit to Phimai, consider staying in the lovely old guest house there, rather than commuting from Khorat.

Ake Nakhon Hotel, 120 Chumphon Rd (☎044/242504). Noisy but adequate rooms from B100.

Chomsurang Hotel, 2701/2 Mahathai Rd, near the night bazaar (☎044/257088). One of Khorat's best, and the usual choice of businesspeople and better-off tourists. Rooms start at B500, including use of the swimming pool.

Doctor's Guest House, 78 Soi 4, Suebsiri Rd, near TAT (☎044/255846). Friendliest and most peaceful place in town, it has a quaint B&B atmosphere, informative notice boards, mounds of local information and a garden seating area; only six rooms (singles B70, doubles B100) and a dorm (B30). On bus routes #1 and #2.

Sri Hotel, 167–168 Pho Klang Rd (☎044/242831). More central than *Doctor's* and a viable alternative; clean, surprisingly quiet and spacious rooms with fan and shower start at B90 (B80 near the road).

Sripattana Hotel, 355/1 Suranari Rd (☎044/242883). Good value, with air-con singles at B380, doubles B420, including use of swimming pool.

Srivijai Hotel, 9–11 Buarong Rd (☎044/242194). Very noisy streetside location near the bus station, with singles from B120, doubles from B170.

Eating

Khorat's time as a US airbase during the Vietnam War has left a legacy of nightclubs, massage parlours and Western **restaurants**. A number of GIs have settled in the city and many frequent the *Veterans of Foreign Wars (VFW) Cafeteria* next to the *Siri Hotel* on Pho Klang Road: a combination of greasy spoon and local pub, it also caters to tourists, dishing up hearty helpings of steak and chips, pork chops, pizzas and sandwiches (drinks only after 7pm). *The Spider* at 221–223 Chumphon Rd serves palatable national and regional dishes (such as duck curry and *larb*) at moderate prices, considering the service and air-conditioned premises, but the beer is expensive. Khorat's youth like to hang out at *SPK Restaurant*, a coffee shop-cum-restaurant near the Thao Suranari Monument at the intersection of Assadang and Chumphon Roads, which does a good range of Thai and Chinese dishes, assorted cakes and twenty blends of coffee. The **"night bazaar"** – as Khorat's night market is ambitiously named – along the *Chomsurang Hotel* end of Mahathai Road is the place to come for cheap Isaan specialities like *kai yang* (barbecued chicken), *khao niaw* (sticky rice) and *somtam* (raw papaya salad), not to mention all manner of spicy sausages. If it's good old *pat thai* you're after, there are cheap and tasty roadside noodle stalls opposite the station.

Dan Kwian

Some of the most sought-after modern pottery in Thailand is produced by the potters of **DAN KWIAN**, a tiny village 15km south of Khorat on Route 224. Buses to the village leave frequently from Khorat's southern city gate; get off as soon as you see the roadside pottery stalls. Inevitably, the popularity of the highly distinctive Dan Kwian ceramics has made the village something of a tourist trap, but the place remains remarkably untacky (and the wares underpriced). The roadside stalls display the whole range of products, from cheap sunbaked clay necklaces to traditional urn-shaped water jars; in the background the potters work the clay without much regard for curious onlookers.

Characteristic of **Dan Kwian pottery** is its unglazed metallic finish. The local clay, dug from the banks of the Mun, has a high iron content, which when fired in wood-burning kilns combines with ash to create the shimmering end result. Different shades are achieved by cramming the pots into the kiln to achieve uneven firing: the greater their exposure to heat, the darker the finish. The usual technique consists of building the pots through the continuous addition of small pieces of clay. From this method comes the most typical Dan Kwian motif, the geometrical latticework pattern, which is incorporated into all sorts of designs, from incense burners and ash trays to vases and storage jars. The potters also mould clay into sets of ceramic tiles and large-scale religious and secular murals – increasingly popular decorations in modern wats and wealthy city homes.

First settled by Mons in the mid-eighteenth century, Dan Kwian has always been a convenient resting place for travellers journeying between the Khorat plateau and Cambodia – hence its name, which means "Cart Place" or "Wagon Station". The tag still applies, as the village is now home to the only **cart museum** in Thailand (always open; free), a ramshackle outdoor collection of traditional vehicles and farming implements assembled at the back of the pottery stalls. Look out for the monster machine with seven-foot wheels, designed to carry two tons of rice, and the covered passenger wagons with their intricately carved shafts. The exhibits aren't all as archaic as they look – Isaan farmers still use some of the sugarcane presses on display, and the fish traps and lobster pots are a common sight in this part of the country.

Phimai

Hemmed in by its rectangular old city walls and encircled by tributaries of the River Mun, the tiny modern town of **PHIMAI**, 60km northeast of Khorat, is completely dominated by one of the most impressive Khmer sites in Thailand – the exquisitely restored temple complex of **Prasat Hin Phimai**. No one knows for sure when the prasat was built or for whom, but as a religious site it probably dates back to the reign of the Khmer King Suriyavarman I (1002–49); the complex was connected by a direct road to Angkor and oriented southeast, towards the Khmer capital. Over the next couple of centuries Khmer rulers made substantial modifications, and by the end of Jayavarman VII's reign (1181–1220) Phimai had been officially dedicated to Mahayana Buddhism. Phimai's other claim to fame is **Sai Ngam** (Beautiful Banyan), reputedly the largest banyan tree in Thailand, still growing a couple of kilometres beyond the temple walls.

Phimai's ruins attract a constant trickle of (mostly Thai) tourists throughout the year, but crowds only really congregate here for the annual **boat races**, held on the Mun's tributaries over a weekend in late October or early November. In common with many other riverside towns throughout Thailand, Phimai marks the end of the rainy season by holding fiercely competitive long-boat races on the well-filled waterways, and putting on lavish parades of ornate barges done up to emulate the Royal Barges of Bangkok.

KHMER RUINS

To make sense of the **Khmer ruins** of Thailand, it's essential to identify their common architectural features. The history of the Khmers in Thailand is covered in *Contexts*; what follows is a brief rundown of the layout of their temple complexes.

At the centre of the rectangular temple compound is always the **main prang**, a pyramidal or corn-cob-shaped tower built to house the temple's most sacred image. Each prang has four entrance chambers or **gopura**, the most important of which (usually the eastern one, facing the dawn) is often extended into a large antechamber. The **lintels** and **pediments** above the gopura are carved with subjects from relevant mythology: typical Hindu reliefs show incidents from the *Ramayana* epic and lively portraits of the Hindu deities Shiva and Vishnu, while Buddhist scenes come from the lives of the Buddha and other *bodhisattva*s. **Antefixes** on the roof of the prang are often carved with the Hindu gods of direction, some of the most common being: east, Indra on the three-headed elephant; south, Yama on a buffalo; west, Varuna on a naga or a *hamsa* (sacred goose); north, Brahma on a *hamsa*; and northeast, Isaana on a bull.

Originally, the prang would have sheltered a **shiva lingam**, continuously bathed by lustral water dripping from a pot suspended over it; the water then flowed out of the inner chamber by means of a stone channel, a process which symbolised the water of the Ganges flowing from the Himalayan home of Shiva. In most prasats, however, the lingam has disappeared or been replaced with Hindu or Buddhist statues.

One or two **minor prangs** usually flank the main prang: often these were added at a later date to house images of less important gods, though in some cases they predate the main structure. Concentric sets of walls shield these shrines within an inner courtyard. In many temples, the innermost wall – the **gallery** – was roofed, either with wood (none of these have survived) or stone, and some galleries have gopuras at their cardinal points. These gopuras also have carved lintels and pediments and are usually approached by staircases flanked with **naga balustrades**; in Khmer temples, nagas generally appear as symbolic bridges between the human world and that of the gods. Most prangs enclose ponds between their outer and inner walls, and many are surrounded by a network of moats and reservoirs: historians attribute the Khmers' political success in part to their skill in designing highly efficient irrigation systems.

The ruins

Built mainly of dusky pink and greyish white sandstone, **Prasat Hin Phimai** (daily 7.30am–6pm; B20) is a seductive sight for so solemn a set of buildings. Even from a distance, the muted colours give off a far from austere glow; closer inspection reveals a mass of intricate carvings.

From the main southeastern gate, a staircase ornamented with classic naga balustrades leads to a gopura in the **outer walls**, which are punctuated on either side by false balustraded windows – a bit of sculptural sleight-of-hand to jazz up the solid stonework without piercing the defences. A raised pathway bridges the space between these walls and the inner gallery that protects the prangs of the **inner sanctuary**. The minor prang to the right, made of laterite, is attributed to the megalomaniac twelfth-century King Jayavarman VII – a statue of him, now kept in the National Museum in Bangkok, was found here – while the pink sandstone prang to the left, which is connected to a Brahmin shrine where seven stone linga were found, was probably built around the same time.

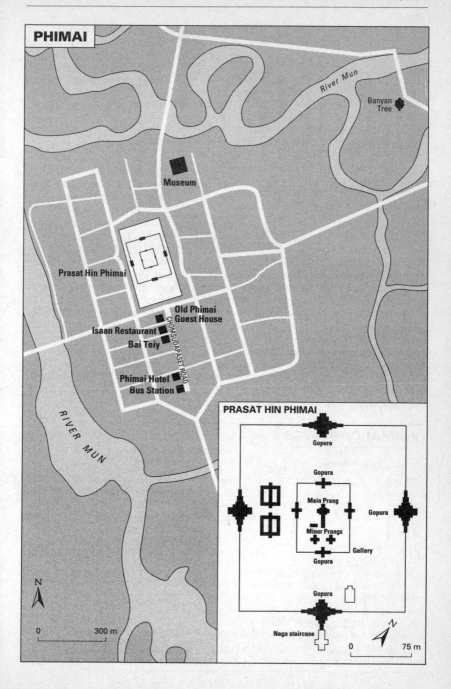

PHIMAI

River Mun

Banyan Tree

Museum

Prasat Hin Phimai

Old Phimai Guest House

CHOMSUDAPASET ROAD

Isaan Restaurant

Bai Teiy

Phimai Hotel

Bus Station

RIVER MUN

N

0   300 m

PRASAT HIN PHIMAI

Gopura

Gopura

Main Prang

Gopura

Minor Prangs

Gallery

Gopura

Gopura

Naga staircase

N

0   75 m

A false window

After more than twenty years of archaeological detective work and painstaking reassembly, the magnificent **main prang** has now been restored to its original cruciform groundplan and conical shape, complete with an almost full set of carved lintels, pediments and antefixes, and capped with a stone lotus bud. The **carvings** around the outside of the prang depict predominantly Hindu themes. Shiva – the Destroyer – dances above the main entrance to the southeast antechamber: his destruction dance heralds the end of the world and the creation of a new order, a supremely potent image that warranted this place over the most important doorway. Most of the other external carvings pick out momentous episodes from the *Ramayana*, starring heroic Rama, his brother Lakshaman, and their band of faithful monkeys in endless battles of strength, wits and magical powers against Ravana, the embodiment of evil. Inside, more sedate Buddhist scenes give evidence of the conversion from Hindu to Buddhist faith, and the prasat's most important image, Buddha sheltered by a seven-headed naga, sits atop a base that once supported a Hindu shiva lingam.

Much of the carved stonework discovered at Phimai but not fitted back into the renovated structure can be seen at the open-air **museum** (Wed–Sun 8am–4.30pm; free) northeast of the ruins, just inside the old city walls. They're easier to appreciate here, being at eye-level, well-labelled, and backed up by a photographic lesson on the evolution of the different styles.

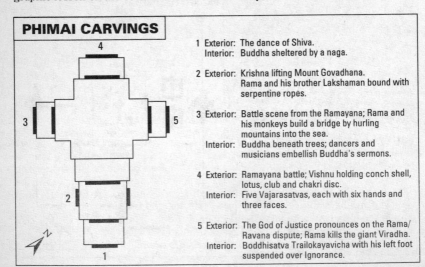

PHIMAI CARVINGS

1 Exterior: The dance of Shiva.
  Interior: Buddha sheltered by a naga.

2 Exterior: Krishna lifting Mount Govadhana.
  Rama and his brother Lakshaman bound with serpentine ropes.

3 Exterior: Battle scene from the Ramayana; Rama and his monkeys build a bridge by hurling mountains into the sea.
  Interior: Buddha beneath trees; dancers and musicians embellish Buddha's sermons.

4 Exterior: Ramayana battle; Vishnu holding conch shell, lotus, club and chakri disc.
  Interior: Five Vajarasatvas, each with six hands and three faces.

5 Exterior: The God of Justice pronounces on the Rama/Ravana dispute; Rama kills the giant Viradha.
  Interior: Boddhisatva Trailokayavicha with his left foot suspended over Ignorance.

Sai Ngam

Two kilometres northeast of the museum – get there by bicycle or samlor – **Sai Ngam** is a banyan tree so enormous that it's reputed to cover an area about half the size of a football pitch (approximately 25,000 square feet). It might look to you like a grove of small banyans, but Sai Ngam is in fact a single plant whose branches have dropped vertically into the ground, taken root and spawned other branches, thereby growing further and further outwards from its central trunk. Banyan trees are believed to harbour animist spirits and you can make merit here by releasing fish into the artificial lake which surrounds Sai Ngam. The tree has become a popular recreation spot, and several restaurants have sprung up alongside it. If you go by bike you'll pass a large-scale model of the Thungsunrit Irrigation Project, an indication of the northeast's dependence on a well-regulated water supply.

Practicalities

Direct **buses** to Phimai from Khorat's main bus station take about an hour and stop within sight of the ruins. Buses between Khorat and towns further north will drop you on Highway 2, about 10km west of Phimai, where you'll have to change (count on waiting a half hour or so).

Though most people visit the ruins as a day trip, Phimai's one very friendly **guest house** makes it a serviceable stopover between Khorat and points north. A lovely old wooden house with a roof garden and sun rooms, *Old Phimai Guest House* (☎044/471725) is just off Chomsudasapet Road, a couple of minutes from the ruins; singles cost B80, doubles B100, and rooms with extra cots are also available. Slightly more upmarket but nowhere near as atmospheric, the *Phimai Hotel* (☎044/471306), next to the bus station, is worth considering only for its air conditioning; singles (with a/c and shower) go for B240, doubles for B300 (basic rooms with no extras are B100).

Bai Teiy on Chomsudasapet Road, the town's most popular **restaurant**, serves tasty Thai dishes, including fresh fish from the river. For typical northeastern fare try around the corner at *Isaan Excellent Taste*, but if you prefer a meal with a view go to the string of interchangeable restaurants alongside Sai Ngam – their food is good enough, though prices are pitched high because of the location.

Bai Teiy also rents **bicycles** – note that these aren't allowed inside the ruins – and runs a tourist information desk where you can pick up a bus timetable and a free map showing cycling routes around the town.

Phanom Rung and Muang Tham

East of Khorat the bleached plains roll blandly on, broken only by the occasional small town and, if you're travelling along Highway 24, the odd tantalising glimpse of the smoky Phanom Dongkrek mountain range above the southern horizon. That said, it's well worth jumping off the Surin-bound bus for a detour to the fine Khmer ruins of **Prasat Hin Khao Phanom Rung** and **Prasat Muang Tham**. Built during the same period as Phimai, and for the same purpose, the temple complexes form two more links in the chain that once connected the Khmer capital with the limits of its empire. Sited dramatically atop an extinct volcano, Phanom Rung has now been beautifully restored, while the still wild ruins of Muang Tham lie on the plains below.

Buses plying between Khorat and Surin will let you off at BAN TAKO, roughly midway between the two towns on Highway 24; from there it's 12km south to Phanom Rung and another 8km south to Muang Tham. There's no public transport direct to the ruins so unless you hitch you'll have to hire a **motorbike taxi**, which should cost B80–100 per person for a return trip with as much time as you like at both prasats. It's worth the money, especially for the exhilarating views as you climb up to Phanom Rung and then drop down again to Muang Tham.

Prasat Hin Khao Phanom Rung

Prasat Hin Khao Phanom Rung (daily 8am–5pm; B20) stands as the finest example of Khmer architecture in Thailand, its every surface ornamented with exquisite carvings and its buildings so perfectly aligned that on the morning of April's full-moon day you can stand at the westernmost gopura and see the rising sun through all fifteen doors. This day marks Songkhran, the Thai new year, which is celebrated with a day-long **festival** of huge parades all the way up the hill to the prasat – a tradition believed to go back 800 years. As at most Khmer prasats, building at Phanom Rung was a continuous process that spanned several reigns: the earliest structures are thought to date to the beginning of the tenth century and final additions were probably made 300 years later, not long before it was abandoned. Restoration work, started in 1971, was completed in 1988.

The **approach** to the temple compound is one of the most dramatic of its kind. Symbolic of the journey from earth to the heavenly palace of the gods, the ascent to the inner compound is freighted with metaphorical import: by following the 200-metre-long avenue, paved in laterite and sandstone and flanked with lotus-bud pillars, you are walking to the ends of the earth. Ahead, Mount Meru, home of the gods, looms large above the gallery walls, accessible only via the first of three **naga bridges**, a raised cruciform structure with sixteen naga balustrades, each naga having five heads. You have now crossed the abyss between earth and heaven. A series of stairways ascends to the eastern entrance of the celestial home, first passing four small ponds, thought to have been used for ritual purification. A second naga bridge crosses to the **east gopura**, entrance to the inner sanctuary, which is topped by a lintel carved with Indra (god of the east) sitting on a lion throne. The gopura is the main gateway through the **gallery** which runs right round the inner compound and has one main and two minor entranceways on each side. Part of the gallery has been restored to its original covered design, with arched roofs, small chambers inside and false windows. The chambers may have been used for exhibiting as well as storing artifacts.

Phanom Rung is surprisingly compact, so the east gopura leads almost directly into the **main prang**, separated from it only by a final naga bridge. A dancing Shiva, nine of his ten arms intact, and a lintel carved with a relief of a reclining Vishnu preside over the eastern entrance to the prang. The Vishnu image has a somewhat controversial history: stolen from the site in the early 1960s, it mysteriously reappeared as a donated exhibit in the Art Institute of Chicago; for over ten years the curators refused to return it to Thailand, but as restoration work on Phanom Rung neared completion in 1988, the public took up the cause and the institute finally relented. Of the other recurring figures decorating the prang, one of the most important is the lion head of Kala, also known as Kirtimukha, symbolic of both the lunar and the solar eclipse and – because he's able to "swallow" the sun – considered far superior to other planetary gods. Inside the prang you can still see the base of the once all-powerful shiva lingam, for which the prang was originally built.

Two rough-hewn laterite libraries stand alongside the main prang, in the northeast and southeast corners, and there are remains of two early-tenth-century brick prangs just northeast of the main prang. The unfinished **prang noi** (little prang) in the southwest corner now contains a stone Buddha footprint, which has become the focus of the merit-making that underlies the annual April festivities, thus neatly linking ancient and modern religious practices.

Prasat Muang Tham

Tumbledown and dishevelled **Prasat Muang Tham** (daily 8am–5pm; B20) makes a wonderful counterpoint to Phanom Rung – at least until the Fine Arts Department gets to work on it. Like Phanom Rung, it was probably built in stages between the tenth and thirteenth centuries, but it hasn't weathered nearly so well. Walls and windows lean gracefully at 45-degree angles, balustrades lie in collapsed heaps, and blocks of carved sandstone litter the grassy compound. At the heart of the prasat, the main prang has crumpled into a forlorn pile, but the four smaller prangs surrounding it are sturdier and almost complete; parts of the gallery protecting them remains recognisable too, pierced by shaky gopuras displaying some of their original carvings. Between the gallery and the outer wall, the four L-shaped ponds still hold water, though the stone rims are slipping beneath the surface. Having seen Phanom Rung, it's quite easy to make out the layout from this partial evidence, but it's an evocative site even without an imaginative effort to reconstruct it.

Surin province

Best known for its highly hyped elephant round-up, the provincial capital of **SURIN**, 197km east of Khorat, is an otherwise typical northeastern town, a good place to absorb the easygoing pace of Isaan life, with the bonus of some atmospheric Khmer ruins nearby. The elephant tie-in comes from the local Suay people, whose prowess with pachyderms is well known and can be seen firsthand in the nearby village of Ta Klang (see below). Thais, Laotians and Khmers make up the remainder of the population of Surin province – the Khmer population was boosted during the Khmer Rouge takeover of Cambodia in the 1970s, when many upper-class Cambodians fled here.

Surin's **elephant round-up**, held every year on the third weekend of November, draws some 40,000 spectators to watch elephants play football, engage in tugs of war, and parade in full battle garb. These shows give both trainers and animals the chance to practise their skills, but however well-controlled the elephants appear, you should always approach them with caution – an American woman was trampled to death in 1991 when her camera flash frightened one. If you miss the Surin show, you might catch one of the lesser roundups in Chaiyaphum or Ayutthaya – or better still, take a trip out to Ta Klang.

Seven **trains** a day make the Bangkok–Surin connection (though only two arrive at a sensible hour), stopping at the station on the northern edge of town, less than ten minutes' walk from the central market area on Krungsrinai Road.

The **bus** terminal is one block east of the railway station. Extra trains and buses are laid on to cope with the crowds that flock here for the elephant round-up and these can be booked through TAT; alternatively you could join one of the overnight packages organised by Bangkok tour agencies.

Surin town

Surin's only official sight is its **museum** (Mon–Fri 8.30am–4.30pm; free), a tiny one-room exhibition on Chitramboong Road featuring stacks of carved antefixes and, more interestingly, several sacred elephant ropes formerly used by the Suay in their hunts to capture wild elephants for taming. Made of buffalo hide and measuring up to 100m, these ropes were considered so special by the men who handled them that women weren't allowed to touch them and, as the essential tools of the hunt, they were blessed by ancestral spirits before every expedition. As added protection the hunters wore the specially inscribed protective clothing on display here: the *yantra* designs are produced by combinations of letters and numbers arranged in such a way as to invoke magic and ward off evil.

SILKWORMS

Most hand-woven **Thai silk** is produced by Isaan village women, some of whom oversee every aspect of sericulture, from the breeding of the silkworm through to the dyeing of the fabric. "Silk-tours" give you a good insight into the weaving and subsequent processes, but guides rarely dwell on the fascinating stages that precede them.

A principal reason for Isaan's pre-eminence in the silk industry is that its soils are particularly suitable for the growth of mulberry tree, the leaves of which are the silkworms' favoured diet. The cycle of production commences with the female silkmoth, which lives just a few days but lays around 300–500 eggs in that time. In three to four weeks each egg expands from a microscopic speck into a six-centimetre-long silkworm – gorging itself on mulberry leaves, it finally attains a weight ten thousand times its original size, ready for the cocoon-building **pupal** stage.

The silkworm constructs its **cocoon** from a single white or yellow fibre that it secretes from its mouth at a rate of 12cm a minute, sealing the filaments with a gummy substance called sericin. The metamorphosis of the pupa into a moth may take as few as two days or as many as seven, but the sericulturist must anticipate the moment at which the new moth is about to break out of the cocoon, in order to prevent the destruction of the precious fibre – which at this stage is often 900 metres long. At the crucial point the cocoon is dropped into boiling water, killing the moth and softening the sericin, so that the unbroken filament can be unravelled. The fibres from several cocoons are "reeled" into a single thread, and two or three threads are subsequently twisted or "thrown" into the yarn known as **raw silk**. (Broken threads from damaged cocoons are worked into a second-rate yarn called "spun silk".) In most cases, next comes the "degumming process", in which the raw silk is soaked in soapy water to entirely dissolve the sericin, reducing the weight of the thread by as much as thirty percent and leaving it soft and lustrously semitransparent.

Extremely absorbent and finely textured, finished silk is the perfect material for dyeing. It's also one of the strongest natural textiles, able to sustain a dead weight of as much as 28 grammes on a single fibre – which is why it's used to make parachutes as well as £700 shirts from Gianni Versace.

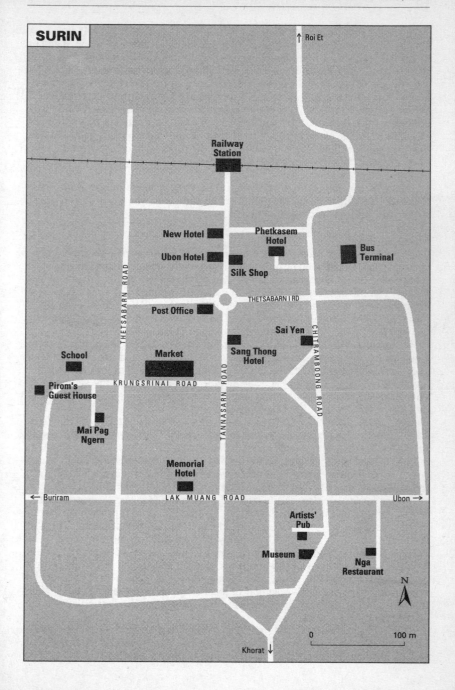

SURIN

↑ Roi Et

Railway
Station

New Hotel

Phetkasem
Hotel

Bus
Terminal

Ubon Hotel

Silk Shop

THETSABARN ROAD

THETSABARN I RD

Post Office

Sai Yen

School

Market

Sang Thong
Hotel

CHITRAMBOONG ROAD

Pirom's
Guest House

KRUNGSRINAI ROAD

TANNASARN ROAD

Mai Pag
Ngern

Memorial
Hotel

← Buriram

LAK MUANG ROAD

Ubon →

Artists'
Pub

Museum

Nga
Restaurant

N

0   100 m

Khorat ↓

You won't find "magic" clothing on sale in Surin, but the local **silk** weave is famous for its variety: 700 designs are produced in Surin province alone, many of them of Cambodian origin, including the locally popular rhomboid pattern. A shop opposite the *Ubon Hotel* on Tannasarn Road stocks a huge selection of silks and cottons, though prices are of course cheaper on the street; there are usually four or five women selling their wares around the Tannasarn–Krungsrinai intersection. Most of these women come from surrounding villages, and while it is possible to visit these villages, you'll need to go with a guide, not only to understand the weavers' explanations of what they do, but also to get a more behind-the-scenes look at the less obvious aspects of the process, like the breeding of the silkworms and the extracting of the thread; *Pirom's Guest House* should be able to arrange a guide for you.

Timing is also important if you want to see the weavers in action, the best months to see them are between November and June, when the women aren't required to work day and night in the fields.

Practicalities

During the elephant round-up, **accommodation** in Surin gets extremely tight and rates double, but at other times you'll have no trouble finding a place to stay. First choice has to be *Pirom's Guest House*, one block west of the market at 242 Krungsrinai Rd: quintessentially Thai in its stylish simplicity, it's one of the best establishments in Isaan, with singles for B60, doubles B100 (dorm beds B40). Pirom himself is a highly informed social worker who genuinely enjoys conversing with foreigners and leading informal tours around the area.

Phetkasem Hotel at 104 Chitramboong Rd (☎045/511274) offers much more conventional digs, with sizeable rooms with shower, fan and use of swimming pool starting at a bargain B200 (B300 with a/c). Other less luxurious hotels offering clean rooms with fan and shower include *New Hotel* , near the station at 22 Tannasarn Rd (☎045/511341), B90 single, B150 double; *Sang Thong Hotel*, near the post office at 155-161 Tannasarn Rd (☎045/512099), B130 single, B170 double; and *Memorial Hotel*, at 186 Lak Muang Rd (☎045/511288), singles from B140. Bottom of the range, and a last resort, is the *Ubon Hotel* at 156 Tannasarn Rd (☎044/511133), with singles for B70, doubles for B80.

For the best in Isaan **food**, make for *Sai Yen* on Chitramboong Road, which serves a constant stream of local office workers and families in traditional style: roll the sticky rice into little balls and dip them into assorted chilli sauces, *larb* curries and spicey *somtam* salads. Try the (unsigned) *Mai Pag Ngern* restaurant, off the western end of Krungsrinai Road, for good food from central Thailand – curries, noodle soups and the like – and cheap beer in a garden setting. The *Nga* restaurant off Lak Muang Road, instantly recognizable by the two huge tusks outside its gates, offers a much more touristy and expensive experience, with weekend dinner shows featuring – you guessed it – performing elephants. Surin's lively **night market** on Krungsrinai Road is one of Isaan's best, boasting a remarkably large and tasty selection of local food. More prosaically, the restaurant and bowling alley in the forecourt of the *Phetkasem Hotel* specialises in ice creams and Western food.

Aspiring local musicians and their friends hang out in the *Artist's Pub* down a small soi just north of the museum, where the atmosphere is laid-back and welcoming, if not always exactly bustling, and the beer is cheap.

Ta Klang

Some 50km north of Surin, the "elephant village" of **TA KLANG** is the main settlement of the Suay people and training centre for their elephants. A visit to the village could be worthwhile if you time it right: although Suay mahouts and their herd now spend most of their time doing shows around the country, they are likely to be home during the rice-growing season from July to October and for the period just before the Surin round-up on the third weekend in November. For the ten days prior to the Surin show they train intensively in their village and then walk to Surin for the round-up; you'll see them in a healthier state if you make the trip just before the big weekend rather than after.

Traditionally regarded as the most expert hunters and trainers of elephants in Thailand, the **Suay** tribe migrated to the region from Central Asia before the rise of the Khmers in the ninth century. It was the Suay who masterminded the use of elephants in the construction of the great Khmer temples, and a Suay chief who in 1760 helped recapture a runaway white elephant belonging to the king of Ayutthaya, earning the hereditary title "Lord of Surin". Surin was governed by members of the Suay tribe until Rama Vs administrative reforms of 1907.

The role of the elephant has diminished with the advent of modern machinery and the 1989 ban on teak logging, but other Asian governments occasionally ask for their help as hauliers, and one of the stranger Thai superstitions provides the Suay with a handy money-spinner. Many Thais believe that it's good luck to walk under an elephant's belly (pregnant women who do so are guaranteed an easy birth), so it's not unheard of for a Suay mahout to walk his elephant the 450km from Surin to Bangkok, charging around B20 per limbo en route.

Local **buses** to Ta Klang depart approximately hourly from the Surin terminal and take about two hours. Although there are no hotels in Ta Klang, **overnight visits** can be arranged through *Pirom's Guest House* – even if you don't want to stay, it might be a good idea to get advice on timing.

Ta Muen Toj, Prasat Ta Muen Tam and Bay Kream

The cluster of Khmer ruins called **Ta Muen Toj**, **Prasat Ta Muen Tam** and **Bay Kream**, close to the Cambodian border east of Surin, are best visited on a tour from *Pirom's Guest House*, for this is not a zone to explore unguided. The two-hour drive to the frontier area passes through several checkpoints along the way, and as the road nears Phanom Dongrek – the mountains that divide Thailand from Cambodia – it runs through villages whose inhabitants live under the daily threat of unexploded land-mines whenever they go fishing in remote parts of the river or wood-cutting off the main forest paths. These legacies from the war in Cambodia continue to claim lives and limbs, and not a village in this area is without its disabled victims. The pathways to the ruins have of course been cleared, but when you arrive at Ta Muen Toj an armed escort joins the tour – with tensions still unresolved in Cambodia, the area is a sensitive one.

It's thought that the tiny **Ta Muen Toj** was a resting place for worshippers at the nearby **Prasat Ta Muen Tam**, a walled temple compound in the clutches of enormous trees – a testament to the age of the place and to the durability of the materials with which the temple was built. A kilometre or so further, **Bay Kream** stands on a mound, like an island in the suffocating jungle. This is the largest and the most recognisable of the three sites, with carved lintels and large stone blocks strewn between the dilapidated walls; piled-up earth now fills many of the rooms to ceiling height and the window frames have subsided beneath ground level, giving the whole complex a wonderful air of decomposition. Beyond Bay Kream, the unconquered Cambodian jungle stretches to the horizon, a vista accompanied by the sound of sporadic shelling.

Ubon Ratchathani and around

East of Surin, Highway 226 and the rail line run in tandem through dessicated, impoverished plains before coming to a halt at **UBON RATACHATANI** (Royal City of the Lotus), a provincial capital which, despite its name, is of neither regal nor botanical distinction. Almost always referred to simply as Ubon – not to be confused with Udon (Udon Thani) to the north – Thailand's fifth largest city holds little in the way of atmosphere or attraction beyond a couple of wats, a decent museum and a lingering hangover from its days as a US airbase site. It's only really worth visiting in order to make trips out: eastwards to the prehistoric cliff paintings at Pha Taem, or southwest to the ruins of Khao Phra Viharn.

If you're near Ubon in early July, you should definitely consider coming into town for the local **Asanha Puja** festivities, an auspicious Buddhist holiday celebrated all over Thailand to mark the beginning of Khao Pansa (the annual three-month Buddhist retreat). Ubon's version of this festival is the most spectacular in the country: local people make huge wooden or plaster sculptures, coat them in orange beeswax and then carve intricate decorations in the wax. The sculptures are mounted on floats around enormous candles and paraded through the town – hence the tourist name for the celebrations, the **Ubon Candle Festival** – before being presented to various wats. In most wats the candle is kept burning throughout the retreat period.

The most painless way to get to Ubon from Bangkok (and most places in between) is by **train** – the rail line terminates at WARINCHAMRAB, Ubon's suburban alter ego just across the sluggish Maenam Mun. City buses #1, #2, #3, #6 and #7 will get you across the river to Ubon, #2 and #7 carrying on to Kaenthani and Auparat roads for the main hotels and TAT office. Regular long-distance **buses** from Bangkok and points west, and Kong Chiam to the east, pull into the Warinchamrab terminal, one block east of the train station; those from the north (Yasothon, Khon Kaen, Udon) arrive at a terminal north of the town centre on Jaengsanit Road. The several air-con bus companies connecting Ubon with other cities (Bangkok, Chiang Mai, Phitsanulok, Khorat, Surin) have various arrival and departure points near TAT on Kaenthani Road and opposite the Monument of Merit on the parallel Phalochai Road.

The city

Aside from its confusing number of arrival points, central Ubon is easy enough to negotiate. The main hotel and eating area is confined to a compact area between Sumpasit Road in the north and the Mae Nam Mun in the south. Of the city's eight main wats, **Wat Thung Si Muang**, in the middle of this zone near the post office, is the most noteworthy, mainly for its unusually well-preserved teak library – raised on stilts over an artificial pond to keep book-devouring insects at bay.

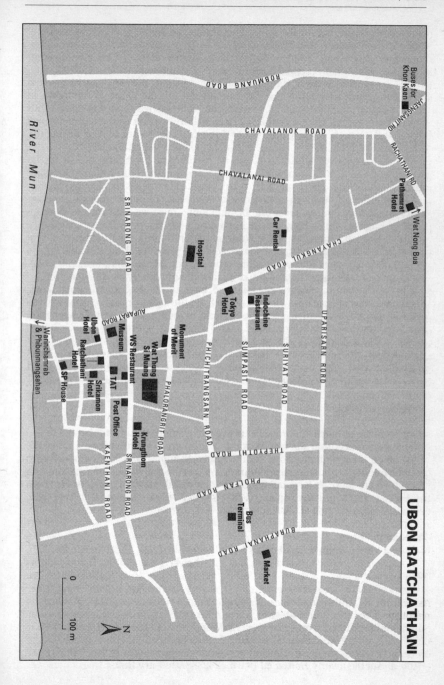

The murals in the bot, to the left of the library, have also survived remarkably well: the lively scenes of everyday nineteenth-century life include musicians playing *khaen* pipes and devotees performing characteristic Isaan merit-making dances, as well as conventional portraits of city life in Bangkok.

Off Chayangkun Road at the northern edge of town, the much more modern **Wat Nong Bua** (city bus #2 or #3) is modelled on the stupa at Bodhgaya in India, scene of Buddha's enlightenment. The whitewashed replica is carved with scenes from the *Jataka* and contains a scaled-down version of the stupa covered in gold leaf. Of more interest, especially if you don't happen to be here during the candle festival, is the wax float kept in a small building behind the chedi.

For an overview of all things to do with southern Isaan, pay a visit to the **museum** (Wed–Sun 8.30am–4.30pm; free) housed in the blue and grey building opposite the *Ubon Hotel* on Kaenthani Road. This is a real something-for-everyone offering, with thematic displays on the region's geology, ancient history, folk crafts, musical instruments and more, most with informative descriptions in English. Particularly worth looking out for are a ninth-century Khmer statue of Ganesh, examples of the star-embroidered fabric that is a speciality of Ubon, and a pre-fourth-century bronze bell and ceremonial drum found in the vicinity. Also on show is a serviceable reproduction of the Pha Taem cliff paintings – much easier to get to than the originals, though hardly as atmospheric.

Silk, cotton and silverware are all good buys in Ubon. Several shops along Kaenthani Road specialise in clothes made from the stripey rough **cotton** weaves peculiar to the Ubon region. Fifty metres east of the museum, just off Kaenthani Road, an (unsigned) upmarket Isaan crafts shop sells interesting antique implements as well as lengths of **silk** and clothes made to local designs. Fashionable at the moment with middle-class Thai women are Laotian-style **silver filigree** belts and accessories (best worn with top-quality Isaan silk sarongs); there's a good selection at the jewellery shop just north of *SP House* near the main night market.

Practicalities

Ubon's choice of hotels and restaurants is fair enough, though to date there are no guest houses within the city to act as a focal point for travellers. Staff at the **TAT office** on Kaenthani Road (daily 8.30am–4.30pm) will help you out with specific queries on bus and train departures, but all their local information is in Thai. If you're thinking of going out to the cliff paintings, then consider renting a **motorbike** (B200 per day) or **car** (B800 per day with or without a driver) from *Watana* (☎045/242202) at 39/8 Suriyat Rd.

Accommodation

The best and friendliest of Ubon's **cheap hotels** is *Tokyo Hotel* (☎045/241739), 178 Auparat Rd, where rooms with fan and shower go for B100. Double rooms with fan and shower at the *Ubon Hotel*, 333 Kaenthani Rd (☎045/254952), are overpriced at B220, but clean and quiet. The very similar *Ratchathani Hotel* at 229 Kaenthani Rd (☎045/254599) has bigger singles starting at B150. *Krungthom Hotel*, near the post office at 24 Si Narong Rd (☎045/241609), also has spacious singles from B180. Ubon's cheapest, *Decha Hotel* on Kaenthani Road (☎045/254270), has very basic rooms from B50. Unless everywhere else is full, avoid the two dingy places on Suriyat Road: rooms at *Suriyat Hotel* (☎045/241144) are B100, and at the nearby *Homsa-ad* (☎045/242368) they are B80.

Moving up to **more expensive places**, the central *Srikamon Hotel* at 22 Ubonsak Rd (☎045/241136) has comfortable rooms from B500 and also organises day and overnight trips to Pha Taem and other local attractions. Top of the range is *Pathumrat Hotel* at 173 Chayangkun Rd (☎045/241501) on the northern outskirts of town, where air-conditioned rooms start at B600, including use of the swimming pool.

Eating and drinking

One of Ubon's more interesting **eating** experiences is the *Indochine Restaurant* on Sumpasat Road – there's no English sign, but it's easily recognisable by the photos of speciality dishes on the walls. The predominantly Vietnamese food is based around stuffed rice-noodle pancakes with spicy sauces and lashings of fresh mint. A set meal of two or three dishes costs about B60; unfortunately the place closes at 6pm. Also reasonably priced, *WS Restaurant*, round the corner from TAT, serves a large range of Thai and Chinese dishes – the ribs in black bean sauce are a treat. *Chiokee* on Kaenthani Road seems to get the most breakfast business: farangs come for the ham and eggs, local office workers for rice gruel. If you hanker after Western food at other times of the day, try the pizzas and steaks in *Sky Restaurant* on Auparat Road, across the way from the *lak muang*, or the coffee and cakes at *SP House*, round the corner from the *Ratchathani Hotel* near the river. The Maenam Mun makes a great setting for Ubon's main **night market**, which serves particularly good *hawy thawt* (mussel omelettes), among other standard fare; a smaller market sets up next to the *Tokyo Hotel* every evening.

The massage parlours and whisky joints of the Vietnam War days have mostly disappeared, and while Ubon's few remaining **bars** bear absolutely no resemblance to the brash neon horrors of other former R&R spots, they still don't make very congenial places to drink. Several typical "pubs" are clustered around the *Ubon Hotel*, each offering a studiously bland ambience with leather chairs, pretty hostesses and pricey drinks.

East of Ubon

Highway 217, the main road east from Ubon, roughly follows the River Mun for 45km before splitting into two at Phibunmangsahan, where Route 2222 continues along the river to its confluence with the Mekhong at **Kong Chiam** – worth a trip for the nearby prehistoric paintings at Pha Taem. Contrary to what TAT will tell you, it is possible to get to Kong Chiam by bus, and the village has a couple of inviting guest houses, but with your own transport you'd also be able to explore **Kaeng Tana National Park** on the way. It's also possible to organise two-day river trips through the park: for more information contact Prapat Seetong of *Chaiseng Computer* in Ubon (☎045/254087).

The Maenam Mun and Kaeng Tana National Park

Whether travelling by bus, car or bike, your first stop will be **PHIBUNMANGSAHAN** (known locally as Phibun), 45km east of Ubon at the turbulent point of the Mun known as **Kaeng Saphue** (*kaeng* means rapids), a popular fishing and picnic spot. Buses leave every half-hour or so from the Warinchamrab bus station and terminate at Phibun, so you'll have to change here if heading on to Kong Chiam. Just before the town, there's a signpost for **Wat**

Phokakaew, an unusually attractive modern wat, worth a look for its eye-catchingly tiled exterior and its interior reliefs of twelve of Thailand's most revered wats, including the Golden Mount in Bangkok and Nakhon Pathom's monumental chedi.

Continuing eastwards, there's a choice of two routes to Kong Chiam: buses follow the more direct Highway 2222 (30km), while the more scenic Highway 217 passes through Kaeng Tana National Park (37km). After about 30km on 217, you'll reach the **Srindhorn Dam**, which holds in one of the largest reservoirs in Isaan. The landscape around here looks set to change drastically over the next few years, thanks to a new hydroelectric dam under construction a few kilometres north of the highway. The resulting reservoir will cover 117 square kilometres of farmed and inhabited land, forcing 250 families to relocate – local villagers and environmentalists have been protesting for several years but despite some international support have failed to stop the project.

KAENG TANA NATIONAL PARK headquarters are 7km down a dirt track signposted off Highway 217 just northwest of the dam. Although the park offers only a couple of short trails from the headquarters through predominantly scrubby vegetation to waterfalls and caves, it does make a pleasant place to break your journey. The best picnic spot is beside **Kaeng Tana**, a much wilder set of rapids than those at Kaeng Saphue, less than 1km beyond the headquarters. If desperate you can also stay here: six-berth national park bungalows go for B700. To get from here to Kong Chiam you'll have to cross the Mun by vehicle ferry, which pulls in about 4km away from the headquarters – ask at the headquarters for directions. Once on the other bank, follow the road until the signpost for Kong Chiam, a couple of kilometres further.

Kong Chiam

The small wooden village of **KONG CHIAM** isn't immediately the most seductive place in Isaan. Its fancifully named "two-coloured river" is created by the merging of the muddy brown Mun with the muddy brown Mekhong, and its cliff-side **Wat Tamkohasawan**, with its huge and ugly modern Buddha staring down on the inhabitants, doesn't invite you to linger on the road to Pha Taem either.

Nonetheless, Kong Chiam makes a very pleasant overnight stopover point, for it's well off the beaten track, and rarely do you get the opportunity to stay in such a well-appointed **guest house** in a typical Thai village. The *Apple Guest House*, opposite the post office and about five minutes' walk from the bus stop and the riverbank, has clean wooden rooms with good beds and is run by a very convivial family who extend a warm welcome to the smattering of travellers who make it this far. The other guest house, *Kong Chiam*, lies buried in the heart of the village (ask at the bus stop for directions) and has slightly less comfortable rooms for the same price. For **restaurants** you're limited to a string of similar riverside places, which are reasonably priced if not very exciting, though you might be lucky enough to coincide with a good fish catch, in which case you should ask if they have any *pla duk*, the catfish which is very much a local speciality.

The Pha Taem paintings

Clear proof of the antiquity of the fertile Mekhong Valley, the **Pha Taem paintings** – 18km up the Mekhong from Kong Chiam – are believed to be between 3000 and 4000 years old. The work of rice-cultivating settlers who lived in huts rather than caves, the bold and childlike paintings cover a 170-metre stretch of cliff face.

Protected from the elements by an overhang, the red paint – a mixture of soil, tree gum and fat – has kept its colour so well that the shapes and figures are still clearly discernible. Human forms and geometric designs appear in groups alongside massive depictions of animals and enormous fish – possibly the prized catfish still caught in the Mekhong. Most awesome of all is a thirty-metre string of hand prints, giving an uncannily emphatic sense of prehistoric human presence.

Pha Taem (Taem Cliff) is clearly signposted from Kong Chiam, but if you're reliant on public transport you'll have to hitch or charter a tuk-tuk or taxi from the village – ask at *Apple Guest House* for advice. The road ends at the cliff, passing weird mushroom-shaped rock formations known as Sao Chaliang; from the car park, follow the unsigned path down the cliff face and along the shelf in the rock to the paintings. If you continue along the path past the paintings, you'll eventually

climb back up to the top of the cliff again, taking in fine views of the fertile Mekhong valley floor and glimpses of hilly western Laos. Having reached surface level again, double back across the rocky scrub to reach the car park, a couple of kilometres away.

Pha Taem cliff paintings

Khao Phra Viharn and Wat Pa Nanachat Beung Rai

Perched atop a 547-metre-high spur of the Dongkrek mountains about 80km southwest of Ubon, the Khmer ruins of **Khao Phra Viharn** (daily 8am–4pm; B50) surpass even the spectacularly set Phanom Rung. A magnificent avenue over 500 metres long rises to the sanctuary, lined at intervals with naga balustrades and punctuated by four pavilions which afford views from each cardinal point – east and west over jungle-clad hills, north to Thailand, and south up to the main temple sited right on the cliff edge.

Accessible only by this promenade which starts just inside Thailand's southern border, Khao Phra Viharn nevertheless stands on Cambodian land – and until January 1992 it was officially out of bounds, due both to the territorial struggles between the two neighbours and the continuing fighting in Cambodia. The ruins should now be open (half the entrance fee goes to each national government), but before attempting to reach them you should check with the Khorat or Bangkok TAT office on the current situation – you may need to obtain written permission beforehand. **Buses** from Ubon's Warinchamrab station will get you as far as KANTHARALAK (1hr 30min), but from there you'll have to arrange a motorbike taxi to the ruins.

Seventeen kilometres west of Ubon, a short walk off Highway 226, a group of foreign monks have established the forest monastery of **Wat Pa Nanachat Beung Rai** specifically for farangs who want to immerse themselves in meditation. Short- and long-term visitors are welcome, but the atmosphere is serious and intense and not for curious sightseers. Nearly all west-bound buses from the Warinchamrab bus station in Ubon will pass close by the monastery; ask to be let out at the village of BEUNG RAI and follow the signs for the wat. (For general information on meditation centres, see p.37.)

Yasothon and Roi Et

By the beginning of May, Isaan is desperate for rain; there may not have been significant rainfall for six months and the rice crops need to be planted. In northeastern folklore, rain is the fruit of sexual encounters between the gods, so at this time villagers all over Isaan hold the bawdy **Bun Bang Fai** – a merit-making **rocket festival** – to encourage the gods to get on with it. The largest and most public of these festivals takes place in **YASOTHON**, 98km northwest of Ubon, on a weekend in mid-May. Not only is the firework display a spectacular affair, but the rockets built to launch them are superbly crafted machines in themselves, beautifully decorated and carried proudly through the streets before blast-off. Up to 25kg of gunpowder may be packed into the nine-metre-long rockets and, in keeping with the fertility theme of the festivities, performance is everything. Sexual innuendo, general flirtation and dirty jokes are essential components of Bun Bang Fai; rocket builders compete to shoot their rockets the highest, and anyone whose missile fails to leave the ground gets coated in mud as a punishment. At other times of the year, Yasothon is a dud, with a faceless high street full of motorbike-part shops and not even a worthwhile wat to look at.

All Khon Kaen-bound **buses** from Ubon stop in Yasothon, as do some buses heading for Chaiyaphum. If you want to **stay** here during festival time, book well in advance and be prepared to pay double what the room's worth. *Yot Nakhon* at 141–143 Uthai-Ramrit Rd (☎045/711122) is the biggest hotel in town and has rooms from B100 (B200 a/c). Otherwise, there's not much to choose between the following, which all have adequate rooms with fan and shower for B70–100: *Udomphon*, 82/3 Uthai-Ramrit Rd (☎045/711564); *Surawet Watthana*, 128/1–3 Jaengsanit Rd (☎045/711690); and *Suk Niran* , 278–86 Jaengsanit Rd (☎045/711196).

If Yasothon's booked out you could commute from either Ubon or **ROI ET**, a pleasant if unarresting town 71km further northwest and also on the Ubon–Khon Kaen bus route. The best value here is the very large *Si Chumphon* on Haisok Road (☎043/511741), where air-conditioned rooms start at B130. The more central *Sai Thip* at 133 Suriyadet Bamrung Rd (☎043/511365) has rooms for B100 with fan, and similar rooms at the nearby *Banchong*, 99–101 Suriyadet Bamrung Rd (☎043/511235), start at B80. *Mai Thai*, 99 Haisok Rd (☎043/511136), is Roi Et's poshest hotel, with air-conditioned rooms from B340 to B950.

CENTRAL ISAAN

The more northerly branch of the northeastern railway line bypasses Khorat, heading straight up through **central Isaan** to the Laotian border town of Nong Khai via Khon Kaen and Udon Thani, paralleling Highway 2 most of the way. West of these arteries, the smaller Highway 201 is shadowed by the thickly wooded Phetchabun and Dong Phrayayen mountain ranges, the westernmost limits of Isaan, chunks of which have been turned into the **national parks** of Phu Kradung, Phu Reua and Phu Hin Rongkla. But hills play only a minor part in central Isaan's landscape, most of which suffers from poor-quality soil that sustains little in the way of profitable crops and, quite apart from what it does to the farmers who work it, makes for drab views from the bus or train window. Nevertheless, there are a handful of towns worth stopping off at: **Chaiyaphum**, where guest houses provide the opportunity to visit silk weavers in a nearby village; **Khon Kaen** for its excellent museum of local history; **Udon Thani**, a departure point for the Bronze Age settlement of **Ban Chiang**; and **Loei**, for its access to the mountainous national parks.

Trains connect only the larger towns, **buses** link all the above centres, also conveniently servicing the town of Phitsanulok (see p.153), the springboard for a tour of the ruins of Sukhothai and a junction for onward travel to Chiang Mai.

Chaiyaphum

The few travellers who stop off at **CHAIYAPHUM** generally come for the organised silk tours, but even if you're not interested in cocoons, dye vats and hand looms, you could spend a couple of enjoyable days here. It's a relaxing town, compact enough to walk easily from end to end in half an hour, and only gets really lively in January, when it holds a week-long celebration in honour of Phraya Phakdi Chumphon, the nineteenth-century founder of the modern town, whose statue graces the main roundabout at its southern end. Recently an **elephant round-up** has been held on the two days preceding the festival – a scaled-down version of the famous Surin show that's a lot less crowded than its prototype.

The only notable sight in town is **Prang Ku**, a ruined Khmer temple probably built in the late twelfth century at the site of a resting place along the route between Phimai and northern outposts of the Khmer empire. All that's left here is the central prang, now housing a sandstone Dvaravati-era Buddha, and the remnants of a surrounding wall. Prang Ku is on Bannakarn Road, about 2km east of the main roundabout. If you go by bike (rentable from the guest houses) you can make a pleasant round-trip by continuing past the prang, through rice fields interspersed with villages, eventually ending up on Niwet Rat Road, 1km east of the bus station at the northern edge of the town centre.

While it's easy enough to cover the 15km west to the **silk-weaving** village of BAN KHWAO by songthaew from Nonmuang Road (on the west side of town), you're likely to have a much more rewarding time if you go with a tour from one of the two guest houses. These cost about B50 per person and include an overview of the whole process from breeding through spinning, dyeing and weaving. Buying silk direct from the weavers makes economic sense for both parties as it cuts out the middle merchants – six yards of good-quality silk can cost as little as B1000. Tailors in Chaiyaphum will make up the cloth for you, but for complicated designs you should wait until you reach the savvy stitchers of Chiang Mai or Bangkok.

Finally, for a therapeutic shower and peaceful jungle picnic you could make the trip to **Nam Tok Pa Eung**, 26km to the northwest. From the bus station take a songthaew bound for NONG BUA DAENG and ask to get out at the waterfall, 45 minutes on. Follow the dirt track on the right to a car park (1500m), cross the river and continue for 1km to the next pair of bridges – the falls are just beyond.

Practicalities

From Bangkok, **buses** to Chaiyaphum leave at least once an hour and take about six hours. There are also connections from Phitsanulok in the central plains, Chiang Mai and Chiang Rai in the north, and Khorat, Surin, Ubon, Khon Kaen, Loei and Chiang Khan in Isaan. All ordinary buses stop at the station on Niwet Rat Road at the eastern edge of town; air-con tour buses stop on Nonmuang Road at the western edge.

There's not much to choose between Chaiyaphum's two basic but quiet, friendly and laid-back **guest houses**. *Yin's Guest House*, the longer established, has simple rooms (singles B50, doubles B90) in three houses at the edge of a swampy lake opposite the ordinary bus terminal. *Chaiyaphum Guest House*, on Nonmuang Road, ten minutes' walk west of the air-con bus station, has singles at B40, doubles B80, plus a large garden and cooking facilities. If you prefer a **hotel**, try the typical Thai-Chinese *Sirichai Hotel* (☎044/811461) just south of *Chaiyaphum Guest House* on Nonmuang Road, where rooms start from B130, or the *Lert Nimit* (☎044/811522) opposite the bus station at 447 Niwetrat Rd, which has rooms from B115.

For value and variety the best place to **eat** is, as usual, the **night market**, which starts from about 6pm along the roads running east and west of the main roundabout; alternatively, the **curry stalls** in front of the department store on Ratchathani Road serve through the evening and during most of the day as well. If you prefer to eat inside, there are **noodle shops** on Ratchathani and Nonmuang roads, but avoid the grim and overpriced café in the *Sirichai Hotel*.

Khon Kaen

Geographically at the virtual centre of Isaan, **KHON KAEN** has been the focus of government plans to regenerate the northeast, and is now the base of a highly respected university as well as the Channel 5 television studios; its province, however, still has the lowest per capita income in the country, at just B4000 per year. Considering its size and importance, the city is surprisingly uncongested and spacious, and its location 188km northeast of Khorat on the Bangkok–Nong Khai railway and Highway 2, makes it a convenient resting point, even though the provincial museum is just about the only sight here.

In keeping with its status as a university town, Khon Kaen has several fine collections in its **museum**, two blocks north of the bus station on Lung Soon Rachakarn Road (Wed–Sun 10am–noon & 1–4pm; B10). The star attraction on the ground floor is a *sema* carved with a sensuous depiction of Princess Bhimba wiping the Buddha's feet with her hair on his return to Kabilabasad after years of absence in search of enlightenment. In the same room, the scope of the **Ban Chiang** collection of reassembled pots, bronze tools and jewellery rivals those held in Bangkok's National Museum and at Ban Chiang itself (see p.309), and is put into context by a map showing the distribution of contemporaneous settlements in the region. The display of **folk art** in one of the smaller ground floor galleries includes traditional fish traps and animal snares, and a selection of betel trays that run the gamut of styles from crude wooden vessels carved by Isaan farmers to more intricate silver sets given by the better-off as a dowry. Upstairs, the displays of Buddha sculptures feature the most perfect small bronze Lanna-style images outside of northern Thailand.

If you have an evening to fill, you could take a samlor tour of **Beung Kaen Nakhon** (B70 from the *Kaen Inn*), the artificial lake 1500m south of the bus station on the southern outskirts of town, and then eat at one of the lakeside restaurants. Aside from a couple of wats and some upmarket residences on its shores, there's nothing else much here, but it's the nearest Khon Kaen has to a public park and as such attracts families and kids on weekends and holidays. You can walk the perimeter in an hour and a half.

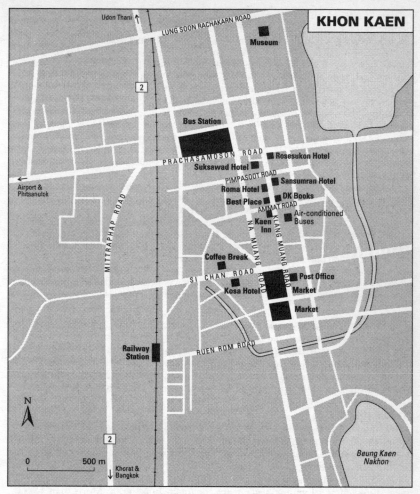

The other moderately interesting way of killing a few hours in Khon Kaen is to make a trip out into the countryside north of town, to visit the revered *that* (reliquary tower) which gave the town and province its name, and to take in some typical northeastern hamlets. The monument, called **Phra That Kham Kaen**, is located within the compound of Wat Chediyaphum in a hamlet of NAN PONG, 30km north of Khon Kaen, and large yellow songthaews make the ninety-minute journey from Khon Kaen bus station about every half-hour. On the way you'll pass through a string of settlements consisting of little more than a few wooden houses raised on stilts to provide shelter for livestock and storage space for looms and ox-carts, and surrounded by small groves of banana and areca palm trees. Outside every house you'll see at least one enormous *ohng*, the all-important water storage jars that are left to collect rainwater for use during the

---

BETEL

Betel-chewing is a habit indulged in all over Asia, and in Thailand nowhere more enthusiastically than in the northeast, where the three essential ingredients for a good chew – **betel leaf, limestone ash** and **areca palm fruit** – are found in abundance. You chew the coarse red flesh of the narcotic fruit (best picked when small and green-skinned) first, before adding a large heart-shaped betel leaf, spread with limestone ash paste and folded into manageable size. For a stronger kick, you can include tobacco and/or marijuana at this point. It's an acquired and bitter taste that numbs the mouth and generates a warm feeling around the ears. Less pleasantly, constant spitting is necessary: in traditional houses you spit through any hole in the floorboards, while in more elegant households a spittoon is provided. It doesn't do much for your looks either: betel-chewers are easily spotted by their rotten teeth and lips stained scarlet from the habit.

When travelling long distances, chewers carry basketloads of the ingredients with them; at home, guests are served from a **betel set**, comprising at least three small covered receptacles, and sometimes a tray to hold these boxes and the knife or nutcracker used to split the fruit. Betel-chewing today is popular mainly with elderly Thais, particularly northeastern women, but it used to be a much more widespread social custom, and a person's betel tray set was once a Thai's most prized possession and an indication of rank: royalty would have sets made in gold, the nobility's would be in silver or nielloware, and poorer folk wove theirs from rattan or carved them from wood. Betel sets still feature as important dowry items in Isaan, with tray-giving processions forming part of northeastern engagement ceremonies.

---

debilitating annual drought. The journey to Nan Pong is more rewarding than the arriving: the whitewashed *that* looks too inconsequential to merit such a significant place in local mythology. The story goes that two monks once rested here beneath a dead tamarind tree (*kham* in Thai); when they returned to the spot a couple of months later it had sprung back into life, so they had the miraculous tree enshrined – and the name Khon Kaen followed from the Kham Kaen shrine.

Practicalities

Khon Kaen is easily reached by road or rail from Bangkok and most other major towns in the northeast. **Trains** from Bangkok leave five times daily, taking between seven and eight hours; two of these go via Khorat and continue as far as Udon Thani; the other three bypass Khorat en route to the end of the line at Nong Khai. The **train station** is just off Highway 2 on the southwestern edge of town, about fifteen minutes' walk from the main hotel area. More than twenty daily **buses** come from Bangkok, taking six to seven hours; regular bus connections also serve Chaiyaphum, Nong Khai via Udon Thani, Khorat, Ubon and Phitsanulok. The main **bus station** is on Prachasamoson Road, a five-minute walk southeast of the Klang Muang Road hotels; the air-con bus terminal is right in the town centre, at the junction of Ammat and Klang Muang roads.

Accommodation is plentiful and reasonably priced, with most of the hotels along Klang Muang Road. Best value of the cheapies here is *Suksawad*, set back from the road and therefore quiet, with singles with fan and shower for B90, doubles B120. Rooms at *Sansumran* (☎043/239611) start at B80 without shower, while those at *Roma* (☎043/236276) cost a standard B140 including shower. *Kaen Inn* (☎043/236866) has the best value air-conditioned doubles at B400 including shower, TV and fridge.

Khon Kaen has a reputation for very spicey **food**, particularly sausages, *sai krog isaan*, which are served with cubes of raw ginger, onion, lime and plenty of chilli sauce, at stalls along Klang Muang Road between the *Suksawad* and *Kaen Inn*. You can also sample these and other local favourites – such as pigs' trotters, roast duck and shellfish – at the stalls along the northern edge of Bueng Kaen Nakhon. There's quite a choice of restaurants around the lake as well, including one that actually juts out over it, which makes a pleasant spot to spend the evening. For cheap *pat thai* and *khao pat*, with air conditioning, go to *Coffee Break*, west of Klang Muang Road off Sri Chan Road.

For a town with no real tourist sights, Khon Kaen has a surprising number of shops selling Isaan **arts and crafts**. There are several on the left-hand side of Klang Muang Road as you walk south towards the lake, where you'll find triangular "axe" pillows of all sizes, *mut mee* cotton and silk weaves, and *khaen* pipes.

Udon Thani and Ban Chiang

Economically important but charmless, **UDON THANI** looms for most travellers as a misty, early-morning sprawl of grey cement seen from the window of the overnight train to Nong Khai. The capital of an arid rice-growing province, 137km north of Khon Kaen, Udon was given an economic shot in the arm during the Vietnam War with the siting of a huge American military base nearby, and despite the American withdrawal in 1976, the town has maintained its rapid industrial and commercial development. The only conceivable reason to alight here would be to satisfy a lust for archaeology at the excavated Bronze Age settlement of **BAN CHIANG**, 50km to the east in sleepy farming country.

The village of Ban Chiang is unremarkable nowadays, though its fertile setting is attractive. It achieved worldwide fame in 1966, when a rich seam of archaeological remains was accidentally discovered: clay pots, uncovered in human graves alongside sophisticated **bronze** objects, were dated to around 3000 BC, implying the same date for the bronze pieces; Ban Chiang was immediately hailed as the vanguard of the Bronze Age, 700 years before Mesopotamia's discovery of the metal. Unfortunately the archaeologists' triumph was spiked by a later, more accurate test that set the date at around 2000 BC. Nevertheless Ban Chiang stands as one of the world's earliest bronze producers, its methods of smelting showing no signs of influence from northern China and other neighbouring bronze cultures, which suggests the area was the birthplace of southeast Asian civilization.

The present village's fine **National Museum** (Wed–Sun 8am–4pm; B10) displays some of the choicest finds from Ban Chiang and provides a richly informative commentary. It also contains the country's best collection of characteristic late-period Ban Chiang clay pots, with their red whorled patterns on a buff background – although not of prime historical significance, these have become an attractive emblem of Ban Chiang, and freely adapted by local souvenir producers – and takes you through the stages of manufacturing them. A single room in the museum is dedicated to the modern village; the story it tells, of the rapid disappearance of traditional ways, is an all-too-familiar lament in Thailand.

In the grounds of **Wat Pho Si Nai**, on the south side of the village, part of an early dig has been canopied over and opened to the public (same times and ticket as the museum). Two burial pits have been left exposed to show how and where artefacts were found.

Practicalities

Udon Thani's **train station** lies an inconvenient 2km east of the town centre; **buses** stop at the station on Sai Uthit Road, also on the eastern side but 1km closer in. To get to Ban Chiang from Udon, catch a Sakhon Nakhon-bound bus (every 20min) at the station, and then a tuk-tuk for the last 5km or so from the main road to the village. Alternatively, songthaews make the one-hour trip direct to Ban Chiang from Talat Mung Thorn (Mung Thorn Market) on Prajak Road, north of the bus station.

There's no **accommodation** in Ban Chiang, but you can get a simple fried lunch at one of the village cafés. In Udon, the *Queen Hotel* at 6–8 Udon–Dussadi Rd is central, with decent rooms for B80 single, B100 double; or you might want to splash out on the *Charoen Hotel* at 549 Phosri Rd (☎042/221331), where air-conditioned rooms with hot showers, and a swimming pool outside, start at B450. Delicious *kai yang* (barbecued chicken) and *khao niaw* (sticky rice) are served at *Weeta*, the best of three similar cafés by the Rama Cinema at the top end of Prajak Road, though you might be put off by the thick, sooty grime which decorates the interior.

Loei and around

Most people carry on from Udon Thani straight north to Nong Khai (see p.317), but making a detour via **LOEI**, 147km to the west, takes you within range of three towering national parks and sets you up for a lazy tour along the Mekhong. The capital of a province renowned for the unusual shapes of its stark, craggy mountains, Loei is, more significantly, the crossroads of one of Thailand's least tamed border regions; from Laos come all manner of illegal goods and refugees, especially Hmong tribespeople, who are still punished for siding with the Americans during the Vietnam War by the communist Pathet Lao, who seized control of Laos at the end of the war in 1975. The border area to the northwest remains sensitive after a major skirmish with Laos in 1987 over disputed territory, and Thai soldiers are often to be seen around Loei town.

Despite its frontier feel, the town, lying along the west bank of the small Loei River, is generally friendly and offers legitimate products of its own: tamarind paste and pork sausages are sold in industrial quantities along Ararree Road (off Charoenrat Road, Loei's main street, which runs roughly parallel to the river), while local quilts and lengths of silk and cotton in strong, simple designs are available at *Dork Fai*, 138/2 Charoenrat Rd, and at the more refined *Chao Sakul*, 4 Ararree Rd. Loei also has its own rain-making festival, **Phi Ta Kon**, held every

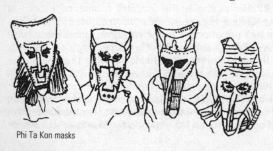
Phi Ta Kon masks

June (dates vary from year to year), which is worth making a special trip to see. In order to encourage the heavens to open, young men dress up as spirits in patchwork rags and fierce, brightly painted wooden masks, and then parade the town's most sacred Buddha image round the streets, while making fun of as many onlookers as they can and generally having themselves a whale of a time.

Beyond these meagre attractions, the town is really only useful as a transport hub. **Buses** run to Loei from Udon Thani and Khon Kaen every half hour, from Phitsanulok in the central plains seven times a day and from Bangkok (via Chaiyaphum) seventeen times a day. An hourly service also links the town to Chiang Kham, two hours to the north at the start of the Mekhong River route. All of these arrive and depart at the **bus terminal** on Ruamjai Road, the main east–west street, about 300m west of the intersection with Charoenrat Road.

Practicalities

Finding a decent **place to stay** in Loei shouldn't be a problem. *Muang Loei Guest House* has two branches, situated on separate unmarked sois just off the north side of Ruamjai Road: turning left out of the bus station towards the river, you'll come across the newer branch first in what looks like a converted garage, where rooms with a double bed, mosquito net and not much else go for B50. The original *Muang Loei*, five minutes' walk further on, has similar rooms above its restaurant at B30 for a dorm bed, B50 for a single and B60 for a double. The owners can help with local information, and hire out bikes for B30 per day and motorbikes for B200 per day. Comfortable and centrally placed, *Thai Udom Hotel*, at 122/1 Charoenrat Rd, charges B150 for a double with hot-water bathroom and fan, B250 with air conditioning. The new, quiet *Sarm-O Hotel*, south of the centre at 191/1–9 Charoenrat Rd, has the same rates.

The **food** at the *Nawng Neung Restaurant*, next to the Thai Military Bank at 8/22 Ruamjai Rd, is delicious and very cheap – *khao man kai* and *khao na pet* (chicken rice and duck rice) and noodle soup are specialities – but it's only open until 3pm. The *Samouan Restaurant* at 13–14 Ruamjit Rd (the next street west from Charoenrat Road) is also a good bet: especially worth trying is the spicy *tom klorng*, crispy salted fish with local tamarind and onions. The market on Charoenrat Road serves up the unusual local delicacy, *khai ping*, barbecued eggs on skewers which end up tasting like coarse, salty souffles. The *Savita Bakery* at 137 Charoenrat Rd does cakes, Western breakfasts, ice cream and good coffee.

Phu Kradung National Park

The most scenic and accessible of the three parks in Loei province, **PHU KRADUNG NATIONAL PARK**, about 80km south of Loei, protects a grassy 1300-metre plateau whose temperate climate supports a number of tree, flower and bird species not normally found in tropical Thailand. Walking trails crisscross much of sixty-square-kilometre Phu Kradung ("Bell Mountain"), and you ought to reckon on spending three days here if you want to explore them fully – at a minimum you'll have to spend one night, as the trip from Loei to the top of the plateau and back can't be done in a day. The park is closed during the rainy season (June–Sept), due to the increased risk of mud-slides and land-slips.

Access and accommodation

To get to the park, take any bus between Loei and Khon Kaen and get off at the village of PHU KRADUNG, then hop on a B10 songthaew for the remaining 5km to the **visitors' centre**, where you can pick up a trail map and pay the B5 admission fee.

The park's primitive **accommodation** is up on the plateau; you can leave your gear at the visitors' centre, or hire a porter to tote it to the top for B5 per kilo. At park headquarters, 8km from the visitors' centre, the cheapest room in a national park bungalow is B200, with enough mattresses and blankets for six; tents can be hired for B40 per day, blankets (needed on cool season nights) for B10. A private concern, *Phu Kradung House*, has opened on the south side of the plateau, 7km from the visitors' centre (Bangkok reservations ☎02/271 3737). Small A-frame huts, packed together in holiday-camp rows, go for B120 single, B160 double, with a light mattress and a decent blanket (B70/B140 with a thin blanket and no mattress). A simple **restaurant** there competes with several at park headquarters and at the rim of the plateau, all of which can rustle up cheap, tasty food from limited ingredients, so there's no need to bring your own provisions.

The park

The gruelling main **trail** leads from the visitors' centre 5km up the eastern side of Phu Kradung, passing occasional refreshment stalls; most people take at least three hours, including rest stops. The path becomes steeper and rockier in the last 1km, with wooden steps over the most difficult parts, but it's worth it for the unbelievable view as your head peeps over the rim: flat as a playing field, the broad plateau is dotted with odd clumps of pine trees, thinned by periodic lightning fires, which give it the appearance of a country park. Several feeder trails fan out from here, including a twelve-kilometre path along the precipitous southern edge that offers sweeping views of Dong Phaya Yen, the untidy range of mountains to the southeast that forms the unofficial border between the northeast and the central plains. Another trail heads along the eastern rim for 2.5km to Pha Nok An – also reached by a two-kilometre path due east from the headquarters – which looks down on neat ricefields and matchbox-like houses in the valley below, an outlook that's especially breathtaking at sunrise.

The attractions of the mountain come and go with the **seasons**. October is muddy after the rains, but the waterfalls which tumble off the northwestern edge of the plateau are in full cascade and the main trail is green and shady. December brings out the maple leaves, but by February the waterfalls have disappeared and the vegetation on the lower slopes has been burnt away. April is good for the rhododendrons and wild roses, which in Thailand are only found at such high altitudes as this.

Among the park's **wildlife**, mammals such as elephants, sambar deer and gibbons can be seen very occasionally, but they generally confine themselves to the evergreen forest on the northern part of the plateau, which is out of bounds to visitors. In the temperate pines, oaks and beeches that dot the rest of the plateau you're more likely to spot resident **birds** such as jays, sultan tits and snowy-browed flycatchers if you're out walking in the early morning and evening.

Phu Reua National Park

About 50km west of Loei, **PHU REUA NATIONAL PARK**, preserves another flat-topped mountain covered with walking trails among pines and waterfalls, with fine views over the hills to Laos. Named "Boat Mountain" after its alleged resemblance to an upturned sampan, Phu Reua isn't as spectacular as Phu Kradung, but it's quieter, higher (1375m) and colder – the lowest temperature in Thailand (–4°C) was recorded here in 1981. A regular songthaew will take you along Highway

203 towards LOMSAK to the Phu Reua turn-off, leaving you with a 4km walk on a paved road to the visitors' centre and from there a further 5km on a trail to the mountaintop. There are simple **bungalows** (from B250 for 5 people) and a restaurant both at the visitors' centre and at the **campground** 3km up the mountain.

Phu Hin Rongkla National Park

Thailand's densely forested hills and mountains have always harboured bandits and insurgents, and the rugged 300-square-kilometre tract of highland known as **PHU HIN RONGKLA NATIONAL PARK** is no exception: for over a decade these mountains, straddling Phitsanulok, Phetchabun and Loei provinces, were the stronghold of the **Communist Party of Thailand**. Founded in 1942 and banned ten years later, the CPT went underground and by 1967 had established a self-contained command centre in Phu Hin Rongkla, complete with a hospital, library and a printing press that even issued birth and death certificates. Despite assaults on the Phu Hin Rongkla base from government forces, numbers swelled in the wake of the murderous suppression of Bangkok pro-democracy demonstrations in 1973 and 1976. Then, in 1978, a policy of amnesty in return for the surrender of weapons was extended to the students and others who had fled to the hills; over the next few years, as CPT members returned to the cities, the party began to crumble. As the threat of insurgence diminished, the government built roads through Phu Hin Rongkla and other inaccessible parts of Isaan; finally, in 1982, Phu Hin Rongkla was declared a national park.

The park's history is a significant part of its appeal but for most visitors Phu Hin Rongkla is principally a refreshing change of scenery – and temperature – from the plains to the east and west. At an elevation that rises to about 1800m, much of the park's vegetation is typical of a tropical mountain forest, with trees growing much further apart than they do in the valleys, leaving occasional expanses of exposed rock peppered by low-lying scrub and montane flowers. Walking through these open forests is relatively easy, and the park's few short trails take you across some of the most attractive parts of the stony terrain.

Access and accommodation

Getting to Phu Hin Rongkla by public transport is a hassle, involving uncertain connections and lengthy journeys. **From Loei**, take a Phitsanulok-bound bus to either NAKHON THAI (130km southwest on the junction of routes 2013 and 2331), or LOMSAK (140km down Highway 203). Route 2331 is the main access road through the park and about three songthaews make the daily 20km run from Nakhon Thai to the park visitors' centre. From Lomsak you'll have to hire a motorcycle taxi to take you the 30km to the vistors' centre (about B100).

All in all, considering you have to hike fair distances along Route 2331 to get between trail heads once you're in the park, you're much better off renting your own transport from either Phitsanulok or Loei. If travelling by **car** or **motorbike** from Loei, your quickest route is west via Route 203, then south on 2013 to Nakhon Thai, and southeast on 2331. From Phitsanulok, follow Highway 12 eastwards towards Lomsak for 68km, then north along Route 2013 to Nakhon Thai.

About 10km after entering the park gates via Nakhon Thai on Route 2331, you'll reach the **visitors' centre**, alongside the park headquarters and a rudimentary restaurant. The centre doubles as a small CPT **museum** and provides free maps giving trail distances and routes. There's not really enough in the park to merit an **overnight stay**, but if you do get stuck, there are bungalows here for B100 per person and two-person tents for B40. It's also possible to stay in Lomsak: *Pen Sin 1* at 33/8 Wachi Rd (☎056/701545) and *Sawang Hotel* at 147/6 Samakkichai Rd (☎056/701642) are both within a few minutes' walk of the bus station and have rooms from B100.

The park

The best of the park's trails is the 3.5-kilometre **Lan Hin Pum Walk** ("One Million Knotty Rocks"), which starts about 5km east of the visitors' centre. It runs through a superb natural rock garden that's particularly pretty in the rainy season when wild orchids and all kinds of hardy flowers bloom amongst the mosses, ferns and lichen. Halfway through the circuit you come to a precipice overlooking dense jungle, usually with plenty of mist to heighten the atmosphere; the route also passes the office of the party's headquarters, as well as Pha Chu Thong, the so-called "flag-raising cliff" where the red flag was unfurled after every CPT victory.

A less dramatic 1500-metre walk across **Lan Hin Daeg** ("One Million Broken Rocks") begins 3km west of the visitors' centre. The rocks here are so deeply fissured that at times it feels like picking your way across a stegosaurus's back; clogged with ferns and mosses, the well-camouflaged crevices made ideal natural hideouts and air-raid shelters for the CPT – with full command of terrain like this, it's hardly surpring that the CPT withstood some fifteen years of persistent battery from the government forces.

ALONG THE MEKHONG

Having descended from its Tibetan sources through China, Burma and Laos, with a brief stint along Thailand's northern frontier, the mighty **Mekhong River** reappears on the scene in Isaan to form 750km of the border between Thailand and Laos. The word is beginning to get out about this remote and dramatic margin, but it's still possible to spend days here without seeing another foreigner.

The guest houses along the upper stretch, east from **Chiang Khan**, are geared towards relaxation and gentle exploration of the rural way of life. **Nong Khai**, the terminus of the railway from Bangkok and the jumping-off point for trips to the Laotian capital of Vientiane, is the pivotal town on the river, but charming and restful nonetheless. East of Nong Khai you're into wild country. The unique natural beauty of **Wat Phu Tok** is well worth the hefty detour, and your Mekhong journey wouldn't be complete without seeing **Wat Phra That Phanom**, a place of pilgrimage for 2500 years. Sights get sparse beyond that, although by continuing south through **Mukdahan** you'll be able to join up with the southern Isaan route at Ubon Ratchathani (see p.298).

A road, served by very slow **buses** and **songthaews**, runs beside or at least parallel to the river as far as Mukdahan. If you've got the time (allow at least a week to do it any sort of justice) you could make the entire marathon journey described in this section, although realistically you'll probably start in Nong Khai and work your way either upstream or downstream from there. **Motorcycle** hire may provide another incentive to base yourself in Nong Khai: having your own transport will give you more freedom of movement in this region, and the roads are quiet and easy to negotiate. There's no long-distance **boat** transport along the river – you'll have to settle for brief forays by chartered boat or inner tube.

Chiang Khan to Tha Bo

Rustic "backpackers' resorts" – and the travelling between them – are the chief draw along the reach of the Mekhong between Chiang Khan and Tha Bo. Highway 211 covers this whole course: songthaews take you as far as Pak Chom, from where buses complete the journey, stopping at all towns en route.

Chiang Khan

The Mekhong route starts promisingly at **CHIANG KHAN**, a friendly town that happily hasn't been converted to concrete yet. Rows of wooden shophouses stretch out in a two-kilometre-long ribbon parallel to the river, which for much of the year runs red with what locals call the "blood of the trees": rampant deforestation on the Laotian side causes the rust-coloured topsoil to erode into the river. The town has only two streets – the main through road (Highway 211) and a quieter riverfront road – with a line of sois connecting them numbered from west to east. Songthaews from Loei and Pak Chom stop at the west end of town on Highway 201 (the road from Loei), 150m south of the junction with Highway 211.

Arguably the most enjoyable thing you can do here is take a **boat trip** upriver along the border (about 20km), a tranquil float between high tree-lined banks of red earth. Heading west towards the lofty mountains of Khao Laem and Khao Ngu on the Thai side and Phu Lane and Phu Hat Song in Laos, you'll glide round a long, slow bend to THA DEE MEE, where the Mekhong is joined by the Heuang River, which forms the border to the west of this point. To arrange a trip, ask at the *Nong Sam Guest House*.

It's also worth taking a walk towards the eastern end of the river road to **Wat Tha Khok**, by Soi 20, for its unobstructed view across the majestic Mekhong. The Laotian viharn shows some odd French influences in its balustrades, rounded arches and elegantly coloured ceiling. Continuing another 2km east along the main highway, a left turn back towards the river will bring you to **Wat Tha Khaek**, a ramshackle temple under the trees. One kilometre further along this side road, the river runs over rocks at a wide bend to form the modest rapids of **Kaeng Kut Khu**. Set against the forested hillside of imaginatively named Phu Yai (Big Mountain), it's a pretty enough spot, and the small, shaded restaurants are popular at weekends.

Practicalities

For **accommodation**, the *Nong Sam Guest House*, on the river road between sois 12 and 13, makes a good base, with decent rooms for B60 single, B80 double; the food's good and you can take it easy on the verandah high above the river. Besides arranging boat trips, the English manager rents out bicycles and can advise on local exploration. The *Souksomboon Hotel*, on the river road between sois 8 and 9, is a more traditional wooden hotel built around a courtyard, with a café on its riverside terrace; clean doubles are B80 with bathroom, B60 without. *Zen Guest House* on quiet Soi 12 weighs in as Chiang Khan's cheapest, with mattresses in rather pokey wooden rooms costing B40 per person.

The most fruitful hunting grounds for **food** are the day market, on the south side of the main through road opposite Soi 10, and the night market (6–8pm), between sois 17 and 18 on the main road. For a hearty *pat thai*, head for the popular café on the east side of Soi 9.

Pak Chom

A poor road through sparsely populated countryside takes you up hill and down dale to **PAK CHOM**, 41km downriver of Chiang Khan. Framed in a gap between hills, the town has swollen into a bustling administrative centre thanks to BAN WINAI, 10km to the south, a refugee camp for 15,000 Laotian Hmong, who have been persecuted in their country since the Pathet Lao took over in 1975. Though conditions in the camp are now stable, casual visitors are not welcome, and the whole operation is due to move soon to Chiang Rai province. Do your bit by visiting the *Refugee Handicraft Store* on the main road through Pak Chom, which sells the trademark blue and white geometric batiks and other simple Hmong cotton pieces. As the Thai authorities don't allow them out of the camps to work (subsistence is provided by the UN), the refugees produce these crafts to bring in a little extra income.

Pak Chom has a couple of **guest houses** – but neither of them will spoil you. The *Pak Chom Guest House*, at the west end of town, is at least set in leafy grounds; primitive bungalows on stilts overlooking the river cost B40 for a single, B60 double. The other option, *Chumpee Guest House*, situated on the riverbank in the middle of town, is singularly unwelcoming; its dingy bamboo rooms start at B40.

Sang Khom and Wat Hin Ma Beng

Beyond Pak Chom the road through the Mekhong valley becomes flatter and straighter. After 50km, a sign in English points down a side road to **Than Tip Falls**, 3km south, which is well worth seeking out. The ten-metre high waterfall splashes down into a rock pool overhung by jungle on three sides; higher up, a bigger waterfall has a good pool for swimming, and if you can face the sticky climb you can explore three higher levels.

Staying in idyllic, tree-shaded **SANG KHOM**, 63km east of Pak Chom, puts you in the heart of an especially lush stretch of the river within easy **biking** distance of several backroad villages and temples. You can rent bicycles and motorbikes at *River Huts*, which outshines the village's other three **guest houses** with its welcoming, sociable atmosphere and excellent food: decent bamboo huts, set in a garden with beautiful views out over the river, start from B50 single, B80 double. They've also got inner tubes to carry you down the Mekhong, and if that sounds too strenuous, there's a herbal sauna tent or you can get yourself massaged.

Another 19km east on Route 211, **Wat Hin Ma Beng** is a famous meditation temple, popular with Thai visitors and pilgrims. The long white boundary wall and huge modern buildings are evidence of the temple's prosperity, but its reputation is in fact based on the asceticism of the monks, who keep themselves in strict poverty and allow only one meal a day to distract them from their meditation. Keep an eye out for the large statue of a tiger, the symbol of hermits. The founder of the wat, Luang Phu Thet, is now well into his eighties and seldom makes public appearances, but visitors have the opportunity to revere a lifelike waxwork of him that has been set up next to the river. Across the narrow stretch of water here, you can get a good look at a much less prosperous Laotian forest wat.

Sri Chiangmai and Tha Bo

Unprepossessing it may be, but **SRI CHIANGMAI**, 38km east of Sang Chom, is known in Chinese catering circles as one of the world's leading manufacturing centres of spring-roll wrappers, which you can see being left out to dry on bamboo racks around the town, and taste in local restaurants. Many of Sri Chiangmai's spring-roll wrapper makers are Vietnamese, victims of the upheavals caused by the two postwar Indochina wars who have fled across Laos to safe haven in Thailand. The town also offers the unique opportunity of gazing at the backstreets of Vientiane, directly across the Mekhong, without having to go through all the expensive red tape to get there. It looks quite unappealing and lifeless, replicating the same concrete architecture as on the Thai side.

Here again, one outstanding **guest house** makes the town accessible to farangs who want to experience its daily life. *Tim Guest House*, situated on the quiet river road, has clean singles starting from B40, doubles from B60, and the Thai and Western food is good; the Swiss manager is hospitable and informative, and can arrange bicycle, motorbike and boat rental.

Thanks to spring-roll traffic, the condition of Highway 211 and the frequency of buses improve noticeably east of Sri Chiangmai. **Wat Nam Mong** can be seen across the fields on the west side of the road, 12km out of Sri Chiangmai and 3km before **THA BO**. A slender Laotian-style viharn makes the perfect setting for the gaunt Phra Ong Thu image inside. Stern but handsome, the 300-year-old bronze image is the brother of a more famous Buddha in Laos – it's much revered, especially by Laotian emigrants, some of whom even send their sons from the United States to serve as monks here. If you need a place to **stay** in Tha Bo, try the cosy *Isan Orchid Guest Lodge*, 87/9 Gaowarawud Rd (☎042/431665), where American standards of comfort start from B500 single, B650 double including breakfast.

Nong Khai and around

The major border town in these parts is **NONG KHAI** (population 25,000), still a backwater but fast developing, with the construction of a huge bridge over the Mekhong due to be getting under way in 1992. Plenty of trade, much of it illegal, goes on quite happily without a bridge, giving Nong Khai a kind of frontier frisson. Occupying a strategic position at the end of Highway 2 and the northeastern railway, and just 24km from Vientiane, Nong Khai acts as a conduit for goods bought and sold by Thais and Laotians, who are allowed to pass between the two cities freely for the day (foreigners have to join a tour). For the souvenir market that's sprung up around the main pier, Tha Sadet, the Laotians ship across wood and cane items, and sundry goods from the old Soviet bloc, such as vacuum cleaners and samovars. They return with noodles, soap powder and toilet rolls.

As with most of the towns along this part of the Mekhong, the thing to do in Nong Khai is just to take it easy, enjoying the riverside atmosphere and the peaceful settings of the good-value guest houses. Before you lapse into a relaxation-induced coma, though, try joining an evening river tour, or make a day trip out to see the sculptures and rock formations in the surrounding countryside. Nong Khai is also the only overland jumping-off point for tours into Laos, but these take a lot of organisation which is best done before you leave Bangkok.

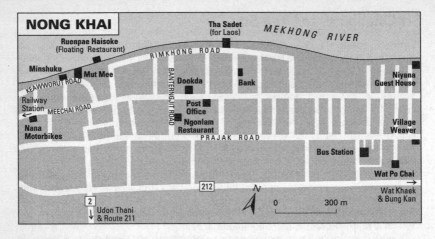

From the capital, you'll most likely be coming to Nong Khai by night **train**, arriving just after dawn at the station 2km west of the centre. Day **buses** from all points in Isaan and night buses from further afield pull in at the terminal on the east side of town off Prajak Road.

The town

Nong Khai lays itself out along the south bank of the Mekhong in a four-kilometre band which is never more than 500m deep. Running from east to west, Meechai Road dominates activity: the main shops and businesses are plumb in the middle around the post office, with more frenetic commerce to the west at the morning Chaiyaporn food market and at the stalls around Haisoke Road, which sell clothes and household goods all day and night. Although most of the buildings have been replaced by concrete boxes, a few weather-beaten wooden houses remain, their attractive balconies, porticoes and slatted shutters showing the influence of colonial architecture, which was imported from across the river before the French were forced out of Laos in 1954.

The most pleasant place for a stroll, however, is the riverside area, which, although built-up in the centre around Tha Sadet, becomes rustic and leafy around the fringes, which are often busy with people bathing, washing their clothes and fishing, especially in the early morning and evening. The largest freshwater fish in the world, the *pla beuk* or **giant catfish**, which can weigh in at 300kg, lives in the Mekhong: instead of the old method of harpooning, fishermen now trawl the river with nets during the catfish season (April–June), when you can occasionally see them struggling with these leviathans on the riverbank. If you're lucky, you might also catch sight of a sunken chedi, **Phra That Nong Khai**, which slipped into the river in 1847 and has since subsided so far that it's only visible in the dry season.

To catch the best of life on the river, take the **boat trip** which sets out from the *Ruenpae Haisoke* floating restaurant behind the temple at the top of Haisoke Road every evening at 5pm. It's the cheapest way of getting onto the Mekhong in Thailand (B20), and runs up and down the length of Nong Khai for an hour, sticking to the Thai side. Drinks are available, as is food if you order twenty minutes before the boat leaves, all at reasonable prices. There's no stunning scenery, but plenty of activity on both riverbanks.

The main temple of the region is **Wat Po Chai** at the east end of Prajak Road. The cruciform viharn with its complex and elegant array of Laotian tiers shelters a venerated solid gold image, the Phra Sai Buddha. Prince Chakri, the future Rama I, is said to have looted the image from Vientiane along with the Emerald Buddha, but the boat which was bringing back the Phra Sai overturned and sank in the Mekhong. Later, the statue miraculously rose to the surface and the grateful people of Nong Khai built this great hangar of a viharn to house it, where the present king, Chakri's descendant, comes every year to pay his respects. It's worth a visit for the Buddha's stagey setting, in front of a steep, flame-covered altar, dazzlingly lit from above and below in green. The solid gold is so highly polished that you have to peer carefully to make out the Sukhothai influence in its haughty expression and beaked nose.

Five minutes' walk east of Wat Po Chai at 786/1 Prajak Rd, *Village Weaver* specialises in **mut mee**, the northeastern method of tie-dyeing which produces white geometrical patterns on an indigo-coloured base. The shop provides an outlet for work produced by local farmers to earn cash through a self-help project run by the Good Shepherd Sisters.

Practicalities

As everything in Nong Khai is so spread out, you might want to consider hopping on a **samlor** (around B10) for getting around. To get to some of the area's remoter spots, small **motorbikes** can be hired for B150–200 at *Nana Motorbikes*, 1160 Meechai Rd, opposite Chaiyaporn Market, but at the time of writing bicycles were unavailable anywhere. If time's running out on your tourist visa, you should be able to get it extended at the **immigration office** by Tha Sadet.

Accommodation

Nong Khai has a good choice of cheap **places to stay**, most of them on the quiet edges of town, with their own simple restaurants overlooking the river. There's nothing upmarket as yet, though a big deluxe hotel is planned to the west of town to coincide with the opening of the bridge. If you're hankering for luxury, consider the *Isan Orchid* in Tha Bo (see above).

Mekong Guest House, Rimkhong Road by Tha Sadet. Good for watching the bustle at the pier, but noisy. Clean, basic rooms for B50 single, B80 double.

Minshuku Guest House, 1038/1 Keawworut Rd. The closest guest house to the railway station, with neat and clean singles from B60, doubles from B80.

Mut Mee Guest House, 1111 Keawworut Rd. The riverside terrace is a magnet for travellers; rooms or bamboo huts sprawled around it go for B60 single, B80 double and up.

Niyana Guest House, 584 Soi Yodkaew 1, Meechai Rd. Earthy and welcoming. Peaceful rooms in ordinary wooden houses by the river start at B40 single, B70 double.

Pongvichit Hotel, 723 Banterngjit Rd. Bland, but clean and efficient concrete block. Doubles with bathrooms B80.

Sawasdee Guest House, 402 Meechai Rd (☎042/412502). Well-equipped, reliable and friendly, though the main road can be a little noisy. Rooms in a grand old wooden house are B60 single, B80 double and B100 twin; the simple air-conditioned rooms (B200/250) are the best in town at the moment.

Eating

The most popular **restaurants** in Nong Khai, amongst locals and tourists alike, are the handful of moderately priced riverside terraces clustered around the pier on Rimkhong Road. *Udom Rot* here has particularly good food and atmosphere, specialising in *paw pia yuan* (Vietnamese spring rolls), *plaa raat phrik* (whole fish cooked in chillies and garlic) and *kai lao daeng* (Laotian-style chicken cooked in red wine), and occasionally serving up giant catfish in season. The *Ruenpae Haisoke* behind Wat Haisoke is also justifiably popular: as well as the boat trip mentioned above, it has a floating restaurant that is permanently moored to the bank, where you can enjoy large, moderately priced portions of standard Thai dishes. For excellent, cheap Vietnamese and Thai food, try the *Ngonlam Restaurant* on Banterngjit Road: there's no sign or number, but you'll know it by the clean, white decor. The *Dookda Bakery* on Meechai Road opposite the GPO is a clean and businesslike café, that serves Western breakfasts, cakes and Thai food.

Around Nong Khai

By far the easiest and most popular day trip out of Nong Khai takes in **Wat Khaek**, with its weird artificial setting, a short songthaew hop to the east. To the southwest of town and also easy to get to, **Wat Phra That Bang Puan** offers classic temple sightseeing, while the natural rock formations at **Ban Phu** require much more effort and a full day out. Some of the sights upstream along the Mekhong described above are also within daytripping distance, and it's also quite possible to get to Ban Chiang and back in a day – change buses at Udon Thani – without having to stay in drab Udon.

TOURS TO LAOS

Although **Laos** has shown signs of a loosening of attitudes towards tourism in recent years, at the time of writing the only way of getting into the country that can be recommended is on an **organised tour** arranged from Bangkok. Tours involve three days in VIENTIANE, the capital, whose major sights are unexceptional wats and some colonial-style architecture, with a further optional three days in much more interesting LUANG PRABANG, an unspoilt town of ancient temples amid the mountain jungle. Bank on paying around B20,000 per person all-in (visa fee, return air ticket to Vientiane, accommodation with full board, guide and local transport in Laos), or B40,000 if you go to Luang Prabang. *STA Travel* in Bangkok (see p.108) organises "no-frills" three-day packages to Vientiane for around B6000 per person, but on these you have to pay for your own transport to Laos, either by air or by crossing the Mekhong at Nong Khai – passenger boats run across from Tha Sadet to the Laotian bank about every half hour during the day, leaving a 16-kilometre taxi ride into Vientiane. You need to book at least a week in advance to allow the travel agent time to get your visa.

As well as organising packages, a number of unreliable travel agents in Nong Khai and Bangkok offer to get you simple three-day visas for **independent travel** in Laos, but these are not advisable – travel is strictly confined to Vientiane, and Laotian immigration officers are temperamental to say the least, often turning back travellers with visas on the grounds that they don't have a tour voucher.

Wat Khaek

Just off the main highway 5km east of Nong Khai, **Wat Khaek** is best known for its bizarre sculpture garden, which looks like the work of an artistic giant on acid. Its proper name is Phutthamamakasamakhom, but even locals have a hard time getting their mouths around that – if you're getting there by songthaew, ask to be let off at SALA KAEOKOO, the stop on the highway five minutes' walk north of the wat.

The temple was founded by **Luang Phu Boonlua Surirat**, an unconventional Thai holy man who studied under a Hindu guru in Vietnam and preached in Laos until he was thrown out by the communists in the late 1970s. His charisma – those who drink water offered by him will, it's rumoured, give up all they own to the temple – and heavy emphasis on morality have attracted many followers among the farmers of Nong Khai. Luang Phu's popularity has suffered, however, since his recent imprisonment for insulting King Bhumibol, a crime alleged by jealous neighbours and probably without foundation.

Viewed to the accompaniment of saccharine piped music, the **sculpture garden** bristles with Buddhist, Hindu and secular figures, all executed in concrete with imaginative abandon by unskilled followers under Luang Phu's direction. The religious statues, in particular, are radically modern. Characteristics that marked the Buddha out as a supernatural being – tight curls and a bump on the crown of the head called the *ushnisha* – are here transformed into beehives, and the flaming *rashmis* on top are depicted as long, sharp spikes. The largest statue in the garden shows the familiar story of the kindly naga king, Muchalinda, sheltering the Buddha, who is lost in meditation, from the heavy rain and floods: here the Buddha has shrunk in significance and the seven-headed snake has grown to twenty-five metres, with fierce, gaping fangs and long tongues.

Many of the statues illustrate **Thai proverbs**. Near the entrance, an elephant surrounded by a pack of dogs symbolises integrity, "as the elephant is indifferent to the barking dogs". The nearby monster with the moon in his mouth – Rahoo, the cause of eclipses – serves as an injunction to oppose all obstacles, just as the people of Isaan and Laos used to ward off eclipses by banging drums and firing guns. In the corner furthest from the entrance, you enter the complex Circle of Life through a huge mouth representing the womb, inside which a policeman, a monk, a rich man, a beggar and even a farang represent different paths in life. A man with two wives is shown beating the older one because he is ensnared by the wishes of the younger one, and an old couple who have made the mistake of not having children now find they have only each other for comfort.

The disturbingly vacant, smiling faces of the garden Buddhas bear more than a passing resemblance to Luang Phu himself, whose picture you can see in the **temple building** – he's the one with the bouffant hair-do, dressed in white. This featureless, two-storey building contains similar, smaller statuary, a random collection of sculpture from all over Southeast Asia and a greenhouse full of prize cacti.

Wat Phra That Bang Phuan

More famous as the site of a now concealed 2000-year-old Indian chedi than for its modern replacement, rural **Wat Phra That Bang Phuan** remains a highly revered place of pilgrimage. The wat is in the hamlet of BAN BANG PHUAN,

22km southwest of Nong Khai on Highway 211 – buses to Pak Chom pass right by the wat (but yellow direct buses to Tha Bo don't: they follow a minor road along the river).

The original **chedi** is supposed to have been built by disciples of the Buddha to hold 29 relics – pieces of chest bone – brought from India. A sixteenth-century king of Vientiane piously earned himself merit by building a tall Laotian-style chedi over the top of the previous stupa; rain damage toppled this in 1970, but it was restored in 1977 to the fine, gleaming white edifice you can see now. The unkempt compound also contains a small museum, crumbling brick chedis and some large open-air Buddhas.

Ban Phu

Deep in the countryside 61km southwest of Nong Khai, the wooded slopes around **BAN PHU** are dotted with strangely eroded sandstone formations which have long exerted a mystical hold over local people. The outcrops, many of which were converted into small temples from the seventh century onwards, together with a stupa enshrining a Buddha footprint that is now an important pilgrimage site, have been rounded up under the auspices of **Phu Phra Bat Historical Park** (daylight hours; free).

Such charming rural isolation is, however, difficult to reach for those relying on **public transport**. The fastest way of getting there from Nong Khai is to take a bus towards Udon Thani for about 35km to BAN NGOI, where you can change onto one of the half-hourly buses to Ban Phu from Udon's Lansina market; from Ban Phu, it's another 13km west to the historical park, which makes a difficult hitch or a hairy ride on a motorbike taxi. The total journey takes a couple of hours. Ten kilometres out of Ban Phu, a right fork in the road leads to the main park entrance, which the Fine Arts Department has helpfully sprinkled with site maps.

A well-signposted network of **paths** has been cleared from the thin forest to connect twenty-five of the outcrops, which would take a good five hours to explore. Among the most interesting are **Tham Wua** and **Tham Khon**, two natural shelters whose paintings of oxen and human stick figures suggest that the area was first settled at least 6000 years ago.

A local legend accounts for the name of nearby **Kok Ma Thao Barot** (Prince Barot's Stable), a broad platform overhung by a huge slab of sandstone. A certain Princess Ussa, banished by her father to these slopes to be educated by a hermit, sent out an SOS which was answered by a dashing prince, Barot. The two fell in love and were married against the wishes of Ussa's father, prompting the king to challenge Barot to a distinctly oriental sort of duel: each would build a temple, and the last to finish would be beheaded. The king lost. Kok Ma Thao Barot is celebrated as the place where Barot kept his horse when he visited Ussa.

More spectacular is **Hor Nang Ussa** (Ussa's Tower), a mushroom formed by a flat slab capping a five-metre-high rock pillar. Under the cap of the mushroom, a shelter has been carved out and walled in on two sides. The *sema* found scattered around the site, and the square holes in which others would have been embedded, indicate that this was a shrine, probably in the Dvaravati period (seventh to tenth centuries). Finally, a huge rock on a flimsy pivot miraculously balances itself against a tree at **Wat Por Ta** (The Father's Temple); the walls and floor have been evenly carved out to form a vaguely rectangular shrine, with Dvaravati Buddha images dotted around.

The left fork on the way to the park entrance leads to **Wat Phra Bat Bua Bok**: a crude reliquary tower (*that*) built in imitation of Wat Phra That Phanom, it's decorated with naive bas-reliefs of divinities and boggle-eyed monsters, which add to the atmosphere of simple, rustic piety. In a gloomy chamber in the tower's base, the only visible markings of the sandstone **Buddha footprint** show the Wheel of the Law. Legend has it that the Buddha made the footprint here for a serpent which had asked to be ordained as a monk, but had been refused because it was not human. Higher up the slope, a smaller *that* perches on a hanging rock that seems to defy gravity.

Downstream to Mukdahan

East of Nong Khai, the land on the Thai side of the Mekhong becomes gradually more arid, while jagged forest-covered mountains loom on the Laos side. Few visitors make it this far, to the northeast's northeast, though the attractions are surprisingly varied, ranging from painterly riverscapes to Isaan's major religious site, **Wat Phra That Phanom**.

Transport along Highway 212 out of Nong Khai is fairly straightforward, requiring just one transfer: five buses a day from Nong Khai run to Bung Kan (2hr) and Nakhon Phanom (6hr), where you have to change onto one of the hourly buses to get to That Phanom (1hr) and Mukdahan (2hr).

Bung Kan and Wat Phu Tok

The concrete lump of **BUNG KAN**, topped with a nest of TV aerials, rises out of a barren plain 137km east of Nong Khai. It's a reasonably prosperous riverside town, but dusty and unfriendly: only consider staying here if you're running out of time. Basic hotels such as the *Santisuk* and the *Neramit* on Prasatchai Road have doubles for B80.

Like it or not, Bung Kan is the closest town to the extraordinary hilltop retreat of **Wat Phu Tok**. One of two sandstone outcrops which jut steeply out of the plain 35km southeast of Bung Kan, Phu Tok has been transformed in the past few years into a meditation wat, its fifty or so monks building their scattered huts on perches high above breathtaking cliffs.

Getting there isn't easy – the location was chosen for its isolation, after all – but the trip out gives you a slice of life in remote countryside which hasn't been developed by the paving of the roads. Coming from Nong Khai, change at Bung Kan, from where regular buses head south along Route 222; get off at BAN SIWILAI to intercept the daily songthaew (at noon) making the hour-long, 25-kilometre trip along a dirt road to Phu Tok. A tuk-tuk also operates in the area, so you might be lucky enough to be in the right place at the right time when it passes by, or you could try hitching – pilgrims go to the wat every day and often pick up other visitors. The outcrop comes into sight long before you get there, its sheer red face sandwiched between green vegetation on the lower slopes and tufts of trees on the narrow plateau above. As you get closer, the horizontal white lines across the cliffs reveal themselves to be painted wooden walkways, built to give the temple seven levels to represent the seven stages of enlightenment.

In an ornamental garden at the base, an elegant, incongruously modern marble **chedi** commemorates Phra Ajaan Juen, the famous meditation master who founded the wat in 1968 and died in a plane crash ten years later. The first part of the ascent takes you to the third level up a series of long, sometimes slippery, wooden staircases, the first of many for which you'll need something more sturdy than flip-flops. A choice of two routes – the left fork is more interesting – leads to the fifth and most important level, where the **Sala Yai** houses the temple's main Buddha image in an airy, dimly lit cavern.

The artificial ledges which cut across the northeast face are not for the faint-hearted, but they are one way of getting to the dramatic northwest tip: here, on the other side of a deep crevice spanned by a wooden bridge, a monk has built a shelter under a huge anvil rock. This spot affords stunning **views** over a broad sweep of countryside and across to the second, uninhabited outcrop. The flat top of the hill forms the seventh level, where you can wander along overgrown paths through thick forest.

As the songthaew timetable is designed for Phu Tok folk going to Ban Siwilai, the daily departure from the wat is at 8am. Most people **stay** at least one night at Phu Tok, and in fact a monk will often approach when you arrive offering some-where to sleep in the temple buildings. You should make a small donation to the temple (about B50 a night), and the monks will usually invite you to share – at a respectable distance – in a hearty breakfast, the only meal they eat each day. Bring your own provisions for other meals. The monks don't speak English, but sign language suffices.

Nakhon Phanom

Beyond Bung Kan, the river road rounds the hilly northeastern tip of Thailand before heading south through remote country where you're apt to find yourself stopping for buffaloes as often as for vehicles. The Mekhong can only be glimpsed occasionally until you reach **NAKHON PHANOM**, 302km from Nong Khai, a clean and prosperous town which affords the finest view of the river in northern Isaan, framed against the giant anthills of the Annamite mountains in Laos.

The town makes a pleasant place to hang out, its broad streets lined with some grand old public buildings, colonial-style houses and creaking wooden shop-houses. During the Indochina wars, Nakhon Phanom was an important gateway for thousands of Vietnamese refugees, whose influence can be seen in the dilapi-dated and atmospheric hybrid, **Wat Or Jak**, opposite the pier for Laos at the northern end of the riverside promenade. The biggest Buddha in Isaan is at **Wat Phra Yai**, but the image is an unattractive 25-metre-high architectural feature covered in rust-coloured tiles, which forms the roof of a small viharn, squeezed in underneath its crossed legs. The temple is west of town on the road to Udon Thani (Highway 22): where the main road begins to rise through a thick wood after 2km, turn left down an unmarked side road along the eastern edge of the trees, and look for the temple on the right after another 2km.

The friendly and informative *River Inn* on Suntorn Vichit Road has the best location of Nakhon Phanom's **hotels**, as well as a good riverside restaurant: quiet air-conditioned rooms overlooking the river cost B300, fan rooms on the other side of the building B120. At the budget end, the *First Hotel* at 370 Sri Thep Rd has clean, decent rooms with attached bathrooms for B80 single, B90 double. A few small, reasonable **restaurants** with riverside terraces are clustered around the pier and the clocktower, at the corner of Suntorn Vichit and Sri Thep roads.

Sakhon Nakhon

Ninety kilometres to the west on Highway 22, unappealing **SAKHON NAKHON** only justifies a detour off the Mekhong River route if you're interested in temples – though if you're travelling by bus from Udon Thani or Khon Kaen to Nakhon Phanom or That Phanom you'll have to pass through here in any case. Separated from the heart of Isaan by the forested Pan mountains, Sakhon Nakhon has developed only recently, and you can still see the fields out of which the town grew in the empty lots and partly paved roads of the town centre. Ironically, the town has the only airport in this part of Isaan, with daily flights from Bangkok.

Top of the wats is **Wat Phra That Choeng Choom**, near Nong Harn Lake, where the angular, white Laotian chedi has been built around and on top of a Khmer laterite prang dating from the eleventh century. The chedi affords glimpses of the prang through its three outer doors and can be entered through a door at the back of the adjacent viharn. Legend has it that the chedi was built to enshrine four pairs of footprints made by the Buddha in his different manifestations. Elsewhere in the spacious grounds is a tower with a huge wooden bell, hollowed from a single tree trunk.

A small, well-restored Khmer prang, **Wat Phra That Narai Cheng Weng** lies 6km northwest of town, 100m to the left off Highway 22 opposite the turning for Nakhon Phanom. The laterite prang, set among coconut palms on a grassy knoll, is said to contain ashes of the Buddha. The lintel above the eastern doorway displays a well-preserved bas-relief of twelve-armed Shiva, dancing a jig to destroy the universe. On the northern pediment is shown the next stage in the never-ending cycle of destruction and rebirth, with Vishnu reclining on a dragon dreaming up the new creation. An umbilical cord topped by a lotus extends from his navel, but the figure of Brahma on top of the lotus, whose job it is to put Vishnu's dream into practice, has been eroded. Beneath is a lively carving of Krishna, one of the incarnations of Vishnu, locked in combat with a toothy lion.

Accommodation in Sakhon Nakhon is pokey, although the *Dusit Hotel*, 1784 Yuvapatana Rd (☎042/711198), probably reigns as the cheapest hotel in Thailand to have a swimming pool: clean, comfortable rooms with hot-water bathrooms are B160 with a fan, B250 with air conditioning. Basic, shabby rooms at the *Krong Thong Hotel*, 645/2 Charoen Muang Rd, start from B60.

That Phanom

Fifty kilometres south of Nakhon Phanom, **THAT PHANOM**, a green and friendly village of weather-beaten wooden buildings, sprawls around Isaan's most important shrine. Popularly held to be one of the four sacred pillars of Thai religion (the other three are Chiang Mai's Wat Phra That Doi Suthep, Wat Mahathat in Nakhon Si Thammarat, and Wat Phra Phuttabat near Lopburi), **Wat Phra That Phanom** is a fascinating place of pilgrimage – especially at the time of the Ngan Phra That Phanom in January, when thousands of people come to pay homage and enjoy themselves in the holiday between harvesting and sowing. That Phanom is only an hour away from Nakhon Phanom, Sakhon Nakhon and Mukdahan, and served by frequent **buses** from each, which stop on Chayangkun Road, immediately outside the wat. The centre of the village is 200m due east of here, clustered around the pier on the Mekhong.

This far northeastern corner of Thailand may seem like a strange location for one of the country's holiest sites, but the wat used to serve both Thais and Laotians, as evidenced by the ample boat landing in the village, now largely disused – since the Pathet Lao took over Laos in 1975, pilgrims have been barred from coming across the river in the huge numbers of former times. The temple reputedly dates back to the eighth year after the death of the Buddha (535 BC), when five local princes built a simple brick chedi to house bits of his breast bone. It's been restored or rebuilt seven times, most recently after it collapsed during a rainstorm in 1975; the latest incarnation is in the form of a Laotian *that*, 57m high, modelled on the That Luang in Vientiane.

The best approach is from the river: a short ceremonial way leads directly from the pier, under a Disneyesque victory arch erected by the Laotians, through the temple gates to the chedi itself, which, as is the custom, faces water and the rising sun. A brick and plaster structure covered with white paint and gold floral decorations, the **chedi** looks like nothing so much as a giant, ornate table leg turned upside down. From each of the four sides, an eye forming part of the traditional flame pattern stares down, and the whole thing is surmounted by an umbrella made of 16kg of gold with precious gems and gold rings embedded in each tier. The chedi sits on a gleaming white marble platform, on which pilgrims say their prayers and leave every imaginable kind of offering to the relics. Look out for the brick reliefs in the shape of four-leaf clovers above three of the doorways in the base: the eastern side shows Vishnu mounted on a garuda; on the western side, the four guardians of the earth putting offerings in the Buddha's alms bowl; and above the south door, a carving of the Buddha entering Nirvana. At the corners of the chedi, brick plaques, carved in the tenth century but now heavily restored, tell the stories of the wat's princely founders.

That Phanom has a limited choice of **accommodation**. The *Sang Thong Hotel* near the river on the south side of the pier is your best bet: a wooden house around a family courtyard, it offers basic rooms with their own bathrooms for B80 single, B120 double. Two inferior options are *Chai Von Hotel*, on the north side of the pier, and *Rim Charoen Hotel*, 100m north of the wat on Chayangkun Road, which have the same prices as *Sang Thong*.

The only excursion you can make out of That Phanom is on one of the regular songthaews to the **weaving village** of RENU NAKHON, 17km northwest. The wat at the centre of the village has a smaller, stubbier imitation of the Phra That Phanom, crudely decorated with stucco carvings and brown paint. Around the wat, stalls and shops sell a huge variety of reasonable cotton and silk, much of it in simple, colourful *mut mee* styles.

Mukdahan – and beyond

Fifty kilometres downriver of That Phanom, **MUKDAHAN** is the last stop on the Mekhong trail before Highway 212 heads off inland to Ubon Ratchathani, 170km to the south. You're really in the Wild East out here: rutted dirt roads and makeshift buildings of wood and corrugated iron bear witness to the fact that this is the capital of Thailand's newest province. Very few visitors – Thai or farang – make it this far.

Half-hourly buses from That Phanom and Ubon Ratchathani stop on Samut Sakdarak Road, the main north–south street. In the heart of town to the east of this road, the main river pier serves the cross-border trade, which accounts for a large part of the local economy. By the pier, a pleasant tree-lined promenade overlooks the big Laotian town of Sawannakhet, and a market, which spills over into the compound of Wat Sri Mongkon, sells household goods and cheap ornaments, such as Vietnamese mother-of-pearl and Chinese ceramics, brought over from Laos.

To **stay**, try the *Hua Nam Hotel* at 20 Samut Sakdarak Rd, with large, clean rooms for B100. The cosy *Phai Rim Khong*, just south of the pier on Samlarn Chai Khong Road, does good Thai **food** at moderate prices. South again and first right is the spotless *Mukdarat Restaurant*, which serves excellent, though expensive, Thai favourites.

Phu Pha Terp National Park

If you're tired of concrete Isaan towns, you can stretch your legs exploring the strange rock formations and beautiful waterfalls of **PHU PHA TERP NATIONAL PARK**, down a minor road along the Mekhong southeast of Mukdahan. Regular songthaews pass the turning for the park 14km out of town, and from there it's a two-kilometre walk uphill to the park headquarters. If he's free, the bustling English-speaking park ranger will guide you around the park for no charge. Just above the headquarters is a hillside of bizarre rocks, eroded into the shapes of toadstools and crocodiles, which is great for scrambling around. The hillside also bears two remnants of the area's prehistory: the red finger-painting under one of the sandstone slabs is reckoned to be 4000 years old, while a small cage on the ground protects a 75-million-year-old fossil. Further up, the bare sandstone ridge seems to have been cut out of the surrounding forest by a giant lawnmower, but in October it's brought to life with a covering of grasses and wildflowers. A series of ladders leads up a cliff to the highest point, on a ridge at the western end of the park, which affords a sweeping view over the rocks to the forests and paddies of Laos. Halfway up the cliff is a cave in which villagers have enshrined scores of Buddha images, and nearby, at least from July to November, you'll find the park's most spectacular waterfall, a thirty-metre drop through thick vegetation.

The park has no bungalows, but **camping** is possible and you can rent tents from park headquarters for a donation of about B50 a night. The simple **food** stalls near HQ, open during daylight hours, will keep you going with fried rice and noodles, but if you're staying overnight you'll want to bring extra provisions.

travel details

Trains

From Khon Kaen to Bangkok (5 daily; 7–8hr); Nong Khai (3 daily; 2hr 45min); Udon Thani (5 daily; 1hr 40min).

From Khorat to Ayutthaya (7 daily; 3hr 30min); Bangkok (9 daily; 4–5hr); Khon Kaen (2 daily; 3hr); Si Saket (7 daily; 4hr–5hr 30min); Surin (7 daily; 2hr 30min–3hr 40min); Ubon Ratchathani (7 daily; 5hr–6hr 40min); Udon Thani (2 daily; 4hr 30min).

From Nong Khai to Bangkok (4 daily; 11hr).

From Pak Chong to Bangkok (7 daily; 3hr 30min); Ubon Ratchathani (7 daily; 6hr 50min–8hr 40min), via Khorat (1hr 30min–2hr) and Surin (4hr 25min–5hr 40min).

From Prachinburi to Bangkok (7 daily; 2hr 30min); Aranyaprathet (2 daily; 2hr 20min).

From Surin to Bangkok (7 daily; 8–10hr); Buriram (7 daily; 55min); Sikhoraphum (6 daily; 30–55min); Si Saket (7 daily; 1hr 35min–2hr 10min); Ubon Ratchathani (7 daily; 2hr 30min–3hr 30min).

From Ubon Ratchathani to Bangkok (7 daily; 10hr 20min–13hr 15min); Si Saket (7 daily; 1hr 10min).

From Udon Thani to Bangkok (6 daily; 10hr); Nong Khai (4 daily; 1hr).

Buses

From Bung Kan to Nakhon Phanom (5 daily; 4hr); Sakhon Nakhon (hourly; 3hr).

From Chaiyaphum to Bangkok (hourly; 6hr); Khon Kaen (10 daily; 2–3hr), Khorat (about every 30min; 2hr), Surin (5 daily; 4hr), Ubon Ratchathani (5 daily; 6–7hr); Phitsanulok (6 daily; 3hr).

From Chiang Khan to Bangkok (6 daily; 11hr).

From Khon Kaen to Bangkok (23 daily; 6–7hr); Chaiyaphum (hourly; 2–3hr); Khorat (hourly; 2hr 30min–3hr); Nong Khai (10 daily; 2–3hr); Phitsanulok (hourly; 5hr); Udon Thani (10 daily; 1hr 30min–2hr); Ubon Ratchathani (15 daily; 6hr).

From Khorat to Bangkok (every 15min; 3–4hr); Chaiyaphum (every 30min; 2hr); Chanthaburi (12 daily; 6hr); Chiang Mai (7 daily; 9–11hr); Khon Kaen (hourly; 2hr 30min–3hr); Lopburi (11 daily; 3hr 30min); Nakhon Phanom (3 daily; 8hr); Nong Khai (3 daily; 6hr); Pattaya (4 daily; 4hr); Phimai (every 30min; 1hr–1hr 30min); Phitsanulok (7 daily; 5–7hr); Rayong (18 daily; 4hr); Sri Chiangmai (4 daily; 6hr 30min); Surin (every 30min; 4–5hr); Ubon Ratchathani (17 daily; 5hr); Udon Thani (39 daily; 3hr 30min).

From Loei to Bangkok (17 daily; 10hr); Chiang Mai (5 daily; 9hr); Khon Kaen (every 30min; 4hr); Nong Khai (7 daily; 6hr); Phitsanulok (6 daily; 4hr); Udon Thani (every 30min; 3hr–3hr 30min).

From Mukdahan to Bangkok (9 daily; 12hr); Nakhon Phanom (hourly; 2hr); Sakhon Nakhon (2 daily; 2hr); Ubon Ratchathani (every 30min; 2–3hr); Udon Thani (5 daily; 4hr–4hr 30min).

From Nakhon Phanom to Bangkok (9 daily; 12hr); Chiang Rai (2 daily; 16hr); Khorat (3 daily; 8hr); Loei (2 daily; 7hr); Phitsanulok (2 daily; 10hr); Ubon Ratchathani (2 daily; 4hr); Udon Thani (5 daily; 5hr).

From Nong Khai to Bangkok (10 daily; 11hr); Bung Kan (5 daily; 2hr); Nakhon Phanom (5 daily; 6hr); Udon Thani (every 30min; 1hr).

From Pak Chom to Nong Khai (hourly; 5hr).

From Pak Chong to Bangkok (every 15min; 3hr); Khorat (every 20min; 1hr 30min).

From Sakhon Nakhon to Bangkok (5 daily; 11hr); Chiang Rai (1 daily; 12hr); Khon Kaen (6 daily; 4hr); Khorat (6 daily; 7hr); Mukdahan (hourly; 3hr); Nakhon Phanom (every 30min; 2hr); That Phanom (every 30min; 1hr 30min); Ubon Ratchathani (9 daily; 5hr); Udon Thani (3 daily; 3hr).

From Sri Chiangmai to Loei (9 daily; 4hr); Nong Khai (hourly; 2hr); Udon Thani (every 30min; 1hr 30min); Bangkok (3 daily; 11hr).

From Surin to Bangkok (up to 20 daily; 8–9hr); Chaiyaphum (5 daily; 4–5hr); Khorat (every 30min; 4hr); Ubon Ratchathani (at least 12 daily; 2hr 30min–3hr); Yasothon (hourly; 2–3hr).

From That Phanom to Nakhon Phanom (every 30min; 1hr).

From Ubon Ratchathani to Bangkok (19 daily; 10–12hr); Chaiyaphum (5 daily; 6–7hr); Chiang Mai (5 daily; 9hr); Kantharalak (8 daily; 1hr 30min); Khon Kaen (16 daily; 6hr); Khorat (17 daily; 5hr); Phibun Mangsahan (every 25min; 1hr); Rayong (7 daily; 9hr); Surin (12 daily; 2hr 30min); Roi Et (16 daily; 2hr 30min–3hr); Yasothon (18 daily; 1hr 30min–2hr).

From Udon Thani to Bangkok (every 20min; 10hr); Chiang Mai (6 daily; 11–15hr); Khon Kaen (every 20min; 1hr 30min–2hr); Phitsanulok (5 daily; 8hr); Sakhon Nakhon (every 20min; 3hr); Ubon Ratchathani (4 daily; 5hr).

From Yasothon to Khon Kaen (hourly; 3hr–3hr 30min); Roi Et (hourly; 1hr).

Flights

From Khon Kaen to Bangkok (2–3 daily; 50min); Chiang Mai (2 weekly; 1hr 25min).

From Khorat to Bangkok (1 daily; 40min); Ubon Ratchathani (1 weekly; 45min).

From Loei to Bangkok (3 weekly; 2hr); Phitsanulok (3 weekly; 40min).

From Sakhon Nakhon to Bangkok (1 daily; 1hr).

From Ubon Ratchatahani to Bangkok (1 daily; 1hr).

From Udon Thani to Bangkok (1–2 daily; 1hr); Sakhon Nakhon (4 weekly; 30min).

CHAPTER SIX

SOUTHERN THAILAND:
THE GULF COAST

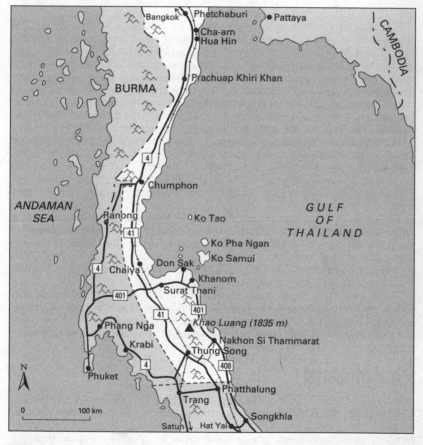

The major part of southern Thailand's **Gulf coast**, gently undulating from Bangkok to Nakhon Si Thammarat, 750km away, is famed above all for the **Samui archipelago**, three small idyllic islands lying off the most prominent hump of the coastline. This is the country's most popular seaside venue for independent travellers, and a lazy stay in a Samui beachfront bungalow is so seductive a prospect that most people overlook the attractions of the mainland, where the sheltered sandy beaches and warm clear water rival the top sunspots in most countries. Added to that you'll find scenery dominated by forested mountains that rise abruptly behind the coastal strip, and a sprinkling of historic sights – notably the crumbling temples of ancient **Phetchaburi**, which offer an atmospheric if less grandiose alternative to the much-visited attractions at Ayutthaya and Lopburi, on the other side of the capital. The stretch of coast south of Phetchaburi, down to the traditional Thai resorts of **Cha-am** and **Hua Hin**, is handy for weekenders escaping the oppressive capital, but you're more likely to be tempted to linger at **Chumphon**, 450km down the coast from Bangkok, a town that's building itself up as a scuba-diving base during the months when the Andaman Coast suffers from the southwest monsoon.

Southeast of Chumphon lies **Ko Samui**, by far the most beautiful of the islands, with its pure white sands, limpid blue waters, and arching fringes of palm trees. The island's beauty has not gone unnoticed by tourist developers of course, but this has marred it only slightly and means you can buy a little extra comfort if you've got the cash. In recent years the next island out, **Ko Pha Ngan**, has drawn increasing numbers of backpackers away from its neighbour: its simple rustic bungalows are cheaper than Ko Samui's, and it offers a few stunning beaches with a more laid-back atmosphere. **Hat Rin** is the distillation of all these features, with back-to-back white sands, hippy flea markets and T'ai Chi classes – though after dusk it swings into action as Thailand's rave capital. For real solitude and the primitive life, you have to go right out to the small rugged, outcrop of **Ko Tao**, where you can explore a network of hilly trails and scramble down to isolated rocky coves. The variety of its coral and fish has also turned it into a well-equipped scuba-diving centre, but this doesn't disturb the island's peace and quiet.

Tucked away beneath the islands, **Nakhon Si Thammarat**, the cultural capital of the south, is well worth a short detour from the main routes down the centre of the peninsula – it's a sophisticated city of grand old temples, delicious cuisine, and highly finished handicrafts, which are found nowhere else in Thailand. With its small but significant Muslim population, and machine-gun dialect, Nakhon begins the transition into Thailand's deep south.

The **railway** from Bangkok connects all the mainland towns, and **coach and bus** services are frequent. Daily boats now run to the islands from two jumping-off points: **Surat Thani**, 650km from Bangkok, has the best choice of routes, but the alternative from **Chumphon** gets you straight to the tranquillity of Ko Tao.

Phetchaburi

Straddling the River Phet about 120km south of Bangkok, the provincial capital of **PHETCHABURI** (aka Phetburi) has been settled ever since the eleventh century, when the Khmers ruled the region, but only really got going six hundred years later, when it began to flourish as a trading post between the Andaman Sea ports, Burma and Ayutthaya. Despite periodic incursions from the Burmese, the town gained a reputation as a cultural centre – as the ornamentation of its older temples testifies – and after the new capital was established in Bangkok it became a favourite country retreat of Rama IV, who

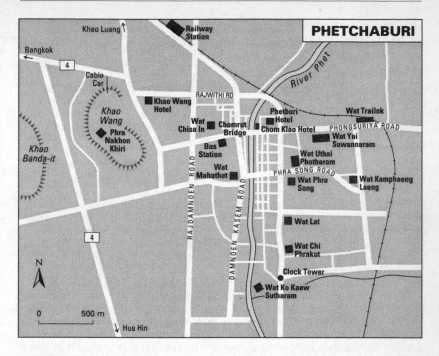

had a hilltop palace built here in the 1850s. Today the town's main claim to fame is as one of Thailand's finest sweet-making centres, the essential ingredient for its assortment of *khanom* being the sugar extracted from the sweet-sapped palms that cover Phetchaburi province. This being very much a cottage industry, modern Phetchaburi has lost relatively little of the ambience that so attracted Rama IV: the central riverside area is hemmed in by historical wats in varying states of disrepair, and wooden rather than concrete shophouses still line the riverbank.

Yet despite the obvious attractions of its old quarter, Phetchaburi gets few visitors and accommodation is poor – most visitors return to Bangkok for the night. It's also possible to combine a day in Phetchaburi with an early morning expedition from Bangkok to the floating markets of Damnoen Saduak, 40km north (see p.118); budget tour operators in the Khao San Road area offer this option as a day trip package for about B300 per person.

Arriving by **bus** from Bangkok, you'll be dropped either at the bus station on Phongsuriya Road, a few minutes' walk west of the town centre or – if it's a bus to Hua Hin and Chumphon – a bit further out, on Rajdamnoen Road. **Trains** pull in on the northern outskirts of town, not far from the hilltop palace of Khao Wang, about 1500m or a B10 samlor ride from the main sight area. Phetchaburi's town centre might look compact, but to see the major temples in a day and have sufficient energy left for climbing Khao Wang and exploring the lesser sights, you're best off hiring a **samlor** for a couple of hours (about B50 per hour) – also, samlor drivers have no qualms about riding through wat compounds, so you can get close-up views of the crumbling facades without getting out.

The town

The pinnacles and rooftops of the town's thirty-odd wats are visible in every direction, but only a few have particular historic or artistic significance. Of this group the most attractive is the still-functioning seventeenth-century **Wat Yai Suwannaram** on Phongsuriya Road, about 700m east of the bus station, across the river. On your right as you enter the compound, the fine old teak *sala* or hall has elaborately carved doors, bearing a gash said to have been made by the Burmese in 1760 as they plundered their way towards Ayutthaya. Across from the *sala*, the windowless Ayutthayan-style bot contains a remarkable set of murals, depicting Indra, Brahma and other lower-ranking divinities ranged in five rows of ascending importance. The bot overlooks a pond in the middle of which stands a well-preserved scripture library or *ho trai*: such structures were built on stilts over water to prevent ants and other insects destroying the precious documents.

The five tumbledown prangs of **Wat Kamphaeng Laeng**, ten minutes' walk south from Wat Yai, mark out Phetchaburi as the probable southernmost outpost of the Khmer empire. Built to enshrine Hindu deities and set out in a cruciform arrangement facing east, the "corncob" prangs were later adapted for Buddhist use, as you can see from the two which now house Buddha images. These days worshippers congregate in the modern whitewashed wat behind these shrines, leaving the decaying prangs to chickens, stray dogs and the occasional tourist.

Continuing west from Wat Kamphaeng Laeng, across the river, you reach Phetchaburi's most fully restored and most important temple, **Wat Mahathat**. Boasting the "Mahathat" title only since 1954, when the requisite Buddha relics were donated by the king, it was probably founded in the fourteenth century, but suffered badly at the hands of the Burmese. The five landmark prangs at its heart are adorned with stucco figures of mythical creatures, though these are nothing compared with those on the roofs of the main viharn and the bot. Instead of tapering off into the usual serpentine *chofa* finials, the gables are studded with miniature *thep* and *deva* figures (angels and gods), which add an almost mischievous vitality to the place. In a similar vein, a couple of gold-embossed crocodiles snarl above the entrance to the bot, and a caricatural carving of the writer and former prime minister Kukrit Pramoj – bare-chested, grimacing and wearing thick-rimmed glasses – rubs shoulders with mythical giants in a relief around the base of the gold Buddha housed in a separate mondop nearby.

Dominating the western outskirts, about thirty minutes' walk from Wat Mahathat, stands Rama IV's hilltop palace, a stew of mid-nineteenth-century Thai and European styles known as **Khao Wang**. During his day, the royal entourage would struggle its way up the steep brick path to the summit, but now there's a **cable car** (Mon–Fri 8am–5.30pm, Sat & Sun 8am–6pm; B35 return including museum entrance) which starts from the base of the hill on Highway 4. Up top, the wooded hill is littered with wats, prangs, chedis, whitewashed gazebos and lots more, in an ill-assorted combination of architectural idioms – the prang-topped viharn, washed all over in burnt sienna, is possibly the ugliest religious building in the country. Whenever the king came on an excursion here, he stayed in the airy summer house, **Phra Nakhon Khiri** (Wed–Sun 9am–4pm; B20 without cable car ticket), with its Mediterranean-style shutters and verandahs. Now a museum, it houses a moderately interesting collection of ceramics, furniture and other artifacts given to the royal family by foreign friends. Besides being cool and breezy, Khao Wang also proved to be a good star-gazing spot, so Rama IV had an open-sided, glass-domed observatory built close to his sleeping quarters. The king's amateur astronomy was not an inconsequential recreation: in August 1868 he predicted a solar eclipse almost to the second, thereby quashing the centuries-old Thai fear that the sun was periodically swallowed by an omnipotent lion god.

If you've got energy to spare, the two cave wats out on the western edges of town make good time-fillers. **Khao Banda-it**, a couple of kilometres west of Khao Wang, comprises a series of stalactite caves filled with Buddha statues and a 200-year-old Ayutthayan-style meditation temple. A bizarre story goes with this wat, attempting to explain its design faults as an intentional whim. The money for the three wat buildings was given by a rich man and his two wealthy wives: the first wife donated the bot, the second wife gave the viharn and the husband stuck the chedi in the middle. The chedi, however, leans distinctly southwards towards the viharn, prompting local commentators to point this out as subtle public acknowledgement of the man's preferences. Five kilometres north of Khao Wang, the caves of **Khao Luang** have the distinction of being a favourite royal picnic spot, and have also been decorated with various Buddha images.

Practicalities

The town's three main **hotels** all offer fairly large, clean rooms of just passable standard. The best-placed is *Chom Klao* at 1–3 Phongsuriya Rd, beside Chomrut Bridge (☎032/425398): rooms cost B80, or B100 with bathroom, and some of them give out onto the riverside walkway. Alternatively, the *Phetburi Hotel*, at 39 Phongsuriya Rd (☎032/425315), has rooms with bathroom for B90. Right over the other side of town, near the base of Khao Wang, rooms with bathroom at the *Khao Wang Hotel*,174/1–3 Rajwithi Rd (☎034/425167), go for B100, or B180 with air conditioning.

Most of Phetchaburi's **restaurants** are near Chomrut Bridge, the best and closest being the open-fronted *Rabieng*, 50m east along Phongsuriya Road from Chomrut Bridge, easily recognised by its glass-topped tables. Popular with young locals, the food here is good, cheap standard Thai, with an English menu for the smattering of farang customers. The nearby *Sri Taleun*, on the corner at 18/7–8 Thanon Surinluechai, is a bit more basic but does a good line in duck and sausage dishes. The best thing about the *Riverside* is its location actually on the bridge, which makes it a scenic spot for a beer.

South to Chumphon

Continuing south from Phetchaburi, road and rail pass through the seaside towns of **Cha-am** (41km), **Hua Hin** (70km) and **Prachuap Khiri Khan** (158km) before arriving at Chumphon, 340km down the coast. In the early 1900s, the royal family "discovered" this stretch of the coast, making summer expeditions here to take the sea air and to go deer- and tiger-hunting in the inland jungle. It soon became a fashionable resort area for the lower echelons of Thai society, and Cha-am and Hua Hin are now very popular weekend holiday spots, while Prachuap Khiri Khan is famed for its seafood if not for its sand. But rampant building is beginning to ruin the shoreline and pollute the sea around Cha-am and Hua Hin, and visually the area is not a patch on seafronts further down the coast, so the towns have little to offer farang travellers, except perhaps as places to break a long journey south.

Cha-am

CHA-AM is a typically Thai resort: almost empty during the week, it gets packed with families on weekends and holidays, when beach life tends to revolve around eating and drinking rather than sunbathing and swimming – Cha-am's beach is long and pleasantly shaded, but disappointingly grey.

Half-hourly **buses** from Bangkok stop in the tiny town centre on Highway 4, 1km west of the beach; **trains** (8 daily) drop passengers at the station one block further west. Most of the **accommodation** is on the beachfront Ruamchit Road and is geared towards family groups. For non-familial travellers, the best options include *Arunthip*, which has large rooms with shower for B200, and *Nirindhorn* (☎032/471038), with adequate rooms from B250.

Phra Ratchaniwet Marukhathaiyawan

Midway between Cha-am and Hua Hin lies the lustrous seaside palace of Rama VI, **Phra Ratchaniwet Marukhathaiyawan** (daily 8am–4pm; free), a rarely visited place despite the easy access – the half-hourly buses from Bangkok to Hua Hin stop within a couple of kilometres' walk of the palace.

Designed by an Italian architect and completed in just sixteen days in 1923, the golden teak building was abandoned to the corrosive sea air after Rama VI's death in 1925. Restoration work began in the 1970s and two-thirds of the structure now looks as it once did: a stylish composition of verandahs and latticework painted in pastel shades of beige and blue, with an emphasis on cool simplicity. The spacious open hall in the north wing, hung with chandeliers and encircled by a first-floor balcony, was once used as a theatre, and the adjacent upstairs rooms, now furnished only with a few black and white portraits from the royal family photo album, were given over to royal attendants. The king stayed in the centre, with the best sea view and access to the promenade, while the south wing (still unrestored) contained the queen's apartments.

Hua Hin

Thailand's oldest beach resort, **HUA HIN** used to be little more than an over-grown fishing village with one exceptionally grand hotel, but now the grotty beachfront flounders under a jungle of half-built upmarket hotels and high-rise condominiums. Around the turn of the century, royalty were Hua Hin's main visitors, but the place became more widely popular in the 1920s, when the opening of the Bangkok–Malaysia railway made short excursions to the beach much more viable. The Victorian-style *Railway Hotel* was built soon after to cater for the leisured classes, and in 1926 Rama VII had his own summer palace, Klai Klangwon ("Far from Worries"), erected at the northern end of the beach. It was here, ironically, that Rama VII was staying in 1932 when the coup was launched in Bangkok against the system of absolute monarchy. The royals still come down to the palace for summer breaks – you'll know if they are in town, because the streets get decked with enormous hand-painted billboard portraits of the king and queen, and all the shops hang out the national flag.

With the beaches of Ko Samui, Krabi and Ko Samet so close at hand, the only reason to make a point of visiting Hua Hin is to stay in the former **Railway Hotel**. Now called the *Hotel Sofitel Central Hua Hin* (☎032/512021; Bangkok ☎02/233 0980), the hotel remains a classic of colonial-style architecture, with cool, high ceilings, heavy-bladed ceiling fans, polished wood-panelling and wide seaview balconies. All is much as it was seventy years ago, except for the swimming pools and tennis courts which were built especially for the filming of *The Killing Fields* – the *Railway* stood in as Phnom Penh's plushest hotel. Prices start at B2178.

If you do find yourself staying here but can't afford those prices, check in at one of the pretty wooden **guest houses** squashed into the back sois behind the sea front. Try *Phuen Guest House* on Soi Binthabat (☎032/512344), where small rooms start at B120 or *Sunee*, which has larger rooms with bathrooms on Naretdamri Road for B150 – bear in mind that all rooms are more expensive at weekends. For **food**, try the night market along Sasong Road, the seafood places on the pier, or the small restaurants on Naretdamri Road – *Nice* serves fresh seafood at night and is also popular for its breakfasts.

Prachuap Khiri Khan

Between Hua Hin and Chumphon there's only one place that makes a decent way-station on the route south, and that's **PRACHUAP KHIRI KHAN**, 90km beyond Hua Hin. It has attractive streets of brightly painted wooden houses and vibrant bougainvillea and hibiscus blossoms, as well as a very good night market, set up alongside the otherwise dismal beach. Prachuap is only 12km east of the Burmese border, and you can see the Burmese mountains clearly if you climb the 417 steps up the monkey-infested Khao Chong Krajok at the northern end of town. For overnight stops, try the *Yutichai Hotel* (☎032/611055) near the train station or the *Inthira Hotel* around the corner near the market square: both have rooms for B100.

Chumphon and around

South Thailand officially starts at **CHUMPHON**, where the main road splits into west and east coast branches, and inevitably the provincial capital saddles itself with the title "gateway to the south". Yet only recently has Chumphon begun to sell itself to tourists, an area of economic potential that assumed vital significance after November 1989, when Typhoon Gay – the worst typhoon to hit Thailand in recent decades – crashed into Chumphon province, killing hundreds of people and uprooting acres of banana, rubber and coconut plantations. With the main-stays of the region's economy in ruins, TAT and other government agencies began billing the beaches 12km east of town as a diving centre for the February to October season, when west-coast seas get too choppy.

Although Chumphon's single diving base offers competitive prices and trips to unpolluted offshore reefs, as a resort it's not in the same league as Ko Samui, with no low-budget guest houses or top-end high-rises either in town or on the beach, and hardly any entertainment facilities. It does however work as a viable departure point for the up-and-coming island destination of Ko Tao, with journey times from Bangkok to Ko Tao via Chumphon being considerably faster than the convoluted Bangkok–Surat Thani–Ko Pha Ngan–Ko Tao route.

Buses from Bangkok arrive at the terminal on Tha Tapao Road, one block west of Chumphon's main thoroughfare Sala Daeng Road; **trains** stop at the station about 500m further north. If you're using Chumphon only as a departure point for **Ko Tao** (see p.356), check the **ferry** times at *Chumphon Travel Service* (☎077/501880) close to the bus terminal: weather permitting, boats should leave daily at around midnight from the port at Pak Nam, 14km southeast of town, with a diminished service operating during the monsoon season.

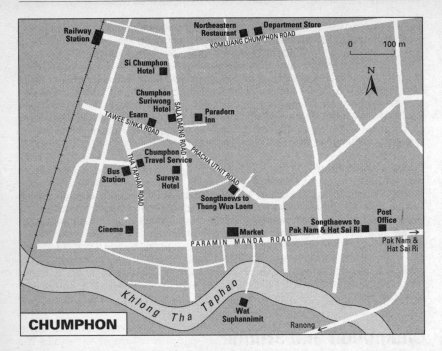

CHUMPHON

Practicalities

The best value and most comfortable **hotel** in town is the *Tha Tapao*, close to the bus station at 66/1 Tha Tapao Rd (☎077/511479), where rooms start at B200. For cheaper, slightly less salubrious accommodation, head for either of the two large characterless, but scrupulously clean places on Sala Daeng Road: *Si Chumphon* (☎077/511379) and *Chumphon Suriwong* (☎077/511397) both have rooms with fan and shower for B120. Cheaper still, but slightly grotty, are the B80 rooms at *Sureya Hotel* also on Sala Daeng Road (☎077/511444). Top of the range is *Paradorm Inn*, across the road from *Suriwong* at 180/12 Paradorm Rd, with air-conditioned rooms for B450, a pool and restaurant.

There are a couple of very good **restaurants** in town – the one next to the department store on Komluang Chumphon Road serves *kai yang, somtam* and sticky rice all day, the other, *Esarn* on Tawee Sinka Road, has basic Thai dishes in the daytime and northeastern fare in the evening. *Paradorm Inn* serves reasonable if pricey breakfasts and the coffee bar on the third floor of the Komluang Chumphon Road department store has a choice of ten different coffee blends.

The beaches and islands

Chumphon's best beach is **THUNG WUA LAEM**, 12km north and served by frequent songthaews from halfway down Pracha Uthit Road, about ten minutes' walk southeast of the Sala Daeng Road hotels. The long sandy stretch is as yet undeveloped, with only one resort, *Chumphon Cabana* (☎077/501990), at the southern end, and a couple of seafood restaurants. Bungalows here range from

B200 to B600. This is the place to come for the diving: *Cabana* runs Chumphon's only **dive centre**, from where you can hire equipment, organise diving trips to the nearby islands, and take NAUI-certified five-day courses for B6000.

If you're keen to go diving or snorkelling independently, then you should make for **HAT SAI RI**, 21km south of town and reached by frequent songthaews from Paramin Manda Road. Though dirtier and busier than Thung Wua Laem, this is the best place to hire boats to the tiny offshore **islands**, some of the best of which are visible from beach: it's well worth exploring the reefs around **Ko Mattra** and **Ko Rat** (the one shaped like a half-submerged rhino), and although nearby **Ko Lang Ka Chiu** is out of bounds because of its birds' nest collecting business, it's quite permissible to dive in the surrounding waters. Further afield, about 18km offshore, the reefs of **Ko Ngam Yai** and **Ko Ngam Noi** are the usual destination of the *Chumphon Cabana* diving expeditions. A day's boat ride around all or some of these islands should cost about B600 per boat (excluding any diving or snorkelling equipment); either negotiate directly with the fishermen on Hat Sai Ri or enlist the help of the amenable manager of *Sai Ri Lodge* at the southern end of the beach.

Chaiya and around

About 140km south of Chumphon, **CHAIYA** was the capital of southern Thailand under the Srivijayan empire, which fanned out from Sumatra between the eighth and thirteenth centuries. Today there's little to mark the passing of the Srivijayan civilisation, but this small, sleepy town has gained new fame as the site of Wat Suan Mokkh, an educational temple whose meditation courses account for the bulk of Chaiya's visitors. Unless you're interested in one of these courses, the town is best visited on a day trip, either as a break in the journey south, or as an excursion from Surat Thani.

Chaiya is 3km from Highway 41, the main road between Chumphon and Surat Thani: buses between the two towns will put you off on the highway, from where you can catch a motorcycle taxi or walk into Chaiya. Although the town lies on the main southern railway, most trains arrive there in the middle of the night. Only the evening trains from Bangkok are useful, getting you to Chaiya first thing in the morning.

The town
The main sight in Chaiya is **Wat Phra Boromathat** on the western side of town, where the ninth-century chedi – one of very few surviving examples of Srivijayan architecture – is said to contain relics of the Buddha himself. Hidden away behind the viharn in a pretty, red-tiled cloister, the chedi looks like an over-sized wedding cake surrounded by an ornamental moat. Its unusual square tiers are spiked with smaller chedis and decorated with gilt, in a style similar to the temples of central Java.

The **National Museum** (Wed–Sun 8am–4pm; B10) on the eastern side of the temple is a disappointment. Although the Srivijaya period produced some of Thailand's finest sculpture, much of it discovered at Chaiya, the best pieces have been carted off to the National Museum in Bangkok. Replicas have been left in their stead, which are shown alongside fragments of some original statues and an exhibition of local handicrafts. The best remaining piece is a serene stone image of the Buddha from **Wat Kaeo**, an imposing chedi on the south side of town. Heading towards the centre from Wat Phra Boromathat, you take the first paved road on the right, which brings you first to the brick remains of Wat Long, and then after one kilometre to **Wat Kaeo**, enclosed by a thick ring of trees. Here you can poke around the murky antechambers of the chedi, taking care not to trip over the various dismembered stone Buddhas that are lying around.

Ban Phum Riang

If you've got some time on your hands, you could take one of the regular songthaews to **BAN PHUM RIANG**, 5km east of Chaiya, a Muslim crab-fishing village of wooden stilted houses clustered around a rickety mosque. The weavers here are famous for their original designs of silk and cotton: although the cottage industry is on the decline, you might still be able to pick up a bargain in the village shop.

Wat Suan Mokkh

The forest temple of **Wat Suan Mokkh** ("Garden of Liberation"), 6km south of Chaiya on Highway 41, was founded by **Buddhadasa Bhikkhu**, southern Thailand's most revered monk. His back-to-basics philosophy, which admits Christian, Zen and Taoist influences, has attracted Thais from all over the country, as well as thousands of farangs. It's not necessary to sign up for one of the wat's courses to enjoy the temple, however – all buses between Chaiya and Surat Thani pass the wat, and there are songthaews and motorcycle taxis too, so it's easy to drop by for a quiet stroll through the wooded grounds.

The layout of the wat is centred on the Golden Hill: scrambling up between trees and monks' huts, you'll reach a hushed clearing on top of the hill which is the temple's holiest meeting-place, a simple open-air platform decorated with nothing more than a stone Buddha with the Wheel of the Doctrine. At the base of the hill, the outer walls of the Spiritual Theatre are lined with bas-reliefs, replicas of originals in India, which depict scenes from the life of the Buddha. Inside, every inch is covered with colourful didactic painting, executed by resident monks and visitors in a jumble of realistic and surrealistic styles.

The **meditation courses** are held by farang and Thai teachers over the first ten days of every month. A rule of silence is maintained, and each day begins before dawn with basic meditation tuition according to the *anapanasati* method, by which the meditator focuses on the movements of his or her own breathing to achieve mindfulness. The fee is B60 per day, which includes two vegetarian meals and a room. Each course has space for about one hundred people – turn up at Suan Mokkh on the last day of the month to enrol, or telephone Khun Supitr in Bangkok (☎02/468 2857) for further information.

Surat Thani

Uninspiring **SURAT THANI**, 60km south of Chaiya, is generally worth visiting only as the jumping-off point for the Samui archipelago (see p.340), though it might be worth a stay when the Chak Phra Festival is in swing, or you might use Surat as a base for seeing the nearby historic town of Chaiya.

Strung along the south bank of the Tapi River, with a busy port for rubber and coconuts near the river mouth, the town is experiencing rapid economic growth and paralysing traffic jams. Its sole attraction is the **Monkey Training College** (daylight hours; B100), a half-hour trip out of town to the east, where young monkeys are trained to pick coconuts from trees which are too tall for humans to reach.

To get there, hire a songthaew, or take a local bus 6km east towards Kanchanadit and Don Sak and then walk the last 2km, following the signpost south from the main road. For anyone who turns up, the owner will put on an exploitative hour-long coconut-picking display with his champion pig-tail macaque, although the serious business of the college is undoubtedly worthy, for coconuts are the province's most important crop, providing a much-needed cash livelihood for small farmers. At the end of the display, the owner will show you the stable at the back where the most laborious parts of the training take place. Graduates of the three-month course are worth B3000 and can farm up to one thousand coconuts a day.

Coconut-picking monkey

Practicalities

All **buses** to Surat Thani arrive at Taladmai Road, in the centre of town. Arriving by **train**, however, means arriving at Phunphin, 13km to the west, from where buses run every ten minutes between 6am and 8pm. (It's also possible to buy express boat tickets to Ko Samui and Ko Pha Ngan from the railway station, including a connecting coach to the pier, Tha Thong.) Arriving by **air**, you can take a B35 minibus for the 27-kilometre journey south into Surat Thani – or a B150 combination ticket to Ko Samui.

THE CHAK PHRA FESTIVAL

At the start of the eleventh lunar month (September or October) the people of Surat Thani celebrate the end of Buddhist Lent with the Chak Phra Festival ("Pulling the Buddha"), which symbolizes the Buddha's return to earth after a monsoon season spent preaching to his mother in heaven. On the Tapi River, tug-boats pull the town's principal Buddha image on a raft decorated with huge nagas, while on land similar floats are hauled across the countryside and through the streets on sleigh-like floats bearing Buddha images and colourful flags and parasols. As the monks have been confined to their monasteries for three months, the end of Lent is also the time to give them generous offerings in the *kathin* ceremony, of which Surat Thani has its own version, called Thot Pha Pa, when the offerings are hung on tree branches planted in front of the houses before dawn. Long-boat races, between teams from all over the south, are also held during the festival.

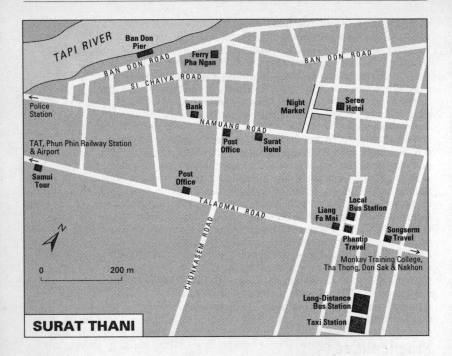

SURAT THANI

TAT have a helpful office at the western end of town at 5 Taladmai Rd (daily 8am–4pm), where they give out free, sketchy maps. Most cheap **accommodation** in Surat Thani is noisy, grotty and over-priced – you would probably be better off on a night boat to Ko Samui or Ko Pha Ngan. The *Surat Hotel* at 496 Namuang Rd has pokey doubles from B80; the *Seree Hotel*, 2/2–5 Tonpor Rd, is clean, quiet and a little upmarket, with fan doubles at B260, and air-conditioned rooms at B310. At the western end of town, the *Wangtai Hotel*, 1 Taladmai Rd (☎077/283020; Bangkok reservations ☎02/253 7947) is the luxury option, and reasonably good value with doubles from B785.

For good, cheap Thai and Chinese **food**, try the *Jarng Pochana* at the top end of Don Nok Road – head west on Taladmai Road past *Samui Tour* and turn left at the *Siam Thara Hotel*. The *Liang Fa Mai* outside the local bus station at 293–41 Taladmai Rd, does cheap and tasty duck, chicken and pork on rice (7am–5pm only). The night market between Si Chaiya and Ban Don roads offers an eye-catching choice of dishes.

Ko Samui

An ever-widening cross-section of visitors, from globetrotting backpackers to suit-case-toting fortnighters, come to southern Thailand just for the beautiful beaches of **KO SAMUI**, 80km from Surat – and at 15km across and down, Samui is large enough to cope, except during the rush at Christmas and New Year, and in July and August. The paradisal beaches and crystal-clear seas have kept their good looks, which are enhanced by a thick fringe of palm trees that gives a harvest of three million coconuts each month. Development behind the beaches, which a local bye-law limits to the height of a coconut tree, has brought the islanders greater prosperity than the crop could bring, but this doesn't seem to have deflected them from their easy-going ways.

For most visitors, the days are spent indulging in a few water sports or just lying on the beach waiting for the next drinks seller, hair braider or masseur to come along. For a day off the sand, you should not miss the almost supernatural beauty of the **Ang Thong National Marine Park**, which comprises many of the eighty islands in the Samui archipelago. A motorbike day trip on the fifty-kilometre round-island road will throw up plenty more gorgeous beaches, and night-time entertainment is provided by a limited number of bars and discos. Buffalo fighting, once a common sport on the island, is now restricted to special festivals such as Thai New Year; the practices and rituals are much the same as those of bull-fighting in Hat Yai (see p.419).

The island's most appealing beaches have seen the heaviest development and are now the most expensive places to stay, while quieter beaches such as Maenam are generally less attractive. **Accommodation** on the island is in bungalow resorts, from the primitive to the very swish: at the lower end of the scale, expect to pay at least B150 per bungalow for a mosquito screen and some degree of comfort, while for the more upmarket places at Chaweng and Lamai, the most beautiful but most developed beaches, you'll pay at least B1500. Many of these resorts have restaurants which are cheap and good, especially if you like seafood.

No particular **season** is best for coming to Ko Samui. The northeast monsoon brings rain between October and January, and sometimes makes the sea on the east coast too heavy for swimming. (The north coast is generally calm enough for swimming all year round.) January is often breezy, March and April are very hot, and then between May and October the southwest monsoon blows mildly onto its west coast and causes a little rain.

Getting to the island

The most obvious way of getting to Ko Samui is on a boat from the Surat Thani area. Of these the cheapest is the ferry which leaves Ban Don pier in **Surat Thani** itself for Na Thon – the main port on Samui – at 11pm every night (6hr; from B40). From **Tha Thong**, 5km east of Surat, three express boats a day run to Na Thon for most of the year, reduced to two from June to October (2hr 30min; B95). Vehicle ferries run five times a day between **Don Sak** pier, 60km east of Surat, and Thong Yang (1hr 30min); a combination ticket including the bus trips from Surat to Don Sak and from Thong Yang to Na Thon costs around B60.

Surat Thani is teeming with touts trying to persuade you onto their employer's service to Ko Samui and offering transport to the embarkation points, where you can buy your tickets. In Surat itself you can buy tickets from the major travel agents, who generally arrange transport to the piers outside of town. *Songserm Travel* (☎077/272928), on Taladmai Road opposite the long-distance bus station, handles the express boats from Tha Thong and the night boats from Ban Don pier; *Samui Tour* (☎077/272452), 1km west along Taladmai Road opposite the Esso petrol station, handles the vehicle ferry from Don Sak pier.

From Bangkok, the State Railway does a train-bus-boat package through to Ko Samui which costs about the same as organising the parts independently –

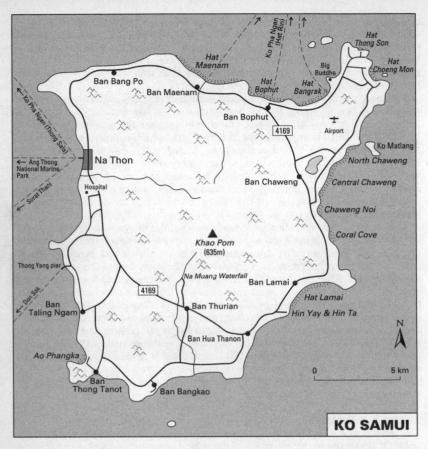

KO SAMUI

about B300 if you travel second-class. Overnight coach-boat packages are especially cheap on Khao San Road, from around B250. A flashier option from Bangkok is **Jumbo Ferry** (☎02/398 1170), which cruises between Bangkok and Songkhla via Ko Samui twice a week in each direction. From Bangkok it takes about sixteen hours and costs from B660; from Songkhla it takes ten hours and costs B300. At the top of the range, you can get to Ko Samui direct **by air** on *Bangkok Airways* (☎02/253 4014); five seventy-minute flights a day leave Bangkok (B1700), and there's even a daily forty-minute flight from Phuket (B1000). Minibuses meet incoming flights (and connect with departures) at the **airport** in the northeastern tip of the island, and run to the north coast, Na Thon, Chaweng and Lamai for B60.

Finally, it's possible to hop to Ko Samui **from Ko Pha Ngan**: two boats a day do the 45-minute trip from Thong Sala to Na Thon, while from Hat Rin one boat a day runs to Bangrak, two to Bophut and one to Maenam – though the Hat Rin routes are likely to be cancelled if there aren't enough takers or if the weather's bad.

Na Thon

The island capital, **NA THON**, at the top of the long western coast, is a frenetic half-built town that is best treated as a service station before hitting the sand: it's stuffed with fix-it **travel agents** and **banks** (often with late-night opening and safe-deposit boxes); the supermarkets are geared up for the basic beachside needs; there's a **post office** at the northern end of the prom with poste restante and international telephone service (daily 8am–midnight); and tourist visas may be extended at the **immigration office**, 25/3 Moo 3, Na Amphoe Rd (☎077/421069). A handful of **bookshops** sell and buy novels, and stock V. Hongsombud's detailed, accurate **map** of Surat and the archipelago (B35). For emergencies, **clinics** operate on Ang Thong Road and Route 4169, the main through road, with the cheaper **hospital** 3km south. The **Tourist Police** (☎077/421281) have a base on the way out of town to the south, first right on Route 4169 after Preedaraj Road.

If you really need a **place to stay** in Na Thon, try the simple *Town Guest House* off Ang Thong Road (from B150) or the more comfortable *Seaside Palace* towards the southern end of the waterfront, where fan rooms start at B300. If you do find yourself staying, don't miss the *Herbal Centre for Health*, one kilometre north along Route 4169 – it dispenses the best massages and herbal saunas on the island. Na Thon provides little in the way of Thai **food**, but all manner of Western places. Justifiably popular, especially for breakfast, is the reasonable *Jelly Roll Bakery* in front of the pier, which also serves Thai food. The *Restaurant New York* (*Il Pescatore*) is a showy Italian place, which serves up good, satisfying home-made pasta and lives up to its subtitle by organizing fishing trips for B1500 a day.

For **getting around the island**, Na Thon is well-served with songthaews: Lamai and Ao Phangka songthaews leave from just south of the pier, songthaews for the other main beaches from just north, with fares ranging from B10 to B20. You can **rent** a motorbike from B150 in Na Thon, but it's hard to find a decent, new bike in the capital, so it's probably safer to rent at one of the main beaches – and dozens are killed on Samui's roads each year, so proceed with caution.

Ang Thong National Marine Park

Even if you don't get your buns off the beach for the rest of your stay, it's worth taking at least a day out to visit the beautiful **ANG THONG NATIONAL MARINE PARK**, a lush, dense group of 41 small islands strewn like dragon's teeth over the deep blue Gulf of Thailand, 25km west of Samui. Once a haven for pirate junks, the islands and their coral reefs, white sand beaches and wooded slopes, along with the monkeys, birds and rare orchids which live there, are now preserved under the watchful eye of the National Parks Department.

Erosion of the soft limestone has dug caves and chiselled out shapes which are variously said to resemble seals, a

Clown Fish

rhinoceros, a Buddha image and even the temple complex at Angkor. The largest in the group is **KO WUA TALAB** (Sleeping Cow Island) where the park head-quarters shelters in a hollow behind the small beach. From there it's a steep 400-metre climb to the island's peak to gawp at the panorama, which is especially fine at sunrise and sunset: in the distance, Ko Samui, Ko Pha Ngan and the mainland; nearer at hand, the jagged edges of the surrounding archipelago; and below the peak, a secret cove on the western side and an almost sheer drop to the clear blue sea to the east. Another climb from the beach at headquarters, only 200m but harder going, leads to Tham Buabok, a cave set high in the cliff face. Some of the stalactites and stalagmites resemble lotuses, the meaning of the cave's name.

The feature which gives the park the name Ang Thong, meaning "Golden Bowl", is a landlocked lake, 250m in diameter, on **KO MAE KO** to the north of Ko Wua Talab. A well-made path leads from the beach to the rim of the cliff wall which encircles the lake, affording another stunning view of the archipelago and the shallow, green water far below, which is connected to the sea by a natural underground tunnel.

Practicalities

Apart from chartering your own boat at huge expense, the only way of **getting to Ang Thong** is on an organized day trip. From Na Thon, boats leave every day at 8.30am, returning at 5pm. In between, there's lunch on the beach at Ko Wua Talab and time to explore the island, some cruising through the archipelago, a visit to the viewpoint over the lake on Ko Mae Ko and a snorkelling stop. Tickets cost B250 per person, available from agencies around Na Thon pier. Similar trips run from Thong Sala pier on Ko Pha Ngan, but less frequently. *Crowded House Pub* on Bangrak beach organizes party tours for B1000, including a beach barbe-cue and overnight camping at the park, and *Seaflower*, at Ao Chaophao on Ko Pha Ngan's west coast, does three-day "treks".

If you want to **stay at Ko Wua Talab**, the National Parks Department main-tains five large, simple bungalows at the headquarters, costing from B400. To book accommodation, contact the Ang Thong National Marine Park Headquarters at PO Box 29, Surat Thani 84000 (☎077/286052) or the Forestry Department in Bangkok (see p.22). Camping is also possible in certain specified areas, and there's a restaurant at headquarters. If you do want to camp, you can go over on a boat trip ticket – it's valid for a return on a later day. For getting around the archipelago from Ko Wua Talab, you should be able to charter a motor boat from the fishermen who live in the park.

Maenam

The most westerly of the beaches on the north coast is **MAENAM**, 13km from Na Thon and now Samui's most popular destination for shoestring travellers. The exposed four-kilometre bay is not the island's prettiest, being more of a broad dent in the coastline, and the sloping beach is relatively narrow and coarse. But Maenam has the cheapest food and beds on the island, unspoilt views of fishing boats and Ko Pha Ngan, and is the quietest of the major beaches. Jet-skis give way to windsurfing here (there are two rental "schools" in the centre of the beach) and there's no sign of videos or anything resembling nightlife – though if you want to go on the razzle, some of the bungalows arrange late-night song-thaews to and from Chaweng or Lamai. The main road is set back far from the beach amongst the trees, and runs through the sizeable fishing village of BAN MAENAM, in the centre of the bay. This has some cheap restaurants and is one of the few places on Samui where life carries on regardless of farangs.

Practicalities

Maenam has over twenty, mostly primitive bungalow complexes, with little to choose between them, although the following can all be recommended. Starting at the far western end of Maenam, *Home Bay* overlooks its own large stretch of untidy beach, tucked in beside a small cliff. The bungalows are set in a quiet, spacious coconut grove, with high season prices starting at B50 for simple two-berth shacks. Smart wooden bungalows with mosquito screens are B200, and big, concrete family cottages go for B400. One kilometre towards the centre of the bay, but still west of the village, *Shangrilah* is a disorderly compound which sprawls onto the nicest, widest stretch of sand along Maenam. Simple bungalows with mosquito nets start at B50 or you can pay B150 or more for mosquito screens and a fan. The restaurant serves good Thai food.

The best clutch of places to stay are at the far eastern end of the bay. The first is *Cleopatra's Palace*, 1km from the village, where, in an orderly though rather cramped compound, clean wooden bungalows with fans and showers go for B100. Laid-back *Rose*, four compounds along to the east, offers basic wooden huts with mosquito nets for B40. Next door but one, *Friendly* is helpful and easy-going; wooden bungalows with bathrooms cost B80, smart concrete ones B120, though the place feels exposed with no trees to provide shade.

Bophut

The next bay to the east is **BOPHUT**, which has a similar look to Maenam but shows a marked difference in atmosphere and facilities. The quiet two-kilometre beach attracts as many families as young travellers, and accommodation is generally more expensive. BAN BOPHUT, at the east end of the bay, caters largely to tourists, with a bank, a clinic, a scuba diving outlet, and bookshops crammed into its two narrow streets along with bars, bungalows and restaurants, two of them French. The part of the beach which stretches from *Peace* to *World* bungalows, at the western end of the bay, is the nicest, but again the sand is slightly coarse by Samui's high standards.

Best of the **cheap accommodation** deals is *Peace*, a large, well-run concern at the mid-point of the beach, but it may be too much like a holiday camp for some. The restaurant serves good food from Thailand and Europe, and the safe-deposit boxes are free. Decent bungalows start at B80 with fan and mosquito net, rising to B250 for a motel-style chalet. In the **moderate** range, *Smile House* has a reliable set of chalets grouped around a small, clean swimming pool, at the western end of Bophut village; B350 gets you a clean bathroom, mosquito screens and a fan, B1000 gets air conditioning. Next-door-but-two west of *Peace*, the *Samui Palm Beach Resort* (☎077/421358; Bangkok reservations ☎02/254 2905) is **expensive** but good value, with a small jacuzzi and swimming pool. The elegant cottages have hints of southern Thai architecture, air conditioning and hot water, and go from B1900 double – with big reductions possible in low season.

For a change from bungalow food, try *The Bird in the Hand*, a simple and busy **restaurant** in the village, which serves good French and Thai food (especially seafood) at reasonable prices.

For more active pursuits, sailboards are available at *Peace* for B100 an hour, and the *Samui Cart Club*, a **go-karting** track on the main road 1km west of town opposite the *Euphoria Hotel*, offers everyone the chance to let off steam without becoming another accident statistic on the roads of Samui (daily 10am–6.30pm; from B200 for 10min).

Bangrak

Beyond the sharp headland with its sweep of coral reefs lies **BANGRAK**, sometimes called Big Buddha Beach, after the colossus which gazes sternly down on the sun worshippers from its island in the bay. The beach is no great shakes, especially during the northeast monsoon, when the sea retreats and leaves a slippery mudflat, but Bangrak still manages to attract the water-sports crowd.

The **Big Buddha** is certainly big and works hard at being a tourist attraction, but is no beauty despite a recent face-lift. A short causeway at the eastern end of the bay leads across to a clump of souvenir shops and food stalls in front of the temple, catering to day-tripping Thai worshippers as well as farangs. Ceremonial dragon-steps then bring you up to the covered terrace around the Big Buddha, from where there's a fine view of the sweeping north coast.

Bangrak's **bungalows** are squeezed together in a narrow, noisy strip between the road and the shore. Best of the cheapies is *Como's*, which fronts a long stretch of beach at the western end: a huge variety of bungalows start at B60 for a basic A-frame hut, with famous Mekhong whisky cocktails in the same price bracket. *LA Resort*, three doors along, is a welcoming family-run place, but their concrete bungalows with bathrooms and mosquito screens (B150 and up) are rather bland. Wooden bungalows with the same trappings go from B100 at *Sunset Song* in the middle of the beach, while next door but one, at *Sunset*, are the cheapest most ramshackle bungalows on the beach, at B40 and up.

Most people who come to Bangrak spend some time at *Crowded House Pub Restaurant*, a chummy beachfront youth club with a pool table and other games. As well as serving cocktails and big portions of decent Western food, the restaurant organizes barbecues and overnight trips to the Ang Thong islands.

The northeastern cape

After Bangrak comes the high-kicking boot of the **northeastern cape**, some of whose quiet, rocky coves have been colonised by a number of upmarket resorts. Songthaews run along the paved road to the largest and most beautiful bay, **CHOENG MON**, whose white sandy beach is lined with casuarina trees which provide shade for the bungalows. To the north of Choeng Mon, sandy lanes connect several secluded inlets, only one of which – **Thong Son** – has been developed at all.

For **cheap accommodation**, try *Choeng Mon Resort*, a relaxing, shady compound with a good restaurant and a big choice of beds: wooden rooms are B50, while bungalows with bathrooms start at B100. The friendly and enthusiastic *Thong Son Bay* has simple bungalows with bathrooms from B100. In the **moderate** range, the *Samui Tongson Resort* in Thong Son has comfy though tightly packed bungalows from B200. Two of Samui's most **expensive** hotels are on Choeng Mon, both run by the reliable *Imperial* group (☎077/421451 for both, Bangkok reservations ☎02/254 0023): the *Boat House Hotel*, so named after the rice barges which have been converted into suites in the grounds (B5324 double), comes a close second to the easy-going *Imperial Tongsai Bay Hotel*, the island's finest – its red-tiled cottages (same price) command beautiful views over a secluded private beach, a vast saltwater swimming pool and the whole bay.

Chaweng

For sheer natural beauty, none of the other beaches can match **CHAWENG**, with its broad, gently sloping strip of white sand sandwiched between the limpid blue sea and a line of palm trees. Such beauty has not escaped attention, which means, on the plus side, that Chaweng can provide just about anything the active beach bum demands – from parascending and water-skiing to thumping nightlife. The negative angle is that the new developments are ever more expensive, building work is always in progress and there's no certainty that it will look lovely when the bulldozers retreat.

The six-kilometre bay is framed between the small island of Ko Matlang at the north end and the 300-metre high headland above Coral Cove in the south. From **Ko Matlang**, where the waters provide some colourful snorkelling, an often exposed coral reef slices southwest across to the mainland, marking out a shallow lagoon and **North Chaweng**. This S-shaped part of the beach has some ugly pockets of development, but at low tide it becomes a wide, inviting playground, and from November to January the reef shelters it from the worst of the northeast winds. South of the reef, the idyllic shoreline of **Central Chaweng** stretches for 2km in a dead straight line, the large village of amenities concealed behind the treeline. Around a low promontory is **Chaweng Noi**, a little curving beach in a rocky bay, which is quiet in its northern part, away from the road. South of Chaweng, the road climbs and dips into **Coral Cove**, a tiny isolated beach of coarse sand hemmed in by high rocks, with some good coral for snorkelling. It's well worth making the trip to the *Beverly Hills Café*, towards the tip of the headland which divides Chaweng from Lamai, for a jaw-dropping view over Chaweng and Choeng Mon to the peaks of Ko Pha Ngan.

Accommodation

Over fifty sets of **bungalows** at Chaweng are squeezed into thin strips running back from the beachfront at right angles. In the **cheap and moderate** range, prices are generally over the odds, although a few places, described here starting at the north end of the beach, offer reasonable value.

IKK, a short walk around the point at the far north end of the beach, has comfortable new bungalows from B200, on an unusually spacious and peaceful stretch of sand. Back round the point at the top end of **North Chaweng**, *Moon* is a friendly set-up, with shaded wooden bungalows at B150 with their own bathrooms. *The Island* (☎077/421288), in the middle of North Chaweng, is a real find, but often full. A spread of well-designed accommodation with en suite bathrooms rises from B200 for a simple room to B1500 for a beachside, air-conditioned bungalow with hot water. A good restaurant and easy-going beach bar are turning this into a popular hangout.

The *Thai Restaurant*, secluded among dense trees at the top end of **Chaweng Central**, ignores the surrounding flash development to offer old-fashioned primitive huts and a friendly, laid-way-back ambience for B100. The four branches of *Charlie's Huts* offer the only cheap deal right in the heart of Chaweng, from B100, but don't expect any character or room to breathe. In the south, opposite the *Reggae Pub*, *Arabian* offers good food and big bungalows with bathrooms around a lush garden, from B400.

Maeo on **Chaweng Noi** is a cute, leafy oasis hemmed in by a giant resort and the main road. A few primitive A-frames go for B50, the cheapest here, but most of the bungalows have bathrooms and start at B150. In the tight squeeze of developments at **Coral Cove**, *Coral Cove Chalets* have grabbed a nice spot and serve good food. Dilapidated A-frames perched over a tiny inlet are B70, while attractive, clean bungalows with mosquito screens and bathrooms on a landscaped slope are B200 and up.

Of the many **expensive** places which are sprouting up, the *Chaweng Regent* at the bottom end of North Chaweng (☎077/286910; Bangkok reservations ☎02/418 4066) is a reasonable deal though conditions are cramped – elegant bungalows, with all mod cons, start at B2100. Right in the centre of Chaweng, *Pansea* (☎077/ 421384; Bangkok reservations ☎02/237 4792), a long-established, sedate place set in spacious gardens, has large cottages suitable for the average family at B2900. Daddy of them all is the *Imperial* (☎077/421390; Bangkok reservations ☎02/254 0023) on Chaweng Noi, a grand but lively hotel with a Mediterranean feel – prices start at B4114 per double, taxes included.

Eating, drinking and other practicalities

It's hard to find Thai **food** here, but if you're determined, head for the alley leading to the *Chicago* nightclub at the north end of Central Chaweng, where a line of cafés serve cheapish food day and night to Thai workers. The *Royal Thai Cuisine*, 200m down the road, is at the other end of the price scale, the delicious food is carefully prepared and beautifully presented, and is cheaper than the second-rate Western food peddled in most places. The restaurant at *The Island* bungalows on North Chaweng is also worth the journey for slightly pricey Western and Thai food and good breakfasts. For lunch on a beachside terrace, try *Arabian* on Central Chaweng, where good eastern Mediterranean snacks and Thai seafood are quite reasonable.

If you're looking for a decent place to **drink**, go to the *Rock Island Pub* on the pretty stretch of beach in front of *The Island* bungalows, which makes a good place to start the evening, as well as hosting all-night bashes, usually on a Saturday. The open-air *Jazz Bar*, at Central Chaweng's busy road junction, is the chic place to be, with live folksy music and a relaxed mood.

The **dance** floor at the *Reggae Pub*, at the south end of Central Chaweng, is a sand pit, made for shuffling to the reggae standards on the chest-thumping sound system. This long-running institution (with a message board) is set to move to a bigger venue further back from the beach. More expensive but livelier is the *Green Mango* videotheque, inland from the *Jazz Bar*, which pumps out the MTV charts. Forget your cool if you make it to *Chicago* (B10), the all-dancing, all-*sanuk* Thai nightclub at the north end of Central Chaweng, which heaves at weekends to Thai pop mixed with a few American imports.

For the necessities, the *Black Cat* complex on the road parallel to the Chaweng shoreline has a **post office**, a **bank** (10am–12.30pm & 1.30–9pm), a **supermarket**, a **travel agent** and a big bookshop. The most established and reliable place for **scuba diving** is *Ko Samui Divers* (☎077/421465); based at the *Malibu Resort* towards the north end of Central Chaweng, it offers certified courses to inexperienced divers and trips for the qualified throughout the year.

Lamai

Samui's nightlife is most intense at messily over-developed **LAMAI**, which boasts the island's most sophisticated nightclub as well as dozens of open-air hostess bars, where the clientele sink buckets of booze slumped in front of boxing videos. Running roughly north to south for 4km, the white palm-fringed beach is still a picture, though it doesn't quite match Chaweng. At the northern end, the quiet spur of land which hooks eastward into the sea is perhaps the prettiest spot: it has more rocks than sand, but the shallow sea behind the coral reef is protected from the high seas of November, December and January.

A farang toytown of bars, restaurants and supermarkets has grown up behind the centre of the beach, packed cheek-by-jowl along the rutted back roads. The original village of BAN LAMAI, set well back at the northern end, remains aloof from these goings-on, and its wat contains a small museum of ceramics, agricultural tools and other everyday objects. Most visitors get more of a buzz from **Hin Yay** ("Grandmother Rock") and **Hin Ta** ("Grandfather Rock"), small rock formations on the bay's southern promontory, which never fail to raise a giggle with their resemblance to the male and female sexual organs. The Tourist Police (☎077/421436) have a branch opposite the slip road to the rocks. Currency can be exchanged there too, and by the main crossroads in central Lamai.

Accommodation

Lamai's **accommodation** is cheaper than Chaweng's, if not quite as good. At the northern end of the bay, the **cheap** bungalow villages on the tree-covered slopes of the headland include *Comfort*, a welcoming place in a pretty garden, where basic bungalows with showers and mosquito screens cost from B250. *Weekender Villa* is sandwiched between the main road and the beach just to the east of Ban Lamai, but is quiet nonetheless, except when it occasionally hosts a rave. The people are friendly and the large, well-equipped bungalows in an airy coconut grove cost B200. The far southern end of the bay towards the Grandparent Rocks has the best concentration of budget bungalows. The long-established and laid-back *White Sand* is very good value with plenty of beachside huts from B50. *Bungalow Bill* has slightly less primitive huts for B80–150, and does good, cheap food. Beyond the headland, the large *Swiss Chalets*, dotted over a sloping lawn, are fully furnished and would sleep three for B200.

On the central stretch of Lamai, the **upmarket** *Pavilion* is just far enough from the pubs and clubs to get some peace, and the atmosphere is friendly and lively with a good beachside pool and restaurant. Rooms start at B650, but if your purse will stretch that far, go for one of the huge thatched cottages at B1800.

Eating and nightlife

The best advice on **eating** is to head for the cheap Thai restaurants in Ban Lamai. Otherwise, try *Tempio* in amongst the beachside sprawl, a grand Italian restaurant which rolls its own good but pricey pasta. If you fancy a walk for your breakfast, *L'Auberge*, on the headland above *Comfort*, bakes excellent bread and croissants.

Lamai's **nightlife** is all within spitting distance of the tourist village's main crossroads. *Bauhaus* features off-centre reggae and cheapish drinks, while chart hits are the staple fare at the sweaty *Flamingo* disco. The best club on the island, though, is *Mix*, a huge psychedelic dovecot, with a big dance floor and plenty of outside tables. The DJs are flown in from England and drinks are expensive.

The south and west coasts

Lacking the long beaches of the more famous resorts, the **south and west coasts** rely on a few charming, isolated spots with peaceful bungalows, which can usually only be reached by renting a motorcycle. Heading south from Lamai, you come first to the Muslim fishing village at **BAN HUA THANON**: *Cosy Resort*, 1km south of the village has some attractive wooden bungalows from B100 in a big, grassy coconut grove, though the beach is nothing to write home about. Half a kilometre down the beach, the *Samui Orchid Resort* (☎077/272222) offers a touch of luxury at a good price: air-con rooms with hot-water bathrooms, set around two large swimming pools, start at B650.

The gentle but unspectacular coast beyond is lined with a good reef for snorkelling, which can be explored most easily from the fishing village of **BAN BANGKAO**. Snorkellers rave about the coral around **Ko Mad Sum**, 4km offshore: an all-day tour from Ban Bangkao, including fishing, snorkelling and lunch, will set you back B300 per person. About 5km inland, near Ban Thurian, the **Na Muang** falls make a popular outing as they're not far off the round-island road. The lower fall splashes and sprays down a twenty-metre wall of rock into a large bathing pool; the more spectacular, shaded cascade of the upper fall is reached by a 1500-metre path which begins 300m back along the road from the lower fall. Best place to stay hereabouts is *Diamond Villa*, 1km west of Ban Bangkao – it's a similar set-up to *Cosy*, with bungalows from B60 to B300.

At the base of the west coast, **AO PHANGKA** (Emerald Cove) is a pretty horseshoe bay, sheltered by the high headland which forms Samui's southwestern tip and by a coral reef which turns it into a placid paddling pool. The beach is poor but, like the whole of the west coast, gives fine views of the tiny offshore islands of Ko Si and Ko Ha with the sun setting over the larger Ang Thong archipelago behind. The best place to stay here is *Seagull* on the north shore of the bay, where the clean bungalows (B80–300, all with showers) are spread out on a flowery slope.

Further up the coast, the flat beaches are unexceptional but make a calm alternative when the northeast winds hit the other side of the island. *Cococabana*, 1500m south of the vehicle ferry pier at Thong Yang, has big thatched bungalows from B200 and a long stretch of beach to itself.

Ko Pha Ngan

In recent years backpackers have begun moving over to Ko Samui's little sibling, **KO PHA NGAN**, 20km to the north, but the island still has a simple atmosphere, mostly because the lousy road system is an impediment to the developers. With a dense jungle covering its inland mountains and rugged granite outcrops along the coast, Pha Ngan lacks the huge, gently sweeping beaches for which Samui is famous, but it does have plenty of coral to explore and some beautiful, sheltered bays: **Hat Khuat** on the north coast; **Thong Nai Pan** and half a dozen remote, virgin beaches on the east coast; and, on an isolated neck of land at the southeast corner, **Hat Rin**, a pilgrimage site for travellers. Most of Pha Ngan's development, however, has plonked itself along the less attractive south and west sides, linked by the only coastal roads on the island, which fan out from Thong Sala, the capital.

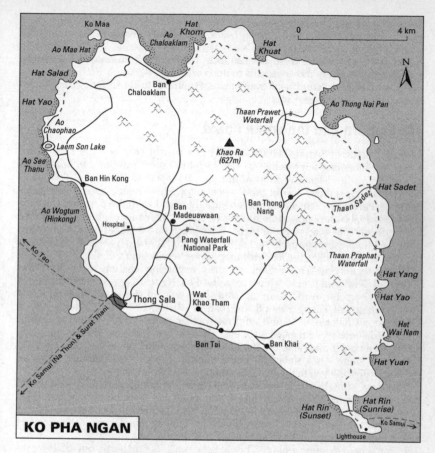

KO PHA NGAN

Pha Ngan's **bungalows**, like most of the buildings, are made of coconut tree trunks and bamboo, and most now have running water, electricity and a few creature comforts. The 150 or so resorts generally have more space to spread out than on Ko Samui and the cost of living is cheaper – the prices given below are standard for most of the year, but they tend to jump when times are busy, especially between December and February.

Getting to Ko Pha Ngan

The cheapest **ferry** from the Gulf coast leaves Ban Don pier in **Surat Thani** at 11pm every night for the ferry pier at Thong Sala (7hr; from B60); tickets for this and for the express boats from Tha Thong (see below) are handled by *Songserm Travel* in Surat Thani (see p.341). A vehicle ferry leaves once a day from **Don Sak**, 60km east of Surat (2hr 30min): a combination ticket including the bus trip to Don Sak, either from Phun Phin railway station (2hr) or from Surat (1hr), costs B95 – buy it in Surat Thani from *Ferry Pha Ngan* (☎077/286461), on Chonkasem Road near the corner of Ban Don Road.

From **Tha Thong**, two express boats a day run to Thong Sala (3hr 30min; B120) via **Ko Samui** (45min; B60). Small boats also shuttle between Samui and the eastern side of Pha Ngan (see p.342).

One boat a day comes **from Ko Tao** (3hr; B150), and from roughly November to May express boats also cover this route (1hr 30min; B200).

From Bangkok, coach and train packages similar to those for getting to Ko Samui are available (see p.341).

Thong Sala and the south coast

Like the capital of Samui, **THONG SALA** is a port of entrance and little more, where the incoming ferry is met by touts sent to escort travellers to bungalows elsewhere on the island. In front of the pier, transport to the rest of the island congregates by a dusty row of travel agents, travellers' restaurants, a supermarket and a currency exchange. If you go straight ahead from the pier, you can turn right onto Pha Ngan's only stretch of paved road, a leafy mix of shops and houses that's ghostly and wind-swept at night. Here you'll find a laundry, a scuba diving outfit and the best motorcycle rental places (from B150 a day) – and, 500m from the pier, the post office, the long-distance phone service and a clinic.

In the vicinity of Thong Sala, an easy excursion can be made to **Pang Waterfall National Park**, which contains Pha Ngan's biggest waterfall and a stunning viewpoint overlooking the south and west of the island. The park lies 4km northeast of Thong Sala off the road to Chaloaklam – if you don't have a bike, take a Chaloaklam-bound songthaew as far as Ban Madeuawaan, and then it's a one-kilometre signposted walk east. A small waterfall near the entrance has an artificial pool for bathing, but the main fall – bouncing down in stages over the hard, grey stone – is a steep 250-metre walk up a forest trail. Another 200m up the path will bring you to the fantastic mountaintop viewpoint.

The long, straight **south coast** is well-served by songthaews and motorcycle taxis from Thong Sala, and is lined with bungalows, especially around BAN KHAI, to take the overspill from nearby Hat Rin. It's hard to recommend staying here, however: the beaches are mediocre by Thai standards, and the coral reef which hugs the length of the shoreline gets in the way of swimming.

If you need to **stay** around Thong Sala, walk 800m north out of town to *Siriphun*. The owner is helpful, the food is good and the bungalows are clean and well-positioned along the beach; B100 gets you a shower and mosquito screens, B300 buys a bit of plush and one of the island's few bathtubs. Alternatively, *Charm Beach Resort*, a friendly place only 1500m south of Thong Sala, has bungalows from B50 and good Thai food. Worth mentioning among the handful of tourist **restaurants** in Thong Sala is *The Meeting Point*, at the only corner in the high street, which serves decent Thai food at reasonable prices and has a terrace overlooking the sea at the back. In the rash of shops by the pier, *Noodle* is a basic Thai café, doing curries on rice and noodle soup at only slightly inflated prices.

Hat Rin

HAT RIN has been getting quite a name for itself as a rave venue over the past few years, especially among British clubbers: the main season at the "new Ibiza" is from November to January, though just about every month people flock in for the Full Moon party – something like *Apocalypse Now* without the war. There's a more sedate side to Hat Rin's alternative scene too, with old and new age hippies packing out the t'ai chi, yoga and meditation classes, and helping consume the drugs that are readily available here. Drug-related horror stories are common currency round here, and many of them are true: "special" omelettes containing the local mushrooms called *hed khi kwai* now put an average of two farangs a month into the local hospital for psychiatric treatment.

Hat Rin occupies the neck of Pha Ngan's southeast headland, which is so narrow that the resort comprises two back-to-back beaches, joined by transverse roads at the north and south ends. The eastern beach, always referred to as **Sunrise**, is what originally drew visitors here and you can see why. It's a classical curve of fine white sand between two rocky slopes, where the swimming's good and there's even some coral at the southern end to explore. This is the centre of the action, with windsurfing and water-skiing, and beachside bars, restaurants and bungalows tucked under the palm trees. **Sunset** beach looks ordinary by comparison but has plenty of quieter accommodation. The flat neck between is crammed with small shops and businesses: there's a clinic, a post office, second-hand bookshops, travel agents, offices with expensive overseas phone and currency exchange facilities, even photo-developers and tattooists. A farang flea market meets at *Tommy's Resort* on Sunrise on Wednesday afternoons.

The awkwardness of **getting to Hat Rin** – it's an hour's walk to the nearest road – helps to maintain its individuality. The cheapest option from Thong Sala is to take one of the **longtail** boats which meet incoming ferries at the main pier. Alternatively, songthaews and motorcycle taxis run to the end of the south coast road at Ban Khai, where longtails are always waiting to take people to Hat Rin. When the tide is at its lowest, pick-ups run to Ban Khai then plunge across the sand into the shallow water to cover the last 4km – more fun for the driver than for the passengers. Finally, if the weather's good and there are enough passengers, one boat a day comes from Thong Nai Pan and Hat Sadet, on Pha Ngan's east coast, and four a day run from Ko Samui (see p.342).

Accommodation

Staying on **Sunrise** is often expensive and noisy, though a few places can be recommended. *Paradise* spreads itself over the far southern end and up the slope behind: simple huts are B60, B200 with a bathroom, and the restaurant does good food. *Had Rin*, three doors along, is as primitive and friendly as the resorts at Hat Rin get: sturdy old wooden bungalows go for B60, which might go up when electricity is put in. A twenty-minute walk from the back of *Paradise*, the last section along a wooden walkway over the rocky shoreline, brings you to *Lighthouse Bungalows*, a friendly haven where wooden bungalows, sturdily built to withstand the wind, start at B70 – and the food is varied and tasty. At the quieter northern end of Sunrise, *Seaview* has a big plot of land with B200 bungalows (bathrooms attached) giving onto the beach, and large B80 bungalows behind among the coconut palms. Prices are the same next door at *Palita* – though only the cheaper bungalows are a good deal – and the food gets rave reviews.

On **Sunset**, the twenty or more resorts are laid out in orderly rows, and are especially quiet and cheap between June and September. *Palm Beach* is typical of the bungalows here, but has a little more room as it spreads onto the tiny headland which marks the centre of the beach. Clean, sturdy wooden bungalows, most of them fronting the sand, start at B50. *Crystal Palace* to the north is clean and friendly, with very smart, tiled bungalows for B300, and a few shacks for

B100. Further north are a number of small places with basic huts from B50. High up on the tree-lined slope above the south end of Sunset, *Sea Breeze* has good food, great views and well-built bungalows for B50, or B150 with showers.

If you get to Hat Rin in the highest season and find all the bungalows full, your last chance is *Black Scene* on the southern transverse road, which keeps cheap tents and has a camping area.

Eating and nightlife

As well as good simple Thai fare at some of the bungalows, Hat Rin sports an unnerving choice of world **foods** for somewhere so remote. All-day breakfasts at the bakery behind the southern end of Sunrise are especially popular, and vegetarians are unusually well provided for in most places. Worth seeking out are *The Shell* on the southern transverse, for reasonably priced pasta, and the Indian food at *Namaste* on the northern transverse.

Casablanca on the northern transverse is the main **dancing** club, with a big covered area, a light show, and outside tables. On the southern transverse, *Sand Bar* is just a small wooden outdoor bar, but it pulls them in with the latest sounds. Down on Sunrise several music bars at the south end have tables on the beach, sometimes with videos inside, but the best of the action is entirely spontaneous – a beach party might break out at any time.

The east coast

North of Hat Rin, the rocky, exposed **east coast** stretches as far as Thong Nai Pan, the only centre of development. No roads run along this coast, only a rough, steep fifteen-kilometre trail, which starts from *Hillside Bungalows* on Hat Rin's northern transverse road and runs reasonably close to the shore, occasionally dipping down into pristine sandy coves.

Steep, desolate **HAT SADET**, 12km up the trail, has a couple of ramshackle bungalow operations, sited here because of their proximity to **Thaan Sadet**, a boulder-strewn brook which runs out into the sea here. The spot was popularised by various kings of Thailand who came here to walk, swim and vandalise the huge boulders by carving their initials on them. A path above and parallel to Thaan Sadet is being bulldozed into a rough road to connect with the main road from Thong Sala to Thong Nai Pan, which is a bumpy nightmare of a dirt track, winding its way for 12km over the steep mountains from Ban Tai on the south coast. Jeeps connect with incoming and outgoing boats at Thong Sala every day, but if there's heavy rain they don't chance it. The weather similarly affects the daily boat service from Thong Sala via Hat Rin.

THONG NAI PAN is a beautiful, semicircular bay backed by steep, green hills, which looks as if it's been bitten out of the island's northeast corner, leaving a tall hump of land dividing the bay into two parts. The southern half has the better sand and a hamlet which now sports a few farang bars and shops, though it's still peaceful enough; the northern half is very quiet, disturbed only by the little bit of surf which squeezes in. Both halves are sheltered and deep enough for good swimming.

Half a dozen resorts line the southern half of Thong Nai Pan, where the friendly *Nice Beach* has simple, standard bungalows from B60. At *Thong Tapan Resort* you pay B100 to have the northern beach to yourself. The beautiful setting on the steep slopes of the central outcrop has been monopolised by the

Panviman Resort, Ko Pha Ngan's only attempt at luxury accommodation. Comfortable huts are B250, rooms B600 and bungalows B800–1200, all with cold-water bathrooms. It's worth making the climb up here for the view from the restaurant perched over the cliff edge.

The north coast

The village at **CHALOAKLAM**, the largest bay on the **north coast**, has long been a famous R & R spot for fishermen from all over the Gulf of Thailand, with sometimes as many as a hundred trawlers at anchor in the broad and sheltered bay. Nowadays it is slowly being turned into a low-key tourist resort, as it can easily be reached from Thong Sala, 10km away, by songthaew or motorcycle taxi along the island's best road. Tourist facilities now include a travel agency, an international phone service and a scuba outfit – the best diving is at **Hat Khom**, a tiny cove dramatically tucked in under the headland to the east, with a secluded strip of sand and good coral. For **accommodation**, try *Fanta*, at the eastern end of Chaloaklam village, a homely and well-run place where bungalows are B50–100 and the food is good. Or walk out to *Coral Bay*, which perches on the promontory dividing Hat Khom from the rest of Chaloaklam, and has the beautiful cove all to itself: basic, flimsy bungalows are B40 and up.

The daily longtail boat from Chaloaklam is the best way of getting to secluded **HAT KHUAT** (Bottle Beach), the best of the beaches on the north coast. Sitting between steep hills in a perfect cup of a bay, Hat Khuat has accommodation at the friendly and helpful *Bottle Beach*, with smart beachfront bungalows from B100 and tightly-packed huts from B40, and at *Bottle Beach II*, where simple bungalows along the beach are B60 and the food is recommended.

On the island's northwest corner, the uninspiring beach at **MAE HAT**, which can be reached on a rented bike along the rough three-kilometre road from Chaloaklam, or by jeep from Thong Sala, might be worth taking in on a day trip for the coral which lines the sand causeway to Ko Maa. The beach also supports several decent bungalow resorts, including *Island View Cabana*, a lively place with a good restaurant, where posh bungalows start at B150.

The west coast

Pha Ngan's **west coast** has almost as much development as the south coast, though the landscape is nothing special and most of the sheltered bays are enclosed by reefs which keep the sea too shallow for swimming. From Thong Sala, motorcycle taxis drive safely as far as Seethanu, whereas jeeps and songthaews get right up to Hat Yao.

The first bay north of Thong Sala, **WOGTUM** (aka Hinkong), yawns wide across a featureless expanse which turns into a mudflat when the sea retreats behind the reef barrier at low tide. In a shady setting at the south end, you'll find *Kiet*, a quiet, family-run place with simple wooden huts for just B30. Beyond the headland, the nondescript bay of **Seethanu** can be recommended only for *Loy Fa*, a lively place which commands good views from its perch on top of the steep southern cape and has access to a tiny, secluded beach below; charges are B50 for a simple wooden bungalow, from B100 for a more comfortable one with bathroom.

Continuing north, there's a surprise in store in the shape of **Laem Son** lake, a beautiful, tranquil stretch of clear water cordoned by pines which spread down to the nearby beach. Under the shade of the pines, boisterous *Bovy Resort* has rudimentary thatched huts along the beach for B70 but all have their own basic bathrooms. Round the next headland, *Seaflower*, on the small bay of **CHAOPHAO**, has thatched bungalows from B40 and serves good food. The owner plays nonstop reggae, except when he's leading trips to Ang Thong National Marine Park (see p.343).

Beyond Chaophao, **Hat Yao** offers a long, gently curved beach and a non-stop line of decent bungalows. *Ibiza* is a good bet here: smart, airy bungalows in a spacious garden are B100 with clean bathrooms, B50 without. The only bay to the north of that, **HAT SALAD**, is probably the best of the bunch: it's pretty and quiet, and snorkelling off the northern tip is highly recommended. The only place to stay here, *My Way*, is a relaxing place for chilling out: primitive bamboo bungalows set in a colourful garden cost B30 – and the owner brings a boat down to Hat Yao every day to pick travellers up.

Ko Tao

KO TAO (Turtle Island) is so named because its outline resembles a turtle nose-diving towards Ko Pha Ngan, 40km to the south. The rugged shell of the turtle, to the east, is crenellated with secluded coves where one or two bungalows hide among the rocks. On the western side, the turtle's underbelly is a long curve of classic beach facing Ko Nang Yuan, a beautiful Y-shaped group of islands offshore. The twenty-one square kilometres of granite in between is topped by dense forest on the higher slopes and dotted with huge boulders that look as if they await some Easter Island sculptor. It's fun to spend a couple of days exploring the network of rough trails, after which you'll probably know all 750 of the island's inhabitants. Ko Tao is also a magnet for scuba divers, with several companies based at Mae Hat, the main village and arrival point: the coral beds and stacks around the island are the finest in the region, and the trip to Sail Rock, a spectacular coral chimney out towards Ko Pha Ngan, can also be arranged.

The island is the last and most remote of the archipelago which continues the line of Surat Thani's mountains into the sea. Because of the difficulties in getting there, life is still close to nature, with no sign of videos or nightclubs. There were thirty-five sets of **bungalows** at the latest count, concentrated along the west and south sides: most provide the bare minimum, with no electricity in the individual bungalows, plain mattresses for beds, and shared bathrooms. **Food** can be a little pricey because most of it is brought across on the ferry boats.

One road good enough for pick-ups runs from the southern beaches along the west coast, but you'll be **getting around** mostly on foot, unless you hitch a ride on one of the pick-ups or boats which congregate at Mae Hat to meet the ferries. If you're just **arriving** it might be a good idea to get picked up by a tout, since at least you'll know that his or her bungalows aren't full or closed – the former is possible in January, the latter from June to August.

The **weather** is much the same as on Pha Ngan and Samui, but being that bit further off the mainland, Ko Tao feels the effect of the southwest monsoon more: August can have strong winds and rain, with a lot of debris blown onto the windward coasts. The south coast is sheltered from the worst of both monsoons, but consequently is being developed into a crowded resort – give it a miss, as you might as well be on one of the larger islands.

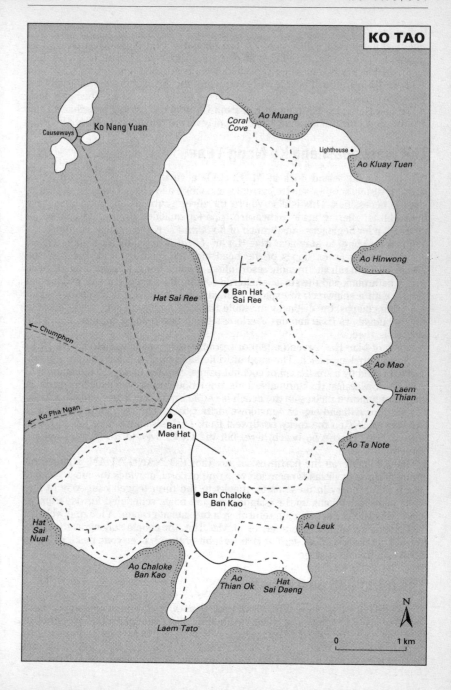

KO TAO

Ko Nang Yuan

Causeways

Coral
Cove

Ao Muang

Lighthouse

Ao Kluay Tuen

← Chumphon

Hat Sai Ree

Ban Hat
Sai Ree

Ao Hinwong

Ao Mao

Laem
Thian

← Ko Pha Ngan

Ban
Mae Hat

Ao Ta Note

Ban Chaloke
Ban Kao

Ao Leuk

Hat
Sai
Nual

Ao Chaloke
Ban Kao

Ao
Thian Ok

Hat
Sai Daeng

Laem Tato

N

0   1 km

Getting to Ko Tao

One boat a day makes the trip to Ko Tao **from Ko Pha Ngan** (3hr; B150), late enough for people who have taken an early morning boat from Surat or Samui to catch; the journey is sometimes cancelled if winds are too high.

From Chumphon, a boat leaves every night for the six-hour crossing (B200), but again departures are sometimes cancelled if the weather's bad. The boats dock at the Pak Nam pier 14km downriver from Chumphon: catch a songthaew from near the post office on Paramin Manda Road (every 10min during daylight hours).

The west coast and Ko Nang Yuan

All boats to the island dock at **MAE HAT**, a small, lively village with a few seafront restaurants, expensive currency exchange and postal facilities, as well as seaside necessities. This is also where the three scuba diving operations have their offices, offering made-to-measure trips for qualified divers and courses of instruction for beginners – the branch of *Ko Samui Divers* specialises in these.

For somewhere **to stay** near Mae Hat, try *Coral Beach*, which occupies a good position on the lower slopes of the headland, ten minutes' walk south of the village; the well-run and friendly resort offers reliable bungalows for B60, or B150 with a bathroom, and the small, sheltered beach offers excellent snorkelling and diving, with a shipwreck to explore. An easy two-kilometre walk further south will bring you past the distinctly missable *Saithong*, to *Siam Cookie* and *Char*; the sturdy bungalows (B50 and up) overlook a small beach and a coral reef, and the kitchen is good.

North of Mae Hat, beyond a blip of a promontory, you'll find **HAT SAI REE**, Ko Tao's only long beach. The strip of white sand stretches for 2km in a gentle curve, backed by a smattering of coconut palms. *Sai Ree Cottage*, a fifteen-minute walk from Mae Hat, has primitive huts from B50 and serves excellent grub. A couple of hundred metres up the beach is *O-Chai*, a friendly place with shacks by the sand for B40 and bigger bungalows further back. The road ends beyond Hat Sai Ree, at *CFT* on the rocky northwest flank of the island, where basic shacks start at B40. There's no beach here, but the views over to Ko Nang Yuan are something else.

One kilometre off the northwest of Ko Tao, **KO NANG YUAN**, a close-knit group of three tiny islands encircled by a ring of coral, provides the most spectacular beach scenery in these parts, thanks to the three-legged causeway of fine white sand which joins up the islands. Longtail boats scheduled for day-trippers leave Mae Hat in the morning, returning in the late afternoon. A longtail will also meet incoming and outgoing ferries at Mae Hat, for people staying at the *Nang Yuan* bungalows – prices start at B80 for a bit of thatch over your head, rising to B500 for a swanky cottage.

The north and east coasts

The sheltered inlets of the **north and east coasts**, few of them containing more than one set of bungalows, are best reached by boat, though each is served by at least one path through the forest. The snorkelling at **AO MUANG**, on the north side, is especially good. Out on its own here, *Coral Cove* has fine views and comfortable A-frame huts for B50, in the tiny cove at the western end of the bay.

In the middle of the east coast, the dramatic tiered promontory of **LAEM THIAN** shelters a tiny beach and a colourful reef on its south side. With the headland to itself, *Laem Thian* offers bungalows for B50 and has decent food. Laem Thian's coral reef stretches down as far as **Ta Note**, a craggy horseshoe bay with the best snorkelling just north of the bay's mouth. The better of the two resorts here is *Ta Note Bay Resort*, which has wooden bungalows from B50, and is well-equipped with snorkelling gear. The last bay carved out of the turtle's shell, **Ao Leuk**, has a white sandy beach fringed with palms and a handful of primitive huts from B30.

The **southeast corner** of the island sticks out in a long, thin mole of land, which shelters the sandy beach on one side if the wind's coming from the northeast, or the rocky cove on the other side if it's blowing from the southwest. *Kiet*, a popular, well-equipped place, straddles the headland and has primitive but colourfully decorated bungalows at B50.

Nakhon Si Thammarat

NAKHON SI THAMMARAT, the south's second largest town, occupies a blind spot in the eyes of most tourists, whose focus is fixed on Ko Samui, 100km to the north. Its neglect is unfortunate, for in its way Nakhon is as absorbing a place as Chiang Mai, although it doesn't have the accommodation and facilities to match. The south's major pilgrimage site, it's a relaxed, self-confident and sophisticated place, well-known for its excellent cuisine and traditional handicrafts – the stores on Thachang Road are especially good for local nielloware, household items elegantly patterned in gold or silver on black, and *yan lipao*, sturdy basketware made from intricately woven fern stems of different colours. Nakhon is also the only place in the country where you can see how Thai shadow plays work, at Suchart Subsin's workshop.

The town is recorded under the name of Ligor (or Lakhon), the capital of the kingdom of Lankasuka, as early as the second century, and classical dance-drama, *lakhon*, is supposed to have been developed here. Well-placed for trade with China and southern India, Nakhon was the point through which the Theravada form of Buddhism was imported from Sri Lanka and spread to Sukhothai, the capital of the new Thai state, in the thirteenth century.

Known as *muang phra*, the "city of monks", Nakhon is still the religious capital of the south, and the main centre for **festivals**. The most important of these are the **Tamboon Deuan Sip**, held during the waning of the moon in the tenth lunar month (either September or October), and the **Hae Pha Khun That** in the third lunar month (either February or March). The purpose of the former is to pay homage to dead relatives and friends. It is believed that during this fifteen-day period all *pret* – ancestors who have been damned to hell – are allowed out to visit the world, and so their relatives perform a merit-making ceremony in the temples, presenting offerings from the first harvest to ease their suffering. A huge ten-day fair takes place on Sanam Na Muang, the town field, at this time, as well as processions, shadow plays and other theatrical performances. The Hae Pha Khun That also attracts people from all over the south, to pay homage to the relics of the Buddha at Wat Mahathat. The ceremonial centrepiece of this festival is the Pha Phra Bot, a strip of yellow cloth many hundreds of metres long, which is carried in a spectacular procession around the chedi.

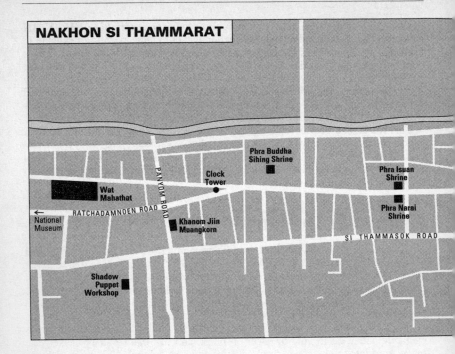

NAKHON SI THAMMARAT

Phra Buddha
Sihing Shrine

Clock
Tower

Phra Isuan
Shrine

PANYOM ROAD

Wat
Mahathat

Phra Narai
Shrine

RATCHADAMNOEN ROAD

← National
Museum

Khanom Jiin
Muangkorn

SI THAMMASOK ROAD

Shadow
Puppet
Workshop

The town

The **town plan** is simple, but puzzling at first sight: it runs in a straight line for
7km from north to south, paralleled by the jagged peaks of 1800-metre-high Khao
Luang to the west, and is never more than a few hundred metres wide, a layout
dictated by the availability of fresh water. The modern centre for businesses and
shops sits at the north end around the railway station. To the south, centred on
the elegant, traditional mosque on Karom Road, lies the old Muslim quarter,
where pictures of the Thai king take their place alongside the Ayatollah
Khomeini. South again is the start of the old city walls, of which a few crumbling
remains can be seen, and the historic centre, with the town's main places of interest now set in a leafy residential area.

Songthaews ply up and down Ratchadamnoen Road, which links the whole
length of the town, for B4 a ride.

Wat Mahathat

Missing out **Wat Mahathat** (daily 8.30am–4.30pm) would be like going to Rome
and not visiting St Peter's, for the Buddha relics in the vast chedi make this the
south's most important shrine.

Inside the temple cloisters, which have their main entrance facing
Ratchadamnoen Road about 2km south of the modern centre, the courtyard looks
like a surreal ornamental garden, with row upon row of smaller chedis, spiked like
bayonets, each surrounded by a box hedge in the shadow of the main chedi, the
Phra Boromathat. This huge, stubby Sri Lankan bell supports a slender, ringed

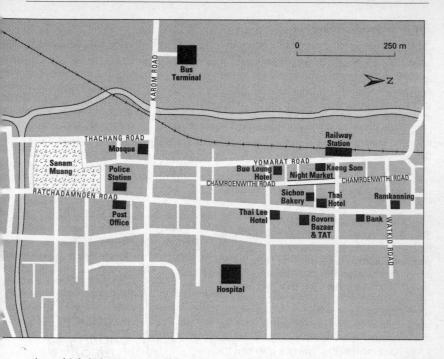

spire, which is in turn topped by a shiny pinnacle said to be covered in 600kg of gold leaf. According to the chronicles, relics of the Buddha were brought here from Sri Lanka 2000 years ago by an Indian prince and princess and enshrined in a chedi. It's undergone plenty of face-lifts since: an earlier Srivijayan version, a model of which stands at one corner, is encased in the present twelfth-century chedi. The most recent restoration work, funded by donations from all over Thailand, rescued it from collapse, although it still seems to be leaning danger-ously to the southeast. Worshippers head for the north side's vast enclosed stair-way, framed by lions and giants, which they liberally decorate with gold leaf to add to the shrine's radiance and gain some merit. In the left-hand shrine at the foot of the stairs here, look out for some fine stuccos of the life of the Buddha.

The **Viharn Kien Museum** (daily 8.30am–noon & 1–4.30pm), which extends north from the chedi, is an Aladdin's cave of bric-a-brac, said to house 50,000 arti-facts donated by worshippers, ranging from ships made out of seashells to gold and silver models of the Bodhi Tree. At the entrance to the museum, you'll pass the Phra Puay, an image of the Buddha giving a gesture of reassurance. Women pray to the image when they want to have children, and the lucky ones return to give thanks and to leave photos of their chubby progeny.

Outside the cloister to the south is the eighteenth-century **Viharn Luang**, raised on elegant slanting columns, a beautiful example of Ayutthayan architec-ture. The interior is austere at ground level, but the red coffered ceiling shines with carved and gilded stars and lotus blooms. Elsewhere in the spacious grounds, cheap and cheerful stalls peddle local handicrafts such as shadow puppets, bronze and basket ware.

The National Museum

South again from Wat Mahathat, the **National Museum** (daily 9am–4pm; B10), houses a small but diverse collection of artifacts from southern Thailand. In the prehistory room downstairs, two impressive ceremonial bronze kettle drums, topped with chunky frogs (local frogs are the biggest in Thailand and a prized delicacy), typify the culture around the fifth century BC. Next door are some interesting Hindu finds and many characteristic Buddha images made in imitation of the Phra Buddha Sihing at the city hall, the most revered image in southern Thailand. Amongst the collections of ceramics and household articles upstairs, you can't miss the seat panel of Rama V's barge, a dazzling example of the nielloware (*kruang tom*) for which Nakhon is famous – the delicate animals and landscapes have been etched onto a layer of gold which covers the silver base, and then picked out by inlaying a black alloy into the background.

The shadow puppet workshop

The best possible introduction to *nang thalung*, southern Thailand's **shadow puppet theatre**, is to head for 110/18 Soi 3, Si Thammasok Rd, ten minutes' walk east of Wat Mahathat: here Suchart Subsin, one of the south's leading exponents of *nang thalung*, has opened up his workshop to the public, and, if you ask, he'll show you a few scenes from a shadow play in the small open-air theatre. You can also see the intricate process of making the leather puppets and can buy the finished products as souvenirs: puppets sold here are of much better quality and design than those usually found on southern Thailand's souvenir stalls.

Nang Thalung puppet

Other shrines and temples

In the chapel of the City Hall on Ratchadamnoen Road sits the **Phra Buddha Sihing**, which according to legend was magically created in Sri Lanka in the second century. In the thirteenth century it was sent by ship to the King of Sukhothai, but the vessel sank and the image miraculously floated on a plank to Nakhon. Two other images, one in the National Museum in Bangkok, one in Wat Phra Singh in Chiang Mai, claim to be the authentic Phra Buddha Sihing, but none of the three is in the Sri Lankan style, so they are all probably derived from a lost original. Although similar to the other two in size and shape, the image in Nakhon has a style unique to this area, distinguished by the heavily pleated flap of its robe over the left shoulder, a beaky nose and harsh features, which sit uneasily on the short, chubby body. The image's plumpness has given the style the name *khanom tom* – "banana and rice pudding".

You're bound to pass the small, red-roofed Hindu shrines of **Phra Isuan** and **Phra Narai** on Ratchadamnoen Road, legacies of Nakhon's ancient commercial links with India. The former – which is usually open to the public – houses a *lingam*, a phallic representation of Shiva worshipped by women who want to

SHADOW PUPPETS

Found throughout southern Asia, **shadow puppets** are one of the oldest forms of theatre, featuring in Buddhist literature as early as 400BC. The art form seems to have come from India, via Java, to Thailand, where it's called *nang*, meaning "hide": the puppets are made from the skins of water buffaloes or cows, which are softened in water then pounded until almost transparent, before being carved and coloured to represent the characters of the play. The puppets are then manipulated on sticks in front of a bright light, to project their image onto a large white screen, while the story is narrated to the audience.

The grander version of the art, **nang yai** – "big hide", so-called because the figures are life-size – deals only with the *Ramayana* story. It's known to have been part of the entertainment at official ceremonies in the Ayutthayan period, but has now almost died out. The more populist version, **nang thalung** – *thalung* is probably a shortening of the town name, Phatthalung – is also in decline now: performances are generally limited to temple festivals, marriages and ordinations, lasting usually from 9pm to dawn. As well as working the two-feet-high *nang thalung* puppets, the puppet master narrates the story, impersonates the characters, chants and cracks jokes to the accompaniment of flutes, fiddles and percussion instruments. Not surprisingly, in view of this virtuoso semi-improvised display, puppet-masters are esteemed as possessed geniuses by their public.

At big festivals, companies often perform the *Ramayana*, sometimes in competition with each other; at smaller events they put on more down-to-earth stories, with stock characters such as the jokers Yor Thong, an angry man with a pot belly and a sword, and Kaew Kop, a man with a frog's head. Yogi, a wizard and teacher, is thought to protect the puppet master and his company from evil spirits with his magic, so he is always the first puppet on at the beginning of every performance.

In an attempt to halt their decline as a form of popular entertainment, the puppet companies are now incorporating modern instruments and characters in modern dress into their shows, and are boosting the love element in their stories. They're fighting a battle they can't win against television and cinemas, although at least the debt owed to shadow puppets has been acknowledged – *nang* has become the Thai word for "movie".

conceive, and in its grounds there's a ritual swing, a smaller version of the Sao Ching Cha at Wat Suthat in Bangkok. The Brahmin community based at these shrines supplies astrologers to the royal court and priests for the Ploughing Ceremony, held every May in Bangkok.

Practicalities

TAT have a very helpful office in the Bovorn Bazaar on Ratchadamnoen Road (daily 8.30am–4.30pm), which is due to move to a permanent home on Thachang Road soon. Though most of Nakhon's limited number of **hotels** are dingy and soulless, there are enough exceptions to get by. For cheap accommodation, the *Thai Lee Hotel* at 1130 Ratchadamnoen Rd (☎075/356948) is a good deal: smart, clean rooms start at B80 single and B120 double (B200/B240 with a/c). The central but quiet *Bue Loung Hotel*, at 1487/19 Soi Luang Muang, Chamroenwithi Rd (☎075/341518), gets the thumbs-up from visiting businessmen, with single rooms with showers at B120, doubles B180 (B200/B260 with a/c). Top of the range is the *Thai Hotel*, 1375 Ratchadamnoen Rd (☎075/356505), a large institutional tower block, with clean, reliable rooms for B200 (B412 with a/c).

Nakhon is a great place for cheap **food**. Most famous, and justifiably so, is *Khanom Jiin Muangkorn* (7am–3.30pm) on Panyom Road near Wat Mahathat: the rough-and-ready outdoor restaurant dishes up one of the local specialities, *khanom jiin*, noodles topped with hot, sweet or fishy sauce, and served with *pak ruam*, a platter of crispy raw vegetables. Also very cheap is *Krua Nakhon* (7am–3pm) in the Bovorn Bazaar on Ratchadamnoen Road, a big, rustic pavilion which offers good *khanom jiin* and other local dishes: *kaeng som*, a mild yellow curry, *kaeng tai plaa*, fish stomach curry, and various *khanom wan*, coconut milk puddings. The *Sichon Bakery*, opposite the *Thai Hotel*, does decent foreign breakfasts.

In the evening, the busy market on Chamroenwithi Road near the *Bue Loung Hotel* is great for cheap food and watching the world go by. In the old Muslim quarter, many stalls near the corner of Karom and Yomarat roads sell good Muslim food, such as *roti* (sweet pancake) and chicken with curried rice. *Kaeng Som* (aka *The Yellow Curry House*), at 1465 Yomarat Rd by the railway station, has a wide menu of interesting Thai dishes, especially seafood, and a relaxing, bistro atmosphere. On the corner of Watkid and Ratchadamnoen roads, *Ramkanning* is one of many cheap and popular restaurants with pavement tables in the area.

travel details

Trains
From Bangkok to Nakhon Si Thammarat (2 daily; 15hr); Surat Thani (8 daily; 11hr).

From Cha-am to Bangkok (8 daily; 3hr 10min–3hr 40min); Hua Hin (8 daily; 25min); Surat Thani (7 daily; 7hr 10min–8hr 25min) via Chumphon (4hr 10min–4hr 55min).

From Chumphon to Bangkok (8 daily; 7hr 30min–8hr); Surat Thani (7 daily; 3–4hr).

From Hua Hin to Bangkok (8 daily; 3hr 35min–4hr 5min); Surat Thani (7 daily; 6hr 45min–8hr) via Chumphon (3hr 45min–4hr 30min).

From Phetchaburi to Bangkok (8 daily; 2hr 45min–3hr 15min); Hua Hin (8 daily; 40min) via Cha-am (20min); Surat Thani (7 daily; 7hr 30min–8hr 45min) via Chumphon (4hr 30min–5hr 15min).

Buses
From Bangkok to Nakhon Si Thammarat (12 daily; 12hr); Surat Thani (11 daily; 12hr).

From Cha-am to Bangkok (every 30min; 2hr 45min–3hr 15min); Chumphon (every 2hr; 4hr 10min–5hr 10min); Hua Hin (every 30min; 40min).

From Chumphon to Bangkok (6 daily; 7hr); Ranong (hourly; 2hr).

From Hua Hin to Bangkok (every 30min; 3hr 15min–3hr 45min); Chumphon (about every 2hr; 3hr 30min–4hr 30min).

From Nakhon Si Thammarat to Hat Yai (12 daily; 3hr); Phuket (7 daily; 7hr); Trang (4 daily; 3hr); Surat Thani (every 30min; 3hr); Phatthalung (every 30min; 3hr); Songkhla (13 daily; 3hr).

From Phetchaburi to Bangkok (every 20min; 2hr–2hr 30min); Chumphon (about every 2hr; 5hr–6hr); Hua Hin (1hr 30min) via Cha-am (50min).

From Surat Thani to Chaiya (hourly; 1hr); Chumphon (every 30min; 3–4hr); Hat Yai (5 daily; 5hr); Krabi (16 daily; 4hr–4hr 30min); Phuket (10 daily; 6hr); Phunphin (every 10min; 30min); Trang (1 daily; 3hr).

Ferries
From Bangkok to Ko Samui (2 weekly; 16hr).

From Chumphon to Ko Tao (1 daily; 6hr).

From Don Sak to Ko Samui (5 daily; 1hr 30min); Ko Pha Ngan (1 daily; 2hr 30min).

From Surat Thani to Ko Samui (1 daily; 6hr); Ko Pha Ngan (1 daily; 7hr).

From Tha Thong to Ko Samui (2–3 daily; 2hr 30min); Ko Pha Ngan (2 daily; 3hr 30min).

Flights
From Bangkok to Ko Samui (5 daily; 1hr 10min).

From Phuket to Ko Samui (1 daily; 40min).

CHAPTER SEVEN

SOUTHERN THAILAND: THE ANDAMAN COAST

s Highway 4 switches from the east flank of the Thailand peninsula to the **Andaman Coast** it enters a markedly different country: nourished by rain nearly all the year round, the vegetation down here is lushly tropical, with forests of trees of up to eighty metres high, and massive rubber and coconut plantations replacing the mundane rice and sugar-cane fields of central Thailand. In this region's heartland the drama of the landscape is enhanced by sheer limestone crags, topographical hallmarks that spike every horizon and make for stunning views from the road. Even more spectacular – and the main crowd-puller – is the Andaman Sea itself: translucent turquoise and in some place so clear that you can see to a depth of thirty metres, it harbours the country's largest **coral reefs** and is far and away the top diving area in Thailand. Unlike the Gulf coast, the Andaman coast is hit by the southwest monsoon, which brings rain and high seas from May to October, rendering some of the islands inaccessible, but generally not so bad as to ruin a beach holiday closer to the mainland – there you'll have only the occasional cloudburst to contend with, and that's offset by the advantages of notably cheaper and less crowded accommodation.

Eager to reach the high-profile beaches of Phuket and Krabi, most people either fly over the first 300-kilometre stretch of the west coast or pass through it on an overnight bus, thereby missing out on the lushly forested hills of **Ranong** province and bypassing three gems: the **Ko Surin** and **Ko Similan** island-chains – whose reefs rate alongside the Maldives and the Great Barrier Reef – and the rarely visited **Khao Sok National Park**, where you can stay in a treehouse beneath the shadows of looming limestone outcrops. Tourism begins in earnest on **Ko Phuket**, one of Thailand's biggest resort islands and the best place in Thailand to learn to dive. The high-rises and consumerist gloss of Phuket don't appeal to everyone however, and many travellers opt instead for the less mainstream but very popular beaches around the former fishing village of **Krabi**. Nearby **Ko Phi Phi** attracts a lot of attention considering its size, yet the island's natural beauty remains pretty much intact both on land and underwater. Solitude seekers have moved on again, searching out hideaways on **Ko Lanta** and bringing custom to the tiny retreats of **Ko Jum** and **Ko Bubu**.

Getting to Andaman coast destinations is made easy by Highway 4, also known as the Phetkasem Highway – and usually called Phetkasem Road when it passes through towns. The road runs from Bangkok to the Malaysian border, and frequent air-con and ordinary **buses** ply this route, connecting all major – and most minor – mainland tourist destinations). **Ferries** to the most popular islands

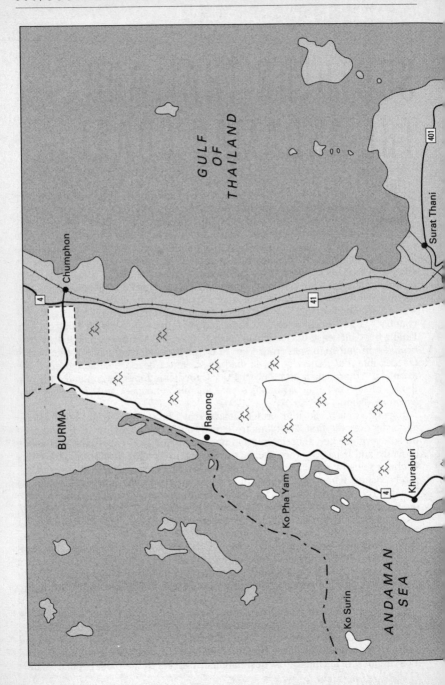

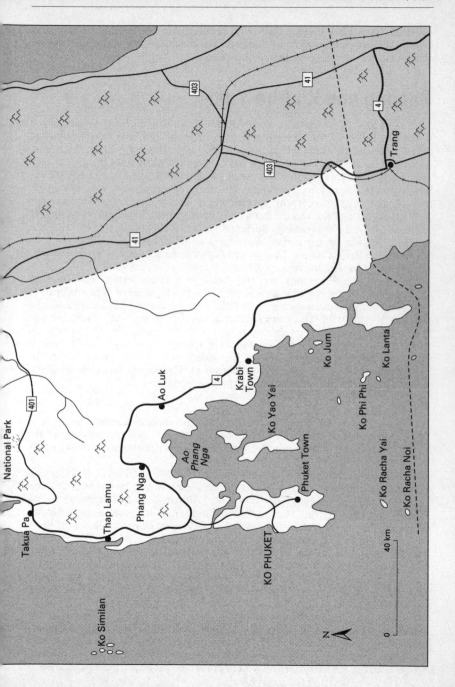

usually leave several times a day (with reduced services during the monsoon season), but for more remote destinations you may have to charter your own or wait for islanders' trading boats to pick you up.

Ranong and Ko Pha Yam

Highway 4 hits the Andaman coast at KRABURI, where a signpost welcomes you to the **Kra Isthmus**, the narrowest part of peninsular Thailand. At this point just 22km separates the Gulf of Thailand from the inlet where the River Chan flows into the Andaman Sea, west of which lies the southernmost tip of Burma. Seventy kilometres south this channel widens out at the small port town of **RANONG**, which thrives – not entirely legitimately – on its proximity to Thailand's neighbour. A black-market economy specialising in timber flourishes alongside the legal import businesses, and the town occasionally makes headlines when its fishing fleet gets caught poaching Burmese waters. Rumours of racketeering are frequent too, but on the surface Ranong is an unexceptional trading town, its population of Thais, Chinese, Malays and Burmese supplemented by tourists who come here for the health-giving properties of the local spring water.

The **geothermal springs** are the focus of a small leisure park just off Phetkasem Road, ten minutes' walk north of the bus terminal or 1km southeast of the town centre – take songthaew #2 (B5) from the central Ruangrat Road or a motorcycle taxi (B10). You can't submerge yourself in the water here, but you can buy eggs to boil in the sulphurous 65°C water, or paddle in the cooler pools that have been siphoned off from the main springs. Picnickers throng here at weekends, but to properly appreciate the springs you need to soak in them: the *Jansom Thara Hotel*, five minutes' walk away on Phetkasem Road, channels the mineral waters into its public bath (B50 for non-guests).

Practicalities

All **buses** from Bangkok to Phuket or Krabi pass through Ranong, stopping at the bus terminal on Highway 4 (Phetkasem Road), 1500m southeast of the centre; a few buses continue on into the tiny nucleus of the town, clustered on each side of Ruangrat Road.

The *Jansom Thara Hotel* at 2/10 Phetkasem Rd (☎077/811511), is the town's best **accommodation**, offering mineral baths and jacuzzis; rooms start at B600, rising to B3000 for a suite. It also has a *Thai Airways* desk and organises thrice-weekly day trips to the Surin islands during the dry season (see below). Otherwise you are limited to the rash of Thai-Chinese places on Ruangrat Road, which are cheap if not particularly cheerful. First choice is *Asia Hotel* (☎077/811113) at 39/9 Ruangrat Road (the southern end): clean and friendly, it has rather dark rooms with fan and shower from B120. Heading northwards up the road, there's *Sin Thawi Hotel* at 81/1 Ruangrat Rd (☎077/811213), with rooms from B150, and then *Rattanasin Hotel* (☎077/811242) at no. 226, at B100. Avoid the superficially plush but cockroach-ridden *Sin Ranong Hotel* at no. 26/23–24.

Ranong's ethnic diversity ensures an ample range of **eating** options, from the Muslim restaurant just south of the *Rattanasin Hotel* to the string of Chinese pastry shops on Ruangrat Road. The seafood restaurant opposite the Kamlangsap/Ruangrat intersection serves up the day's local catch, while at the 24-hour market across from the *Sin Ranong Hotel*, you're guaranteed at least a plate of *khao pat* or a bowl of *kwetiaw nam* day or night. In the evenings, the outdoor bar squashed in between *Sin Ranong* and the petrol station opens up for drinks and snacks.

Ko Pha Yam

For travellers Ranong is of interest chiefly as the departure point for the beaches and coral reefs of **KO PHA YAM**, a small island whose few inhabitants make a tenuous living by growing cashew nuts. At the time of writing there was only one set of bungalows here, so rarely visited that it was in danger of going out of business; check with Mr Tawon, usually found hanging around the lobby of *Sin Ranong Hotel*, to see if it's still operating. If it's not, you could still camp, but take fresh water and food.

Boats to the island go from SAPHAN PLA, 8km west of Ranong: songthaews between Ruangrat Road and Saphan Pla run regularly throughout the day. Boats can be chartered for about B1500 each way, but the cheaper alternative is to get a ride on the thrice-weekly supply boats – again, Mr Tawon will know the latest. The boat ride takes about an hour and costs around B30.

Ko Surin

Sticking close to the coast, but just out of sight of it, Highway 4 speeds southwards from Ranong between lushly forested hills to the east and a strip of mangrove swamps, rubber plantations and casuarina groves to the west – preserved as LAEM SON NATIONAL PARK. One hundred and ten kilometres south of Ranong, it reaches the coastal town of KHURABURI, the main departure point for the national park of **KO SURIN**, a group of five small islands surrounded by spectacular shallow reefs which offer some of the best snorkelling on this coast.

The best and most easily explored reefs lie off the coasts of the two main islands in the group, Ko Surin Nua (north) and Ko Surin Tai (south), which are separated only by a narrow channel. **SURIN NUA**, slightly the larger at about 5km across, holds the national park headquarters, visitors' centre and park bungalows on its southwest coast. The water is so clear here, and the reefs so close to the surface, that you can make out a forest of sea anemones while sitting in a boat just ten metres from the park headquarters' beach. Visibility off the east and west coasts of both islands stretches to a depth of forty metres.

Across the channel, **SURIN TAI** is the site of the official camping ground and the long-established home of a community of *chao ley* (see p.384). Every April, around the time of the Thai new-year festival of Songkhran, hundreds of *chao ley* from nearby islands (including those in Burmese waters) congregate here to celebrate their new year with a ceremony which involves, among other rites, the release of several hundred turtles into the sea.

Practicalities

Of the few regular **boat services** to Ko Surin, the day-trip packages from **Ranong**'s *Jansom Thara Hotel* (see above) are probably the most reliable; they leave at 7am every Friday, Saturday and Sunday, take three hours each way, give you about five hours on the islands, and cost B950 return. If you want to stay over on the islands, you should be able to negotiate a return trip on another day. Some companies in **Phuket** run occasional boats from Patong and Rawai beaches, and several of the diving centres organise excursions from there too.

Alternatively, you could join one of the tourist boats that make day trips to the islands on weekends and holidays from **Ban Hin Lat** pier, 1km west of Highway 4 as it passes through Khuraburi; these take three to four hours and cost about B500 return. It's also possible to charter your own fishing boat from Ban Hin Lat for around B2000 a day (journey time 4–5hr): unless you speak fluent Thai the best way to arrange this is either by calling the provincial governor's office (☎076/411140) or by going to the national park office on Ban Hin Lat pier. If you're stuck in this area waiting for a boat you can put up at the *Hin Lat Port View Hotel* which overlooks Highway 4 at the head of the road leading to the pier and has basic rooms from B100.

For **accommodation** on the islands you have the choice of renting one of the expensive six-person national park bungalows on Surin Nua for B500 (deals for couples may be negotiable) or opting for a B60 two-person tent in the campground on the northeast coast of Surin Tai. Otherwise, you can camp in your own tent anywhere on the islands for B5 per night per person.

Khao Sok National Park

South from Khuraburi, Highway 4 reaches the junction town of TAKUA PA after 40km. Highway 401, which cuts east from here, is the route taken by all Surat Thani-bound buses from Phuket and Krabi, and it's a spectacular journey across the mountains that stretch the length of the peninsula, a landscape of limestone crags and jungle, scarred only by the single, and at times perilous, road. Most of what you see belongs to **KHAO SOK NATIONAL PARK**, a tiny part of which – entered 40km from Takua Pa – is set aside for overnight visitors. Few visitors to south Thailand consider even briefly foregoing the delights of the coast, but Khao Sok definitely merits a couple of land-based days: waking up to the sound of hooting gibbons and the sight of thick white mist curling around the dramatic karst formations is an experience not quickly forgotten.

Practicalities

The park entrance is less than an hour by **bus** from Takua Pa or two hours from Surat Thani. Buses run every ninety minutes or so in both directions; ask to be let off at the park and chances are there'll be someone from one of the park's bungalow outfits waiting to meet the bus and give you a free lift to the park headquarters and accommodation area, 3km away.

The grimly functional national park bungalows (B500) are supplemented by three much more pleasant **accommodation** possibilities, all within easy walking distance of each other, the park headquarters and trail heads, yet each managing to feel quite isolated. *Treetops* (☎02/233 0196) is the most exclusive and caters primarily to tour groups pre-booked from abroad, so their B300 riverside huts may be full up. You should have no problem getting into the other two though, as few travellers break their journey here. *Art's Jungle House*, dramatically located in the shadow of a huge karst formation, has huts for B150 but the real attractions are the two so-called treehouses, large wooden huts built on seven-metre stilts overlooking the river, which are a real bargain at B300. The food is good as well, and there's plenty of information on getting around the park. Simplest but friendliest of the three, *Bamboo House* stands fifteen minutes' walk from *Art's* in a similarly scenic location beside the river. It's run by the family of the park warden, who proffer endless quantities of food, jokes and information. Bungalows here cost B100–200, plus B100 per person for three generous and delicious meals.

The park

Two well-defined **trails** radiate from the park headquarters and visitors' centre; they are marked by blank wooden signposts and the centre has photocopied maps, though they are not exactly a model of accuracy. Both trails follow the course of the stream that flows through the park and take you past beautiful waterfalls and pools through forests of thirty-metre-high bamboos rife with gibbons, gekkoes and frogs. The more energetic hike is the one to **Ton Sai** waterfall, which is over 10km each way and gets quite rugged towards the end, from where the only route back involves retracing your steps.

Longer and less well-tramped forays into the jungle interior can be arranged through your accommodation, for which you'll need a guide (B100 per person per day); if you want to make it a two- or three-day trek, they'll loan you a tent. These itineraries usually take in the park's eleven-tiered waterfall, several bathing pools and a couple of stalactite caves, and possibly a **night safari**, when you might be lucky enough to see some of the park's rarer inhabitants, like elephants, pony-sized black and white tapirs, tigers and clouded leopards. A northwestward trek will eventually get you to Rajaphraba lake, 40km from the headquarters, surrounded by crags and home to a number of fishing families; a shorter hike northeast from the central park area runs to an enormous bat cave.

Ko Similan

The only place of note between Takua Pa and Phuket is THAP LAMU, 30km south of Takua Pa, the mainland harbour closest to the diving and snorkelling destination of Ko Similan, 40km offshore. Even if you're not going to Ko Similan, you should think about stopping here for the *Poseidon Bungalows*, which are superbly located on a wild and rocky shore with jungle and rubber plantations in the background. The bungalows range from B60 to B200 (closed May–Oct), and the owners organise budget trips to the islands too.

Rated by *Skin Diver* magazine as one of the world's top ten spots for both above-water and underwater beauty, the nine islands that make up **KO SIMILAN** are perhaps the most exciting **diving** destination in Thailand. Massive granite boulders set magnificently against turquoise waters give the islands their distinctive character, but it's the thirty-metre visibility that draws the flipper brigade. The underwater scenery is nothing short of overwhelming here. The reefs teem with a host of coral fish, from the long-nosed butterfly fish to the black-, yellow- and white-striped angel fish, and the ubiquitous purple and turquoise parrot fish, which nibble so incessantly at the coral that they are held responsible for much of the fine white sand that rings the Similans. A little further off shore, magnificent mauve and burgundy crown-of-thorns starfish stalk the sea-bed, gobbling chunks of coral as they go – and out here you'll also see turtles, manta rays, moray eels, red grouper and quite possibly white-tip sharks, barracuda and enormous tuna.

As well as suffering from indigenous predators, the Similan reefs also attract idiots who lob home-made bottle bombs to kill the fish and break off the coral for sale as souvenirs. To date though, the damage to the reefs has been limited and, thanks to their relative inaccessibility and national park protection, the islands themselves – except for the two which are inhabited – remain almost undisturbed by tourism.

Practicalities

Getting to the Similans independently can be a lengthy business, involving waiting around at **Thap Lamu pier** (accessible by motorcycle taxi from the bus stop) for a supply boat or an already chartered boat on which you can beg a lift. Chartering your own fishing boat will cost about B11,000 for three days.

There is, however, a fair choice of **organised trips** to the Similans. The informal and well-run **three-day trips** organised by *Poseidon Bungalows* (see above) cost B1600 and include food, hut accommodation and several shuttles between the islands – there's no other inter-island transport. Alternatively, you can join the twice-weekly **day trips** operated by *Songserm* **from Phuket**. Their express boat does the journey in three hours, and the B1500 package deal includes lunch and snorkelling gear, but leaves you with only a few hours to explore the phenomenal underwater scenery. If you want to stay on the Similans and be picked up on their next trip, you should be able to negotiate a one-way ticket for B500. **Divers** should go with one of the dive operators from Phuket; a five-day diving expedition including all equipment, food and accommodation costs about B11,000.

As for accommodation on the islands, Ko Similan hosts the national park headquarters and a few dormitory **huts** (B50 per person), while Ko Miang offers several **bungalows** (B200), tent accommodation (B60 a double) and a restaurant. As these islands aren't really a destination for the independent traveller, it's unlikely that you'll stray from Ko Miang without the support of a well-equipped guide, but should you decide to go it alone come well-prepared as there's no drinking water available outside Ko Miang and campfires are prohibited on all the islands.

KO PHUKET

Thailand's largest island and a province in its own right, **Ko Phuket** has been a well-off region since the last century, when Chinese merchants got in on its tin-mining and sea-borne trade, before turning to the rubber industry. Phuket remains the wealthiest province, with the highest per capita income in Thailand, but what mints the money nowadays is **tourism**: with an annual influx that tops one million, Ko Phuket ranks second in popularity only to Pattaya, and the package-tour traffic has wrought its usual transformations. Thoughtless tourist developments have scarred much of the island, particularly along the west coast, and the trend on all the beaches is upmarket, with very few budget possibilities. As mainstream resorts go, however, those on Phuket are just about the best in Thailand, offering a huge range of **water sports** and magnificent **diving** facilities to make the most of the clear and sparkling sea. Remoter parts of the island are still attractive too, particularly the interior: a fertile, hilly expanse dominated by rubber and pineapple plantations and interspersed with wild tropical vegetation.

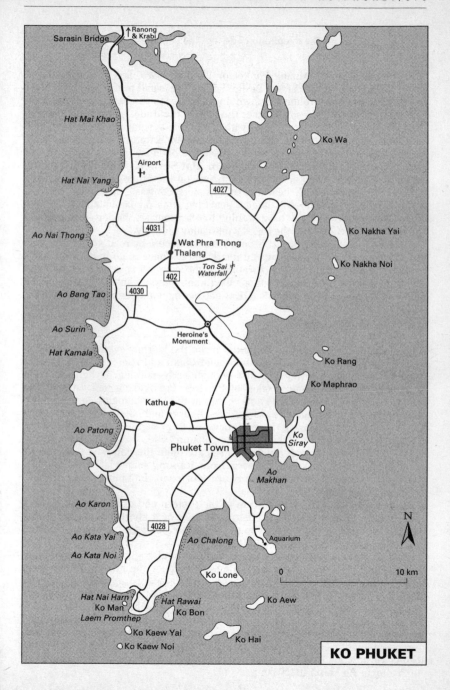

KO PHUKET

The **telephone code** for Phuket is ☎076.

Ko Phuket's capital, Muang Phuket or **Phuket town**, lies on the southeast coast, 42km south of the Sarasin Bridge linking the island to the mainland. Most people pass straight through the town on their way to the beaches on the **west coast**, where three big resorts corner the bulk of the trade: highrise **Ao Patong**, the most developed and expensive, with a nightlife verging on the seedy; similarly unappealing **Ao Karon**; and neighbouring **Ao Kata**, the quietest and least spoilt. Most of the other west-coast beaches have been taken over by one or two upmarket hotels, specifically **Hat Nai Harn**, **Hat Surin** and **Hat Bang Tao**; the northerly **Hat Nai Yang** and **Hat Mai Khao**, on the other hand, are relatively untarnished national park beaches. In complete contrast, the south and east coasts hold one of Thailand's largest seafaring *chao ley* communities, but the beaches along these shores have nothing to offer tourists, having been polluted and generally disfigured by the island's tin-mining industry.

Although the best west-coast beaches are connected by road, to get from one beach to another by **songthaew** you nearly always have to go back into Phuket town; songthaews run regularly throughout the day and cost between B10 and B20 from town to the coast. For those who want complete independence, all the main resorts rent out **motorbikes** (B150–250 per day) and **jeeps** (B700–1000).

Getting to the island

All direct **air-con buses** from **Bangkok** make the journey overnight, leaving at approximately half-hourly intervals between 5.30pm and 7pm and arriving about fourteen hours later, giving you just enough early-morning daylight hours to appreciate the most scenic section of the trip. Pre-booking at least a day in advance is essential, and can be done either at the bus station or, for a commission, through booking agents in some guest houses and hotels. Unless you get a kick out of hard seats, taking the **ordinary bus** from Bangkok only makes sense if you're desperate to see all the intervening countryside.

From more **local towns**, ordinary buses are often the only way to get to Ko Phuket: eight buses make the daily trip **from Ranong** (6hr) via Takua Pa (3hr); hourly buses connect the island with **Krabi** (4hr); and eight buses make the journey from **Surat Thani** (6hr).

All buses arrive at the **bus station** at the eastern end of Phang Nga Road in Phuket town, from where it's a ten-minute walk or a short tuk-tuk ride to the central hotel area, slightly further to the departure point for the beaches in front of the fruit and vegetable market on Ranong Road.

Thai Airways operates up to thirteen **flights** from Bangkok (1hr 15min) every day, though at B2000 a throw that's almost five times the price of the plushest bus. For similar rates, *Thai Airways* also connects the island with Chiang Mai (B3775), Hat Yai (B780), Nakhon Si Thammarat (B690), Surat Thani (B475) and Trang (B435), and *Bangkok Airways* does two daily runs between Ko Phuket and Ko Samui (B600). *Thai Airways* runs a coach service between the **airport** and the town (B50), 32km to the southwest – more reliable than the cheap but very infrequent songthaews. The only way of getting directly from the airport to the west-coast beaches is to take a taxi (about B350), or air-conditioned minivan to Ao Patong or Ao Karon (B150 per person).

DIVING CENTRES

Phuket is one of Thailand's two main diving areas, and the following **diving centres** offer PADI and/or NAUI certified diving courses, rent out equipment, and organise diving excursions to Ko Phi Phi, Shark Point, Ko Surin and Ko Similan. Average costs are from B1650 for a one-day introductory course and B8000 for a five-day open-water course, including equipment. Dive centres usually hire out masks and fins to snorkellers, who are often welcome on dive trips at a reduced rate, as are non-swimmers.

Ao Patong

Fantasea Dives Next to the *Holiday Inn* at the southern end of Patong (☎321309).

Ocean Divers At the *Patong Beach Hotel*, south of Soi Bangla (☎321166).

Phuket International Diving Centre (PIDC) At the *Coral Beach Hotel*, southern end of Patong (☎321106).

South East Asia 89/71 Thavee Wong Rd (☎321292).

Ao Karon

Marina Divers Next to *Marina Cottages* on the headland between Ao Karon and Ao Kata (☎212901).

Siam Diving Centre Opposite *Marina Divers* (☎381608).

Phuket International Diving Centre At the *Le Meridien Hotel*, located at the far northern end of Ao Karon (☎321480).

Phuket town

Phuket Aquatic Safari 62/9 Rasda Centre, Rasda Rd (☎216562).

Phuket Divers 7/70 Poonpon Road (☎215738).

Phuket Town

Though it has plentiful hotels and restaurants, **PHUKET TOWN** stands distinct from the tailor-made tourist settlements along the beaches as a place geared primarily towards its residents. Customers for the diving centres account for a fair proportion of the few tourists who linger here – most visitors hang about just long enough to jump on a beach-bound songthaew. Nevertheless, if you're on a tight budget it can make sense to base yourself in town, as accommodation and food come a lot cheaper, and you can get out to all the beaches with relative ease.

Aside from a manically bustling market on Ranong Road there's not a great deal to see, though a two-hour-wander around the streets will take you past several dilapidated colonial-style residences built by Chinese merchants at the turn of the century. Recognizable by their doors and shutters painted in pastel pinks, blues and greens, a string of these faded mansions lines Yaowarat Road, and others remain on Ranong Road (the *Thai Airways* office), Phang Nga Road (the *On On Hotel*) and Damrong Road, where the town hall stood in for the US embassy in Phnom Penh in the film *The Killing Fields*.

Accommodation

Not only does Phuket town offer a better range of cheap accommodation than any of the beach resorts, its rooms fill up slower during peak periods – so you might

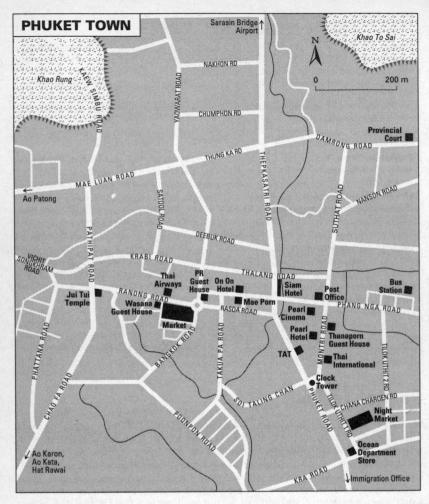

find yourself staying here either through economic choice or until there's space at your preferred beach.

CHEAP AND MODERATE

On On Hotel, 19 Phang Nga Rd (☎211154). Attractive colonial-style building with basic but adequate doubles B80–120.

Pacific Inn, near the night market on Phuket Rd (☎214838). Quaint toy-town building with doubles B220 (fan) and B320 (a/c).

PR Guest House, on the corner of Phang Nga and Bangkok roads. Small, clean singles without attached bathroom for B70, doubles for B120.

Siam Hotel, 13–15 Phuket Rd (☎212328). Above a tape shop, so noise could be a problem, but otherwise good spacious singles and doubles from B150 with fan and shower.

Thanaporn Guest House, 41/7 Montri Road (☎216504). Well-appointed rooms, good value at B350 (with fan) and B450 (a/c).

Wasana Guest House, opposite *Thai Airways* on Ranong Rd (☎211754). Very convenient for songthaews to the beaches; spotless and comfortable doubles with fan and shower for B200.

UPMARKET

The Metropole, 1 Montri Rd (☎215050). The poshest, priciest, newest and largest in town; doubles B1600–7000.

Pearl Hotel, 42 Montri Rd (☎211044). Top-class hotel favoured by Asian package tourists; facilities include rooftop restaurant and swimming pool. Rooms from B787.

Phuket Merlin, 158/1 Yaowarat Rd (☎212866). Swimming pool, nightclub and all the rest; doubles B920–3872.

Eating and nightlife

For authentically cheap and tasty Thai **food** hit any one of the noodle shops along Rasda or Takua Pa roads, or check out the curries, soups and stews at the no-frills food centre on the top floor of the Montri Road *Ocean Department Store* (10am–9.30pm). Alternatively, there's always the night market which materialises around the square off Tilok Uthit 1 Road every evening at about 6pm. Food stalls are also set up at night opposite TAT on Phuket Road, but the prices here are inflated because of the English-language menu. The best of the town's less than stunning array of restaurants are listed below.

Cham Tong, Phang Nga Rd. Early-morning noodle-soup breakfasts a big crowd-puller; also good for *kanom jiin* and sweet rice confections wrapped in banana leaves.

Kanda Bakery, Rasda Rd. The brown bread, cakes and croissants make satisfying if pricey breakfasts and coffee breaks, but the full-blown Thai meals are significantly overpriced.

Mae Porn, Phang Nga Rd. Popular Chinese restaurant with a large English-language menu of curries, seafood, rice and noodle dishes. They also advertise a few illegal dishes such as mouse deer and baked monkey.

Phuket View Restaurant, near the top of Khao Rung, the wooded hill on the western outskirts of town. Middle-class Phuketians drive up here for outdoor seafood with a view. Moderately priced and slightly formal. Bring mosquito repellent.

Tung Ka Café, just above *Phuket View* and very similar.

Apart from the **discos** in the big hotels and the fair smattering of **bars** with hostess service, your choice of **nightlife** is virtually confined to the *Pearl* cinema just off Montri Road, which has English soundtrack headphones.

Listings

Banks and exchange All the main banks have branches on Phang Nga or Rasda roads, with adjacent exchange facilities open till at least 7pm.

Hospitals The private *Mission Hospital* on Thep Kasatri Rd (☎211173) has Phuket's best and most expensive facilities; also in town are *Wachira Hospital* on Yaowarat Rd (☎211114) and *Phuket Ruam Phaet* on Phuket Rd (☎212950).

Immigration At the southern end of Phuket Road, near Ao Makham (Mon–Fri 8.30am–4.30pm).

Tours *Songserm Travel* at 64/2 Rasda Centre, Rasda Rd (☎214272) runs daily trips to Ko Phi Phi for B850 including lunch and snorkelling gear (overnight stays also possible); their twice-weekly day trips to Ko Similan are the fastest way of getting to the islands (see p.371), but at B1500 don't come cheap. The ecologically conscious *Phuket Sea Canoe Center* at 367/3 Yaowarat Rd (☎212172) runs adventurous canoe trips around Ao Phang Nga (see p.386) and

---

NGAN KIN JEH – THE VEGETARIAN FESTIVAL

For nine days every October or November, at the start of the ninth lunar month, the streets of Phuket are enlivened by **Ngan Kin Jeh** – the Vegetarian Festival – which culminates in the unnerving spectacle of men and women parading about with steel rods through their cheeks and tongues. The festival marks the beginning of **Taoist lent**, a month-long period of purification observed by devout Chinese all over the world, but celebrated most ostentatiously in Phuket, by devotees of the island's five Chinese temples. After six days' abstention from meat, alcohol and sex, the white-clad worshippers flock to their local temple, where drum rhythms help induce a trance state in which they become possessed by spirits. As proof of their new-found superiority to the physical world they skewer themselves with any available sharp instrument – fishing rods and car wing-mirrors have done service in the past – before walking over red-hot coals or up ladders of swords as further testament to their otherworldliness. In the meantime there's much singing and dancing and almost continuous firework displays, with the grandest festivities held at Wat Jui Tui on Ranong Road in Phuket town.

The ceremony dates back to the mid-nineteenth century when a travelling Chinese opera company turned up on the island to entertain emigrant Chinese working in the tin mines. They had been there almost a year when suddenly the whole troupe, together with a number of the miners, came down with a life-endangering fever. Realising that they'd neglected their gods somewhat, the actors performed expiatory rites which soon effected a cure for most of the sufferers. The festival has been held ever since, though the self-mortification rites are a later modification, possibly of Hindu origin.

---

beyond: much the best way to observe the undisturbed wildlife of the karst bay. Trips cost from B2500 per person (one day) to B25,000 (seven days).

Post Office Montri Road, with poste restante.

TAT 73–75 Phuket Rd; daily 8.30am–4.30pm (☎212213).

Thai Airways International branch at 41/33 Montri Rd (☎212889); domestic branch at 78 Ranong Rd (☎211195).

Tourist Police In the TAT office on Phuket Road (☎212213).

Telephones For international calls use the 24-hr public phone office on Phang Nga Road. For long-distance calls within Thailand, go to the private office across the road.

Around the island

This account of the island starts at the top of Ko Phuket's most appealing coast and follows an anti-clockwise route around the perimeter, through the chief tourist centres. The west coast boasts a series of long sandy beaches punctuated by sheer rocky headlands, unprotected from the monsoons and consequently quite rough and windswept from May to September, but nevertheless heavily developed and packed with Ko Phuket's best hotels and facilities. Shadowed by the mainland, the east coast is much more sheltered and thus makes a convenient docking point for ships, but there's not a single commendable beach along its entire length. Finally, the interior remains fairly untouched either by industry or by the tourist trade, and can make a refreshing break from the beaches.

Hat Mai Khao and Hat Nai Yang

Phuket's northwest coast kicks off with the island's longest and least-visited beach, the twelve-kilometre **HAT MAI KHAO**, which starts 3km southwest of the airport and 30km northwest of Phuket town, and remains completely unsullied by any touristic enticements, with not a single hut or restaurant standing on its shores. Together with Hat Nai Yang immediately to the south, Hat Mai Khao constitutes a **national park**, chiefly because giant turtles come ashore here between October and February to lay their eggs. A symbol of longevity, turtles are especially precious to Thai and Chinese people, who every April 13, as part of the *Songkhran* festivities, release young turtles into the sea to mark an auspicious beginning to the New Year. Mai Khao is also a prime habitat of a much-revered but non-protected species – the sea grasshopper or sea louse, a tiny crustacean that's considered a great delicacy.

Sheltered by feathery casuarina trees and fronted only by a sandy track, a collection of wooden souvenir stalls and several makeshift open-air restaurants, **HAT NAI YANG** is very much a Thai beach resort, a particular favourite with families who come here to picnic in the shade, eat seafood and go windsurfing or jet-skiing. It's not as unadulterated as Hat Mai Khao, but neither has it been developed to anything like the extent of the farang-oriented resorts further down this coast: the two condominium and hotel blocks that have somehow managed to sneak their way past national park building regulations are discreetly screened by the trees.

Practicalities

An infrequent **songthaew** service runs between Phuket town and Nai Yang via the airport; to get to Mai Khao you have to walk up the beach. **Accommodation** is only available on Hat Nai Yang, where you're limited to four-person B500 national park bamboo huts (☎212901, ext 15), B60 two-person tents, or the expensive *Pearl Village Hotel* (☎311338), with rooms from B1800. But you can pitch your own tent anywhere on both Nai Yang and Mai Khao if you ask permission from the park headquarters on Hat Nai Yang (daily, 8.30am–4.30pm). **Food** options are also confined to Hat Nai Yang, with its half-dozen small open-air seafood restaurants and a handful of itinerant vendors hawking their wares beneath the casuarinas.

Hat Bang Tao, Hat Surin and Ao Kamala

One or two large hotel complexes dominate each of the three beaches south of Nai Yang – **HAT BANG TAO, HAT SURIN** and **AO KAMALA** – and have between them bought up their respective beachfronts, thus leaving the shorelines free of the shops, bars and restaurants that make the resorts further south so frenetic. What's more, the hotels cannot legally restrict access to their strips of sand, so even if you can't afford to stay on these stretches they make good day-trip destinations – though beware of the undertow off the coast here, which confines most guests to the hotel pools. Hat Bang Tao is only accessible via a four-kilometre branch road, but a coastal road links the adjacent Hat Surin and Ao Kamala, running via Laem Singh, a very scenic headland which divides the two.

Practicalities

Songthaews from Phuket town to these beaches (about 24km) run about every thirty minutes. For **accommodation**, *Dusit Laguna* (☎311320), with rooms from B3200, presently holds sway over **Hat Bang Tao**, but is soon to be joined by a *Sheraton* hotel. **Hat Surin** hosts Phuket's most indulgent resort, *Amanpuri* (☎311394), where a minimum of B6500 will get you a personal attendant, a private Thai-style pavilion and unlimited use of the black marble swimming pool. On **Ao Kamala**, *Kamala Beach Estate* (☎01/723 0379) with rooms from B4800 competes with *Phuket Kamala Resort* (☎212901), B1400 and up.

Ao Patong

The most popular and developed of all Phuket's beaches, **AO PATONG** – 5km south of Ao Kamala and 15km west of Phuket town – is where the action is: the three-kilometre beach offers good sand, safe sea, the densest concentration of top hotels, plus the island's biggest choice of water sports and diving centres. On the downside though, a congestion of high-rise hotels and souvenir shops disfigures the beachfront Thavee Wong Road and pollution is becoming a problem as the big hotels persist in dumping their sewage straight into the sea. Signs are that it can only get worse: boasting the most active scene between Bangkok and Hat Yai, Patong's hostess bars and strip joints are attracting an increasing number of single Western men. Before long, this might be a second Pattaya.

Accommodation

Moderately priced accommodation on Patong is very poor value by usual Thai standards: because demand is so great, rudimentary facilities cost twice as much here as they would even in Bangkok. On the other hand, though few of Patong's best hotels are actually on the beach, they all compensate with excellent amenities that compare well with upmarket places all over the country.

MODERATE

Jeep Bungalows, 81/7 Soi Bangla (☎321264). Two lines of terraced huts in a grassy compound at the beach end of the nightlife zone; B300.

Nordic Bungalows, 82/25 Soi Bangla, at far eastern end of Soi Bangla (☎321284). Bungalows and use of swimming pool for B450.

Sipthan Mansion, east of *Nordic Bungalow*, across Raja Uthit Rd. Cheapish unprepossessing doubles in a low-rise from B250.

Skandia Bungalows, close to *Holiday Inn* on Thavee Wong Rd. Bungalows with fan thirty metres from the beach for B400, B500 a/c.

Swiss Garden, beach end of Soi Bangla. Bungalows for B380.

Valentine, Soi Bangla. Bungalows in a garden for B450.

EXPENSIVE

Baan Sukhothai, Soi Bangla. Traditional wooden bungalows, luxuriously outfitted and set in a landscaped garden. B1331–1694.

Casuarina Lodge, 92/9 Thavee Wong Rd (☎321123). Individual bungalows in tree-covered grounds in the least congested part of the resort. B680–1000.

Coral Beach, 104 Traitrang Rd (☎321106). Secluded spot on a cliff at the southernmost end of the beach; all facilities. B2900–4981.

Holiday Inn Phuket, 86/11 Thavee Wong Rd, southern end of the road (☎321020). International standard accommodation and facilities for B2000–8500.

Islet Mansion, 87/29 Thavee Wong Rd, on the central stretch (☎321404). Only ten bunga-lows, and one of the few outfits right on the beach. B500–1500.

Patong Merlin, 99/2 Thavee Wong Rd, southern end (☎321070). Top-quality rooms and service in large chain hotel popular with tour groups. B2000–5000.

Sandy House, central stretch of Thavee Wong Rd. Bungalows on the beach for B500–B1500.

Eating, drinking and nightlife

At night, most people eat in their hotels, snacking during the day at the Western-oriented cafés squashed in amongst the high-rises and shops. Of the hotel **restaurants**, *Baan Sukhothai*'s is worth splashing out on for its fine "Royal Thai" dishes, a sort of Thai *nouvelle cuisine*. For locally caught seafood, particularly Phuket lobster, try either *Number 1 Seafood and Wine Garden* or *Patong Seafood Restaurant*, both on the central stretch of Thavee Wong Road, and both fairly pricey at around B150 for a main dish

Patong's **nightlife** is packed into the strip of neon-lit open-air bar beers along Soi Bangla and the tiny sois that shoot off it, where a few go-go bars add a seam-ier aspect to the zone. If the nightclubs in the big hotels don't appeal, you're otherwise limited to the cavernous *Titanic Disco* at 89/17 Raja Uthit Rd, which plays western pop and shows videos on its huge screen, or *Maxim's* gay bar at 32/9 Raja Uthit Rd, which puts on a nightly transvestite cabaret to a mixed crowd.

Ao Karon

Twenty kilometres southwest of Phuket town, and about 5km south from Patong, **AO KARON** has been developed almost to saturation point: high-rises dominate the central stretch of the beachfront and although only a couple of single-storey bungalow sets stand on the actual beach there are no trees to screen the ugliness from the sea. During the monsoon season the seas can get quite treacherous here, but the weather is suitable for windsurfing throughout the year.

Songthaews from Phuket town run to the north end of Karon along the outer road before doubling back along the beachfront and continuing south as far as *Chao Keun* bungalows on Ao Kata Yai. Karon's main commercial area wells up each side of the landmark *Phuket Arcadia*, halfway down the beach: this is where you'll find the banks, supermarkets and the post office. A second conglomeration of bars and tape shops dominates the headland separating Karon from neighbour-ing Ao Kata Yai to the south. The tiny island of Ko Pu sits just off this headland and makes quite a good place for snorkelling. The tiny bay north of Ao Karon – variously known as Karon Noi and Relax Bay – has effectively become the private beach for guests of the exclusive *Le Meridien* hotel, but non-guests are quite welcome to swim and sunbathe here.

Accommodation

Karon is cheaper than Patong, but during peak season you won't find much **accommodation** for under B200 per person and should be prepared to pay more than that for such luxuries as a fan and attached bathroom. All Karon's low-cost possibilities are listed here.

CHEAP

Dream Hut, north end of the beach. Basic bungalows some way off the seafront; from B180.

Happy Hut, up the hill from *Tropicana*. Pleasantly located in a grassy dip some 300m from the beach, though the staff aren't all that friendly. Bungalows B200.

Kata Tropicana, towards the southern end of the beach (☎211606). Budget travellers' first stop; friendly, with simple huts from B150.

Kata Villa and **Fantasy Hill**, both at the far southern end of Ao Karon, inland from the rocky headland between Karon and Kata; the B200 roadside bungalows stand at the heart of a small but busy shopping and entertainment area.

Much My Friend, north of *Prayoon*. Basic terraced huts near the beach for B300.

Prayoon Bungalows, a short walk north of *Tropicana*. Huts ranged across a grassy slope a little way off the beach; from B150.

MODERATE AND EXPENSIVE

Le Meridien, on Karon Noi (☎321480). Has the tiny bay all to itself and facilities include a huge lake-style swimming pool (with islands), squash and tennis courts and private woods. Singles and doubles B1900–9000.

Phuket Golden Sand Inn (☎381493) and **Phuket Ocean Resort 1** (☎381599), both at the northern end of the beach. Air-conditioned doubles, with swimming pools, in the B500–1200 range.

Thavorn Palm Beach Hotel (☎381034) and **Karon Villa** (☎381149), halfway down the beachfront road. Both offer a high standard of accommodation for B2000–17,000 double.

Eating and nightlife

Karon's **restaurants** pride themselves on their international menus, which means that seafood is often the closest you get to an authentic Thai meal; try the moderately priced *Maxim's* near the *Thavorn Palm Beach Hotel*, or the plush and expensive *Praichart Seafood Inn* inside *Karon Villa*. The fairly low-key **nightlife** here ranges from the bizarre leather fetishist *Easyriders Chopper Pub* at 144/64 Kata Centre, on the Karon-Kata headland, to the ranks of video-bars along the beachfront road.

Ao Kata Yai and Ao Kata Noi

Tree-lined and peaceful **AO KATA YAI** (Big Kata Bay) is only a few minutes' walk around the headland from Karon but both prettier and safer for swimming, thanks to the protective rocky promontories at either end. The northern stretch of Kata Yai is completely given over to the unobtrusive buildings of the *Club Med* resort, and the rest of the beachfront remains fairly uncluttered. A small headland to the south divides Ao Kata Yai from **AO KATA NOI** (Little Kata Bay), a smaller and less attractive beach, though a more secluded spot.

Practicalities

Songthaews from Phuket go as far as the headland between Kata Yai and Kata Noi; to get to Kata Noi, continue walking over the hill for about ten minutes.

There are only a couple of cheap places to stay on **Kata Yai**, both of them down at the far southern end of the beach, where the ground gets rockier: *Shady Bungalows* has simple huts right on the beach for B150, while across the road at *Cool Breeze* you get a choice of bungalows for between B150 and B600. In the more expensive categories, the very large upmarket *Kata Beach Resort*, at the southern end of Kata Yai (☎381521), has a swimming pool and rooms in the hotel from B1500 to B6000, while the adjacent *Chao Keun Bungalows* (☎381403) offers eighteen well-appointed air-conditioned bungalows on the beach from B600 to B1500.

Down on **Kata Noi** you can stay on the beach for around B100 per double at *Island Lodge*, or across the road at *Kata Noi Riviera* or *Jao Tong's*. In the next bracket, *Kata Noi Club*, right at the end of the beach, has bungalows for B600. The most luxurious place on the beach is *Kata Thani Hotel* (☎381417), with a swimming pool and rooms from B2599 to B13,300.

Hat Nai Harn and Laem Promthep

Around the next headland south from Kata Noi, **HAT NAI HARN** – 18km southwest of Phuket town – would be beautiful were it not for the backdrop of tireless bulldozers and ravaged earth. Lording it over the beach and yacht-filled bay is the luxurious *Phuket Yacht Club*, which for the last few years has sponsored a King's Cup Regatta in early December, attracting high-rollers from all over Asia.

Follow the coastal road 2km south and you'll get to a small bay which has coral reefs very close to the shore, though the currents are strong and the sewage pipes uncomfortably close. A further 1km on, you reach the southernmost tip of Ko Phuket at the sheer headland of **Laem Promthep**. Wild and rugged, jutting out into the deep blue of the Andaman Sea, the cape is one of the island's top beauty spots: at sunset, busloads of tour groups get shipped in to admire the scenery – and just to ensure you don't miss the spectacle, a list of year-round sunset times is posted at the viewpoint. Several reefs lie just off the cape, but it's safer to snorkel from a boat rather than attempting the rocky shore.

Practicalities

Songthaews bypass Laem Promthep and follow the direct inland road between Nai Harn and Rawai instead, so you may have to do the lengthy climb round the promontory on foot. It's a popular spot though, so it should be easy enough to hitch.

At the time of writing, only two sets of cheap **bungalows** were in operation on Nai Harn, but more will follow as soon as enough trees have been cleared. *Coconut Bungalows*, on the northern cliffside, shares the same view as the *Yacht Club* and offers basic huts for B70; across the bay, *Sunset Bungalows* monopolises the hillside, boasting equally good sea views for B80 to B250. To find anything else in this range, you have to trudge to the bay 2km south of Nai Harn, where *Nai Harn Ya Noi Bungalows* offers huts for B200. The internationally acclaimed *Phuket Yacht Club* (☎381156) is one of the most exclusive places on the whole island, with superb rooms from B3500. If this is beyond your means but you want a bit of comfort, you could continue a little further round the headland to the *Jungle Beach Resort*, where rooms cost from B1200.

Hat Rawai and its islands

The eastern side of Laem Promthep curves round into **HAT RAWAI**, Phuket's southernmost beach and the first to be exploited for tourist purposes. Twenty years later the developers have moved to the softer sands of Kata and Karon and returned Rawai to its former inhabitants, the *chao ley*. A few bungalow outfits still operate here, but most visitors come either to eat seafood with Phuket's towns-people in one of the nameless open-air seafood restaurants on the beachfront or to hire a longtail out to the **islands** offshore. Of these, Ko Lone, Ko Hai (aka Coral Island), Ko Racha Yai, Ko Racha Noi and Ko Mai Thon are good for snorkelling and diving – the visibility and variety of the reefs around **Ko Racha** in particular compare with those off Ko Similan further up the Andaman coast, and make a popular destination for Phuket's diving centres. You should be able to charter a boat for a day trip to one or more of these islands for between B500 and B1000: ask at the pier.

Hat Rawai boasts an idiosyncratic monument in the shape of the *Henry Wagner*, a very ordinary thirty-eight-foot longtail boat set back from the road just west of the pier. In June 1987, five disabled men set off in this boat to pioneer a course across the Isthmus of Kra, and in just six weeks they navigated the rivers connecting the Andaman Sea to the Gulf of Thailand, without the aid of accurate charts. The captain and inspiration behind the enterprise was 64-year-old amputee Tristan Jones, veteran adventurer and campaigner for the disabled, who told the story of the trip in his book, *To Venture Further*.

Practicalities

Songthaews from Phuket town pass through Rawai on their way to and from Nai Harn. Unless you're keen on desolate beaches, Rawai makes a pretty dismal place to stay. *Rawai Garden Resort*, beyond the far western edge of the beach where the road forks to Laem Promthep and Hat Nai Harn, is the most attractive option, with bungalows in a garden for B250. Much closer to the pier, *Porn Sri* has a range of bungalows from B150 to B500 and *Rawai Plaza* offers the poshest accommodation, from B350 to B900.

THE CHAO LEY

Sometimes called sea gypsies, the **chao ley** or *chao nam* ("people of the sea" or "water people") earn their living from the seas around the west coast of the Malay peninsula, some of them living in established communities, many preferring to move on when the catch dries up or the season changes. The *chao ley* are expert **divers** and make most of their money from **pearls** and **shells**, attaching stones to their waists to dive to depths of 200 feet with only an air-hose connecting them to the surface; sometimes they fish in this way too, taking down enormous nets into which they herd the fish as they walk along the sea bed. Their agility and courage make them good **birds'-nesters** too (see p.400).

Very dark-skinned and with a reddish tinge to their hair because of constant exposure to the sun, the *chao ley* probably originated in Indonesia. They speak their own language and follow animistic beliefs: for example, at the beginning and end of each fishing season, they launch miniature boats filled with tiny weapons onto the sea to placate the spirits of the deep. If the boat returns to the same village it's considered a bad omen and the inhabitants may move to a new location.

As well as being kicked off territory that has been theirs for centuries, the *chao ley* have been subjected to attempts to get them to adopt a recognised religion, and to such insensitive aid schemes as the building of communal toilets close to eating and sleeping areas – shockingly unclean in the eyes of the *chao ley*. As if that weren't enough, coachloads of tourists race through *chao ley* settlements trading cute photo poses for coins and sweets, setting in motion a cycle of dependancy that threatens the very basis of the *chao ley* way of life.

The east coast

Tin mines and docks take up a lot of Phuket's east coast, which is thus neither scenic nor swimmable. East of Rawai, the sizeable offshore island of **Ko Lone** protects the broad sweep of **Ao Chalong**, where many a Chinese fortune was made from the huge quantities of tin mined in the bay. Ao Chalong tapers off eastwards into **Laem Panwa**, at the tip of which you'll find the **Phuket Aquarium** (daily; 8.30am–4.30pm), 9km south of Phuket town and accessible by frequent songthaews. Run by the island's Marine Research Centre, it makes a poor substitute for a day's snorkelling, but not a bad primer for what you might see on a reef. Around the other side of Laem Panwa, the island's main port of **Ao Makham** is dominated by a smelting and refining plant, bordered to the north by **Ko Sirey** (4km east of Phuket town), just about qualifying as an island because of the narrow canal that separates it from Ko Phuket. Tour buses always stop off here to spy on Phuket's largest and longest established *chao ley* community, an example of exploitative tourism at its worst.

The interior

If you have your own transport, exploring the lush, verdant **interior** makes a good antidote to lying on scorched beaches. All the tiny backroads – some too small to figure on tourist maps – eventually link up with the arteries connecting Phuket town with the beaches, and the minor routes south of Hat Nai Yang are especially picturesque, passing through monsoon forest which once in a while opens out into spikey pineapple fields or regimentally ordered **rubber plantations**. Thailand's first rubber trees were planted in Trang in 1901, and Phuket's sandy soil proved to be especially well-suited to the crop. All over the island you'll see cream-coloured sheets of latex hanging out to dry on bamboo racks in front of villagers' houses.

North of Karon, Phuket's minor roads eventually swing back to the central Highway 402, also known as Thep Kasatri Road after the landmark monument that stands on a roundabout 12km north of Phuket town. This **Heroines' Monument** commemorates the repulse of the Burmese army by the widow of the Governor of Phuket and her sister in 1785: the two women rallied the island's womenfolk who, legend has it, cut their hair short and rolled up banana leaves to look like musket barrels to frighten the Burmese away. All songthaews to Hat Surin and Hat Nai Yang pass the monument (as does all mainland-bound traffic), and this is where you should alight for **Thalang Museum** (Wed–Sun 8.30am–4pm; free) five minutes' walk east of here on Route 4027. Phuket's only museum, it has a few interesting exhibits on the local tin and rubber industries, as well as some colourful folkloric history and photos of the masochistic feats of the Vegetarian Festival.

Eight kilometres north of the Heroines' Monument, just beyond the crossroads in the small town of THALANG, stands **Wat Phra Thong**, one of Phuket's most revered temples on account of the power of the Buddha statue it enshrines. The solid gold image is half-buried and no one dares dig it up for fear of a curse that has struck down excavators in the past. After the wat was built around the statue, the image was encased in plaster to deter would-be robbers.

The road east of the Thalang intersection takes you to **Phra Taew National Park** 3km away. Several undemanding paths cross this small hilly enclave, taking you through the forest habitat of gibbons and macaques, to waterfalls at Nam Tok Ton Sai and Nam Tok Bang Pae.

KO PHI PHI AND THE KRABI COAST

East around the mainland coast from Ko Phuket's Sarasin Bridge, the limestone pinnacles that so dominate the landscape of southern Thailand suddenly begin to pepper the sea as well, making **Ao Phang Nga** one of the most fascinating bays in the country. Most travellers, however, head straight for the hub of the region at **Krabi**, springboard for the spectacular mainland beaches of **Laem Phra Nang** and the even more stunning – and very popular – **Ko Phi Phi**. If it's tropical paradise minus the crowds that you're after, opt instead for the sizeable but barely developed **Ko Lanta Yai** or the smaller **Ko Jum**.

All the major islands are served by frequent **ferries** from Krabi except during the rainy season (June–Oct), when convoluted routes via other mainland ports are sometimes possible. Buses and songthaews connect all mainland spots whatever the weather, and you can rent motorbikes in Krabi.

Ao Phang Nga

Protected from the ravages of the Andaman Sea by Ko Phuket, **AO PHANG NGA** has a seascape both bizarre and beautiful. Covering some 400 square kilometres of coast between Ko Phuket and Krabi, the mangrove-lined bay is littered with limestone karst formations of up to 300 metres tall, jungle-clad and craggily profiled. The bay was probably formed about 12,000 years ago when a dramatic rise in sea level flooded the summits of mountain ranges which over millions of years had been eroded by an acidic mixture of atmospheric carbon dioxide and rainwater.

It's possible to join a boat trip around the bay from Ko Phuket or Krabi, but the best way of doing things is to go on one of the tours that leave the town of **Phang Nga** every morning around 8.30am. Day tours return to Phang Nga town at about 2.30pm; overnight tours last till after breakfast the following morning.

Phang Nga town and Tha Don

All buses from Phuket and Takua Pa to Krabi pass through nondescript little **PHANG NGA** about midway along their routes, dropping passengers on Phetkasem Road within five minutes' walk of the clearly signposted cheap hotels. If you want to go straight to the bay, change on to a songthaew bound for the pier at **THA DON**, 9km south and the departure point for trips around Ao Phang Nga.

Because it was the first to run bay tours (see below for details), *Thawisuk Hotel* gets the most custom of Phang Nga's four **cheap hotels**: large clean rooms here are good value at B80. The very similar *Ratanapong Hotel* (☎076/411247), also now a tour arranger, has rooms for B100 and a coffee shop on street level. On the other side of the road, *Muang Tong* (☎076/411132) has doubles with fan and shower for B100 (B200 with a/c), while doubles at the least pleasant of the four, *Rak Phang Nga*, start at B80. For **eating**, the *Ratanapong Coffee Shop* does a satisfying range of breakfasts, and the well-established streetside restaurant near *Ratanapong Hotel* has an English menu and a large selection of rice, noodle and fish dishes. Otherwise plenty of noodle stalls line the Phetkasem Road day and night.

If you're after more **upmarket** accommodation, then you should head to Tha Don, where the *Phang Nga Bay Resort* (☎076/411201) boasts a swimming pool and good facilities, but gives disappointing views considering the bayside location; rooms start at B850.

The bay

The standard itinerary follows a circular or figure-of-eight route around the bay, passing extraordinary karst silhouettes that change character with the shifting light – in the eerie glow of an early-morning mist it can be a breathtaking experience. Many of the formations have nicknames suggested by their weird outlines – like **Khao Machu**, which translates as "Pekinese Rock", and **Khao Tapu** or Nail Rock. Others have titles derived from other attributes – **Tham Nak** (Naga Cave) gets its name from the serpentine stalagmites inside; and a close inspection of **Khao Kien** (Painting Rock) reveals a cliff wall decorated with paintings of elephants, monkeys, fish, crabs and hunting weapons, believed to be between 3000 and 5000 years old.

Ao Phang Nga's most celebrated feature, however, earned its tag from a movie: the cleft **Khao Ping Gan** (Leaning Rock) is better known as **James Bond Island**, after doubling as Scaramanga's hideaway in *The Man With the Golden Gun*. Every boat stops off here and the rock crawls with trinket vendors.

From Khao Ping Gan most boats return to the mainland via the eye-catching settlement of **KO PANYI**, a Muslim village built almost entirely on stilts around the rock that supports the mosque. Nearly all boat tours stop here for lunch, so the island's become little more than a tourists' shopping and eating arcade. If you want to eat here, avoid the expensive and noisy seafood restaurants out front, and head towards the locals' food stalls around the mosque. Overnight visitors stay on at Ko Panyi after lunch and get put up in dormitory-style accommodation in the village.

At some point on your trip you should pass several small brick **kilns** on the edge of a mangrove swamp – once used for producing charcoal from mangrove wood – before being ferried beneath **Tham Lod**, a photogenic archway roofed with stalactites and opening onto spectacular limestone and mangrove vistas.

Bay tours and boat rental

The most affordable way of seeing the bay is to join an **organised tour** from Phang Nga – you can go from Phuket or Krabi too, but the Phuket boats are more expensive and generally too big to manoeuvre the more interesting areas, and Krabi tours go via Phang Nga anyway. The best of the cheapest tours from the town of Phang Nga are the **longtail boat trips** run by the *Thawisuk Hotel* and *Ratanapong Hotel*: starting from the hotels at 8.30am, they charge B100 for a six-hour jaunt, B250 if you stay overnight on Ko Panyi. (Should you be staying at Tha Don, you can join the tours at the pier.) Though the longer trip gives you a chance to appreciate Ko Panyi once the tourist rush is over, and to watch the sun set and rise over the bay, you're confined to the village until a boat picks you up after breakfast, with very little to do during the hours in between.

You could **charter a longtail boat** for upwards of B600 per day from the pier at Tha Don, but this is only really an advantage if your Thai is good enough to specify where you do or don't want to go: otherwise, you'll probably end up covering the same ground as the tours.

If you have the money, the best way to see the bay is by **sea canoe**. *Phuket Sea Canoe Center*, at 367 Yaowarat Rd, Phuket town (☎076/212172), runs day trips around the bay in their vast "sea explorer" canoes for B2500 per person. Everyone gets full paddling instruction and each canoe is piloted by an English-speaking guide and canoeing expert; the special features of these tours are the exploration of lagoons hidden inside the karst outcrops, and of course the chance to see the bay without the constant roar of an engine to scare away the seabirds, kingfishers, crab-eating macaques, mudskippers, fiddler crabs and other wildlife that haunt the mangrove-fringed shores.

Krabi

The compact size and relatively peaceful atmosphere of **KRABI** belie this small fishing town's role as provincial capital and major hub for onward travel to some of the region's most popular islands. Apart from an early-morning flurry when the Bangkok and Surat Thani buses arrive to connect with island-bound boats, the town stays relatively empty of tourists for most of the day, and so efficient are the transport links you don't really need to stop here. It's an attractive spot, though: strung out along the west bank of the Krabi estuary, it provides mangrove-lined shorelines to the east, a harbour filled with rickety old fishing vessels, and dramatically looming limestone outcrops on every horizon. There are plenty of guest houses to enable you to take your time, and it's also possible to base yourself here and make day trips to the Krabi beaches forty-five minutes' boat or song-thaew ride away, though most people prefer to stay at the beaches.

The main Utrakit Road runs north–south along the estuary, veering slightly inland just north of the Tha Reua Chao Fa (Chao Fa boat pier) and forming the eastern perimeter of the tiny **town centre**. Most of the banks on Utrakit Road have exchange facilities, several shops stock a sizeable range of snorkelling equipment and the post office runs an efficient poste restante.

Arrival and information

Direct **air-con buses from Bangkok** leave five times daily between 6pm and 9.30pm, with at least two additional VIP buses departing between 6pm and 7.30pm; they take at least twelve hours and should be booked one day ahead. Three air-con buses make the daily connection with **Surat Thani**, taking three hours. Air-con buses stop in front of the TAT office on Utrakit Road, less than ten minutes' walk north of the Chao Fa pier and five minutes' east of the town centre; touts for guest houses and boat tickets always meet these buses, offering free transport to the pier or guest house, regardless of what you decide, so if you're feeling weary after the long journey, you may as well take advantage of the ride. Arriving by **ordinary bus** from Phang Nga, Phuket or Surat Thani, you'll be dropped at the ordinary bus terminal 5km north of town in the village of TALAT KAO, which stands at the intersection of Utrakit Road and Highway 4. From here there's a frequent songthaew service into Krabi.

Krabi's only independent **tourist information** service is the small TAT branch (Mon–Sat 8.30am–noon & 1–4.30pm; ☎075/611381) housed in a lone white-washed hut on the river side of Utrakit Road. Staff here provide maps, bus timeta-bles and hotel lists, but will send you off to **private tour companies** for beach and island accommodation bookings and ferry tickets. Two of the more reliable

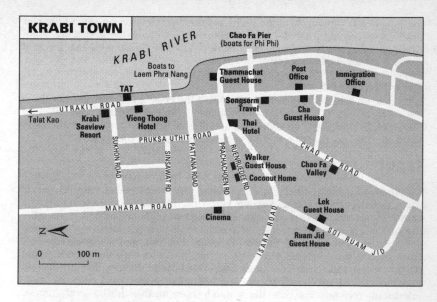

KRABI TOWN

companies are the very helpful *Krabi Seaview Resort* on Utrakit Road (☎075/611648) and *Lanta Independence Tour* on Prachachoen Road (☎075/611717). There's actually no need to buy ferry tickets in advance as none of the boats have reserved seats, but it may be worth booking your first night's island or beach accommodation through one of these agents, as Ko Phi Phi especially gets packed out during peak season.

Accommodation

Of the town's **guest houses**, *Chao Fa Valley*, five minutes' walk west along Chao Fa Road from the pier, is by far the prettiest and most comfortable: spacious bungalows arranged around a colourful flower garden start at B200. All the other guest houses offer cheaper accommodation, often cramped and windowless but good enough for one night. Budget travellers tend to head for the garden compound of *Cha Guest House*, opposite the post office on Utrakit Road, where rock bottom huts go for B50 single, B60 double. Otherwise, try *B&B Guest House* on Pruksa Uthit Road (☎075/612538) for B50 single, B80 double, or any of the three Ruenruedee Road guest houses: *Coconut Home* (☎075/612601) at B60 double; *Walker Guest House* (☎075/612756) at B100 single, B120 double; or *KL Guest House* (☎075/612511), at the same price. If you'd rather stay in a **hotel**, *Vieng Thong* on Utrakit Road (☎075/611188) has doubles from B250 and *Thai Hotel* on Issara Road (☎075/611122) has them from B200.

Eating

Most people eat in the guest house **restaurants**, which serve the standard travellers' fare of milk shakes, pizzas, hamburgers, fish and chips and of course *pat thai* and *khao pat*. It might have grotty rooms but the *Thammachat Guest House* near Chao Fa pier has the best menu in town and is particularly strong on unusual Thai and adventurous vegetarian dishes. For a cheaper Thai meal in a more authentic setting, eat at the **night market**, which is set up around the pier head every evening from about 6pm. The river views are the best thing about Krabi's floating restaurant, just south of the TAT office off Utrakit Road: the food is expensive and nothing special.

Day trips from Krabi

With time on your hands you'll soon exhaust the possibilites in Krabi, but there are a couple of trips to make out of town apart from the popular excursion to Ao Phang Nga. Most Krabi guest houses and tour companies rent out **motorbikes** for about B250 per day, or you can use public or chartered transport.

THE MANGROVES

For about B100 per hour, the boatmen who hang around near the floating restaurant will take you deep into the **mangrove swamps** that infest the Krabi River estuary, giving you a close up view of the wildlife and stopping off at a couple of riverside caves on the way. It's best to set off at fairly low tide when the mangroves are at their creepiest, their aerial roots fully exposed to form gnarled and knotted archways above the muddy banks. Not only are these roots essential parts of the tree's breathing apparatus, but they also reclaim land for future mangroves, trapping and accumulating water-borne debris into which the metre-long mangrove seedlings can fall. Mangrove swamp mud harbours some interesting creatures too, like the instantly recognisable **fiddler crab**, named after the male's single outsized reddish claw which it brandishes for communication and defense purposes – the claw is so powerful it could open a can of baked beans. If you keep your eyes peeled you should be able to make out a few **mudskippers**; these specially adapted fish can absorb atmospheric oxygen through their skins as long as they keep their outsides damp, which is why they spend so much time slithering around in the sludge. As you'd imagine from the name, on land they move in tiny hops by flicking their tails, aided by their extra strong pectoral fins. Of the bigger creatures who patrol the mangrove swamps in search of food, you might well come across **kingfishers** and white-bellied **sea eagles**, but you'd be very lucky indeed to encounter the rare crab-eating macaque.

WAT THAM SEUA

Set beautifully amidst limestone cliffs twelve kilometres northeast of Krabi, the tropical forest of **Wat Tham Seua** (Tiger Cave Temple) can be reached on a songthaew from Utrakit Road, which should take about twenty minutes. The main bot – on your left under the cliff overhang – might come as a bit of a shock: alongside portraits of the abbot, a renowned teacher of Vipassana meditation, close-up photos of human entrails and internal organs are also on display – reminders of the impermanence of the body. Any skulls and skeletons you might come across in the compound serve the same educative purpose.

The most interesting part of Wat Tham Seua lies beyond the bot, past the large tacky statue of the Chinese fertility goddess Kuan Im, where a staircase takes you over the cliff and down into a deep dell encircled by high limestone walls. Here the monks have built themselves self-sufficient meditation cells, linked by paths across through the lush ravine, which is home to squirrels and monkeys as well as a pair of remarkable trees with overground triangular roots over ten metres high.

SUSAAN HOI

Thais make a big deal out of **Susaan Hoi** (Shell Cemetery), 17km west around the coast from Krabi, but it's hard to get very excited about a shoreline of metre-long beige-coloured rocks that could easily be mistaken for concrete slabs. Nevertheless, the facts of their formation are impressive: these stones are 75 million years old and are made entirely from compressed shell fossils. You get a distant view of them from any longtail boat travelling between Krabi and Ao Phra Nang; for a closer look take a songthaew from Utrakit Road.

THAN BOKKHARANI

Fifty kilometres northwest of Krabi, on the road to Phang Nga, the botanical gardens of **Than Bokkharani** make a small-scale contrast to the severe and rugged drama of Krabi's powerful limestone landscapes. Called Than Bok for short, the tiny park is a glade of emerald pools, grottoes and waterfalls enclosed in a ring of lush forest, and lies 1km south of AO LUK. All west-bound songthaews stop here and the journey takes about an hour; from the Ao Luk intersection either walk or take a songthaew. Chances are that if you come here during the week you'll have the place to yourself, but because it's so small Than Bok quickly gets congested on holidays. Tours to Ao Phang Nga from Krabi sometimes take in Than Bok on the return journey.

Krabi beaches

Although the two mainland beach areas west of Krabi can't compete with the local islands for snorkelling or seclusion, the stunning headland of **Laem Phra Nang** is accessible only by boat, so staying on one of its three beaches can feel like being on an island, albeit a crowded one. In contrast, a road runs right along the **Ao Nang** beachfront, which has enabled an upmarket resort to thrive around its far from exceptional beach. Don't bother coming to Ao Nang between May and October, when the beach gets covered in sea-borne debris and most accommodation is closed. The Laem Phra Nang beaches, on the other hand, don't change much year-round, though a few places close up for the rainy season.

Laem Phra Nang

Seen from the close quarters of a longtail boat, the combination of sheer limestone cliffs, pure white sand and emerald waters at **LAEM PHRA NANG** is spectacular – and would be even more so without the hundreds of other admirers gathered on its beaches. Almost every inch of buildable land on the cape has now been taken over by bungalows, but at least high-rises don't feature yet, and developers have so far favoured natural materials over concrete. Even if you don't want to stay, it's worth coming for the day to gawp at the scenery and scramble down into the lushly vegetated area around the cape's enclosed lagoon. For more ambitious explorations, several bungalows on Laem Phra Nang organise **snorkelling trips** to the nearby islands of Hua Kwan and Ko Poda. So-called **nautical treks** are also becoming popular: often led by *chao ley*, these are three-day snorkelling and shell-hunting forays around islands, with camp fire meals and nights under the stars. Prices average out at about B1000 per person.

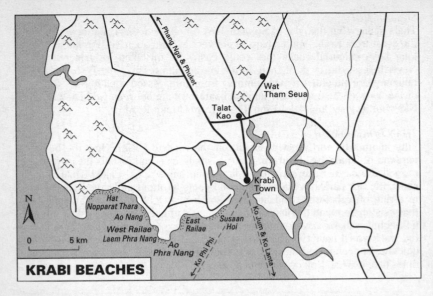

KRABI BEACHES

Longtail **boats** to Laem Phra Nang depart from beside the floating restaurant on the Krabi riverfront (45 min; B45), leaving throughout the day as soon as they fill up. From November to April the boatmen pull in at Ao Phra Nang, on the tip of the cape, and can usually be persuaded to continue round to west Railae; during the rainy season they'll only go as far as east Railae. Except during the monsoon season, longtails connect Ao Nang, further west around the coast, with west Railae (10 min; B20).

The beaches

The headland has three beaches within ten minutes' walk of each other: **Ao Phra Nang** graces the southwestern edge, and is flanked by **Hat Railae**, technically one bay but in fact composed of distinct **east** and **west** beaches.

AO PHRA NANG

Set against a magnificent backdrop of cliffs and palms, diminutive **AO PHRA NANG** (aka Hat Tham Phra Nang) is the loveliest spot on the cape despite the noisy longtail traffic, attracting sunbathers to its luxuriously soft sand and snorkellers to the reefs some 200m offshore.

The beach and cape are named after a princess (*phra nang* means "revered lady"), whom the local fisherfolk believe lives here and controls the fertility of the sea. If you walk past the entrance to **Tham Phra Nang** (Princess Cave), hollowed out of the huge karst outcrop at the eastern edge of the bay, you'll see a host of red-tipped wooden phalluses stacked as offerings to her, by way of insurance for large catches.

The numerous passageways and rocks around the cave are fun to scramble over, but getting down into **Sa Phra Nang** (Princess Lagoon) is more of a challenge. Buried deep inside the same rock, the lagoon is accessible only via a steep 45-minute descent that starts at the "resting spot" halfway along the wooden walkway connecting the east edge of Ao Phra Nang with east Railae. After an initial ten-minute clamber, with the help of ropes, the path forks: go left for a panoramic view over the east and west bays of Hat Railae, or right for the lagoon. (For the strong-armed, there's the third option of hauling yourself up ropes to the top of the cliff for a bird's-eye view.) Taking the right-hand fork, you'll pass through the tropical dell dubbed "big tree valley" before eventually descending to the murky lagoon. The muddy banks have spawned a lagoonside gallery of clay models fashioned by visitors.

Tham Phra Nang

EAST RAILAE

The least attractive of the cape's beaches, **EAST RAILAE** is not suitable for swimming because of its fairly dense mangrove growth, a tide that goes out for miles, and sand that's littered with building rubble. As compensation, bungalows come cheaper here, and none is more than ten minutes from the much cleaner sands of West Railae and Ao Phra Nang. To get to east Railae from Ao Phra Nang, follow the wooden walkway from the eastern edge; from west Railae walk through the *Railae Beach* bungalow compound.

The northern end of east Railae backs on to a rocky hillside which, behind *Diamond Cave* bungalows, hides another set of caves. Referred to as **Tham Phra Nang Nai** (Inner Princess Cave) or Diamond Cave, these are said to shimmer with stalactite formations, but at the time of writing a tour operator had grabbed the keys to the entrance gate and would only open up for certain groups.

WEST RAILAE

Sometimes known as Sunset Beach, **WEST RAILAE** comes a close second to Ao Phra Nang, with similarly dramatic scenery and a much longer stretch of good sand. Longtails sometimes dock here, otherwise you can walk from Ao Phra Nang via the walkway to east Railae, cutting across to west Railae through *Queen* bungalow compound.

Accommodation

There's no air conditioning on the cape, and most accommodation is budget traveller oriented: Ao Phra Nang beach has the most expensive bungalow operations and east Railae the cheapest, but facilities don't vary much. Some bungalow outfits charge more for a sea view, though no room on the cape is more than 200m from the sea. All bungalow operations have restaurants where food is pricey and unremarkable; entertainment consists of either watching the restaurant videos – most have twice-nightly viewings – or going to one of the beachfront bars.

AO PHRA NANG

Phra Nang Bay Village (☎075/611944). Good value considering its prime location on the best beach, but screened from it by trees; bungalows with shower start at B200.

Phra Nang Place (☎075/611944). The classiest operation on the cape, its tastefully laid-out bungalows covering an area that stretches from Ao Phra Nang to east and west Railae beaches. B350 per bungalow.

EAST RAILAE

Coco. Small compound of standard bungalows with shower for B200.

Diamond Cave. The best value huts on the cape, at B100 with shower (B70 without).

Hillside II. Bungalows set on the hillside, with great views out over the bay and early morning gibbon calls; B60 without shower.

Queen. Average huts with shower from B200.

Sunrise. Almost identical to *Queen*; from B200.

Ya Ya's. Unusual three-storey bamboo towers with a shared bathroom on the ground floor go for B80 per two-person storey; regular huts with shower cost B120.

WEST RAILAE

Railae Beach. Adequate bungalows, with shower – on the beachfront B300, away from the beach B150.

Railae Village. Very similar to *Railae Beach*; B150–300.

SandSea (☎075/611944). Well-spaced seafront huts with shower for B200; those further back for B150.

Starlight. Occupies the land between east and west Railae (no sea views): clean, comfortable bungalows B150 with shower.

Ao Nang and Hat Nopparat Thara

The scene at **AO NANG**, just around the rocky outcrop from west Railae, is much more middle-aged than at Laem Phra Nang, with the emphasis on air-conditioned opulence rather than beach life. Developers have moved in en masse, so that the narrow and unprepossessing beach now has a road running right along its length, with the resort area stretching back over a kilometre from the shore. Yet the expansive seaward view of crystal clear water dotted with limestone monoliths remains pretty amazing, and it's easy enough to escape when the atmosphere gets too stifling – a short walk takes you to the unadulterated stretch of Hay Nopparat Thara, and it's a dramatic ten-minute boat ride to the beaches of Laem Phra Nang. Access is easy, as songthaews run from Krabi regularly throughout the day and take about 45 minutes, and in terms of facilities Ao Nang is quite well set up, with diving equipment rental close to the beachfront at *Baby Shark Divers* and a couple of official money-exchanges just off the beach.

Continue for about a kilometre along the road west and you come to the eastern end of two kilometre-long **Hat Nopparat Thara**. Invariably deserted, this beach is part of the national marine park that encompasses Ko Phi Phi, and has the park headquarters about halfway along. At low tide it's almost impossible to swim here, but the sands are enlivened by millions of starfish and thousands of hermit crabs, and you can walk out to the small offshore island if you tire of the supine life.

Accommodation

For **cheap bungalows** on the beach at Ao Nang your only option is *PS Cottages* (☎01/211 4860) at B120 per double – all the others are on the wrong side of the road. Failing that, you could try for a B100 bungalow with sea view and shower at the nearby *Coconut Garden* or pay B200 for a similar deal at *Gift* – both are in the central beachfront area; whether or not you stay at *Gift*, check out their French-inspired restaurant which serves up great food, especially fish dishes and home-baked cakes. On the road leading up the hill and away from the beach, *Peace Bungalows* (☎075/611944) is predominantly upmarket, but keeps a few fan-cooled bungalows set around a small ornamental lake for B150. Off the same road some way from the beach, the friendly *Dum's Guest House* has the cheapest rooms in Ao Nang: simple doubles in a house go for B50. Proper treehouses at the next door *Jungle Hut* are well worth B70; *Jungle Hut*'s grounded bungalows with shower are also good value at B100.

In the **upmarket** category, *Krabi Resort* (☎075/611389) is the poshest, set in a large tropical garden in a tiny bay just north of the main beachfront, with top-class bungalows and rooms in a low-rise hotel from B800 to B1540. On the main beachfront, the very elegant wooden *Phra Nang Inn* (☎075/612173) has doubles from B999 and the nearby resort-style *Ao Nang Villa* (☎075/611129) has attractive air-conditioned bungalows just off the beach for B750.

Ask permission and you should be able to **camp** on **Hat Nopparat Thara**, though there's very little shelter and the road is visible along most of it. Alternatively you could stay in the national park **bungalows** next to the head-quarters, though at B500 they're not really worth it.

Ko Phi Phi

Now well-established as one of southern Thailand's most popular destinations for budget travellers, the two **KO PHI PHI** islands lie 40km south of Krabi and 48km east of southern Phuket, encircled by water so clear that you can see almost to the sea bed from the surface, easily making out the splayed leaves of cabbage coral and the distinctively yellow-striped tiger fish from the boat as you approach the islands. The action is concentrated on the larger **Ko Phi Phi Don**, packed with bungalow operations and tourist enterprises serving the burgeoning ranks of divers, snorkellers and sybarites who just come to slump on the long white beaches. No less stunning is the uninhabited sister island of **Ko Phi Phi Leh**, whose sheer cliff faces get national marine park protection, on account of the lucra-tive birds' nest business.

Getting to the islands

During peak season, **ferries** to Ko Phi Phi Don run at least three times daily **from Krabi** (1hr 30min–2hr; B125) and from **Ko Phuket** (1hr 30min–2hr 30min; B180–250). In the rainy season the service from both is reduced to twice daily. From November to May, there are also once-daily boats to Phi Phi Don from **Ao Nang** (2hr; B135) and **Ko Lanta Yai** (1hr 30min; B150). The only way you can get to Phi Phi Leh is by longtail from Phi Phi Don or as part of a tour.

If you're short of time, you could join one of the **day cruises** run by Phuket's *Songserm Travel Center*, 64/2 Rasada Centre, Rasada Rd. The trips include two hours' snorkelling, visits to Phi Phi Don and Phi Phi Leh, plus lunch – the main

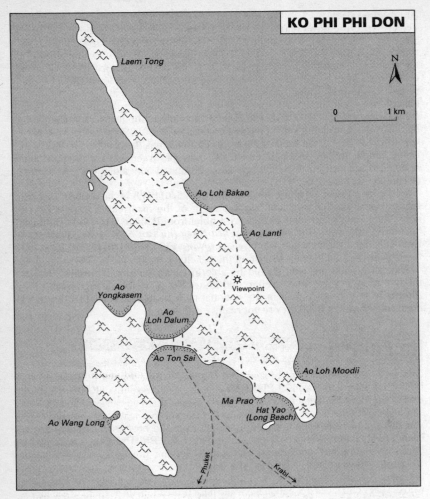

KO PHI PHI DON

Laem Tong

N

0   1 km

Ao Loh Bakao

Ao Lanti

Ao
Yongkasem

Viewpoint

Ao
Loh Dalum

Ao Ton Sai

Ao Loh Moodii

Ma Prao

Hat Yao
(Long Beach)

Ao Wang Long

Phuket→

Krabi→

disadvantage being that the *Songserm* ferries are huge. They cost B850 (B600 for under 12s) and depart from major Phuket hotels around 7am, returning at 5.30pm.

Ko Phi Phi Don

KO PHI PHI DON would itself be two islands were it not for the tenuous palm-fringed isthmus that connects the hilly expanses to east and west, separating the stunningly symmetrical double bays of Ao Ton Sai to the south and Ao Loh Dalum to the north. So steep is the smaller western half that the small population lives in isolated clusters across the slopes of the densely vegetated eastern stretch, while the tourist bungalows stick mainly to the intervening sandy flats, with a few developments on the beaches fringing the cliffs east and north of the isthmus.

All boats dock at **Ao Ton Sai**, the busiest bay on the island. From here you can catch a longtail to any of the other beaches or walk – there are no roads or vehicle tracks on Phi Phi Don, just a series of paths across the steep and at times rugged interior, at points affording superb views over the bays. **Accommodation** on Phi Phi Don ranges from the exclusive to the tacky, but it's expensive in all categories: reckon on paying up to fifty percent more than you'd pay on the mainland.

Ao Ton Sai

The constantly expanding village at **AO TON SAI** has the feel of a pop festival. Makeshift stalls selling everything you could possibly need for a few days on a beach form convoluted rows alongside money changers, diving schools, bars and restaurants serving the gamut of tourist fare – and at the western end there's even an open-air arena for weekly bouts of Thai boxing. Eastwards and northwards the village merges with residential areas, and the port gives way to sunbathing spots.

Most of the **accommodation** around here is packed between the Ao Ton Sai and Ao Loh Dalum beaches and at the foot of the hills to the east and west. Ten minutes east of the pier, at the edge of the village, *Chao Ko* has beachfront bungalows for B250 with bathroom. Inland from here, in the thick of the residential scrum, *Twin Palm Guest House* is one of the cheapest places on the island: small rooms with thin walls start at B90. The nearby *Ruen Tai* bungalows are just about worth B150, but forget about the rip-off *Tara Inn* and *Rim Na*. The top-end place to stay on Ao Ton Sai is the well-organised *Phi Phi Cabana* (☎075/612132) on the seafront just west of the pier, which has resort-like facilities and air-conditioned bungalows from B726.

DIVING AND SNORKELLING OFF KO PHI PHI

More accessible than Ko Similan and Ko Surin, Ko Phi Phi and its neighbouring islands rate very high on the list of Andaman coast **diving and snorkelling** spots, offering depths of up to thirty-five metres, visibility touching thirty metres, and the possibility of seeing white-tip sharks, moray eels and stingrays. **Diving centres** on Ko Phuket run daily excursions here, and there are several centres closer to hand, at Ao Ton Sai and at *Phi Phi International Resort* on Laem Tong, all of which rent equipment, organise excursions and run courses. The Phi Phi centres are less established than those on Ko Phuket, so although prices are slightly lower than at Phuket – about B1000 for an introductory one-day diving course and B7500 for the five-day open water course – you may feel better entrusting yourself to the Phuket operators.

Nearly all the bungalow operations on Phi Phi Don organize day and half-day **snorkelling** trips. Prices vary slightly, but they average out at B150 for a day trip including lunch and snorkelling gear; try *Long Beach Bungalows* first, for the most competitive rates. In the case of snorkelling, the longtails that run from Ko Phi Phi are better than the cruise ships that make day trips from Phuket, which are so popular you can rarely see the fish for the swimmers.

Diving and snorkelling **tours** generally take in the same reefs and islands. At uninhabited **Ko Pai** (or Bamboo Island), off the northeast coast of Phi Phi Don, much of the reef lies near the shore and close to the surface, and gives you a chance of seeing the occasional turtle and the harmless purple- and black-striped sea snake – not to be confused with the poisonous red and black one. Fewer day-trippers are brought to the adjacent **Ko Yung**, whose offshore reef plunges into a steep-sided and spectacular drop. Off the west coast of Phi Phi Don, **Ao Yongkasame** also has good reefs as do the tranquil waters at **Ao Maya** on the west coast of Phi Phi Leh.

East along the coast from *Chao Ko*, the scenically positioned bungalows at *Phi Phi Don Resort* command good views over Ao Ton Sai and go for between B180 and B450. Set even higher up, the nearby bungalows of *Bay View Resort* have massive windows and very comfortable rooms for B450.

New **restaurants** spring up as old ones fold, but at the time of writing the seafront *Siam Seafood*, next to the jetty, was serving delicious red snapper, tuna and shark, and French-run *Mama's*, on the main track from the pier, was offering high quality seafood meals and good cakes, at a price.

Hat Yao

With its deluxe sand and large reefs packed with polychromatic marine life just twenty metres offshore, **HAT YAO** (Long Beach) is the best of Phi Phi's three main beaches. Unperturbed by the longtail traffic, shoals of golden butterfly fish, turquoise and purple parrot fish, and hooped angel fish scour the coral for food, escorted by brigades of small cleaner fish who live off the parasites trapped in the scales of larger species. For the best of the coral and the biggest reef in the vicinity, you should make for the submerged rock known as **Hin Pae** off the southern end of Hat Yao – novice divers get ferried out there by boat, but if you're a strong swimmer you can easily reach it from the beach.

Longtail boats do the ten-minute shuttle between here and Ao Ton Sai from about 8am to 10.30pm, or you could walk between the two in half an hour, either along the hillside path or, at low tide, around the rocks and along the beach.

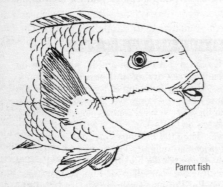
Parrot fish

Several other paths connect Hat Yao to the beaches of Ao Loh Dalum to the north and the tiny bay of Loh Moodii to the northeast: the trails start behind the last of the *Long Beach Bungalows*.

The most attractive of Hat Yao's **accommodation** is tucked away in a little cove just west of Hat Yao itself, with easy access via a rocky path. This is the small, secluded and friendly *Ma Prao* (aka *Funny Land*), where bungalows range from B150 to B250. Of the two bungalow operations on Hat Yao, most budget travellers head first for the simple but atmospheric B100 huts at *Long Beach Bungalows*, communal bathrooms and limited electricity and water supplies notwithstanding. The larger but more sparse-looking bungalows at *Paradise Pearl* (☎01/723 0484) all have attached bathrooms, and range in price from B150 to B550 for the ones on the front row, which aren't really worth the extra as they get the worst of the noise from the longtails.

Ao Loh Dalum

Though less attractive than Hat Yao, **AO LOH DALUM**, affords a magnificent wrap around panorama from the **viewpoint** beyond the *chao ley* settlement at the eastern edge of the beach. Photographers slog up the steep half-hour climb for sunset shots of Ao Loh Dalum and Ao Ton Sai, but early morning is an equally good time to go, as the summit's *Mountain View Café* serves simple breakfasts as well as cold drinks. From the viewpoint you can descend the rocky and at times almost sheer path to **Ao Lanti**, a tiny bay on the east coast with choppy surf and a couple of resident *chao ley*. Theoretically, it should also be possible to reach the northeastern bay of Ao Loh Bakao (see below) by path from near the viewpoint, but the two-kilometre route is unsignposted and overgrown.

The cheapest **place to stay** on Ao Loh Dalum is *Chang Kao* at the western edge of the beach, where basic huts start at B100. The rest of the accommodation is fairly upmarket: beachfront bungalows at *Krabi Phi Phi Resort* (☎075/611484) start from B300, while next door at *Phi Phi Charlie Resort* (☎01/723 0495), similar bungalows range from B400 to B700. Both resorts are fully equipped with bars, restaurants and tour information. Strung out across the hillside at the eastern edge of Ao Loh Dalum are the attractive but pricey bungalows of *Viewpoint Bungalows*, where for B650 you get great views out over the bay.

Ao Loh Bakao and Laem Tong

Far removed from the hustle of Ao Ton Sai and its environs, a few exclusive resorts have effectively bought up the secluded northern beaches of Phi Phi Don. This is primarily package-holiday territory – you're unlikely to find a room free if you turn up unannounced. There are no regular boats from Ao Ton Sai, but long-tail boats will take you for about B200; the trip takes about an hour to Ao Loh Bakao and a further half-hour north to Laem Tong.

Phi Phi Island Village (☎076/215014) has the beach of **Ao Loh Bakao** all to itself; resort-standard bungalows here range from B850 to B1200. The beach at the northernmost tip, **Laem Tong**, is dominated by the top-of-the-range *Phi Phi International* (☎076/214297), whose bungalows range from B1900 to B9000; cruises in fully kitted-out old-fashioned sailing junks are a speciality.

Ko Phi Phi Leh

More rugged than its twin Ko Phi Phi Don, and a quarter the size, **KO PHI PHI LEH** is home only to the **sea swift**, whose valuable nests are gathered by intrepid *chao ley* for export to specialist Chinese restaurants all over the world. Tourists descend on the island not only to see the nest-collecting caves but also to snorkel off its sheltered bays, and the anchoring of their boats has damaged much of the coral in the best spots. Most snorkelling trips out of Phi Phi Don include Phi Phi Leh, which is only twenty minutes south of Ao Ton Sai, but you can also get there by renting a longtail from Ao Ton Sai or Hat Yao (B200–B400 per six-person boat). If you do charter your own boat, go either very early or very late in the day, to beat the tour-group rush.

Most idyllic of all the bays in the area is **Ao Maya** on the southwest coast, where the water is still and very clear and the coral extremely varied – a perfect snorkelling spot and a feature of most day trips. Unfortunately the discarded lunch boxes and water bottles of day-trippers now threaten the health of the marine life in **Ao Phi Leh**, an almost completely enclosed east-coast lagoon of breathtakingly turquoise water. Not far from the cove, the **Viking Cave** gets its misleading name from the scratchy wall paintings of Chinese junks inside, but more interesting than this 400-year-old graffiti is the **bird's-nesting** that goes on here: rickety bamboo scaffolding extends hundreds of feet up to the roof of the cave, where the harvesters spend the day scraping the tiny sea swift nests off the rock face.

Prized for its aphrodisiac and energising qualities, **bird's nest soup** is such a delicacy in Taiwan, Singapore and Hong Kong that ludicrous sums of money change hands for a dish whose basic ingredients are tiny twigs glued together with bird's spit. Collecting these nests is a lucrative but life-endangering business: sea swifts build their nests in rock crevices hundreds of feet above sea level, often on sheer cliff faces or in cavernous hollowed-out karst. **Nest-building** begins in January and the harvesting season usually lasts from February to May, during which time the female sea swift builds three nests on the same spot, none of them more than 12cm across, by secreting an unbroken thread of saliva which she winds round as if making a coil pot. **Gatherers** will only steal the first two nests made by each bird, prizing them off the cave walls with special metal forks. Gathering the nests demands faultless agility and balance, skills that seem to come naturally to the *chao ley*, whose six-man teams bring about 400 nests down the perilous bamboo scaffolds each day, weighing about 4kg in total. At a market rate of B20–50,000 per kilo, so much money is at stake that a government franchise must be granted before any collecting commences, and armed guards often protect the sites at night. The *chao ley* themselves seek spiritual protection from the dangers of the job by making offerings to the spirits of the cliff or cave at the beginning of the season; in the Viking Cave, they place buffalo flesh, horns and tail at the foot of one of the stalagmites.

Ko Lanta Yai, Ko Bubu and Ko Jum

East and southeast of Ko Phi Phi, three of the more inhabitable of the 130 islands lying off the Krabi coast have started to divert budget travellers from the crowds on Ko Phi Phi. Much closer to the mainland, neither **Ko Lanta Yai**, **Ko Bubu** nor **Ko Jum** can compete with Phi Phi's stupendous scenery or its prolific reef life, but they do offer good sandy beaches, safe seas, and the much greater likelihood of solitude and seclusion. Of the three, Ko Lanta Yai is by far the largest – some 25km long as compared with Phi Phi's 8km – and the most tourist-oriented, with nine bungalow operations to date. The minuscule Ko Bubu, only 7km off Lanta Yai's east coast is the preserve of just one bungalow outfit, but in contrast to many one-resort islands, this is not an exclusive upmarket operation. The same is true of Ko Jum, which is slightly larger than Phi Phi Don but nevertheless offers only one accommodation option.

Ko Lanta Yai

Development on **KO LANTA YAI** is in its embryonic stage and has so far been confined to the west-coast beaches; as a result the island still feels like it belongs to its residents (something which can't be said of Ko Phi Phi, Ko Phuket or Ko Samui), the majority of whom are mixed-blood Muslim descendants of Malaysian and *chao ley* peoples. Aside from fishing, many of the islanders support themselves by cultivating the land between the beaches and the forested ridges that dominate the central and eastern parts of Lanta Yai.

The local *chao ley* name for the island is *Paulao Satak*, "Island of Long Beaches", an apt description of the six beaches of the rocky western coast. The northerly ones tend to be more developed than others, but deserted spots are not hard to find and they all offer good sand and clear water, while the bungalow outfits advertise day trips to reefs off the islands further south, where the snorkelling is better than on Ko Lanta Yai itself. Much of the east coast is fringed with mangrove swamps and unsuitable for swimming.

There's no regular songthaew service on Ko Lanta, so once you're established on the island you either have to hire a motorbike from your accommodation or hitch – which is pretty easy, though you'll probably be expected to pay.

Getting to the island

From November to May **ferries** run **from Krabi to Ban Sala Dan** on the northern tip of Ko Lanta Yai (3 daily; 2hr 30min). During the rest of the year, the rainy season, you can get the daily ferry from **Bo Muang**, about 80km southeast of Krabi, to **Lanta** on the island's east coast (1hr), from where motorbike taxis will take you to the beaches. You should be able to get a direct songthaew from Krabi to Bo Muang: check with Krabi tour agencies about the songthaew and boat departure times.

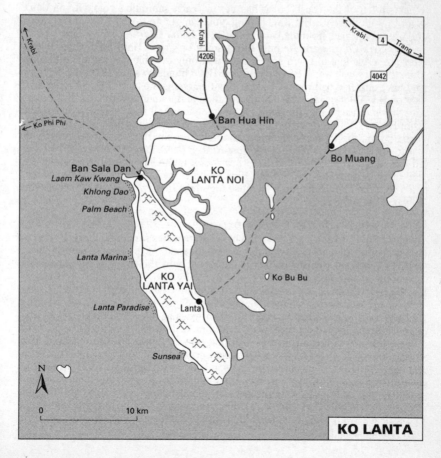

KO LANTA

Around the island

Although a hundred farang tourists must pass through **BAN SALA DAN** every day, it remains surprisingly intact as a Muslim fishing port, where concessions to the tourist trade don't stretch much further than a money exchange (poor rates) and a French restaurant. Vociferous touts always meet the boats, competing to take you from the village to your chosen bungalows free of charge, but be prepared for the price bracket you agreed on to be suddenly unavailable.

HAT KAW KWANG AND HAT KHLONG DAO

The tip of the northwest coast, 500m west of Ban Sala Dan, begins with the island's least picturesque beach, **HAT KAW KWANG**, whose 2km stretch of grey shoreline turns mostly to mud at low tide. But things get better at the far western end, where a five-minute walk round the neck of **Laem Kaw Kwang** (Deer Neck Cape) brings you to the best beach on the island, **HAT KHLONG DAO**. The sand is soft and golden here, and there's a good choice of discreet bungalows, so not surprisingly Hat Khlong Dao attracts more visitors than any other stretch of the coast, but it has yet to reach saturation point. If you don't want to walk there via Hat Kaw Kwang, you can get on to Hat Khlong Dao from the west coast road, from the back entrance of *Lanta Charlie Beach Resort*.

Deer Neck Cabana are the only **bungalows** on grotty Hat Kaw Kwang, but as they are at the foot of Laem Kaw Kwang and only five minutes from Hat Khlong Dao, they are well worth considering: the B100 bungalows are all on the seafront and have attached bathrooms. *Golden Bay Cottages* is the pick of the accommodation on Hat Khlong Dao, with a prime location in the middle of the bay and expansive views to each side; the well-spaced bungalows all have showers and range from B60 to B150. A bit farther south, *Lanta Sea House* has the cheapest accommodation on the island with simple bamboo huts for B30 and larger ones with bathroom for B120. Similar huts at *Kaw Kwang Beach Bungalow* start at B50 and all have a sea view. *Lanta Charlie Beach Resort* is the largest resort on Lanta Yai and offers **motorbike and jet-ski hire** and a **restaurant** specialising in barbecued fish; the bungalows are a bit close together though, and cost B300 near the beach, B150 at the back.

BEACHES SOUTH OF HAT KHLONG DAO

South of Hat Khlong Dao lies a string of silken beaches separated by rocky points and accessible only by tracks off the west-coast road. At the time of writing these beaches remained officially nameless, known only by the single set of bungalows operating on each one.

PALM BEACH, about two kilometres south of Khlong Dao, is a beautiful long strip of almost deserted white sand, slightly disfigured by the ugly concrete huts of *Palm Beach Bungalows* among the palm trees at the back; they start at B60 with bathroom, or you can pitch your own tent for B30.

Five kilometres south, the B50 bamboo huts of *Lanta Marina* are built to a traditional A-frame design and are well spaced in the thick of a coconut grove. A further six kilometres on come the fine sands of **PARADISE BEACH**, where the *Lanta Paradise* bungalows – packed uncomfortably close together but spacious inside – ranging from B100 in the back row to B150 on the beachfront. Furthest away from Ban Sala Dan, almost at the southernmost end of Lanta Yai, *Sunsea* is set against a lovely hilly backdrop 5km south of Paradise Beach; the huts are a bit ugly, but cheap at B70.

Ko Bubu

The only reason to venture round to Lanta Yai's east coast would be to make the short hop across to **KO BUBU**, a minuscule dot of an island about twenty minutes' longtail ride from the small town of LANTA (B150). With a radius of not much more than 500m, wooded Ko Bubu has room for just one set of thirty bungalows, which cost from B200 for two people, or B80 per person sleeping dormitory style; if all the rooms are full you should be allowed to pitch your own tent here.

You can also reach Ko Bubu direct **from Krabi**, by following the rainy season route for Ko Lanta Yai and chartering a longtail from Bo Muang for about B250. Krabi's *Thammachat Guest House* acts as an agent for the Ko Bubu bungalow resort and might be persuaded to organise through-transport from Krabi.

Ko Jum

Situated halfway between Krabi and Ko Lanta Yai, **KO JUM** (or Ko Pu) is the sort of laid-back and simple spot that people come to for a couple of days then can't bring themselves to leave. Its mangrove-fringed east coast holds the island's only fishing village and a beachfront school, while across on the sandy west coast there's just one small bungalow operation down towards the southern tip; much of the north is made inaccessible by the breastbone of forested hills. So there's little to do here except hunt for shells, stroll the kilometre across the island to buy snacks in the village or roast on the beach and then plunge into the sea. The sole **place to stay** is *Joy Bungalows* where simple bamboo huts go for B70 (B150 with bathroom), and where you can camp for a small fee. At night the paraffin-lit **restaurant** serves food that's expensive but surprisingly varied considering the distance it has to come.

Joy Bungalows sends a longtail **boat** out to meet the Krabi–Ko Lanta ferries as they pass the west coast (1hr 30min from Krabi); in the rainy season they organise a daily songthaew and longtail to cover the alternative mainland route, which runs from Krabi via the pier at LAEM KRUAT, 40km southeast, from where the boat takes you out to Ko Jum's east coast – ask any Krabi tour operator for songthaew departure times.

travel details

Buses

From Krabi to Bangkok (at least 3 daily; 12–14hr); Hat Yai (2 daily; 4hr); Nakhon Si Thammarat (8 daily; 3hr); Surat Thani (hourly; 3–4hr); Trang (8 daily; 3hr).

From Phang Nga to Bangkok (4 daily; 11hr–12hr 30min); Krabi (every 30min; 1hr 45min); Phuket (6 daily; 2hr–2hr 30min).

From Phuket to Bangkok (at least 10 daily; 14–16hr); Hat Yai (7 daily; 7–8hr); Krabi (hourly; 4hr) via Phang Nga (2hr); Nakhon Si Thammarat (8 daily; 8hr); Surat Thani (9 daily; 5–6hr); Trang (8 daily; 6hr).

From Ranong to Bangkok (7 daily; 9–10hr); Chumphon (every 90min; 2hr); Phuket (8 daily; 6hr) via Khuraburi (2hr) and Takua Pa (2hr 30min–3hr).

Ferries

From Ko Phi Phi Don to Ao Nang (Nov–May 1 daily; 2hr); Ko Lanta Yai (Nov–May 1 daily; 1hr 30min).

From Krabi to Ko Phi Phi Don (2–4 daily; 1hr 30min–2hr); Ko Lanta Yai (Nov–May 3 daily; 2hr 30min), via Ko Jum (1hr 30min).

From Phuket to Ko Phi Phi Don (2–4 daily; 1hr 30min–2hr 30min); Ko Similan (Nov–May 2 weekly; 3hr).

From Ranong to Ko Surin (Nov–May 3 weekly; 3hr).

Flights

From Phuket to Bangkok (8–13 daily; 1hr 15min); Chiang Mai (4 weekly; 2hr 5min); Hat Yai (1–2 daily; 55min); Ko Samui (2 daily; 40min); Nakhon Si Thammarat (3 weekly; 1hr 40min); Surat Thani (1 daily; 35min); Trang (2 weekly; 45min)

CHAPTER EIGHT

THE DEEP SOUTH

The frontier between Thailand and Malaysia carves across the peninsula six degrees north of the equator, but the cultures of the two countries shade into each other much further north. According to official divisions the southern Thais – the *thai pak tai* – begin around Chumphon, and as you move further down the peninsula you'll see ever more sarongs, yashmaks and towering mosques, and hear with increasing frequency a staccato dialect that baffles many Thais. In **Trang** and **Phatthalung** – the most northerly of the distinctly different southern provinces – the Muslim population is generally accepted as being Thai, but the inhabitants of the four southernmost provinces – **Satun**, **Pattani**, **Yala** and **Narathiwat** – are ethnically more akin to the Malaysians: most of the 1,500,000 followers of Islam here speak Yawi, an old Malay dialect, and many yearn for secession from Thailand. And to add to the ethnic confusion, the deep south has a large urban population of Chinese, whose comparative wealth stands them out sharply from the Muslim farmers and fishermen.

On a journey south, the first thing you might be tempted by is an atmospheric boat trip through the **Waterbird Park** near Phatthalung. The easiest route after that is to hop across to the great natural beauty of the **west coast**, with its sheer limestone outcrops, pristine sands and fish-laden coral stretching down to the Malaysian border. The spread of tourism around from Phuket has halted at Ko Lanta for the moment, so from **Trang** southwards – where the peaceful and spectacular islands of **Ko Tarutao National Park** are the most obvious attraction – you'll get the beaches and islands to yourself, though you'll have to work harder to get there and stay there.

On the less attractive **east** side of the peninsula, you'll probably pass through the ugly, modern city of **Hat Yai** at some stage, as it's the transport capital for the south and for connections to Malaysia, but a far more sympathetic place to stay is the old town of **Songkhla**, an hour away on the seashore. The region southeast of here is where you'll experience Malay Muslim culture at its purest, though there's nothing compelling to do there.

As well as the usual bus services and the railway line, which forks at Hat Yai to Butterworth on the Malaysian west coast and Sungai Kolok on the eastern border, the deep south is the territory of **share taxis** – often grand old 1950s Mercs, which connect all the major towns for about twice the fare of ordinary buses. Each town has several taxi ranks, divided according to destination, and the cars leave when they're full, which usually means seven passengers plus a babe-in-arms and livestock. They are a quick way of getting around and you should get dropped off at the door of your destination.

There are at least half a dozen **border crossings** to Malaysia, which are outlined below. At any of them you can nip across and back to get a fifteen-day Thai visa or to begin the second part of a double-entry visa. For buying longer visas, Thailand has consulates at Penang on the west side of Malaysia and at Kota Baru on the east side.

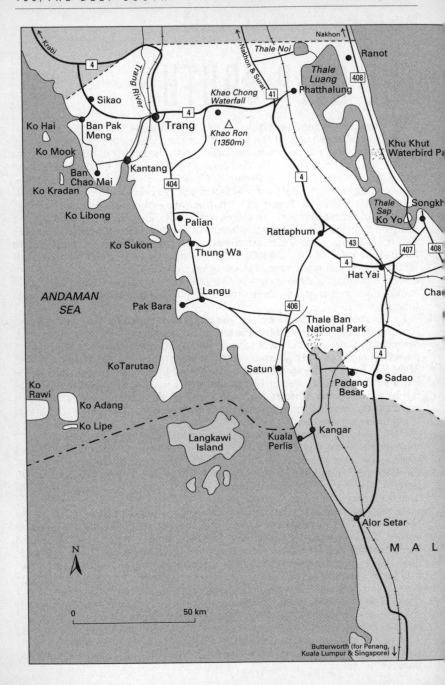

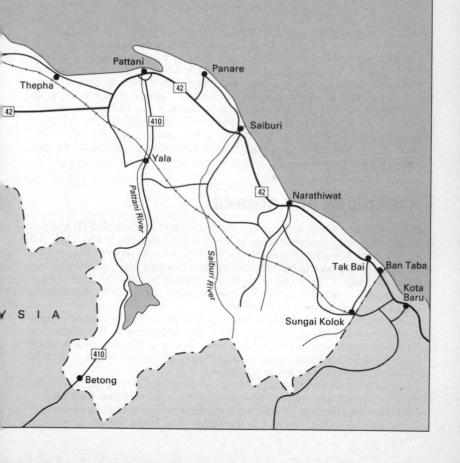

Some history

The central area of the Malay Peninsula first entered Thai history when it came under the rule of Sukhothai, probably around the beginning of the fourteenth century. Islam was introduced to the area by the end of that century, by which time Ayutthaya was taking a firmer grip on the peninsula. **Songkhla** and **Pattani** then rose to be the major cities, prospering on the goods passed through the two ports across the peninsula to avoid the pirates in the Straits of Malacca between Malaysia and Sumatra. More closely tied to the Muslim Malay states to the south, Pattani began to **rebel** against the central power of Ayutthaya in the sixteenth century, but the fight for self-determination only weakened Pattani's strength. The town's last rebellious fling was in 1902, and seven years later Pattani was isolated from its allies, Kedah, Kelantan and Trengganu, when they were transferred into the suzerainty of the British in Malaysia.

During World War II the **Communist Party of Malaysia** made its home in the jungle around the Thai border to fight the occupying Japanese. After the war they turned their guns against the British colonialists, but having been excluded from power after independence, descended into general banditry and racketeering around Betong. The Thai authorities have largely succeeded in breaking up the bandit gangs through a combination of pardons and bribes, but the stability of the region now faces disruption from another source, as the aggressive stance of the Muslim rulers of Malaysia has been paralleled by a rise in **Islamic militancy** in the deep south. Many Muslims feel alienated by what they see as the Bangkok government's colonial-style prejudices, and feel excluded from the recent consumer boom and the economic benefits of tourism. The government is pumping money into development projects but hasn't changed the law which prevents those educated in Muslim universities from becoming teachers. Thai teachers, who are paid danger money to come to the south, have recently been the object of attacks by separatists of the Pattani United Liberation Organization, the militant edge of Muslim disaffection.

Phatthalung and around

Halfway between Nakhon and Hat Yai, the hot, dusty town of **PHATTHALUNG** is worth a stop only if you're tempted by a boat trip through the nearby Thale Noi Waterbird Park, a beautiful watery landscape, rich in exotic birds and vegetation. Although its setting among limestone outcrops is dramatic, the town itself is drab and unwelcoming: its only claims to fame are *nang thalung*, the Thai shadow puppet theatre to which it probably gave its name (see p.363), and bandits, though it's cleaned up its act in recent years.

Phatthalung is served by frequent buses from north and south and from Trang, 57km to the west, and is on the major railway line, which crosses the main street, Ramet Road, in the centre of town. Most buses stop near the train station, which is on the north side of Ramet Road; through buses only stop on Highway 4, to the west, leaving a short songthaew hop into town.

Going to the waterbird park is the main reason for coming to Phatthalung, but if you've got time to kill before or after a visit there, head for **Khao Hua Taek** or "Broken-Headed Mountain", the limestone outcrop with a dent in its peak which rises abruptly out of the west end of the centre. **Wat Kuha Sawan**, on the east side, has been built around a large cool, cave in the base of the outcrop, where a crude Buddha image is sheltered by a model of the bodhi tree hung with delicate brass leaves. Climb the concrete steps to the right of the cave, then follow the path to the left to reach the summit, where you'll get a good view over Phatthalung and the surrounding ricefields. To the east, you'll also be able to see **Khao Ok**

Rice planting

Taloo, "Broken-Hearted Mountain", so called because of the natural tunnel through its peak: according to legend, Hua Taek and Ok Taloo were the wife and the mistress of a third mountain to the north, Khao Muang, over whom they had a fierce fight, leaving them with these wounds.

If a visit to Khao Hua Taek still leaves you with time on your hands, you could make a short trip out of town towards the resort of Lam Pam, half an hour away to the northeast: take one of the frequent songthaews from the railway crossing on Ramet Road. About 6km out on the right-hand side, stop off at the 200-year-old bot of **Wat Wang** to see a series of elegant and dynamic murals, depicting the life of the Buddha – ask a monk for the key to the formidable cloisters which surround it. Two former **governor's palaces**, appealing examples of traditional southern Thai architecture, overlook a picturesque canal 200m beyond Wat Wang on the same side of the road. Nearer to the road, the "old" residence, which dates from the middle of the last century, is built entirely of wood on inward-sloping stilts, a design whose tensile properties mean that it can be held together with tongue-and-groove joints rather than nails. In the so-called "new" palace, built in 1889 with a raised stone courtyard around a large tree, look out for the intricate traditional carvings on the main house, especially the "sunrise" gable, sometimes called the "crest of a monk's robe" because it resembles the edge of the robe gathered into pleats by a monk's hand.

At **LAM PAM** itself there's nothing to do but eat and drink cheaply, while sitting in a relaxing deck chair on the shady banks of the Thale Luang, the lagoon adjoining Thale Noi (see below). A cheap way of getting onto the lake is to take one of the morning boats across to RANOT, ninety minutes away, which is connected to Songkhla and Nakhon by hourly buses.

Practicalities

Out of a poor selection of **hotels**, best value is the friendly *Thai Hotel*, at 14 Disara Sakarin Rd, behind the *Bangkok Bank* on Ramet Road; clean, reasonably quiet rooms with attached bathrooms start at B120 with fan, B200 with air conditioning. *Koo Hoo*, at 9 Prachabamrung Rd (parallel to and south of Ramet) is an excellent, moderately priced **restaurant** – try the chicken with lemon sauce on a bed of fried seaweed.

Thale Noi Waterbird Park

Thale Noi Waterbird Park isn't just for bird-spotters – even the most recalcitrant city-dweller can appreciate boating through the bizarre freshwater habitat formed at the head of the huge lagoon that spills into the sea at Songkhla. Here, in the "Little Sea" (Thale Noi), the distinction between land and water breaks down: the lake is dotted with low, marshy islands, and much of the intervening water is so thickly covered with water vines, lotus pads and reeds that it looks like a field. But the real delight of this area are the hundreds of thousands of birds which breed here – brown teals, loping purple herons, white cattle egrets, and nearly two hundred other species. Most are migratory, arriving here from January onwards from as far away as Siberia – March and April provide the widest variety of birds, whereas from October to December you'll spot just a small range of native species. Early morning and late evening are the best times to come, when the heat is less searing and when, in the absence of hunters and fishermen, more birds are visible.

To get from Phatthalung to **BAN THALE NOI**, the village on the western bank, take one of the frequent **songthaews** from Nivas Road, which runs north off Ramet Road near the station – they take one hour. If you're coming from Nakhon or points further north by bus, you can save yourself a trip into Phatthalung by getting out at BAN CHAI KHLONG, 15km from Ban Thale Noi, and waiting for a songthaew there. Look out for the water-reeds being dried by the side of the road: the locals weave them into mats, bags, fans and hats, which are on sale in Ban Thale Noi – a good buy, as the sun on the lake is fierce.

Longtail boats can be hired at the pier in the village: for B150, the boatman will give you a two-hour trip around the lake, taking in the best spotting areas and, usually, a spur of land where a local artist has built a thoroughly modern spirit house from found materials. If you want to get a dawn start, *Thale Noi Villa* has a restaurant and secluded lakeside **bungalows** for B200, 1km from the village (free boat from the pier).

Trang province

From Phatthalung, Highway 4 heads south for 100km to Hat Yai, but if you want to have a thorough look around the deep south, with as little backtracking as possible, it's easiest first to visit Trang, 60km west. From there you can go down the west coast, with its pristine beaches and unspoilt islands, before heading across to Hat Yai to begin your journey down the east coast. The attractive route to Trang, served by half-hourly buses, climbs out of Phatthalung's plain of ricefields to a pass over the Khao Ron range of mountains before descending a series of hairpin bends through forest and rubber plantations past the **Khao Chong waterfall**, 18km from Trang. A three-kilometre walk through the park on the south side of the road leads to the bathing pool and the cascades, which cut a broad path down the hillside through thick, humming jungle. The fall has only a weak flow of water from around January to July but is spectacular during and after the rainy season.

A detour at BAN NA YONG NEUA, 10km east of Trang, will take you to **BAN NA MUEN SRI**, a famous weaving village, 5km to the north (motorcycle taxis wait at the crossroads). The women of the village use a wide variety of colours but stick to intricate traditional patterns, each of which has its own name: *lai look khaew*, a diagonal weave which is used for women's and men's scarves and other accessories, is the best known. The cloth is sold very cheaply in the village shop at the bend in the road.

Trang town

The town of **TRANG** (aka Taptieng), which prospers on rubber, oil palms and fisheries, is a sociable place whose wide, clean streets are dotted with crumbling, wooden-shuttered houses. In the evening, restaurant tables sprawl onto the main Rama VI Road and Wisetkul Road, and during the day, many of the town's Chinese inhabitants hang out in the cafés, drinking the local Khao Chong coffee. Trang's Chinese population make the **Vegetarian Festival** at the beginning of October almost as frenetic as Phuket's – and for veggie travellers it's an opportunity to feast at the stalls set up around the temples.

Getting there is easy, as Trang is ninety minutes from Phatthalung and well-served by **buses** from all the surrounding provinces. Most of these arrive at the square in front of the train station, from which the town's main street, Rama VI Road, runs eastward; buses from Satun and Palian stop on Ratsada Road, which runs south from the eastern end of Rama VI Road. *Thai Airways* has **flights** to the airport every day from Bangkok, and one overnight **train** from the capital runs down a branch of the southern line to Trang.

Practicalities

Hotels in Trang are concentrated along Rama VI Road and the busy V-shaped street just above it, Ratchadamnoen Road. The latter has the cheapest, the *Phetch Hotel* (the sign says *Pecth*), a decaying place with no frills, where rooms are B60 without a bathroom, B80 with. The best budget choice, though, is the *Ko Teng Hotel* on Rama VI Road, where large clean rooms with their own bathrooms start at B120. The friendly couple who run the hotel can help with local info and the restaurant downstairs is a meeting place for any travellers in town. The slightly upmarket *Trang Hotel* (☎075/218944), on Rama VI Road overlooking the clock tower, has large, comfortable rooms from B250. *Thumrin Hotel* (☎075/211011; Bangkok reservations ☎02/437 0136), on Rama VI near the station, is the deluxe option, with carpets and a Japanese restaurant: fan rooms are B600, air-con B900.

Trang's **food** comes into its own in the evenings, when two good **night markets** open for business. One is in the station square, serving a mean *pat thai* with fresh prawns; the other is on Wisetkul Road north of the clock tower, where you can try very cheap *khanom jiin*, soft noodles topped with hot, sweet or fishy sauces, and eaten with crispy greens. *Khao Tom Bui*, 111 Rama VI Rd, is a very popular and reasonable pavement restaurant on the north side of the street.

Diagonally opposite *Thumrin Hotel* on Rama VI, *Bor Daeng* serves the ubiquitous Khao Chong coffee with *patongkoh* (Chinese doughnuts) and *ahaan det diap*, plates of assorted tasty titbits such as spring rolls, baby corn and sausage. For breakfasts, cakes and posh food all day, try *Richy Restaurant and Bakery*, a friendly but slightly pricey place on Ratchadamnoen Road.

Dodgy **motorcycles** can be rented for B200 a day from the yellow-vested motorbike-taxi riders at the north corner of the market on Ratchadamnoen Road. **Scuba diving** off the coast of Trang is handled by the environmentally conscious *Rainbow Divers*, at 63/6 Soi 2, Wisetkul Rd (☎075/218820), the only dive operator in the area. On offer are courses for beginners at B1500 for a one-day introduction, as well as trips for qualified divers starting from B2500 per day.

The Trang coast

From Pak Meng, 40km due west of Trang town, to the mouth of the Trang River runs a thirty-kilometre stretch of gorgeous **beaches**, broken only by dramatic limestone outcrops which are pitted with explorable caves. If you're just looking for a day at the beach, go to Pak Meng, the most accessible part of the coast and a popular weekend picnic spot for Thais; if you want a good root around the quietest beaches, you'll have to hire a motorbike or taxi in Trang, try your luck at hitching along the quiet coastal lanes, or be prepared for some long walks.

Most of the **islands** off this coast are blessed with blinding white beaches, fantastic coral and amazing marine life, but they too are difficult to reach, and are not cheap to stay on. If you just fancy a day exploring the islands, *Trang Travel* on Rama VI Road opposite *Thumrin Hotel* organise day trips on their own boat, taking in Ko Kradan, Ko Mook and Ko Cheuak, for B400 including lunch. They also rent out snorkelling equipment and will drop you off at one of the islands if you wish.

Pak Meng

The beach at **PAK MENG** is typical of the area, a long, gently curving strip strewn with small shells, which has a fine outlook to the headlands and islands to the west. Getting there takes about an hour over an hour on the hourly air-con mini-buses from the northwestern end of Ratchadamnoen Road in Trang. Plenty of drink and food stalls line the back of the beach, and if you're stuck here, *Nong Dam Guest House* has pokey rooms for B150 at the back of the restaurant.

The unpaved road south from Pak Meng passes Hat Chang Lang, which is famous for its oysters, before reaching the headquarters of **Hat Chao Mai National Park** after 7km. For B60 a night, two-person tents can be rented here which you can pitch under the casuarina trees at the back of the sandy beach. You can use the bathrooms here, but bring your own food.

Ko Hai, Ko Cheuak, Ko Mook and Ko Kradan

The easiest island to get to is **KO HAI** (aka Ko Ngai), 16km southwest of Pak Meng: a boat leaves the pier 1km north of Pak Meng every morning as soon as it has passengers, and charges around B100 per person for the one-hour crossing. The beaches are nice and there's a reef off the southeast tip – though be careful of the sharp stag coral. Of the three resorts on the island, the cheapest is *Ko Hai Villa*, with primitive bamboo huts for B300. The best, though, is *Ko Hai Village*, with wooden, stilted bungalows set among coconut palms from B1000; it has an office in Trang at 145 Huay Yot Rd (☎075/218674). All three resorts also offer tents for B150 per night. For the best snorkelling in the region you can rent a longtail on Ko Hai to get to **Ko Cheuak**, just off Ko Hai to the east, where you can swim into caverns and explore a fantastic variety of multi-coloured coral.

To get to Ko Mook and Ko Kradan, the two islands on the south side of Ko Hai, you'll need to hire a longtail at Pak Meng pier for around B500. **KO MOOK**, about 8km southeast of Ko Hai, is renowned for **Tham Morakhot**, the beautiful "Emerald Cave" which can be entered by boat at low tide. The beaches around the cave are good, but the side facing the mainland, with the fishing village, can get rather dirty. *Ko Mook Resort* (☎075/219499) has crowded bungalows from B125.

About 6km to the southwest of Ko Mook, the beautiful island of **KO KRADAN** is good snorkelling territory, as its clear waters contain a great variety of hard coral, especially on the east side. The resort on the east coast has unattractive bungalows with bathrooms from B500.

Ban Chao Mai

The mainland beaches around **BAN CHAO MAI** just shade Pak Meng for beauty and, if anything, are even quieter, although getting there requires a rented motorbike or a taxi from Trang. This Muslim village, a straggle of simple thatched houses on stilts, exists on fishing, especially for crabs, and has a few shops where visitors can buy food and drink. On the canal running behind the village you'll find mangrove swamps and a large cave containing huge rock pillars and a natural theatre, its stage framed by rock curtains. **Hat Yao** (Long Beach) runs north in a broad five-kilometre strip that's exposed enough to see occasional high surf; immediately beyond comes **Hat Yong Ling**, an attractive convex beach with another large cave which you can swim into at high tide or walk into at low tide.

Ko Tarutao National Marine Park

The unspoilt **KO TARUTAO NATIONAL MARINE PARK** is probably the most beautiful of all Thailand's accessible beach destinations. Occupying 1400 square kilometres of the Andaman Sea, the park covers 51 mostly uninhabited islands, of which three – Ko Tarutao, Ko Adang and Ko Lipe – are easy to reach and offer accommodation for visitors. The area's forests and seas support an incredible variety of **fauna**: langurs, crab-eating macaques and wild pigs are common on the islands, which also shelter several unique subspecies of squirrel, treeshrew and lesser mouse deer; among over a hundred bird species which occur here, reef egrets and hornbills are regularly seen, while white-bellied sea eagles, frigate birds and pied imperial pigeons are more rarely encountered; and the park is the habitat of about twenty-five percent of the world's fish species, as well as marine mammals such as the dugong, sperm whale and three species of migratory sea turtle. To help conserve the park's natural resources, it has been nominated as a UNESCO World Heritage Site, but plans have been mooted to set up regular boat connections with the highly developed Malaysian resort on Langkawi Island, 8km from Ko Tarutao, a scheme that would inevitably lead to disastrous disturbance from tourism, which at the moment is kept at a bearable level.

The park is closed to tourists during the monsoon season, roughly June to October; at other times of the year, you should have no problem finding somewhere to stay except at the three New Years (Thai, Chinese and the end of December), when it's best to book ahead in Bangkok (see p.22). The *Traveler's Adventure Handbook* to Tarutao is a must-buy at only B10, available at the park offices at Pak Bara and Ao Pante.

Getting to Tarutao

Boats leave **PAK BARA**, 60km north of Satun, twice a day for the ninety-minute trip to Ao Pante on Ko Tarutao, the largest of the park's islands. To get there **from Trang**, take a bus (2hr 30min) or a share taxi (1hr 30min) to the inland town of LANGU and change to a red songthaew for the ten-kilometre hop to the port. From the clock tower in front of the *President Hotel* in **Hat Yai**, one bus a day (at 7.45am) goes all the way through to Pak Bara in two and half hours, to connect with the first boat to Tarutao – otherwise take a share taxi to Langu, or a Satun-bound bus to CHALUNG and change onto a bus from Satun to Langu. From **Satun**, frequent buses and taxis make the fifty-kilometre trip to Langu.

Pak Bara has simple **accommodation** for people who miss the boat to Tarutao. *Adesorn* by the jetty will provide a dirty mattress for B50, and *Marena*, 300m along the tree-lined beach, has decent bungalows with bathrooms for B120.

Ko Tarutao

KO TARUTAO offers the greatest natural variety of all the islands: mountains covered in semi-evergreen rainforest rise steeply to a high point of 700m; limestone caves and mangrove swamps dot the shoreline; and the west coast is lined with perfect beaches for most of its 26-kilometre length. It's also where you'll find the park's best facilities for visitors.

Boats dock at **Ao Pante**, on the northwestern side of the island, where the admission fee is collected (B5) and where the **park headquarters** is situated. Here you'll find the only shop on the island, selling basic supplies, as well as a visitor centre and a well-stocked library. The **bungalows**, which are spread over a large, quiet park behind the beach, are National Park standard issue, simple, hygienic concrete affairs with cold water bathrooms; each room sleeps four and costs B400. **Beds** in the bamboo longhouses cost B70 per person, and two-person **tents** can be hired for B40 a night. Ao Pante has two **eateries**: the café does cheap, simple dishes, while the restaurant has a more varied and expensive menu.

Behind the settlement, the steep, half-hour climb to **To-Boo Cliff** is a must, especially at sunset, for the view of the surrounding islands and the crocodile's-head cape at the north end of the bay. A fun boat trip can also be made near Ao Pante, up the canal which leads 2km inland from the pier, through the lush leaves and dense roots of a bird-filled mangrove swamp, to **Crocodile Cave**. Inside the cave a walkway extends through stalagmites for about 1km, where you can glimpse a ray of light from the distant cave-mouth at Ao Jak – though it's not possible to walk all the way through. Contact the information centre at headquarters to hire a boat (B150) for the one-hour round trip – and bring a flashlight.

A half-hour walk south from Ao Pante will bring you to the two quiet bays of **Ao Jak** and **Ao Malae**, fringed by coconut palms and filled with fine white sand. Behind the house at the south end of Ao Malae, a road leads over the headland to **Ao Sone** (2hr from Ao Pante), where a pretty freshwater stream runs past the ranger station at the north end of the bay, making this a good place for peaceful camping. The main part of the bay is a three-kilometre sweep of flawless sand, with a ninety-minute trail leading up to a waterfall in the middle and a mangrove swamp at the far south end.

On the east side of the island, **Ao Taloh Wow** is a rocky bay with a ranger station, connected to Ao Pante by a twelve-kilometre road through old rubber plantations and evergreen forest. If you have a tent, you might want to set off along the overgrown, five-hour trail beyond Taloh Wow, which cuts through the forest to **Ao Taloh Udang**, a sandy bay on the south side. Here the remnants of a penal colony for political prisoners are just visible: the plotters of two failed coup attempts were imprisoned here in the 1930s before returning to high government posts. The ordinary convicts, who used to be imprisoned at Ao Taloh Wow, had a much harsher time, and during World War II, when supplies from the mainland dried up, prisoners and guards ganged together to turn to piracy. Pirates and smugglers still occasionally hide out in the Tarutao archipelago, but the main problem now is illegal trawlers fishing in National Park waters.

Ko Adang and Ko Lipe

The only way to reach the park's two other principal islands – Ko Adang and Ko Lipe – is on the mail boat which leaves Ao Pante three times a week for the three-hour journey, coming back on the following day. The return ticket costs a hefty B350, but it's an open return, so you can stay on the islands as long as you want.

At **KO ADANG**, a wild, rugged island covered in tropical rainforest, the boat pulls in at the **Laem Sone** park station on the southern shore, where the beach is steep and narrow and backed by a thick canopy of pines. **Beds** in the bamboo longhouses here are B70 per person, and the **restaurant** is limited and a bit pricey. The half-hour climb to **Sha-do** cliff on the steep slope above Laem Sone gives good views over the sand spit of the harbour and Ko Lipe to the south. About 2km west along the coast from the park station, the small beach is lined with coconut palms and an abandoned customs house, behind which a twenty-minute trail leads to the small **Pirate Waterfall**. For more ambitious explorations, the author of the park handbook recommends **"snork-hiking"**, an amphibious method of reaching distant attractions. Up the east coast, you can make a day trip like this to Rattana Waterfall, 3km from the park station, and to the *chao ley* (see p.384) village of **Taloh Puya**, 1km further, which has a fine coral reef directly offshore and a nice beach to the north.

KO LIPE, 2km south of Adang, makes a busy contrast to the other islands. A small, flat triangle, it's covered in coconut plantations and inhabited by *chao ley,* with shops, a school and a health centre in the village on the eastern side – from where longtail boats come out to meet the mail boat. The *chao ley* have opened several **bungalow** outfits in the village, with dorm beds for B50 and simple bungalows from B200: the best of these is *Laem Sone Oun* at the north end, which has bamboo bungalows by the beach under shady pine trees. The owner has longtail boats if you want to visit the coral reefs around Ko Jabang and Ko Yang, on the west side of Adang, but there's rewarding water around tiny **Ko Gra**, 200m out to sea from the village, which has a beautiful coral reef. **Pattaya Beach**, about 1km from the village on the south side of the island, has a similar set of bungalows and a good offshore reef to explore.

Satun and around

Remote **SATUN** nestles in the last wedge of Thailand's west coast and is served by just one road, Highway 406, which approaches the town through forbidding karst outcrops. Set in a green valley bordered by limestone hills, the town is leafy and relaxing but not especially interesting: the boat service to and from Malaysia are the main reason for farangs to come here, though some use the town as an approach to Ko Tarutao (see above) or Thale Ban National Park (see below).

Frequent **buses** depart from Ratsada Road in Trang, and regular buses also come from Phattalung and from Hat Yai – if you don't get a direct bus from there to Satun, it's easy to change at RATTAPHUM, on the junction of highways 4 and 406. The bus depot is at the north end of town, but most buses also make a stop in the centre.

Rian Thong, by the town pier at 4 Saman Pradit Rd (☎074/711036) is the best cheap **hotel** in Satun; the owners are friendly and speak English, and some of the clean, well-furnished rooms (from B100) overlook the canal. *Farm Gai*, more or less in open country ten minutes' west of the centre (take a motorbike taxi), is run by a Swiss who was once a pioneering bungalow-builder on Ko Samui. Very comfortable, well-designed huts and rooms in a quiet garden start at B60; the family prefer guests who will stay for a while to sample Thai country life, but don't insist on it. In complete contrast, *Wangmai Hotel*, out towards the bus depot at 43 Satun Thani Rd (☎074/711607), is a typical "deluxe" hotel in a modern concrete block, with a/c rooms from B460. For evening **food**, try *Yim Yim* on Saman Pradit Road by the Chinese temple, a clean and popular restaurant which serves good, simple Chinese food.

Crossing the border

For travel across the border, longtail boats take one hour (B30) to reach **Kuala Perlis** on Malaysia's northwest tip, from where there are plentiful transport connections down the west coast. When Khlong Bambang is high enough, the boats can reach the pier in the town centre – otherwise they use **Tammalang** pier, 10km south at the mouth of the river, site of the main customs and immigration offices. Frequent songthaews and motorcycle taxis run to Tammalang from the town centre in around half an hour.

Thale Ban National Park

Spread over rainforested mountains along the Malaysian border, **THALE BAN NATIONAL PARK** is a pristine nature reserve which shelters a breathtaking variety of wildlife: from gibbons, tapirs, Malayan sun bears and a few rarely sighted elephants and tigers, to unusual birds such as bat hawks, booted eagles and flamboyant argus pheasants. Unfortunately for naturalists and casual visitors alike, few trails have been marked out through the jungle, but the lush, peaceful setting of the headquarters and the views and bathing pools of the Yaroy waterfall are enough to justify the trip. From BAN KHWAN SATOR, 19km north of Satun on Highway 406, irregular songthaews make the twenty-kilometre journey south to the park headquarters, which lies just 2km from Malaysia. The songthaews continue to the border, where share taxis wait to ferry you south.

Hemmed in by steep, verdant hills and spangled with red water lilies, the **lake** by the headquarters is central to the story that gives the park its name. Local legend tells how a villager once put his *ban* (headscarf) on a tree stump to have a rest; this caused a landslide, the lake appeared from nowhere, and he, the stump and the *ban* tumbled into it. The water is now surrounded by **bungalows**, which start at B500 for six people, but lower rates can be negotiated on weekdays, when business is slow. A decent open-air **canteen** also overlooks the lake.

The most interesting **jungle walk** runs east along the border to the summit of Khao Chin, 12km away, but the trail is overgrown and easy to lose – someone at headquarters might be free to guide you. A less strenuous trip is the one to **Tham Tondin**, a low, sweaty stalactite cave which gradually slopes down for 800m to deep water. It's about 2km north of headquarters back along the road to Khwan Sator – look out for the wooden sign in Thai, on the west side of the main road just north of the 18km post, then climb 30m up the slope to see the tiny entrance at your feet. If you time your visit so that you emerge just before dusk, you'll see hundreds of bats streaming out of the hole for the night. It's best to consult the detailed map at headquarters before you visit the cave, and you'll need a torch.

The one essential jaunt, though, is to **Yaroy Waterfall** – bring swimming gear for the pools above the main fall. Take the main road north from the headquarters through the narrow, idyllic valley for 6km (beyond the village of Wang Prachan) and follow the sign to the right. After 700m, you'll find the main, lower fall set in screeching jungle. By climbing the path on the left side, you reach what seems like the top, with fine views of the steep, green peaks to the west. However, there's more: if you carry on up the stream, you'll find a series of gorgeous shady pools, where you can bathe and shower under the six-metre falls.

Hat Yai

HAT YAI, the transport axis of the deep south, was given a dose of instant American-style modernization in the 1950s, since when it's commercially usurped its own provincial capital, Songkhla. The resulting concrete mess, reminiscent of Bangkok without the interesting bits, attracts half a million tourists a year, nearly all of them Malaysians who nip across the border to shop and get laid. On any extended tour of the south you are bound to end up in Hat Yai, and you may as well take the opportunity to call in at the TAT office for the whole deep south at 1/1 Soi 2, Niphat Uthit Rd 3 (☎074/243747). If the concrete and the sleaze turns you off a protracted stay, remember that Songkhla is only 25km away.

If you're leap-frogging into the deep south via Hat Yai **airport** you'll arrive 12km from town, then be shuttled into the centre on the *Thai Airways* minibus to their office at 166/4 Niphat Uthit Rd 2 (☎074/245851). The **railway station** is on the west side of the centre at the end of Thamnoon Vithi Rd, whereas all air-con **buses** and ordinary buses from Sungai Kolok and Bangkok arrive at the main bus station to the southeast of town, leaving you with a songthaew ride to the centre. Other ordinary buses stop at the smaller Plaza station on Petchkasem Road, on the north side of the centre. **Share taxis** should drop you off at your destination; for departure, they have a number of different ranks around town (marked on the map) according to where you want to go. Recently, a variety of **air-con minibus** companies have sprung up, each serving a particular town, as shown on the map. They cost about the same as taxis and are much more comfortable.

Practicalities

Hat Yai has a huge range of **hotels**, none of them very good value and most worked by prostitutes. A few in the budget range are geared to travellers: the friendly *Cathay Guest House* at 93 Niphat Uthit Rd 2 (☎074/243815) is falling apart, but the movable parts are reasonably clean and the information board is a guide book in itself. Dorm beds are B60 and double rooms start at B120 – try to get one away from the street. Beside the ordinary bus station, *Sorasilp Guest House*, 251/7–8 Petchkasem Rd (☎074/232635) is also friendly and helpful; dorm beds are B60, singles B140, doubles B180, and air-con rooms start at B200.

The best of many typical Chinese hotels around the central Niphat Uthit roads is *Laem Thong*, 46 Thamnoon Vithi Rd (☎074/244893), where fan rooms start at B180 and air-con rooms are B370. For more comfort, try *Lada Guest House*, by the railway station at 13–15 Thamnoon Vithi Rd (☎074/243770); carpeted air-con rooms with bathrooms and an overdose of pink paint are B290 single, B320 double. Hat Yai's top hotel is the *J B Hotel*, 99 Jootee-Anusorn Rd (☎074/234300), recently taken over by the ever reliable *Dusit* group; luxury rooms start at B1100.

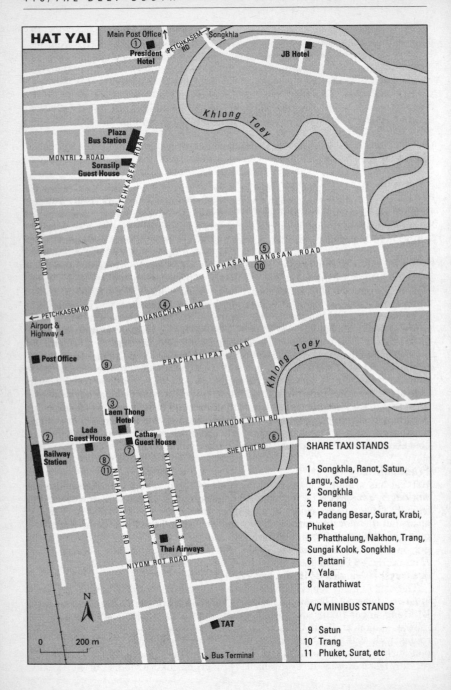

HAT YAI

Main Post Office ↑
① President Hotel
PETCHKASEM RD
Songkhla
JB Hotel

Khlong Toey

Plaza Bus Station
PETCHKASEM ROAD
MONTRI 2 ROAD
Sorasilp Guest House

RATAKARN ROAD

⑤
SUPHASAN RANGSAN ROAD
⑩

← PETCHKASEM RD
Airport & Highway 4

④
DUANGCHAN ROAD

Post Office

PRACHATHIPAT ROAD

⑨

Khlong Toey

③ Laem Thong Hotel

②
Lada Guest House
Cathay Guest House

THAMNOON VITHI RD

⑥

⑦

SHE UTHIT RD

② Railway Station

⑧
⑪

NIPHAT UTHIT RD 1
NIPHAT UTHIT RD 2
NIPHAT UTHIT RD 3

Thai Airways

NIYOM ROT ROAD

N

0   200 m

TAT

Bus Terminal

SHARE TAXI STANDS

1 Songkhla, Ranot, Satun, Langu, Sadao
2 Songkhla
3 Penang
4 Padang Besar, Surat, Krabi, Phuket
5 Phatthalung, Nakhon, Trang, Sungai Kolok, Songkhla
6 Pattani
7 Yala
8 Narathiwat

A/C MINIBUS STANDS

9   Satun
10 Trang
11 Phuket, Surat, etc

Hat Yai's **restaurants** offer a choice of Thai, Chinese, Muslim and Western food. On the corner of Thamnoon Vithi and Niphat Uthit 3, try the bustling *Ko Yao* for cheap and tasty Chinese food in the evening. *Muslim O-Cha*, at 117 Niphat Uthit 1 (closes 8.30pm), is a simple, clean restaurant which serves curried chicken and rice and other cheap Muslim food in small portions. A reasonable place for all-day breakfasts, Western food and some interesting Thai dishes is the cool and comfortable *Nakorn Nai* at 166/7 Niphat Uthit 2. If you want to splurge out, the *Jye Beer and Bakery* at the bottom of Ratakarn Road does posh Thai and American food in a cosy, rustic atmosphere. Finally, the sprawling night market, near the ordinary bus station on Montri 2 Road, has something for everyone: seafood and beer, Thai curries, deep fried chicken, and the Muslim speciality *khao neua daeng*, tender cured beef in a sweet red sauce.

For a quiet **drink**, head for *Sugar Rock*, 114 Thamnoon Vithi Rd, a pleasant café bar with low-volume Western music, or *Camp*, 27 Niyom Rot Rd, a small, easy-going bar done out like a wild west saloon.

Hat Yai is one of the south's major centres for **bullfighting**, which in its Thai version involves bull tussling with bull, the winner being the one which forces the other to retreat. Fights can last anything from a few seconds to half an hour, in which case the frantic betting of the audience becomes more interesting than the deadlock in the ring. On the first Saturday of every month, a day-long competition, beginning at 10am, is held at a stadium 8km south of town on the road to Sadao. It's best to get there in the early afternoon as the big fights, involving prize money of up to B200,000, are lower down the card. A special entrance fee of B100 is charged to farangs; to get there charter a songthaew and ask for *klong wa*.

Crossing the border

Hat Yai is only 50km from the border with **Malaysia**. The fastest way of getting across is to take a **share taxi** to **Penang**, where you can renew your visa at the Thai consulate; taxis depart every morning for about B220. Tickets for the more comfortable and slightly cheaper **air-con buses** can be bought at travel agents, such as *Magic Tour*, under the *Cathay Guest House*. These buses depart every day for Penang (6hr), as well as Kuala Lumpur (12hr) and Singapore (18hr). More comfortable again are the **trains**, though they're not very convenient: seven a day run to Sungai Kolok on the east-coast border, while one a day heads via Padang Besar to Butterworth deep inside Malaysia. The cheapest but most time-consuming method is to take a **bus** from Plaza station to Padang Besar, walk 800m across the border and take a share taxi for the half-hour journey to Kuala Perlis – avoid the obvious route straight down Highway 4 to Sadao, because there's a long stretch between the opposing border posts which there's no cheap way of covering.

Songkhla and around

Known as the "big town of two seas" because it sits on a north-pointing peninsula between the Gulf of Thailand and the Thale Sap lagoon, **SONGKHLA** provides a sharp contrast to Hat Yai. A small, sophisticated provincial capital, it retains many historic buildings – such as the elegant Wat Matchimawat and the Chinese mansion that now houses the national museum – and its broad, quiet streets are planted with soothing greenery. When you add some fine restaurants and decent accommodation, and the proximity to the wonderful Southern Folklore Museum at Ko Yo, Songkhla makes a stimulating place to hole up in for a few days.

The settlement was originally sited on the north side of the mouth of the Thale Sap, where a deepwater port has now been built, and flourished as a **trading port** from the eighth century onwards. The shift across the river came after 1769, when a Chinese merchant named Yieng Hao was granted permission by the Thai ruler, Taksin, to collect swallows' nests from Ko Si Ko Ha – now part of Khu Khut Waterbird Park. Having made a packet from selling them for their culinary and medicinal properties, he was made governor of Songkhla by Taksin and established the city on its present site. For seven generations the **Na Songkhla dynasty** he founded kept the governorship in the family, overseeing the construction of many of the buildings you see today. The town is now an unhurried administrative centre, which maintains a strong central Thai feel – most of the province's Muslim population live in the hinterland.

Modern Songkhla's central landmark is a modern clock tower, where Ramwithi Road meets Jana Road and where most **buses** arrive. People usually come here straight from Hat Yai, 25km to the west, but buses also run direct from Nakhon and Chana. **Taxis** for these towns and places further afield congregate on the south side of the clock tower. The scenic route to Songkhla is the **Jumbo Ferry**, which cruises down from Ko Samui twice a week in ten hours (see p.342).

The town

The town which the Na Songkhlas built has expanded to fill the headland, and makes a great place for strolling around – or, if the distances involved put you off, riding around on a bicycle hired from the *Narai Hotel* (see below). The western side, where the town first developed, shelters a fishing port which presents a vivid, smelly scene in the mornings. Two abrupt hills – **Khao Tung Kuan** and the smaller **Khao Noi** – border the north side of the centre, while in the heart of town lie the main tourist attractions, the **National Museum** and the extravagantly decorated **Wat Matchimawat**. Sitting on the fringe of town at the bottom end of Hat Samila – the 8km of beach along the eastern shore – **Khao Saen** is an impoverished but vibrant fishing village, whose multi-coloured boats provide Songkhla's most hackneyed postcard image.

Khao Tung Kuan

To get your bearings, preferably in the cool of the morning or evening, climb up **Khao Tung Kuan** at the northwestern end of town. From Laem Sai Road, on the western side of the hill, steps rise past simple monks' huts which surround what looks like a red-brick Wendy house – Rama V ordered the pavilion to be built at the height of his Westernization programme, but the local artisans clearly couldn't get their heads round the monarch's conception. From the chedi at the top of the hill, you can look south over the town and the fishing port, and west over the Thale Sap to the island of Ko Yo. Further up Laem Sai Road, you can visit **Laem Sai Fort**, with its low walls and cannon, which was built by the French in the seventeenth century, when they held favour with the kings of Ayutthaya.

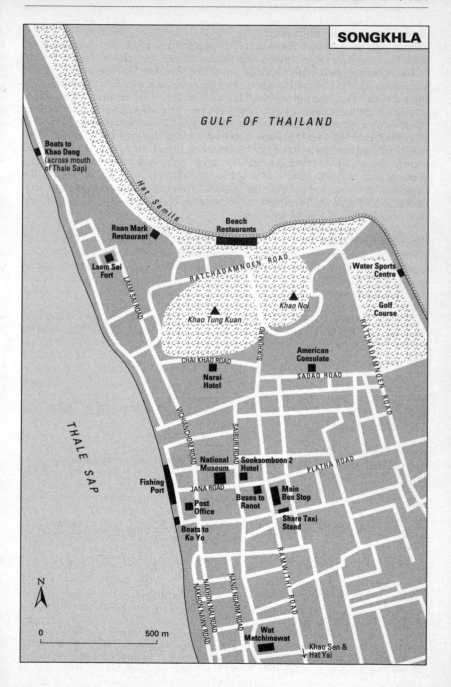

SONGKHLA

GULF OF THAILAND

Boats to
Khao Dang
(across mouth
of Thale Sap)

Hat Samila

Raan Mark
Restaurant

Beach
Restaurants

Laem Sai
Fort

RATCHADAMNOEN ROAD

Water Sports
Centre

LAEM SAI ROAD

Khao Noi

Khao Tung Kuan

Golf
Course

SUKHUM RD

RATCHADAMNOEN ROAD

CHAI KHAO ROAD

American
Consulate

Narai
Hotel

SADAO ROAD

THALE SAP

VICHIANCHOM ROAD

SAIBURI ROAD

National
Museum

Sooksomboon 2
Hotel

PLATHA ROAD

Fishing
Port

JANA ROAD

Post
Office

Buses to
Ranot

Main
Bus Stop

Boats to
Ko Yo

Share Taxi
Stand

RAMWITHI ROAD

N

NAKHON NAI ROAD

NANG NGARM ROAD

NAKHON NAWK ROAD

0   500 m

Wat
Matchimawat

Khao Sen &
Hat Yai

Songkhla National Museum

The **Songkhla National Museum** (Wed–Sun 8.30am–4.30pm) on Jana Road, the main east–west street, is worth a visit for its architecture alone. Built in 1878 in south Chinese style, this graceful mansion was first the residence of the Governor of Songkhla and Nakhon, then the city hall, and later the local poorhouse before being converted into a museum in the 1970s. Its best side faces the garden at the back: from here you can see how the ornamental staircases and the roof were constructed in shapely curves to disorientate straight-flying evil spirits.

A jumble of folk exhibits, such as masks for the *manohra* (the southern Thai dance-drama) and agricultural implements, are strewn around the garden, while inside the wildly diverse collection includes well-preserved examples of Ban Chiang pottery, early Hindu statues and Mahayana Buddhist images from the Srivijaya period, and a selection of beautiful Chinese ceramics. Upstairs everything is upstaged by overblown Chinese and Thai furniture, all lacquer and mother-of-pearl and bas-relief carving.

Wat Matchimawat

From the museum, you can explore the atmospheric old streets of Nakhon Nai and Nakhon Nawk, which show European influence in their colonnaded pavements and crumbling stucco, on your way south to **Wat Matchimawat**, a grand, attention-grabbing affair set in ornamental grounds on Saiburi Road. What stands out most of all is the bot, a florid mixture of Chinese and Thai styles, which was apparently modelled on Wat Phra Kaeo in Bangkok. Fetching stone bas-reliefs decorate the low walls around the bot, depicting leafy scenes from *The Romance of The Three Kingdoms*, a Chinese historical novel which served as a handbook of manners and morals in the middle of the nineteenth century, when the temple was built. Every inch of the lofty interior is covered with colourful *Jataka* murals, telling of the previous lives of the Buddha, mixed in with vivacious tableaux of nineteenth-century Songkhla life. The bot is usually locked, but you can get the key from the adjacent museum (Wed–Sun 8.30am–4.30pm), which is filled with ceramics, votive tablets, stuffed animals and other clutter.

Khao Saen

To see the best of the Muslim shanty village of **Khao Saen** – set against a rocky headland on the southern edge of Songkhla's tide of development – you should visit in the late afternoon, when the boisterous fish market is in full swing (except Fridays). Songthaews from Saiburi Road, south of the junction with Jana Road, make the trip in fifteen minutes. The crowded, rotting shacks of the village make a bleak contrast with the objects for which Khao Saen is most celebrated – its decorated prawn-fishing vessels. Drawn up in rows on the beach, these immaculate small boats have dragon prows wrapped in lucky garlands and hulls brightly painted with flags and intricate artwork. These pictures, which mostly depict mosques and idyllic landscapes, are the work of an artist at Saiburi, further down the coast, and cost each fisherman a month's income.

Practicalities

Narai, at 14 Chai Khao Rd (☎074/311078), is Songkhla's outstanding budget **hotel**: situated in a quiet, rambling wooden house at the foot of Doi Tung Kuan, its singles are B80, doubles B90. *Narai* also rents out **bicycles** for B40 a day. In the same price bracket as *Narai* is the seedier and noisier *Holland House* on Ramwithi Road, just north of the clock tower. *Sooksomboon 2*, at 18 Saiburi Rd, is divided in two: the cavernous old wing (☎074/311149) has clean, ordinary rooms for B140 single, B240 double; the new wing (☎074/323808) is good value, with comfortable air-con rooms for B270 single, B405 double, all with hot-water bathrooms. The same facilities as in this new wing are offered at the *Lake Inn Hotel*, 301 Nakhon Nawk Rd (☎074/314240); double rooms (B450), the ground-floor restaurant and the rooftop beer garden in this tastefully furnished tower block all face the lake, whereas single rooms (B350) face the town.

Songkhla's top hotel is the *Samila Beach*, 1/11 Ratchadamnoen Rd (☎074/311310), which has an unbeatable location at the northeast corner of town with sprawling gardens overlooking the beach, as well as a swimming pool, tennis courts and a golf course; singles in the slightly run-down but homely modern building start at B600, doubles at B700. Across the mouth of the Thale Sap, 6km along the road to Nakhon, the swish, upmarket *Haad Kaew Resort* (☎074/331059; Bangkok reservations ☎02/249 9305) is near the beach, has a swimming pool and offers mod-con bungalows from B600.

For somewhere to eat in the daytime, pull up a deck chair and relax at the cheap, shaded **restaurants** by the end of Sukhum Road on Hat Samila. Where the beach starts curving to the north near the top of Laem Sai Road, you'll find a posher open-air restaurant, *Raan Mark*, which serves good seafood. Songkhla's most famous restaurant, *Raan Tae*, at 85 Nang Ngarm Rd, is spotlessly clean and justly popular, serving especially good seafood – but it closes at 8pm. An excellent and stylish alternative is *Choeng Thian*, at 70/2 Raman Rd (turn left south of *Raan Tae* and look for the rosette outside). The interior is cosy and slightly surreal – bric-a-brac stares up at you from under the glass-topped tables – while the food is moderately-priced and imaginative. Try the *plaa samli song kleuang*, cottonfish with a salad of mango, peanuts and dried squid. The night market, south of the post office on Nakhon Nai Road, is the place for budget-conscious travellers.

Songkhla's **nightlife** is tame, apart from the *Offshore Pub* on Sadao Road, a roistering drinking-hole where oilmen and ex-pats gather.

Ko Yo

KO YO, the small island in the Thale Sap to the west of Songkhla, has long been a destination for day-trippers, and the road link with the land on both sides of the lagoon has accelerated the transformation of BAN NOK – the island's main settlement – into a souvenir village, selling durian cakes and the high-quality fabrics for which Ko Yo is famous. The best way of **getting there from Songkhla** is to take one of the frequent Ranot-bound buses from Jana Road, which take half an hour to get to Ko Yo, and then continue to Khu Khut Waterbird Park. If you fancy a more scenic but costly route, longtail boats from the pier behind the post office on Nakhon Nai Road cost B100 per person. If you're coming **from Hat Yai**, there's no need to go into Songkhla first: take a Songkhla-bound bus but get off on the edge of the suburbs at the junction with Highway 408, and catch a songthaew or bus across the bridge to Ko Yo.

Cakes or cloth apart, the chief appeal of Ko Yo is the **Southern Folklore Museum** (daily 8am–6pm; B10 with a free pamphlet in English), which sprawls over twelve acres of hillside on the northern tip of Ko Yo just before the northern bridge. Giving stunning views over the water to Songkhla and of the fishing villages on the western side of the island, the park is strewn with all kinds of boats and wooden reproductions of traditional southern houses, in which the collections are neatly set out. The exhibits inside, such as the shadow-puppet paraphernalia and the *kris* – long knives with intricately carved handles and sheaths – show the strong influences of Malaysia and Indonesia on southern Thailand. Also on show are the elaborate dance costumes for the *manohra*, but probably the most fascinating objects are the *lek kood* or coconut scrapers, which are set into seat-blocks carved into an offbeat variety of shapes – rabbits, elephants, phalluses, beauty queens. The museum occasionally stages free cultural shows, which are well worth going to (for details ring ☎074/239899 or ask at TAT in Hat Yai).

One hundred metres south of the museum, a slip road leads to a good seafood restaurant, *Suan Kaeo*, passing a **weaving workshop** where you can watch the work in progress in the mornings and early afternoons, and buy the finished product at a cheap rate.

Khu Khut Waterbird Park

About 40km up Highway 408 from Songkhla, a left turn by the police station leads after 3km to the headquarters of **Khu Khut Waterbird Park**, a conservation area on the Thale Luang where over 140 species of mostly migratory birds are found. The park is similar to Thale Noi near Phatthalung, though not as impressive and more expensive, but if you're not planning to visit Phatthalung, it's worth coming here on a day trip from Songkhla. A longtail boat trip to view the birds costs B150 for an hour, or for B250 you get a two-hour jaunt across the shallow lake – weaving between water reeds and crayfish traps – to Ko Si Ko Ha, the dramatic limestone islands where birds' nests are gathered for Chinese gourmets. *Kukon Guest House*, 50m back from the headquarters, has very basic rooms for B100.

Pattani

PATTANI, the traditional centre of the Muslim south, is a rather forbidding town, but presents a fascinating cultural clash embodied by the discord between its polychrome Chinese temples and the remains of its sixteenth-century mosque. Founded around the beginning of the fifteenth century, not long after the introduction of Islam to the area, Pattani soon became an important port for trade in the Gulf of Thailand. From the time of its founding, Pattani owed allegiance to the Thai kings at Ayutthaya, and after the capital was moved to Bangkok the city state was fully integrated into Thailand. However, having close ties with fellow Islamic states to the south, it has always chafed against the central power and is even now the focus of Muslim antipathy towards the Thai government. Although the port has declined, the industry and fisheries which in recent years have been established around the town have turned it into a busy, though rather ugly, commercial centre.

Pattani is also home to a sizeable Chinese community, whose rivalry with Islam is enshrined in the town's most famous legend. In the 1570s a certain Lim Toh

Khiem, a notorious Chinese pirate, married a local woman and was converted to Islam. To show his conviction in his new faith, he began a mosque – at which point, legend has it, his sister Lim Ko Niaw sailed from China to persuade him to renounce Islam and return to his homeland. When her mission failed she hanged herself from the nearest cashew nut tree, now preserved at the **San Jao Lim Ko Niaw** on Arnoaru Road, a side street off the northern stretch of Yarang Road, the main north–south street. It's a gaudy, dimly lit shrine, groaning with rich offerings and grimy with the soot of endless joss-sticks, with a child's doll, representing Lim Ko Niaw, as its centrepiece. During the annual Lim Ko Niaw festival, held in the mini-stadium opposite at the beginning of March, the doll is carried through a raging bonfire by entranced devotees, who by this and other masochistic feats seek to prove their purity to their heroine goddess.

Lim Ko Niaw's suicide put a curse on her brother's mosque, the **Masjid Kreu Se**, which confounded his and his successors' attempts to finish it. Located 5km east of town towards Narathiwat, the roofless brick shell was recently renovated by the Thai authorities as a historical and touristic site, causing great offence among the local population – in May 1990 a crowd of 10,000 people gathered here to vent their anger. An unofficial Muslim guard is now stationed near the entrance at all times, to prevent non-Muslims from walking onto the holy ruins. Next door to the mosque the Chinese have built an ostentatious shrine around the horseshoe burial mound of Lim Ko Niaw. The mosque can be visited by songthaew or bus from Ramkomud Road, the eastern continuation of Rudee Road, whose intersection with Yarang Road marks the centre of town.

Facilities for visitors are very limited, though at a pinch the town could be visited on a long day trip from Hat Yai or as a break in the journey south. The pick of a pitiful choice of **hotels** in Pattani is the *Palace*, on Preeda Road, between Pipit and Rudee roads (☎073/349171); fairly clean singles are B130 with fan (B200 air-con), doubles are B180 (B270 air-con). The best place to **eat** is the busy night market on the north side of Pipit Road.

South to Yala and the border

From Pattani, Highway 410 heads due south to Yala, a dull but efficient town 43km across the coastal plain, then on for 140km through the mountains to Betong, the most southerly point on the Thai-Malaysian border. This makes a quiet, scenic route into Malaysia but otherwise has little to offer.

Yala

YALA is the business and education centre of the Muslim border provinces, a town of tree-lined boulevards that's won awards as the cleanest town in Thailand. An uninspiring place, its liveliest time is during the the the **ASEAN Barred Ground Dove Festival** at the beginning of March, when hundreds of competitors flock here from all over Southeast Asia. The breeding of luck-bringing Java doves is an obsession among the Muslim population of the south, where most houses have a cage outside and many villages feature fields of metal poles on which to hang the cages at competition time, which is usually March and April. The birds are judged on the pitch, melody and volume of their cooing and on their appearance, and the most musical specimens change hands for as much as two million baht at the Yala jamboree.

Though staunchly Islamic, Yala attracts coachloads of Buddhist pilgrims, who come to revere the twenty-five-metre-long reclining Buddha at **Wat Tham**, 6km out of town on the road to YAHA. The image's aura of holiness comes from its atmospheric setting in a broad, dank cave, and from its great age: it's said that the image was constructed and the temple founded by a king of Palembang (Sumatra), some time around the end of the eighth century. To get there, take a bus from behind the *Thepvimarn* hotel (see below), which will leave you with a 500-metre walk south to the temple.

The railway station is on the east side of the centre; buses from Pattani stop on Siriros Road, north of the station and east of the tracks – those from Hat Yai stop 500m west on the same road. If you need somewhere **to stay**, the best budget deal is *Thepvimarn* (☎073/212400) at 31 Sribumrung Rd, where clean rooms cost from B70; coming from the railway station, it's the first left off Pipitpakdee Road. For an evening **meal** of simple, reasonable seafood, try the popular *Talat Restaurant* at the corner of Sribumrung and Pipitpakdee roads.

Betong

Perched on the tip of a narrow tongue of land reaching into Malaysia, **BETONG** is only worth considering if you're heading out of the country – the town is notorious for its fog, and most of Betong's visitors come across the border for shopping and brothel-creeping. The mountainous route from Yala is largely the preserve of share taxis and air-con minibuses, as only one sluggish bus a day makes the journey, taking around six hours; taxis and minibuses leave from in front of the railway station, taking three hours to reach Betong. From here you can **cross the border** to Keroh in Malaysia, which gives access to Sungai Petani and the west coast.

Along the coast from Pattani

The coastal region between Pattani and the Malaysian border is one of the least developed areas of the deep south, but it contains a couple of stunning beaches and its towns – **Saiburi** and **Narathiwat** – are appealingly ramshackle. The best way of getting around within this area is on the regular local buses, although the train stations at the border crossing of Sungai Kolok and at Tanyongmat (for Narathiwat) are useful if you're coming into the region from the north.

Saiburi and around

SAIBURI, 50km from Pattani on the bus route to Narathiwat, is a relaxing, leafy town of dilapidated wooden mansions, with pleasant accommodation at the quiet, tree-lined beach of **Hat Wasukri**, about 2km from the centre, across the Saiburi River and behind the fishing port; the bungalows here cost B200. The best of this area, however, lies along the minor road back up the coast towards PANARE. About 17km up this road – which after 2km, at BAN BON, passes a fascinating open-air workshop which builds and decorates fishing boats – you'll come to **Hat Kae Kae**, an idyllic seaside hamlet which gets its onomatopoeic name from the sound the sea makes when it hits the smooth boulders on the small, steeply sloping beach. To get this far, you'll need to take a songthaew bound for Panare – ask to be let off at Hat Kae Kae and you'll be left with a 500-metre walk over a low rocky rise to reach the seashore. Among the shady palm trees, two sturdy **bungalows** can be rented for B150 a night (fresh water is sometimes a problem) and there's a beachside restaurant.

Narathiwat and around

NARATHIWAT, 50km on from Saiburi, feels like an outsized village, with goats and cows roaming its quiet, potholed streets, but the violently modern mosque which casts a huge shadow over the northern end gives away the town's status as the provincial capital. An easy-going place to soak up the atmosphere for a couple of days, Narathiwat also offers the opportunity of a day at the beach and an excursion to the beautiful Wat Chonthara Sing He, and has a decent range of hotels and restaurants. The town is set on the west bank of the slowly curving Bang Nara River, at the mouth of which, just five minutes' walk north of the centre, sits a shanty fishing village fronted by fantastically painted boats. It's worth getting up early on a Friday morning for the bustling, colourful **market** which sprawls over the north end of Thanon Na (the main riverbank road) by the fishing village. Local batiks are sold here, as well as all kinds of food, including the local replacement for fish sauce, a beige concoction called *budu*: it's made from lemon, chilli, onion and raw sugar. Just beyond the village, you could easily while away an afternoon at one of the deck chair restaurants under the casuarina trees overlooking Hat Narathat – but this beach is too dangerous for swimming.

The two main streets run from north to south: Thanon Na (aka Puphapugdee Road) and the inland Pichit Bamrung Road, where most **buses** make a stop to the south of the clock tower – though the bus terminal is on the southwest side of town. **Trains** on the line to Sungai Kolok stop at TANYONGMAT, a half-hour bus ride from the centre. The best of the town's cheap **hotels**, *Narathiwat*, occupies a characterful wooden building overlooking the river at 341 Thanon Na, with rooms for B80. On a cross street towards the north end of town, the friendly *Tanyong Hotel* at 16/1 Sopapisai Rd (☎073/511477) is highly recommended for a splurge: comfortable rooms start at B500. The top **restaurant** is the swish *Mankornthong* on Thanon Na, fronted by Chinese dragons with a floating platform at the back – the varied food is pricey but very good. If you're counting your baht, head for the night market on Pichit Bamrung Road. For **lunch**, try the *kai ko lay* (chicken in a mild thick curry) at the cheap restaurant opposite the *Tanyong Hotel*.

The best **beach** in the area is within easy reach of Narathiwat: lined with trees and a few seafood restaurants, **Ao Manao** (Lemon Bay) takes its name from its long, gentle curve. It's 3km south towards Tak Bai, then 3km left down a paved side road – getting there by motorcycle taxi is easiest.

Wat Chonthara Sing He
One of the finest bots in Thailand lies about 30km further down the coast in **TAK BAI**, which can either be visited as an easy day trip from Narathiwat or on your way to the border at Ban Taba – take one of the frequent songthaews from the south end of Thanon Na, on the corner of Jaturongrussamee Road. (About 7km into the one-hour trip, you can't miss the Taksin Ratchaniwet, the king's palace which stands on a wooded hill overlooking the sea.)

Standing in a sandy, tree-shaded compound by the river, the bot at **Wat Chonthara Sing He** (Wat Chon) was built in the middle of the last century, as an emblem of Thai sovereignty to prove that Narathiwat was an integral part of Thailand, at a time when the British were claiming the area as part of Malaya. The building's brightly coloured fifteen-tiered roof exemplifies the fashion for curvaceous Chinese styles, here mixed with typical southern Thai features, such as the spiky white nagas, to produce an elegant, dynamic structure. Ask a monk for the key, to look at the lively, well-preserved murals which cover every inch of the interior, portraying bawdy love scenes as well as many typical details of southern life – bull- and goat-fighting, and men dressed in turbans and long sarongs.

Crossing the border

South of Narathiwat, you can cross to Malaysia at one of two frontier posts, both of which have plenty of share taxis to take you to Kota Baru, the nearest town on the other side. The slower, less direct route takes you inland via **SUNGAI KOLOK**, a seedy brothel town, popular with Malaysian weekenders. The longer established of the border posts, Sungai Kolok is the end of the **rail** line from Bangkok, and air-con buses make the four-hour trip from Hat Yai via Pattani and Narathiwat, from where the ride takes two hours. There should be no reason for you to stay in Kolok, but if you need a **hotel**, the best of the town's many budget places is the *Thanee*, at 4/1 Cheunmanka Rd (5min south from the railway station), where clean rooms go for B130 with fan, B220 with air-con.

BAN TABA, a small town with a couple of mediocre hotels if you're really stuck, lies on the quicker coastal route between Narathiwat and Kota Baru. Frequent buses from Narathiwat make the ninety-minute trip to the riverside frontier post, where a ferry will shuttle you across to your taxi.

travel details

Trains

From Bangkok to Hat Yai (4 daily; 16hr); Padang Besar (1 daily; 17hr); Phatthalung (4 daily; 15hr); Sungai Kolok (2 daily; 20hr); Trang (1 daily; 16hr); Yala (3 daily; 18hr).

From Hat Yai to Bangkok (4 daily; 16hr); Padang Besar (1 daily; 3hr); Phatthalung (7 daily; 2hr); Sungai Kolok (6 daily; 4hr 30min); Surat (5 daily; 6hr); Yala (6 daily; 2hr)

From Sungai Kolok to Hat Yai (6 daily; 4hr 30min); Nakhon (1 daily; 9hr); Phatthalung (5 daily; 7hr); Surat (3 daily; 12hr); Yala (7 daily; 2hr 30min).

Buses

From Bangkok to Hat Yai (9 daily; 14hr); Narathiwat (3 daily; 17hr); Pattani (2 daily; 16hr); Phatthalung (4 daily; 13hr); Satun (2 daily; 16hr); Sungai Kolok (3 daily; 18hr); Trang (8 daily; 14hr); Yala (3 daily; 16hr).

From Hat Yai to Krabi (7 daily; 4–5hr); Nakhon (9 daily; 2–3hr); Narathiwat (8 daily; 3–4hr); Padang Besar (every 30min; 1hr); Pak Bara (1 daily; 2hr 30min); Pattani (every 30min; 2–3hr); Phatthalung (every 30min; 1hr 30min); Phuket (7 daily; 6–8hr); Satun (every 30min; 1hr 30min); Songkhla (every 15min; 30min); Sungai Kolok (4 daily; 4hr); Surat Thani (6 daily; 4hr); Trang (hourly; 3hr); Yala (every 30min; 2–3hr).

From Narathiwat to Ban Taba (every 30min; 1hr 30min); Pattani (every 30min; 2hr); Sungai Kolok (every 30min; 2hr); Tak Bai (every 30min; 1hr).

From Songkhla to Chana (every 30min; 30min); Nakhon (9 daily; 2hr 30min–3hr); Pattani (2 daily; 2hr); Ranot (every 30min; 1hr).

From Sungai Kolok to Hat Yai (4 daily; 4hr) via Narathiwat (1hr) and Pattani (2hr).

From Trang to Krabi (hourly; 2hr); Nakhon Si Thammarat (hourly; 2hr); Phatthalung (hourly;

1hr); Phuket (11 daily; 4hr 30min); Satun (every 30min; 3hr).
From Yala to Betong (1 daily; 4hr).

Ferries

From Pak Bara to Ko Tarutao (2 daily; 1hr 30min).

Flights

From Bangkok to Hat Yai (5 daily; 1hr 30min); Narathiwat (3 weekly; 2hr 40min); Pattani (2 weekly; 2hr 30min); Trang (1 daily; 3hr).

From Hat Yai to Narathiwat (3 weekly; 40min); Pattani (2 weekly; 30min); Phuket (11 weekly; 1hr).

PART THREE

THE

CONTEXTS

THE HISTORICAL FRAMEWORK

BEGINNINGS

As long as forty thousand years ago, Thailand was inhabited by **hunter-gatherers** who lived in semi-permanent settlements and used tools made of wood, bamboo and stone. By the end of the last Ice Age around ten thousand years ago, these groups had become **farmers**, keeping chickens, pigs and cattle, and – as evidenced by the seeds and plant husks which have been discovered in caves in northern Thailand – cultivating rice and beans. This drift into an agricultural society gave rise to further technological developments: the earliest **pottery** found in Thailand has been dated to 6800BC, while the recent excavations at **Ban Chiang** in the northeast have shown that **bronze** was being worked at least as early as 2000BC, putting Thailand on a par with Mesopotamia, which has traditionally been regarded as the earliest Bronze Age culture. By two thousand years ago, the peoples of Southeast Asia had settled in small villages among which there was regular communication and trade, but they had split into several broad families, differentiated by language and culture. At this time, the ancestors of the Thais, speaking proto-Thai languages, were still far away in southeastern China, whereas Thailand itself was inhabited by Austroasiatic speakers, among whom the Mon were to establish the region's first distinctive civilization, Dvaravati.

DVARAVATI AND SRIVIJAYA

The history of **Dvaravati** is ill-defined to say the least, but the name is applied to a distinctive culture complex which shared the **Mon** language and **Theravada Buddhism**. This form of religion probably entered Thailand during the second or third centuries BC, when Indian missionaries were sent to Suvarnabhumi, "land of gold", which seems to correspond to the broad swathe of fertile land stretching from southern Burma across the north end of the Gulf of Thailand.

From the discovery of monastery boundary stones (*sema*), clay votive tablets and Indian-influenced Buddhist sculpture it's clear that Dvaravati was an extensive and prosperous Buddhist civilization which had its greatest flourishing between the sixth and ninth centuries AD. No strong evidence has turned up, however, for the existence of a single capital – rather than an empire, Dvaravati seems to have been a collection of city states, which, at least in their early history, came under the lax suzerainty of **Funan**, a poorly documented kingdom centred in Cambodia. Nakhon Pathom, Lopburi, Si Thep and Muang Sema were among the most important Dvaravati sites, and their concentration around the Chao Phraya valley would seem to show that they gained much of their prosperity, and maintained religious and cultural contacts with India, via the **trade route** from the Indian Ocean over the Three Pagodas Pass.

Although they passed on aspects of their heavily Indianized art, religion and government to later rulers of Thailand, these Mon city states were politically fragile and from the ninth century onwards succumbed to the domination of the invading Khmers from Cambodia. One northern outpost, the state of **Haripunjaya** centred on Lamphun, which had been set up on the trade route with southern China, maintained its independence probably until the beginning of the eleventh century.

Meanwhile, to the south of Dvaravati, the shadowy Indianized state of Lankasuka had grown up in the second century, centred on Ligor (now Nakhon Si Thammarat) and covering an area of the Malay peninsula which included the important trade crossings at Chaiya and

Trang. In the eighth century, it came under the control of the **Srivijaya** empire, a Mahayana Buddhist state centred on Sumatra which had strong ties with India and a complex but uneasy relationship with neighbouring Java. Thriving on seaborne trade between Persia and China, Srivijaya extended its influence as far north as Chaiya, its regional capital, where discoveries of temple remains and some of the finest stone and bronze statues ever produced in Thailand have borne witness to the cultural vitality of this crossroads empire. In the tenth century the northern part of Lankasuka, under the name **Tambralinga**, regained a measure of independence, although it seems still to have come under the influence of Srivijaya as well as owing some form of allegiance to Dvaravati. By the beginning of the eleventh century, however, peninsular Thailand had come under the sway of the Khmer empire, with a Cambodian prince ruling over a community of Khmer settlers and soldiers at Tambralinga.

THE KHMERS

The history of central southeast Asia comes into sharper focus with the emergence of the **Khmers**, vigorous empire-builders whose political history can be pieced together from the numerous stone inscriptions they left. Originally vassal subjects of Funan, the Khmers of **Chenla** – to the north of Cambodia – seized power in the latter half of the sixth century during a period of economic decline in the area. Chenla's rise to power was knocked back by a punitive expedition conducted by the Srivijaya empire in the eighth century, but was reconsolidated during the watershed reign of **Jayavarman II** (802–50), who succeeded in conquering the whole of Kambuja, an area which roughly corresponds to modern-day Cambodia. In order to establish the authority of his monarchy and of his country, Jayavarman II had himself initiated as a *chakravartin* or universal ruler, the living embodiment of the **devaraja**, the divine essence of kingship – a concept which was adopted by later Thai rulers. Taking as the symbol of his authority the phallic *lingam*, the king was thus identified with the god Shiva, although the Khmer concept of kingship and thus the religious mix of the state as a whole was not confined to

Hinduism – elements of ancestor worship were also included, and Mahayana Buddhism gradually increased its hold over the next four centuries.

It was Jayavarman II who moved the Khmer capital to **Angkor** in northern Cambodia, which he and later kings, especially after the eleventh century, embellished with a series of prodigiously beautiful temples. Jayavarman II also recognized the advantages of the lakes around Angkor for irrigating ricefields and providing fish, and thus for feeding a large population . His successors developed this idea and gave the state a sound economic core with a remarkably complex system of **reservoirs** (*baray*) and water channels, which were copied and adapted in later Thai cities.

In the ninth and tenth centuries, Jayavarman II and his imperialistic successors, especially **Yasovarman I** (889–900), confirmed Angkor as the major power in southeast Asia. They pushed into Vietnam, Laos, southern China and into northeastern Thailand, where the Khmers left dozens of Angkor-style temple complexes, as seen today at Prasat Phanom Rung and Prasat Hin Phimai. To the west and northwest, Angkor took control over central Thailand, with its most important outpost at Lopburi, and even established a strong presence to the south on the Malay peninsula. As a result of this expansion, the Khmers were masters of the most important trade routes between India and China and indeed nearly every communications link in the region, from which they were able to derive huge income and strength.

The reign of **Jayavarman VII** (1181–1219), a Mahayana Buddhist who firmly believed in his royal destiny as a *bodhisattva*, a Buddha-to-be, sowed the seeds of Angkor's downfall. Nearly half of all the extant great religious monuments of the empire were erected under his supervision, but the ambitious scale of these building projects and the upkeep they demanded – some 300,000 priests and temple servants of 20,000 shrines consumed 38,000 tons of rice per year – along with a series of wars against Vietnam, terminally exhausted the economy.

In subsequent reigns, much of the life-giving irrigation system around Angkor turned into malarial swamp through neglect, and the rise of the more democratic creed of Theravada

Buddhism undermined the divine authority which the Khmer kings had derived from the hierarchical Mahayana creed. As a result of all these factors, the Khmers were in no position to resist the onslaught between the thirteenth and fifteenth centuries of the vibrant new force in southeast Asia, the Thais.

THE EARLIEST THAIS

The earliest traceable history of the **Thai people** picks them up in southern China around the fifth century AD, when they were squeezed by Chinese and Vietnamese expansionism into sparsely inhabited northeastern Laos and neighbouring areas. The first entry of a significant number of Thais onto what is now Thailand's soil seems to have happened in the region of Chiang Saen, where it appears that some time after the seventh century the Thais formed a state in an area then known as **Yonok**. A development which can be more accurately dated and which had immense cultural significance was the spread of Theravada Buddhism to Yonok via Dvaravati around the end of the tenth century, which served not only to unify the Thais but also to link them to Mon civilization and give them a sense of belonging to the community of Buddhists.

The Thais' political development was also aided by **Nan-chao**, a well-organized military state comprising a huge variety of ethnic groups, which established itself as a major player on the southern fringes of the Chinese empire from the beginning of the eighth century. As far as can be gathered, Nan-chao permitted the rise of Thai *muang* or small principalities on its periphery, especially in the area immediately to the south known as **Sipsong Panna**.

Thai infiltration continued until, by the end of the twelfth century, they seem to have formed the majority of the population in Thailand, then under the control of the Khmer empire. The Khmers' main outpost, at Lopburi, was by then regarded as the administrative capital of a land called "Syam" (possibly from the Sanskrit *syam*, meaning swarthy) – a mid-twelfth-century bas-relief at Angkor Wat portraying the troops of Lopburi preceded by a large group of self-confident Syam Kuk mercenaries, shows that the Thais were becoming a force to be reckoned with.

SUKHOTHAI

By the middle of the thirteenth century, the Thais, thanks largely to the decline of Angkor and the inspiring effect of Theravada Buddhism, were poised on the verge of autonomous power. The final catalyst was the invasion by Qubilai Khan's Mongol armies of China and Nan-chao, which began around 1215 and was completed in the 1250s. Demanding that the whole world should acknowledge the primacy of the Great Khan, the Mongols set their hearts on the "pacification" of the "barbarians" to the south of China, which obliged the Thais to form a broad power base to meet the threat.

The founding of the first Thai kingdom at **Sukhothai**, now popularly viewed as the cornerstone of the country's development, was in fact a small-scale piece of opportunism which almost fell at the first hurdle. At some time around 1238, the princes of two small Thai principalities in the upper Chao Phraya valley joined forces to capture the main Khmer outpost in the region at Sukhothai. One of the princes, **Intradit**, was crowned king, but for the first forty years Sukhothai remained merely a local power, whose existence was threatened by the ambitions of neighbouring princes. When attacked by the ruler of Mae Sot, Intradit's army was only saved by the grand entrance of Sukhothai's most dynamic leader: the king's nineteen-year-old son, Rama, held his ground and pushed forward to defeat the opposing commander, earning himself the name **Ramkhamhaeng**, "Rama the Bold".

When Ramkhamhaeng came to the throne around 1278, he saw the south as his most promising avenue for expansion and, copying the formidable military organization of the Mongols, seized control of much of the Chao Phraya valley. Over the next twenty years, largely by diplomacy rather than military action, Ramkhamhaeng gained the submission of most of the rulers of Thailand, who entered the **new empire**'s complex tributary system either through the pressure of the Sukhothai king's personal connections or out of recognition of his superior military strength and moral prestige. To the east, Ramkhamhaeng pushed as far as Vientiane in Laos; by marrying his daughter to a Mon ruler to the west, he obtained the allegiance of parts of southern Burma; and to the south his vassals stretched down the peninsula at least as far as Nakhon Si Thammarat. To the north, Sukhothai concluded an alliance with the parallel Thai states of Lanna and Phayao in 1287 for mutual protection against the Mongols – though it appears that Ramkhamhaeng managed to pinch several *muang* on their eastern periphery as tribute states.

Meanwhile **Lopburi**, which had wrested itself free from Angkor sometime in the middle of the thirteenth century, was able to keep its independence and its control of the eastern side of the Chao Phraya valley – having been first a major cultural and religious centre for the Mons, then the Khmers' provincial capital, and now a state dominated by migrating Thais, Lopburi was a strong and vibrant place mixing the best of the three cultures, as evidenced by the numerous original works of art produced at this time.

Although the empire of Sukhothai extended Thai control over a vast area, its greatest contribution to the Thais' development was at home, in cultural and political matters. A famous **inscription** by Ramkhamhaeng, now housed in the Bangkok National Museum, describes a prosperous era of benevolent rule: "In the time of King Ramkhamhaeng this land of Sukhothai is thriving. There is fish in the water and rice in the fields . . . [The King] has hung a bell in the opening of the gate over there: if any commoner has a grievance which sickens his belly and gripes his heart . . . he goes and strikes the bell . . . [and King Ramkhamhaeng] questions the man, examines the case, and decides it justly for him.." Although this plainly smacks of self-promotion, it seems to contain at least a kernel of truth: in deliberate contrast to the Khmer god-kings, Ramkhamhaeng styled himself as a **dhamma-raja**, a king who ruled justly according to Theravada Buddhist doctrine and made himself accessible to his people. To honour the state religion, the city's temples were lavishly endowed: as original as Sukhothai's political systems were its religious **architecture and sculpture**, which, though bound to borrow from existing Khmer and Sri Lankan styles, shows the greatest leap of creativity at any stage in the history of art in Thailand. A further sign of the Thais' new self-confidence was the invention of a new **script** to make their tonal language understood by the non-Thai inhabitants of the land.

All this was achieved in a remarkably short period of time. After the death of Ramkhamhaeng around 1299, his successors took their Buddhism so seriously that they neglected affairs of state. The empire quickly fell apart, and by 1320 Sukhothai had regressed to being a kingdom of only local significance.

LANNA

Almost simultaneous with the birth of Sukhothai was the establishment of a less momentous but longer-lasting kingdom to the north, called **Lanna**. Its founding father was **Mengrai**, chief of Ngon Yang, a small principality on the banks of the Mekhong near modern-day Chiang Saen. Around 1259 he set out to unify the squabbling Thai principalities of the region, first building a strategically placed city at Chiang Rai in 1262, and then forging alliances with Ngam Muang, the Thai king of Phayao, and with Ramkhamhaeng of Sukhothai.

In 1281, after ten years of guileful preparations, Mengrai conquered the Mon kingdom of Haripunjaya based at Lamphun, and was now master of northern Thailand. Taking advice from Ngam Muang and Ramkhamhaeng, in 1292 he selected a site for an impressive new capital of Lanna at **Chiang Mai**, which remains the centre of the north to the present day. Mengrai concluded further alliances in Burma and Laos, making him strong enough to successfully resist further Mongol attacks, although he was eventually obliged to bow to the superiority of the Mongols by sending them small tributes from 1312 onwards. When Mengrai died after a sixty-year reign in 1317, supposedly struck by a bolt of lightning, he had built up an extensive and powerful kingdom. But although he began a tradition of humane, reasonable laws, probably borrowed from the Mons, he had found little time to set up sound political and administrative institutions. His death severely destabilized Lanna, which quickly shrank in size and influence.

It was only in the reign of **Ku Na** (1355–85) that Lanna's development regained momentum. A well-educated and effective ruler, Ku Na enticed the venerable monk Sumana from Sukhothai in 1369, to establish an ascetic Sri Lankan sect in Lanna. Sumana brought a number of Buddha images with him, inspiring a new school of art that flourished for over a century, but more importantly his sect became a cultural force that had a profound unifying effect on the kingdom. The influence of Buddhism was further strengthened under **King Tilok** (1441–87), who built many great monuments at Chiang Mai and cast huge numbers of bronze seated Buddhas in the style of the central image at Bodhgaya in India, the scene of the Buddha's enlightenment. Tilok, however, is best remembered as a great warrior, who spent most of his reign resisting the advances of Ayutthaya, by now the strongest Thai kingdom.

Under continuing pressure both from Ayutthaya and from Burma, Lanna went into rapid decline in the second quarter of the sixteenth century. For a short period after 1546, Chiang Mai came under the control of Setthathirat, the king of Lan Sang (Laos), but, unable to cope with Lanna's warring factions, he then abdicated, purloining the talismanic Emerald Buddha for his own capital at Luang Prabang. In 1558, Burma decisively captured Chiang Mai and the Mengrai dynasty came to an end. For most of the next two centuries, the Burmese maintained control through a succession of puppet rulers, and Lanna again became much as it had been before Mengrai, little more than a chain of competing principalities.

AYUTTHAYA

While Lanna was fighting for its place as a marginalized kingdom, from the fourteenth century onwards the seeds of a full-blown Thai nation were being sown to the south at **Ayutthaya**. The city of Ayutthaya itself was founded on its present site in 1351 by U Thong, "Prince Golden Cradle", when his own town, Lopburi, was ravaged by smallpox. Taking the title **Ramathibodi**, he soon united the principalities of the lower Chao Phraya valley, which had formed the western provinces of the Khmer empire. When he recruited his bureaucracy from the urban elite of Lopburi, Ramathibodi set the **style of government** at Ayutthaya – the elaborate etiquette, language and rituals of Angkor were adopted, and, most importantly, the conception of the ruler as *devaraja*. The king became sacred and remote, an object of awe and dread, with none of the accessibility of the kings of Sukhothai: when he processed through the town, ordinary people were forbid-

den to look at him and had to be silent while he passed. This hierarchical system also provided the state with much-needed manpower, as all freemen were obliged to give up six months of each year to the crown either on public works or military service.

The site chosen by Ramathibodi turned out to be the best in the region for an international port and so began Ayutthaya's rise to prosperity, based on its ability to exploit the upswing in **trade** in the middle of the fourteenth century along the routes between India and China. Flushed with economic success, Ramathibodi's successors were able to expand their control over the ailing states in the region. After a long period of subjugation, Sukhothai became a province of the Kingdom of Ayutthaya in 1438, six years after Borommaracha II had powerfully demonstrated Ayutthaya's pre-eminence by capturing the once-mighty Angkor, enslaving large numbers of its subjects and looting the Khmer royal regalia. (The Cambodian royal family were forced to abandon the palace forever and to found a new capital near Phnom Penh.)

Although a century of nearly continuous warfare against Lanna was less decisive, success generally bred success, and Ayutthaya's increasing wealth through trade brought ever greater power over its neighbouring states. To streamline the functioning of his unwieldy empire, **Trailok** (1448–88) found it necessary to make reforms of its administration. His **Law of Civil Hierarchy** formally entrenched the inequality of Ayutthayan society, defining the status of every individual by assigning him or her an imaginary number of rice fields – for example, 25 for an ordinary freeman and 10,000 for the highest ministers of state. Trailok's legacy is found in today's unofficial but fiendishly complex status system, by which everyone in Thailand knows his place.

Ramathibodi II (1491–1529), almost at a loss as to what to do with his enormous wealth, undertook an extensive programme of public works. In the 1490s he built several major religious monuments and between 1500 and 1503 cast the largest standing metal image of the Buddha ever known, the Phra Si Sanphet, which gave its name to the temple of the Royal Palace. By 1540, the Kingdom of Ayutthaya had grown to cover most of the area of modern-day Thailand.

BURMESE WARS AND EUROPEAN TRADE

In the sixteenth century recurring tensions with Burma led **Chakkraphat** (1548–69) to improve his army and build brick ramparts around the capital. This was to no avail however: in 1568 the Burmese besieged Ayutthaya with a huge army, said by later accounts to have consisted of 1,400,000 men. The Thais held out until August 8, 1569, when treachery within their own ranks helped the Burmese to break through the defences. The Burmese looted the city, took thousands of prisoners and installed a vassal king to keep control.

The decisive character who broke the Burmese stranglehold twenty years later and re-established Ayutthaya's economic growth was **Naresuan** (1590–1605), who defied the Burmese by amassing a large army to defend Ayutthaya. The enemy sent a punitive expedition which was conclusively defeated at Nong Sarai near modern-day Suphanburi on January 18, 1593, Naresuan himself turning the battle by killing the Burmese crown prince. Historians have praised Naresuan for his personal bravery and his dynamic leadership, although the chronicles of the time record a strong streak of tyranny – in his fifteen years as king he had 80,000 people killed, excluding the victims of war. A favoured means of punishment was to slice off pieces of the offender's flesh, which he was then made to eat in the king's presence.

The period following Naresuan's reign was characterised by a more sophisticated engagement in **foreign trade**. In 1511 the Portuguese had become the first Western power to trade with Ayutthaya, and Naresuan himself concluded a treaty with Spain in 1598; relations with Holland and England were initiated in 1608 and 1612 respectively. For most of the seventeenth century, European merchants flocked to Thailand, not only to buy Thai products, but also to gain access to Chinese and Japanese goods on sale there. The role of foreigners at Ayutthaya reached its peak under **Narai** (1656–88), but he overstepped the mark in cultivating close links with Louis XIV of France, who secretly harboured the notion of converting Ayutthaya to Christianity. On Narai's death, relations with Westerners were severely cut back.

Despite this reduction of trade and prolonged civil strife over the succession to the throne whenever a king died – then, as now, there wasn't a fixed principle of primogeniture – Ayutthaya continued to flourish for much of the eighteenth century. The reign of **Borommakot** (1733–58) was particularly prosperous, producing many works of drama and poetry. Furthermore, Thai Buddhism had by then achieved such prestige that Sri Lanka, from where the Thais had originally imported their form of religion in the thirteenth century, requested Thai aid in restoring their monastic orders in 1751.

However, immediately after the death of Borommakot the rumbling in the Burmese jungle to the north began to make itself heard again. Alaunghpaya of Burma, apparently a blindly aggressive country bumpkin, first recaptured the south of his country from the Mons, then turned his attentions on Ayutthaya. A siege in 1760 was unsuccessful, with Alaunghpaya dying of wounds sustained there, but the scene was set. In February 1766 the Burmese descended upon Ayutthaya for the last time. The Thais held out for over a year, during which they were afflicted by famine, epidemics and a terrible fire which destroyed ten thousand houses. Finally, in **April 1767**, the walls were breached and the city taken. The Burmese razed everything to the ground and tens of thousands of prisoners were led off to Burma, including most of the royal family. The king, Suriyamarin, is said to have escaped from the city in a boat and starved to death ten days later. As one observer has said, the Burmese laid waste to Ayutthaya "in such a savage manner that it is hard to imagine that they shared the same religion with the Siamese." The city was abandoned to the jungle, but with remarkable speed the Thais regrouped and established a new seat of power, further down the Chao Phraya River at Bangkok.

THE EARLY BANGKOK EMPIRE

As the bulk of the Burmese army was obliged by war with China to withdraw almost immediately, Thailand was left to descend into banditry. Out of this lawless mess several centres of power arose, the most significant being at Chanthaburi, commanded by **Phraya Taksin**. A charismatic, brave and able general who had been unfairly blamed for a failed counter-attack against the Burmese at Ayutthaya, Taksin had anticipated the fall of the besieged city and quietly slipped away with a force of 500 men. In June 1767 he took control of the east-coast strip around Chanthaburi and very rapidly expanded his power across central Thailand.

Blessed with the financial backing of the Chinese trading community, to whom he was connected through his father, Taksin was crowned king in December 1768 at his new capital of Thonburi, on the opposite bank of the river from modern-day Bangkok. One by one the new king defeated his rivals, and within two years he had restored all of Ayutthaya's territories. More remarkably, by the end of the next decade Taksin had outdone his Ayutthayan predecessors by bringing Lanna, Cambodia and much of Laos into a huge new empire. During this period of expansionism, Taksin left most of the fighting to Thong Duang, an ambitious soldier and descendant of an Ayutthayan noble family, who became the *chakri*, the military commander, and took the title **Chao Phraya Chakri**.

However, by 1779 all was not well with the king. Being an outsider, who had risen from an ordinary family on the fringes of society, Taksin became paranoid about plots against him, a delusion that drove him to imprison and torture even his wife and sons. At the same time he sank into religious excesses, demanding that the monkhood worship him as a god. By March 1782, public outrage at his sadism and dangerously irrational behaviour had reached such fervour that he was ousted in a coup.

Chao Phraya Chakri was invited to take power and had Taksin executed. In accordance with ancient etiquette, this had to be done without royal blood touching the earth; the mad king was duly wrapped in a black velvet sack and struck on the back of the neck with a sandalwood club. (Popular tradition has it that even this form of execution was too much: an unfortunate substitute got the velvet sack treatment, while Taksin was whisked away to a palace in the hills near Nakhon Si Thammarat, where he is said to have lived until 1825.)

RAMA I

With the support of the Ayutthayan aristocracy, Chakri – reigning as **Rama I** (1782–1809) – set about consolidating the Thai kingdom. His first act was to move the capital across the river to Bangkok, a better defensive position against

any Burmese attack from the west. Borrowing from the layout of Ayutthaya, he built a new royal palace and impressive monasteries, and enshrined in the palace wat the Emerald Buddha, which he had snatched during his campaigns in Laos.

As all the state records had disappeared in the destruction of Ayutthaya, religious and legal texts had to be written afresh and historical chronicles reconstituted – with some very sketchy guesswork. The monkhood was in such a state of crisis that it was widely held that moral decay had been partly responsible for Ayutthaya's downfall. Within a month of becoming king, Rama I issued a series of religious laws and made appointments to the leadership of the monkhood, to restore discipline and confidence after the excesses of Taksin's reign. Many works of drama and poetry had also been lost in the sacking of Ayutthaya, so Rama I set about rebuilding the Thais' literary heritage, at the same time attempting to make it more cosmopolitan and populist. His main contribution was the *Ramakien*, a dramatic version of the Indian epic *Ramayana*, which is said to have been set to verse by the king himself, with a little help from his courtiers, in 1797. Heavily adapted to its Thai setting, the *Ramakien* served as an affirmation of the new monarchy and its divine links, and has since become the national epic.

In the early part of Rama I's reign, the Burmese reopened hostilities on several occasions, the biggest attempted invasion coming in 1785, but the emphatic manner in which the Thais repelled them only served to knit together the young kingdom. Trade with China revived, and the king addressed the besetting problem of manpower by ordering every man to be tattooed with the name of his master and his town, so that avoiding royal service became almost impossible. On a more general note, Rama I put the style of government in Thailand on a modern footing: while retaining many of the features of a *devaraja*, he shared more responsibility with his courtiers, as a first among equals.

RAMA II AND RAMA III

The peaceful accession of his son as **Rama II** (1809–24) signalled the establishment of the **Chakri dynasty**, which is still in place today. This Second Reign was a quiet interlude, best

remembered as a fertile period for Thai literature. The king, himself one of the great Thai
poets, gathered round him a group of writers
including the famous Sunthorn Phu, who
produced scores of masterly love poems, travel
accounts and narrative songs.

In contrast, **Rama III** (1824–51) actively
discouraged literary development – probably in
reaction against his father – and was a vigorous
defender of conservative values. To this end, he
embarked on an extraordinary redevelopment of
Wat Po, the oldest temple in Bangkok.
Hundreds of educational inscriptions and mural
paintings, on all manner of secular and religious
subjects, were put on show, apparently to
preserve traditional culture against the rapid
change which the king saw corroding the country. In foreign affairs, Rama III faced a serious
threat from the vassal states of Laos, who in
1827 sent an invading army from Vientiane,
which got as far as Saraburi, only three days'
march from Bangkok. The king's response was
savage: having repelled the initial invasion, he
ordered his army to destroy everything in
Vientiane apart from Buddhist temples and to
forcibly resettle huge numbers of Lao in Isaan.
Shortly after, the king was forced to go to war in
Cambodia, to save Buddhism and its traditional
institutions from the attentions of the newly
powerful, non-Buddhist Vietnamese. A series of
campaigns in the 1830s and 1840s culminated
in the peace treaty of 1845–46, which again
established Thailand as the dominant influence
in Cambodia.

More significant in the long run was the
danger posed by the increase in Western influence which began in the Third Reign. As early
as 1825, the Thais were sufficiently alarmed at
British colonialism to strengthen Bangkok's
defences by stretching a great iron chain across
the mouth of the Chao Phraya River, to which
every blacksmith in the area had to donate a
certain number of links. In 1826 Rama III was
obliged to sign a limited trade agreement with
the British, the **Burney Treaty**, by which the
Thais won some political security in return for
reducing their taxes on goods passing through
Bangkok. British and American missions in 1850
unsuccessfully demanded more radical concessions, but by this time Rama III was seriously ill,
and it was left to his far-sighted and progressive successors to reach a decisive accommodation with the Western powers.

MONGKUT AND CHULALONGKORN

Rama IV, more commonly known as **Mongkut**
(1851–68), had been a Buddhist monk for 27
years when he succeeded his brother. But far
from leading a cloistered life, Mongkut had
travelled widely throughout Thailand, had
maintained scholarly contacts with French and
American missionaries, and, like most of the
country's new generation of leaders, had taken
an interest in Western learning, studying
English, Latin and the sciences. He had also
turned his mind to the condition of Buddhism in
Thailand, which seemed to him to have
descended into little more than popular superstition; indeed, after a study of the Buddhist
scriptures in Pali, he was horrified to find that
Thai ordinations were probably invalid. So in
the late 1830s he set up a rigorously fundamen-
talist sect called *Thammayutika*, the "Order
Adhering to the Teachings of the Buddha", and
as abbot of the order he oversaw the training
of a generation of scholarly leaders for Thai
Buddhism from his base at Bangkok's Wat
Bowonniwet, which became a major centre of
Western learning.

When his kingship faced its first major test,
in the form of a threatening British mission in
1855 led by **Sir John Bowring**, Mongkut was
able to deal with it confidently. Realizing that
Thailand was unable to resist the military
might of the British, the king reduced import
and export taxes, allowed British subjects to
live and own land in Thailand and granted them
freedom of trade. Of the **government monop-
olies**, which had long been the mainstay of the
Thai economy, only that on opium was
retained. After making up the loss in revenue
through internal taxation, Mongkut quickly
made it known that he would welcome diplo-
matic contacts from other Western countries:
within a decade, agreements similar to the
Bowring Treaty had been signed with France,
the United States and a score of other nations.
Thus by skilful diplomacy the king avoided a
close relationship with only one power, which
could easily have led to Thailand's annexation.

While all around the colonial powers were
carving up southeast Asia amongst themselves,
Thailand suffered nothing more than the weakening of its influence over Cambodia, which in
1863 the French brought under their protection.
As a result of the open-door policy, foreign

trade boomed, financing the redevelopment of Bangkok's waterfront and, for the first time, the building of paved roads. However, Mongkut ran out of time for instituting the far-reaching domestic reforms which he saw were needed to drag Thailand into the modern world.

THE MODERNISATION OF THAILAND

Mongkut's son, **Chulalongkorn**, took the throne as Rama V (1868–1910) at the age of only fifteen, but he was well prepared by an excellent education which mixed traditional Thai and modern Western elements – provided by Mrs Anna Leonowens, subject of *The King and I*. When Chulalongkorn reached his majority after a five-year regency, he set to work on the reforms envisioned by his father. One of his first acts was to scrap the custom by which subjects were required to prostrate themselves in the presence of the king, which he followed up in 1874 with a series of decrees announcing the gradual abolition of slavery. The speed of his financial and administrative reforms, however, proved too much for the "**Ancients**" (*hua boran*), the old guard of ministers and officials inherited from his father. Their opposition culminated in the Front Palace Crisis of 1875, when a show of military strength almost plunged the country into civil war, and although Chulalongkorn skilfully defused the crisis, many of his reforms had to be quietly shelved for the time being.

An important administrative reform which did go through, necessitated by the threat of colonial expansionism, concerned the former kingdom of Lanna. British exploitation of teak had recently spread into northern Thailand from neighbouring Burma, so in 1874 Chulalongkorn sent a commissioner to Chiang Mai to keep an eye on the Prince of Chiang Mai and make sure that he avoided any collision with the British. The commissioner was gradually able to limit the power of the princes and integrate the region more fully into the kingdom.

In the 1880s prospects for reform brightened as many of the "Ancients" died or retired. This allowed Chulalongkorn to **restructure the government** to meet the country's needs: the Royal Audit Office made possible the proper control of revenue and finance; the Department of the Army became the nucleus of a modern armed services; and a host of other departments were set up, for justice, education, public

health and the like. To fill these new positions, the king appointed many of his younger brothers, who had all received a modern education, while scores of foreign technicians and advisers were brought in to help with everything from foreign affairs to railway lines.

Throughout this period, however, the Western powers maintained their pressure on the region. The most serious threat to Thai sovereignty was the **Franco-Siamese Crisis** of 1893, which culminated in the French, based in Vietnam, sending gunboats up the Chao Phraya River to Bangkok. Flouting numerous international laws, France claimed control over Laos and made other outrageous demands, which Chulalongkorn had no option but to concede. In 1907 Thailand was also forced to relinquish Cambodia to the French, and in 1909 three Malay states fell to the British. In order to preserve its independence, the country ceded almost half of its territory and forewent huge sums of tax revenue. But from the end of the Fifth Reign, the frontiers were fixed as they are today.

By the time of the king's death in 1910, Thailand could not yet be called a modern nation state – corruption and nepotism were still grave problems, for example. However, Chulalongkorn had made remarkable advances, and, almost from scratch, had established the political institutions to cope with twentieth-century development.

THE END OF ABSOLUTE MONARCHY

Chulalongkorn was succeeded by a flamboyant, British-educated prince, **Vajiravudh** (1910–25), who was crowned as Rama VI. The new king found it difficult to shake the dominance of his father's appointees in the government, who formed an extremely narrow elite, comprised almost entirely of members of Chulalongkorn's family. In an attempt to build up a personal following, Vajiravudh created, in May 1911, the **Wild Tigers**, a nationwide paramilitary corps recruited widely from the civil service. However, in 1912 a group of young army lieutenants, disillusioned by the absolute monarchy and upset at the downgrading of the regular army in favour of the Wild Tigers, plotted a **coup**. The conspirators were easily broken up before any trouble began, but this was something new in Thai history: the country was used to in-fighting amongst the royal family, but not to military intrigue from men from comparatively ordinary backgrounds.

Vajiravudh's response to the coup was a series of modernizing **reforms**, including the introduction of compulsory primary education and an attempt to better the status of women by supporting monogamy in place of the widespread practice of polygamy. His huge output of writings invariably encouraged people to live as modern Westerners, and he brought large numbers of commoners into high positions in government. Nonetheless, he would not relinquish his strong opposition to constitutional democracy.

When **World War I** broke out in 1914, the Thais were generally sympathetic to the Germans out of resentment over their loss of territory to the French and British. The King, however, was in favour of neutrality, until the United States entered the war in 1917, when Thailand followed the expedient policy of joining the winning side and sent an expeditionary force of 1300 men to France in June 1918. The goodwill earned by this gesture enabled the Thais, between 1920 and 1926, to negotiate away the unequal treaties which had been imposed on them by the Western powers. Foreigners on Thai soil were no longer exempted from Thai laws, and the Thais were allowed to set reasonable rates of import and export taxes.

Yet Vajiravudh's extravagant lifestyle – during his reign, royal expenditure amounted to as much as ten percent of the state budget – left severe financial problems for his successor. Vajiravudh died without leaving a son, and as three better-placed contenders to the crown all died in the 1920s, **Prajadhipok** – the seventy-sixth child and last son of Chulalongkorn – was catapulted to the throne as Rama VII (1925–1935). Young and inexperienced, he responded to the country's crisis by creating a Supreme Council of State, seen by many as a return to Chulalongkorn's absolutist "government by princes".

Prajadhipok himself seems to have been in favour of constitutional government, but the weakness of his personality and the opposition of the old guard in the Supreme Council prevented him from introducing it. Meanwhile a vigorous community of Western-educated intellectuals had emerged in the lower echelons of the bureaucracy, who were increasingly dissatisfied with the injustices of monarchical government. The final shock to the Thai system came with the Great Depression, which from 1930 onwards ravaged the economy. On **June 24, 1932**, a small group of middle-ranking officials, led by a lawyer, Pridi Phanomyong, and an army major, Luang Phibunsongkhram, staged a **coup** with only a handful of troops. Prajadhipok weakly submitted to the conspirators, or "Promoters", and 150 years of absolute monarchy in Bangkok came to a sudden end. The King was sidelined to a position of symbolic significance and in 1935 he abdicated in favour of his ten-year-old nephew, **Ananda**, then a schoolboy living in Switzerland.

TO THE 1957 COUP

The success of the 1932 coup was in large measure attributable to the army officers who gave the conspirators credibility, and it was they who were to dominate the constitutional regimes that followed. The Promoters' first worry was that the French or British might attempt to restore the monarchy to full power. To deflect such intervention, they appointed a government under a provisional constitution and espoused a wide range of liberal Western-type reforms, including freedom of the press and social equality, few of which ever saw the light of day.

The regime's first crisis came early in 1933 when **Pridi Phanomyong**, by now leader of the government's civilian faction, put forward a socialist economic plan based on the nationalization of land and labour. The proposal was denounced as communistic by the military, Pridi was forced into temporary exile and an anti-communist law was passed. Then, in October, a royalist coup was mounted which brought the kingdom close to civil war. After intense fighting, the rebels were defeated by Lieutenant-Colonel **Luang Phibunsongkhram** (or Phibun), so strengthening the government and bringing Phibun to the fore as the leading light of the military faction.

Pridi was rehabilitated in 1934 and remained powerful and popular, especially among the intelligentsia, but it was Phibun who became prime minister after the decisive **elections of 1938**, presiding over a cabinet dominated by military men. Phibun encouraged a wave of nationalistic feeling with such measures as the official institution of the name Thailand in 1939 – Siam, it was argued, was a name bestowed by external forces, and the new title made it clear that the country belonged to the Thais rather than the economically dominant Chinese. This latter sentiment was reinforced with a series of harsh laws against the Chinese, who faced discriminatory taxes on income and commerce.

WORLD WAR II

The outbreak of **World War II** gave the Thais the chance to avenge the humiliation of the 1893 Franco-Siamese Crisis. When France was occupied by Germany in June 1940, Phibun seized the opportunity to invade western Cambodia and the area of Laos lying to the west of the Mekong River. In the following year, however, the threat of a Japanese attack on Thailand loomed. On December 8, 1941, almost at the same time as the assault on Pearl Harbour, the Japanese invaded the country at nine points, most of them along the east coast of the peninsula. The Thais at first resisted fiercely, but realizing that the position was hopeless, Phibun quickly ordered a ceasefire. Meanwhile the British sent a force from Malaysia to try to stop the Japanese at Songkhla, but were held up in a fight with Thai border police. The Japanese had time to establish themselves, before pushing down the Peninsula to take Singapore.

The Thai government concluded a military alliance with Japan and declared war against the United States and Great Britain in January 1942, probably in the belief that the Japanese would win the war. However, the Thai minister in Washington, Seni Pramoj, refused to deliver the declaration of war against the US and, in cooperation with the Americans, began organising a resistance movement called **Seri Thai**. Pridi, now acting as regent to the young king, furtively co-ordinated the movement under the noses of the occupying Japanese, smuggling in American agents and housing them in a European prison camp in Bangkok.

By 1944 Japan's final defeat looked likely, and Phibun, who had been most closely associated with them, was forced to resign by the National Assembly in July. A civilian, Khuang Aphaiwong, was chosen as prime minister, while *Seri Thai* became well established in the government under the control of Pridi. At the end of the war, Thailand was forced to restore the annexed Cambodian and Lao provinces to French Indochina, but American support prevented the British from imposing heavy punishments for the alliance with Japan.

POSTWAR UPHEAVALS

With the fading of the military, the election of January 1946 was for the first time contested by organized political parties, resulting in Pridi's becoming prime minister. A new constitution was drafted and the outlook for democratic, civilian government seemed bright.

Hopes were shattered, however, on June 9, 1946, when King Ananda was found dead in his bed, with a bullet wound in his forehead. Three palace servants were hurriedly tried and executed, but the murder has never been satisfactorily explained, and public opinion attached at least indirect responsibility for the killing to Pridi, who had in the past shown strong antiroyalist feeling. He resigned as prime minister, and in April 1948 the military made a decisive return: playing on the threat of communism, with Pridi pictured as a red bogey man, Phibun took over the premiership.

After the bloody suppression of two attempted coups in favour of Pridi, the main feature of Phibun's second regime was its heavy involvement with the United States. As communism developed its hold in the region, with the takeover of China in 1949 and the French defeat in Indochina in 1954, the US increasingly viewed Thailand as a bulwark against the red menace. Between 1951 and 1957, when its annual state budget was only about $200 million a year, Thailand received a total $149 million in American economic aid and $222 million in military aid. This strengthened Phibun's dictatorship, while enabling leading military figures to divert American money and other funds into their own pockets.

In 1955, his position threatened by two rival generals, Phibun experienced a sudden conversion to the cause of democracy. He narrowly won a general election in 1957, but only by blatant vote rigging and coercion. Although there's a strong tradition of foul play in Thai elections, this is remembered as the dirtiest ever: after vehement public outcry, **General Sarit**, the commander-in-chief of the army, overthrew the new government in September 1957.

TO THE PRESENT DAY

Believing that Thailand would prosper best under a unifying authority, an ideology that still has its supporters, Sarit set about re-establishing the monarchy as the head of the social hierarchy and the source of legitimacy for the government. Ananda's successor, **King Bhumibol** (Rama IX), was pushed into an active role while Sarit ruthlessly silenced critics and pressed ahead with a plan for economic development. These policies achieved a large measure of stability and prosperity at home, although from 1960 onwards the international situation worsened. With the Marxist Pathet Lao making considerable advances in Laos and Cambodia's ruler, Prince Sihanouk, drawing into closer relations with China, Sarit turned again to the United States. The Americans obliged by sharply increasing military aid and by stationing troops in Thailand.

THE VIETNAM WAR

Sarit died in 1963, whereupon the military succession passed to **General Thanom**, closely aided by his deputy prime minister, **General Praphas**. Neither man had anything of Sarit's charisma and during a decade in power they followed his political philosophies largely unchanged. Their most pressing problem was the resumption of open hostilities between North and South Vietnam in the early 1960s – the **Vietnam War**. Both Laos and Cambodia became involved on the side of the communists by allowing the North Vietnamese to supply their troops in the south along the Ho Chi Minh Trail, which passed through southern Laos and northeastern Cambodia. The Thais, with the backing of the US, quietly began to conduct military operations in Laos, to which North Vietnam and China responded by supporting antigovernment insurgency in Thailand.

The more the Thais felt threatened by the spread of communism, the more they looked to the Americans for help – by 1968 around 45,000 US military personnel were on Thai soil, which became the base for US bombing raids against North Vietnam and Laos, and for covert operations into Laos and beyond.

The effects of the **American presence in Thailand** were profound. The economy swelled with dollars, and hundreds of thousands of Thais became reliant on the Americans for a living, with a consequent proliferation of corruption and prostitution. What's more, the sudden exposure to Western culture led many to question the traditional Thai values and the political status quo.

THE DEMOCRACY MOVEMENT AND CIVIL UNREST

At the same time, poor farmers were becoming disillusioned with their lot and during the 1960s many turned against the Bangkok government. At the end of 1964, the **Communist Party of Thailand** and other groups formed a **broad left coalition** which soon had the support of several thousand insurgents in remote areas of the northeast. By 1967, the problem had spread to Chiang Rai and Nan provinces, and a separate threat had arisen in southern Thailand, involving **Muslim dissidents** and the Chinese-dominated **Communist Party of Malaysia**, as well as local Thais.

Thanom was now facing a major security crisis, especially as the war in Vietnam was going badly. In 1969 he held elections which produced a majority for the government party but, still worried about national stability, the general got cold feet and in November 1971 he reimposed repressive military rule. However, the 1969 experiment with democracy had heightened expectations of power-sharing among the middle classes, especially in the universities. **Student demonstrations** began in June 1973, and in October as many as 500,000 people turned out at Thammasat University in Bangkok to demand a new constitution. Clashes with the police ensued but elements in the army, backed by King Bhumibol, prevented Thanom from crushing the protest with troops. On October 14, 1973, Thanom and Praphas were forced to resign and leave the country.

In a new climate of openness, **Kukrit Pramoj** managed to form a coalition of seventeen elected parties and secured a promise of US withdrawal from Thailand, but his government was riven with feuding. Meanwhile, the king and much of the middle class, alarmed at the unchecked radicalism of the students, began to support new, often violent, right-wing organizations. In **October 1976**, the students demonstrated again, protesting against the return of Thanom to Thailand to become a monk at Wat Bowonniwet. This time there was no restraint: supported by elements of the military and the government, the police and reactionary students launched a massive assault on Thammasat University. On October 6, hundreds of students were brutally beaten, scores were lynched and some even burnt alive; the military took control and suspended the constitution.

GENERAL PREM

Soon after, the military-appointed prime minister, **Thanin Kraivichien**, imposed rigid censorship and forced dissidents to undergo anti-communist indoctrination, but his measures seem to have been too repressive even for the military, who forced him to resign in October 1977. General Kriangsak Chomanand took over, and began to break up the insurgency with shrewd offers of amnesty. His power base was weak, however, and although Kriangsak won the elections of 1979, he was displaced in February 1980 by **General Prem Tinsulanonda**, who was backed by a broad parliamentary coalition.

Untainted by corruption, Prem achieved widespread support, including that of the monarchy, which was to prove crucial. In April 1981, a group of disaffected military officers seized government buildings in Bangkok, forcing Prem to flee the capital. However, the rebels' attempt to mobilize the army was hamstrung by a radio message from Queen Sirikit in support of Prem, who was easily able to retake Bangkok. Parliamentary elections in 1983 returned the military to power and legitimized Prem's rule.

Strong foreign investment played a major role in restoring rapid growth to the economy at this time, but Thailand faced problems from communist Indochina. Early in 1979, the Vietnamese had invaded **Cambodia** to oust the brutal Khmer Rouge, and continued to fight them into the 1980s, crossing into Thailand to attack their bases. In response to this perceived threat, Prem supported and supplied the Khmer Rouge and a wide variety of other Cambodian guerilla groups sheltering on Thai soil, and worked through the United Nations and the Association of Southeast Asian Nations (ASEAN) to persuade the Vietnamese to withdraw their troops. At the time of writing, the continuation of Prem's policy seems to have paid off for the Thais: after the withdrawal of Vietnamese forces, a UN-sponsored peace plan has been signed by the rival factions, which provides for the repatriation of all refugees on Thai soil. However, it remains to be seen whether the UN can successfully monitor the disarming of the Khmer Rouge and ensure the fairness of promised elections.

Prem maintained the premiership until 1988, with a unique mixture of dictatorship and democracy sometimes called Premocracy: although never standing for parliament himself, Prem was asked by the legislature after every election to become prime minister. He eventually stepped down because, he said, it was time for the country's leader to be chosen from among its elected representatives.

THE 1992 DEMONSTRATIONS

The man chosen for the job in 1988 was **Chatichai Choonhavan**, a retired general with a long civilian career in public office. Chatichai pursued a vigorous policy of economic development, filling his cabinet with businessmen and encouraging rampant foreign investment. The resultant economic boom, however, fostered widespread corruption, in which members of the government were often implicated. Following an economic downturn and Chatichai's attempts to downgrade the political role of the military, the armed forces staged a bloodless **coup on February 23, 1991**, led by Supreme Commander **Sunthorn** and General **Suchinda**, the army commander-in-chief.

Perhaps recognizing that coups were no longer a viable means of seizing power in Thailand, Sunthorn and Suchinda immediately installed a civilian caretaker government, led by a former diplomat, **Anand Panyarachun**, and promised elections within six months. A poll was eventually held on March 22, 1992, but the new constitution permitted the unelected Suchinda to barge his way to the premiership. Opposition to the move was organized around the former Mayor of Bangkok, Chamlong Srimuang, culminating in **mass demonstrations** between May 17 and 20. Hopelessly misjudging the mood of the country, Suchinda brutally crushed the protests, leaving at least 100 people dead. Having justified the massacre on the grounds that he was protecting the king from communist agitators, Suchinda was forced to resign when King

Bhumibol expressed his disapproval in a ticking-off that was broadcast on world television. Anand was again invited to form an interim government, and quickly moved to restructure the armed forces. New elections are in the offing at the time of writing, but it remains to be seen whether Anand's reforms will remove the military from their hitherto dominant position in Thai politics, and thus accelerate the country's transformation into a true democracy.

ART AND ARCHITECTURE

Aside from pockets of Hindu-inspired statuary and architecture, the vast majority of historical Thai culture takes its inspiration from Theravada Buddhism, and though the country does have some excellent museums, to understand fully the evolution of Thai art you have to visit its temples. For Thailand's architects and sculptors, the act of creation was an act of merit and a representation of unchanging truths, rather than an act of expression, and thus Thai art history is characterised by broad schools rather than individual names. This section is designed to help you make sense of the most common aspects of Thai art and architecture at their various stages of development.

THE BASICS

To appreciate the plethora of temples and religious images in Thailand, you first need a grasp of the fundamental architectural forms and the iconography of Buddhism. Only then can you begin to appreciate the differences in the creations of different eras.

THE WAT

The **wat** or Buddhist temple complex has a great range of uses, as home to a monastic community, a place of public worship, a shrine for holy images and a shaded meeting place for townspeople and villagers. Wat architecture has evolved in ways as various as its functions,

but there remain several essential components which have stayed constant for some fifteen centuries.

The most important wat building is the **bot** (sometimes known as the *ubosot*), a term most accurately translated as the "ordination hall". It usually stands at the heart of the compound and is the preserve of the monks: lay persons are rarely allowed inside. There's only one bot in any wat complex, and often the only way to distinguish it from other temple buildings is by the eight **sema** or boundary stones which always surround it. Positioned at the four corners of the bot and at the cardinal points of the compass, these stone *sema* define the consecrated ground and usually look something like upright gravestones, though they can take many forms. They are often carved all over with symbolic Buddhist scenes or ideograms, and sometimes are even protected within miniature shrines of their own. (One of the best *sema* collections is housed in the National Museum of Khon Kaen.)

Often almost identical to the bot, the **viharn** or assembly hall is for the lay congregation, and as a tourist this is the building you're most likely to enter, as it usually contains the wat's **principal Buddha image**, and sometimes two or three minor images as well. Large wats may have several viharns, while strict meditation wats, which don't deal with the laity, may not have one at all.

Thirdly, there's the **chedi** or stupa (known as a **that** in the north), a tower which was originally conceived as a monument to enshrine relics of the Buddha, but has since become a place to contain the ashes of royalty – and anyone else who can afford it. Of all Buddhist structures, the chedi has undergone the most changes and as such is often the most characteristic hallmark of each period.

Less common wat buildings include the small square **mondop**, usually built to house either a Buddha statue or footprint or to contain holy texts, and the **ho trai** or scripture library.

BUDDHIST ICONOGRAPHY

In the early days of Buddhism, image-making was considered inadequate to convey the faith's abstract philosophies, and thus the only approved iconography comprised doctrinal **symbols** such as the *Dharmachakra* (Wheel of Law). Gradually these symbols were displaced by **images of the Buddha**, construed chiefly as physical embodiments of Buddha's teachings rather than as portraits of the man. Sculptors took their guidance from the Pali texts which ordained the Buddha's most common postures (*asanha*) and gestures (*mudra*).

Of the **four postures** – sitting, standing, walking and reclining – the **seated Buddha**, which represents him in meditation, is the most common in Thailand. A popular variation shows Buddha seated on a coiled serpent, protected by the serpent's hood – a reference to the story about Buddha meditating during the rainy season, when a serpent offered to raise him off the wet ground and shelter him from the storms. The **reclining** pose symbolises Buddha entering Nirvana at his death, while the **standing** and **walking** images both represent Buddha's descent from Tavatimsa heaven.

The most common **hand gestures** include: *Dhyana Mudra* (Meditation), in which the hands rest on the lap, palms upwards; *Bhumisparsa Mudra* (Calling the Earth to Witness, a reference to Buddha resisting temptation), with the left hand upturned in the lap and the right-hand fingers resting on the right knee and pointing to the earth; *Vitarkha Mudra* (Teaching), with one or both hands held at chest height with the thumb and forefinger touching; and *Abhaya Mudra* (Dispelling Fear), showing the right hand (occasionally both hands) raised in a flat-palmed "stop" gesture.

All three-dimensional Buddha images are objects of reverence, but some are more esteemed than others. Some are alleged to have displayed human attributes or reacted in some way to unusual events, others have performed miracles, or are simply admired for their beauty, their phenomenal size, or even their material value – if made of solid gold or of jade, for example. Most Thais are familiar with these exceptional images, all of which have been given special names, always prefixed by the honorific "Phra", and many of which have spawned thousands of miniaturised copies in the form of amulets. Pilgrimages are made to see the most famous originals.

It was in the Sukhothai era that the craze for producing **Buddha footprints** really took off. Harking back to the time when images were allusive rather than representative, these footprints were generally moulded from stucco to depict the 108 auspicious signs (which included references to the sixteen Buddhist heavens, the traditional four great continents and seven great rivers and lakes) and housed in a special mondop. Few of the Sukhothai prints remain, but Ratanakosin era examples are found all over the country, the most famous being Phra Phuttabat near Lopburi, the object of pilgrimages throughout the year.

HINDU ICONOGRAPHY

Hindu images tend to be a lot livelier than Buddhist ones, partly because there are more gods to choose from, and partly because these gods have more mischievous personalities and re-appear in all sorts of bizarre incarnations. Though pure Hinduism receded from Thailand with the collapse of the Khmers, its iconography has endured, as Buddhist Thais have incorporated some Hindu and Brahmin concepts into the national belief system and have continued to create statues of the three chief Hindu deities – Brahma, Vishnu and Shiva – as well as using lesser mythological beasts in modern designs.

Vishnu (the Preserver) has always been especially popular, because his avatar or human manifestation is **Rama**, the super-hero of the epic story the *Ramayana*, who appears in story-telling reliefs in every Hindu temple in Thailand. Vishnu himself generally has four arms, his hands holding a conch shell, a disc, a club and a lotus, and he's often depicted astride a **garuda**, a half-man, half-bird. Even without Vishnu on his back, the garuda is a very important beast – a symbol of strength, it's often shown "supporting" temple buildings.

Statues and representations of **Brahma** (the Creator) are very rare. Confusingly he too has four arms, but you should recognise him by the fact that he holds no objects, has four faces, and is generally borne by a goose-like creature called a *hamsa*.

Shiva (the Destroyer) usually has eight arms and is often shown dancing, while **Indra** is generally only distinguished by his mount, the three-headed elephant **Erawan**. Depictions of the elephant-headed deity **Ganesh** abound, both as statues and, because he is the god of knowledge and overcomer of obstacles, as the symbol of the Fine Arts Department – which crops up on all entrance tickets to museums and historical parks.

Lesser mythological figures, which originated as Hindu symbols but feature frequently in wats and other Buddhist contexts, include the **yaksha** giants who ward off evil spirits (like the enormous freestanding ones guarding Bangkok's Wat Phra Kaeo); the graceful half-woman, half-bird **kinnari**; and finally, the ubiquitous **naga**, or serpent king of the underworld – often the proud owner of as many as seven heads, whose reptilian body most frequently appears as staircase balustrades in Hindu and Buddhist temples.

THE SCHOOLS

In the 1920s art historians and academics began compiling a classification system for Thai art and architecture which was modelled along the lines of the country's historical periods – these are the guidelines followed below. The following brief overview starts in the sixth century, when Buddhism began to take a hold on the country – a point before which very few examples of art and no known architectural relics have survived.

DVARAVATI
[SIXTH–ELEVENTH CENTURIES]

Centred around Nakhon Pathom, U Thong and Lopburi in the Chao Phraya basin and in the smaller northern enclave of Haripunjaya (modern-day Lamphun), the **Dvaravati** state was populated by Theravada Buddhists who were strongly influenced by Indian culture.

Only one, fairly late, known example of a Dvaravati-era **building** remains standing: the pyramidal laterite chedi in the compound of Lamphun's Wat Kukut, which is divided into five tiers with niches for stucco Buddha images on each row. Dvaravati-era **artefacts** are much more common, and the national museums in Nakhon Pathom and Lamphun both house quite extensive collections of Buddha images from that period. In an effort to combat the defects inherent in the poor-quality limestone at their disposal, sculptors made their Buddhas quite stocky, cleverly dressing the figures in a sheet-like drape that dropped down to ankle level from each raised wrist, forming a U-shaped hemline – a style which they used when casting in bronze as well. Nonetheless many **statues** have cracked, leaving them headless or limbless. Where the faces have survived, Dvaravati statues display some of the most naturalistic features ever produced in Thailand, distinguished by their thick lips, flattened noses and wide cheekbones.

Nakhon Pathom, a target of Buddhist missionaries from India since before the first century AD, has also yielded a substantial hoard of **dharmachakra**, originating in the period when Buddha could not be directly represented. These metre-high carved stone wheels depict the cycles of life and reincarnation, and in Dvaravati examples are often accompanied by a small statue of a deer, which refers to Buddha preaching his first sermon in a deer park.

SRIVIJAYA
[EIGHTH–THIRTEENTH CENTURIES]

While Dvaravati's Theravada Buddhists were influencing the central plains and, to a limited extent, areas further north, southern Thailand was paying allegiance to the Mahayana Buddhists of the **Srivijayan** empire. The key distinction between Theravada and Mahayana strands of thought is that Mahayanists believe that those who have achieved enlightenment should postpone their entry into Nirvana in order to help others along the way. These stay-behinds, revered like saints both during and after life, are called **bodhisattva**, and **statues** of them were the mainstay of Srivijaya art.

The finest Srivijayan *bodhisattva* statues were cast in bronze and show such grace and sinuosity that they rank among the finest sculpture ever produced in the country. Usually shown in the **tribunga** or hipshot pose, with right hip thrust out and left knee bent, many are lavishly adorned, and some were even bedecked in real jewels when first made. By far the most popular *bodhisattva* subject was **Avalokitesvara**, worshipped as compassion incarnate. Generally shown with four or more arms and with an animal skin over the left shoulder or tied at the waist, Avalokitesvara is also sometimes depicted with his torso covered in tiny Buddha images. Bangkok's National Museum holds the most beautiful Avalokitesvara, found in Chaiya; most of the other best Srivijayan sculptures have been snapped up by Bangkok's curators as well.

As for Srivijayan **temples**, quite a number have been built over, and so are unviewable. The most typical intact example is the Javanese-style chedi at Chaiya's Wat Phra Boromathat, heavily restored but distinguished from contemporaneous Dvaravati structures by its highly ornamented stepped chedi, with mini chedis at each corner.

KHMER AND LOPBURI
[TENTH–FOURTEENTH CENTURIES]

By the end of the ninth century the **Khmers** of Cambodia were starting to expand from their capital at Angkor into the Dvaravati states, bringing with them the Hindu faith and the cult of the god-king (*devaraja*). As lasting testaments to the sacred power of their kings, the Khmers built hundreds of imposing stone **sanctuaries** across their newly acquired territory: the two top examples are both in southern Isaan, at Phimai and Phanom Rung, though there is also an interesting early one at Muang Singh near Kanchanaburi.

Each magnificent castle-temple – known in Khmer as a **prasat** – was constructed primarily as a shrine for a *shiva lingam*, the phallic representation of the god Shiva. They followed a similar pattern, centred on at least one towering structure, or **prang**, which represented Mount Meru (the gods' heavenly abode), and surrounded by concentric rectangular enclosures, within and beyond which were dug artificial lakes and moats – miniature versions of the primordial ocean dividing heaven from earth.

The prasats' most fascinating and superbly crafted features, however, are the **carvings** that ornament almost every surface. Usually gouged from sandstone, but frequently moulded in stucco, these exuberant reliefs depict Hindu deities, incarnations and stories, especially episodes from the *Ramayana*. Towards the end of the twelfth century, the Khmer leadership became Mahayana Buddhist, commissioning Buddhist carvings to be installed alongside the Hindu ones, and simultaneously replacing the *shiva lingam* at the heart of each sanctuary with a Buddha or *bodhisattva* image.

The temples built in the former Theravada Buddhist principality of **Lopburi** during the Khmer period are much smaller affairs than those in Isaan, and are best represented by the triple-pranged temple of Phra Prang Sam Yot. The Lopburi classification is most usually applied to the Buddha statues that emerged at the tail-end of the Khmer period, picking up the Dvaravati sculptural legacy. Broad-faced and muscular, the classic Lopburi Buddha wears a diadem or ornamental headband – a nod to the Khmers' ideological fusion of earthly and heavenly power – and the *ushnisha* (the sign of enlightenment) becomes distinctly conical rather than a mere bump on the head. Early Lopburi Buddhas come garlanded with necklaces and ornamental belts; later examples eschew the jewels. As you'd expect, Lopburi National Museum houses a good selection.

SUKHOTHAI
[THIRTEENTH–FIFTEENTH CENTURIES]

Capitalising on the Khmers' weakening hold over central Thailand, two Thai generals established the first real Thai kindom in **Sukhothai** in 1238, and over the next two hundred years the artists of this realm produced some of Thailand's most refined art. Sukhothai's artistic reputation rests above all on its **sculpture**. More sinuous even than the Srivijayan images, Sukhothai Buddhas tend towards elegant androgyny, with slim oval faces that show little of the humanistic Dvaravati features or the strength of Lopburi statues, and slender curvaceous bodies usually clad in a plain skin-tight robe that fastens with a tassle close to the navel. The sculptors favoured the seated pose, with hands in the *Bhumisparsa Mudra*, most expertly executed in the Phra Buddha Chinnarat image, now housed in Phitsanulok's Wat Si Ratana Mahathat (replicated at Bangkok's Wat Benchamabophit) and in the enormous Phra Sri Sakyamuni, now enshrined in Bangkok's Wat Suthat. They were also the first to represent the **walking Buddha**, a supremely graceful figure with his right leg poised to move forwards and his left arm in the *Vitarkha Mudra*, as seen in the compounds of Sukhothai's Wat Sra Si.

The cities of Sukhothai and nearby Si Satchanalai were already stamped with sturdy relics of the Khmers' presence, but rather than pull down the sacred prangs of their predecessors, Sukhothai builders added bots, viharns and chedis to the existing structures, as well as conceiving quite separate **temple complexes**. Their viharns and bots are the earliest halls of worship still standing in Thailand (the Khmers didn't go in for large public assemblies), but in most cases only the stone pillars and their platforms remain, the wooden roofs having long since disintegrated. The best examples can be seen in the historical park at Sukhothai, with less grandiose structures at the parks in nearby Si Satchanalai and Kamphaeng Phet.

Most of the **chedis**, though, are in much better shape. Many were modelled on the Sri Lankan bell-shaped reliquary tower (symbolising the Buddha's teachings ringing out far and wide), often set atop a one- or two-tiered square base surrounded by elephant buttresses – Si Satchanalai's Wat Chang Lom is a stylish example. The architects also devised a new type of chedi, as elegant in its way as the images their sculptor colleagues were producing. This was the **lotus-bud chedi**, a slender tower topped with a tapered finial that was to become a hallmark of the Sukhothai era. In Sukhothai both Wat Mahathat and Wat Trapang Ngoen display good samples.

Ancient Sukhothai is also renowned for the skill of its potters, who produced a **ceramic ware** known as Sawankhalok, after the name of one of the nearby kiln towns. Most museum ceramics collections are dominated by Sawankhalok ware, which is distinguished by its grey-green celadon glazes and by the fish- and chrysanthemum-like motifs used to decorate bowls and plates.

LANNA
[THIRTEENTH–SIXTEENTH CENTURIES]

Meanwhile, to the north of Sukhothai, the independent Theravada Buddhist kingdom of Lanna was flourishing. Its art styles – known interchangeably as Chiang Saen and Lanna – evolved from an eclectic range of precursors, building on the Dvaravati heritage of Haripunjaya, copying direct from Indian sources and incorporating Sukhothai and Sri Lankan ideas from the south.

The earliest surviving Lanna **monument** is the Dvaravati-style Chedi Si Liem in Chiang Mai, built to the pyramidical form characteristic of Mon builders in fairly close imitation of the much earlier Wat Kukut in Lampang. Also in Chiang Mai, Wat Jet Yot replicates the temple built at Bodhgaya in India to commemorate the seven sites where Buddha meditated in the first seven weeks after attaining enlightenment – hence the symbolic seven pyramidal chedis, and hence also the name, which means "The temple of seven spires".

Lanna **sculpture** also drew some inspiration from Bodhgaya: the early Lanna images tend to plumpness, with broad shoulders and prominent hair curls, which are all characteristics of the main Buddha at Bodhgaya. The later

works are slimmer, probably as a result of Sukhothai influence, and one of the most famous examples of this type is the Phra Singh Buddha, enshrined in Chiang Mai's Wat Phra Singh. Other good illustrations of both styles are housed in Chiang Mai's National Museum.

AYUTTHAYA
[FOURTEENTH–EIGHTEENTH CENTURIES]

Although the Sukhothai era was artistically fertile, the kingdom had only a short political life and from 1351 Thailand's central plains came under the thrall of a new power centred on **Ayutthaya** and ruled by a former prince of Lopburi. Over the next four centuries, the Ayutthayan capital became one of the most prosperous and ostentatious cities in Asia, its rulers commissioning some 400 grand wats as symbols of their wealth and power. Though essentially Theravada Buddhists, the kings also adopted some Hindu and Brahmin beliefs from the Khmers – most significantly the concept of *devaraja* or god-kingship, whereby the monarch became a mediator between the people and the Hindu gods. The religious buildings and sculptures of this era reflected this new composite ideology, both by fusing the architectural styles inherited from the Khmers and from Sukhothai and by dressing their Buddhas to look like regents.

Retaining the concentric layout of the typical Khmer **temple complex**, Ayutthayan builders played around with the component structures, most notably the prang, which they refined and elongated into a **corncob-shaped tower**, rounding it off at the top and introducing vertical incisions around its circumference. As a spire they often added a bronze thunderbolt, and into niches within the prang walls they placed Buddha images. In Ayutthaya itself, the ruined complexes of Wat Phra Mahathat and Wat Ratburana both include these corncob prangs, but the most famous example is Bangkok's Wat Arun, which though built during the subsequent Bangkok period is a classic Ayutthayan structure.

Ayutthaya's architects also adapted the Sri Lankan **chedi** so favoured by their Sukhothai predecessors, stretching the bell-shaped base and tapering it into a very graceful conical spire, as at Wat Sri Sanphet in Ayutthaya. The **viharns** of this era are characterised by walls pierced by slit-like windows, designed to foster a mysterious atmosphere by limiting the amount of light inside the building. As with all of Ayutthaya's buildings, few viharns survived the brutal 1767 sacking, with the notable exception of Wat Na Phra Mane. Phitsanulok's Wat Phra Ratana Si Mahathat was built to a similar plan – and in Phetchaburi, Wat Yai Suwannaram has no windows at all.

From Sukhothai's Buddha **sculptures** the Ayutthayans copied the soft oval face, adding an earthlier demeanour to the features and imbuing them with a hauteur in tune with the *devaraja* ideology. Like the Lopburi images, early Ayutthayan statues wear crowns to associate kingship with Buddhahood; as the court became ever more lavish, so these figures became increasingly adorned, until – as in the monumental bronze at Wat Na Phra Mane – they appeared in earrings, armlets, anklets, bandoliers and coronets. The artists justified these luscious portraits of the Buddha – who was, after all, supposed to have given up worldly possessions – by pointing to an episode when the Buddha transformed himself into a well-dressed nobleman to gain the ear of a proud emperor, whereupon he scolded the man into entering the monkhood.

While a couple of wats in Sukhothai show hints of painted decoration, religious **painting** in Thailand really dates from the Ayutthayan era. Unfortunately most of Ayutthaya's own paintings were destroyed in 1767 and others have suffered badly from damp, but several temples in other parts of the country still have some well-preserved murals, in particular Wat Yai Suwannaram in Phetchaburi. By all accounts typical of late seventeenth-century painting, Phetchaburi's murals depict rows of *thep* or divinities paying homage to Buddha, in scenes presented without shadow or perspective, and mainly executed in dark reds and cream.

RATANAKOSIN
[EIGHTEENTH CENTURY TO THE PRESENT]

When **Bangkok** emerged as Ayutthaya's successor in 1782, the new capital's founder was determined to revive the old city's grandeur, and the **Ratanakosin** (or Bangkok) period began by aping what the Ayutthayans had done. Since then neither wat architecture nor religious sculpture has evolved much further.

The first Ratanakosin **building** was the bot of Bangkok's Wat Phra Kaeo, built to enshrine the Emerald Buddha. Designed to a typical Ayutthayan plan, it's coated in glittering mirrors and gold leaf, with roofs ranged in multiple tiers and tiled in green and orange. To this day, most newly built bots and viharns follow a more economical version of this paradigm, whitewashing the outside walls but decorating the pediment in gilded ornaments and mosaics of coloured glass. Tiered temple roofs – an Ayutthayan innovation of which few examples remain in that city – still taper off into the slender bird-like finials called *chofa*, and naga staircases – a Khmer feature inherited by Ayutthaya – have become an almost obligatory feature of any major temple. The result is that modern wats are often almost indistinguishable from each other, though Bangkok does have a few exceptions, including Wat Benchamabophit, which uses marble cladding for its walls and incorporates Victorian-style stained glass windows, and Wat Rajapobhit, which is covered all over in Chinese ceramics. The most dramatic chedi of the Ratanokosin era – the tallest in the world – was constructed in the mid-nineteenth century in Nakhon Pathom to the original Sri Lankan style, but minus the elephant buttresses that you find in Sukhothai.

Early Ratanokosin sculptors produced adorned **Buddha images** very much in the Ayutthayan vein, sometimes adding real jewels to the figures, and more modern images are notable for their ugliness rather than for any radical departure from type. The obsession with size, first apparent in the Sukhothai period, has plumbed new depths, with graceless concrete statues up to 60m high becoming the norm (as in Roi Et's Wat Burapha), a monumentalism made worse by the routine application of browns and dull yellows. Most small images are cast from or patterned on older models, mostly Sukhothai or Ayutthayan in origin.

Painting has fared much better, with the *Ramayana* murals in Bangkok's Wat Phra Kaeo a shining example of how Ayutthayan techniques and traditional subject matters could be adapted into something fantastic, imaginative and beautiful. Though for the last sixty years artists and sculptors have experimented with secular themes and Western-influenced styles, no strong movement has emerged to decisively bring secular Thai art into competition with its spiritually inspired antecedents.

RELIGION: THAI BUDDHISM

Over ninety percent of Thais consider themselves Theravada Buddhists, followers of the teachings of a holy man usually referred to as Buddha ("Enlightened One"), though more precisely known as Gautama Buddha to distinguish him from three lesser-known Buddhas who preceded him and from the fifth and final Buddha who is predicted to arrive in the year 4457 AD. Theravada Buddhism is one of the two main schools of Buddhism practised in Asia, and in Thailand it has absorbed an eclectic assortment of animist and Hindu elements into its beliefs as well. The other ten percent of Thailand's population comprises Mahayana Buddhists, Muslims, Hindus, Sikhs and Christians.

BUDDHA: HIS LIFE AND LEGENDS

Buddhists believe that Gautama Buddha was the five-hundredth incarnation of a single being: the stories of these five hundred lives, collectively known as the **Jataka**, provide the inspiration for much Thai art. (Hindus also accept Gautama Buddha into their pantheon, perceiving him as the ninth manifestation of their god Vishnu.)

In his last incarnation he was born in Nepal as **Prince Gautama Siddhartha** in either the sixth or seventh century BC, the son of a king and his hitherto barren wife, who finally became pregnant only after having a dream that a white elephant had entered her womb. At the time of his birth astrologers predicted that Gautama was to become universally respected, either as a worldly king or as a spiritual saviour, depending on which way of life he pursued. Much preferring the former idea, the prince's father forbade anyone to let the boy out of the palace grounds, and took it upon himself to educate Gautama in all aspects of the high life. Most statues of Buddha depict him with elongated earlobes, which is a reference to this early pampered existence, when he would have worn heavy precious stones in his ears.

The prince married and became a father, but at the age of 29 he flouted his father's authority and sneaked out into the world beyond the palace. On this fateful trip he encountered successively an old man, a sick man, a corpse and a hermit, and thus for the first time was made aware that pain and suffering were intrinsic to human life. Contemplation seemed the only means of discovering why this should be so – and therefore Gautama decided to leave the palace and become a **Hindu ascetic**.

For six or seven years he wandered the countryside leading a life of self-denial and self-mortification, but failed to come any closer to the answer. Eventually concluding that the best course of action must be to follow a "**Middle Way**" – neither indulgent nor overly ascetic – Gautama sat down beneath the famous riverside bodhi tree at **Bodhgaya** in India, facing the rising sun, to meditate until he achieved enlightenment. For 49 days he sat crosslegged in the "lotus position", contemplating the causes of suffering and wrestling with temptations that materialised to distract him. Most of these were sent by **Mara**, the Evil One, who was finally subdued when Gautama summoned the earth goddess **Mae Toranee** by pointing the fingers of his right hand at the ground – the gesture known as *Bhumisparsa Mudra*, which has been immortalised by hundreds of Thai sculptors. Mae Toranee wrung torrents of water from her hair and engulfed Mara's demonic emissaries in a flood, an episode that also features in several sculptures and paintings, most famously in the one standing in Bangkok's Sanam Luang.

Temptations dealt with, Gautama soon came to attain **enlightenment** and so become a Buddha. As the place of his enlightenment, the **bodhi tree** (or bo tree) has assumed special significance for Buddhists: not only does it appear in many Buddhist paintings and a few sculptures, but there's often a real bodhi tree planted in temple compounds as well. Furthermore, the bot is nearly always built facing either a body of water or facing east (preferably both).

Buddha preached his **first sermon** in a deer park in India, where he characterised his *Dharma* (doctrine) as a wheel. From this episode comes the early Buddhist symbol the **Dharmachakra**, known as the Wheel of Law or the Wheel of Life, which is often accompanied by a statue of a deer. Thais celebrate this first sermon with a public holiday in July known as *Asanha Puja*. On another occasion 1250 people spontaneously gathered to hear Buddha speak, an event remembered in Thailand as *Maha Puja* and marked by a public holiday in February.

For the next forty-odd years Buddha travelled the region converting non-believers and performing miracles. One rainy season he even ascended into the Tavatimsa heaven ("Heaven of the thirty-three gods") to visit his mother and to preach the doctrine to her. His descent from this heaven is quite a common theme of paintings and sculptures, and the Standing Buddha pose of numerous Buddha statues comes from this story. He also went back to his father's palace where he was temporarily reunited with his wife and child: the Khon Kaen museum houses a particularly lovely carving of this event.

Buddha "died" at the age of eighty on the banks of a river at Kusinari in India – an event often dated to 543 BC, which is why the Thai calendar is 543 years out of synch with the Western one. Lying on his side, propping up his head on his hand, the Buddha passed into **Nirvana** (giving rise to another classic pose, the Reclining Buddha), the unimaginable state of nothingness which knows no suffering and from which there is no reincarnation. Buddhists believe that the day Buddha entered Nirvana was the same date on which he was born and he achieved enlightenment, a triply significant day that Thais honour with the *Visakha Puja* festival in May.

BUDDHIST DOCTRINE

After Buddha entered Nirvana, his **doctrine** spread relatively quickly across India, and probably was first promulgated in Thailand in about the third century BC. His teachings, the *Tripitaka*, were written down in the Pali language – a derivative of Sanskrit – in a form that became known as Theravada or "The Doctrine of the Elders".

As taught by Buddha, **Theravada Buddhism** built on the Hindu theory of perpetual reincarnation in the pursuit of perfection, introducing the notion of life as a cycle of suffering which could only be transcended by enlightened beings able to free themselves from earthly ties and enter into the blissful

state of Nirvana. For the well-behaved but unenlightened Buddhist, each reincarnation marks a move up a vague kind of ladder, with animals at the bottom, women figuring lower down than men, and monks coming at the top – a hierarchy complicated by the very pragmatic notion that the more comfortable your lifestyle the higher your spiritual status.

The Buddhist has no hope of enlightenment without acceptance of the **four noble truths**. In encapsulated form, these hold that desire is the root cause of all suffering and can be extinguished only by following the eightfold path or Middle Way. This **Middle Way** is essentially a highly moral mode of life that includes all the usual virtues like compassion, respect, and moderation, and eschews vices such as self-indulgence and anti-social behaviour. But the key to it all is an acknowledgement that the physical world is impermanent and ever-changing, and that all things – including the self – are therefore not worth craving. Only by pursuing a condition of complete **detachment** can human beings transcend earthly suffering.

By the beginning of the first millennium, a new movement called **Mahayana** ("Great Vehicle") had emerged within the Theravada school, attempting to make Buddhism more accessible by introducing a Hindu-style pantheon of *bodhisattva* or Buddhist saints who, although they had achieved enlightenment, nevertheless postponed entering Nirvana in order to inspire the populace. Mahayana Buddhism subsequently spread north into China, Korea, Vietnam and Japan, also entering the southern Thai kingdom of Srivijaya around the eighth century and parts of Khmer Cambodia in about the eleventh century. Meanwhile Theravada Buddhism (which the Mahayanists disparagingly renamed "Hinayana" or "Lesser Vehicle") established itself most significantly in Sri Lanka, Thailand and Burma.

THE MONKHOOD

In Thailand it's the duty of the 200,000-strong **Sangha** (monkhood) to set an example to the Theravada Buddhist community by living a life as close to the Middle Way as possible and by preaching the *Dharma* to the people. A monk's life is governed by 227 strict rules that include celibacy and the rejection of all personal possessions except gifts.

Each day begins with an alms round in the neighbourhood so that the laity can donate food and thereby gain themselves merit (see below), and then is chiefly spent in meditation, chanting, teaching and study. The stricter of the Thai *Sangha*'s two sects, the **Thammayutika**, places strong emphasis on scholarship and meditation, but the much larger and longer established **Mahanikai** sect encourages monks to pursue wider activities within the community. Always the most respected members of any community, monks act as teachers, counsellors and arbiters in local disputes and, in rural areas, they often become spokesmen for villagers' rights, particularly on environmental and land ownership issues. Although some Thai women do become nuns, they belong to no official order and aren't respected as much as the monks.

Monkhood doesn't have to be for life: a man may leave the *Sangha* three times without stigma and in fact every Thai male (including royalty) is expected to **enter the monkhood** for a short period at some point in his life, ideally between leaving school and marrying, as a rite of passage into adulthood. So ingrained into the social system is this practice that nearly all Thai companies grant their employees paid leave for their time as a monk. The most popular time for temporary ordination is the three-month Buddhist retreat period – **Pansa** – which begins in July and lasts for the duration of the rainy season. (The monks' confinement is said to originate from the earliest years of Buddhist history, when farmers complained that perambulating monks were squashing their sprouting rice crops.) **Ordination ceremonies** take place in almost every wat at this time and make spectacular scenes, with the shaven-headed novice usually clad entirely in white and carried about on friends' or relatives' shoulders. The boys' parents donate money, food and necessities such as washing powder and mosquito repellent, processing around the temple compound with their gifts, often joined by dancers or travelling players hired for the occasion.

BUDDHIST PRACTICE

In practice most Thai Buddhists aim only to be **reborn** higher up the incarnation scale rather than set their sights on the ultimate goal of Nirvana. The rank of the reincarnation is directly related to the good and bad actions performed in the previous life, which accumulate to determine one's **karma** or destiny – hence the Thai obsession with "making merit".

Merit-making (*tham bun*) can be done in all sorts of ways, from giving a monk his breakfast to attending a Buddhist service or donating money to the neighbourhood temple, and most festivals are essentially communal merit-making opportunities. For a Thai man, temporary ordination is a very important way of accruing merit not only for himself but also for his mother and sisters – wealthier citizens might take things a step further by commissioning the casting of a Buddha statue or even paying for the building of a wat. One of the more bizarre but common merit-making activities involves **releasing caged birds**: worshippers buy one or more tiny finches from vendors at wat compounds and, by liberating them from their cage prove their Buddhist compassion towards all living things. The fact that the birds were free until netted earlier that morning doesn't seem to detract from the ritual at all. In riverside and seaside wats, birds are sometimes replaced by fish or even baby turtles.

SPIRITS AND NON-BUDDHIST DEITIES

The complicated history of the area now known as Thailand has, not surprisingly, made Thai Buddhism a strangely syncretic faith, as you'll realise when you enter a Buddhist temple compound to be confronted by a statue of a Hindu deity. While regular Buddhist merit-making ensures a Thai for the next life, there are certain **Hindu gods and animist spirits** that most Thais also cultivate for help with more immediate problems. Sophisticated Bangkokians and illiterate farmers alike will find no inconsistency in these apparently incompatible practices, and as often as not it's a Buddhist monk who is called in to exorcise a malevolent spirit. Even the Buddhist King Bhumibol employs Brahmin priests and astrologers to determine auspicious days and officiate at certain royal ceremonies and, like his royal predecessors of the Chakri dynasty, he also associates himself with the Hindu god Vishnu by assuming the title Rama IX – Rama, hero of the Hindu epic the *Ramayana*, having been Vishnu's seventh manifestation on earth.

If a Thai wants help in achieving a short-term goal, like passing an exam, becoming pregnant or winning the lottery, then he or she will quite likely turn to the **Hindu pantheon**, visiting an enshrined statue of either Brahma, Vishnu, Shiva, Indra or Ganesh, and making offerings of flowers, incense and maybe food. If the outcome is favourable, devotees will probably come back to show thanks, bringing more offerings and maybe even hiring a dance troupe to perform a celebratory *lakhon chatri* as well. Built in honour of Brahma, Bangkok's Erawan Shrine is the most famous place of Hindu-inspired worship in the country.

Whereas Hindu deities tend to be benevolent, **spirits** (or *phi*) are not nearly as reliable and need to be mollified more frequently. They come in hundreds of varieties, some more malign than others, and inhabit everything from trees, rivers and caves to public buildings and private homes – even taking over people if they feel like it. So that these *phi* don't pester human inhabitants, each building has a special **spirit house** in its vicinity, as a dwelling for spirits ousted by the building's construction. Usually raised on a short column and designed to look like a wat or a traditional Thai house, these spirit houses are generally about the size of a dolls'-house, but their ornamentation is supposed to reflect the status of the humans' building – thus if that building is enlarged or refurbished, then the spirit house should be improved accordingly. Daily offerings of incense, lighted candles and garlands of jasmine are placed inside the spirit house to keep the *phi* happy – a disgruntled spirit is a dangerous spirit, liable to cause sickness, accidents and even death.

THE ENVIRONMENT

Set in the heart of southeast Asia's tropical zone, Thailand encloses a vast range of habitats: dry tropical **pine forests** in the mountainous north; wet **evergreen forests** in the steamy south; **flood plains** in the central region; **mangrove swamps** along its coasts; and some of the world's most beautiful coral reefs off each coastline. The country boasts some 916 species of birds and an estimated 27,000 flower species – some ten percent of the world's total. These statistics, however, mask a situation that has deteriorated rapidly since World War II. Before then, Thailand's landscapes were virtually unspoiled and were teeming with wild animals such as elephants, wild boars, rhinoceroses, bears and deers. So numerous were these species, in fact, that they were regarded as little more than an impediment to economic progress, an attitude which resulted in a calamitous reduction of Thailand's wildlife and its habitats.

Only in the 1970s did some sort of environmental awareness emerge, when the politicisation of the poor rural areas began to catch up with the powerbrokers in Bangkok. For years farmers had been displaced from land on which they had long established a thriving ecological balance, to be resettled out of the way of the Bangkok-based logging interests. Discontent with this treatment finally led some of the farmers to join the student protests of 1973, and in the subsequent right-wing backlash many political ringleaders fled the capital to seek refuge in the north. Many have since returned under amnesty, and their experiences among the nation's dispossessed have ensured that the environment plays a major role in the mainstream politics of Thailand.

DEFORESTATION

Undoubtedly the biggest crisis facing Thailand's environment is **deforestation**, the effects of which are felt all over the country. As well as providing shelter and sustenance for birds and animals, trees prevent water from dispersing and binds the soil together. When they are cut down, water and topsoil are both rapidly lost, as was demonstrated tragically in 1988, when villages in the south were devastated by mudslides that swept down deforested slopes, killing hundreds of people. A formal **ban on most commercial logging** was finally established in the following year, but much illegal activity has continued.

There was little likelihood that the ban would ever be fully observed, as nothing has been done to change the pattern of wood consumption and the government has instituted no supervisory body to ensure the cessation of illegal logging. To make matters worse, there's the endemic problem of "influence": when the big guns from Bangkok want to build a golf course on a forest reserve, it is virtually impossible for a lowly provincial civil servant to resist their money. On top of that, there's the problem of precisely defining a role for the Royal Forestry Department, which was set up early this century to exploit the forest's resources, but now is charged with the maintenance of the trees. In order to boost its profile the RFD classifies as "forest" virtually anything that looks green from an aeroplane – rubber plantations, eucalyptus farms and even ricefields. Even employing this extraordinary lax criterion, the RFD acknowledges that the percentage of Thailand's territory covered by "forest" has fallen from 53 percent in 1961 to just 28 percent in 1988. Environmental groups think the true figure is even lower.

The timber firms and their financial backers and political protectors have various ways of circumventing the law. Much skulduggery goes on close to the **Burmese border**, where the lawbreakers can claim that the felled timber came from outside the country. Some of it does indeed come from Burma, where the vicious and greedy military regime has set up deals with some of the less scrupulous Thai timber merchants – a racket put in motion by a former chief of the Thai army.

Another favourite trick involves the legal concession granted for the clearance of the hardwood whenever a dam or road condemns an area of forest. Invariably what then happens is that trees are felled outside the designated area and mixed in with the legitimately cut logs. A notorious case concerned the concession to remove trees destroyed by Typhoon Gay in Chumphon and Ranong provinces in 1989 when thousands of healthy trees were felled by the logging company while the local government officials looked on helplessly.

The environmental vandals are not slow to profit from the misfortunes of **Cambodia** either. There the Khmer Rouge have benefitted from Thailand's logging ban, which came at the same time as the withdrawal of support from China, previously the Khmer Rouge's chief military backer. When Thailand cast its eye on the tracts of forests controlled by the Khmer Rouge, the Khmers saw a source of funding for its war against the Vietnamese puppet government in Phnom Penh. Secretive deals were done and the result is that Thailand now imports untold quantities of hardwood from the Khmer Rouge.

REFORESTATION SCHEMES

Commercial **reforestation** has actually worsened the situation. Backed by vested interests, the RFD has classified several areas as "degraded" forest, even though some of these are ancient virgin forest. Once thus designated, the hardwood forests are felled and cleared for commercial development. This usually takes the form of the plantation of fast-growing species such as **eucalyptus**, which are vital to the economically important – but grossly polluting – pulp and paper industries, but suck nutrients and water from the soil at a terrible rate, and are also impossible to mix with other crops. Moreover, some ten million people happen to live in these "degraded" forests.

Under the **khor jor kor** plan, part of Thailand's National Forest Policy of 1985, it's intended that some 25 percent of the country's land area is to remain covered with forest (including rubber plantations), while a further 15 percent will be set aside for commercial planta-

tion by the private sector and government agencies. The first phase of *khor jor kor* targets some 250,000 Isaan families – labelled "encroachers" – for relocation from about 2500 villages, thereby reducing their living space by about one third. Some 2000 families have already been uprooted to make way for new plantations. Without warning, soldiers arrived at two villages in Khon Khaen province, ordered their inhabitants to leave and proceeded to demolish their dwellings. Each family was given temporary food rations and a nominal sum of money before being dumped in resettlement sites that had not been finished and had no attached farmland. Villagers were forced to kill their most valuable possessions – their buffalo – for food. As a result of the subsequent furore, the future of the *khor jor kor* plan is in doubt.

INFRASTRUCTURE PROJECTS

Another major cause of deforestation is development of the country's infrastructure. The expanding **road network**, essential to Thailand's emergence as an industrialised nation, has inevitably damaged the ecology of the country, as have the **quarries** that supplied the construction boom of the 1980s. But nothing has stirred as much controversy as Thailand's **hydro-electric schemes**, which might be a lot cleaner than the production and burning of lignite – the low-grade coal that's Thailand's major source of energy – but destroys vast areas and, of course, displaces countless people.

The latest proposed dam is on the **Pak Mun River** in Isaan. Scheduled for completion in 1994, it will flood the Kaeng-Tana park and forest, and remove an estimated 1000 families from their farmlands. Furthermore, the Mun is a major tributary of the Mekhong River, and is vital to the breeding patterns of various species of edible fish that live in the Mekhong: the proposed dam could thus deprive the population in the southern reaches of the Mekhong of their chief source of protein. The initiation of this project has not been plain sailing for the Thai government, who applied to the World Bank for partial funding for the project, more to legitimise its construction than to compensate for a lack of funding. The decision on funding was to be taken at the 1991 annual meeting of the World Bank and International Monetary Fund, held in Bangkok. To the embarrassment of the Thais, the meeting was preceded by the release of an international report showing that the electricity company's environmental impact study on the dam was deficient, and that bacteria likely to multiply in the reservoir would cause disease amongst the local inhabitants.

Protestors used the opening of the meeting – which was Thailand's most prestigious event of the year and inaugurated the much-vaunted Queen Sirikit National Convention Centre – as a platform to voice their opposition, and were temporarily heartened when the World Bank announced a postponement on the decision. In Thailand such "postponements" usually mean cancellation, with face-saving for all. Unfortunately, notwithstanding its new "green image", the Bank approved the loan a few months later, perhaps influenced by the Thai government's defiant announcement that it would press ahead with the dam with or without funding. The battle is not yet lost, but local protest would have carried more weight if the World Bank had pulled out.

MANGROVES AND CORAL REEFS

Mangrove swamps grow along the 2500 kilometres of both southern coasts of Thailand, and are the key to an ecosystem which protects and nourishes an enormous variety of plant and animal species. In the past the swamps were used by rice farmers to raise **prawns**, using the tides to wash the larvae into prepared pools. Some rice farmers even converted their paddies into prawn farms, but generally the scale of this aquaculture was small and sustainable.

Then, in 1972, the Department of Fisheries began to promote modern technology, enticing many people to invest all they could afford – and sometimes more – in this growth sector. It looked like good money, with farmers initially reporting profits of 300 percent, which for people used to living on the breadline was a gift from the gods. However, big business swiftly moved in, so that today almost all prawn farming in Thailand is in the hands of a few companies.

This was bad for the local farmers, and disastrous for the ecology of the mangroves. Large-scale prawn farming uses vast amounts of sea water, which salinates the neighbouring land to the extent that rice farmers who used to produce two crops a year are now reduced to one small harvest. Furthermore, the chemicals used to feed the prawns and ward off disease are allowed to wash back into the swamps, damaging not only the mangroves themselves, but also the water used for irrigation, drinking and washing. Pollution also kills the very industry that produces it, forcing farmers to move their breeding pools along the coast, damaging yet more mangrove. This destruction of the mangrove forests to make way for new breeding pools is exemplified by the case of the Wen River National Forest Reserve in Kanchanaburi, where the RFD's own figures show that a mere ten percent of the fertile mangrove forest has survived intact.

Tourism, the country's biggest single foreign exchange earner since 1975, has played a significant part in the damaging of Thailand's **coral reefs**. Huge areas of reef are being destroyed at a frightening rate by factors attributable to the tourist explosion, the main cause being pollution emanated by the host of hotels and bungalows which have multiplied unchecked at many of the most beautiful sites on the coasts. The demand for coral souvenirs is exploited by unscrupulous divers and local traders, and many irresponsible dive leaders allow their customers to use harpoon guns, which cause terrible damage to reefs. However, the destruction of coral by tourists is dwarfed by the practice of **dynamite fishing**, which goes on in areas away from the normal tourist haunts.

ENDANGERED SPECIES AND WILDLIFE TRADE

Having hunted many of its indigenous species to extinction – such as Schomburgk's Deer, the Javan Rhinoceros and the Sumatran Rhinoceros – Thailand now acts as the "wildlife supermarket of the world", to quote the World Wide Fund for Nature, which also condemned Thailand as "probably the worst country in the world for the illegal trade in endangered wildlife". Thailand signed the Convention on the International Trade in Endangered Species – **CITES** – in 1973, but for years afterwards the Thais exploited the uncertainty as to whether CITES covered trade in species originating outside the trading country. Even now that it has been established that CITES applies to all commerce in all listed species, Thailand continues to make money out of imported animals and animal products.

Cambodia – not a signatory of CITES – is the major supplier of **live animals**. The main action is focused on border towns such as Aranyaprathet, where Thai middlemen can easily acquire monkeys, deer, wildcats, monitor lizards and various other reptiles, secure in the knowledge that official intervention will be minimal. The RFD, which is charged with the suppression of wildlife trade, has a budget for only thirty wildlife officers nationwide, and doesn't have the money to train them properly, so even if they do intercept a transaction in an endangered species, they probably won't know what they're looking at.

Several animal traders deal quite openly in Bangkok, chiefly at the Weekend Market, but the capital's trade is weighted towards **animal products**. One of the most serious problems is the business in crocodile skins, many of which come from South America, and are sold in huge numbers in Bangkok and other tourist areas. The other critical area is the trade in ivory, most of which is imported from Burma and Laos, although some is native – despite the fact that the Asian elephant has long been protected by law in Thailand.

Thailand's own legislation – the Wild Animals Reservation and Protection Act – is notoriously weak at protecting native Thai species not listed by CITES. For example, the WWF has accused Thailand of showing little interest in protecting its **orchid** species, which grow here in a profusion unmatched anywhere else. And although Thailand's politicians are sensitive to international disapproval when it comes to conservation issues, it seems that there is still a lack of real will to clamp down on the people who profit from the destruction of rare animals. After the WWF made its "supermarket" comment, several highly publicised raids were made on traders who were breeding endangered species for commercial purposes – as well as on a restaurant serving exotic and endangered dishes. The fines, however, were relatively small, and it soon became clear that the raids had served their cosmetic purpose once they had been reported on television.

Gavin Lewis

BOOKS

The following books should be readily available in the UK, US and/or Bangkok. We have given the publishers and prices for most of the in-print titles, though with some Thai titles it's impossible to give an accurate price in baht. The currency indicates the country of publication – where a price appears without a publisher, this means that the book is produced by the publisher previously cited in that listing. The titles listed as being out of print (o/p) should be easy enough to find in secondhand bookstores.

TRAVEL

Carl Bock, *Temples and Elephants* (Oxford University Press, o/p; $9.95). Nineteenth-century account of a rough journey from Bangkok to the far north, dotted with vivid descriptions of rural life and court ceremonial.

Ian Buruma, *God's Dust* (Vintage, £5.99; Noonday, $8.95). Modern portraits of various southeast and east Asian countries, of which only 40 pages are devoted to Thailand – worthwhile nevertheless for its sharp, unsentimental and stylish observations.

Tristan Jones, *To Venture Further* (Grafton, £5.99; Hearst Marine Books, $19). Amazing tale of how the author, a veteran adventurer and an amputee, pioneered the crossing of the Isthmus of Kra in a longtail boat staffed by a disabled crew. Unusually forthright perspective on Thailand and its people.

Charles Nicholl, *Borderlines* (Picador, £5.99; Viking Penguin $8.95). Entertaining adventures and dangerous romance in the "Golden Triangle" form the core of this slightly hackneyed traveller's tale, interwoven with stimulating and well-informed cultural diversions.

Alistair Shearer, *Thailand: the Lotus Kingdom* (John Murray, £14.95). Amusing, sensitive and well-researched contemporary travelogue: a cut above the competition.

Eric Valli and Diane Summers, *Nest Gatherers of Tiger Cave* (Thames and Hudson, £19.95); published in Thailand under the title *The Shadow Hunters* (Suntree, B1350). Beautifully photographed large format photo-essay on the birds' nest collectors of southern Thailand. The authors spent over a year with the harvesters, scaling the phenomenal heights of the sheer limestone walls with them.

William Warren, *Bangkok's Waterways: An Explorer's Handbook* (Asia Books, B395). A cross between a useful guide and an indulgent coffee table book: attractively produced survey of the capital's riverine sights, spiced with cultural and historical snippets.

Richard West, *Thailand: The Last Domino* (Michael Joseph, £16.99). Worthy attempt to get under the skin of "enigmatic Thailand", with a heady mix of political analysis, travelogue and anecdote. The author focuses on Thailand's relationships with neighbouring countries to show how it failed to become the "last domino" in the spread of communism.

CULTURE AND SOCIETY

Michael Carrithers, *The Buddha* (Oxford University Press, £4.99; $6.95). Clear, accessible account of the life of the Buddha, and the development and significance of his thought.

Robert and Nanthapa Cooper, *Culture Shock! Thailand* (Kuperard, £6.95). Widely available but in every respect inferior to Denis Segaller's books on Thai culture (see below) – seems chiefly intended for prospective employers worried about how to deal with the Thia maid.

John R. Davies, *A Trekkers' Guide to the Hilltribes of Northern Thailand* (Footloose, £5.95; B150). Bite-sized but well-informed insight into hill-tribe cultures, including some practical information and a small dictionary of hill-tribe languages.

Sanitsuda Ekachai, *Behind the Smile* (Thai Development Support Committee, £5; B200). Collected articles of a *Bangkok Post* journalist highlighting the effect of Thailand's sudden economic growth on the country's rural poor.

William J. Klausner, *Reflections on Thai Culture* (Siam Society, Bangkok). Humorous accounts of an anthropologist living in Thailand since 1955. Entertaining mixture of the academic and the anecdotal; especially good on everyday life and festivals in Isaan villages.

Elaine and Paul Lewis, *Peoples of the Golden Triangle* (Thames and Hudson, £24; $35). Hefty, exhaustive work illustrated with excellent photographs, describing every aspect of hill-tribe life.

John McKinnon (ed.), *Highlanders of Thailand* (Oxford University Press, £19.50; o/p in the US). A rather dry but enlightening collection of essays on the hill tribes.

Trilok Chandra Majupuria, *Erawan Shrine and Brahma Worship in Thailand* (Tecpress, Bangkok). The most concise introduction to the complexities of Thai religion, with a much wider scope than the title implies.

Phya Anuman Rajadhon *Some Traditions of the Thai* (DK Books, Bangkok). Meticulously researched essays written by one of Thailand's leading scholars, republished to commemorate the centenary of the author's birth.

Denis Segaller, *Thai Ways* and *More Thai Ways* (Asia Books, Bangkok). Fascinating collections of short pieces on Thai customs and traditions written for the former *Bangkok World* by a long-term English resident of Bangkok.

Pira Sudham, *People of Esarn* (Shire Books, Bangkok). Wry and touching potted life-stories of villagers who live in, leave and return to the poverty-stricken northeast, compiled by a northeastern village lad turned author.

Thanh-Dam Truong, *Sex, Money and Morality: Prostitution and tourism in South-East Asia* (Zed Books, £10.95; $17.50). Hard-hitting analysis of the marketing of Thailand as sex-tourism capital of Asia.

William Warren, *Living in Thailand* (Thames and Hudson, £25). Luscious coffee table volume of traditional houses and furnishings, with an emphasis on the homes of Thailand's rich and famous; seductively photographed by Luca Invernizzi Tettoni.

HISTORY

Anna Leonowens, *The Original Anna and the King of Siam* (Chalermnit, B120). The menda-cious memoirs of the nineteenth-century English governess that inspired the infamous Yul Brunner film *The King and I*; low on accuracy, high on inside-palace gossip.

Michael Smithies, *Old Bangkok* (Oxford University Press, £8.95). Brief, anecdotal history of the capital's early development, emphasizing what remains to be seen of bygone Bangkok.

John Stewart, *To the River Kwai: Two Journeys – 1943, 1979* (Bloomsbury, £3.99). A survivor of the horrific World War II POW camps along the River Kwai, the author returns to the region, interlacing his wartime reminiscences with observations on how he feels and what he sees 36 years later.

William Warren, *Jim Thompson: the Legendary American of Thailand* (Jim Thompson Thai Silk Co, Bangkok). The engrossing biography of the ex-OSS agent, art collector and Thai silk magnate whose disappearance in Malaysia in 1967 has never been satisfactorily resolved.

Joseph J. Wright Jr, *The Balancing Act: A History of Modern Thailand* (Asia Books, B395). Detailed analysis of the Thai political scene from the end of the absolute monarchy in 1932 until the February 1991 coup; plenty of anecdotes and wider cultural references make it a far from dry read.

David K. Wyatt, *Thailand: A Short History* (Yale University Press, £14; $14.95). The only comprehensive history of Thailand that's up-to-date and accurate. An excellent treatment, scholarly but highly readable, with a good eye for witty, telling details. Good chapters on the story of the Thais before they reached what's now Thailand, and on recent (up to 1984) developments.

ART AND ARCHITECTURE

Steve van Beek, *The Arts of Thailand* (Thames and Hudson £24; $45). Lavishly produced and perfectly pitched introduction to the history of Thai architecture, sculpture and painting, with superb photographs by Luca Invernizzi Tettoni.

Jean Boisselier, *The Heritage of Thai Sculpture* (Asia Books, Bangkok). Weighty but accessible seminal tome by influential French art historian.

Susan Conway, *Thai Textiles* (British Museum Press, £16.95); Uiversity of Washington Press, $30). A fascinating, richly illustrated work which draws on the evidence of sculptures and temple murals to trace the evolution of Thai weaving techniques and costume styles, and to examine the functional and ceremonial uses of textiles.

Dorothy H. Fickle, *Images of the Buddha in Thailand* (Oxford University Press, £6.95; $11.95). Clear, concise, though rather arid examination of Thai Buddha images of all periods, and the historical and religious influences which have shaped their development. Well-illustrated, with a short introduction on the life of the Buddha himself.

Betty Gosling, *Sukhothai: Its History, Culture and Art* (Oxford University Press, £30). Overpriced but thoroughy researched dissection of the ruins of Sukhothai and the kings who commissioned them.

Sumet Jumsai, *Naga: Cultural Origins in Siam and the West Pacific* (Oxford University Press, £32; $45). Wide-ranging discussion of water symbols in Thailand and other parts of Asia, offering a stimulating mix of art, architecture, mythology and cosmology.

NATURAL HISTORY AND ECOLOGY

Ashley J. Boyd and Collin Piprell, *Thailand: the Kingdom Beneath the Sea* (Artasia Press, B220). Stunningly photographed documentation of marine life annotated with accounts of diving expeditions. Useful tips on good diving spots, identification of fish and coral, and underwater health and safety.

Philip Hurst, *Rainforest Politics* (Zed Books, £10.95; $17.50). Case studies of alarming ecological destruction in six southeast Asian countries, sponsored by Friends of the Earth, which clearly and powerfully assesses the causes and offers pragmatic solutions.

Insight Guide to Southeast Asian Wildlife (Geocentre, £11.95; Prentice Hall $19.95). Adequate introduction to the flora and fauna of the region, with a fairly detailed focus on several of Thailand's national parks. Full of gorgeous photos, but not very useful for identifying species in the field.

LITERATURE

Kampoon Boontawee, *A Child of the Northeast* (DK Books, B150). Overly sentimental prizewinning novel set in 1930s Isaan, but well worth reading for its wealth of local colour and insights into northeastern folklore and customs.

Kukrit Pramoj, *Si Phaendin: Four Reigns* (DK Books, 2 vols, B90 each). A kind of historical romance spanning the four reigns of Ramas V to VIII (1892–1946) as experienced by a heroine called Ploi. Written by former prime minister Kukrit Pramoj, the story has become a modern classic in Thailand, made into films, plays and TV dramas, with Ploi as the archetypal feminine role model.

Rama I, *Thai Ramayana* (Chalermnit, B80). Slightly stilted abridged prose translation of King Rama I's version of the epic Hindu narrative, full of gleeful descriptions of bizarre mythological characters and supernatural battles. Essential reading if you want anything like a full appreciation of Thai painting, carving and classical dance.

J.C. Shaw, *The Ramayana through Western Eyes* (DK, Bangkok). The bare bones of the epic tale are retold between tenuously comparable excerpts from Western poets, including Shakespeare, Shelley and Walt Whitman. Much more helpfully, the text is interspersed with key scenes from the murals at Bangkok's Wat Phra Kaeo.

Khamsing Srinawk, *The Politician and Other Stories* (Oxford University Press, £10.99). A collection of brilliantly satiric short stories, full of pithy moral observation and biting irony, which capture the vulnerability of peasant farmers in the north and northeast, as they try to come to grips with the modern world. Written by an insider from a peasant family, who was educated at Chulalongkorn University, became a hero of the left, and joined the communist insurgents after the 1976 clampdown.

THAILAND IN FOREIGN LITERATURE

Botan, *Letters from Thailand* (DK, B135). Probably the best introduction to the Chinese community in Bangkok, presented in the form of letters written over a twenty-year period by a Chinese emigrant to his mother. Branded both as anti-Chinese and anti-Thai, this 1969 prizewinning book is now mandatory reading in school social studies' classes.

Pierre Boulle, *The Bridge Over the River Kwai* (Fontana, o/p; Bantam, $4.50). The World War II novel which inspired the David Lean movie and kicked off the Kanchanaburi tourist industry.

Spalding Gray, *Swimming to Cambodia* (Picador £5.99; Theatre Communications Group, $7.95). Hugely entertaining and politically acute account of the actor and monologuist's time in Thailand on location for the filming of the *The Killing Fields*.

FOOD AND COOKERY

Vatcharin Bhumichitr, *The Taste of Thailand* (Pavilion, £10.99; Macmillan,. $34.95). Another glossy introduction to this eminently photogenic country, this time through its food. The author runs a Thai restaurant in London and provides background colour as well as about 150 recipes adapted for Western kitchens.

Jacqueline M. Piper, *Fruits of South-East Asia* (Oxford University Press, £6.95). An exploration of the bounteous fruits of the region, tracing their role in cooking, medicine, handicrafts and rituals. Well-illustrated with photos, watercolours and early botanical drawings.

LANGUAGE

Thai belongs to one of the oldest families of languages in the world, Austro-Thai, and is radically different from most of the other tongues of southeast Asia. Being tonal, Thai is extremely difficult for Westerners to master, but by building up from a small core of set phrases, you'll soon get the hang of enough to get by. Most Thais who deal with tourists speak some English, but once you stray off the beaten track you'll probably need at least a few words in Thai. Anywhere you go, you'll impress and get better treatment if you at least make an effort to speak a few words.

Distinct dialects are spoken in the north, the northeast and the south, which can increase the difficulty of comprehending what's said to you. **Thai script** is even more of a problem to Westerners, with 44 consonants to represent 21 consonant sounds and 32 vowels to deal with 48 different vowel sounds. However, street signs are nearly always written in Roman script as well as Thai, and in other circumstances you're better off asking than trying to unscramble the swirling mess of symbols, signs and accents. Transliteration into Roman script leads to many problems – see the note in the introduction.

For the basics, the most useful **language books** on the market are *Thai at your Fingertips* (Routledge, £5.99) and *Robertson's Practical English-Thai Dictionary* (Asia Books, B229), which is available only in Thailand. Both cover the essential phrases and expressions, as well as dipping into grammar and providing a fuller vocabulary in dictionary format – the former probably has the edge in having a Thai-English section, arranged by subject area. Lonely Planet's *Thai Phrasebook* (£1.95/$3.95) is cheap and portable.

The best **teach-yourself course** is *Linguaphone Thai* (£159.90); for a more traditional text book, try *The Fundamentals of the Thai Language* (Bailey Bros & Swinfen, £12.95), which is comprehensive, though hard going; G.H. Allison's *Easy Thai* (Tuttle, £4.95) is best for those who feel the urge to learn the alphabet.

PRONUNCIATION

Mastering **tones** is probably the most difficult part of learning Thai. Five different tones are used – low, middle, high, falling, and rising – by which the meaning of a single syllable can be altered in five different ways. Thus, using four of the five tones, you can make a sentence just from just one syllable: *mái mài mâi mãi* – "New wood burns, doesn't it?" As well as the natural difficulty in becoming attuned to speaking and listening to these different tones, Western efforts are complicated by our tendency to denote the overall meaning of a sentence by modulating our tones – for example, turning a statement into a question through a shift of stress and tone. Listen to native Thai speakers and you'll soon begin to pick up the different approach to tone.

The pitch of each tone is gauged in relation to your vocal range when speaking, but they should all lie within a narrow band, separated by gaps just big enough to differentiate them. The **low tones** (syllables marked with ` below), **middle tones** (unmarked syllables), and **high tones** (syllables marked ´) should each be pronounced evenly and with no inflection. The **falling tone** (syllables marked ^) is spoken with an obvious drop in pitch, as if you were sharply emphasizing a word in English. The **rising tone** (marked ~) is pronounced as if you were asking an exaggerated question in English.

As well as the unfamiliar tones, you'll find that, despite the best efforts of the transliterators, there is no precise English equivalent to many **vowel and consonant sounds** in the Thai language. The lists below give a rough idea of pronounciation.

VOWELS

a as in dad.

aa has no precise equivalent, but is pronounced as it looks, with the vowel elongated.

ae as in there.

ai/ay as in buy.

ao as in now.

aw as in awe.

e as in pen.

eu as in sir, but heavily nasalised.

i as in tip.

ii as in feet.

o as in knock.

oe as in hurt, but more closed.

oh as in toe.

u as in loot.

uu as in pool.

CONSONANTS

r as in rip, but with the tongue flapped quickly against the palate – in everyday speech, it's often pronounced like "l".

kh as in keep.

ph as in put.

th as in time.

k is unaspirated and unvoiced, and closer to "g".

p is also unaspirated and unvoiced, and closer to "b".

t is also unaspirated and unvoiced, and closer to "d".

THAI WORDS AND PHRASES

GREETINGS AND BASIC PHRASES

Whenever you speak to a stranger in Thailand, you should end your sentence in *khráp* if you're a man, *khâ* if you're a woman – these untranslatable politening syllables will gain good will, and should always be used after *sawàt dii* (hello/goodbye) and *khàwp khun* (Thank you). *Khráp* and *khâ* are also often used to answer "yes" to a question, though the most common way is to repeat the verb of the question (precede it with *mâi* for "no"). *Châi* (yes) and *mâi châi* (no) are less frequently used than their English equivalents.

Hello	*sawàt dii*	My name is	*phõm (men)/ diichãn (women) chêu . . .*
Where are you going? (not always meant literally, but used as a general greeting)	*pai nãi*	I come from . . .	*phõm/diichãn maa jàak . . .*
		I don't understand	*mâi khão jai*
		Do you speak English?	*khun phûut phasãa angkrìt dâi mãi?*
I'm out having fun/I'm travelling (answer to *pai nãi*, almost indefinable pleasantry)	*pai thîaw*	Do you have . . . ?	*mii . . . mãi?*
		Is there . . . ?	*. . . mii mãi?*
Goodbye	*sawàt dii/la kàwn*	Is . . . possible?	*. . . dâi mãi?*
Good luck	*chôk dii*	Can you help me?	*chûay phõm/diichãn dâi mãi?*
Excuse me	*khãw thâwt*		
Thank you	*khàwp khun*	(I) want . . .	*ao . . .*
It's nothing/it doesn't matter/no problem	*mâi pen rai*	(I) would like to . . .	*yàak jà . . .*
		(I) like . . .	*châwp . . .*
How are you?	*sabai dii reũ ?*	What is this called in Thai?	*níi phasãa thai rîak wâa arai?*
I'm fine	*sabai dii*		
What's your name?	*khun chêu arai ?*		

GETTING AROUND

Where is the . . . ?	*. . . yùu thîi nãi?*	What time does the bus arrive in . . . ?	*rót thẽung . . . kìi mohng?*
How far?	*klai thâo rai?*	Stop here	*jàwt thîi nîi*
I would like to go to . . .	*yàak jà pai . . .*	here	*thîi nîi*
Where have you been?	*pai nãi maa?*	over there	*thîi nâan/thîi nôhn*
Where is this bus going?	*rót níi pai nãi?*	right	*khwãa*
When will the bus leave?	*rót jà àwk mêua rai?*	left	*sái*

GETTING AROUND (cont.)

straight	*trong*	ticket	*tŭa*
north	*nŭea*	hotel	*rohng raem*
south	*tâi*	post office	*praisanii*
east	*tawan àwk*	restaurant	*raan ahăan*
west	*tawan tòk*	shop	*raan*
near/far	*klâi/klai*	market	*talàat*
street	*thanŏn*	hospital	*rohng phayaabaan*
train station	*sathàanii rót fai*	motorcycle	*rót mohtoesai*
bus station	*sathàanii rót meh*	taxi	*rót táksîi*
airport	*sanăam bin*	boat	*reua*

ACCOMMODATION AND SHOPPING

How much is …?	*… thâo rai/kìi bàat?*	Can I store my bag here?	*fàak krapăo wái thîi nîi dâi măi?*
How much is a room here per night?	*hâwng thîi nîi kheun lá thâo rai?*	cheap/expensive	*thùuk/phaeng*
Do you have a cheaper room?	*mii hâwng thùuk kwàa măi?*	air-con room	*hăwng ae*
Can I/we look at the room?	*duu hâwng dâi măi?*	ordinary room	*hăwng thammadaa*
I/We'll stay two nights	*jà yùu săwng kheun*	telephone	*thohrásàp*
Can you reduce the price?	*lót raakhaa dâi măi?*	laundry	*sák phâa*
		blanket	*phâa hòm*
		fan	*phát lom*

GENERAL ADJECTIVES

alone	*khon diaw*	easy	*ngâi*
another	*ìik … nèung*	fun	*sanùk*
bad	*mâi dii*	hot	*ráwn*
big	*yài*	hungry	*hĭu khâo*
clean	*sa-àat*	ill	*mâi sabai*
closed	*pìt*	open	*pòet*
cold (object)	*yen*	pretty	*sŭai*
cold (person or weather)	*năo*	small	*lek*
delicious	*aròi*	thirsty	*hĭu nám*
difficult	*yâak*	tired	*nèu-ai*
dirty	*sokaprok*	very	*mâak*

GENERAL NOUNS

Nouns have no plurals or genders, and don't require an article.

bathroom/toilet	*hâwng nám*	friend	*phêuan*
boyfriend or girlfriend	*faen*	money	*ngoen*
foreigner	*fàràng*	water	*nám*
food	*ahăan*		

GENERAL VERBS

Thai verbs do not conjugate at all, and also often double up as nouns and adjectives, which means that foreigners' most unidiomatic attempts to construct sentences are often readily understood.

come	*maa*	give	*hâi*	sleep	*nawn làp*
do	*tham*	go	*pai*	take	*ao*
eat	*kin/thaan khâo*	sit	*nâng*	walk	*doen pai*

NUMBERS

zero	*sūun*	eight	*pàet*	twenty two,	*yîi sìp sǎwng, yîi*
one	*nèung*	nine	*kâo*	twenty three, etc	*sìp sǎam . . .*
two	*sǎwng*	ten	*sìp*	thirty, forty, etc	*sǎam sìp, sìi sìp . .*
three	*sǎam*	eleven	*sìp èt*	one hundred, two	*nèung rói, sǎwng*
four	*sìi*	twelve, thir-	*sìp sǎwng, sìp*	hundred, etc	*rói . . .*
five	*hâa*	teen, etc	*sǎam . . .*	one thousand	*nèung phan*
six	*hòk*	twenty	*yîi sìp/yiip*	ten thousand	*nèung mèun*
seven	*jèt*	twenty one	*yîi sìp èt*		

TIME

The commonest system for telling the time, as outlined below, is actually a confusing mix of several different systems. The state railways and government officials use the 24-hour clock (9am is *kâo naalikaa*, 10am *sìp naalikaa*, and so on), which is always worth trying if you get stuck.

1am–5am	*tii nèung–tii hâa*	minute	*naathii*
6am–11am	*hòk mohng cháo–sìp èt mohng cháo*	hour	*chûa mohng*
		day	*waan*
noon	*thîang*	week	*aathít*
1pm	*bài mohng*	month	*deuan*
2pm–4pm	*bài sǎwng mohng– bài sìi mohng*	year	*pii*
		today	*wan níi*
5pm–6pm	*hâa mohng yen–hòk mohng yen*	tomorrow	*phrûng níi*
		yesterday	*mêua wan*
7pm–11pm	*nèung thûm–hâa thûm*	now	*dǐ aw níi*
		next week	*aathít nâa*
midnight	*thîang kheun*	last week	*aathít kàwn*
What time is it?	*kìi mohng láew?*	morning	*cháo*
How many hours?	*kìi chûa mohng?*	afternoon	*bài*
How long?	*naan thâo rai?*	evening	*yen*
		night	*kheun*

A THAI GLOSSARY

AO Bay.

ASPARA Female deity.

AVALOKITESVARA Bodhisattava representing compassion.

AVATAR Earthly manifestation of a deity.

BAN Village or house.

BENCHARONG Polychromatic ceramics made in China for the Thai market.

BHUMISPARSA MUDRA Most common gesture of Buddha images; symbolises Buddha's victory over temptation.

BODHISATTVA In Mahayana Buddhism, an enlightened being who postpones his or her entry into Nirvana.

BOT Main sanctuary of a Buddhist temple.

BRAHMA One of the Hindu trinity: "the Creator". Usually depicted with four faces and four arms.

CHAO LEY/CHAO NAM "Sea gipsies" – nomadic fisherfolk of southern Thailand.

CHEDI Reliquary tower in Buddhist temple.

CHOFA Finial on temple roof.

DEVA Mythical deity.

DEVARAJA God-king.

DHARMA The teachings or doctrine of the Buddha.

DHARMACHAKRA Buddhist Wheel of Law.

DOI Mountain.

ERAWAN Mythical three-headed elephant; Indra's vehicle.

FARANG A foreigner; a corruption of the word *français*.

GANESH Hindu elephant-headed deity, remover of obstacles and god of knowledge

GARUDA Mythical Hindu creature – half-man half-bird; Vishnu's vehicle.

GOPURA Entrance pavillion to temple precinct (especially Khmer).

HAMSA Sacred mythical goose; Brahma's vehicle.

HANG YAO Longtail boat.

HANUMAN Monkey god and chief of the monkey army in the *Ramayana*; ally of Rama.

HAT Beach.

HIN Stone.

HINAYANA Pejorative term for Theravada school of Buddhism , literally " Lesser Vehicle".

HO TRAI A scripture library.

INDRA Hindu king of the gods and, in Buddhism, devotee of Buddha; usually carries a thunderbolt.

ISAAN Northeast Thailand.

JATAKA Stories of the 500 lives of the Buddha.

KHAEN Reed and wood pipe; the characteristic musical instrument of Isaan.

KHAO Hill, mountain.

KHLONG Canal.

KHON Classical dance-drama.

KINNARI Mythical creature – half-woman, half-horse.

KIRTIMUKHA Very powerful deity depicted as a lion-head.

KO Island.

KU The Laotian word for *prang*; a tower in a temple complex.

LAEM Headland or cape.

LAKHON Classical dance-drama.

LAK MUANG City pillar; revered home for the city's guardian spirit.

LAKSHANA Auspicious signs or "marks of greatness" displayed by the Buddha.

LAKSHAMAN/PHRA LAK Rama's younger brother.

LIKAY Popular folk theatre.

LONGYI Burmese sarong.

MAENAM River.

MAHATHAT Chedi containing relics of the Buddha.

MAHAYANA School of Buddhism now practised mainly in China, Japan and Korea; literally " the Great Vehicle".

MARA The Evil One; tempter of Buddha.

MERU/SINERU Mythical mountain at the centre of Hindu and Buddhist cosmologies.

MONDOP Small, square temple building to house minor images or religious texts.

MUDRA Symbolic gesture of the Buddha.

MUT MEE Tie-dyed cotton or silk.

MUANG City or town.

MUAY THAI Thai boxing.

NAGA Mythical dragon-headed serpent in Buddhism and Hinduism.

NAKHON Honorific title for a city.

NAM Water.

NAM TOK Waterfall.

NANG THALUNG Shadow puppet entertainment, found in southern Thailand.

NIRVANA Final liberation from the cycle of rebirths; state of non-being to which Buddhists aspire.

PAK TAI Southern Thailand.

PALI Language of ancient India; the script of the original Buddhist scriptures.

PHRA Honorific term for a person – literally "excellent".

PHU Mountain.

PRANG Central tower in a Khmer temple.

PRASAT Khmer temple complex or central shrine.

RAMA Human manifestation of Hindu deity Vishnu; hero of the *Ramayana*.

RAMAKIEN Thai version of the *Ramayana*.

RAMAYANA Hindu epic of good versus evil: chief characters include Rama, Sita, Ravana, Hanuman.

RAVANA Rama's adversary in the *Ramayana*; represents evil. Also known as Totsagan.

RISHI Ascetic hermit.

ROT AE/ROT TUA Air-conditioned bus.

ROT THAMMADA Ordinary bus.

SALA Meeting hall.

SAMLOR Passenger tricycle; literally "three-wheeled".

SANSKRIT Sacred language of Hinduism, also used in Buddhism.

SEMA Boundary stone to mark consecrated ground within temple complex.

SHIVA One of the Hindu trinity – "The Destroyer".

SHIVA LINGAM Phallic representation of Shiva.

SOI Alley or side-road.

SONGKHRAN Thai New Year.

SONGTHAEW Pick-up used as public transport; literally "two rows", after the vehicle's two facing benches.

TAKRAW Game played with a rattan ball.

TALAT Market.

TALAT NAM Floating market.

TALAT YEN Night market.

TAVATIMSA Buddhist heaven.

THALE Sea or lake.

THAM Cave.

THAT Chedi.

THEP A divinity.

THERAVADA Main school of Buddhist thought in Thailand; also known as Hinayana.

TOTSAGAN Rama's evil rival in the *Ramayana*; also known as Ravana.

TUK-TUK Motorised three-wheeled taxi.

UMA Shiva's consort.

USHNISHA Cranial protuberance on Buddha images, signifying an enlightened being.

VIHARN Temple assembly hall for the laity; usually contains the principal Buddha image.

VIPASSANA Buddhist meditation technique; literally " insight".

VISHNU One of the Hindu trinity – "The Preserver". Usually shown with four arms, holding a disc, a conch, a lotus and a club.

WANG Palace.

WAT Temple.

WIANG Fortified town.

YAKSHA Mythical giant.

YANTRA Magical combination of numbers and letters, used to ward off danger.

INDEX

Accommodation 21–22
Addresses 42
Amulets 75
Antiques, exporting 42
Ao Nang 394
Ao Phang Nga 386–388
Ao Phra Nang 392
Art and architecture 447–452
Ayutthaya 138–147

Ban Chao Mai 413
Ban Chiang 309
Ban Na Muen Sri 410
Ban Phu 322
Ban Phum Riang 338
Ban Taba 428
Bang Pa-In 137
BANGKOK 45–111
  Accommodation 54–60
  Airlines 108
  Amulet market 74
  Antique shops 105
  Arriving in Bangkok 47
  Barge Museum 81
  Bars 100
  Bookshops 106
  Boxing, Thai 102
  Buddhaisawan Chapel 73
  Bus routes 48
  Bus stations 49
  Canal rides 80
  Chatuchak Weekend Market 92
  Chinatown 76–78
  Cinemas 102
  City transport 52–54
  Counterfeit Culture 104
  Culture shows 101
  Democracy Monument 73
  Don Muang airport 48
  Dusit 82
  Eating 97–99
  Embassies, Asian 109
  Embassies, Western 110
  Emerald Buddha 63
  Erawan Shrine 86
  Express boat stops 53
  Gay bars 101
  Gem shops 104
  Giant Swing (Sao Ching Cha) 76
  Golden Buddha 77

Golden Mount 74
Grand Palace 62–66
  Handicraft shops 105
  History 46
  Hualamphong Station 49
  Human Imagery Museum 96
  Jim Thompson's House 84
  Kamthieng House 86
  Kite flying 70
  Lak Muang 69
  Listings 109
  Loh Prasat 74
  Lumphini Park 90
  Mae Toranee 70
  Marble Temple (Wat Benjamabophit) 83
  Muang Boran Ancient City 95
  Museum of Imaging Technology 89
  Museum of the Department of Corrections 94
  National Gallery 73
  National Museum 70–73
  Nightlife and entertainment 100–102
  Nonthaburi 93–95
  Pahurat 79
  Patpong 91
  Ploughing Ceremony 69
  Pratunam Market 88
  Ratanakosin 60–73
  Reclining Buddha 69
  Sampeng Lane 78
  Sanam Luang 69
  Shopping 103–106
  Siam Square 84
  Silk shops 103
  Silpakorn University Gallery 73
  Snake Farm 89
  Suan Pakkad Palace Museum 87
  Thieves' Market (Nakhon Kasem) 78
  Thonburi 79–82
  Tourist information 52
  Travel agents 108
  Travel from Bangkok 106
  Victory Monument 88
  Vimanmek Palace 82
  Wang Na 72
  Wat Arun 80
  Wat Chakrawat 78
  Wat Chalerm Phra Kiat 94
  Wat Phra Kaeo 62–65
  Wat Po 67
  Wat Prayoon 81
  Wat Rajabophit 76
  Wat Rajnadda 74
  Wat Saket 74
  Wat Suthat 75

  Wat Traimit 77
  Zoo 82
Banks 12
Bay Kream 297
Betel 308
Betong 426
Bird's-Nesting 400
Books 461–464
Boxing, Thai 36
Bung Kan 323
Burmese Junta and the Karen 173
Buses 16

Camping 22
Car rental 19
Catfish, giant 253
Cha-am 334
Chaiya 337
Chaiyaphum 305
Chak Phra Festival 339
Chanthaburi 270–272
Chiang Khan 315
Chiang Khong 252
CHIANG MAI 188–210
  Accommodation 193–195
  Arriving 189
  Doi Suthep 206
  Eating 203
  Festivals 195
  Information 192
  Listings 205
  Mae Sa 210
  National Museum 197
  Night Bazaar 200
  Nightlife 204
  San Kamphaeng 200
  Shopping 200–203
  Transport 192
  Wat Bupparam 200
  Wat Chedi Luang 197
  Wat Chiang Man 197
  Wat Jet Yot 198
  Wat Phra Singh 196
  Wat Suan Dork 199
  Wat Umong 199
  Wiang Kum Kam 208
  Zoo 198

Chiang Rai 240–244
Chiang Saen 250
Chinese in Thailand 77
Chom Thong 222
Chumphon 335–337
Costs 13
Credit cards 12
Crime 30

Currency 12
Customs restrictions 13, 42

Damnoen Saduak 118
Dan Kwian 286
Death Railway 124, 129
Disabled travel 41
Diving 39
Doi Inthanon National Park 221–223
Doi Phukha National Park 220
Doi Suthep 206
Doi Tung 247
Drama 34
Drinks 25
Durians 95

Elephant Training Centre 215
Elephants 216
Elephants, white 83
Embassies, Thai 10
Emergencies 9
Endangered species 93
Environment 457–460
Erawan National Park 128

Fang 238
Ferries 18
Festivals 32
Films 36
Flight agents in Australasia 8
Flight agents in North America 7
Flight agents in the UK and Ireland 4
Flights from Australasia 8
Flights from North America 6
Flights from the UK and Ireland 3
Flights in Thailand 18
Food 23–27

Gay life 41
Glossary 469
"Golden Triangle" 249
Guest houses 21

Hat Nopparat Thara 394
Hat Yai 417
Health 14
Hill tribes 182–187
History of Thailand 433–446

Hitchhiking 20
Holidays, national 31
Hotels 21
Hua Hin 334
Huai Khom 245

Immigration 9
Inoculations 14
Insurance 14

Kaeng Tana National Park 302
Kamphaeng Phet 168–171
Kanchanaburi 119–126
Khao Phra Viharn 303
Khao Sok National Park 370
Khao Yai National Park 281–283
Khlong Yai 273
Khmer ruins 288
Khon 34
Khon Khaen 306–309
Khorat 283–286
Khruba Srivijaya 207
Khu Khut Waterbird Park 424
Khun Yuam 226
Kite flying 70
Ko Adang 415
Ko Bubu 403
Ko Chang 274–277
Ko Hai 412
Ko Jum 403
Ko Kradan 412
Ko Lanta Yai 400–402
Ko Lipe 415
Ko Mook 412
Ko Panyi 387
KO PHA NGAN 350–356
  Chaloaklam 355
  Getting to Ko Pha Ngan 351
  Hat Khuat 355
  Hat Rin 352
  Hat Sadet 354
  Hat Salad 356
  Mae Hat 355
  Pang Waterfall National Park 352
  Thong Nai Pan 354
  Thong Sala 352
  Wogtum 355
Ko Pha Yam 369
Ko Phi Phi 395–400
Ko Phi Phi Don 396–399
Ko Phi Phi Leh 399
KO PHUKET 372–385

Ao Kamala 379
Ao Karon 381
Ao Kata Noi 382
Ao Kata Yai 382
Ao Patong 380
Chao Ley 384
Diving Centres 375
East coast 385
Getting to Ko Phuket 374
Hat Bang Tao 379
Hat Mai Khao 379
Hat Nai Harn 383
Hat Nai Yang 379
Hat Rawai 383
Hat Surin 379
Interior 385
Laem Promthep 383
Ngan Kin Jeh – the Vegetarian Festival 378
Phuket Town 375–378
Ko Samet 265–270
KO SAMUI 340–350
  Ang Thong National Marine Park 343
  Ao Phangka 350
  Ban Bangkao 350
  Ban Hua Thanon 350
  Bangrak 346
  Bophut 345
  Chaweng 347
  Choeng Mon 346
  Getting to Ko Samui 341
  Lamai 349
  Maenam 344
  Na Thon 343
Ko Si Chang 255–258
Ko Similan 371
Ko Surin 369
KO TAO 356–359
  Ao Muang 358
  Getting to Ko Tao 358
  Hat Sai Ree 358
  Ko Nang Yuan 358
  Laem Thian 359
  Mae Hat 358
Ko Tarutao 414
Ko Tarutao National Marine Park 413–415
Ko Yo 423
Kok River 239
Kong Chiam 302
Krabi 388–391
Kuomintang 245

Laem Ngop 273
Laem Phra Nang 391–394
Lakhon 34
Lampang 211–216

Lamphun 209
Language 465–468
Laos, tours to 320
Likay 35
Local transport 18
Loei 310
Long-neck women 231
Lopburi 147–152
Loy Krathong 162

Mae Aw 233
Mae Hong Son 226–234
Mae Ko Vafe 226
Mae Lana 235
Mae Sa 210
Mae Sai 248
Mae Salong 245
Mae Sam Laeb 224
Mae Sariang 224
Mae Sot 172
Mae Suya 234
Malaria 15
Maps 11
Meditation centres 37
Mekhong River 314–327
Mon people 134
Monarchy 37
Motorbike rental 19
Mrabri 220
Mukdahan 326
Music 35

Nai Soi 231
Nakhon Pathom 113–118
Nakhon Phanom 324
Nakhon Ratchasima, see
  Khorat
Nakhon Si Thammarat
  359–364
Nam Tok 130
Nan 216–220
Nang 35
Narathiwat 427
National Park
  accommodation 22
National Parks 40
Newspapers 29
Nong Khai 317–320
Northern history 178

Opening hours 31
Opium and the Golden
  Triangle 188
Overland routes from Asia 8

Package holidays from North
  America 7
Package holidays from the
  UK 5
Pai 236
Pak Bara 413
Pak Chom 316
Pak Meng 412
Pamalor 224
Pattani 424
Pattaya 258–264
Pha Taem cliff paintings 302
Phang Nga 386
Phatthalung 408
Phayao 240
Phetchaburi 330–333
Phibunmangsahan 301
Phimai 287–291
Phitsanulok 153–157
Phra Ratchaniwet
  Marukhathaiyawan 334
Phu Hin Rongkla National
  Park 313
Phu Kradung National Park
  311
Phu Pha Terp National Park
  327
Phu Reua National Park 312
Police, Tourist 31
Post offices 28
Prachuap Khiri Khan 335
Prasat Hin Khao Phanom
  Rung 292
Prasat Hin Phimai 287
Prasat Muang Singh 129
Prasat Muang Tham 293
Prasat Ta Muen Tam 297

Radio 29
Railae, east 393
Railae, west 393
Ramayana 65
Ranong 368
Religion 453–456
River Kwai, Bridge over 125
Roi Et 304
Rubies and sapphires 272

Sai Yok National Park 132
Saiburi 426
Sakhon Nakhon 325
Sang Khom 316
Sangkhlaburi 133
Satun 415

Sawankhalok kilns 167
Sex industry 90
Sexual harassment 31
Shadow Puppets 363
Si Satchanalai 165
Silkworms 294
Snake's blood 89
Snorkelling 39
Songkhla 419–423
Songthaews 17
Sop Ruak 249
Soppong 235
Spirits of the Yellow Leaves
  220
Sri Chiangmai 317
Stupas 117
Sukhothai 157–165
Sukhothai Buddha 160
Sungai Kolok 428
Surat Thani 338–340
Surin 294–296

Ta Klang 297
Ta Muen Toj 297
Tak 171
Tak Bai 427
Takraw 36
Telephone codes,
  international 29
Telephones 28
Television 29
Tha Bo 317
Tha Don 386
Tha Ton 238
Thale Ban National Park 416
Thale Noi Waterbird Park
  410
Tham Lot 235
Than Bokkharani 391
That Phanom 325
Thompson, Jim 85
Three Pagodas Pass 135
Tourism Authority of
  Thailand (TAT) 10
Tourist information 10
Trains 17
Trang 411
Trat 273
Travellers' cheques 12
Trekking 178–188

Ubon Ratchathani 298–
  301
Udon Thani 309

Video 36
Visas 9

Wat Hin Ma Beng 316
Wat Khaek 321
Wat Pa Nanachat Beung Rai 303
Wat Phra Phutthabat

(Temple of the Buddha's Footprint) 151
Wat Phra That Bang Phuan 321
Wat Phra That Lampang Luang 214
Wat Phu Tok 323

Wat Suan Mokkh 338
Wat Tham Seua 390
Wiang Kum Kam 208
Women's groups 42

Yala 425
Yasothon 304

HELP US UPDATE

We've gone to a lot of effort to make sure that the **Rough Guide: Thailand** is thoroughly up-to-date and accurate. However things do change, and we'd very much appreciate any comments, corrections or additions for the next edition of the book. For the best letters, we'll send a copy of the new edition or any other Rough Guide. Send your comments along to:

Paul Gray and Lucy Ridout, The Rough Guides, 1 Mercer Street, London WC2H 9QL.

BEFORE YOU TRAVEL THE WORLD, TALK TO AN EXPERIENCED STAMP COLLECTOR.

At STA Travel we're all seasoned travellers so we should know a thing or two about where you're headed. We can offer you the best deals on fares with the flexibility to change your mind as you go – without having to pay over the top for the privilege. We operate from 120 offices worldwide. So call in soon.

74 and 86 Old Brompton Road, SW7, 117 Euston Road, NW1. London.
Manchester. Leeds. Oxford. Cambridge. Bristol.
North America 071-937 9971. Europe 071-937 9921. Rest of World 071-937 9962
(incl. Sundays 10am-2pm). OR 061-834 0668 (Manchester)

WHEREVER YOU'RE BOUND, WE'RE BOUND TO HAVE BEEN. STA

 Retail Agents for ATOL Holders

STA TRAVEL